RESOURCE BOOK

*F*ACING *H*ISTORY *AND* *O*URSELVES

HOLOCAUST AND HUMAN BEHAVIOR

Margot Stern Strom

Facing History and Ourselves National Foundation, Inc.

Brookline, Massachusetts

Acknowledgment of the many quotations included in each chapter of this book can be found at the end of the chapter. Every effort has been made to trace and acknowledge owners of copyrighted materials, but in some cases this has proved impossible. Facing History would be pleased to add, correct, or revise any such acknowledgments in future printings.

For permission to reproduce the photographs in this book, grateful acknowledgment is made to the following:
Pages 3–7: Illustrations from *The Bear That Wasn't* reprinted by permission of the heirs to the Frank Tashlin Trust. **Page 125:** Reproduced from the Collections of the Library of Congress. **Page 134:** (top left) Bruno Voigt, *Street Scene*, from the Collection of Marvin and Janet Fishman, Milwaukee. (top right) George Grosz, *Street Scene*, from the Collection of Marvin and Janet Fishman, Milwaukee. (bottom) Albert Birkle, *Street Scene*, from the Collection of Marvin and Janet Fishman, Milwaukee. **Page 302:** Martin Gilbert, *Atlas of the Holocaust*, second edition, William Morrow USA (New York), 1992. **Page 344:** Arnold Kramer; United States Holocaust Memorial Museum. **Page 349:** Martin Gilbert, *Atlas of the Holocaust*, second edition, William Morrow USA (New York), 1992. **Page 477:** Arnold Kramer; United States Holocaust Memorial Museum. **Page 515:** FAYFOTO.

ISBN 0-9615841-4-9 Printed in the United States of America

11   14 13 12

The contents of this resource book are being distributed in part under a grant from the United States Department of Education. However, those contents do not necessarily represent the policy of the Department of Education nor should the reader assume an endorsement by the Federal Government.

Samuel J. Baskin,
1911-1989

*This new edition of the Facing History and Ourselves Resource Book
is dedicated to the memory of Samuel J. Baskin.*

Samuel Baskin was a creative and successful trial lawyer with extraordinary skills in negotiation, mediation, and arbitration. Throughout his lifetime, he held innumerable positions of leadership and trust in organizations devoted to religious and secular education, justice, and world peace.

It was written of him by a prominent educator that "he had rare professional skills. He had deep personal concerns; always available to others. He was one of the most articulate of men. He spoke with a felicity and eloquence before which we could only stand in awe. His verbal fluency was the window of an analytical mind which quickly penetrated and ordered the world of ideas and issues. And all was informed by a warm humanity, a love of people, all people, the oppressed of the earth, the victims of injustice, intolerance, and war."

Memories are the alchemy which can transmute sorrow into comfort. Thus, we are comforted to be able to dedicate this book to a man who would have been so enthusiastic about the contribution it makes to the cause of education, harmony, and peace. He would have been especially excited about the role this book will play in helping teachers motivate young people to make a difference in our society.

MRS. SAMUEL J. (HADASSAH) BASKIN

Facing History and Ourselves is a nonprofit foundation with international headquarters in Brookline, Massachusetts, and regional offices in Chicago, Cleveland, Los Angeles, Memphis, New York, the San Francisco Bay Area, and Switzerland. Facing History provides teachers throughout the world with professional development in the form of workshops, institutes, and seminars. Facing History teachers also have access to an assortment of books, periodicals, speakers, videotapes, and online resources. In addition, ongoing research into twentieth-century history and adolescent development has resulted in a number of Facing History publications, many of which are referenced in this resource book and are available from the Facing History resource library or website.

Facing History and Ourselves
16 Hurd Road
Brookline, Massachusetts 02445
(617) 232-1595
(617) 232-0281 (fax)
www.facinghistory.org

Contents

Many individuals quoted in this book use the terms *man* and *men* to refer to women as well as men. This usage reflects the era in which they lived.

2. We and They   56-108

Democracy is becoming rather than being. It can easily be lost,
but never is fully won. Its essence is eternal struggle.

WILLIAM H. HASTIE

3. Germany in the 1920s   109-153

The shadowy figures that look out at us from the tarnished
mirror of history are—in the final analysis—ourselves.

DETLEV J. K. PEUKERT

4. The Nazis Take Power   154-208

Anyone who interprets National Socialism as merely a political movement knows almost nothing about it. It is more than a religion. It is the determination to create the new man.

ADOLF HITLER

5. Conformity and Obedience   *209-251*

When you think of the long and gloomy history of man, you find
more hideous crimes have been committed in the name of obedience
than have ever been committed in the name of rebellion.

C. P. SNOW

6. Escalating Violence   *252-306*

And what was said long ago is true: Nations are made not of
oak and rock but of men, and, as the men are,
so will the nations be.

MILTON MAYER

7. *The Holocaust*   *307-362*

*The more we come to know about the Holocaust,
how it came about, how it was carried out, etc., the greater the
possibility that we will become sensitized to inhumanity and
suffering whenever they occur.*

EVA FLEISCHNER

8. Bystanders and Rescuers   *363-417*

*The world is too dangerous to live in—not because
of the people who do evil, but because of
the people who sit and let it happen.*

ALBERT EINSTEIN

11. Choosing to Participate   523-567

*Each time a man stands up for an ideal, or acts to improve
the lot of others, or strikes out against injustice, he sends forth
a tiny ripple of hope.*

ROBERT F. KENNEDY

Preface
by Margot Stern Strom

According to anthropologist Marcelo Suárez-Orozco, "globalization defines our era." He defines globalization as the "movement of people, goods, or ideas among countries and regions." While globalization is not new, transnational exchanges continue to accelerate, even in the aftermath of the terrorist attacks in the United States on September 11, 2001. These exchanges are dramatically changing the world in which we live. How we respond to those changes will shape future generations. Suárez-Orozco notes that, "Education is at the center of this uncharted continent."

How will classrooms across the world help students negotiate the challenges that come with the unfamiliar? Often uncertainty is coupled with change. How can we help our students live with uncertainty without compromising their values? Across much of the world, communities find themselves challenged by visible signs of difference—new faces, new customs, and new ideas. Each day newspapers report on religious and ethnic tensions both within and across borders, whether it is about the placement of a new church or the religious dress of new arrivals. What can educators do to help promote tolerance, respect, and understanding? Sociology Professor David Shoem points out:

> The effort it takes for us to know so little about one another across racial and ethnic groups is truly remarkable. That we can live so closely together, that our lives can be so intertwined socially, economically, and politically, and that we can spend so many years of study in grade school and even in higher education and yet still manage to be ignorant of one another is clear testimony to the deep-seated roots of this human and national tragedy. What we do learn along the way is to place heavy reliance on stereotypes, gossip, rumor, and fear to shape our lack of knowledge.

The success of that "reliance on stereotypes, gossip, rumor, and fear" can be seen and heard in classrooms across the world. Students express a universal knowledge of negative words and hostile images of "the other." When asked what they know about "them," the answers too often reveal virulent stereotypes: "Asians are...," "Blacks are...," "Jews are...," "Muslims are..." Even very young children have managed to acquire a store of racial and religious epithets. Although we teach our children that "sticks and stones may break my bones, but words can never hurt me," they know a different reality. They are well aware that words of hate degrade, dehumanize, and eventually destroy. Indeed, much of the violence that threatens our society has its roots in bigotry and hate.

How did our children acquire the language of bigotry? One answer lies in the lyrics to a song from the musical *South Pacific*: "You've got to be taught to hate and fear. You've got to be taught from year to year. It's got to be drummed into your dear little ear. You've got to be carefully taught, you've got to be carefully taught." Our children have indeed been carefully taught and far too many of them have mastered the lesson. If we are to win the struggle for the world's conscience and future, we must counter lessons of hate with lessons that promote understanding and caring. We must help students examine their thoughts and feelings and then confront not only their own potential for passivity and complicity but also for their courage and resilience. And we must teach them to value their rights as citizens and take responsibility for their actions. To do so, they must know not only the triumphs of history but also the failures, the tragedies, and the humiliations.

Why is it necessary to study evil in the past to understand freedom, value difference, and seek justice today? Hannah Arendt, one of the foremost political philosophers of our time, offered one answer to that question. She argued that we can put past evils into the service of a future good only by squarely facing reality. She wrote, "The methods used in the pursuit of historical truth are not the methods of the prosecutor, and the men who stand guard over the facts are not the officers of interest groups—no matter how legitimate their claim—but the reporters, the historians, and finally the poets." The facts, no matter how horrifying must be preserved, not "lest we forget," but so that we may judge.

Joseph Brodsky, a Nobel Prize-winning poet from what was once Yugoslavia, agrees. In his view, evil is not an aberration that stands apart from ourselves but a mirror—"a reflection of ourselves: of human negative potential." And he maintains that we will never be able to combat evil unless we honestly examine the negative as well as the positive aspects of our nature. History matters for other reasons too. It fosters perspective-taking, critical thinking, and moral decision-making. Our students must learn that the world they live in did not just happen. It is the result of choices made by countless individuals and groups. Even the smallest of those decisions can have enormous consequences for both good and evil. Journalist Bill Moyers proudly notes that every school he attended was a legacy created "brick by brick, dollar by dollar, classroom by classroom, book by book" by people he had never met, many of whom had died long before he was born. In *Before the Mayflower*, Lerone Bennett, Jr., uses a similar metaphor to describe how communities throughout the United States came to be segregated. He likens it to the building of a wall "brick by brick, bill by bill, fear by fear." After World War II, a German professor described a similar process when he confessed:

> If the last and worst act of the whole [Nazi] regime had come immediately after the first and smallest, thousands, yes millions, would have been sufficiently shocked…. But of course this isn't the way it happens. In between come all the hundreds of little steps, some of them imperceptible, each of them preparing you not to be shocked by the next. Step C is not so much worse than Step B, and, if you did not make a stand at Step B, why should you at Step C? And so on to Step D.

In a Facing History course, students examine each of those small steps. As they do so, they discover that history is not inevitable. They also come to realize that there are no easy answers to the complex problems of racism, antisemitism, hate, and violence, no quick fixes for social injustices, and no simple solutions to moral dilemmas. Meaningful change takes patience and commitment. Still, as one student said of the course, "The more we learn about why and how people behave the way they do, the more likely we are to become involved and find our own solutions." Another writes:

> Life used to be so easy. There always seemed to be an answer to everything. Everything fit into place, getting up at seven o'clock, going to school at eight, coming home at four, doing homework at eight, and finally going to bed at eleven. In my tightly scheduled life I left no time to reflect. In these past four months, however, I've been forced to think. It hasn't been easy.

She's right. It is not easy. Facing History began for me in 1976, at a time when I was both teacher and student. I taught history and English to junior high school students in a suburb of Boston in the morning and studied moral development theory at Harvard University's Graduate School of Education in the afternoon. That spring, I attended my first workshop on the Holocaust and discovered a history of which I was totally ignorant. As I listened to the speakers and reflected on the issues they raised, I began to feel a sense of disquiet about my own education and that of my students. As my uneasiness intensified, I came upon a letter that a principal sent to his teachers on the first day of school:

> Dear Teacher:
> I am a survivor of a concentration camp. My eyes saw what no man should witness:
> Gas chambers built by learned engineers.
> Children poisoned by educated physicians.
> Infants killed by trained nurses.
> Women and babies shot and burned by high school and college graduates.
> So I am suspicious of education.
> My request is: Help your students become human. Your efforts must never produce learned monsters, skilled psychopaths, educated Eichmanns.
> Reading, writing, arithmetic are important only if they serve to make our children more human.

That letter provided the impetus for me to face my own history. My journey began with newly awakened memories of my childhood. I grew up in Memphis, Tennessee, at a time when separate never meant equal. I grew up in a city where "colored" water fountains did not spout brightly colored water as a child might expect but stood instead as symbols of the unchallenged dogmas of racism. I grew up in a city where black children could visit the zoo only on Thursdays and where "their" library housed discarded books from "our" library. I grew up knowing there would always be empty seats at the front of the bus for young white girls while those with a darker skin color would stand crowded at the back of the bus. I grew up knowing all this, but it was never addressed at school.

Conspicuous by its absence from my formal schooling was any study of the ethical or moral dimensions of history or human behavior. Our teachers didn't trust my classmates or me with the complexities of history. The dogmas were easier to teach. There were, on occasion, inspirational teachers who encouraged dialogue, risked inquiry, or introduced controversy. But I am hard pressed to remember any discussion of race or any explanation of the water fountains, zoo admission policies, the separate libraries, or the way seats were allocated on the buses. What my teachers neglected or elected not to teach, I ultimately learned at home. My real education was family centered. My parents taught me the meaning of social justice, the importance of political participation, and the value of faith. Those lessons nurtured my development and gave impulse to my life's work. Later as a teacher, I tried to ensure that my students learned what my own teachers failed to teach—that history is largely the result of human decisions, that prevention is possible, and that education must have a moral component if it is to make a difference.

Facing History and Ourselves is based on those beliefs. It is also based on the conviction that education in a democracy must be what Alexis de Tocqueville once called an "apprenticeship in liberty." That is, it must promote the attitudes, values, and skills needed to live in freedom. In an article entitled "America Skips School," Benjamin R. Barber, a political science professor, said of that process:

> The claim that all men are born free, upon which America was founded, is at best a promising fiction . . . . We acquire our freedom over time, if at all. Embedded in families, clans, communities, and nations, we must learn to be free. We may be natural consumers and born narcissists, but citizens have to be made.

Early leaders of the United States understood the connection between freedom and moral education. After all, liberty, equality, and justice are assertions of right and wrong; they raise moral issues that require the ability not only to reason but also to make judgments and then take appropriate action. Only a people that truly values its own freedom will respond to injustice with moral outrage. That is why abolitionist and author Harriet Beecher Stowe viewed the mid-nineteenth century, the age in which she lived, as a time when "nations are trembling and convulsed." When asked if the United States was safe from those convulsions, she replied, "Every nation that carries in its bosom great and unredressed injustice has in it the elements of this last convulsion." Poet Langston Hughes expressed it more directly when he wondered what happens to a "dream deferred." "Does it sag like a heavy load?" he asked. "Or does it explode—like a raisin in the sun?"

Barber warns that we have been "nominally democratic for so long that we presume it is our natural condition rather than the product of persistent effort and tenacious responsibility. We have decoupled rights from civic responsibilities and severed citizenship from education on the false assumption that citizens just happen." He describes civic literacy as the "fundamental literacy by which we live in a civil society. It encompasses the competence to participate in democratic communities, the ability to think critically and act with deliberation in a pluralistic world, and the empathy to identify sufficiently with others to live with them despite conflicts of interest and differences in character. At the most elementary level, what our children suffer from most, whether they're hurling racial epithets from fraternity porches or shooting one another down in schoolyards, is the absence of civility."

Barber and others have defined *civility* as "a work of the imagination, for it is through the imagination that we render others sufficiently like ourselves for them to become subjects of tolerance and respect, if not always affection." Former President of the Czech Republic Vaclav Havel has called the building of a civil society the "greatest challenge of our time." Facing History and Ourselves seeks to meet that challenge by reviving the time-honored idea that history is a branch of moral philosophy with lessons that can serve as guidelines for prudent thinking and moral behavior. With the guidance and support of the Facing History staff and resource speakers, teachers and students explore the roots of religious, racial, and ethnic hatreds and their consequences. And they come to recognize that "the shadowy figures that look out at us from the tarnished mirror of history are—in the final analysis—ourselves."

Facing History holds up "the tarnished mirror of history" by asking students to analyze events that threatened democracy in one of the most murderous centuries in history—the twentieth century, a century marked by the Nazis' attempt to exterminate the Jews of Europe solely because of their ancestry. That history, like every history, is both universal and particular. As Catholic historian Eva Fleischner has noted, "We can attain universality only through particularity: there are no shortcuts. The more we come to know about the Holocaust, how it came about, how it was carried out, etc., the greater the possibility that we will become sensitized to inhumanity and suffering whenever they occur." She therefore views the history of the events that led to the Holocaust not as *their* history but as *our* history. In her view, it touches us all.

Important connections can be made with the events that led to the genocide of the Armenian people during World War I; the enslavement of Africans; the destruction of Native American nations in the years that followed European colonization of the Americas; and mass murders during World War II in Nanking, China, and the Soviet Union and more recently in Cambodia, Laos, Tibet, Rwanda, and Sudan. However, the series of events that led to the Holocaust is the focus of this book for a number of reasons.

Perhaps the most important is that it helps students better understand the modern world and ultimately themselves. In no other history are the steps that resulted in totalitarianism and ultimately genocide so carefully documented not only by the victims but also by perpetrators and by-standers. It is a history that clearly shows the deadly consequences of un-examined prejudices, unfaced fears, and unchallenged lies. It shows too the dangers of charismatic leaders who manipulate the young by appealing to prejudice, fear, and ignorance. We do not want yet another generation of young people influenced by propaganda to march blindly in someone else's parade.

It is a history that shattered what historian Ronnie Laudau calls in his book *The Nazi Holocaust,* "Europe-centered, liberal dreams of Western reason and culture as forces that necessarily sensitize and humanize us and which promote genuine tolerance of difference. It also destroyed, once and for all, the tottering belief that science and technology were securely harnessed for the good of humanity, as scientists, politicians, bureaucrats and generals found the means progressively to give destructive expression to their decisions and fantasies."

Landau notes that the Holocaust was, "in part, the outcome of problems of identity—the alienation and isolation of the individual in our modern mass societies, which have become so depersonalized and conformist."

> Nazism appealed to people's need for a sense of belonging, loyalty and community, a need left dangerously unfulfilled by modern, vast, centralized society. It encouraged a psychological state whereby they could easily be sucked into the entire bureaucratic process. Bureaucracy is a human invention which can subjugate its inventor, undermine human conscience and allow individuals to abdicate personal moral responsibility.

Thus the events that led to the Holocaust raise profound and disturbing questions about the consequences of our actions and our beliefs, of how we as individuals make distinctions between right and wrong, good and evil. Those questions are universal even though the Holocaust is unique. Many of these questions center on the ways we as individuals and as members of groups define what Helen Fein calls our "universe of obligation"—the circle of persons "toward whom obligations are owed, to whom rules apply and whose injuries call for [amends] by the community."

This history also forces us to consider the consequences of what it means to be pushed outside that "universe of obligation." In *The Cunning of History,* scholar Richard Rubenstein describes such individuals as "superfluous." As he puts it, "Political rights are neither God-given, auto-nomous nor self-validating. The Germans understood that no person has any rights unless they are guaranteed by an organized community with the power to defend such rights." And in the 1930s and 1940s, no organized community was willing to defend the rights of Jews, "Gypsies," and other groups the Nazis regarded as "subhuman."

The racism that permeated Nazi Germany was not an isolated occur-rence. As Rubenstein explains, Auschwitz is linked, although not exclu-sively, to a cultural tradition of slavery "which stretches back to the Middle Passage from the coast of Africa, and beyond, to the enforced servitude in

Ancient Greece and Rome. If we ignore this linkage, we ignore the existence of the sleeping virus in the bloodstream of civilization, at the risk of our future."

Facing History and Ourselves confronts that issue and others like it by offering a rigorous study of the events that led to the Holocaust and a thoughtful examination of universal themes inherent in that history. Like many people, we regard the Holocaust itself as a unique event for which comparisons are inappropriate. Yet we also believe it is essential to explore connections between the events that led to the Holocaust and the world today. In the TV series, *The Ascent of Man*, Jacob Bronowski explained why: "When the future looks back on the 1930s, it will think of them as a crucial confrontation of culture..., the ascent of man, against the throwback to the despots' belief that they have absolute certainty." He then gave his viewers a glimpse of Auschwitz:

> This is the concentration camp and crematorium at Auschwitz. This is where people were turned into numbers. Into this pond were flushed the ashes of [over a million and a half] people. And that was not done by gas. It was done by arrogance. It was done by dogma. It was done by ignorance. When people believe they have absolute knowledge, with no test in reality, this is how they behave. This is what men do when they aspire to the knowledge of the gods...
>
> I owe it as a scientist..., as a human being to the many members of my family who died at Auschwitz, to stand here by the pond as a survivor and a witness. We have to cure ourselves of the itch for absolute knowledge and power. We have to close the distance between the push-button order and the human act. We have to touch people.

Racism and antisemitism, scapegoating and stereotyping, a propensity to violence, intellectual and cultural arrogance, a failure of empathy are all issues that are difficult to confront. But in a book written soon after World War II ended, Bronowski urged that they be faced. He began by describing the ashy, clinical remains of Nagasaki, Japan, and told of "a universal moment." "On an evening like that evening, some time in 1945, each of us in his own way learned that his imagination had been dwarfed. We looked up and saw the power of which we had been proud loom over us like the ruins of Nagasaki." The experience convinced him that all decisions about issues which weigh the fate of nations "should be made within the forbidding context of Nagasaki: only then could statesmen make realistic judgments of the problems which they handle on our behalf." Confronting those issues is profoundly uncomfortable. Yet if we deny students access to them, we fail to honor their potential to confront, to cope, and to make a difference today and in the future.

Introduction

*F*acing History and Ourselves is devoted to teaching about the dangers of indifference and the values of civility by helping schools confront the complexities of history in ways that promote critical and creative thinking about the challenges we face and the opportunities we have for positive change. Facing History is unique in that it is not a program of one-week seminars that are all-too-easily forgotten, a packaged curriculum, or a prescribed set of lessons. Rather, it offers dynamic, long-term intervention. It is designed to have a lasting effect on the life of a school.

THE FACING HISTORY APPROACH

With the help of the Facing History staff and resource speakers, teachers who participate in the program learn to use the tools of the humanities—inquiry, analysis, and interpretation—to supplement or enrich existing courses. At workshops and follow-up sessions, those teachers are offered materials that engage and challenge their students' most advanced thinking and promote individual reflection and group discussion.

Adolescence is a time when many young people struggle with issues of independence, trust, freedom, and responsibility. It is also a time when life centers around peer groups and mutual relationships. The readings and films recommended by Facing History support and challenge students in their efforts to define their own identity and their relationship to society as a whole. Thus many of those materials promote an understanding of differing perspectives, competing truths, and the need to comprehend not only one's own motives but also those of others. By offering a framework for examining issues students regard as important, Facing History helps them find meaning in their education and empowers them to make positive changes in their lives.

Adolescence is a time of major developmental transitions. Students need to think about their thinking in order to become aware of their moral development. As a student explained, "One thing this course has done, it has made me more aware—not only of what happened in the past but also of what is happening today, now, in the world and in me." Facing History seeks to foster cognitive growth and historical understanding through a content and methodology that induces conflict and continually complicates students' simple answers to complex questions. The readings and activities included in the Resource Book, the recommended videos, and the guest speakers encourage students to view the world from more than one perspective, to place themselves in someone else's shoes, and to express their ideas freely. They are stimulated to think about the choices they have as individuals within a society and the consequences of those decisions.

At a time when many are urging that students learn to think critically without paying much attention to what those students are to think about, Facing History stresses compelling content. This is not a program that is mired in relativism. Facing History has a strong bias. It is committed to content that furthers democratic values and beliefs. It is also committed to prevention. We believe that unexamined prejudices, myths, and misinformation are threatening the nation and its future. The violence in our streets is but one sign of the danger. We therefore must teach our students to look, listen, read, and think critically. And they must be constantly challenged to complicate their thinking by not accepting simple solutions to complex questions. Many of the readings and films used in Facing History courses were deliberately selected with that aim in mind. Some focus on the choices open to various individuals. Others draw attention to aspects of society or human behavior that affect the kinds of decisions groups and even nations make. Each reading helps students realize that "life is almost always more complicated than we think. Behind the gleaming ranks of those who seem totalitarian robots stand men and women, various and diverse, complex and complicated, some brave, some cowardly, some brainwashed, some violently idiosyncratic, and all of them very human."

As students engage in thinking about thinking, they develop a vocabulary of decision-making and justice as aids to their reasoning. And as they grapple with the range of choices individuals actually had in the decades before the Nazis took power, many find it harder and harder to defend simple explanations of why democracy failed in Germany. They also begin to see critical connections between past and present. And they begin to wonder. As a Facing History student from South Africa wrote in her journal, "We learnt lessons that cannot be found in any textbook. The discussions and stories held me spellbound. Now my mind is like a probing satellite and I can ask more than 'who, how many and where.' I can ask 'why and how could.'" In time she may also begin to raise questions of "should and would."

The fundamental concerns of Facing History and Ourselves figure prominently in the works of Hannah Arendt. She has traced her own impulse to think about thinking to the trial of Adolf Eichmann, the Nazi official in charge of the deportation and extermination of Jews. She expected the trial to reveal that he acted out of ideological conviction, evil motives, or stupidity. Instead she concluded that he never gave much thought to what he did. Indeed, he was protected from thinking by routines, cliches, and the constant pressure to conform. Arendt therefore wondered, "Could the activity of thinking as such, the habit of examining. . . be among the conditions that make men abstain from evil-doing or even condition them against it?"

In the end, Arendt decided that even though the activity of thinking breaks down preconceived ideas, thinking in and of itself does not lead to action. In her view, informed judgment is the bridge between thought and action. Thus, she did not consider judgment the mechanical process of applying a rule or law to a particular case but rather an art that can be carried out only within the realm of choice.

The writings of Jacob Bronowski have also influenced Facing History's approach to the process of thinking, judging, and ultimately taking action. "There is no way of exchanging information that does not demand an act of judgment," he wrote. "All knowledge, all information between human beings can only be exchanged within a play of tolerance. And that is true whether the exchange is in science, or in literature, or in religion, or in politics, or even in any form of thought that aspires to dogma." For Bronowski, the ability to tolerate divergent views is what distinguishes humans from all other creatures.

The Facing History program incorporates both Arendt's ideas and Bronowski's by offering students a variety of perspectives and helping them sift through differing, and at times conflicting, points of view before asking them to make wise judgments. It is, writes one high school teacher, a program that "honors duality; process and product, head and heart, history and ethics."

The importance of pushing students to form judgments was brought to light by the research Betty Bardige conducted for the thesis she wrote under the direction of Professor Carol Gilligan. Bardige discovered that unless students are encouraged to make moral judgments, they are likely to become paralyzed by their own thinking and therefore unable to respond to injustice. She maintains that it is essential that students examine the consequences of actions as well as analyze the causes.

Facing History and Ourselves does both. It helps teachers move their students from thought to judgment and ultimately to participation. Through that process, students and their teachers build a community of thinkers. As Hannah Arendt once observed, the activity of thinking is a solitary endeavor—a dialogue with oneself in order to formulate moral principles. Judgment, however, requires dialogue with others. Arendt stressed the importance of that discourse.

> The world is not humane because it is made by human beings, and it does not become humane just because the human voice sounds in it, but only when it has become the object of discourse. However much we are affected by the things of the world, however deeply they may stir and stimulate us, they become human for us only when we can discuss them with our fellows. . . . We humanize what is going on in the world and in ourselves only by speaking of it, and in the course of speaking of it we learn to be human.

In a Facing History classroom, teachers and students chronicle their learning in journals. They use their journals to reflect on who they are and to re-examine their goals, values, and beliefs. Only then do they come together to share insights and responses to complex questions. That sharing requires trust and mutual respect. Building that kind of classroom community is hard work and requires a new relationship between students and teacher. Many teachers make contracts with their students to underscore the importance of that new relationship. One teacher wrote:

> I told the students that the curriculum touches on a great many things that could hurt us all if we were not sensitive to one another's feelings. I stated that I was uncomfortable teaching the unit unless we could maintain an atmosphere of mutual respect. The contract included that each person could express his or her feelings without being put down by others.

The materials provided in this Resource Book are designed to stimulate and inform that interaction by reinforcing the idea that learning is a collaborative endeavor that benefits every participant. It guides both the teacher and the student. Thus Facing History seeks to:

- develop an educational model that helps students move from thought to judgment to participation as they confront the moral questions inherent in a study of violence, racism, antisemitism, and bigotry;
- reveal the universal connections of history through a rigorous examination of a particular history;
- further a commitment to adolescents as the moral philosophers of our society and help them build a "civil society" through an understanding that turning neighbor against neighbor leads to violence.

Educators learn the Facing History approach by experiencing it in workshops, retreats, and institutes, where they encounter scholars who challenge their thinking not only about ethics and history but also about the process of teaching. As one administrator has noted "the material is so powerful and so significant that it calls to question why we teach and how we teach. It calls for mastery of teaching skills, learning how to pose the significant questions and how to complicate the thinking of those who would be content with simple solutions."

The Facing History staff helps educators acquire those skills as they explore the opportunities new approaches can provide to challenge students and stimulate their thinking. Later teachers meet individually with a Facing History program associate to design a Facing History course that meets their students' needs and the needs of their particular school.

Teachers who participate in Facing History programs have access not only to the program staff and resource speakers but also to the Facing History Resource Center, a lending library of relevant videos and films, books, slides, tape recordings, posters, and articles on a broad range of topics. They also receive newsletters, invitations to Facing History conferences, and an opportunity to join a community of teachers in their region who meet regularly to continue learning. In addition, Facing History offers adult education programs and community-wide events that help link the work of Facing History to the larger community.

For nearly two decades, Facing History and Ourselves has been documenting the effectiveness of these efforts. Reports of those evaluations, which are available from the Facing History Resource Center, show that the program is achieving its goals. Students are indeed capable of handling a rigorous course that demands their best thinking. And they are able to make connections between the past and their own lives. And although each student seems to feel the impact in a slightly different way, few participants are able to avoid comparisons with issues close to home; any discussion of prejudice, discrimination, or violence almost invariably draws parallels to similar problems in the students' own schools and neighborhoods. Henry Zabierek, the director of social studies in Brookline at the time Facing History was founded, summarized the program in this way:

> This curriculum is about more than the Holocaust. It's about the reading and the writing and the arithmetic of genocide, but it's also about such R's as rethinking, reflecting, and reasoning. It's about prejudice, discrimination and scapegoating; but it's also about human dignity, morality, law, and citizenship. It's about avoiding and forgetting, but it's also about civic courage and justice. In an age of "back to basics" this curriculum declares that there is one thing more basic, more sacred, than any of the three R's; namely, the sanctity of human life.

In all probability, Facing History will not end prejudice, discrimination, scapegoating, or even fights on the playground. Nevertheless, program evaluations demonstrate that students and teachers in a Facing History program have heightened awareness of the causes and consequences of those issues. In some cases, the impact has been subtle, with students observing that they have begun to think differently about stereotypes and racial slurs. As one student explained, "This unit showed me that as a young black man my race is not the only race that has suffered. . . .We are all simply human beings. . . .This course made me look inside myself. I for one know that I have felt prejudice toward someone of some other group. These things are all a part of being a human being, but cooperation, peace and love are ingredients also." Achieving that degree of awareness is a meaningful objective for many students.

In other instances, participants in the program have shown more dramatic changes. A young Chicagoan who found the courage to leave his gang said of the program, "Facing History showed me that there are people, teachers and other students concerned about teenagers' well-being in this world of violence. Facing History showed me that yes, people do know we have problems growing up in today's society and no, we are not turning our backs on it."

In another community, a school recently reported the way its students responded when teachers discovered that someone had written "KKK" and "Nigger go home" on the washroom walls. When those students were confronted with what had happened, the room was silent for a moment and then a white student turned to a black classmate and said, "Valita, I'm sorry that's written on the walls; it's no different than what we've been studying. This is how it begins. I'm going to go and take it off, and anyone who wants to join me, can." One by one, students rose and followed her to the washroom where they erased the graffiti.

Parents have also observed measurable differences. One parent wrote, "In no other course was [my daughter] exposed to real dilemmas as complex and challenging. In no other course has she been inspired to use the whole of her spiritual, moral, and intellectual resources to solve a problem. In no other course has she been so sure that the task mattered seriously for her development as a responsible person."

Just as many students find that the program has altered their perceptions and compelled them to think more about their behaviors, many teachers find that it has changed not only the way they teach but also the way they think. Ron Gwiazda, the assistant to the headmaster of Boston Latin School, described that process when he spoke of the impact the program had on one of his students.

> Bedelia is an excellent student, runs 400 meters in under 60 seconds, has a radiant smile, and is one of the most sweet and gentle human beings I know. We like each other very much, but when Bedelia thinks through the complex issues of race and violence and writes in her journal "we," I realize that I'm not part of that "we." And I don't have simple answers to the conflicting emotions that she feels, nor to this invisible but present distance that arises in that "we."
>
> What I can offer Bedelia, because of Facing History and Ourselves, is ways of thinking about complex issues and ways of coming to know herself and me better, which is essentially the core of Facing History and Ourselves. What Facing History and Ourselves does so well is to avoid substituting one set of simple solutions, one polemic, one propaganda, for another. Instead it aims to teach teachers to teach young people to think critically and independently, to know the past as fact and to confront its implications in ways that make us all seek to change the future for the better. If there are no simple answers to the hatred and violence from the past or in the present, there are the countering forces of intellectual honesty, integrity, justice, and empathy.

A CLOSER LOOK AT THE RESOURCE BOOK

This new edition of the Facing History Resource Book is similar to the previous one in many respects. Like the earlier edition, it is not a textbook—a series of discreet lessons with goals and objectives. Rather, it provides students and teachers with a meaningful but flexible structure for examining complex events and ideas. It also fosters original and thoughtful responses by encouraging students to reflect on difficult questions and issues. The new edition, like the earlier one, helps students make connections between historical events and their own lives. And it too can be used not only in social studies classes but also in combination with English, art, and science classes.

There are differences between the two editions. The "Using" sections that followed readings in the earlier edition are now known as "Connections." Films and key quotations no longer appear as readings. Films are now referenced in Connections along with suggestions for their use in the classroom. Key quotations appear as sidebars. And the new book, unlike the earlier one, contains a detailed table of contents, an index of audio-visual resources, and an index.

The readings in the new edition are somewhat longer and provide more context. Many were selected to help students better understand the links between the past and their own lives today. The new edition also contains more social history and reflects the insights of current scholarship, particularly scholarship on issues related to violence and racism. Two important chapters in the earlier edition have been deleted and their content added to other chapters. As a result, anti-Judaism and antisemitism are discussed within the context of particular eras rather than in an isolated chapter. The same is true of the Armenian Genocide. It too has been placed within a chronological framework.

The new edition is cross-referenced to two other Facing History publications: *Elements of Time* and *Choosing to Participate*. *Elements of Time* is a companion manual to the Facing History videotape collection of Holocaust testimonies—the result of a five-year collaborative project between Facing History and the Fortunoff Video Archive at Yale University made possible through the vision and support of Eli Evans and the Charles H. Revson Foundation. The book includes transcriptions of the videos along with essays and readings from some of the many scholars and resource speakers who have addressed Facing History conferences. *Choosing to Participate* is an outgrowth of the last chapter of the Resource Book. It addresses students' questions about how they can make a difference by introducing them to traditions of care and models for participation in American democracy. The book provides a history of the voluntary sector and traces the way individuals and groups have used the First Amendment to the Constitution as an avenue of outrage and advocacy.

AN OVERVIEW

The first two chapters in the Resource Book use literature to introduce the key concepts developed in Facing History. Those ideas are then applied to real individuals and real events in history. The opening chapters engage students in thinking about behavior and introduce them to the principles of decision-making. They also help students build a vocabulary of morality. In Chapter 1, for example, students explore the connections between individuals and the society in which they live. And they discover why Martha Minow argues that "when we identify one thing as like the others, we are not merely classifying the world; we are investing particular classifications with consequences and positioning ourselves in relation to those meanings. When we identify one thing as unlike the others, we are dividing the world; we use our language to exclude, to distinguish—to discriminate."

Chapter 1 also begins an exploration of many of the central questions developed in the program:

- How is our identity formed?
- How do our attitudes and beliefs influence our thinking? How does our thinking affect our actions?
- How can we keep our individuality and still be a part of a group?
- How does our tendency to see us as unique but them as members affect our behavior as well as our attitudes?

Chapter 2 then outlines the ways various nations, including the United States, have defined their identity. And it helps students understand the significance of those definitions. After all, those who define a nation's identity determine who is a part of its "universe of obligation." Early in the chapter, the focus is on the United States and the way three sets of ideas shaped those definitions in the nineteenth and early twentieth centuries: *democracy*, *race*, and *nationalism*. All three concepts have had tremendous appeal to people all over the world. And all three, when carried to an extreme, have been abused. False ideas about "race" have on occasion turned nationalism into ethnocentrism and chauvinism. At the same time, some democrats have confused equality with conformity. Others have viewed differences as proof that "they" are less human than "we" are.

The next few chapters focus primarily on the decisions that resulted in the Holocaust and relate those decisions to issues important to students' lives today—particularly to issues of racism, antisemitism, violence, conformity, and power. Chapter 3, which marks the beginning of the case study, examines the choices people in Europe and the United States made after World War I. The chapter highlights German efforts to build a lasting democracy after the humiliation of defeat and explores the values, myths, and fears that threatened those efforts. Chapters 4 through 8 examine *how* the Nazis turned Germany into a totalitarian state by turning neighbor against neighbor in order to break the moral backbone of a citizenry and *why* the German people allowed them to do so. Students also consider the way individuals and nations defined their "universe of obligation" in the 1930s and 1940s and the consequences of those definitions. It is in these chapters that students begin to wonder, "What might I have done?" And it in these chapters that students see connections to their own world and come to understand why Cynthia Ozick warns that "when a whole population takes on the status of bystander, the victims are without allies; the criminals, unchecked, are strengthened; and only then do we need to speak of heroes. When a field is filled from end to end with sheep, a stag stands out. When a continent is filled from end to end with the compliant, we learn what heroism is."

As they read these chapters, some teachers and students emphasize the acts of courage that rekindle hope in humanity. But, to study only heroes and speak solely of human dignity is to distort and distract from the painful reality of this history. Thinking about the victims and perpetrators of mass murder requires a new "vocabulary of annihilation." The "choiceless choices" of this history of human behavior in extremity do not reflect options between right and wrong but between one form of abnormal response and another.

In the last three chapters, students move from thought to judgment, and then to action. As students think about judgment in moral and legal terms, they consider such questions as:

- What is the difference between crimes against humanity and killings sanctioned by war?

- What is the purpose of a trial? Is it to punish evil-doing or set a precedent for the future?

- Are individuals responsible for their crimes if they have obeyed the laws of their nation? Or are there higher laws?

- How does one determine punishment? Is everyone equally guilty? Or do some bear more responsibility than others? Can an entire nation be guilty?

Chapters 10 and 11 consider issues related to prevention by returning to themes developed in the first two chapters of the book. Chapter 10 explores how we remember the past and considers the ways those memories shape the present. It also focuses on the ways individuals and nations avoid, revise, deny, or rewrite their history. In the words of journalist Judith Miller, "Knowing and remembering the evil in history and in each of us might not prevent a recurrence of genocide. But ignorance of history or the suppression of memory removes the surest defense we have, however inadequate, against such gigantic cruelty and indifference to it." What then fosters memory? For Miller, it is anything that makes the past more real and encourages empathy and caring. As part of this chapter, students examine the way we memorialize the past through monuments, museums, and schooling.

Chapter 11 further develops the idea of prevention by considering what it takes to be a good citizen. The chapter is organized around the idea that "people become brave by doing brave acts. People become compassionate by doing compassionate acts. People become good citizens by engaging in acts of good citizenship." Many of the individuals highlighted in Chapter 11 help us understand what it takes to keep democracy alive. The chapter also promotes participation through acts of community service.

STRUCTURE AND ORGANIZATION

Each chapter in the Resource Book has a similar structure. Each begins with an overview that outlines key concepts and themes. The readings that follow allow students to explore those concepts and themes in greater depth. Many are primary sources that capture the ideas, assumptions, and observations of those living through a particular age in history. As Jacob Bronowski once wrote, those sources help us "draw conclusions from what we see to what we do not see" and "recognize ourselves in the past, on the steps to the present." Teachers are encouraged to select the ones that match their objectives and the needs and interests of their students. Readings that develop important concepts are identified in the sidebars and should not be omitted.

At the end of each reading, students encounter a number of activities, quotations, and questions grouped under the heading, "Connections." These are designed to build curiosity, develop habits of inquiry, promote critical thinking, encourage research, and foster an understanding of the relationship between various ideas and concepts. Many ask students to make inferences or think about attitudes and consequences. Others provide practice in expressing ideas orally, visually, or in writing.

Some activities are set off with a special symbol ➤. These activities refer to videos, books, and other materials available from the Facing History Resource Center. These materials can be used in place of a reading or along with it. A number of these materials present ideas critical to the program and suggestions for using them are provided.

The activities provided in the Connections are only a starting point for helping students confront the past and themselves. Teachers should always select the activities that relate the history most directly to the lives of their particular students and add new questions and activities as appropriate.

Acknowledgments

*L*earning is always a collaborative process, one that blurs the line separating student from teacher. It is also a process that has no ending. Preparing this resource book has truly been a learning experience—one that mirrors the ways we have tried to develop Facing History as a team of colleagues who collaborate in the very best sense of the word.

I would like to thank everyone who has taken part in that process, particularly the many teachers, students, and scholars who informed our progress. We heard their voices and felt their influence as we researched, wrote, edited, revised, and wrote yet again. We are profoundly grateful to each of them. It was especially gratifying for us to discover that some of our former students have become teachers who are now transmitting the lessons of Facing History to yet another generation.

I should also like to express my deep affection for the staff of Facing History. As we worked on the Resource Book, individually and as a group, they shared their knowledge and expertise and demonstrated their caring and commitment in ways that have come to mark their approach to every endeavor whether it is direct service to educators, interaction with students in a classroom or study group, docent training for an exhibit, or preparation for a conference or benefit. I would like to particularly acknowledge the contributions of our editor, Phyllis Goldstein, who pulled the resource book together and wrote with me the final draft. I so enjoyed the process of working with her, exchanging ideas and then watching those ideas take shape in the book itself. We value her collaboration, her patience, and her friendship. A very special thank you goes to Steve Cohen whose research launched the first revision of this book and to Mary Johnson, Alan Stoskopf, and Marc Skvirsky who guided the book through the revision process by providing drafts, ideas, resources, critiques, and support. The book would not have been possible without them. We also recognize the contributions of Tracy O'Brien who handled everything from research to permissions with enthusiasm and creativity and of Cathy McCarney who typed much of the original manuscript. And special mention must also go to Joe Wiellette whose friendship and devotion to Facing History, its mission, and publications has quietly sustained us all.

I would also like to acknowledge the support we received from the many scholars who worked with us at institutes, conferences, seminars, and workshops. We are especially appreciative of the contributions made by Philip Johnson and Benjamin Ferencz who drafted early chapters that informed our thinking and Carol Gilligan, who gave us ideas, advice, and special expertise. I am also grateful for the thoughtful reviews we received from Betty Bardige, an educational consultant; Michael Berenbaum, director of the research department at the United States Memorial Holocaust Museum; and Paul Bookbinder, professor of history at the University of Massachusetts. I should also like to acknowledge my gratitude to the following individuals and groups:

- the senior staff that helps me direct Facing History: Marc Skvirsky, Bonnie Meltzer, Joe Wiellette, Terry Tollefson, Chris Stokes, Alan Stoskopf, Ted Scott and Marty Sleeper. Our national and international growth would have been impossible without their leadership. They embody the very best of Facing History.

- Father Robert Bullock, the former chair of the Board of Facing History and now chair of the Board of Trustees, for his loyalty, wisdom, faith, scholarly advice, and unfailing support. His vision guided Facing History from the beginning and allowed it to grow and prosper. He has been our most constant teacher.

- Richard A. Smith, chair of the board of both Harcourt General, Inc. and of Facing History and Ourselves, for his early commitment to Facing History and his willingness to nurture our development and foster our growth. He epitomizes the rare devotion our entire board of directors makes to Facing History and to the nation's students and teachers. His leadership and philanthropy are a model for everyone who serves on the board of directors of a non-profit organization.

- Sandra and Philip Gordon who gave Facing History the support necessary to open our first regional office and who continue to play a special role in the support of our national staff.

- Patricia Ceasar, a consultant, board member, and friend who has understood the potential of Facing History to make a difference and has helped guide its growth.

- Harcourt General, Inc. for its many services including copy editing the final manuscript, designing the overall look of the book, and providing for its printing and binding.

- Sam Bak for the thought-provoking paintings that appear on the cover of this resource book as well as the covers of *Choosing to Participate* and *Elements of Time*.

- Hadassah Baskin for the generous gift she gave us to complete the Resource Book in memory of her husband Samuel Baskin; her son Sheldon Baskin and her daughter-in-law Judith Wise, without whom Facing History would not have been able to open a Chicago office.

- AARTPACK for all of its design help, production advice, and most especially the dedication that allowed us to produce the book on an extremely tight schedule.

- the many individuals and groups whose ideas and approaches informed the original resource book. We particularly wish to acknowledge the contributions of William S. Parsons who co-authored the first edition of the resource book as well as those of Henry Zabierek, Barbara Halley, Judy Botsford, Robert Sperber, Kenneth B. Schwartz, Margaret Drew, Barbara Perry, Lisa Colt, Zezette Larsen, and Sonia Weitz.

- the National Diffusion Network for its recognition of Facing History and Ourselves as an "exemplary model program worthy to be replicated across the nation." There are NDN facilitators in each state whose role is to advise and support those educators interested in adopting the program. We also value and appreciate the leadership shown by Max McConkey, the executive director of the National Dissemination Association.

I must also thank my first Facing History classes at Runkle School and my colleagues there who helped me create Facing History. My students knew they were part of something important. Indeed their journals became my guide. Although the journeys those early classes made are elaborated on in this Resource Book, the journey itself remains essentially unchanged: Facing History remains committed to understanding the world we live in and changing that world for the better.

I want to make special mention of my brother Gerald Stern and my sister Paula Stern, both of whom have practiced what our parents, Fan and Lloyd, taught us—things must and can change. Their courage, loyalty, honesty, and commitment to quality reflect the expectations our parents had for us. Gerald's early work in the civil rights division of the Justice Department expanded my understanding of social justice and courage and Paula's writings on the place of women in the world and her achievements in government and the corporate world have paved roads for me and for many others.

And finally, I want to thank my husband Terry Strom who shares my love of study and whose advice and support I have sought in every area of my personal and professional development. He is a caring and compassionate teacher, doctor, and parent. Our son Adam, his wife Sandy, and our daughter Rachel have expressed their pride and belief in us. Each has studied Facing History and has given me unique insights into the ways Facing History is taught and understood. I have been truly privileged to develop in this family; our children have brought out the best in me and like the children in classrooms everywhere, they are the true moral philosophers.

Margot Stern Strom
Executive Director
Facing History and Ourselves

1. The Individual and Society

"All the people like us are we, and everyone else is they."

RUDYARD KIPLING

OVERVIEW

We begin to learn our culture—the ways of our society—just after birth. That process is called socialization and it involves far more than schooling. It affects our values, what we consider right and wrong. Our religious beliefs are therefore an integral part of our culture. So is our racial or ethnic heritage. Our culture also shapes the way we work and play. And it makes a difference to the way we view ourselves and others. Psychologist Deborah Tannen warns of our tendency to generalize about the things we observe and the people we encounter. "Generalizations, while capturing similarities," she points out, "obscure differences. Everyone is shaped by innumerable influences such as ethnicity, religion, class, race, age, profession, the geographical regions they and their relatives have lived in, and many other group identities—all mingled with individual personality and predilection."[1]

The United States is home to hundreds of different groups, each with its own culture and traditions. It would be impossible to study each group's history in depth. But by focusing on the links between particular individuals and society, Chapter 1 reveals a number of universal principles. In doing so, it raises a number of questions:

- How is our identity formed? To what extent are we defined by our talents, tastes, and interests? By our membership in a particular ethnic group? Our religion? By the nation in which we live?

- Are we limited by the groups to which we belong or can we expand our horizons? What opportunities do individuals have in our society to expand their horizons? How does one make the most of those opportunities?

- How do our attitudes and beliefs influence our thinking? How does our thinking affect our actions?

- How can we keep our individuality and still be a part of a group?

- How does our tendency to see *us* as unique but *them* as members of groups affect our behavior as well as our attitudes? Do we welcome or fear *them*? When does fear turn to hate?

In exploring these and many of the other questions you will encounter in Facing History and Ourselves, it is useful to keep a journal. Unlike a finished work, a journal documents the process of thinking. Much like history itself, it always awaits further entries. A journal also allows a writer to witness his or her own history and consider the way ideas grow and change. For author Joan Didion and many others, writing is a way of examining ideas. She explains, "I write entirely to find out what I'm thinking, what I'm looking at, what I see and what it means."

A complete lesson plan for using a journal with this course is available from the Facing History Resource Center, as are copies of journals kept by two teachers and their students.

R E A D I N G 1

The Bear That Wasn't

No two people are exactly alike. Each is an individual with unique talents, interests, and values. At the same time, each also belongs to many different groups. Everywhere, to be human means to live with others. In groups, we meet our most basic needs. In groups, we learn a language, customs, and values. We also satisfy our yearning to belong, receive comfort in times of trouble, and find companions who share our dreams and beliefs. Even as we struggle to define our unique identity, those groups attach labels to us that may differ from those we would choose for ourselves. In the book, *the bear that wasn't*, Frank Tashlin uses words and pictures to describe that process.

the bear that wasn't introduces themes and concepts central not only to this chapter but also to subsequent chapters. The reading is abridged from a children's book with many more illustrations. Multiple copies of the book are available in English and French from the Facing History Resource Center.

Once upon a time, in fact it was on a Tuesday, the Bear saw that it was time to go into a cave and hibernate. And that was just what he did. Not long afterward, in fact it was on a Wednesday, lots of workers arrived near that cave. While the Bear slept, they built a great, huge factory.

As winter turned to spring, the Bear awoke and stepped out of his cave. His eyes popped.

Where was the forest?
Where was the grass?
Where were the trees?
Where were the flowers?
WHAT HAD HAPPENED?

"I must be dreaming," he said. "Of course, I'm dreaming." But it wasn't a dream. It was real. Just then the Foreman came out of the factory. "Hey, you get back to work," he said.

The Bear replied, "I don't work here. I'm a Bear."

The Foreman laughed, "That's a fine excuse for a man to keep from doing any work. Saying he's a Bear."

The Bear said, "But, I am a Bear."

The Foreman stopped laughing. He was very mad.

"Don't try to fool me," he said. "You're not a Bear. You're a silly man who needs a shave and wears a fur coat. I'm going to take you to the *General Manager*."

The General Manager also insisted the Bear was a silly man who needs a shave and wears a fur coat.

The Bear said, "No, you're mistaken. I am a Bear."

The General Manager was very mad, too.

The Bear said, "I'm sorry to hear you say that. You see, I am a Bear."

The Third Vice President was even madder.

The Second Vice President was more than mad or madder. He was furious.

The First Vice President yelled in rage.

He said, "You're not a Bear. You're a silly man who needs a shave and wears a fur coat. I'm going to take you to the *President*."

The Bear pleaded, "This is a dreadful error, you know, because ever since I can remember, I've always been a Bear."

And that is exactly what the Bear told the President.

"Thank you for telling me," the President said. "You can't be a Bear. Bears are only in a zoo or a circus. They're never inside a factory and that's where you are; inside a factory. So how can you be a Bear?"

The Bear said, "But I am a Bear."

The President said, "Not only are you a silly man who needs a shave and wears a fur coat, but you are also very stubborn. So I'm going to prove it to you, once and for all, that you are *not* a Bear."

The Bear said, "But I *am* a Bear."

The President packed his vice presidents and the Bear into a car and drove to the zoo. The Bears in the zoo said the Bear was not a Bear, because if he were a Bear, he would be inside a cage.

The Bear said, "But I am a Bear."

So they all left the zoo and drove to the nearest circus.

"Is he a Bear?" the President asked the circus Bears.

The Bears said no. If he were a Bear he would be wearing a little hat with a striped ribbon holding onto a balloon and riding a bicycle.

The Bear said, "But I am a Bear."

When the President and his vice presidents returned to the factory, they put the Bear to work on a big machine with a lot of other men. The Bear worked on the big machine for many, many months.

After a long, long time, the factory closed and all the workers went away. The Bear was the last one left. As he left the shut-down factory, he saw geese flying south and the leaves falling from the trees. Winter was coming, he thought. It was time to hibernate.

He found a cave and was about to enter when he stopped. "I can't go in a cave. I'm NOT a Bear. I'm a silly man who needs a shave and wears a fur coat."

As the days grew colder and the snow fell, the Bear sat shivering with cold. "I wish I were a Bear," he thought.

Then suddenly he got up and walked through the deep snow toward the cave. Inside it was cozy and snug. The icy wind and cold, cold snow couldn't reach him here. He felt warm all over.

He sank down on a bed of pine boughs and soon he was happily asleep and dreaming sweet dreams, just like all bears do, when they hibernate. So even though the

FOREMAN
and the
GENERAL MANAGER
and the
THIRD VICE PRESIDENT
and the
SECOND VICE PRESIDENT
and the
FIRST
VICE PRESIDENT
and the
PRESIDENT
and the
ZOO BEARS
and the
CIRCUS BEARS
had said, he was a silly man who needed a shave and wore a fur coat, I don't think he really believed it. Do you? No indeed, he knew he wasn't a silly man, and he wasn't a silly Bear either.[2]

The Individual and Society **7**

"Who am I?" is a question that each of us asks at some time in our life. In answering, we define ourselves. The word *define* means "to separate one thing from all of the others." What distinguishes the Bear from all other bears? From all other workers at the factory? Create an identity chart for the Bear. The diagram below is an example of an identity chart. Individuals fill it in with the words they call themselves as well as the labels society gives them. What phrases does the Bear use to define himself? What words did others use to define him? Include both on the diagram.

Identity Chart

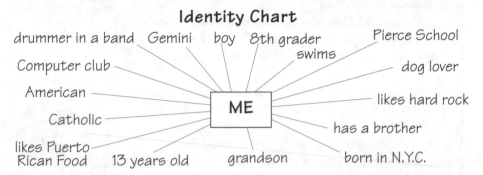

drummer in a band   Gemini   boy   8th grader   Pierce School

swims

Computer club   dog lover

American   **ME**   likes hard rock

Catholic   has a brother

likes Puerto

Rican Food   13 years old   grandson   born in N.Y.C.

Create an identity chart for yourself. Begin with the words or phrases that describe the way you see yourself. Add those words and phrases to your chart. Most people define themselves by using categories important to their culture. They include not only gender, age, and physical characteristics but also ties to a particular religion, class, neighborhood, school, and nation.

Compare your chart with those of your classmates. Which categories were included on every chart? Which appeared on only a few charts? As you look at other charts your perspective may change. You may wish to add new categories to the one you created. This activity allows you to see the world through multiple perspectives. What labels would others attach to you? Do they see you as a leader or a follower? A conformist or a rebel? Are you a peacemaker, a bully, or a bystander? How do society's labels influence the way you see yourself? The kinds of choices you and others make each day? For example, if a person is known as a bully, how likely is he or she to live up to that label?

Throughout this course, you will encounter words that you know but have difficulty explaining. Instead of relying only on a dictionary to define these words, develop your own working definitions. Doing so will help you make those words an integral part of your vocabulary. The following is an example of a working definition that builds to encompass more and more information:

Bureaucracy:
- like a tree or an organization
- a structure that organizes the work of business or government

- the system set up in the factory described in *the bear that wasn't* (foreman—general manager—3rd vice president — and so on.)

You may want to include pictures in your working definition. Often they reveal more about a complex idea than a definition that relies only on words. Draw a picture of a bureaucracy and add it to your working definition. Then create a working definition for the word *identity*. A useful reference is *Visual Thinking* by Rudolf Arnheim (University of California Press, 1969). It suggests new ways of looking at ideas.

What does the title *the bear that wasn't* mean? Why didn't the factory officials recognize the Bear for what he was? Why did it become harder and harder for him to maintain his identity as he moved through the bureaucracy of the factory? What is Tashlin suggesting about the relationship between an individual and society? About the way a person's identity is defined? About the way powerful individuals and groups shape the identity of those with less power and authority?

How does our need to be a part of a group affect our actions? Why is it so difficult for a person to go against the group? Have you ever experienced a similar problem to that of the Bear? How did you deal with it? Were you able to maintain your independence? How difficult was it to do so?

➤ The film, *After the First*, tells of a 12 year-old boy's first hunting trip and the way he and other members of his family responded to the event. It is available from the Facing History Resource Center. The film explores how Steve and each of his parents viewed the trip. This film is the first of many included in the course. Each was chosen to prompt discussion of sophisticated and complex moral issues. As you watch this film and others like it, try not to take sides until you have looked at the issue from each character's perspective. The following questions can be used to guide class discussion or journal writing.

- What does the scene in the kitchen reveal about Steve's personality? His parents' values? How does the viewer know what Steve thinks?

- What is Steve's mood at the beginning of the film? At the end? At what point does his attitude begin to change?

- The relationship between Steve and his father is essential to the film. How is that relationship revealed in these scenes: in the truck on the way to the woods, when Steve learns to use a rifle, when he decides whether to shoot the rabbit, and when the film ends?

- What dilemma did Steve face? What options did he have? What values were associated with each option? How did Steve resolve his dilemma? What motivated his decision? What part did cultural values play in his decision? What other factors influenced it? How hard is it to go against the group? To stand up for the things you believe in?

➤ indicates key videos, books, and other resources. The use of these materials is highly recommended.

- What does the word *values* mean? How do Steve's values affect the way he views the world? The way he acts?

- *After the First* is a parable—a story that has a moral or teaches a lesson. To figure out the moral of the film, ask yourself what lesson Steve's father wanted him to learn. What lesson did his mother want him to learn? How do you know her feelings? What did Steve actually learn? Then decide what the film taught you.

- What do people mean when they say, "Don't be so quick to judge?" How does it apply to the film?

- Make an identity chart for Steve. What words or phrases would he use to describe himself? What words or phrases might his father add to the chart? What might his mother add?

- How does the father's attitude toward hunting apply to violence on a larger scale? (To war, for example.) Are there forms of violence that are not physical?

- Most cultures have rites of passage—ceremonies that mark the beginning of a new stage in a person's life. Many of those rites focus on the passage from childhood to adulthood. A hunting trip is a rite of passage in Steve's family. What event, if any, seems to mark the end of childhood in your family? In your community? Is that rite of passage the same for boys as it is for girls? You may want to research and then compare rites of passage in several different cultures. What do they all have in common? What differences seem most striking? Is there a universal rite of passage?

Sigmund Freud once posed a fateful question for humankind: To what extent can culture overcome the violence caused by the human instincts of aggression and self-destruction? Is there a human instinct of aggression? What insights does *After the First* provide?

READING 2

"Little Boxes"

Categories and labels can help us understand why we act the way we do. But sometimes those labels obscure what is really important about a person. Student Anthony Wright's difficulties in filling in the "little boxes" on an application form explains why reducing individuals to a category can be misleading.

Little Boxes. "How would you describe yourself? (please check one)" Some aren't as cordial. "Ethnic Group": These little boxes and circles bring up an issue for me that threatens my identity. Who am I?

Unlike many others, I cannot answer that question easily when it comes to ethnicity. My mother is Hispanic (for those who consider South American as Hispanic) with an Asian father and my father is white with English and Irish roots. What does that make me? My identity already gets lost when my mother becomes a "Latino" instead of an "Ecuadorean." The cultures of Puerto Rico and Argentina are distinct, even though they are both "Hispanic." The same applies to White, Asian, Native American or Black, all vague terms trying to classify cultures that have sometimes greater disparities inside the classification than with other cultures. Yet I can't even be classified by these excessively broad terms.

My classification problem doesn't stop with my ethnicity. My father is a blue-collar worker, yet the technical work he does is much more than manual labor. My family, through our sweat, brains and savings, have managed to live comfortably. We no longer can really be classified as poor or lower class, but we really aren't middle class. Also, in my childhood my parents became disillusioned with the Catholic religion and stopped going to church. They gave me the option of going or not, but I was lazy and opted to stay in bed late Sunday mornings. Right now I don't even know if I am agnostic, atheist or something else, like transcendentalist. I just don't fit into categories nicely.

My biggest conflict of identity comes from another source: education. In the seventh grade, I was placed in a prep school from P.S. 61. The only similarity between the two institutions is that they are both in the Bronx, yet one is a block away from Charlotte Street, a nationally known symbol of urban decay, while the other is in one of the wealthiest sections of New York City. Prep for Prep, a program for disadvantaged students that starts in the fifth grade, worked with me for fourteen months, bringing me up to the private-school level academically and preparing me socially, but still, the transition was rough. Even in my senior year, I felt like I really did not fit in with the prep school culture. Yet I am totally separated from my neighborhood. My home happens to be situated there, and I might go to the corner bodega for milk and bananas, or walk to the subway station, but that is the extent of my contact with my neighborhood. I regret this, but when more than half the teen-agers are high-school dropouts, and drugs are becoming a major industry there, there is no place for me. Prep for Prep was where I would "hang out" if not at my high school, and it took the place of my neighborhood and has been a valuable cushion. At high school, I was separate from the mainstream majority, but still an inextricable part of it, so I worked there and put my effort into making it a better place.

For a while, I desperately wanted to fit into a category in order to be accepted. Everywhere I went I felt out of place. When I go into the neighborhood restaurant to ask for *arroz y pollo*, my awkward Spanish and gringo accent makes the lady at the counter go in the back for someone who knows English, even though I think I know enough Spanish to survive a conversation. When I was little, and had short straight black hair, I appeared to be one of the few Asians in my school, and was tagged with the stereotype. I went to Ecuador to visit relatives, and they could not agree about whether I was Latino or gringo. When the little boxes appeared on the Achievements, I marked Hispanic even though I had doubts on the subject. At first sight, I can pass as white, and my last name will assure that I will not be persecuted as someone who is dark and has "Rodriguez" as his last name. I chose Hispanic because I most identified with it, because of my Puerto Rican neighborhood that I grew up in, and my mother, who has a big influence on me. However, many people would not consider me a Latino. And by putting just "Hispanic," "White," or "Asian," I felt as if I was neglecting a very essential side of me, and lying in the process. I now put "Other" in those little boxes, and when possible indicate exactly what I am.

I realize now the problem is not with me but with the identification system. The words *Black*, *White*, *Hispanic*, *Asian*, and *Native American*, describe more than one would expect. They describe genealogy, appearance and culture, all very distinct things, which most people associate as one; but there exists many exceptions, like the person who grows up in the Black inner city and adopts that culture, but is white by birth; or the Puerto Rican immigrant with blue eyes and blond hair. Religion can also obscure definitions, as is the case in Israel recently with the label "Jewish," which can be a race, culture or religion, and the definition of being Jewish by birth. The classifications especially get confused when appearance affects the culture, as with non-White cultures due to discrimination. Defining what is "culture;" and the specifics also confuses the issue. For example, it can be argued that almost every American, regardless of race (genealogy), is at least to some degree of the white culture, the "norm" in this country. With more culturally and racially mixed people like myself entering society, these classifications have to be addressed and defined.

My mixture helps me look to issues and ideas from more than one viewpoint, and I like that. Racial, economic, social and religious topics can be looked upon with a special type of objectivity that I feel is unique. I am not objective. I am subjective with more than one bias, so I can see both sides of an argument between a black militant and white conservative, a tenant and a landlord or a Protestant and a Catholic. I will usually side with the underdog, but it is necessary to understand opposing viewpoints in order to take a position. This diversity of self that I have, I enjoy, despite the confusion caused by a society so complex that sweeping generalizations are made. I cannot and don't deserve to be generalized or classified, just like anybody else. My background and position have affected me, but I dislike trying to be treated from that information. I am Anthony E. Wright, and the rest of the information about me should come from what I write, what I say and how I act. Nothing else.[3]

CONNECTIONS

Construct an identity chart for Anthony Wright. How does it help explain why he called his essay "Little Boxes"? Why does he find it so difficult to classify himself? When does a special designation become a box that limits a person?

Psychologist Deborah Tannen writes, "We all know we are unique individuals, but we tend to see others as representatives of groups. It's a natural tendency, since we must see the world in patterns in order to make sense of it; we wouldn't be able to deal with the daily onslaught of people and objects if we couldn't predict a lot about them and feel that we know who and what they are. But this natural and useful ability to see patterns of similarity has unfortunate consequences. It is offensive to reduce an individual to a category, and it is also misleading."[4]

Give examples of the ways that generalizing can be useful. Give examples of its "unfortunate consequences." How does Wright's essay support Tannen's observation?

What is Wright's dilemma? Do you or people you know share that dilemma? If so, how do you or they resolve it? Does the reverse of Wright's dilemma ever cause problems? That is, do people ever feel hurt because their membership in a group is not acknowledged?

How do Tannen's comments help explain why Wright concludes that "I cannot and don't deserve to be generalized or classified, just like anybody else"? Do you share his feelings?

READING 3

"Race" and Science

What things objectively *are* is often less significant to human beings than what things *mean* in cultural frameworks of beliefs, values, and attitudes.

Race is one of the categories people use to identify themselves and others. In biology, *race* refers to those who share a genetic heritage. Most biologists today believe that it is a meaningless concept. As one scientist noted, "Human 'racial' differentiation is, indeed, only skin deep. Any use of racial categories must take its justification from some other source than biology. The remarkable feature of human evolution and history has been the very small degree of divergence between geographical populations as compared with the genetic variation among individuals."[5] Yet these findings have had little effect on popular opinion. Sociologist Allan G. Johnson offers an example to describe the importance individuals and groups in American society have placed on the concept of "race."

Imagine that you apply for a copy of your birth certificate one day, and when you receive it, you discover that it lists your "race" as something other than what you and everyone else always considered it to be. You are black, and the certificate says you are white; or you are white, and it says you are black. How would you feel?

This is exactly what happened in 1977 to Susie Guillory Phipps—a New Orleans resident who had always been white, both to herself and to everyone who encountered her. She had twice married white men, and her family album was filled with pictures of blue-eyed, white ancestors. The state of Louisiana, however, defined her as "colored."

When she protested to state authorities, they carefully traced her ancestry back 222 years, and found that although her great-great-great-great grandfather was white, her great-great-great-great grandmother was black. Under Louisiana law, anyone whose ancestry was at least 3 percent black was considered black. Thus, even with an ancestry 97 percent white, the state defined her as black.

Susie Phipps spent $20,000 to force Louisiana to change her birth certificate, and in 1983 Louisiana repealed the law. Why did she go to such expense? Beyond the obvious shock to her identity, there are larger issues. Why does the state have a formula for officially deciding what each person's race is? Why would a tiny percentage of black ancestry cause her to be considered black, while an overwhelmingly white ancestry would not mean she is white?

The key lies in the word "mean" in the previous sentence, for . . . what things objectively <u>are</u> is often less significant to human beings than what things <u>mean</u> in cultural frameworks of beliefs, values, and attitudes.[6]

Susie Phipps' dilemma has nothing to do with biology and everything to do with the way her society uses the term *race*. Until the mid-1800s, the word had a number of meanings. Sometimes it referred to a whole species—as in "the human race." Sometimes it meant a nation or tribe—as in "the Japanese race or the French race." And sometimes it referred to a family—"the last of his or her race." These usages all imply ties of kinship and suggest that shared characteristics are somehow passed from one generation to the next. These usages also lack precision. So did the way biologists used the term in the mid-1800s.

Nineteenth-century scientists defined *race* as "kind," an identifiably different form of an organism within a species. But as knowledge of genetics expanded, that definition became less and less useful. As a result, one writer wondered why we "have no difficulty at all in telling individuals apart in our own group, but 'they' all look alike." He went on to ask, "[If] we could look at a random sample of different genes, not biased by our socialization, how much difference would there be between major geographical groups, say between Africans and Australian aborigines, as opposed to the differences between individuals within these groups?"[7] To answer that question, a number of scientists have studied genetic variations both within a population and among different populations. Their findings?

> Of all human genetic variation known for enzymes and other proteins, where it has been possible to actually count up the frequencies of different forms of the genes and so get an objective estimate of genetic variation, 85 percent turns out to be between individuals within the same local population, tribe, or nation; a further 8 percent between tribes or nations within a major "race" and the remaining 7 percent is between major "races." That means that the genetic variation between one Spaniard and another, or between one Masai and another, is 85 percent of all human genetic variation, while only 15 percent is accounted for by breaking people into groups.[8]

CONNECTIONS

Like the Bear in *the bear that wasn't*, Susie Phipps was told that she wasn't who she thought she was. Who told her that? How important is that opinion? What does Johnson mean when he says "what things objectively <u>are</u> is often less significant to human beings than what things <u>mean</u> in cultural frameworks of beliefs, values and attitudes"? As you continue reading, look for other examples that support that point of view. Look, too, for evidence that calls it into question.

Anthony Appiah, a professor who teaches Afro-American Studies, points out that even though scientists have proven that the concept of race is invalid, it persists in not only popular culture but also such academic disciplines as history and literature. He maintains, however, that the idea of a collective identity is not inherently wrong. He sees a problem *only* when we begin to assign moral or social rankings to those collective identities. Then, he argues, we must rethink why we divide ourselves into races. How do you explain the continuing acceptance of a meaningless idea? What kind of power do ideas—even mistaken ideas—have to shape the way we see ourselves and others?

Why do you think we have no difficulty in telling individuals apart in our own group, but *they* all look alike—even though there are more genetic variations among *us* than there are between *us* and *them*?

Create a working definition of *race*. Begin with what the word means to you. Then add the meanings explored in this reading. Write a working

Many students use their journals to record their answers to questions raised in Connections. Some keep a "double-entry" journal in which they write responses to key questions on the left side of the page, leaving room on the right for later observations. In this way, they conduct a conversation with themselves.

definition of *racism.* Keep in mind that the ending *ism* refers to a doctrine or principle. You will want to expand both definitions as you complete this chapter and those that follow.

READING 4

Stereotyping

Some sociologists study the effects of the idea of "race" on human behavior. They also explore the impact of ethnicity. An ethnic group is a distinctive group of people within a country. Members share a cultural heritage. Ethnicity can be the basis for feelings of pride and solidarity. But, like race, it can also be the basis for prejudice and discrimination.

The word *prejudice* comes from the word *pre-judge.* We pre-judge when we have an opinion about a person because of a group to which that individual belongs. A prejudice has the following characteristics.

1. It is based on real or imagined differences between groups.

2. It attaches values to those differences in ways that benefit one group at the expense of others.

3. It is generalized to all members of a target group.

Discrimination occurs when prejudices are translated into action. For example, a person who says that all Mexicans are lazy is guilty of prejudice, but one who refuses to hire a Mexican is guilty of discrimination. Not all prejudices result in discrimination. Some are positive. But, whether positive or negative, prejudices have a similar effect—they reduce individuals to categories or stereotypes. A stereotype is a judgment about an individual based on the real or imagined characteristics of a group. Joseph H. Suina, a professor of education and a member of the Cochiti Pueblo, recalls the effects stereotyping had on his behavior in the Marines.

> From the moment my comrades in the military discovered I was an Indian, I was treated differently. My name disappeared. I was no longer Suina, Joseph, or Joe. Suddenly, I was Chief, Indian, or Tonto. Occasionally, I was referred to as Geronimo, Crazy Horse or some other well-known warrior from the past. It was almost always with an affection that develops in a family, but clearly, I was seen in the light of stereotypes that my fellow Marines from around the country had about Native Americans.
>
> Natives were few in the Marine Corps. Occasionally, I'd run across one from another battalion. Sure enough, just like me, each of them was "Chief" or "Indian." Machismo is very important in the Corps and names such as Chief and Crazy Horse were affirmations of very

desirable qualities for those entering combat situations. Good warriors, good fighting men, we were to be skilled in reading the land, notable for our physical prowess, renowned for our bravery. In addition, we were to drink to the point of total inebriation or to be in the midst of a barroom brawl before the night was over. Never permitted to assume leadership, but always in the role of supportive and faithful companion, just like the Lone Ranger's Tonto.

Personally, I was anything but combatant, and my experiences with alcohol had been limited to two or three beers prior to my enlistment. Never in my wildest dreams had I imagined that I would be accorded the characteristics of a noble and reckless warrior. Since these traits were held in such high esteem, I enjoyed the status and acceptance they afforded me among the men. My own platoon commander singled me out to compete in a rope-climbing event at a regimental field meet. After I easily won that contest (my Pueblo life had included a great deal of wood chopping), my stature as chief increased.

I actually began to believe that I had those qualities and started behaving in accord with the stereotypes. Later during my two tours of duty in Vietnam, I played out my expected role quite well. I went on twice as many search and destroy missions as others; I took "the point" more often than anyone else. After all, couldn't I hear, see, smell, and react to signs of the enemy better than any of my comrades? On shore leave, I learned to drink with the best of them and always managed to find trouble.

Almost a full year beyond my four years of enlistment, I was recovered from my second set of wounds and finally discharged. I had earned two purple hearts, a bronze star, the Gallantry Cross (Vietnam's highest military award), and numerous other combat expedition medals. I also had, on my record, time in jails in Japan, the Philippines, and Mexico.[9]

Over twenty years later, Jeanne Park, a student at Stuyvesant High School in New York City, had a similar experience with stereotypes.

Who am I?

For Asian-American students, the answer is a diligent, hard-working and intelligent young person. But living up to this reputation has secretly haunted me.

The labeling starts in elementary school. It's not uncommon for a teacher to remark, "You're Asian, you're supposed to do well in math." The underlying message is, "You're Asian and you're supposed to be smarter."

Not to say being labeled intelligent isn't flattering, because it is, or not to deny that basking in the limelight of being top of my class isn't ego-boosting, because frankly it is. But at a certain point, the pressure became crushing. I felt as if doing poorly on my next spelling quiz would stain the exalted reputation of all Asian students forever.

So I continued to be an academic overachiever, as were my friends. By junior high school I started to believe I was indeed smarter. I became condescending toward non-Asians. I was a bigot; all my friends were Asians. The thought of intermingling occurred rarely if ever.

My elitist opinion of Asian students changed, however, in high school. As a student at what is considered one of the nation's most competitive science and math schools, I found that being on top is no longer an easy feat.

I quickly learned that Asian students were not smarter. How could I ever have believed such a thing? All around me are intelligent, ambitious people who are not only Asian but white, black and Hispanic.

Superiority complexes aside, the problem of social segregation still exists in the schools. With few exceptions, each race socializes only with its "own kind."

Students see one another in the classroom, but outside the classroom there remains distinct segregation.

Racist lingo abounds. An Asian student who socializes only with other Asians is believed to be an Asian Supremacist or, at the very least, arrogant and closed off. Yet an Asian student who socializes only with whites is called a "twinkie," one who is yellow on the outside but white on the inside.

A white teenager who socializes only with whites is thought of as prejudiced, yet one who socializes with Asians is considered an "egg," white on the outside and yellow on the inside.

These culinary classifications go on endlessly, needless to say, leaving many confused, and leaving many more fearful than ever of social experimentation. Because the stereotypes are accepted almost unanimously, they are rarely challenged. Many develop harmful stereotypes of entire races. We label people before we even know them.

Labels learned at a young age later metamorphose into more visible acts of racism. For example, my parents once accused and ultimately fired a Puerto Rican cashier, believing she had stolen $200 from the register at their grocery store. They later learned it was a mistake. An Asian shopkeeper nearby once beat a young Hispanic youth who worked there with a baseball bat because he believed the boy to be lazy and dishonest.

We all hold misleading stereotypes of people that limit us as individuals in that we cheat ourselves out of the benefits different cultures can contribute. We can grow and learn from each culture whether it be Chinese, Korean or African-American.

Just recently some Asian boys in my neighborhood were attacked by a group of young white boys who have christened themselves the Master Race. Rather than being angered by this act, I feel pity for this generation that lives in a state of bigotry.

It may be too late for our parents' generation to accept that each person can only be judged for the characteristics that set him or her apart as an individual. We, however, can do better.[10]

CONNECTIONS

In 1993, the *Los Angeles Times* printed an interview with a group of teenagers on their use of stereotypes. A high-school freshman told the reporter, "I don't mean to stereotype but sometimes I judge people by first impressions. Once, I stereotyped a white girl because I thought she was acting black to make friends. Once I got to know her, I learned she was a sweet person and that she acted the way she did because she had grown up around blacks. That changed my mind." How is a stereotype like a first impression? How is it different? How do stereotypes affect relationships at your school? At home? On the street? How do they affect the way you see yourself? The way you view others?

What did Suina learn from his experiences with stereotyping? What did Jeanne Park learn? How did their experiences shape their identity?

This reading describes three characteristics of prejudice. Which characteristic or characteristics are reflected in Suina's experiences as a Marine? In Park's experiences? In your own experiences?

In *The House on Mango Street,* Sandra Cisneros writes of "those who don't know better." What is she saying about the way prejudices shape our perceptions of *us* and *them*?

Those who don't know any better come into our neighborhood scared. They think we're dangerous. They think we will attack them with shiny knives. They are stupid people who are lost and got here by mistake.

But we aren't afraid. We know the guy with the crooked eye is Davey the Baby's brother, and the tall one next to him in the straw brim, that Rosa's Eddie V. and the big one that looks like a dumb grown man, he's Fat Boy, though he's not fat anymore nor a boy.

All brown all around, we are safe. But watch us drive into a neighborhood of another color and our knees go shakity-shake and our car windows get rolled up tight and our eyes look straight. Yeah. That is how it goes and goes.[11]

Write a working definition of the following terms: *ethnic group, prejudice, discrimination, stereotype.* You will want to add to those definitions throughout the course.

➤In *The Survival of Sontheary Sou,* a Cambodian immigrant describes the difficulties she faced as a result of the assumptions people made about her. The video is available from the Facing History Resource Center, as is a bibliography of multicultural literature.

➤The video, *Eye of the Storm* documents a unique lesson taught by a third-grade teacher in a small Iowa town. Jane Elliott divided her students into two groups based on the color of their eyes. The film details what happened next. *A Class Divided*, an expanded version of *Eye of the Storm*, includes a meeting Elliott had with her former students in 1985 to discuss how the experiment affected their lives. It also shows the outcome of a similar experiment, this time with adults at a correctional facility. Both videos are available from the Facing History Resource Center. As you watch either film, think about the lesson the experiment teaches. What does it suggest about the meanings we assign to differences? About the way stereotypes shape our view of ourselves and others?

READING 5

Legacies

Maya Angelou is an artist whose life defies labels. She is a novelist, poet, actor, composer, director, and civil rights activist. She is also a woman with a strong sense of identity. In an interview, she spoke of the people who helped her make the most of her unique talents and skills. She particularly recalled her uncle Willie.

I think that the courage to confront evil and turn it by dint of will into something applicable in the development of our evolution, individually and collectively is exciting, honorable.

> I was sent to him when I was three from California and he and my grandmother owned the only black-owned store in the town. He was obliged to work in the store, but he was severely crippled. So he needed me to help, and my brother. So at about four he started us to learn to read and write and do our times tables. In order to get me to do my times tables, he would take me behind my neck—my clothes—and stand me in front of a pot-bellied stove. And he would say, "Now, sister, do your sixes." I did my sixes. I did my sevens. Even now, after an evening of copious libation, I can be awakened at eleven o'clock at night and asked, "Will you do your elevenses?" I do my elevenses with alacrity.
>
> A few years ago my uncle died, and I went to Little Rock and was met by Miss Daisy Bates. She told me, "Girl, there's somebody who wants to meet you." I said that I'd be glad to meet whoever. She said, "Good looking man." I said, "Indeed, yes, certainly." So that evening she brought a man over to the hotel. He said, "I don't want to shake your hand. I want to hug you." And I agreed. He said, "You know, Willie has died in Stamps [Arkansas]." Well, now Stamps is very near to Texas. And Little Rock, when I was growing up, was as exotic as Cairo, Egypt, Buda and Pest. This man knew where Stamps was, and my crippled uncle?

He said, "Because of your uncle Willie I am who I am today." He said, "In the '20s, I was the only child of a blind mother. Your uncle gave me a job in your store, made me love to learn, and taught me my times tables." I asked him how did he do that and he said, "He used to grab me [by the neck]." He said, "I guess you want to know who I am today."

"Yes, sir."

He said, "I'm Bussick, vice-mayor of Little Rock, Arkansas." He went on to become the first black mayor of Little Rock, Arkansas.

He said, "When you get down to Stamps, look up" and he gave me the name of a lawyer. He said, "He's a good old boy. He will look after you properly." I went down expecting a middle-aged black man, and a young white man leapt to his feet. He said, "Miss Angelou, I am just delighted to meet you. Why you don't understand. Mr. Bussick called me today. Mr. Bussick is the most powerful black man in the state of Arkansas, but more important than that, he's a noble man. Because of Mr. Bussick, I am who I am today." I said, "Let me sit down first."

He said, "I was an only child of a blind mother, and when I was eleven years old, Mr. Bussick got hold of me and made me love to learn. And I'm now in the State Legislature."

That which lives after us. I look back at Uncle Willie: crippled, black, poor, unexposed to the worlds of great ideas, who left for our generation and generations to come a legacy so rich. . . .

We need the courage to create ourselves daily. To be bodacious enough to create ourselves daily. As Christians, as Jews, as Muslims, as thinking, caring, laughing, loving human beings. I think that the courage to confront evil and turn it by dint of will into something applicable to the development of our evolution, individually and collectively is exciting, honorable.[12]

CONNECTIONS

What is a *legacy*? What legacy did Uncle Willie leave? How did it affect Maya Angelou? The first black mayor of Little Rock? The young white lawyer Uncle Willie never met? Has anyone in your life left a similar legacy? If so, what difference has that legacy made in your life? In the lives of others in your community?

What does Angelou mean when she says, "I think that the courage to confront evil and turn it by dint of will into something applicable in the development of our evolution, individually and collectively is exciting, honorable"? What does the statement suggest about the way she defines *courage*? The ways she defines *creativity*?

➤The interview with Maya Angelou is included on a video entitled *Facing Evil with Bill Moyers*. It is available from the Facing History Resource

Center. Moyers also interviewed Angelou for a television series on creativity. It, too, can be ordered from the Resource Center. At one point in the program, Moyers reminds his audience of all the people who have made a difference in Angelou's life. "They signified her worth. They said, 'You matter,' they turned her suffering rage upward and brought the poet to life. It is not a scientifically certifiable fact that each child born into the world comes with the potential to create. It is rather a statement of faith. But I can't imagine any declaration more important for our society to make. Where our heart is, so too perhaps our treasure." What is Moyers saying about the relationship between an individual and society? About their mutual responsibilities?

Among the people who made a difference in Angelou's life was a neighbor that young Maya knew as "Mrs. Flowers." She helped the child regain the voice she lost as a result of a trauma. Who are the people who have helped you find your voice? How is one's voice related to his or her self-esteem?

If you were to interview Maya Angelou, what questions would you like to ask about her uncle and his legacy? What experiences would you share with her? Record both in your journal. You may want to read her books and poems to see if you can find answers to your questions.

R E A D I N G   6

Finding One's Voice

*I*n a series of television programs that explore creativity, Bill Moyers states that "in classrooms and in schools everywhere, the urge to create is lying in each [child] like a seed in the spring soil." In how many, he wonders, will the ground "never be touched by the season's warmth." He goes on to say, "I think it is true, as wiser men than I have noted, that the suppression of this life within us lies at the base of so much of today's waste, violence and mindless cruelty, for the artist, the craftsman, is not necessarily the more gifted among us but the more fortunate."[13]

Julius Lester, a noted author and college professor, has also reflected on the way violence and humiliation affected his own life.

> I grew up in the forties and fifties in Kansas City, Kansas, and Nashville, Tennessee, with summers spent in Arkansas. The forties and fifties were not pleasant times for blacks and I am offended by white people who get nostalgic for the fifties. I have no nostalgia for segregation, for the "No Colored Allowed" signs covering the landscape like litter on the smooth, green grass of a park, I have no nostalgia for a time when I endangered my life if, while downtown

Who we are by the sociological and political definitions of society has little to do with who we are.

shopping with my parents, I raised my eyes and accidentally met the eyes of a white woman. Black men and boys were lynched for this during my childhood and adolescence.[14]

Lester describes the way he survived those years.

I grew up in a violent world. Segregation was a deathly spiritual violence, not only in its many restrictions on where we could live, eat, go to school, and go after dark. There was also the constant threat of physical death if you looked at a white man in what he considered the wrong way or if he didn't like your attitude. There was also the physical violence of my community. . . . What I have realized is that on those nights I lay in bed reading westerns and detective novels, I was attempting to neutralize and withstand the violence that was so much a part of my dailiness. In westerns and mysteries I found a kind of mirror in which one element of my world—violence—was isolated and made less harmful to me."

Not surprisingly, Lester found his voice in a book.

One of the pivotal experiences of my life came when I was eighteen. I wandered into a bookstore in downtown Nashville one frosted, gray day in late autumn aware that I was looking for something: I was looking for myself, and I generally find myself while wandering through a bookstore, looking at books until I find the one that is calling me. On this particular day I wandered for quite a while until I picked up a paperback with the word *Haiku* on the cover. What is that? I wondered. I opened the book and read,

On a withered branch
a crow has settled—
autumn nightfall.

I trembled and turned the pages hastily until my eyes stopped on these words:

A giant firefly;
that way, this way, that way, this—
and it passes by.

I read more of the brief poems, these voices from seventeenth-century Japan, and I knew: This is my voice. This simplicity, this directness, this way of using words to direct the soul to silence and beyond. This is my voice! I exulted inside. Then I stopped. How could I, a little colored kid from Nashville, Tennessee—and that is all I knew myself to be in those days like perpetual death knells—how could I be feeling that something written in seventeenth-century Japan could be my voice?

I almost put the book back, but that inner prompting which had led me to it would not allow such an act of self-betrayal. I bought the book and began writing haiku, and the study of haiku led to the study of Zen Buddhism, which led to the study of flower arranging, and I suspect I am still following the path that opened to me on that day when I was eighteen, though I no longer write haiku.

I eventually understood that it made perfect sense for a little colored kid from Nashville, Tennessee, to recognize his voice in seventeenth-century Japanese poetry. Who we are by the sociological and political definitions of society has little to do with who we are.

In the quiet and stillness that surrounds us when we read a book, we are known to ourselves in ways we are not when we are with people. We enter a relationship of intimacy with the writer, and if the writer has written truly and if we give ourselves over to what is written, we are given the gift of ourselves in ways that surprise and catch the soul off guard.[15]

CONNECTIONS

Lester says, "Who we are by the sociological and political definitions of society has little to do with who we are." Review your identity chart (Reading 1). Does your chart support his view?

Why does Lester describe segregation as a "deathly spiritual violence"? Some people believe that violence is only physical. Can words be violent? Can they cause violence?

What does Lester mean when he says he found his "voice in seventeenth-century Japanese poetry"? What kind of voice is it? Is it his conscience telling him the right thing to do or a voice that defines who he is? What is the connection between one's voice and his or her identity? What part does one's voice play in shaping an identity?

What lessons did Lester learn from the society in which he grew up? What barriers did society place in the way of his becoming the kind of person he wanted to be? How did he overcome those barriers?

To what degree are we bound by our culture? By the way we were socialized? The way we were educated?

What book has had an impact on you? What film?

Like Lester, Jimmy Santiago Baca is a writer who has experienced prejudice and discrimination. He is a Chicano who has lived amid violence for much of his life. But unlike Lester, he spent little time reading or writing until he went to prison. There he began to do both. When an interviewer asked what prompted him to change, Baca replied, "If I hadn't written in prison, I would still be in prison. . . . I had to go back to my tablet and write in order to find a deeper understanding than the immediate satisfaction or gratification." He went on to say, "The only way to learn is to write and write until you are able to come really close to the way you see life." The word *see* has special meaning for Baca.

> The way the Indians say "seeing" is how close you can come to the way things really are, the way a deer sees a rock, or the way a frog sees water; we call that "seeing." Every human being has that seeing in them, and someone who gets up and writes every day, all he or she is trying to do is to get close to his or her seeing capabilities; that's where the good poems come, when you are able to see. No class is going to teach you that. Luci Tapahonso is a good example. Her poetry could not have been written by anyone but her. She sees things and she has to use her Navajo culture and this other culture and the English language. She has to put them together in such a way that is Luci Tapahonso and only her. She can read all the books she likes to, but nothing is going to teach her her own voice.[16]

How is Baca's use of the word *see* similar to what Julius Lester calls *voice*? How is *seeing*, in Baca's sense of the word, like *empathy*—the ability to walk in someone else's shoes? Are you able to "see" in Baca's sense of the word? If so, describe the experience. How did it make you feel? Did it take courage?

James F. Gilligan, a professor of psychiatry and the clinical director of a prison mental heath service, states, "I have yet to see a serious act of violence that was not provoked by the experience of feeling shamed and humiliated, disrespected and ridiculed, and that did not represent the attempt to prevent or undo this 'loss of face'—no matter how severe the punishment, even if it includes death."[17] How do his comments relate to Lester's description of segregation? Look for other examples as you read. What do they suggest about the relationship between respect and self-esteem?

READING 7

Fear

Not everyone is able to find his or her voice. In a short story entitled "Fear," Gary Soto writes about a boy who had to deal with shame.

> A cold day after school. Frankie T., who would drown his brother by accident that coming spring and would use a length of pipe to beat a woman in a burglary years later, had me pinned on the ground behind a backstop, his breath sour as meat left out in the sun. "*Cabron*," he called me and I didn't say anything. I stared at his face, shaped like the sole of a shoe, and just went along with the insults, although now and

then I tried to raise a shoulder in a halfhearted struggle because that was part of the game.

He let his drool yo-yo from his lips, missing my feet by only inches, after which he giggled and called me names. Finally he let me up. I slapped grass from my jacket and pants, and pulled my shirt tail from my pants to shake out the fistful of dirt he had stuffed in my collar. I stood by him, nervous and red-faced from struggling, and when he suggested that we climb the monkey bars together, I followed him quietly to the kid's section of Jefferson Elementary. He climbed first, with small grunts, and for a second I thought of running but knew he would probably catch me—if not then, the next day. There was no way out of being a fifth grader—the daily event of running to teachers to show them your bloody nose. It was just a fact, like having lunch.

So I climbed the bars and tried to make conversation, first about the girls in our classroom and then about kickball. He looked at me smiling as if I had a camera in my hand, his teeth green like the underside of a rock, before he relaxed his grin into a simple gray line across his face. He told me to shut up. He gave me a hard stare and I looked away to a woman teacher walking to her car and wanted very badly to yell for help. She unlocked her door, got in, played with her face in the visor mirror while the engine warmed, and then drove off with the blue smoke trailing. Frankie was watching me all along and when I turned to him, he laughed, *"Chale!* She can't help you, *ese."* He moved closer to me on the bars and I thought he was going to hit me; instead he put his arm around my shoulder, squeezing firmly in friendship. "C'mon, chicken, let's be cool."

I opened my mouth and tried to feel happy as he told me what he was going to have for Thanksgiving. "My Mamma's got a turkey and ham, lots of potatoes, yams, and stuff like that. I saw it in the refrigerator. And she says we gonna get some pies. Really, *ese."*

Poor liar, I thought, smiling as we clunked our heads softly like good friends. He had seen the same afternoon program on TV as I had, one in which a woman in an apron demonstrated how to prepare a Thanksgiving dinner. I knew he would have tortillas and beans, a round steak, maybe, and oranges from his backyard. He went on describing his Thanksgiving, then changed over to Christmas—the new bicycle, the clothes, the G.I. Joes. I told him that it sounded swell, even though I knew he was making it all up. His mother would in fact stand in line at the Salvation Army to come away hugging armfuls of toys that had been tapped back into shape by reformed alcoholics with veined noses. I pretended to be excited and asked if I could come over to his place to play after Christmas. "Oh, yeah, anytime," he said, squeezing my shoulder and clunking his head against mine.

When he asked what I was having for Thanksgiving, I told him that we would probably have a ham with pineapple on the top. My family was slightly better off than Frankie's, though I sometimes walked around with cardboard in my shoes and socks with holes big enough to be ski masks, so holidays were extravagant happenings. I told him about the candied yams, the frozen green beans, and the pumpkin pie.

His eyes moved across my face as if he were deciding where to hit me—nose, temple, chin, talking mouth—and then he lifted his arm from my shoulder and jumped from the monkey bars, grunting as he landed. He wiped sand from his knees while looking up and warned me not to mess around with him any more. He stared with such a great meanness that I had to look away. He warned me again and then walked away. Incredibly relieved, I jumped from the bars and ran looking over my shoulder until I turned onto my street.

Frankie scared most of the school out of its wits and even had girls scampering out of view when he showed himself on the playground. If he caught us without notice, we grew quiet and stared down at our shoes until he passed after a threat or two. If he pushed us down, we stayed on the ground with our eyes closed and pretended we were badly hurt. If he riffled through our lunch bags, we didn't say anything. He took what he wanted, after which we sighed and watched him walk away after peeling an orange or chewing big chunks of an apple.

Still, that afternoon when he called Mr. Koligian, our teacher, a foul name—we grew scared for him. Mr. Koligian pulled and tugged at his body until it was in his arms and then out of his arms as he hurled Frankie against the building. Some of us looked away because it was unfair. We knew the house he lived in: The empty refrigerator, the father gone, the mother in a sad bathrobe, the beatings, the yearnings for something to love. When a teacher manhandled him, we all wanted to run away, but instead we stared and felt shamed. Robert, Adele, Yolanda shamed; Danny, Alfonso, Brenda shamed; Nash, Margie, Rocha shamed. We all watched him flop about as Mr. Koligian shook and grew red from anger. We knew his house and, for some, it was the same one to walk home to: The broken mother, the indifferent walls, the refrigerator's glare which fed the people no one wanted.[18]

CONNECTIONS

Some psychologists believe that bullies victimize others because they have been victimized. Does Soto's short story support that theory?

If bullies and their victims are linked, is it fear that connects them? Is it shame? Or is it anger? Gary Soto calls his story "Fear." Why do you think he chose that title?

When Professor James Gilligan asked prisoners why they committed a particular assault, he was frequently told that it was "because he disrespected me" or "he disrespected my visit" (meaning "visitor"). He goes on to say, "In fact, the word 'disrespect' is so central in the vocabulary, and therefore in the moral value system and the psychodynamics, of these chronically violent people, that they have abbreviated it into the slang term, 'he dis'ed me.' "[19] How do his comments apply to Frankie? What title do you think Gilligan would choose for this story?

Gary Soto's short stories are based on his memories of his youth in a primarily Mexican American community. To what extent are his experiences unique? To what extent are they universal? How does this story support Julius Lester's belief that "who we are by the sociological and political definitions of society has little to do with who we are"? (Reading 6)

A student named Jonah Kadish reflects on the links between victims and victimizers:

> When I was younger, my best friend and I knew this other kid who wanted to be with us and have us like him. We pushed him around a lot and sometimes beat him up, we teased him and even went so far as to call him the Evil Alien in stories we wrote and read in front of the whole class. He did absolutely nothing back at us and that made us feel even stronger and as though we could keep on doing it, until he said stop. Even though the teachers and our parents tried to get us to stop, we felt justified in continuing, until he stood up for himself, which he never, ever did.
>
> The funny thing was that when I was alone with him, walking from school, I would say "Sorry" and he'd just shrug his shoulders. I would think then that he was actually stronger and more mature than we were, and I still think that, because then he would still talk to me after the day was over and seemed to like me. But the next day, I would join in with my friend again, teasing him and trying not to lose my place as one of the strongest boys in the class.
>
> This still bothers me, that I was so mean to him. I really feel guilty now when I am mean to someone. But this taught me some hard lessons helping me to understand that the physically strong are not always the strongest; what you see on the outside is not the whole truth about a person. Just looking at the outside not the inside makes a person prejudiced and prejudice in turn is a form of hate.[20]

In reflecting on his behavior, Kadish calls it a "funny thing" that he is sorry for teasing and pushing "the other kid" and yet continued to do so. How do you explain his behavior?

Kadish asks if there is a connection between power and hatred. How do you think Gary Soto would respond to that question? How would you answer it? You may wish to record your responses in your journal so that you can refer to them later in the course.

Kadish doesn't want to lose his place "as one of the strongest boys in the class." Yet he believes the "other kid" is stronger than he is. What does he mean? Do you agree with his assessment?

The students in Frankie's class feared him. Yet they felt only shame when their teacher attacked him. How do you account for their response? How might you have felt?

How did his classmates see Frankie? How did their teacher see him? Which came closest to what Jimmy Baca meant when he called seeing "how close you can come to the way things really are"?

➤Is it true that "sticks and stones can break my bones but names can never hurt me"? In the film *Names Can Really Hurt Us*, New York City teens talk about their experiences as victims of bigotry. Within the safety of the group, they share their anger at being victimized and their guilt for the times they hurt others with thoughtless or cruel remarks. The video can be ordered from the Facing History Resource Center. Also available is a similar video featuring a group of students in Chicago. That video is entitled *Facing History and Ourselves: Chicago Students Confront Hatred and Discrimination.*

➤Kadish appears on a videotape entitled *A Discussion with Elie Wiesel: Facing History Students Confront Hatred and Violence.* The tape and a study guide are available from the Facing History Resource Center.

READING 8

The "In" Group

*E*ve Shalen, a high-school student, reflected on her need to belong.

My eighth grade consisted of 28 students most of whom knew each other from the age of five or six. The class was close-knit and we knew each other so well that most of us could distinguish each other's handwriting at a glance. Although we grew up together, we still had class outcasts. From second grade on, a small elite group spent a large portion of their time harassing two or three of the others. I was one of those two or three, though I don't know why. In most cases when children get picked on, they aren't good at sports or they read too much or they wear the wrong clothes or they are of a different race. But in my class, we all read too much and didn't know how to play sports. We had also been brought up to carefully respect each other's races. This is what was so strange about my situation. Usually, people are made outcasts because they are in some way different from the larger group. But in my class, large differences did not exist. It was as if the outcasts were invented by the group out of a need for them. Differences between us did not cause hatred; hatred caused differences between us.

Often being accepted by others is more satisfying than being accepted by oneself, even though the satisfaction does not last. Too often our actions are determined by the moment.

The harassment was subtle. It came in the form of muffled giggles when I talked, and rolled eyes when I turned around. If I was out in the playground and approached a group of people, they often fell silent. Sometimes someone would not see me coming and I would catch the tail end of a joke at my expense.

I also have a memory of a different kind. There was another girl in our class who was perhaps even more rejected than I. She also tried harder than I did for acceptance, providing the group with ample material for jokes. One day during lunch I was sitting outside watching a basketball game. One of the popular girls in the class came up to me to show me something she said I wouldn't want to miss. We walked to a corner of the playground where a group of three or four sat. One of them read aloud from a small book, which I was told was the girl's diary. I sat down and, laughing till my sides hurt, heard my voice finally blend with the others. Looking back, I wonder how I could have participated in mocking this girl when I knew perfectly well what it felt like to be mocked myself. I would like to say that if I were in that situation today I would react differently, but I can't honestly be sure. Often being accepted by others is more satisfying than being accepted by oneself, even though the satisfaction does not last. Too often our actions are determined by the moment.[21]

CONNECTIONS

How important is peer pressure to the way we see ourselves and others? How did Eve Shalen's need to belong shape her identity? How did it affect the way she responded when another girl was mocked? Why does her response still trouble her? How do you like to think you would have responded to the incident?

Shalen concludes, "Often being accepted by others is more satisfying than being accepted by oneself, even though the satisfaction does not last." What does she mean? How is her story like that of the Bear in *the bear that wasn't*? How is it different?

"Hatred begins in the heart and not in the head. In so many instances we do not hate people because of a particular deed, but rather we find that deed ugly because we hate them."[22] How do Shalen's experiences support the statement? What experiences might call the statement into question?

In Japan, students labeled as *"itanshi"*—odd or different—are often subject to bullying by classmates. In 1992, the Japanese reported at least thirteen bullying-related murders at junior and senior high schools. "Children bully other children everywhere, of course," said Masatoshi Fukuda, head of the All-Japan Bullying Prevention Council. "But in Japan it is worse because the system itself seems to encourage the punishment of anyone who does not conform to social norms." A fifteen-year-old girl, for example, was beaten to death in Toyonaka City after months of enduring insults for wearing hand-me-down public school uniforms. Her assailant told police, "She was an irritation in our faces. . . she dressed poorly when all other students have new uniforms every year."[23]

What does the girl's assailant mean when he says "She was an irritation in our faces"? Who is most likely to be a victim of bullying in our society?

A high-school student who was born in Cambodia wrote the following stanza in a poem called "You Have to Live in Somebody Else's Country to Understand." Compare it with the views expressed in this reading.

> What is it like to be an outsider?
> What is it like to sit in the class where everyone has blond hair and you have black hair?
> What is it like when the teacher says, "Whoever wasn't born here raise your hand."
> And you are the only one.
> Then, when you raise your hand, everybody looks at you and makes fun of you.
> You have to live in somebody else's country to understand.[24]

➤The animated film, *Up Is Down*, looks at the world from the vantage point of a boy who walks on his head. It describes the attempts of the adults to make the boy conform to their point of view. The video is available from the Facing History Resource Center. Also available is another animated video, *Is It Always Right to Be Right?* It explores what happens to a society when various groups claim to be "right." Eve Shalen appears in the video, *A Discussion with Elie Wiesel: Facing History Students Confront Hatred and Violence.*

READING 9

Conformity and Identity

Most people want to belong, but for some, like Brandon Carson, the price of membership is too high. He writes:

> I like who I am. I have come to accept myself on psychological as well as physical terms. I not only like myself, I like everyone around me. Today, for some gays and especially our youth, that is really hard to say. To learn to accept yourself as you are, and then to start liking yourself completely, is an obstacle some people never overcome. That alone is tough, but to finally do that and then start living a complete and fulfilling life is really too much, isn't it? Is it really too much to ask, for us to be able to go out into society and hold jobs and pursue careers and live the "American Dream"? Should we stay closeted and have to

hide our feelings, forever living in a make-believe world, hoping that no one finds out about us? The pressure is inevitably on at full force, and even the smallest decisions could radically change our lives.

At sixteen, Carson decided to stop pretending and accept himself. His family and friends had more difficulty doing so. Carson still recalls the way a close friend responded. At the time, the two boys were sharing a post-office box.

I received a package one day that was torn at the edges. [My friend] didn't really think any harm could be done by opening the package, so he did. The package contained some books on gay youth that I had ordered. Now the cat was out of the bag.

He asked me about it and I decided to stop denying it. I came out to my best friend. I told him I was a homosexual, and that I was receiving literature about it. At this stage of my life it is still too painful to discuss the consequences of his rejection. I haven't gotten over the loss of my friend yet, and I probably never will. But I've learned some real valuable lessons about life, and I've learned them early, hopefully to prevent any further losses. I've learned people are unique in their own peculiar ways and I've learned that most people are more readily able to accept old ways than they are able to accept new ones.

I could go on and discuss the loss of my friend, the painful nights crying and wondering, the disgusted looks he gave me at school, and the fact that I had to face pain too early. But why should I tell what each person has to learn by himself. . . . Everyone experiences pain, the emptiness of losing someone you love very much. But why should we be tormented and ridiculed? There are so many unanswered questions. Maybe someday, someone will realize what a ridiculous predicament society puts homosexuals in. Until then, I guess we must keep the faith and never stop fighting.[25]

CONNECTIONS

Make an identity chart for Brandon Carson. How does it explain why he found it so painful to come to terms with his identity?

Carson wonders, "Why should we be tormented and ridiculed?" How would you answer his question? What does it suggest about the way society shapes an individual's identity? About the difficulty of going against the group?

Eve Shalen (Reading 8) maintains that "usually people are made outcasts because they are in some way different from the larger group." Do you agree? How do Carson's experiences support your view? How do his experiences call your opinion into question?

Carson writes of the pain of rejection. It is a universal experience in that almost everyone experiences that pain at one time or another. Why does it hurt to be rejected? Are all rejections equally painful? Or do some hurt more than others? How did Carson handle rejection? How do you and your friends handle it? What strategies seem to be most effective?

READING 10

In the Barrio

*I*n reflecting on his experiences with stereotypes, Professor Joseph Suina wrote, "It was clear that I had become what I was expected to become. The power of stereotypes on those they are directed at is not minimal in its effect. I often wonder what happens to the many children in classrooms who are expected not to succeed because of their racial or ethnic heritage."[26] Amelia Valdez, a college student, provides an answer to that question:

> Growing up in the barrio was a protected life. It protected me from the dangers of the outside world. The outside world did not exist, but the oppression of it did. The barrio was a family within a family. Everyone around me was either an aunt or uncle or some distant cousin. The rest of the barrio was just there. We never spoke to each other except to say hello.
>
> There were always boundaries that I could not cross within the barrio. We were all from the same race, but there was a constant struggle for possession. There was a territory called the "ghost town," an area that everyone was afraid of. It had nothing to do with ghosts, but the people that lived there were seen as ghosts. There was a gang in the ghost town made up of Chicanos, and these people did not fear death. Every weekend someone would be shot or killed because someone overstepped the boundaries. The whole barrio did not have time to get scared because the violence was happening so fast. It was a place that felt like time was passing it by, and the fighting was a constant struggle for survival. It reminded me of a place that has no ending, like falling into a black hole.
>
> We live on the side of the "Casianos" because this is the name of the park that we live in front of. The ghost town Chicanos did not mix with the Casianos Chicanos. The Casianos also had a gang, and these two groups did not mix or talk to each other. My brothers and cousins were in the Casianos gang. There is a creek with a bridge that separated the two areas, and there was always trouble between the two groups. There was one incident that I will never forget. My mother and I were

taking a shortcut through the ghost town. We crossed the bridge over to our side, and the Casianos Chicanos on our side were watching us cross. My house was about a half mile from the bridge, and in order to get to my house you needed to cross the park. As we were walking along, the ghost town Chicanos (the gang) started shooting at us, but my mother kept saying, "Run and don't stop until you reach the house." I kept hearing the bullets hitting the ground next to me. My heart kept beating faster as we approached the house, and my mother kept dragging me until we got to the house. I felt my mother sweat as she held my hand. But she held on and did not show any signs of fear. The guys on our side were returning fire, which led to some injuries on the other side. My mother called the police, but they never arrived, which was typical of them. The only way fights got resolved was by revenge. The next strike would be ours. These kinds of incidents always happened, and we lived in fear day by day. I never knew why these gangs were always fighting, but the fights were carried on from past generations. The gangs were at their strongest while I was growing up, and the only way to survive was to be in one. My brothers were always being pressured into joining. It was a sign of being "macho." The gang members were always angry, and their faces were so tight from the anger. I remember my brother being shot once and nearly dying. There were always fights and gangs seeking revenge. The fights were endless, and I lost cousins and uncles, killed by other gangs. It is sad to know that even within the same race problems still existed.

The barrio taught me to survive in a world where you don't know what is going to happen. It prepared me for the struggles of daily life and the unexpected. It taught me to be strong when there was crisis. It also taught me to believe in myself. In the barrio you do not plan your goals; you just take them as they come. It is a constant struggle with life because you do not know what is going to happen the next day. It was a prep school for life, and the experiences were your grades. Nobody pays for this school but you. . . .

The barrio always made me feel safe, but sometimes I felt the anger of being trapped. Even though I survived this seclusion, I did not know how the rest of the world lived. As a child, I felt the frustration of the barrio. Jobs were very limited, and the people did not have very many skills. There were always constant fights within families due to lack of income. There were some alcohol problems, which made things worse. It helped the people forget the problems and the frustrations. . . .

Living in the barrio was a no-win situation because when someone tried to improve themselves or learn something different they would be hated. This was part of growing up in the barrio; you either learn to deal with it or get out. I hated that fact that people would actually get beaten up for trying to improve themselves. If you were caught reading or showing any interest in school, you were considered a "sissy." I can't believe the things I had to put up with living in the barrio. Some days I would love it, and some days I would hate it. In junior high school I remember being chased after school by a girl who hated my guts.

She actually waited to beat me up and chase me around this fenced-in swimming pool. Around and around I went like a fool trying to escape from this madwoman. And, of course, no one was around to save me. Finally, I would get away on my own, but I did not look forward to the next day because of the fear of being beaten again. I don't know how I survived, but it was not easy.

I was always angry at myself for not running away farther. How could I escape from an angry barrio that protected itself from invasion by others? The barrio protected what was theirs and then some. So sometimes people took what was not theirs, but there were reasons why. Did we get a raw deal because we were different? Did we deserve to be isolated from others? I think the barrio had the right to be angry ever since the land got divided and was given to someone else. I am talking about the history of oppression of past generations. The land was taken away from my ancestors by the dividing of Mexico and Texas. The fighting continues on a sublevel; we make it better for future generations to survive without struggle. . . .

I believe in myself and my people, who are rising very rapidly. My family had a lot to do with my beliefs and about how much we should join together to help one another. *La Raza* (the people) can accomplish and succeed what they set out to accomplish. The way to do this is to believe in yourself and forget the past because the future is already here. My family has supported me, and I have learned more about who I am. It gave me strength to survive in an unpredictable world.

Sometimes I feel confused about who I am and how I have come this far and survived. Before I came to the university I would not identify myself as Chicana. I seemed to want to assimilate into the white society, but only until I learned that being Mexican was not bad. It seemed that in the barrio there was always trouble, and the Mexicans were always looked upon as lazy. This was a label that other people gave us. For some Chicanos it is safe to remain in the barrio. For me I feel that getting away and learning about why we were labeled is frustrating, and understanding it is all I can do. There are certain questions I feel could never be answered. Why are Chicanos concentrated in one area? Why is there so much segregation? How far can we go before we, as Chicanos, catch up? After I learned that it was not bad to be a Chicana, I felt stronger. The anger was making me aware and helping me to understand. The more I learn about myself, the more I identify myself as Chicana. The only way I could do this was to understand the barrio. Being raised in the barrio was more a positive than a negative experience. I think the times are right to learn about being a Latino. It is important to me that I can always go back to the barrio and share my learning experience with the rest of the barrio.[27]

Amelia Valdez makes a number of contradictory statements. She says, for example, that she felt safe in the barrio. Yet she describes it as a violent place. How can both statements be true? Find other contradictions in her account. Have you ever had similar feelings about a place? About an individual or a group? How did you resolve your contradictory feelings? How does she seem to resolve hers?

Does seeing one's own group as "good" mean that other groups are "evil" or "bad"? In the last few readings, people have moved from seeing others as "different" to seeing them as "dangerous" to viewing them as unworthy of life. How does each step in that process tend to dehumanize individuals? How does each step in the process pave the way for the next?

Make two identity charts for Valdez: one for the years she lived in the barrio and one for her college years. What similarities are there between the two charts? What differences seem most striking? How do you account for those differences?

Belonging is as important to Amelia Valdez as it is to Eve Shalen (Reading 8) and Brandon Carson (Reading 9). How did Valdez respond to group pressures to conform? Why did she value the support of the barrio? Why did she feel loyalty toward it? How did her response affect her identity? Her struggle for independence? Did it take courage for her to go against the group?

How did stereotypes shape life in Amelia Valdez's barrio? How did they shape the way she sees herself? The way others see her?

Valdez speaks of gang members as "angry." Compare their anger with the anger described in Gary Soto's short story (Reading 7). What similarities do you notice? What differences seem most striking?

How does Amelia Valdez define the word *barrio*? Why is it important for her and others in the community to know exactly where its boundaries lay? Why did she feel safe within those borders? Why did she come to find that safety stifling?

How can the isolation Valdez describes be broken? In your experience, what kinds of interaction destroy barriers? What kinds enhance existing barriers or raise new ones? Record your ideas in your journal.

How do you account for the fact that the word *neighborhood* is a positive term, but words like *ghetto* and *barrio* carry other connotations? What is a *ghetto*? Is a *barrio* a ghetto?

In its *Summary Report*, the American Psychological Association Commission on Violence and Youth states that young people are motivated to join gangs to "meet the same developmental needs that all youth are seeking—a sense of connection, belonging, and self-definition. In the gang, they hope to find peer friendship, pride, an identity separate from their families, self-esteem enhancement, status, excitement, and the acquisition of resources. The positive social identity they gain from group membership partly depends on the group's perceived status and rank."[28] How does Valdez's account support the commission's findings?

The *Summary Report* further states, "In a sense, gangs have formed a subculture with their own values and standards of behavior. Incidents others might think trivial—'disrespecting' someone, stepping on his shoes, insulting his girlfriend—are seen as violations of a code of honor, and taking a life is often seen as not only reasonable, but expected."[29] A subculture is a group set apart from the larger community by a distinctive set of cultural ideas. What ideas set gangs apart from the larger community? What attracts young people to gangs? How do you account for the fact that most young people do not belong to gangs?

➤ The *Summary Report* points out that 90 percent of all gang members are ethnic minorities. Why is the percentage so high? The report suggests one answer. "Part of the explanation . . . may lie in the stressful environment of poverty, unemployment, and economic and social inequality in which these ethnic minority youth live. These stressful conditions may limit youth's access to positive means of meeting developmental needs. As needs increase under difficult life conditions, the satisfaction gained from connection with a gang also increases." What insights does Valdez offer into the question of why minority youth join gangs? Compare those insights to those provided in "Lives in Hazard," a documentary about Latino gangs in East Los Angeles. The video is available from the Facing History Resource Center.

READING 11

The Power of Separation

Much as separation encouraged myths and misinformation in minority neighborhoods, it has also fostered myths and misinformation in white communities. Daniel Dyer, a white teacher, offers some insights into the power of those myths.

> I was nearly 20 years old before I spoke to a black person.
> In 1944, I was born in Enid, Oklahoma, a small city whose racial divisions were codified in law and observed in daily life with a fierce devotion. In my boyhood I never questioned segregation, it was merely a fact of my existence, a fact as unremarkable to me as the blazing prairie heat in August.

I cannot claim to be free of all racism; after all, there is something unpleasantly permanent about many experiences and lessons of our childhood.

The Individual and Society **37**

At the time, I saw nothing immoral, or even extraordinary, about the divided city I lived in. If the backs of the city buses bore painted signs that said COLORED ONLY; if the department stores featured separate drinking fountains and restrooms (WHITE and COLORED); if black citizens of Enid swam in different pools, played in different parks, attended different churches and schools (whites went to Enid High School, blacks to Booker T. Washington); well, that was the way it was supposed to be. That's all. . . .

My racial beliefs were confirmed by everything I read, saw, and heard. Comic books contained racial stereotypes; movies and cartoons featured black characters who were superstitious, cowardly, dirty, ignorant, and incapable of speaking "real" English. The Bing Crosby-Fred Astaire Christmas classic, *Holiday Inn*, includes a blackface musical number that is never shown on TV these days. And would it be possible even to count the times I saw black characters in cartoons whose facial characteristics included puffy lips, broad noses, and—perhaps most common—eyes and teeth so white that they glowed in the dark?

When I left Oklahoma in the summer of 1956, my elementary school still had not complied with the *Brown* v. *Board of Education* guidelines [outlawing segregation] from two years before. And I still had never spoken to a black person.

My father joined the faculty of Hiram College in 1956, and I entered the seventh grade at the Hiram [Ohio] Local Schools. Racially, things were not all that different from Enid. There were no black students in the school system, not during the entire six years I attended it.

But for the first time in my life, I did participate in an activity with blacks: high-school basketball. Although most of the little rural schools in Portage County had few if any blacks in those years (1958-1962), both Windham and Ravenna township high schools had blacks on their teams. Although I recall no racial incidents at those games, I do remember being frightened before tip-off. I was playing, you see, against aliens.

Racist jokes and behavior were normal during my high school years. Wetting the end of your cigarette was called "nigger-lipping"; black recording artists were rarely played at school sock-hops. As a sophomore, I performed in blackface in the school play, enacting crude racial caricatures to the great amusement of the all-white audience.

And it is with great embarrassment that I remember driving with my equally brainless buddies through a black neighborhood in Ravenna, car windows down, yelling vile insults at black pedestrians. Those moments are the most unforgivable of my life.

My years as a student at Hiram College (1962-1966) changed my life. For the first time, I was attending classes with blacks, eating with them, living with them. There were not many, mind you, but their excellence in virtually every area of college life began quietly to invade the roots of my racism; before long, the entire tree was sick. And dying. . . . .

As the 1960s progressed, I was caught up in the civil rights movement, and though Malcom X alarmed me (as he did many other white liberals), I was inspired by Martin Luther King, Jr., as I was instructed by black writers like James Baldwin, Ed Bullins, Leroi Jones, and Ralph Ellison.

After I began my career in education, many black students and colleagues—especially musician Bill Appling (formerly of Western Reserve Academy)—confirmed in actuality what my reason had told me: My white skin is neither a badge of merit nor a divine birthmark. It is simply an accident.

I cannot claim to be free of all racism; after all, there is something unpleasantly permanent about many experiences and lessons of our childhood.

In the 1950s in Oklahoma, a shoe store had a machine called a fluoroscope. You could stick your feet inside; look in the view-finder, and, in a ghostly greenish glow, see how your new shoes fit.

I remember going into that store all the time in the summer and sticking my feet repeatedly into that machine. I was fascinated by the X-ray image of the bones in my feet. I could see what at least part of me would look like as a skeleton.

The countless doses of radiation that machine so innocently gave on those long-ago summer days will always be with me and may even have permanently damaged me, even though shoe-store fluoroscopes are now as illegal as . . . well, as segregation.[30]

CONNECTIONS

What caused Daniel Dyer to change the way he viewed African Americans? How did that change in attitude alter his behavior? What chances do you have to widen your perspective? What barriers are there to your doing so as an individual? As a member of a group?

What did Dyer learn about the *other* as a child? How did that learning distort his view of the world? How might it have led to violence? What does Dyer mean when he says, "I cannot claim to be free of all racism; after all, there is something unpleasantly permanent about many experiences and lessons of our childhood"?

One goal of education is to expose individuals to other ideas so that they weigh alternatives and make wise decisions. How did Dyer's education affect his ability to reach that goal? How did Dyer eventually break his isolation? How have you broken yours?

Dictionaries define *superstition* as an irrational belief, act, or prejudice that can be injurious. Are Dyer's views of African Americans based on superstition? On myth? Misinformation?

Cornel West, a professor of religion and the director of an Afro-American Studies program, asks, "How does one affirm oneself without reenacting negative black stereotypes or overreacting to white supremacist ideals? The difficult and delicate quest for black identity is integral to any talk about racial equality. Yet it is not solely a political or economic matter. The quest for black identity involves self-respect and self-regard, realms inseparable from, yet not identical to, political power and economic status."[31] How would you answer the questions he raises? How are those questions related to the legacy Dyer describes?

➤ *Eyes on the Prize*, a television series about the American civil rights movement, alternates rare historical footage with contemporary interviews. All six segments are available from the Facing History Resource Center. The second, "Fighting Back", traces the effects of the 1954 Supreme Court ruling that "separate but equal" schools and other public institutions are not equal. How does Dyer's story support the court's view of segregation?

READING 12

What's in a Name?

*L*abeling affects even those who have never experienced segregation. Miriam Thaggert described the impact it has had on her.

W. E. B. Du Bois [the African American writer and civil rights activist] called it "double-consciousness": the feeling of "always looking at oneself through the eyes of others". . . . History is inevitably connected to double-consciousness, for as the old analogy goes, a person without knowledge of himself is like a tree without roots: nothing to draw upon for the strength to live. I have two histories, one which denies the significance of the other, and the struggle I endure is a frustrating attempt to unite the two. Double-consciousness affects all minorities in America, but I believe it is different for each person. There is a history that merges people together, but a unique perception of double-consciousness distinguishes the individual.

My own history lesson occurred the first time I was called a nigger and began, appropriately enough, at school while I was waiting for my mom to pick me up. I decided to play pick up sticks with a group of girls, and I won the few games we played. This was disturbing for one girl, Angela, who seemed to be accustomed to winning. According to her, I couldn't have won on my own merits. I was cheating, she thought, which of course, I denied. My efforts to convince her of my innocence were in vain, since she seemed to have her own idea about why I had won.

"Nigger!" she cried. "Get away from me!"

The word came as a jolt and paralyzed my throat. I was tempted to launch an attack, but I thought it would be safer to flee. I did get away from her crying as I left. Fortunately, my mom arrived within a few minutes.

When I got into the car, my mother looked at my face and asked what was wrong. I told her what Angela said. Her immediate response was to ask, "Where is she?"

I attempted to dry my eyes and pointed her out. The car door opened with a force and slammed shut. "Stay in the car," Mom said. I looked up in interest, my distress forgotten in childlike curiosity about what my mother would do.

I saw Mom walk up to the girl and point to the car. I ducked down as the girl looked over in my direction. When I came up, Mom had the girl by the shoulders and was shaking her back and forth.

"Don't you ever call my daughter a nigger again? Do you hear me? Do you hear?" Amazingly, no one felt it was necessary to rescue the girl from my mother's grip.

Later at home in the kitchen, my mom stood before me with her hands on her hips. "Tell me," she said, "what does the word 'nigger' mean?"

I looked at the floor and thought. It suddenly occurred to me that I had no idea what the word meant. I searched my brain, looking for an incident in which I had heard someone say it, I tried to see where and when I had heard that awful word before, but I couldn't. No one, within the hearing range of my-eight-year old ears had ever uttered the word. But why, then, did I react to that one word instantly, so violently, as if the word was familiar, but unspeakable, to my young lips?

"It's a bad person," I managed.

"Bad in what way?"

"It's a person who is bad and mean and evil in every way."

"Are you a nigger?"

"No."

Here my mother got on her knees before me and gently took my small hands in her much larger ones. Softly, she questioned, "Then, Miriam, baby, why did you cry?"

That was a good question. I didn't know. My mom's question remained unanswered.

"All right," she sighed. She got up, pulled a chair next to me, and sat down. "It's time you learn something about yourself." And there at the kitchen table, Mom proceeded to tell me about white and Black folks. I learned that I had a history that went further than the day I was born and a heritage that was a golden link between two distant continents. I realized that to be Black is not just to be a color. It is to have an attitude, a feeling. And now when I hear the word "nigger," I am amazed at how such a small and simple word can contain so much violence and racism, yet also summon intense self-respect in my certain and unquavering knowledge of what I am and what I am not.[32]

CONNECTIONS

➤Words have tremendous power, particularly words that are used to define our identity or label us in some way. What names have you been called? What labels have been applied to you? What have you learned about the power of the spoken word? How do your experiences explain why Miriam Thaggert knew the word *nigger* was a derogatory term the first time she heard it? The video *Names Can Really Hurt* explores concepts related to stereotyping. It is available from the Facing History Resource Center.

The words *black* and *white* are loaded words in the English language. Ossie Davis, an African American author and actor, made a detailed study of the way each is treated in his copy of *Roget's Thesaurus*. There he found 120 synonyms for black, most with negative connotations. They included words like *blight, smut, smudge, sully, begrime, soot, dingy, murky, threatening, frowning, foreboding, forbidden, sinister, baneful, dismal, evil, wicked, malignant, deadly, secretive, unclean, unwashed, foul, blacklist, black book, black-hearted,* and so on. Incorporated in the same listing were such words as *Negro, nigger,* and *darky.*

In the same thesaurus, Davis found 134 synonyms for *white,* almost all of them with positive connotations: *purity, cleanness, bright, shining, fair, blonde, chaste, innocent, honorable, upright, just, straightforward, genuine, trustworthy, honesty,* and so on. *White* as a racial designation was, of course, included in the list. What power do words have to shape our attitudes? Values? Behavior?

Draw an identity chart for Miriam Thaggert. How is it like the one you made for Amelia Valdez? What differences seem most striking? How do you account for those differences?

Miriam Thaggert learned her history from her mother. Why wasn't that history taught in school? Whose history is taught at your school? How does our knowledge of our past shape the way we see ourselves? The way we view others?

It would be impossible to teach everyone's history in school. How then can we learn to find universal lessons in someone else's story? Record your ideas in your journal so that you can add to them as you continue reading this chapter and those that follow.

A poster published by a group called Concerned American Indian Parents shows four banners for baseball teams. The top one reads "Pittsburgh Negroes." The next one says "Kansas City Jews." The third one is "San

Diego Caucasians." The last one reads "Cleveland Indians." Under the four banners the group writes, "Maybe Now You Know How Native Americans Feel." What message does the poster convey? What does it suggest about the power of names?

R E A D I N G   1 3

The Effects of Religious Stereotyping

Like race, our religion is part of our identity. The word *religion* comes from a Latin word that means "to tie or bind together." Modern dictionaries define *religion* as "an organized system of beliefs and rituals centering on a supernatural being or beings." Those "beliefs and rituals" unite followers into a community of believers who share not only a faith but also a worldview.

Each of the world's religions offers its followers a way of explaining the mysterious and the marvelous. Each also provides a code of conduct that guides individuals in their dealings with the people around them. They all have something else in common, too—they all teach respect for individual differences. Indeed, it has been said that Judaism, Christianity, and Islam are more alike than they are different. Yet, often, in practicing their faith, individuals tend to stress the differences rather than focusing on the similarities. As a result, some come to regard those who choose to follow another religion as suspicious, different, and dangerous.

In reflecting on his experiences with religious stereotypes, Major General Robert Bailey Solomon told of the Friday night he found a fellow soldier sitting on his bunk.

> He says, "Hey Solomon, where were you?" I said, "I've been out." And he says, "Well, yeah, where were you?" I said, "Well, I went to religious services." He looked at me and said, "Well, what are you, a Seventh Day Adventist?" I said, "No." He said, "Well, what are you?" With a little trepidation, I said, "I'm Jewish." He said, "Are your parents Jewish?" And he is looking at me very intently. I said, "Yes, both my father and my mother and my grandparents are Jewish." And he said, "You don't look Jewish." And he is still looking at me. You remember the haircuts we had. Everybody looked alike. And so I finally said, "Well, why would you say I don't look Jewish?" because I always thought I did. He said, "Well," and he's looking at my head, he says, "You don't have horns." I said, "Pardon me!" You see I had led a very sheltered life, and I said, "Are you kidding me?" He said, "Well, Jews have horns." I said, "How many Jews do you know who have horns?" He said, "I never met a Jew before." So I found out that of the

probably 220 people in that company, there weren't more than five of them that ever met a Jew. The only ones that had were a couple of kids who had lived in Chicago, a couple in Milwaukee.

Now, the interesting phenomenon is that I spent sixteen weeks in basic training and had probably somewhere between twenty and thirty prizefights. Usually it was some fellow who wanted to beat my brains out because I was Jewish. I didn't lose a fight. I got knocked on my keester a few times, but I think the fact that I was willing to fight sort of let them know that I was not a spindly little Jew that they could walk up to and push over.

As opposed to making me more Christianized, the military service, if anything, has made me more Jewish. I found nothing difficult about being in the army and I found nothing to compromise my faith in the army from the first day. I did find a lot of people who were anti-Semitic. And I also found out that many of those were anti-Semitic because they didn't have the foggiest notion of what Jews were, where they came from, what they might be, what they believed. They simply believed popular myths about Jews.[33]

Over forty years after Solomon's experience with myths and misinformation in the armed forces, Chana Schoenberger had a similar encounter. Hers took place in Wisconsin in the summer of 1993. She and a number of other students from high schools across the nation participated in the National Science Foundation Young Scholars program. She writes:

Represented among us were eight religions: Jewish, Roman Catholic, Muslim, Hindu, Methodist, Mormon, Jehovah's Witness and Lutheran. It was amazing, given the variety of backgrounds, to see the ignorance of some of the smartest young scholars on the subject of other religions.

On the first day, one girl mentioned that she had nine brothers and sisters. "Oh, are you Mormon?" asked another girl, who I knew was a Mormon herself. The first girl, shocked, replied, "No, I dress normal!" She thought Mormon was the same as Mennonite and the only thing she knew about either religion was that Mennonites don't, in her opinion, "dress normal."

My friends, ever curious about Judaism, asked me about everything from our basic theology to food preferences. "How come, if Jesus was a Jew, Jews aren't Christian?" my Catholic roommate asked me in all seriousness. Brought up in a small Wisconsin town, she had never met a Jew before, nor had she met people from most of the other "strange" religions (anything but Catholic or mainstream Protestant). Many of the other kids were the same way.

"Do you all still practice animal sacrifices?" a girl from a small town in Minnesota asked me once. I said no, laughed, and pointed out that this was the 20th century, but she had been absolutely serious. The only Jews she knew were the ones from the Bible.

Nobody was deliberately rude or anti-Semitic, but I got the feeling that I was representing the entire Jewish people through my actions. I realized that many of my friends would go back to their small towns thinking that all Jews liked Dairy Queen Blizzards and grilled cheese sandwiches. After all, that was true of all the Jews they knew (in most cases, me and the only other Jewish young scholar, period).

The most awful thing for me, however, was not the benign ignorance of my friends. Our biology professor had taken us on a field trip to the [Environmental Protection Agency] field site where he worked, and he was telling us about the project he was working on. He said that they had to make sure the EPA got its money's worth from the study—he "wouldn't want them to get Jewed."

I was astounded. The professor had a doctorate, various other degrees and seemed to be a very intelligent man. He apparently had no idea that he had just made an anti-Semitic remark. The other Jewish girl in the group and I debated whether or not to say something to him about it, and although we agreed we would, neither of us ever did. Personally, it made me feel uncomfortable. For a high-school student to tell a professor who taught her class that he was a bigot seemed out of place to me, even if he was one.

What scares me about the experience, in fact about my whole visit to Wisconsin, was that I never met a really vicious anti-Semite or a malignantly prejudiced person. Many of the people I met had been brought up to think that Jews (or Mormons or any other religion that's not mainstream Christian) were different and that difference was not good.[34]

CONNECTIONS

Write a working definition of *religion*. How does religion shape your identity? Your views of other people? Record your ideas in your journal.

What stereotypes about Jews shaped the way Solomon's fellow soldiers regarded him? How did those stereotypes affect the way he saw himself? Compare his responses to those stereotypes with those of Joseph Suina (Reading 4). What similarities do you notice? What differences seem most striking?

Chana Schoenberger says of her experience, "Ignorance was the problem I faced this summer. By itself, ignorance is not always a problem, but it leads to misunderstandings, prejudice, and hatred." Would Solomon agree with her assessment of the problem? Do you agree? If so, for what reasons? If not, what was the problem? Have you ever had an experience like the one she describes? If so, how did you respond? How did it make you feel?

Schoenberger writes, "Represented among us were eight religions: Jewish, Roman Catholic, Muslim, Hindu, Methodist, Mormon, Jehovah's Witness and Lutheran." Members of all eight have encountered the kinds of myths and misinformation Schoenberger confronted. Choose one of the eight and research that faith's history. What prejudices have members experienced in the United States? How has ignorance led "to misunderstandings, prejudice, and hatred?"

How are ignorance, misunderstanding, prejudice and hatred related? Use examples from your research as well as your own experiences and those of people you know to support your answer.

Martha Minow, a professor of law, writes, "When we identify one thing as unlike the others, we are dividing the world; we use our language to exclude, to distinguish—to discriminate."[35] How do her comments apply to Solomon's experience? To Schoenberger's experience?

➤In her novel, *A Boy of Old Prague,* Sulamith Ish-Kishor describes the effects of separation on Tomas, a young Christian boy who lived in the city of Prague in 1556, who learned to view the world through a lens distorted by hate, superstition, and rumor. He grows up accepting without question all that he heard about the Jews until the day his master sends the frightened boy to work for one. Only then are his beliefs challenged. For an excerpt from the novel, see Chapter 6. Multiple copies of the book are available from the Facing History Resource Center. After reading *A Boy of Old Prague,* compare Tomas' views of Jews with those Robert Solomon and Chana Schoenberger encountered. What do your comparisons suggest about the factors that encourage myths and misinformation? About the factors that encourage people to widen their perspective and respect others?

READING 14

Anti-Judaism: A Case Study in Discrimination

This reading is a brief case study that reveals a number of concepts that can be applied to any religious group. After all, every group has at one time or another been the victim of discrimination.

Robert Solomon and Chana Schoenberger were surprised to learn that others saw them only as members of a group. They were even more surprised at the qualities attributed to them as a result of myths and misinformation associated with that group. Where did those myths come from?

Individuals are always affected by the way their group is perceived. If the group is regarded as "outside" society, its members are vulnerable not only to stereotyping and prejudice but also to discrimination. For over two thousand years, Jews were considered outsiders. Their history reveals the relationships between the individual, the group, and the larger society.

Historians have traced many of those myths back over two thousand years to the time of the Roman Empire and the beginnings of Christianity. Historian Robert S. Wistrich writes, "Jesus was born, lived and died as a Jew in first-century Roman Palestine. He never conceived nor dreamed of a Christian Church. His father, mother, brothers and first disciples were all Jews, so that early Christianity can be said to have been essentially a rebellious Jewish sect that emerged out of . . . Judaism and had to define itself against the mother religion."[36]

Jesus lived at a time of crisis for Jews in Palestine. After the Romans conquered their country, they insisted that the Jews not only obey Roman laws but also worship Roman gods just as other conquered peoples did. When the Jews refused to do so, they were labeled "stubborn," "clannish," and "hostile." As pressure to accept Roman culture mounted, Jews searched desperately for a way to maintain their religious identity. Some urged open rebellion against Rome. Others, including Jesus, argued that Jews must reform their religious practices and atone for their sins.

As each side marshaled arguments in defense of its position, the debate increased in intensity. Still, all of the attacks and counterattacks took place within the context of Judaism. Only when Jesus' disciples separated themselves from Judaism did their words take on new meaning. They became, in the words of Krister Stendahl, a professor of Christian Studies, missiles hurled from a "mainly gentile Church toward the Synagogue across the street, from which now those Jews who followed Jesus had been excommunicated. And by that shift Christian anti-Judaism was born." He goes on to say:

> Much has been written and more can be said about why and how that parting of the ways happened. No one factor was decisive. No one action or doctrine did it. As only a small number of Jews but an ever-increasing number of gentiles [or non-Jews] joined the Jesus movement, the outcome was Christian Churches, which, for all practical purposes, were gentile communities.
>
> At the same time, Judaism, having lost its center in Jerusalem and its temple [after the failure of the Jewish revolt against Roman rule in 70 AD], found a new identity in the leadership of its sages and their interpretation of Torah [the Scriptures]. . . . The Rabbinic consolidation of Judaism and the increasingly gentile constituency of Christianity transformed what had begun as a division within the Jewish community into two distinct communities, the Synagogue and the Church.
>
> Once established, these two entities felt the necessity to define themselves by sharpening their differences. These differences appeared even greater once the Greek-speaking Jewish communities all over the Roman Empire partly died out and partly were absorbed into Christianity, while at the same time the language and thinking of Christianity was enlivened by Greek and Roman culture. Yet it was

when Christianity became the official religion of the Roman Empire in the fourth century that Christian anti-Judaism first became a serious threat to Jewish existence. Political power plus religion was and is a dangerous brew.[37]

By the fourth century, the word *Jew* had become an expression of contempt among Christians. Laws now protected Christians from "contamination" by not allowing them to eat or engage in sexual relations with Jews. By the sixth century, Jews could not hold public office, employ Christian servants or slaves, or even show themselves in the streets during Holy Week—the week that commemorates the time between Jesus' "Last Supper" and the crucifixion.

By the eleventh century, Jews were a small vulnerable minority in Western Europe. How vulnerable they truly were became clear in 1096, when Church leaders launched a series of crusades against the Muslims to win control of Palestine. On their way to the Middle East, the crusaders attacked Jewish communities throughout Western Europe. Abba Eban, a scholar and former Israeli diplomat, said of those attacks, "To understand the ferocity of the Christian assault on the Jews during this period, we must grasp the tight interrelationship of power and ideas. Political legitimacy was linked to religious belief. A man's creed defined his social identity."[38]

As persecutions mounted, thousands of Jews fled to Eastern Europe, where they found more freedom for a time. But whether they stayed behind or ventured further east, Jews increasingly found that they could not escape violence based on myths and misinformation. By the thirteenth century, church leaders in what is now Germany required that all Jews wear cone-shaped hats. In Latin countries, they were expected to sew a badge (usually a yellow disk) onto their clothing.

As outsiders Jews faced other restrictions as well. Peter Abelard, a twelfth-century philosopher and priest, described some of them in his *Dialogue between a Philosopher, a Jew, and a Christian*. It says of the Jews, "Heaven is their only place of refuge. If they want to travel to the nearest town, they have to buy protection with high sums of money from the Christian rulers who actually wish for their death so that they can confiscate their possessions. The Jews cannot own land or vineyards because there is nobody to vouch for their safekeeping. Thus, all that is left to them as a means of livelihood is the business of money lending, and this in turn brings the hatred of Christians upon them."

Jews were allowed to become bankers, because the Church considered it a sin for a Christian to charge interest for a loan. Money lending was also contrary to Jewish laws. But Jews had few other ways of earning a living, so many were forced to become bankers. That occupation led to a new stereotype: that of the Jew as a greedy moneylender. It was a stereotype that would linger long after the French and Italians forced the Jews from the banking industry.

[Hatred] may spread throughout the land like the plague, so that a class, a religion, a nation, will become the victim of popular hatred without anyone knowing exactly how it all began; and people will disagree, and even quarrel among themselves, about the real reason for its existence; and no one foresees the inevitable consequences.

By the sixteenth century, except for a few business encounters, Jews were totally isolated from their Christian neighbors. In many countries, people of the Jewish faith were now confined to a ghetto, a section of a city or town that was enclosed by high walls and guarded by Christian gate-keepers. With more rigid separation came new myths and misinformation. Increasingly Jews were portrayed as agents of the devil responsible for every catastrophe from random crime to plague and drought. Artists now portrayed Jews with horns, tails, and evil faces. Priests and scholars elaborated on the idea that Jews were evil creatures who were less than human in sermons and lectures.

By the sixteenth century, there were divisions within Christian Europe. In 1517, in what is now Germany, Martin Luther protested corruption in the Catholic Church by calling on Church leaders to reform. Instead they branded him a heretic and excommunicated him from the Church. The result was the Protestant Reformation, which ultimately led to the founding of new Christian churches in Western Europe. It also led to religious wars, this time between Catholics and Protestants.

Luther had hoped to convert many Jews to Christianity. In 1523, he told his followers that "we in our turn ought to treat the Jews in a brotherly manner in order that we might convert some of them. . . we are but Gentiles, while the Jews are of the lineage of Christ."[39] But when Jews refused to convert, an angry Luther wrote in part:

> First, their synagogues or churches should be set on fire, and whatever does not burn up should be covered or spread over with dirt so that no one may ever be able to see a cinder or stone of it. . . . Secondly, their homes should likewise be broken down and destroyed. For they perpetrate the same things there they do in their synagogues. For this reason they ought to be put under one roof or in a stable, like gypsies, in order that they may realise that they are not masters in this land, as they boast, but miserable captives.[40]

Other Protestant leaders were more tolerant of Jews, in part because their quarrel was with Catholics. But even among those Protestants, the old stereotypes lingered on. Indeed they survived long after the gradual emancipation of the Jews in the 1700s and 1800s. As Malcolm Hay, a Catholic historian, explains: "Men are not born with hatred in their blood. The infection is usually acquired by contact; it may be injected deliberately or even unconsciously, by parents, or by teachers. . . .The disease may spread throughout the land like the plague, so that a class, a religion, a nation, will become the victim of popular hatred without anyone knowing exactly how it all began; and people will disagree, and even quarrel among themselves, about the real reason for its existence; and no one foresees the inevitable consequences."[41]

Rabbi Akiba, a great teacher who lived in Palestine in the days of Roman rule, was once asked to define Judaism. He replied, "What is distasteful unto you, do not do unto your neighbors. All else is commentary." What is he suggesting is the essence of his faith? That teaching is basic to most other religions as well. If it is part of the teaching of most religions, how do you account for the myths and misinformation that often surround the way individuals regard people of other faiths?

Historian Robert S. Wistrich describes the stereotype of the Jews as being "divorced completely from the real, concrete Jews of everyday life." What allows such a stereotype to flourish? What part do leaders play in keeping them alive? What part does segregation play? Why do people cling to stereotypes, even when they have no basis in reality? Record your ideas in your journal. You may wish to test those ideas by researching another religion. Are your answers equally true of the group you researched?

How does a quarrel within a group differ from one between groups? Are there things you can say to a friend or family member that you would not say to outsiders? What happens when words used in a "family quarrel" move outside the family?

Why do leaders choose to stir up hatred? At what times are appeals to hatred most likely to succeed? In times of war? Economic stress? Change?

Write a working definition of the word *disciple.* What are the differences between a disciple and other followers? What is the relationship between a disciple and the founder of a faith?

By the seventh century, both Christians and Jews were defining themselves in relation to yet another religion, one that developed in the deserts of the Arabian Peninsula. Although it was profoundly influenced by both Christianity and Judaism, Islam is a separate faith based on the teachings of Muhammed, its founder. Within a hundred years of his death, his disciples had built a huge empire in Southwest Asia and North Africa. Within that empire, Jews and Christians were viewed as "outsiders." As early as the eighth century, the Muslims required both groups to identify themselves through the color of their clothing. Jewish men were forced to wear yellow and Christians blue. Non-Muslim women had to wear shoes that did not match, in combinations of black with white or red. Why do you think outsiders in Christian Europe and the Muslim Empire were required to wear distinctive clothing? How do you think such clothing shaped the way those individuals were perceived? The way they viewed themselves?

What did Abba Eban mean when he said that power and ideas are interrelated? Do you agree? What is the legacy of that interrelationship?

What part does language play in the level of tolerance one group has for another? In stirring hatred? In dehumanizing a group of people? In the way victims of that process may view themselves?

In October, 1965, the Roman Catholic Church issued the now famous *Nostra Aetate*. In it, the Church condemns "all forms of antisemitism and discrimination." The document states that "liturgical passages that show the Jewish people will be carefully interpreted by the Church to avoid prejudice." In 1994, the Lutheran Church issued a similar statement.

Father Robert Bullock, pastor of Our Lady of Sorrows Church in Sharon, Massachusetts, and a member of the Facing History and Ourselves Board of Directors, observes that to be *ecumenical* is to respect differences among people. Write a working definition for the word *ecumenical*. It comes from a Greek word meaning "of the whole world." Why is that an appropriate name?

Hostility toward a particular person can usually be resolved through a confrontation that leads to dialogue. But hostility toward a group is much harder to resolve—how can one confront a group? Although many students have little or no contact with people who follow other religions, they can find answers to their questions through research or by inviting speakers to class. Professor Krister Stendahl offers a few suggestions for making such encounters more meaningful.

1. Let the others define themselves. We all tend to define or describe the other in negative contrast to ourselves. Hence our descriptions of the other often are a breach of the commandment, "You shall not bear false witness against your neighbor."

2. Compare equal to equal. If you compare the ideal of your own with the average of the other, not to say the best of your own with the worst of the other, you will score false victories and truth will suffer. . . .

3. The highest and indispensable stage of dialogue is what I like to call Holy Envy: to see something in the other that one finds beautiful, but it is not one's own; to want to learn; to want the other to tell more about it, tell us so that we get enriched, warmed, fascinated.[42]

What would happen if Stendahl's rules were applied to *all* dialogues—not just religious ones? What effect might they have on discussions at your school? In your community?

Unlike the other readings in this chapter, this one is a historical case study. It introduces ideas and concepts important to Facing History. After completing this reading, some students may ask, "What does this history have to do with me?" How would you answer them? Record your response in your journal so that you can refer to it later.

The Principle of Tolerance

*T*he readings in this chapter are at least in part about identity and the consequences of being defined by others. Much of world history documents the struggle of people to build societies that include and protect everyone. The concept of a tolerant society is a complicated one. Within every society are many competing ideas, values, and perspectives. Professor Cornel West suggests one way that people who disagree on fundamental issues can learn to live together.

> The interplay of individuality and unity is not one of uniformity and unanimity imposed from above but rather of conflict among diverse groupings that reach a dynamic consensus subject to questioning and criticism. As with a soloist in a jazz quartet, quintet or band, individuality is promoted in order to sustain and increase the *creative* tension with the group—a tension that yields higher levels of performance to achieve the aim of the collective project. This kind of critical and democratic sensibility flies in the face of any policing of borders and boundaries of "blackness," "maleness," "femaleness," or "whiteness."[43]

In the television series, *The Ascent of Man*, and in the book based on that series, scientist Jacob Bronowski expressed that idea a little differently. He based his argument on the idea that tolerance is not just a desirable quality but an essential one. He insisted that without it, society is doomed. Bronowski went on to define *tolerance* by describing the work of scientists in the early 1900s. They made tremendous advances by being open to new ideas and willing to challenge old truths.

> Did physics in the 1920s really consist of argument, seminar, discussion, dispute? Yes, it did. Yes, it still does. The people who met here, [in the university town of Goettingen, Germany] the people who meet in laboratories still, only end their work with a mathematical formulation. They begin it by trying to solve conceptual riddles. The riddles of the sub-atomic particles—of the electrons and the rest—are mental riddles.[44]

Those riddles eventually led to a new theory.

> …Werner Heisenberg gave a new characterization of the electron. Yes, it is a particle, he said, but a particle which yields only limited information. That is, you can specify where it is at this instant, but then you cannot impose on it a specific speed and direction at the setting-off. Or conversely, if you insist that you are going to fire it at a certain

speed in a certain direction, then you cannot specify exactly what its starting-point is—or, of course, its end-point.

That sounds like a very crude characterization. It is not. Heisenberg gave it depth by making it precise. The information that the electron carries is limited in its totality. That is, for instance, its speed and its position fit together in such a way that they are confined by the tolerance of the quantum. This is the profound idea: one of the great scientific ideas, not only of the twentieth century, but in the history of science.

Heisenberg called this the Principle of Uncertainty. In one sense, it is a robust principle of the everyday. We know that we cannot ask the world to be exact. If an object (a familiar face, for example) had to be exactly the same before we recognized it, we would never recognize it from one day to the next. We recognize the object to be the same because it is much the same; it is never exactly like it was, it is tolerably like. In the act of recognition, a judgment is built in—an area of tolerance or uncertainty. So Heisenberg's principle says that no events, not even atomic events, can be described with certainty, that is, with zero tolerance. . . .

Yet the Principle of Uncertainty is a bad name. In science or outside it, we are not uncertain; our knowledge is merely confined within a certain tolerance. We should call it the Principle of Tolerance. And I propose that name in two senses. First, in the engineering sense. Science has progressed step by step, the most successful enterprise in the ascent of man, because it has understood that the exchange of information between man and nature, and man and man, can only take place with a certain tolerance. But second, I also use the word passionately about the real world. All knowledge, all information between human beings can only be exchanged within a play of tolerance. And that is true whether the exchange is in science, or in literature, or in religion, or in politics, or even in any form of thought that aspires to dogma.[45]

CONNECTIONS

What is certainty and why do people seek it? Is certainty the opposite of tolerance? Or is it a "comfortable myth"? If so, does living with tolerance mean living with discomfort? Write working definitions of both *tolerance* and *absolute certainty*.

Some people object to the word *tolerate*. They note that one meaning of the word is "to put up with or endure." They argue that people ought to do more than tolerate each other. Do you agree? If so, what word would you substitute for toleration? If not, how would you respond to the argument? What lies beyond tolerance?

How can people who disagree on fundamental issues live together? What is West's response to that question? How is it similar to Bronowski's? To your own response? How does it differ?

How do you build a society that recognizes differences? That is fair to everyone? What part do rules play in creating such a society? What compromises do individuals have to make?

Do you agree with Bronowski when he insists that without tolerance, society is doomed? Record your opinion in your journal so that you can refer back to it as you read the chapters that follow.

NOTES

[1] Deborah Tannen, preface to *You Just Don't Understand* (Morrow, 1990), 16.

[2] Frank Tashlin, *the bear that wasn't* (1946; reprint, Dover Publications, 1962). Reprinted by permission of the heirs to the Frank Tashlin Trust.

[3] Anthony Wright, "Little Boxes," *Points of View* (Amherst College) 1990.

[4] Tannen, preface to *You Just Don't Understand*, 16.

[5] Richard Lewontin, et al. *Not in Our Genes* (Pantheon, 1990), 127.

[6] Allan G. Johnson, *Human Arrangements* (Harcourt Brace, 1986), 353.

[7] Lewontin, *Not in Our Genes*, 121.

[8] Ibid., 126.

[9] Joseph H. Suina, "Preserving Many Worlds: The Cultural Dimension Since 1492" (paper presented at the ISAM Annual Conference: 1492-1992 Reconsidered, Dana Hall School, 5 May, 1992), 20-21.

[10] "Letter to the Editor" by Jeanne Park, *New York Times*, 20 April, 1990. Copyright © 1990 by The New York Times Company. Reprinted by permission.

[11] From *The House on Mango Street*. Copyright © Sandra Cisneros, 1984. Published in the United States by Vintage Books, a division of Random House, Inc., New York. Reprinted by permission of Susan Bergholz Literary Services, New York.

[12] Maya Angelou, interview by Bill Moyers, *Facing Evil*, (Public Affairs Television).

[13] *Creativity with Bill Moyers*, "A Portrait of Maya Angelou," (Public Broadcasting System, 1985).

[14] Julius Lester, *Falling Pieces of the Broken Sky* (Little Brown, 1990), 69. Reprinted by permission.

[15] Ibid., 71-73.

[16] Quoted in *This Is About Vision: Interviews with Southwestern Writers,* ed. John F. Crawford and Annie O. Eysturoy, (University of New Mexico Press, 1990), 189.

[17] James Gilligan, "Shame and Humiliation: The Emotions of Individual and Collective Violence" (paper presented at the 1991 Erikson Lectures, Harvard University), 11.

[18] Gary Soto,"Fear," in *Living Up the Street; Narrative Recollections,* (Strawberry Hill Press, 1985), 59–62.

[19] Gilligan, "Shame and Humiliation," 8.

[20] Jonah Kadish, *A Discussion with Elie Wiesel: Facing History Students Confront Hatred and Violence.* (Facing History and Ourselves, 1993).

[21] Eve Shalen, Ibid.

[22] Dagobert D. Runes, *The Jew and the Cross* (Citadel Press, 1966), 30-31.

[23] Colin Nickerson, "In Japan, 'Different' Is Dangerous," *The Boston Globe,* 24, January 1993.

[24] Noy Chou, "You Have to Live in Somebody Else's Country to Understand." In *A World of Difference,* Resource Guide (Anti-Defamation League of B'nai B'rith and Facing History and Ourselves, 1986).

[25] From *One Teenager in Ten: Writings by Gay and Lesbian Youth,* ed. Ann Heron, (Alyson Publications, 1983), 15, 17–18.

[26] Joseph H. Suina, "Preserving Many Worlds," 22.

[27] Amelia Valdez, "Surviving in the Barrio." In *Inside Separate Worlds,* ed. David Schoem (University of Michigan Press, 1991), 21-33.

[28] The American Psychological Association Commission on Violence and Youth, *Violence & Youth: Psychology's Response.* Vol. 1 Summary Report (American Psychological Association, 1993), 28-29.

[29] Ibid., 29.

[30] Daniel Dyer, "Racial Background Is Not a Halo But an Accident," *The Cleveland Plain Dealer,* 7 January 1993. Reprinted by permission.

[31] Cornel West, *Race Matters* (Beacon Press, 1993), 65-66.

[32] "Double Vision" by Miriam Thaggert from *The HarperCollins Guide to Writing with Sourcebook* by Nancy Sommers and Linda Simon, 29–32. Copyright © 1993 by Nancy Sommers and Linda Simon. Reprinted by permission of HarperCollins College Publishers.

[33] Howard Simons, *Jewish Times: Voices of the American Jewish Experience* (Houghton Mifflin, 1988), 239-240.

[34] Chana Schoenberger, "Getting to Know About You and Me," *Newsweek,* September 20, 1993, 8.

[35] Martha Minow, *Making All the Difference* (Cornell University Press, 1990), 3.

[36] Robert Wistrich, *Antisemitism: The Longest Hatred* (Pantheon, 1991), 7.

[37] Krister Stendahl, "Can Christianity Shed Its Anti-Judaism?" *Brandeis Review,* Spring, 1992, 26.

[38] Abba Eban, *Heritage: Civilization and the Jews* (Summit Books, 1984), 160.

[39] Robert Wistrich, *Antisemitism,* 39.

[40] Ibid., 39-40.

[41] Malcom Hay, *Thy Brother's Blood: The Roots of Antisemitism* (Hart Publishing Co., 1975), 3.

[42] Krister Stendahl, "Can Christianity Shed Its Anti-Judaism?" 27.

[43] Cornel West, *Race Matters, 105.*

[44] From THE ASCENT OF MAN by Jacob Bronowski, 362. Copyright © 1973 by J. Bronowski. By permission of Little, Brown and Company.

[45] Ibid, 364–365.

2. We and They

Democracy is becoming rather than being. It can easily be lost, but never is fully won. Its essence is eternal struggle.

WILLIAM H. HASTIE

OVERVIEW

Chapter 1 focused on factors that shape an individual's identity. It also described how those factors are sometimes used to exclude people from membership in various groups. Chapter 2 considers the ways a nation's identity is defined. That definition has enormous significance. It indicates who holds power in the nation. And it determines who is a part of its "universe of obligation"—the name Helen Fein has given to the circle of individuals and groups "toward whom obligations are owed, to whom rules apply, and whose injuries call for [amends]."[1]

For much of world history, birth determined who was a part of a group's "universe of obligation" and who was not. As Jacob Bronowski once explained, "The distinction [between self and other] emerges in pre-history in hunting cultures, where competition for limited numbers of food sources requires a clear demarcation between your group and the other group, and this is transferred to agricultural communities in the development of history. Historically this distinction becomes a comparative category in which one judges how like us, or unlike us, is the other, thus enabling people symbolically to organize and divide up their worlds and structure reality."[2]

This chapter explores the power of those classifications and labels. As legal scholar Martha Minow has pointed out, "When we identify one thing as like the others, we are not merely classifying the world; we are investing particular classifications with consequences and positioning ourselves in relation to those meanings. When we identify one thing as unlike the others, we are dividing the world; we use our language to exclude, to distinguish—to discriminate."[3]

The chapter begins with a short story that imagines a society in which differences have been outlawed so that everyone is truly equal. That story introduces the key concepts and themes of the chapter. The readings that follow apply those ideas to the real world by examining the way three nations—the United States, France, and Germany—"divided up their worlds and structured reality" in the 1700s and 1800s. The chapter shows how those divisions led to a world war. It also describes what it meant to be *them*. Were *they* tolerated? Exploited? Feared? Under what conditions could *they* become full members of a nation? Under what conditions did *they* become outcasts—individuals beyond *our* "universe of obligation?" What opportunities did *they* have to alter their status? To protect it?

A number of ideas have shaped the way such questions were answered. One was *nationalism*. Sociologist Theodore Abel defines it as "a strong positive feeling for the accomplishments of the nation, its position of power, the men and institutions and the traditions which are associated with the glorified events of its history."[4] Another set of ideas stressed similarities rather than cultural differences. Those ideas are most eloquently stated in the Declaration of Independence: "We hold these truths to be self-evident, that all men are created equal; that they are endowed by their Creator with certain unalienable rights; that among these rights are life, liberty, and the pursuit of happiness. That to secure these rights, governments are instituted among men, deriving their just power from the consent of the governed."

Both sets of ideas have had tremendous appeal to people all over the world. And both, when carried to an extreme, have been abused. Abel warns that nationalism almost always involves "a certain amount of ethnocentricism, a feeling of superiority of one's nation over other nations, which might turn a nationalistic sentiment into chauvinism when the claim for superiority becomes associated with a claim for exclusiveness and consequent hostility to all other nations."[5] In the nineteenth century, false ideas about "race" gave legitimacy to ethnocentrism and chauvinism. Democratic principles can also be perverted. In their zeal for equality, some people viewed differences with suspicion or used differences to deny *their* humanity.

Like the chapters that follow, this one uses primary sources to capture the ideas, assumptions, and observations of those living through a particular age in history. As Bronowski once wrote, those sources help us "draw conclusions from what we see to what we do not see" and "recognize ourselves in the past, on the steps to the present."

Harrison Bergeron

This reading introduces the key themes and concepts developed in this chapter.

S uppose the government were to use its power to ensure that no one was superior to anyone else. Would such a society be fair to individuals? Would it be just? In the story, "Harrison Bergeron," Kurt Vonnegut, an American author, offers answers to such questions.

The year was 2081 and everyone was finally equal. They were not only equal before God and the law. They were equal in every possible way. Nobody was smarter than anybody else. Nobody was better looking than anybody else. Nobody was stronger or quicker than anybody else. All this equality was due to the 211th, 212th, and the 213th Amendments to the Constitution, and to the unceasing vigilance of agents of the United States Handicapper General.

Some things about living still weren't quite right, though. April, for instance, still drove people crazy by not being springtime. And it was in that clammy month that the H-G men took George and Hazel Bergeron's fourteen-year-old son, Harrison, away.

It was tragic, all right, but George and Hazel couldn't think about it very hard. Hazel had a perfectly average intelligence, which meant she couldn't think about anything except in short bursts. And George, while his intelligence was way above normal, had a little mental handicap radio in his ear. He was required by law to wear it at all times. It was tuned to a government transmitter. Every twenty seconds or so, the transmitter would send out some sharp noise to keep people like George from taking unfair advantage of their brains.

George and Hazel were watching television. There were tears on Hazel's cheeks, but she'd forgotten for the moment what they were about.

On the television screen were ballerinas.

A buzzer sounded in George's head. His thoughts fled in panic, like bandits from a burglar alarm.

"That was a real pretty dance, that dance they just did," said Hazel.

"Huh?" said George.

"That dance—it was nice," said Hazel.

"Yup," said George. He tried to think a little about the ballerinas. They weren't really very good—no better than anybody else would have been, anyway. They were burdened with sash-weights and bags of birdshot, and their faces were masked, so that no one, seeing a free and graceful gesture or a pretty face, would feel like something the cat drug in. George was toying with the vague notion that maybe dancers shouldn't be handicapped. But he didn't get very far before another noise in his ear radio scattered his thoughts.

George winced. So did two out of the eight ballerinas.

Hazel saw him wince. Having no mental handicap herself, she had to ask George what the latest sound had been.

"Sounded like somebody hitting a milk bottle with a ball peen hammer," said George.

"I'd think it would be real interesting, hearing all the different sounds," said Hazel, a little envious. "All the things they think up."

"Um," said George.

"Only, if I was Handicapper General, you know what I would do?" asked Hazel. Hazel, as a matter of fact, bore a strong resemblance to the Handicapper General, a woman named Diana Moon Glampers. "If I was Diana Moon Glampers," said Hazel, "I'd have chimes on Sunday—just chimes. Kind of in honor of religion."

"I could think, if it was just chimes," said George.

"Well—maybe make 'em real loud," said Hazel. "I think I'd make a good Handicapper General."

"Good as anybody else," said George.

"Who knows better'n I do what normal is?" said Hazel.

"Right," said George. He began to think glimmeringly about his abnormal son who was now in jail, about Harrison, but a twenty-one-gun salute in his head stopped that.

"Boy!" said Hazel, "that was a doozy, wasn't it?"

It was such a doozy that George was white and trembling, and tears stood on the rims of his red eyes. Two of the eight ballerinas had collapsed to the studio floor, and were holding their temples.

"All of a sudden you look so tired," said Hazel. "Why don't you stretch out on the sofa, so's you can rest your handicap bag on the pillows, honeybunch." She was referring to the forty-seven pounds of birdshot in a canvas bag, which was padlocked around George's neck. "Go on and rest the bag for awhile," she said. "I don't care if you're not equal to me for awhile."

George weighed the bag with his hands. "I don't mind it," he said. "I don't notice it any more. It's just part of me."

"You've been so tired lately—kind of wore out," said Hazel. "If there was just some way we could make a little hole in the bottom of the bag, and just take out a few of them lead balls. Just a few."

"Two years in prison and two thousand dollars fine for every ball I took out," said George. "I don't call that a bargain."

"If you could just take a few out when you come home from work," said Hazel. "I mean—you don't compete with anybody around here. You just set around."

"If I tried to get away with it," said George, "then other people'd get away with it—and pretty soon we'd be right back to the dark ages again, with everybody competing against everybody else. You wouldn't like that, would you?"

"I'd hate it," said Hazel.

"There you are," said George. "The minute people start cheating on laws, what do you think happens to society?"

If Hazel hadn't been able to come up with an answer to this question, George couldn't have supplied one. A siren was going off in his head.

"Reckon it'd fall apart," said Hazel.

"What would?" said George blankly.

"Society," said Hazel uncertainly. "Wasn't that what you just said?"

"Who knows?" said George.

The television program was suddenly interrupted for a news bulletin. It wasn't clear at first as to what the bulletin was about, since the announcer, like all announcers, had a serious speech impediment. For about half a minute, and in a state of high excitement, the announcer tried to say, "Ladies and gentlemen—"

He finally gave up, handed the bulletin to a ballerina to read.

"That's all right—" Hazel said of the announcer, "he tried. That's the big thing. He tried to do the best he could with what God gave him. He should get a nice raise for trying so hard."

"Ladies and gentlemen—" said the ballerina, reading the bulletin. She must have been extraordinarily beautiful, because the mask she wore was hideous. And it was easy to see that she was the strongest and most graceful of all the dancers, for her handicap bags were as big as those worn by two-hundred-pound men.

And she had to apologize at once for her voice, which was a very unfair voice for a woman to use. Her voice was a warm, luminous, timeless melody. "Excuse me—" she said, and she began again, making her voice absolutely uncompetitive.

"Harrison Bergeron, age fourteen," she said in a grackle squawk, "has just escaped from jail, where he was held on suspicion of plotting to overthrow the government. He is a genius and an athlete, is underhandicapped, and should be regarded as extremely dangerous."

A police photograph of Harrison Bergeron was flashed on the screen—upside down, then sideways, then upside down again, then right side up. The picture showed the full length of Harrison against a background calibrated in feet and inches. He was exactly seven feet tall.

The rest of Harrison's appearance was Halloween and hardware. Nobody had ever borne heavier handicaps. He had outgrown hindrances faster than the H-G men could think them up. Instead of a little ear radio for a mental handicap, he wore a tremendous pair of earphones, and spectacles with thick wavy lenses. The spectacles were intended to make him not only half blind, but to give him whanging headaches besides.

Scrap metal was hung all over him. Ordinarily, there was a certain symmetry, a military neatness to the handicaps issued to strong people, but Harrison looked like a walking junkyard. In the race of life,

Harrison carried three hundred pounds.

And to offset his good looks, the H-G men required that he wear at all times a red rubber ball for a nose, keep his eyebrows shaved off, and cover his even white teeth with black caps at snaggle-tooth random.

"If you see this boy," said the ballerina, "do not—I repeat, do not—try to reason with him."

There was the shriek of a door being torn from its hinges.

Screams and barking cries of consternation came from the television set. The photograph of Harrison Bergeron on the screen jumped again and again, as though dancing to the tune of an earthquake.

George Bergeron correctly identified the earthquake, and well he might have—for many was the time his own home had danced to the same crashing tune. "My God—" said George, "that must be Harrison!"

The realization was blasted from his mind instantly by the sound of an automobile collision in his head.

When George could open his eyes again, the photograph of Harrison was gone. A living, breathing Harrison filled the screen.

Clanking, clownish, and huge, Harrison stood in the center of the studio. The knob of the uprooted studio door was still in his hand. Ballerinas, technicians, musicians, and announcers cowered on their knees before him, expecting to die.

"I am the Emperor!" cried Harrison. "Do you hear? I am the Emperor! Everybody must do what I say at once!" He stamped his foot and the studio shook.

"Even as I stand here—" he bellowed, "crippled, hobbled, sickened—I am a greater ruler than any man who ever lived! Now watch me become what I can become!"

Harrison tore the straps of his handicap harness like wet tissue paper, tore straps guaranteed to support five thousand pounds.

Harrison's scrap-iron handicaps crashed to the floor.

Harrison thrust his thumbs under the bar of the padlock that secured his head harness. The bar snapped like celery. Harrison smashed his headphones and spectacles against the wall.

He flung away his rubber-ball nose, revealed a man that would have awed Thor, the god of thunder.

"I shall now select my Empress!" he said, looking down on the cowering people. "Let the first woman who dares rise to her feet claim her mate and her throne!"

A moment passed, and then a ballerina arose, swaying like a willow.

Harrison plucked the mental handicap from her ear, snapped off her physical handicaps with marvelous delicacy. Last of all, he removed her mask.

She was blindingly beautiful.

"Now—" said Harrison, taking her hand, "shall we show the people the meaning of the word dance? Music!" he commanded.

The musicians scrambled back into their chairs, and Harrison stripped them of their handicaps, too. "Play your best," he told them, "and I'll make you barons and dukes and earls."

The music began. It was normal at first—cheap, silly, false. But Harrison snatched two musicians from their chairs, waved them like batons as he sang the music as he wanted it played. He slammed them back into their chairs.

The music began again and was much improved.

Harrison and his Empress merely listened to the music for a while— listened gravely, as though synchronizing their heartbeats with it.

They shifted their weights to their toes.

Harrison placed his big hands on the girl's tiny waist, letting her sense the weightlessness that would soon be hers.

And then, in an explosion of joy and grace, into the air they sprang!

Not only were the laws of the land abandoned, but the law of gravity and the laws of motion as well.

They reeled, whirled, swiveled, bounced, capered, gamboled, and spun.

They leaped like deer on the moon.

The studio ceiling was thirty feet high, but each leap brought the dancers nearer to it.

It became their obvious intention to kiss the ceiling.

They kissed it.

And then, neutralizing gravity with love and pure will, they remained suspended in air inches below the ceiling, and they kissed each other for a long, long time.

It was then that Diana Moon Glampers, the Handicapper General, came into the studio with a double-barreled ten-gauge shotgun. She fired twice, and the Emperor and the Empress were dead before they hit the floor.

Diana Moon Glampers loaded the gun again. She aimed it at the musicians and told them they had ten seconds to get their handicaps back on.

It was then that the Bergerons' television tube burned out.

Hazel turned to comment about the blackout to George. But George had gone into the kitchen for a can of beer.

George came back in with the beer, paused while a handicap signal shook him up. And then he sat down again. "You have been crying?" he said to Hazel.

"Yup," she said.

"What about?" he said.

"I forget," she said. "Something real sad on television."

"What was it?" he asked.

"It's all kind of mixed up in my mind," said Hazel.

"Forget sad things," said George.

"I always do," said Hazel.

"That's my girl," said George. He winced. There was the sound of a riveting gun in his head.

"Gee—I could tell that one was a doozy," said Hazel.

"You can say that again," said George.

"Gee—" said Hazel, "I could tell that one was a doozy."[6]

CONNECTIONS

Would you want to live in the society Vonnegut describes? Would your opinion change if you could alter one thing in that society? If so, what would you change? What difference would that change make?

What is the "race of life?" How important is it that everyone approach it equally?

How would Harrison Bergeron define *freedom*? *Democracy*? *Equality*? How would Diana Moon Glampers define these terms? How do you define them? Record your working definitions in your journal.

Was Diana Moon Glampers a censor? Add a working definition of the word *censor* to your journal.

Why were the people in the story so obedient? So willing to conform? What could they have done to change things? Why didn't they do so? What were the consequences of their failure to act?

Make an identity chart for Harrison Bergeron. What things influenced him? Did Harrison have the power to define himself or did society do it for him? Harrison tried to break the rules of his society. Should an individual go against society? If so, under what circumstances? What might the consequences be?

Does it take courage to fight for the things you believe in? What opportunities have you had to stand up for what you think is right? How difficult was it? What might have made it easier? Should it be easier? Record your answers in your journal so that you can refer to them later.

Many individuals and families have a "grand plan" for their future. It may involve sending their children to college, buying a home, or starting a business. Nations also devise "grand plans." Often those plans aim at improving society. If you were to design a "perfect" society, what would it be like? What rights would you give individuals? How would you balance their rights with the rights of others?

Before you share your "grand plan" with the class, develop a list of criteria for critically evaluating ideas. In creating a list, consider the following questions:

- How can one judge whether an idea is good or bad?
- What values are assumed in the plan?
- What are the implications for those who do not share those values?
- Is a popular idea always a good one?
- What would the world be like if everyone accepted this plan?
- What strategies would you use to convince others that this plan is the "right" one?
- How can one keep the ideas that inspired this plan from being abused?

Post your list so that you can refer to it as you read about the "grand planners" of history.

READING 2

First Encounters in North America

When two people meet for the first time, each takes stock of the other, often focusing on differences. Martha Minow warns that difference always "implies a reference: difference from whom? I am no more different from you than you are from me. A short person is different only in relation to a tall one; a Spanish-speaking student is different in relation to an English-speaking one. But the point of comparison is often unstated."[7] By identifying unstated points of comparison, we can examine the relationships between those who have the power to assign labels of difference and those who lack that power.

The first meetings between Europeans and Native Americans illustrate Minow's argument. Historians Peter N. Carroll and David W. Noble have used primary sources to describe those encounters:

> [On] an otherwise ordinary autumn day shortly after sunrise, the Arawak inhabitants of the Caribbean Islands noticed strange ships sailing on the horizon, much larger than their dugout canoes. As these ships moved closer and closer, they saw strange-looking people with light skins aboard, making odd gestures. The Arawak youths stood at the banks hesitantly, and then some of the braver men began swimming toward the mysterious boats.

In describing the "Indians," Europeans focused not on who they were but on who they were not.

These strangers offered the Arawak red-colored caps, glass beads, and other curious trifles. In exchange, the Arawak brought parrots, cotton skeins, darts, and other items. Then the strangers drew out swords, which the Arawak, in ignorance, grasped by the blades, cutting themselves. It was a symbolic act, this inadvertent drawing of blood. For the Arawak and the strangers looked at the world from opposite angles, and both were fascinated by what the other was not.

That first contact between Native Americans and Europeans was repeated with increasing frequency as other enterprising Europeans followed those first ships across the Atlantic Ocean. Whether the voyagers were Spanish, English, French, or Portuguese in origin, whether the Native Americans were Arawak, Yurok, Iroquois, Natchez, or Aztec, the initial confrontation was usually the same—two cultures looking at each other from opposite ends of the sword, each awed by the mystery of the other.[8]

> Each group of Europeans drew from its own experiences in defining Native Americans as the *other.*

To the Arawak, the newcomers were so obviously different in language, dress, color that the Native Americans doubted that they were human beings. "They believe very firmly," wrote Christopher Columbus after his first voyage to the Americas, "that I, with these ships and people, came from the sky." Other native peoples reacted in similar ways to their first encounters with Europeans.

Columbus and other Europeans had their own misconceptions. They mistakenly believed that the Americans were "Indians." Carroll and Noble write, "This misconception originated in Columbus's basic error (which he himself never realized) in thinking that in sailing westward from Europe he had reached the Indies, which were the true object of his voyage. To Columbus, it was literally inconceivable that he had found previously unknown lands. Like other Europeans of his time, he believed firmly in the completeness of human knowledge. What he saw, therefore, he incorporated into his existing worldview, and the Native Americans thereby became, to the satisfaction of most Europeans, simply Indians."[9]

In describing the "Indians," Europeans focused not on who they were but on who they were not. They then went on to describe what the indigenous peoples did *not* have. Amerigo Vespucci, for whom the Americas are named, described the "Indians" as neither Muslims nor Jews. He noted that they are "worse than heathen; because we did not see that they offered any sacrifice, nor yet did they have a house of prayer." John Winthrop, an Englishman who helped found Massachusetts Bay Colony, justified his claims to the Indians' land by arguing that they "enclose no land, neither have they any settled habitations, nor any tame cattle."

Each group of Europeans drew from its own experiences in defining Native Americans as the *other.* At about the time the first English settlers were arriving in the Americas, England was also colonizing Ireland. Not surprisingly, historian Ronald Takaki finds that "the English projected the familiar onto the strange, their images of the Irish onto the native people of

America." He goes on to say that in Virginia, they viewed the Indians as "brutal and backward, but they were not yet seen as incapable of becoming civilized because of their race, or 'descent.' Their heathenism had not yet been indelibly attached to their distinctive physical characteristics such as their skin color."[10]

In New England, the story was somewhat different. Although early explorers described the Wampanoag, Pequot, Narraganset and other Native American groups in New England as farmers, many English colonists in the region denied the fact. Instead they viewed them as a lazy, idle people who would rather starve than work. They claimed that like "the foxes and wild beasts," Indians did nothing "but run over the grass."[11]

To the newcomers, the Native Americans were not only "backward" but also dangerous. In Takaki's words, "they represented what English men and women in America thought they were not—and, more important, what they must not become. As exiles living in the wilderness far from 'civilization,' the English used their negative images of Indians to delineate the moral requirements they had set up for themselves." In doing so, they dehumanized Native Americans. Increasingly, "to be 'Indianized' meant to serve the Devil." To be "Indianized" also meant to be "decivilized, to become wild men."[12] After all, the English viewed Indians as people living outside of "civilization."

Such ideas were rooted at least in part in religious beliefs. As Carroll and Nobel point out in their description of Spanish explorers, "Europeans in the age of Columbus saw themselves as Christians, the most spiritually pure people in creation. This ethnocentric idea found reinforcement in the ideals of the Roman Catholic Church, which claimed to be a universal spiritual community. Yet this ideology clearly excluded such religiously different people as Muslims, against whom Christians had waged holy wars for centuries, and Jews, who remained outsiders throughout European society. Believing in a single unitary religion, members of the Catholic Church viewed [nonbelievers] as suitable either for conversion to the true faith or worthy only of death or enslavement. Such religious attitudes shaped the Europeans' relations with Africans as well as Native Americans."[13] Such attitudes were not limited to Europeans who were Catholic. They were shared by Protestants as well.

Relations between the Americans and the Europeans were also shaped by the fierce competition among European nations for wealth and power. As Europeans took control of more and more of the Americas, millions of Native Americans were killed. Countless others were pushed into the interior of both continents. Still others were forced into slavery.

Carroll and Nobel write of Columbus, "Like other Europeans of his time, he believed firmly in the completeness of human knowledge. What he saw, therefore, he incorporated into his existing worldview." How did Columbus's voyage ultimately affect that view? Do people today still hold it?

Sociologist Kai Erikson has noted that one of the surest ways to "confirm an identity, for communities as well as for individuals, is to find some way of measuring what one is *not*."[14] What are the effects of a negative identity—of defining someone by what he or she is not? What did it mean to Native Americans? To Europeans? Have you ever been defined by what you are not? If so, how did it affect the way you viewed yourself? Why do you think that individuals focus on differences rather than similarities when they meet someone for the first time? How does doing so encourage myths and misinformation?

Write working definitions of *savage* and *heathen*. Both words tend to make *them* seem less human and therefore more threatening. Alex Bein suggests that to understand anti-Judaism, we must look at the language of Jew-hatred. How does his comment apply to "anti-Native American" sentiments? How does language affect the tolerance one group has for another? How can language lead to dehumanization?

Carroll and Nobel note that Europeans in the age of Columbus considered themselves "as Christians, the most spiritually pure people in creation." Why do the two historians consider that belief ethnocentric? Compare their definition of ethnocentrism to Abel's in the overview to this chapter. What similarities seem most striking?

A young Native American told an interviewer, "Imagine growing up an American Indian halfbreed with the blood of Caddo, Choctaw, and Chickasaw tribes in you. . . Imagine growing up. . . knowing that you belong to a culture long native to this land before the white man 'discovered' it. Imagine trying to assert your identity when the majority of society affirms that 'Indians are a dead race.' Imagine constantly dealing with people who try their hardest to convince you that you are not an Indian. Imagine."[15] What does he suggest about the power of labels? About the power of those who assign labels? How is his problem similar to that of the Bear in *the bear that wasn't* (Chapter 1, Reading 1)? How is it unique? Why do you think he calls himself a "half-breed"? What does that label imply?

Slavery and Freedom

[The struggle for freedom] forced upon [the slave] a need that no other human beings have felt so acutely: the need for disenslavement, for disalienation, for negation of social death, for recognition of his inherent dignity.

*I*n some parts of the Americas, Europeans enslaved indigenous peoples and used them to exploit the riches of the two continents and enhance their own power. In other places—particularly in what is now the United States—Indian slavery was relatively rare for several reasons. Great numbers of Native Americans died of diseases Europeans unknowingly brought to the Americas. And those who survived fought hard for their freedom. Even those captured in battle did not remain slaves for long. They knew the land too well and had too many places where they could find refuge.

To meet their ever-growing need for workers, the English relied at first on "indentured servants"—men and women who were bound by contract to serve a master for four to seven years. Few came to the Americas voluntarily. Takaki notes:

> Some of the servants were victims of the Irish "slave-trade." English poor laws for the correction and punishment of rogues and idle people were enforced in Ireland, and this led to the wholesale kidnapping of young Irish women and men to supply the labor needs of the colonies. One of them, John King, recalled how he and others were "stolen in Ireland" by English soldiers. Taken from their beds at night "against their Consents," they were put on a ship. "Weeping and Crying," the Irish captives were kept on board until "a Lord's day morning" when the ship set sail for America.[16]

By the early 1600s, the English were importing "servants" not only from England and Ireland but also from Africa. At first, they were treated similarly. But by mid-century, Africans were being degraded into "a condition of servitude for life and even the status of property." Slavery was not a new idea to the people of any continent. According to Orlando Patterson, a sociologist, it has existed "from before the dawn of human history right down to the twentieth century, in the most primitive of human societies and in the most civilized. There is no region on earth that has not at some time harbored the institution. Probably there is no group of people whose ancestors were not at one time slaves or slaveholders."[17]

Although Patterson sees similarities between slavery and other relationships based on the power of one individual over another, he regards slavery as unique in three important ways. The first is that slaves were always powerless. Secondly, they were considered "social nonpersons." That is, they were almost always outsiders—people with no ties to others in the community. So they were outside one's *universe of obligation*—the circle of persons "toward whom obligations are owed, to whom rules apply, and whose injuries call for [amends] by the community."

In every society, the treatment of newly acquired slaves accentuated their isolation. They were usually dressed in special clothing or given a distinctive haircut. Many were also tatooed or branded. Few were permitted to keep their own name, language, customs, or religious beliefs. In the United States, according to historian Winthrop D. Jordan, the powerlessness and social isolation of slaves led to a "generalized conception of 'us'— white, English, free—and 'them'—black, heathen, slave."[18] Patterson explains how such attitudes affected a slave's identity and self-esteem.

> [A slave] had a past, to be sure. But a past is not a heritage. Everything has a history, including sticks and stones. Slaves differed from other human beings in that they were not allowed freely to integrate the experience of their ancestors into their lives, to inform their understanding of social reality with inherited meanings of their natural forebears, or to anchor the living present in any conscious community of memory. That they reached back for the past, as they reached out for the related living, there can be no doubt. Unlike other persons, doing so meant struggling with and penetrating the iron curtain of the master, his community, his laws, his policemen or patrollers, and his heritage.[19]

Slavery was distinctive in yet another way too. Slaves were always dishonored. In his autobiography, Frederick Douglass, a former slave and an abolitionist, described the relationship between dishonor and powerlessness when he wrote of his master's attempts to break his spirit. By fighting back, Douglass regained "a sense of my own manhood. . . . I was nothing before, I was a man now." He added, "A man without force is without the essential dignity of humanity. Human nature is so constituted that it cannot honor a helpless man, although it can pity him; and even that it cannot do long, if the signs of power do not arise." Patterson stresses the importance of acts of resistance:

> The slave resisted . . . in countless ways, only one of which, rebellion, was not subtle. Against all odds he strove for some measure of regularity and predictability in his social life. Because his kin relations were illegitimate, they were all the more cherished. Because he was considered degraded, he was all the more infused with the yearning for dignity. Because of his formal isolation . . . he was acutely sensitive to the realities of community. The fierce love of the slave mother for her child is attested to in every slaveholding society; everywhere the slave's zest for life and fellowship confounded the slaveholder class; and in all slaveholding societies the existential dignity of the slave belied the slaveholder's denial of its existence.[20]

I have yet to see a serious act of violence that was not provoked by the experience of feeling shamed and humiliated, disrespected and ridiculed, and that did not represent the attempt to prevent or undo this "loss of face" — no matter how severe the punishment, even if it includes death.

Patterson notes that "the struggle itself forced upon [the slave] a need that no other human beings have felt so acutely: the need for disenslavement, for disalienation, for negation of social death, for recognition of his inherent dignity." He goes on to say: "And so it was that freedom came into the world. Before slavery people simply could not have conceived of the thing we call freedom. Men and women in premodern, nonslaveholding societies did not, could not, value the removal of restraint as an ideal."

CONNECTIONS

How does Patterson define *slavery*? *Freedom*? Write a working definition of each in your journal. What is the relationship between slavery and freedom? Between slavery and power? How does slavery differ from other relationships based on power? How important are those differences?

What is a "social nonperson"? In the mid-1900s, Ralph Ellison wrote of himself and other African Americans as "invisible men." What do you think the term means? How might it be connected to Patterson's description of a slave as a "social nonperson"?

How does Patterson's view of slavery explain why few Native Americans were enslaved in English colonies? How does it explain why white indentured servants did not become slaves?

James F. Gilligan has said that he has yet to see a serious act of violence that was "not provoked by the experience of feeling shamed and humiliated, disrespected and ridiculed, and that did not represent the attempt to prevent or undo this 'loss of face'—no matter how severe the punishment, even if it includes death." How do his remarks relate to slavery? Research sabotage and other acts of resistance during the years of slavery. What does your research suggest about the relationship between violence and the loss of self-esteem? What other factors encourage violence?

How would an identity chart for a slave be similar to one for a free man or woman? What would be the most significant differences?

Orlando Patterson writes that slaves and other oppressed peoples wear "masks" in their dealings with those who have power over them. What are the masks he refers to? Why were they worn? Do you know of anyone today who wears a "mask"? If so, who?

A *paradox* is a seemingly contradictory statement that is true. Why is it a paradox that the "first men and women to struggle for freedom, the first to think of themselves as free in the only meaningful sense of the term, were freedmen"?

How do you account for the fact that slaves were almost always out-siders—individuals whose race, religion, or nationality differed from that of the slaveholder?

Research slavery in Europe, Asia, Africa, or South America. Who was enslaved? By whom? How were slaves treated? How were they defined by slaveholders? How did they define themselves?

In *Race and Slavery in the Middle East*, historian Bernard Lewis points out that slavery has been "accepted and even endorsed by Judaism, Christianity, and Islam, as well as other religions of the world." How do you account for the widespread acceptance of the institution? What atti-tudes had to change before slavery was viewed as an evil rather than as an accepted part of society?

READING 4

Membership in the United States

*I*n 1776, thirteen of Britain's North American colonies declared their inde-pendence. Soon after, the people who lived in those colonies formed a nation. They then had to decide who was an American and who was not. Would everyone who lived in the new United States be included in the nation? If not, how would citizenship be determined?

In the Declaration of Independence, Thomas Jefferson of Virginia voiced the nation's ideals. Americans acknowledged those ideals in their state constitutions, or plans of government. But no state lived up to them. Each excluded a large number of Americans from citizenship. Everywhere, indigenous peoples were viewed as outsiders, as members of separate but inferior nations. Jefferson referred to them as "merciless savages" in the Declaration of Independence. And most other Americans agreed. Few respected the cultures of indigenous peoples or their property rights. If Native Americans refused to sell their land, they were pushed out, cap-tured, or killed. Most white settlers were too eager for these lands to con-cern themselves with rights or agreements. And most state leaders, and later national leaders, reflected the prejudices of white Americans.

African Americans were also excluded even though many of them had fought for the nation's independence. Slavery was the law of the land throughout the new nation. Still many black Americans were heartened by the ideals expressed in the Declaration of Independence. They repeatedly quoted the document in their demands for the abolition of slavery and the same rights other citizens enjoyed. Indeed, a few slaves successfully sued for their freedom by claiming that slavery went against the Declaration of

If destruction be our lot, we must ourselves be its author and finisher. As a nation of freemen, we must live through all time, or die by suicide.

Independence. In deciding one such case, the Massachusetts Supreme Court noted that the state's constitution declared that "all men are born free and equal." The judges therefore ruled that slavery would "no longer be tolerated" in the state. A few other states also outlawed slavery, but none gave African Americans equal rights. Free blacks were rarely permitted to serve on juries, vote, or hold office. The prejudices that made slavery possible before the Revolution continued after it ended.

Many white Americans did not enjoy all of the rights of citizenship either. In a few states, only Christians could vote or hold office. And every state required that potential voters and officeholders own considerable property. However, no woman, no matter how much property she owned, could participate in government. Indeed, when a woman married, she lost control of her property. According to the laws of every state in the new nation, a married woman's property belonged to her husband—including her wages if she took a job.

Yet even as state constitutions limited citizenship, they also offered individuals more freedom than people had almost anywhere else. Every state protected freedom of speech, press, and religion as well as the right to peacefully assemble and to petition, or formally ask, the government to right a wrong. Indeed many Americans in 1787 refused to support a new national Constitution unless it included a formal listing or "bill" of rights. Therefore soon after the new government was formed, ten amendments were added to the Constitution. They became the nation's Bill of Rights.

Yet neither the new Constitution nor the Bill of Rights addressed the issue of slavery, partly because most white Americans in the late 1700s thought it would not survive for long in a free society. That belief was reflected in the debates at the Constitutional Convention in Philadelphia in 1787. The delegates made several compromises that affected slavery. In a compromise, everyone involved in a dispute gives up something to reach an agreement. For example, the convention was deadlocked for a time over the issue of representation in Congress. Delegates from the smaller states wanted equal representation. Those from larger states argued that a state's representation ought to be based on its population. They compromised by creating a Senate in which each state was equally represented and a House of Representatives with representation based on population. The delegates then had to decide *who* would be counted in a state's population. Northern delegates argued that slaves were not citizens and therefore should not be included. Representatives from the South insisted that slaves were a part of the population. Again, the delegates compromised: a slave would be counted as "three-fifths of a person."

When a few northern delegates tried to abolish the slave trade, southerners tried to block the move. As a result, the convention chose to let the trade continue for another twenty years before officially ending it. The delegates also agreed to a clause calling for the return of runaway slaves. Opponents of slavery went along with such measures, because they saw them as temporary. They thought slavery would soon disappear. Instead, the number of slaves in the nation exploded.

There were only about half a million slaves in the United States in 1790. By 1860, there were over four million and few Americans still believed that the institution would disappear on its own. Too many white Americans now regarded slave labor as essential to their power and prosperity. Increasingly, the right to own slaves was guarded by the nation's laws, supported by the nation's courts, and backed not only by American soldiers but also by the prejudices of white Americans throughout the United States. What caused the change? Historians attribute much of it to the skyrocketing demand for cotton. As sales boomed, so did the need for workers to plant and harvest the crop. Many white southern farmers feared that the abolition of slavery would jeopardize their ability to meet the growing demand for cotton.

Some Americans—both black and white—vigorously opposed the expansion of slavery. They believed it was morally wrong and saw it as proof that the nation was sliding backward rather than moving forward. Theodore Parker, a Boston minister, wrote, "At first, Slavery was an exceptional measure, and men tried to apologize for it, and excuse it. Now it is a normal principle, and the institution must be defended and [celebrated]." For Parker, the last straw came in 1857, when the United States Supreme Court declared slavery legal even in states that had abolished it. The justices ruled that Dred Scott, a slave, did not become a free man when his master brought him to a free state. Indeed the majority argued that he had "no rights which the white man was bound to respect and the negro might justly and lawfully be reduced to slavery for his benefit."

Parker was not the only American horrified by the ruling. The following year, the decision was hotly debated in a number of elections. In Illinois, both candidates for the U.S. Senate, Abraham Lincoln and Stephen Douglas, discussed the future of slavery at every campaign stop. In one speech, Lincoln declared:

> I, as well as Judge Douglas, am in favor of the race to which I belong having the [socially] superior position. I have never said anything to the contrary, but I hold that, notwithstanding all this, there is no reason in the world why the negro is not entitled to all the natural rights enunciated in the Declaration of Independence, the right to life, liberty, and the pursuit of happiness. I hold that he is as much entitled to these as the white man.
>
> I think the authors of [the Declaration] intended to include *all* men, but they did not intend to declare all men equal in *all respects*. They did not mean to say all were equal in color, size, intellect, moral development, or social capacity. They defined, with tolerable distinctness, in what respects they did consider all men created equal— equal in "certain unalienable rights, among which are life, liberty, and the pursuit of happiness."[21]

Democracy is becoming, rather than being. It can easily be lost, but never is fully won. Its essence is eternal struggle.

Lincoln recognized that most white Americans believed in both the ideals expressed in the Declaration and slavery. He insisted that they would eventually have to give up one or the other. In an earlier speech in 1838, he explained why:

> At what point shall we expect the approach of danger? By what means shall we fortify against it? Shall we expect some transatlantic military giant to step the Ocean, and crush us at a blow? Never! All the armies of Europe, Asia, and Africa combined, with all the treasure of the earth (our own excepted) in their military chest; with a Bonaparte [the military leader, Napoleon, who destroyed the French Republic and conquered much of Europe] for a commander, could not by force, take a drink from the Ohio, or make a track on the Blue Ridge, in a trial of a thousand years. At what point then is the approach of danger to be expected? I answer, if it ever reach us, it must spring up amongst us. It cannot come from abroad. If destruction be our lot, we must ourselves be its author and finisher. As a nation of freemen, we must live through all time, or die by suicide.[22]

Lincoln's words were prophetic. In 1861, the year he became President, eleven states left the Union because they wanted to protect slavery. In the bloody Civil War that followed, the nation and its ideals were tested as never before. At first, many Northerners believed that they were fighting only to save the Union. By 1863, the war had a new focus. On January 1, Lincoln issued the Emancipation Proclamation, freeing slaves in the rebellious states.

The following year, he reflected on the war's meaning at the dedication of a cemetery for Union soldiers in Gettysburg, Pennsylvania. "Four score and seven years ago our fathers brought forth, upon this continent, a new nation, conceived in Liberty, and dedicated to the proposition that all men are created equal. Now we are engaged in a great civil war, testing whether that nation, or any nation, so conceived, and so dedicated, can long endure." Lincoln ended his speech by urging "that we here highly resolve that these dead shall not have died in vain; that this nation, under God, shall have a new birth of freedom; and that this government of the people, by the people, for the people, shall not perish from the earth."

After the war, three amendments were added to the Constitution. The Thirteenth Amendment abolished slavery. The Fourteenth stated that anyone born in the United States was a citizen and entitled to all of the rights and responsibilities of citizenship. The Fifteenth Amendment guaranteed every citizen the right to vote. But prejudice and discrimination continued throughout the nation. Everywhere African Americans were treated as second-class citizens.

Nations, like individuals, have an identity. Make an identity chart for the United States. What values and beliefs were central to the nation's identity in 1776? In 1860? Today?

Find out more about the men who served as delegates to the Constitutional Convention in 1787. Who were they? How were they selected? Whose interests did they represent? How did they decide who was "in" and who was "out"? You may also want to research the voices that were not heard at the Convention. Who was excluded? And how did their exclusion affect the final document?

Few delegates to the Constitutional Convention considered the concessions they made to reach agreement as important as their goal— a strong, national government. Were they right? What is the legacy of the compromises Americans made in 1787? For example, how were the compromises that involved slavery related to the decision in the Dred Scott case? To the Civil War? To racism in the United States today?

How important is compromise to democracy? Are there ever issues on which one should never compromise?

The Constitution recognizes and protects slavery. Yet the words *slave* or *slavery* do not appear in the document. Instead the document refers to persons "held to service or labour." Why do you think they went to such lengths to avoid calling a slave a "slave"?

Investigate the federal laws that protected slavery. What do those laws suggest about the power of the majority in a democracy? About the vulnerability of minorities? How are vulnerable minorities protected today? How effective are those safeguards?

Why did Lincoln think that a dictator like Napoleon Bonaparte could conquer European nations but not the United States? What was the only thing that could destroy the nation in his opinion? What events in the United States in the early 1800s might have prompted his warning? What events today support his argument?

Lincoln made the speech in 1838 at a school for young men. It emphasized education as critical to the nation's future. You will find the complete speech in *The Collected Works of Abraham Lincoln* (available at most libraries). What does he say about the dangers of mobs and violence? About the purpose of law in a society? About the dangers of a history that is not remembered or taught?

By the mid-1800s, many states in the South had laws that limited free speech. Those laws did not allow people to publish or distribute books, newspapers, or pamphlets that opposed slavery. They also banned meetings that "interfered" with slavery. How do such limitations on dissent support Lincoln's argument that the nation could not achieve its goals as long as it supported slavery?

Abraham Lincoln once said, "As I would not be a slave, so I would not be a master. This expresses my idea of democracy. Whatever differs from this, to the extent of the difference, is no democracy." To others, democracy was not a condition but a process. Judge William H. Hastie once said of democracy, "It is becoming, rather than being. It can easily be lost, but never is fully won. Its essence is eternal struggle." How do you define democracy? Is it equality as Lincoln suggests? Or is it a process?

The prejudices that made slavery possible did not end when slavery itself was abolished. Laws alone are not enough to ensure a democratic society. In 1993, President Vaclav Havel of the Czech Republic reflected on the need not only for democratic institutions but also for what he calls a "civil society"—one that encourages people "to act as citizens in the best sense of the word and drive out manifestations of intolerance." He called the building of such a society the "biggest challenge of our time."[23] How does one build a civil society? How is the idea related to Bronowski's definition of tolerance (Chapter 1, Reading 15)? To Lincoln's definition of democracy?

After the Civil War, Sojourner Truth, a former slave and an abolitionist, argued that the fight for equality was not yet over. In her view, unless women could vote, slavery was only partly destroyed. What do you think she meant? Do you agree?

In 1963, Dr. Martin Luther King, Jr., spoke to a crowd of over two hundred thousand people who gathered in Washington, D.C., to demand equal rights for all Americans. He told them, "I have a dream that one day this nation will rise up and live out the true meaning of its creed: 'We hold these truths to be self-evident that all men are created equal.' I have a dream that one day on the red hills of Georgia, the sons of former slaves and sons of former slaveholders will be able to sit together at the table of brotherhood."

According to historian Garry Wills, Lincoln viewed the Declaration of Independence as a pledge "to people of all colors everywhere." What do you think he meant? How is that pledge related to King's dream? To what extent had that pledge been fulfilled in 1963, the year King gave his speech? What were the legacies of the failure to keep that pledge in 1963? What are the legacies today? How do they threaten Havel's "civil society"?

Thomas Jefferson, the author of the Declaration of Independence, considered slavery immoral. Yet he himself was a slaveholder who considered Africans a threat to "white racial purity." In reflecting on efforts to free the slaves, he wrote, "This unfortunate difference in color, and perhaps of faculty, is a powerful obstacle to the emancipation of these people." Despite such beliefs, Jefferson has inspired generations of African Americans. In a speech, Julian Bond, a civil rights activist, tried to explain why:

Martin Luther King didn't care whether the . . . author of the Declaration of Independence thought he was inferior. The man may have thought so, but his words belied the thought.

For King and his audiences, the significant Thomas Jefferson was not the Ambassador to France or the Secretary of State, the farmer or the slaveholder; as did Jefferson, they thought his chief virtue was as author of the Declaration of Independence, specifically of those self-evident truths that all are created equal.

The promise of the words—for King, for those before him and us—became the true measure of the man.[24]

Are Jefferson's most famous words the "true measure of the man"? Or should he be judged by his deeds?

Lincoln believed in "progress." He, like others of his time, did not expect the nation to realize its ideals all at once. Lincoln was killed in 1865. Use an American history book or an encyclopedia to research the progress the nation made in his lifetime. To what accomplishments could he point with pride? What work remained?

Do individuals also "progress"? As a young man, Lincoln regarded Africans as inferior. Use a biography or an encyclopedia to find out how his views had changed by the time he ran for the Senate. How had they changed by the time he became President? What prompts people to change their views of other people?

For more information about the efforts of abolitionists to bring about social equality, see Chapter 2 of *Choosing to Participate*.

R E A D I N G 5

Nationalism, Power, and Identity in Europe

*E*uropeans eagerly watched as the Americans experimented with democracy. People there were struggling with similar issues. They, too, were deciding how power should be divided in their nations and what rights individuals ought to have. In 1789, the French replaced their king with a government that allowed individuals a say in their own future. In their Declaration of the Rights of Man and Citizen, they expressed the ideals that inspired their revolution:

I. Men are born, and always continue, free and equal in respect of their rights . . . .

IV. Political liberty consists in the power of doing whatever does not injure another . . . .

Nationalism is a feeling more positive than patriotism, or love for one's country for its "beautiful streams, valleys, and mountains". . . . It involves a certain amount of ethnocentricism, a feeling of superiority of one's nation over other nations.

> X. No man ought to be molested on account of his opinions, not even on account of his religious opinions, provided his avowal of them does not disturb the public order established by the law.

Like the Americans, the French had to decide how their new government would reflect their ideals. Would citizenship be open to all or limited to a few individuals and groups? In the end, the National Assembly took a democratic approach to citizenship. It eliminated distinctions between nobles and ordinary people. Then it turned its attention to religious minorities within the nation—particularly to Protestants and Jews. The assembly declared that both were citizens and entitled to the rights other citizens enjoyed.

France's new republic did not last long. Within a few years, Napoleon Bonaparte, a general in the French army, had destroyed it and made himself emperor. He then set out to conquer neighboring countries. As he took over one nation after the other, his armies spread the ideals of the revolution, particularly the ideals of liberty and equality. They also unknowingly unleashed a new force in the world: nationalism. As Europeans struggled to drive the French army from their land, they began to see themselves in a new way. In the past, people expressed loyalty to their ruler, not to their country. Now many began to see themselves as Germans, Austrians, Hungarians, Slavs, or Italians. It was an idea that lived on long after Napoleon was defeated in 1815 and traditional rulers regained their thrones.

Historian Hans Kohn stresses the importance of membership to the idea of a nation. He defines *nationalism* as "a state of mind inspiring the large majority of a people and claiming to inspire all its members. It asserts that the nation-state is the ideal and the only legitimate form of political organization and that the nationality is the source of all cultural creative energy and of economic well-being."[25] Sociologist Theodore Abel views *nationalism* as a feeling "more positive than patriotism, or love for one's country for its 'beautiful streams, valleys, and mountains'" and warns that it may involve "a certain amount of ethnocentricism, a feeling of superiority of one's nation over other nations."[26]

By the early 1800s, many Europeans were defining a *nation* as a people who share traditions and a history. Among the leaders of this movement were a number of Germans who argued that the character of a people is expressed through its *Volksgeist*—its unchanging spirit as refined through history. They insisted that a common language, history, and culture are essential to national identity. In 1810, one German nationalist wrote, "A state without *Volk* is nothing, a soulless artifice; a *Volk* without a state is nothing, a bodiless airy phantom, like the Gypsies and the Jews. Only state and *Volk* together could form a *Reich*, and such a *Reich* cannot be preserved without *Volkdom*."[27]

Many German students responded to such ideas by organizing patriotic fraternities dedicated to uniting the German people. They were inspired by history books that pictured their ancestors as a pure people who were self-reliant, courageous, free, and loyal. Those who did not share that ancestry were increasingly viewed not only as outsiders but as an evil force that threatened the unity of the nation. In 1817, many of these young men assembled at Wartburg to celebrate the three hundredth anniversary of Martin Luther's break with the Catholic church and the start of Protestantism. The students regarded Luther as more than a religious leader. To them, he was also a German nationalist. After vowing that they would never fight other Germans, become censors, or join the secret police, the students threw dozens of books into a huge bonfire. A witness reported:

> A big basket was then brought to the fire filled with books, which were then publicly, in the presence of the German people, consigned to the flames in the name of Justice, the Fatherland, and the Spirit of the Community. This was supposed to be a righteous judgement over the wicked books, which dishonoured the Fatherland and destroyed the spirit of community; it was supposed to frighten the evil-minded and all those who, with their banal superficiality had—alas!—marred and attenuated the ancient and chaste customs of the Volk. The title of each of those books was read out by a herald, and every time a great cry rose from those present, expressive of their indignation: Into the fire! Into the fire! Let them go to the devil! Upon which the corpus delicti was delivered up into flames.[28]

To the young men who gathered around the bonfire, nationalism was a crusade. Its aim was not only to create a German nation but also to protect its purity. It was an idea that also attracted such scholars as Friedrich von Schlegel, who imagined the founders of the German *Volk* as a gifted "race" that left India in the distant past and carried its language and culture westward. Schlegel did not have a name for this ancient people. But others called them Indo-Europeans. It was not until later in the century that they were known as "Aryans."

Throughout the 1800s, the "Aryans" were romanticized. One German writer pictured their route from east to west as the route of civilization. He wrote, "The march of culture, in its general lines, has always followed the sun's course." A French scholar agreed, but he saw the route as leading "from India to France." The British had their own myth. They had already linked their ancestors—"free Anglo Saxons"—to Germanic tribes. Now they traced a journey through the forests of Germany to the British Isles. [29]

Those who burn books may some day burn people.

Whom did the French consider part of their "universe of obligation"? Whom did the young German nationalists regard as part of theirs?

The way a people define their "universe of obligation" determines who has the power to make the rules or laws. It also determines who will be protected by those laws and who will not.

If the United States had a *Volksgeist*, what would it be? Whose culture would it include?

In 1807, Napoleon called together seventy-one rabbis and other Jewish religious leaders to help him decide whether the Jews of France were members of the French nation. He asked:

> In the eyes of Jews, are Frenchmen considered as their brethren? Or are they considered as strangers?
>
> Do Jews born in France, and treated by the laws as French citizens, consider France their country? Are they bound to defend it? Are they bound to obey the laws and to conform to the dispositions of the civil code?

By 1807, Jews had been living in France for about two thousand years. What do the questions suggest about the way they were viewed? About the way Napoleon, in particular, regarded them? How would you feel if the President of the United States were to ask a group you belonged to similar questions? How would you respond?

The Jews Napoleon questioned offered the following response:

> The love of country is in the heart of Jews a sentiment so natural, so powerful, and so consonant to their religious opinions, that a French Jew considers himself in England, as among strangers, although he may be among Jews; and the case is the same with English Jews in France.
>
> To such a pitch is this sentiment carried among them, that during the last war, French Jews have been seen fighting desperately against other Jews, the subjects of countries then at war with France.

What point were the French Jews trying to make? What were they trying to tell the emperor about the way they defined themselves? About their loyalty? Why do you think that loyalty was questioned?

Chapter 1 explored the need individuals have to belong. How did Napoleon decide who belonged and who did not? How did the German students make those decisions? What similarities do you notice? What differences seem most striking?

Nationalism is a positive idea. It is a way of uniting people. At what point is it dangerous? Can any idea, no matter how positive, be abused?

What is censorship? How are the students at Wartburg who condemned censors and then burned books like Diana Moon Glampers (Reading 1)? How are they different? What part does censorship play in a free society? What is the role of free thought?

Heinrich Heine, a great German poet who lived in the nineteenth century, once wrote that those who burn books may someday burn people. What do you think he meant? How do you think the students would have responded to his remark? How might Diana Moon Glampers respond? Why do you think individuals sometimes choose to cast the things they fear or regard as evil into flames?

Why did German students regard Martin Luther as a German nationalist? What does that suggest about whom they regarded as a "true" German and whom they did not? Were Germans who belonged to the Catholic Church included? What about Germans who followed other religions? What do your answers suggest about the reason that many consider the separation of church and state critical to democracy? Investigate how church and state came to be separated in the United States. How does that separation safeguard democratic institutions? How does that separation promote Havel's "civil society"—one that encourages people "to act as citizens in the best sense of the word and drive out manifestations of intolerance"?

In the journal you began in Chapter 1, describe how you feel about your country and its people. Do you regard yourself as a patriot? A nationalist? Or a chauvinist? What is the difference between those terms? Some people are naturalized citizens. How do they reconcile their loyalty to their new country with their feelings for the country of their birth?

Schlegel's notion of the origins of the "Aryan" race is fiction rather than fact. Yet in 1904, a French writer noted, "Today, out of 1,000 educated Europeans, 999 are convinced of the authenticity of their Aryan origins."[30] What effect do you think such beliefs had on the way a nation viewed its citizens? On the ways individuals regarded themselves and others? Historians maintain that what people perceive as true can be more important than the truth itself. Do you agree?

➤How do immigrants become citizens of the United States? Observe a naturalization ceremony. One such ceremony, *Arn Chorn: Naturalization Ceremony, 1993,* is available on videotape from the Facing History Resource Center. It includes a speech by Chorn, a survivor of the Cambodian Genocide.

Nation Building in Germany

Democracy is not an ideal state, but simply a state in which the forces of good have a free field against the forces of evil.

Debates over freedom and equality continued in the United States, France, and Germany throughout the early 1800s. Those debates had a particular urgency in Germany. During those years, the country was not a united nation but a confederation of more than thirty autocratic states, each jealously guarding its independence. (In an autocracy, a few individuals hold almost unlimited power.) German rulers agreed only on the need to outlaw democratic ideas and maintain their own power. As a result, censorship was a part of life in each German state. Yet in every state, a few individuals managed to spread democratic ideas, even as others vigorously defended authoritarian rule. In the mid-1800s, two Germans came to symbolize those two points of view. Although both were born in Prussia, the largest of the German states, their backgrounds were quite different. Carl Schurz came from a family of peasants, while Otto von Bismarck was a *Junker* or noble. Yet there were peasants who defended autocracy and nobles who were committed to democracy.

The two men came to public notice in 1848. That year, a new revolution began in France and spread to the various German states. Carl Schurz, then a nineteen-year-old university student, was among the first to join the rebels. He later wrote, "Republican ideas were at first only sparingly expressed. But the word democracy was soon on all tongues and many, too, thought it a matter of course that if the princes should try to withhold from the people the rights and liberties demanded, force would take the place of petition."[31]

By the time word of the revolution reached Otto von Bismarck's country estate, fighting had already begun in Berlin. Bismarck immediately rushed to the support of his king. His response grew out of a distaste for what he called "mob interference with political authority." He insisted that when people vote for their leaders, "arithmetic and chance take the place of logical reasoning."[32]

In 1848, Bismarck's position was not a popular one. In one German state after another, rulers frightened for their lives turned power over to the people. By May, an elected assembly was meeting in the city of Frankfurt to write a constitution that would unite Germany. It was not an easy task. Northern Germany was mainly Protestant and southern Germany, Catholic. The country was also home to dozens of ethnic groups. Were all of these people Germans? Should they all be citizens? In the end, the delegates were guided by democratic principles. They allowed men of various ethnic and religious groups to fully participate in the life of the nation for the first time. Women, however, no matter what their ethnicity, continued to be excluded.

Yet even as delegates were planning a new government, the mood in the country was changing—particularly the mood of educated and well-to-do German citizens. They were beginning to realize that in a democratic nation, they would have to share power not only with people who were less educated and less well-to-do but also with those whose economic and political beliefs differed from their own. As a result of their fears, most of Germany's kings and princes regained power.

Many rebels, including Schurz, were forced to flee the country or face prison. Schurz settled in the United States, where he took part not only in the debate over the future of slavery but also in the Civil War as a general in the Union army. After the war, he served the nation as a United States Senator from the state of Missouri and as Secretary of the Interior. His experiences convinced him that a democracy "is not an ideal state, but simply a state in which the forces of good have a free field against the forces of evil."[33]

Bismarck remained in Prussia and served his king. And he continued to believe that "it is not by speeches and majority decisions that the great questions of the age will be decided—that was the big mistake of 1848 and 1849—but by blood and iron." He used Prussia's military might to unite the nation. Under his leadership, Prussia allied with Austria in 1864 to defeat Denmark and win control of the German-speaking areas of Schleswig-Holstein. A quarrel with Austria over the future of the Danish territory led to a second war in 1866. That victory gave Prussia control over most of Germany and parts of Central Europe. By 1868, Bismarck's employer, the king of Prussia, was the most powerful man in Germany.

That year, Schurz returned to Prussia for a brief visit. To his amazement, he was invited to dine with Bismarck. Schurz later recalled that Bismarck had wondered how a government could keep order if the people had no respect for "authority." In reply, Schurz noted that "the Americans would hardly have become the self-reliant, energetic, progressive people they were, had there been . . . a police captain standing at every mud-puddle in America to keep people from stepping into it. " Schurz firmly believed that democracy is not an orderly system of government. He pointed out "that in a democracy with little government, things might go badly in detail but well on the whole, while in a monarchy with much and omnipresent government, things might go very pleasingly in detail but poorly on the whole."

Bismarck was not persuaded. He told Schurz, "I am not a democrat and cannot be. I was born an aristocrat and brought up an aristocrat. To tell you the truth, there was something in me that made me instinctively sympathize with the slaveholders as the aristocratic party in your civil war. But this vague sympathy did not in the least affect my views as to the policy to be followed by our government."[34]

Bismarck supported the North because it was richer and more powerful—not because he believed it was in the right. In his view might made right. As he put it, "Great crises form the weather that fosters Prussia's growth in that we exploit them fearlessly, perhaps even quite ruthlessly." In 1870, he went to war again, this time with France. During that war, King William of Prussia, now known as Kaiser Wilhelm I, proclaimed the German Empire in Versailles, France, on January 18, 1871. Four months later, Bismarck became the kaiser's chancellor, or chief adviser.

Once Germany was united, Bismarck and Wilhelm prepared a constitution. Like the one drafted in 1848, it gave all German men the right to vote. But the Reichstag, Germany's parliament, had very little authority. The French ambassador compared its meetings to a play:

> [The] rules are correctly applied, the customs observed . . . in short everything is done that can give the illusion and make one believe in the gravity of the debates or the importance of the votes; but behind this scenery, at the back of the stage, intervening always at the decisive hour and having their way, appear Emperor and Chancellor, supported by the vital forces of the nation—the army dedicated to the point of fanaticism, the bureaucracy disciplined by the master's hand, the [courts] no less obedient, and the population, skeptical occasionally of their judgments, quick to criticize, quicker still to bow to the supreme will.[35]

Bismarck's response to the growth of the Socialist party suggests how the system worked. The Socialists wanted a government that would foster economic and political equality. Bismarck vigorously opposed their goals but took no action against the group until it posed a political threat. In 1871, the Socialists had two delegates in the Reichstag; just six years later they had twelve. Bismarck was now determined to eliminate the group. His initial efforts to suppress the party, however, only increased its popular appeal. So he decided to move in a more roundabout way. When several attempts were made on the emperor's life in 1878, Bismarck blamed the Socialists even though he had no evidence they were involved. But the charge was enough to persuade the Reichstag to pass a law calling for the abolishment of any group with "social-democratic, socialistic, or communist tendencies" and the closing of any newspaper that supported such a group.

Bismarck then focused his attention on voters who supported the Socialists. Realizing that most were workers, he offered them a well-thought-out program of benefits, including pensions and health insurance. Bismarck was gambling on the idea that they would be willing to accept restrictions on their political rights in exchange for economic security. In the late 1800s, that gamble paid off.

Write working definitions of *democracy* and *autocracy*. What do the two forms of government have in common? What differences seem most striking? Why do you think Bismarck and Wilhelm hid authoritarian rule behind the illusion of a parliamentary government?

What are the strengths and weaknesses of Schurz's arguments? Of Bismarck's? On what issues did they agree? On what issues did they clash? Record your ideas in your journal. Later, you will see how the ideas of both men affected the course of history.

When the revolution began, Schurz wrote that "if the princes should try to withhold from the people the rights and liberties demanded, force would take the place of petition." The Declaration of Independence takes a similar stand. It states that if a government abuses the right of the people to "life, liberty, and the pursuit of happiness," people have not only the right but also the duty "to throw off such a government, and to provide new guards for their safety." What do those who share this view consider a government's main responsibility? Would Bismarck agree?

Make identity charts for Bismarck and Schurz. How did each man's values and beliefs affect the way he responded to the Revolution of 1848? To ideas like democracy and equality? Lincoln became more democratic in his views over the years. If he changed, could someone like Bismarck also change?

Schurz claimed that democracy is "a state in which the forces of good have a free field against the forces of evil." If so, do the "forces of good" always win? Or does might make right? What do Bismarck's remarks about the American Civil War suggest about the way he defines his "universe of obligation"? About the way he perceives himself and others?

Bismarck was always quick to find someone to blame for Germany's problems. Sometimes it was the Socialists; at other times it was the Catholics or the Jews. Each was labeled an "enemy of the state." What are the consequences of uniting a nation by creating enemies? It is a question that a number of German scholars have tried to answer in assessing Bismarck's legacy. In Max Weber's view, it left the German nation "without any political will whatever." Theodor Mommsen, a contemporary of Bismarck and an early supporter, argued that "Bismarck has broken the nation's back." What does it mean to leave a nation without "political will"? To "break the back of a nation"?

Suppose you were present for the conversation between Schurz and Bismarck. What questions might you have asked? What might you have added to their discussion? Record your ideas in your journal.

A Changing World

In a rootless society, it was easy to blame someone else for all that was new and disturbing. *They* were responsible for society's ills. *We* are blameless.

*I*n the 1800s, the world seemed to be changing faster than ever before. Many people were bewildered by those changes. They longed for the "good old days" when life was safe and secure. Stefan Zweig, a writer who grew up in Austria-Hungary, described such a time:

> Everyone knew how much he possessed or what he was entitled to, what was permitted and what forbidden. Everything had its norm, its definite measure and weight. He who had a fortune could accurately compute his annual interest. An official or an officer, for example, could confidently look up in the calendar the year when he would be advanced in grade, or when he would be pensioned. Each family had its fixed budget, and knew how much could be spent for rent and food, for vacations and entertainment; and what is more, invariably a small sum was carefully laid aside for sickness and the doctor's bills, for the unexpected. Whoever owned a house looked upon it as a secure domicile for his children and grandchildren; estates and businesses were handed down from generation to generation. When the babe was still in its cradle, its first mite was put in its little bank, or deposited in the savings bank, as a "reserve" for the future. In this vast empire everything stood firmly and immovably in its appointed place, and at its head was the aged emperor; and were he to die, one knew (or believed) another would come to take his place, and nothing would change in the well-regulated order. No one thought of wars, of revolutions, or revolts. All that was radical, all violence, seemed impossible in an age of reason.[36]

Long before Zweig was born, the old ways were beginning to change. Many of those changes were a result of the Industrial Revolution. It began in England in the 1700s with the invention of machines powered by steam. That innovation quickly led to thousands of others. People everywhere felt the impact of the changes, whether they worked at home or took a job in one of the many new factories that were springing up throughout Europe and North America.

The Industrial Revolution changed not only the way goods were made but also where they were made. More and more people were now leaving the countryside for jobs in large urban centers. Some mourned the change. Friedrich Tonnies, a sociologist, accentuated the differences between the old and the new by comparing a society rooted in tradition with a modern, rootless society in which the old ways were no longer respected. Traditional society was exemplified by the small, rural communities that dotted Europe and much of the United States. In those communities, every family was linked in some way to every other family. People knew their neighbors. Modern society, on the other hand, was exemplified by large industrial cities where people lived and worked among strangers.

In a rootless society, it was easy to blame someone else for all that was new and disturbing. *They* were responsible for society's ills. *We* are blameless. Who were *they*? Sometimes, *they* were people who held unpopular ideas. *They* were communists, socialists, even feminists. Often, *they* were people who were different in some way. In the Ottoman Empire that straddled Europe and Asia, *they* were Armenians, a Christian minority in a Muslim empire. In the United States, *they* were immigrants, African Americans, and Native Americans. In much of Europe, *they* were Jews.

CONNECTIONS

How is the society Zweig describes like the one Harrison Bergeron (Reading 1) lived in? What differences seem most striking? What does Zweig mean when he writes that "all that was radical, all violence, seemed impossible in an age of reason"? What is he implying about the age that followed it?

Write a working definition of the word *revolution*. Was the Industrial Revolution a revolution?

According to Martha Minow, a legal scholar, "Human beings use labels to describe and sort their perceptions of the world. The particular labels often chosen . . . can carry social and moral consequences while burying the choices and responsibility for those consequences. The labels point to conclusions about where an item, or an individual, belongs without opening for debate the purposes for which the label will be used."[37] How do those labels affect who is "tolerated" and who is not?

Why are periods of rapid change often followed by periods of intolerance? What conditions seem to encourage racism? What conditions foster tolerance? Find examples from current events.

READING 8

"Race Science" in a Changing World

*I*ncreasingly, in this new more modern world, people looked to science to justify their ideas about who was "in" and who was "out." The first scientists to respond were not Europeans but Americans. In the United States, dozens of scientists set out to prove the superiority of the "white race" over all others. Such research allowed some to insist that *they* are less than

> Human beings use labels to describe and sort their perceptions of the world. The particular labels often chosen. . . can carry social and moral consequences while burying the choices and responsibility for those consequences.

human and therefore less deserving of having their rights protected or being granted full citizenship than *we* are.

In the early 1800s, for example, a white surgeon from Philadelphia, Samuel Morton, hypothesized that there was a link between brain size and race. He maintained that it was therefore possible to rank races "objectively." After measuring a vast number of skulls, he concluded that his findings "proved" that whites were "superior" to other races. He was not sure if blacks were a separate race or a separate species, but he did insist that they were different from and inferior to whites. He also added a new twist to racist thinking—the idea that each race is fixed, intrinsically different from all others, and incapable of being changed. Although he gathered data just before the Civil War, Morton claimed the debate over slavery had no bearing on his research.

Frederick Douglass disagreed. He claimed that Morton was one who "reasons from prejudice rather than from facts." He went on to say, "It is the province of prejudice to blind; and scientific writers, not less than others, write to please, as well as to instruct, and even unconsciously to themselves, (sometimes,) sacrifice what is true to what is popular. Fashion is not confined to dress; but extends to philosophy as well—and it is fashionable now, in our land, to exaggerate the differences between the Negro and the European."[38]

It was also fashionable in Europe. Many people there were also intrigued with the idea that they belonged to a superior race. A French anthropologist, Paul Broca, later built upon Morton's theories. Broca believed that only "compatible" races would produce fertile or what he called "eugensic" offspring. He therefore warned against "race mixing." These ideas had powerful effects when governments applied them to everyday life.

In the years before the Civil War, Americans used such research to force indigenous peoples onto tiny reservations in the West. After the Civil War, they used it to defend the separation of African Americans from others in the community. In 1896, Homer Plessy, an African American, decided to challenge a Louisiana law that kept blacks separated from whites on public transportation. After deliberately taking a seat in the "white" section of a train, he was arrested, tried, and found guilty. He appealed the verdict, arguing that John Ferguson, the Louisiana judge who convicted him, had violated his rights as stated in the Fourteenth Amendment to the United States Constitution. That amendment guarantees every citizen equal protection under the law. The Supreme Court, however, sided with Ferguson, who argued that as long as the railroad offered "separate but equal" seating for whites and blacks, Plessy's rights were protected. Broca's research supported that ruling. It also encouraged other states to pass similar laws. By the early 1900s, those laws affected every aspect of American life. African Americans were kept apart in schools, factories, churches, theaters, hospitals, and even cemeteries.

It is the province of prejudice to blind; and scientific writers, not less than others, write to please, as well as to instruct, and even unconsciously to themselves, (sometimes,) sacrifice what is true to what is popular.

Racists also found support for their arguments in work that seemed unrelated to human societies. In 1859, Charles Darwin, a British biologist, published *The Origin of the Species*. It explained how various species of plants and animals physically change, or evolve, over time. Darwin's work suggested that each competes for space and nourishment and only those with a selective advantage survive to reproduce themselves. A number of Europeans and Americans, including a British writer named Herbert Spencer, began to apply Darwin's ideas to human society. Referring to Darwin's work but using his own phrases such as "the struggle for existence" and "the survival of the fittest," Spencer helped popularize a new doctrine known as *Social Darwinism*.

Social Darwinists saw their ideas at work everywhere in the world. Those who were fit were at the top of the social and economic pyramid. Those at the bottom were "unfit," they reasoned, because competition rewards "the strong." Many Social Darwinists therefore questioned the wisdom of extending the right to vote to groups who were "less fit." They argued that if the laws of natural selection were allowed to function freely, everyone would find his or her rightful place in the world. Increasingly that place was based on race.

In every country, people interpreted Social Darwinism a little differently. In Germany, Ernst Haeckel, a biologist, popularized the idea by combining it with romantic ideas about the German *Volk*. In a book called *Riddle of the Universe*, he divided humankind into races and ranked each. Not surprisingly "Aryans" were at the top of his list and Jews and Africans at the bottom.

Haeckel was also taken with the idea of eugenics—breeding "society's best with best"— as a way of keeping the "German race" pure. That idea also came from England. Its originator was Francis Galton, a cousin of Charles Darwin. Galton's ideas were popular not only in Germany but also in the United States. American eugenicists used them to advocate restrictions on marriage and immigration as well as laws that would sterilize the "socially unfit."

Scientists who tried to show that there was no "pure" race were ignored. In the late 1800s, the German Anthropological Society, under the leadership of Rudolph Virchow, conducted a study to determine if there really were racial differences between Jewish and "Aryan" children. After studying nearly seven million students, the society concluded that the two groups were more alike than they were different. Historian George Mosse said of the study:

> This survey should have ended controversies about the existence of pure Aryans and Jews. However, it seems to have had surprisingly little impact. The idea of race had been infused with myths, stereotypes, and subjectivities long ago, and a scientific survey could change little. The idea of pure, superior races and the concept of a racial enemy solved too many pressing problems to be easily discarded. The

The idea of pure, superior races and the concept of a racial enemy solved too many pressing problems to be easily discarded.

survey itself was unintelligible to the uneducated part of the population. For them, Haeckel's Riddle of the Universe was a better answer to their problems.[39]

CONNECTIONS

What do you think motivated Morton and other scientists to rank "races"? Morton's work had far-reaching effects mainly because he was considered a scientist—one who judges from evidence. What does *objective* mean? Was Morton objective? Are modern scientists objective?

Define the word *scientific*. Is Social Darwinism scientific? Are scientific proofs more convincing than other proofs? In the 1800s, Social Darwinism and other ideas about "race" were preached from the pulpit and taught in universities. In the United States, those ideas triggered a debate that forced some to question both the message and the messenger. In other societies that debate was censored. Why is the freedom to debate ideas essential to a free society?

What is the danger in linking nationalism with race? How does it increase the vulnerability of minorities? The fragility of democracy?

In the early 1800s, Congress debated whether to break its treaties with the Cherokee and other Native American nations to open more land for white Americans. During the debate, Theodore Frelinghuysen of New Jersey asked his fellow senators, "Do the obligations of justice change with the color of the skin?" What does the question suggest about the way Americans in the early 1800s defined their "universe of obligation"? How would the work of Morton and Broca affect the way Frelinghuysen's fellow senators might answer that question?

Think of times when prejudice has blinded you or someone you know. How did you react? How did you feel? What are the consequences of allowing prejudices to become "fashionable"? How do Mosse's comments support the view that what people believe is true is more important than the truth itself?

What problems did the idea of "pure races" solve in the United States? How does your answer explain why people were so reluctant to disregard the idea? What are the legacies of those solutions?

What are the legacies of Social Darwinism? How can it be used to explain some attitudes toward welfare recipients, for example? Toward work? Toward the rich and the poor? To gather information to answer these questions, see *Choosing to Participate*, Chapter 3.

Citizenship and European Jews

The tightening link between nationalism and race in the late 1800s had a profound effect on the ways European Jews defined their identity. Michael A. Meyer, a professor of Jewish history, writes:

> Long before the word became fashionable among psychoanalysts and sociologists, Jews in the modern world were obsessed with the subject of *identity*. They were confronted by the problem that Jewishness seemed to fit none of the usual categories. Until the establishment of the state of Israel, the Jews were not a nation, at least not in the political sense; being Jewish was different from being German, French, or American. And even after 1948 [the year the state of Israel was declared] most Jews remained nationally something other than Jewish. But neither could Jews define themselves by their religion alone. Few could ever seriously maintain that Judaism was, pure and simple, a religious faith on the model of Christianity. The easy answer was that Jewishness constituted some mixture of ethnicity and religion. But in what proportion? And was not the whole more than simply a compound of those two elements?
>
> Martin Buber, surely one of the most profound of twentieth-century Jewish religious thinkers, argued that the Jews eluded all classification.[40]

The problem was a new one. In the past, Jews had known exactly who they were. Their identity was defined by Jewish law and reinforced by both the Jewish community and the larger Christian society. Meyer notes, "Parents implanted in children the same values that they had absorbed in growing up, values sanctioned by a spiritually self-sufficient Jewish society. Continuity prevailed across the generations." Meyer went on to explain, "Conversion was the only pathway out of the ghetto. Within its walls, clear models of Jewish identity were instilled in the home, in the school, in the community. There were no significant discontinuities, no occasions for severe crises of identity."[41]

In those days, Jews who converted, or so the reasoning went, were no longer outsiders. They belonged. Many Christians who favored equal rights for Jews believed that once Jews had those rights they would abandon their faith and end the "Jewish problem." Indeed many Jews did respond to freedom by assimilating—by becoming more like the majority. They were confident that once they were "more German," "more French," or "more British," discrimination would end.

Instead, racists turned the "Jewish problem" into a permanent problem. Neither assimilation nor conversion to Christianity altered one's race. Jews would always be Jews, because they belonged to a different "race." This new view of the Jew combined older stereotypes with the pseudo-scientific thinking of the age. In 1879, Wilhelm Marr, a German journalist, published a pamphlet entitled *The Victory of Judaism over Germanism*. In it, he used the word *antisemitism* for the first time. It meant, and still means, hatred of Jews. Marr attacked Jews as a separate, evil, and inferior race.

Antisemitism found a home everywhere in Europe. In Germany, it became particularly popular. In 1883, Theodor Fritsch published *The Racists' Decalogue* to explain how a good "German" should treat "Jews." It stated in part:

> Thou shalt keep thy blood pure. Consider it a crime to soil the noble Aryan breed of thy people by mingling it with the Jewish breed. For thou must know that Jewish blood is everlasting, putting the Jewish stamp on body and soul unto the farthest generations. . . .
>
> Avoid all contact and community with the Jew and keep him away from thyself and thy family, especially thy daughters, lest they suffer injury of body and soul.

Two years later, Hermann Ahlwardt, a member of the German Reichstag, urged that Germany's borders be closed to "Israelites who are not citizens of the Reich." His arguments were based on the idea that "Semites" [Jews] were racially different from Germans whom he referred to as "Teutons."

Ahlwardt was concerned by the growing number of Jews moving to Germany and Austria-Hungary to avoid religious persecution in Russia. In 1886, Germans elected their first deputy from an antisemitic party. By 1893, such parties had sixteen deputies in the lower house of parliament; by 1895, they held a majority there.

By the late 1800s, German Jews were increasingly aware that assimilation did not free them to define their own identity nor did it protect them from antisemitism. Walter Rathenau, a prominent businessman and politician, wrote, "In the youth of every German Jew there comes the painful moment which he will remember for the rest of his life, when for the first time he becomes conscious that he has come into the world as a second-class citizen, and that no ability or accomplishment can liberate him from this condition."[42]

Some German Jews tried to ignore the attacks. Others tried to prove that they were more "German" than the Germans. But no matter what they did, the attacks continued and even intensified. One group of prominent Jews in Berlin decided to appeal to the kaiser for help. Raphael Loewenfeld was among those who vigorously opposed the idea. He argued that as "citizens we neither need nor demand any protections beyond our legal rights."

Many German Jews supported Loewenfeld's stand. They formed groups that publicly refuted antisemitic attacks and pressed charges against anyone who infringed upon their civil or political rights. Eugen Fuchs, a leader of the largest of these groups—the *Centralverein* (C.V.) defended its efforts by asking: "Should one always preach caution and patience? Should one console the Jews by holding out hopes for a future when the social question will have been solved? And should one, in the meantime, stand by in idleness because in favorable cases a petty fine results and in the majority of cases the wrongdoer is acquitted? Should one graciously leave in peace the broadsheets which awaken and stir up the fanaticism of the masses and continually try to convince the people that the Jews commit perjury for religious reasons, adulterate foodstuffs, and slaughter Christian children? Is it any wonder if these accusations are raised again and again without a hand or a voice moving against them, that then the people finally believe these fairy tales?"[43] In Fuchs' view, to do less "would mean to despair in the German state and in humanity."

CONNECTIONS

By the late 1800s, membership in a nation required more than residence. A would-be national had to adopt the language and culture of the nation. How did that pressure to conform affect Jewish identity in the late 1800s? What groups today face similar pressures?

Write a working definition of the word *assimilation*. How is it like *conformity*? How does it differ?

What was the "Jewish problem"? Why was it a problem? For whom was it a problem? Does our society face similar "problems" today?

What are the underlying themes of Fritsch's *Racists' Decalogue*? How does the language he uses affect your understanding of his message? What steps did he urge all Germans to take? What was his solution to the "Jewish problem"?

Jakob Wassermann, a Jewish writer from Vienna, Austria, saw no way of combating negative stereotypes:

> Vain to seek obscurity. They say: the coward, he is creeping into hiding, driven by his evil conscience. Vain to go among them and offer one's hand. They say: why does he take such liberties with his Jewish pushiness? Vain to keep faith with them as a comrade-in-arms or as a citizen. They say: he is a Proteus, he can assume any shape or form. Vain to help them strip off the chains of slavery. They say: no doubt he found it profitable. Vain to counteract the poison.[44]

Orlando Patterson (Reading 3) writes that slaves and other oppressed peoples wore "masks" in their dealings with those who had power over them. Did Wassermann wear a mask? Did Rathenau?

Compare the moment Rathenau describes with the one Miriam Thaggert writes of in Chapter 1, Reading 12. What similarities do you notice? What differences seem most striking?

What is the difference between a citizen and a subject? Why did Loewenfeld believe it was unnecessary for citizens to demand protection beyond their legal rights? Do you agree? Compare Loewenfeld's definition of nationality with the one French Jews developed in response to Napoleon's questions (Reading 5). What differences do you detect? What similarities seem most striking?

Have you ever been stereotyped? What is the most effective way to fight a stereotype? What is the least effective way?

➤Father Robert Bullock talks to students about the difference between *antisemitism* written with and without a hyphen. A person can be anti-Catholic, anti-Protestant, anti-Jewish, because these refer to group labels. But since there is no such group as *semites* there should be no hyphen. William Marr used the word with a hyphen, because he assumed that the Jews belonged to the "Semitic race." There is no such thing. The word *semitic* refers to a group of languages, not to a people. Therefore, Facing History and Ourselves uses the word *antisemitism* without a hypen to refer to attitudes of hatred toward Jews. Two videos are available from the Facing History Resource Center. In one Father Bullock discusses the spelling of antisemitism. In the other, he traces its Christian roots.

READING 10

Citizenship and African Americans

As racist thinking became more and more "respectable," incidents of violence increased sharply.

*I*n Europe, *they* were Jews; in the United States, *they* were African Americans. As in Germany, "race science" in the United States gave legitimacy to old myths and misinformation. By the late 1800s, white historians such as Philip A. Bruce were claiming that the abolition of slavery had cut off African Americans from "the spirit of White society." Emancipated slaves regressed to a primitive and criminal state. According to Bruce, middle-class black men posed the greatest danger. They were the "most likely to aim at social equality and to lose the awe with which, in slavey times, Black men had learned to respect the women of the superior race." Popular magazines called the phenomenon "The New Negro Crime."

The negative images evoked by such stories affected the way African Americans saw themselves and others. In his poem, "We Wear the Mask,"

Paul Laurence Dunbar, a noted poet, expressed the way he and other African Americans responded to those stereotypes.

> We wear the mask that grins and lies,
> It hides our cheek and shades our eyes—
> This debt we pay to human guile;
> With torn and bleeding hearts we smile,
> And mouth with myriad subtleties.
>
> Why should that world be overwise,
> In counting all our tears and sighs?
> Nay, let them only see us, while
>   We wear the mask.
>
> We smile, but, O great Christ, our cries
> To Thee from tortured souls arise.
> We sing, but oh, the clay is vile
> Beneath our feet, and long the mile;
> But let the world dream otherwise,
>   We wear the mask.

Whenever African Americans failed to wear "the mask," many white Americans took it upon themselves to keep blacks "in their place." As racist thinking became more and more "respectable," incidents of violence against blacks increased sharply. Only a handful of people had the courage to demand that such crimes be punished. One of them was an African American woman named Ida B. Wells. At a time when few blacks and even fewer women could vote, she led a national campaign to stop the violence associated with racism. Her crusade began after a mob in Memphis, Tennessee, murdered Thomas Moss, a grocer whose only crime was running a successful business. His murder convinced Wells that no one was safe as long as the lynchings went unpunished.

Wells set out to awaken the nation's conscience by gathering information about the 728 lynchings that took place in the United States between 1882 and Moss's death in March of 1892. The more she investigated those murders the more convinced she became that the deaths were linked to racist teachings. Her research revealed that many of the victims were successful businesspeople who posed a threat to notions of white supremacy. She also discovered that a number of women and even children were murdered. Most of the lynchings were for such "crimes" as "testifying against whites in court," "race prejudice," "quarreling with whites," and "making threats." Although a third of the victims were accused of rape, many of them were black men who had long-standing relationships with white women. At the time, it was a crime in most states for a black man to have relations with a white woman. Very few states would allow such a couple to marry. The reverse was also a crime but rarely enforced.

Wells quickly discovered that lynch mobs had widespread support. At times, whole towns turned out to watch the execution and cheer on the mob. Wells's research also suggested that even though most of the slayings took place in the South, the silence of white Americans in other parts of the nation allowed the crimes to continue. Wells set out to break that silence by exposing the truth. White Americans were so threatened by her campaign that she was forced to carry a gun to protect herself. After her newspaper office was burned, she had to leave Memphis for her own safety. Wells continued her campaign in New York. With the active support of black women's clubs, black newspapers, and a few white supporters, she turned lynching into a national issue. After she completed a speaking tour through Britain, it became an international issue as well. At the time of her death in 1931, Congress had not yet passed a lynch law. But at least thirteen states, including Tennessee, now had one and the number of lynchings was declining throughout the nation. Her campaign inspired the African Americans who led the civil rights movement of the 1950s and 1960s.

CONNECTIONS

What is the purpose of a mask? How does the one that Paul L. Dunbar refers to in his poem accomplish that purpose? Why is it a mask that "grins and lies"? Why is it one that "hides our cheek and shades our eyes"? Paul Dunbar was a contemporary of Walter Rathenau and Jakob Wassermann. Did the two wear the "mask" Dunbar described? Do people today wear it? If so, who?

How do Lincoln's warnings about the dangers of mob violence (Reading 4) relate to the experiences of African Americans in the late 1800s? How did that violence threaten democracy?

How were the experiences of African Americans similar to those of European Jews? What differences seem most striking? Was assimilation possible for African Americans?

In 1849, Frederick Douglass wrote, "If there is no struggle there is no progress." He went on to state, "the struggle may be a moral one; or it may be a physical one; or it may be both moral and physical, but it must be a struggle. Power concedes nothing without a demand. It never did and it never will." How do Wells's efforts support his view? Was her struggle moral, physical, or both?

➤Often we think of an historical event in terms of a simple cause and an immediate effect. How does Ida B. Wells's long crusade complicate that view? To fully appreciate who she was, what she did, and what her work means for our lives today, you may want to investigate life in the South during and after Reconstruction, focusing on the Ku Klux Klan, Black Codes, the Freedmen's Bureau, or the presidential election of 1876. You may also want to explore the effect her work had on education and the civil rights movement of the 1950s and 1960s. More information can be found in

Choosing to Participate. Also available is a documentary entitled *A Passion for Justice: The Life of Ida B. Wells.*

➤Maya Angelou (Chapter 1, Reading 5) wrote a variation on Dunbar's poem. She can be heard reading it on the videotaped conference *Facing Evil* available from the Facing History Resource Center.

R E A D I N G 1 1

"Race" and Identity in France

In the late 1800s, Germany and the United States excluded many individuals and groups from their "universe of obligations." In both nations, "race" increasingly determined who "belonged" and who did not. Many people believed that France was different. It seemed free of the racism they observed in the United States and Germany. African Americans often felt freer there than they did at home. And French Jews experienced none of the open antisemitism that marked German life. Yet the French also struggled with issues related to racism. The intensity of that struggle was revealed in the nation's response to the Dreyfus case. It exposed ancient hatreds and fostered angry exchanges over who was a citizen and who was not.

In November, 1894, Alfred Dreyfus, a French army officer, was accused of selling secret documents to the Germans. Two months later, he was convicted of treason. At a special ceremony, the army publicly degraded Dreyfus. He was brought before a group of officers and told, "Alfred Dreyfus, you are unworthy to bear arms. In the name of the French people we degrade you!" A senior officer then cut off his badges and buttons and broke his sword in half. The prisoner was then marched around a courtyard as his fellow soldiers watched silently. Dreyfus himself was not silent. He repeatedly shouted that they were degrading an innocent man. A huge crowd gathered outside. When they heard Dreyfus's cries, the spectators responded by whistling and chanting "Death to Dreyfus! Death to the Jews!"

In describing the trial, reporters repeatedly referred to Dreyfus as a Jew even though his religion had no bearing on the case. Antisemites like Leon Daudet wrote, "Above the wreckage of so many beliefs, a single faith remains authentic and sincere: that which safeguards our race, our language, the blood of our blood, and which keeps us all in solidarity. The closed ranks are our own. This wretch is not French. We have all understood as much from his act, his demeanor, his physiognomy."

At first Dreyfus's family and friends fought the conviction on their own. In time, others joined the struggle. Their efforts divided the nation. For some, the issue was clearly antisemitism. They argued, "Because he

Through hatred, the anti-Semite seeks out the protective community of men of bad faith, who reinforce each other through a collective uniformity of behavior.

was a Jew he was arrested, because he was a Jew he was convicted, because he was a Jew the voices of justice and of truth could not be heard in his favor." For others, the honor of the army and the nation were more important than any individual Jew's rights. They believed that it would weaken the army—and ultimately the nation—to reconsider the case or suggest a mistake had been made. When an officer found proof that Dreyfus was innocent, the army transferred the man to North Africa to keep him quiet. Others interpreted French honor differently. They believed that it required a retrial.

As more and more evidence of Dreyfus's innocence came to light, tempers flared. Debates often ended in fights, duels, and even riots. Finally, in 1899, Dreyfus was retried and once again convicted. But the day after his second conviction, he was pardoned. The courts did not vindicate him until 1906—twelve years after the case began.

> Not my country right or wrong, but, my country: may she always be in the right, and if in the wrong, may I help to set her right.

C O N N E C T I O N S

What themes and issues turned the Dreyfus case into a national debate? Why did that debate touch off rioting and violence? What does the case suggest about the effects of racism on democracy? How does it support the concerns that Abraham Lincoln expressed in the 1838 speech (Reading 4)? What trials in recent years have divided people the way the Dreyfus case did? What themes and issues underlie those cases?

How did the French in the late 1800s define their "universe of obligation"? Who came to Dreyfus's aid? Who did not?

Jean-Paul Sartre, a French philosopher, tried to describe the choices an individual makes when he or she becomes an antisemite. "Through hatred, the anti-Semite seeks out the protective community of men of bad faith, who reinforce each other through a collective uniformity of behavior. . . . The phrase 'I hate the Jews' is one that is uttered in chorus; in pronouncing it one attaches himself to a tradition and a community—the tradition and community of the mediocre."[45] How do those choices apply to the individuals described in this reading? To those described in previous readings?

Carl Schurz responded to patriots who shouted, "My country, right or wrong!" by saying, "Not my country right or wrong, but, my country: may she always be in the right, and if in the wrong, may I help to set her right." How would he answer those who argue that nations cannot admit mistakes? Where do you stand on the issue?

Theodore Herzl attended Dreyfus's trial as a reporter for an Austrian newspaper. Although a Jew, he was not religious. Indeed, he had once considered converting to Christianity. Now shocked by the hatred of Jews the case touched off, Herzl changed his views dramatically. In 1896, he wrote *Der Judenstaat* (The Jewish State). In it, he argued:

The Jewish question still exists. It would be foolish to deny it. It is a remnant of the Middle Ages, which civilized nations do not even yet seem able to shake off, try as they will. They certainly showed a generous desire to do so when they emancipated us. The Jewish question exists wherever Jews live in perceptible numbers. Where it does not exist, it is carried by Jews in the course of their migrations. We naturally move to those places where we are not persecuted, and there our presence produces persecution. This is the case in every country, and will remain so, even in those highly civilized—for instance, France—until the Jewish question finds a solution on a political basis.

Herzl's solution was to create a Jewish state in Palestine, the ancient homeland of the Jewish people. He hoped that European leaders would help the Jews set it up. Zionism, the Jewish form of nationalism, said Herzl, was to everyone's advantage. Evaluate Herzl's idea. How do you think an antisemite like Marr would respond to it?

READING 12

Nationalism, "Race," and Empires

Nationalism and "race" affected not only the way people regarded each other but also the way leaders defined their nation's universe of obligation. Every country wanted to be the strongest and the most powerful. By the late nineteenth century, European nations were competing for power in a variety of ways. They vied economically for resources and markets for their goods. And they contended politically and militarily for territory both in Europe and abroad. By all measures, Britain was the richest and most powerful. Yet, some people there were concerned about the growing economic and political might of the newly united Germany, which had also begun to build an empire.

Earlier in history, nations justified their conquest of other countries on economic, religious, or political grounds. Now Social Darwinism provided a new rationale for imperialism. Many Europeans and Americans now believed that as a superior people, they had a responsibility to "uplift" those who were less advanced. What made Native Americans, Asians, or Africans "less advanced"? Increasingly, the answer was their "race."

In 1884, Otto von Bismarck called an international meeting known as the Congress of Berlin. Fifteen western nations gathered to establish rules for dividing up the continent of Africa. By agreeing to abide by a set of rules, European leaders hoped to avoid a war at home. They paid little or no attention to the effects of their decision on the peoples of Africa. Those

Earlier in history, nations justified their conquest of other countries on economic, religious, or political grounds. Now Social Darwinism provided new rationale for imperialism.

who did consider the effects on Africans tended to share the attitudes expressed in a poem by Rudyard Kipling. He wrote it in 1898 to persuade the United States to make the Philippines a colony.

> Take up the White Man's burden—
> > Send forth the best ye breed—
> Go bind your sons to exile
> > To serve your captives' need;
> To wait in heavy harness,
> > On fluttered folk and wild—
> Your new-caught, sullen peoples,
> > Half-devil and half-child.

The poem ends with the following verse:

> Take up the White Man's Burden—
> > Have done with childish days—
> The lightly proffered laurel,
> > The easy, ungrudged praise.
> Comes now, to search your manhood
> > Through all the thankless years,
> Cold, edged with dear-bought wisdom,
> > The judgment of your peers!

A nation is ready to give up much of its domestic freedom if, in return, it gains more power and prestige in the foreign field.

CONNECTIONS

Labels once applied to groups within a nation were now being applied to whole nations. What did Kipling mean when he spoke of the "White Man's Burden"? Why was it the "white man's" to bear?

In 1863, a law limiting freedom of the press went into effect in Prussia. A newspaper editor responded to the law by saying, "A nation is ready to give up much of its domestic freedom if, in return, it gains more power and prestige in the foreign field." What are the dangers in such an attitude? What happens when people in other countries feel the same way about their nation?

Look carefully at a map of the world in 1900. Who were the strongest nations in the world? How did you reach that conclusion?

Ali A. Mazrui, an African scholar, asks, "Africa might have been denied its full credentials as part of human civilization, but must it also be denied its size in square miles? Can we not begin to experiment in schools with maps and globes that are less distorting?"[46] It is impossible to portray a round Earth on a flat map without distortion. Compare the way Africa looks on two different world maps and a globe. What differences are most striking?

What effect do those differences have on your perception of Africa? Of other continents?

Which countries are powerful today? On what basis did you rate those countries as "strong"? Is your rating based on military might? What other sources of strength does a nation have?

➤ *The World on Display,* available from the Facing History Center, shows how nationalism and race were taught at the 1904 World's Fair in St. Louis, Missouri.

READING 13

The Eve of World War

As the competition among nations increased, the world became a more and more dangerous place to live. One nation could expand its empire only at another's expense. As tensions mounted, nations built more and more ships, stockpiled more and more weapons, and trained more and more soldiers. They also looked for allies. As a result, a conflict between any two nations could draw almost the entire world into war. That is exactly what happened in the summer of 1914.

On June 28, a Serbian nationalist shot the heir to the Austrian throne and his wife. One month later, Austria-Hungary declared war on Serbia. So did Germany, an ally of Austria-Hungary. Russia was also drawn into the fighting, as an ally of Serbia. Within days, France, an ally of Russia, was invaded. Britain entered when Germany began its invasion of France by marching through Belgium, a neutral nation that Britain had pledged to defend. By 1915, the Ottoman Empire had entered the war on Germany's side. Italy now supported France and Britain. A "world war" had indeed begun. By the time it ended in 1918, thirty countries were involved.

In 1914, most people greeted the war with enthusiasm. Many young men viewed it as the adventure of a lifetime and feared only that it would end before they had a chance to fight. Just before the war began, Rupert Brooke, a young British poet, wrote "The Soldier."

> If I should die, think only this of me:
>   That there's some corner of a foreign field
> That is for ever England. There shall be
>   In that rich earth a richer dust concealed;
> A dust whom England bore, shaped, made aware,
>   Gave, once, her flowers to love, her ways to roam,
> A body of England's, breathing English air,
>   Washed by the rivers, blest by suns of home.

The First World War proved to be neither a glorious adventure nor a quick fight.

> And think, this heart, all evil shed away,
>   A pulse in the eternal mind, no less
> Gives somewhere back the thoughts by England given;
>   Her sights and sounds; dreams happy as her day;
> And laughter, learnt of friends; and gentleness,
>   In hearts at peace, under an English heaven.

The First World War proved to be neither a glorious adventure nor a quick fight. On Germany's western front, the two sides faced one another across lines of trenches. Victories were measured in yards rather than miles. As the weeks became months, each side introduced ever newer and more technologically advanced weapons in an effort to break the stalemate. Poison gas, machine guns, aerial bombings, and tanks increased the number of casualties but did not result in a clear-cut victory for either side. After a visit to the front, a British commander said, "I don't know what this is. It isn't war."

CONNECTIONS

What does Rupert Brooke mean when he says "some corner of a foreign field that is for ever England"? How does he picture war? How does he imagine his death? Why do you think young people responded to the war with such enthusiasm? How was their response to war similar to that of German students in 1848 to news of a revolution in France? How was their response different?

European alliances were based on the principle that "the enemies of my enemy are my friends." What are the problems of an alliance system based on that principle? Do nations still use it?

➤ *The Great War,* a series of eight videos, provides a detailed account of World War I. It is available from the Facing History Resource Center.

This reading is a brief case study. It introduces concepts that will be expanded upon in later chapters.

READING 14

Creating Enemies of the State: The Armenians

Under the stresses of war, prejudices are often heightened and tolerance toward vulnerable minorities forgotten. As United States President Woodrow Wilson told a friend a few weeks before the United States entered the war, "Once lead this people into war and they'll forget there ever was such a thing as tolerance. . . . A nation cannot put its strength into a war and keep its head level; it has never been done." [47] The president may have been thinking of a war within a war that was taking place in the Ottoman Empire, then an ally of Germany.

In 1915, soon after the war began, Turkey, which then ruled the Ottoman Empire, turned against the Armenians, a Christian minority that had lived for generations within the Muslim Ottoman Empire. The Armenians were accused of divided loyalties, because there were Armenians in Russia as well as in the Ottoman Empire and Russia was now the enemy. In April, the Turks arrested six hundred Armenian leaders. But these arrests were just the beginning. On April 28, the *New York Times* wrote:

> An appeal for relief of Armenian Christians in Turkey, following reported massacres and threatened further outrages, was made to the Turkish government today by the United States.
>
> Acting upon the request of the Russian Government, submitted through Ambassador Bakhmeteff, Secretary [of State William Jennings] Bryan cabled to Ambassador [Henry] Morgenthau at Constantinople to make representations to the Turkish authorities asking that steps be taken for the protection of imperiled Armenians and to prevent the recurrence of religious outbreaks.

Instead of preventing more outbreaks, the Ottoman government moved against the Armenians. On July 12, the *New York Times* carried that story on page four under the headline "TURKS ARE EVICTING NATIVE CHRISTIANS." By October 4, the story appeared on the front page of the *New York Times* under the headline "TELL OF HORRORS DONE IN ARMENIA." The subheadings outlined the story. "Report of Eminent Americans Says They Are Unequaled in a Thousand Years." "Turkish Record Outdone." "A Policy of Extermination Put in Effect Against a Helpless People." "Entire Villages Scattered." "Men and Boys Massacred, Women and Girls Sold as Slaves and Distributed Among Moslems."

Even as reporters were filing their stories, Morgenthau was sending a "private and confidential" memo to Washington.

> I am firmly convinced that this is the greatest crime of the ages. The repeated advice of some of the Ambassadors not to have any massacres may have led the Turks to adopt this fearful scheme of deportations which they turned into such diabolical massacres, accompanied with rape, pillage, and forced conversions. The Turkish authorities claim that they could not spare more than one battalion to escort this people and that therefore they were exposed to attacks by Kurds, etc. If that is true, they had no right to deport them, because they knew they would be pillaged and murdered on the way, unless properly protected. Halil Bey himself admitted that even the gendarmes that had been assigned to act as escort to the deported Armenians committed some of the worst crimes against them.

Once lead this people into war and they'll forget there ever was such a thing as tolerance . . . . A nation cannot put its strength into a war and keep its head level; it has never been done.

SLAY ALL ARMENIANS IN CITY OF KERASUNT

Turks Wipe Out Entire Population in Town on the Black Sea.

LONDON. Tuesday, Oct. 26.- A dispatch to The Daily Mail from Odessa says:

"The Turks have massacred the entire Armenian population of Kerasunt, on the Black Sea."

Kerasunt is a seaport in Asiatic Turkey, about seventy miles west of Trebizond. It is situated on a rocky promontory with a spacious bay on the east side. The heights surrounding are covered with luxurious vegetation. The population of Kerasunt is about 24,000

LONDON. Oct. 25 — An eyewitness story of Armenian atrocities, given to the British staff at the Dardanelles by an Armenian prisoner who was serving in the Turkish Army, is sent by the Reuter correspondent with the Dardanelles fleet. This Armenian says the declaration of martial law at 7th in

Unfortunately the previous Armenian massacres were allowed to pass without the great Christian Powers punishing the perpetrators thereof; and these people believe that an offense that has been condoned before, will probably be again forgiven. Their success in deporting in May and June of 1914 about 100,000/150,000 Greeks without any of the big nations, then still at peace with them, seriously objecting thereto, led them to the conclusion that now, while four of the great Powers were fighting them and had unsuccessfully attempted to enter their country, and the two other Great Powers were their Allies, it was a great opportunity for them to put into effect their long cherished plan of exterminating the Armenian race and thus finish once for all the question of Armenian Reforms which has so often been the cause of European intervention in Turkish affairs.[48]

Abraham Hartunian, an Armenian Protestant minister, told the story from a more personal point of view:

> On August 6 a terrible order was given: "All Armenians must surrender to the government whatever firearms they have; if a gun is found anywhere during the ensuing search, the owner will be shot instantly." At the same time preparations were being made to deport us the very next day.
>
> Saturday, August 7, had come! The day of hell! The prison gates were thrown open, and about a hundred captives [Armenians] from Zeytoon and Fundejak were brought out. Chained together, they were

led to their slaughter through the streets, to the shouts and joyous outcries of the Turks. Some were hanged from scaffolds in the populous centers of the city. The rest were driven to the foot of Mount Aghur and there were shot in the presence of a great multitude . . . .

These hundred corpses were still lying on the ground when suddenly hell's harbingers ran through the streets shouting, "All Armenian men, seventeen years old and above, must go out of the city and gather in the Field of Marash, to be deported; those who disobey will be shot."

As I now recall that day, there is a trembling in my body. The human mind is unable to bear such heaviness. My pen cannot describe the horrors. Confusion! Chaos! Woe! Wailing! Weeping! The father kissed his wife and children and departed, sobbing, encrazed. The son kissed his mother, his old father, his small sisters and brothers, and departed. Those who went and those who remained sobbed. Many left with no preparation, with only the clothes on their backs, the shoes on their feet, lacking money, lacking food, some without even seeing their loved ones. Already thousands of men had gathered in the appointed place, and like madmen, others were joining them.

The scene was so dreadful that even the hardened Turkish heart could not stand it, and a second order was given: "Those who have gone, have gone; the rest may remain. Let them not go."

Thus the thousands who had given themselves over to the hands of the bloodthirsty gendarmes were driven out to the desert slaughter houses. The remainder, crushed, pale, hopeless, were left in the city to await their turn. It was no more a secret that the annihilation of the nation had been determined.

How can I describe my mental anguish, the agonies of my heart, my emotions! The scenes of that day had bereft me of mind and strength and will. But in this thrice-exhausted condition I still had to comfort my family, to encourage my remaining people, and to do my possible best. I had to visit houses to give consolation. I had to appeal to the governor and to other officials—bowing before them, to beg and cry for mercy for the Armenians. And I too was waiting to walk the road of deportation.

I had all the furnishings of my house packed in boxes and bundles and sent to the American buildings. For the journey I brought together the absolutely necessary things: a tent, water jugs, a cradle! All the money I had was eight liras. How was it possible to travel with my wife and five small children? My God! The very thought makes me shudder!

On Sunday, August 8, the subject for our thought at church was the crucifixion. The nation was on the cross.

From this day on, the work of deportation was carried out systematically. Every day new lists were prepared, and successively, the convoys were put on their way. Everyone knew that in a little while his turn would come. There was not a glimmer of hope. Indeed the

> bitter scenes daily enacted in the city rendered the people willing to go out and face death as soon as possible. Innocent Armenians by the dozens were hanged from scaffolds in different sections of the city, and their corpses dangling in the air wrought horror upon the people. On different days and in different places, nearly five hundred Armenians were either shot or hanged.
>
> On Sunday, August 15, the subject of our spiritual meditation was the burial of Jesus. My people were being entombed.[49]

The word *genocide* was coined during World War II to describe the murder of an entire people. Although the word did not yet exist in 1915, the crime took place nonetheless.

CONNECTIONS

The Turkish government singled out the Armenians as "enemies of the state." They were accused of divided loyalties. What does that mean? What factors allowed the Turks to scapegoat them? What does your answer suggest about what happens to a "tolerated minority" in time of war?

What did the press report about the horrors that were taking place? What could the United States and other countries have done? What should they have done?

In 1915, most Europeans and Americans believed that a genocide like the one in the Ottoman Empire could not have taken place anywhere else in the world. Do you agree?

➤ *The Armenian Genocide*, available from the Facing History Resource Center, highlights the events of 1915-1923 and relates them to other atrocities throughout history. The video shows the steps that may lead to genocide and encourages discussion of human rights violations. Reading materials and other films, including video tapes prepared by survivors as well as a lecture by scholar Richard Hovannisian are also available from the resource center. Chapter 10 (Readings 10-12) contains more information on the Armenian Genocide.

NOTES

[1] Helen Fein, *Accounting for Genocide,* (Free Press, 1979), 4.

[2] From THE ASCENT OF MAN by Jacob Bronowski. Copyright © 1973 by J. Bronowski. By permission of Little, Brown and Company.

[3] Martha Minow, *Making All the Difference, 3.*

[4] Theodore Abel, *Why Hitler Came to Power* (Prentice-Hall, 1938), 29.

[5] Ibid., 29.

[6] Kurt Vonnegut, Jr., "Harrison Bergeron," *Welcome to the Monkey House* (Delacorte Press/Seymour Lawrence). Copyright © 1961 by Kurt Vonnegut, Jr. Originally published in *Fantasy and Science Fiction.* Reprinted by permission.

[7] Martha Minow, *Making All the Difference, 22.*

[8] Peter N. Carroll and David W. No,ble *The Free and the Unfree; A New History of the United States,* Second Edition, (Penguin Books, 1977, 1988), 34.

[9] Ibid., 35-36.

[10] Ronald Takaki, *A Different Mirror: A History of Multicultural America* (Little Brown & Company, 1993), 34.

[11] Ibid., 38.

[12] Ibid., 40-41.

[13] Peter N. Carroll and David W. Noble, *The Free and the Unfree,* 37.

[14] Quoted in Ronald Takaki, *A Different Mirror,* 41.

[15] Carol Hampton, "A Heritage Denied," *Sojourners,* January, 1991.

[16] Ronald Takaki, *A Different Mirror,* 54.

[17] Orlando Patterson, *Slavery and Social Death* (Harvard University Press, 1982), vii.

[18] Winthrop D. Jordan, *White Over Black: American Attitudes Toward the Negro, 1550-1812,* (Norton & Co., 1968), 94.

[19] Orlando Patterson, *Slavery and Social Death,* 5.

[20] Ibid., 340.

[21] Abraham Lincoln, "Reply to Stephen Douglas, August 21," *Created Equal? The Complete Lincoln-Douglas Debates of 1858,* ed. Paul Angle, (University of Chicago Press, 1958), 11.

[22] "Address before the Young Men's Lyceum, January 27, 1838, "*The Collected Works of Abraham Lincoln,* ed. Roy P. Basler (Rutgers University Press, 1953), 109.

[23] Henry Kamm, "Havel Calls the Gypsies 'Litmus Test,' *New York Times,* 10 December, 1993.

[24] Julian Bond, "Address," (Jefferson Conference, October 16, 1992), 19-20.

[25] Hans Kohn, *Nationalism* (D. Van Nostrand, 1955), 9.

[26] Theodore Abel, *Why Hitler Came to Power,* 29.

[27] Quoted in *The War Against the Jews, 1933-1945* by Lucy S. Dawidowicz (Holt, Rinehart & Winston, 1975), 27.

[28] Quoted in *The Course of German Nationalism* by Hagen Schulze (Cambridge University Press, 1991), 57.

[29] Quoted in Reginald Horsman, *Race and Manifest Destiny* (Harvard University Press, 1981), 35-36.

[30] Quoted in Leon Poliakov, *The Aryan Myth* (Basic Books, 1974), 277.

[31] *The Autobiography of Carl Schurz: An Abridgement in One Volume of The Reminiscences of Carl Schurz,* 26.

[32] Otto von Bismarck, *Reflections and Reminiscences* (Harper & Row, 1968), 32.

[33] *The Autobiography of Carl Schurz*, 26.

[34] Ibid., 28.

[35] Comte de St. Vallier, quoted in Fritz Stern, *Gold and Iron* (Alfred Knopf, 1977), 205-206.

[36] Stefan Zweig, *The World of Yesterday, An Autobiography* (Viking, 1945), 1-2.

[37] Martha Minow, *Making All the Difference*, 4.

[38] *The Life and Writings of Frederick Douglass*, Vol. 2, ed. Philip S. Foner, (International Publishers, 1950), 298.

[39] George Mosse, *Toward the Final Solution, A History of European Racism* (Fertig, 1978), 92.

[40] Michael A. Meyer, *Jewish Identity in the Modern World* (University of Washington Press, 1990), 3.

[41] Ibid., 6.

[42] Quoted in Paul Johnson, *A History of the Jews*, (Harper & Row, 1987), 407.

[43] Quoted in Sanford Ragins, *Jewish Responses to Anti-Semitism in Germany 1870-1914*, (Hebrew Union College Press, 1980), 61.

[44] Jakob Wassermann, *Mein Weg als Deutscher und Jude*, (Berlin: Verlag, 1921).

[45] Jean-Paul Sartre, *Anti-Semite and Jew*, trans. G. J. Becker (Schocken, 1948), 22.

[46] Ali A. Mazrui, *The Africans: A Triple Heritage* (Little Brown & Company, 1986), 24.

[47] Quoted in *Cobb of "The World"* by John L. Heaton (E.P. Dutton & Co., 1924).

[48] Henry Morgenthau, *Ambassador Morgenthau's Story* (New Age Publishers, 1919), 301-304.

[49] Abraham Hartunian, *Neither to Laugh nor to Weep, A Memoir of the Armenian Genocide*, trans. Vartan Hartunian (Beacon, 1968), 63-65.

3. *Germany in the 1920s*

The shadowy figures that look out at us from the tarnished mirror of history are—in the final analysis—ourselves.

DETLEV J. K. PEUKERT

OVERVIEW

F ew events in history are inevitable. Most are determined by real people making real decisions. At the time, those choices may not seem important. Yet together, little by little, they shape a period in history and define an age. Those decisions also have consequences that may affect generations to come. Chapter 2 looked at the way three nations—the United States, France, and Germany—decided who belonged in the nineteenth century and who did not. It also considered the outcomes of those choices. This chapter marks the beginning of a case study that examines the choices people made after World War I. It highlights Germany's efforts to build a democracy after the humiliation of defeat and explores the values, myths, and fears that threatened those efforts. It focuses in particular on the choices that led to the destruction of the republic and the rise of the Nazis.

The 1920s were a time of change everywhere in the world. Many of those changes began much earlier and were speeded up by the war. Others were linked to innovations in science that altered the way people saw the world. In 1905, Albert Einstein, a German physicist, published his theory of relativity. By 1920, other scientists had proved that time and space are indeed relative and not absolute. The theory quickly became a part of the way ordinary people viewed the world. As one historian explained, "At the beginning of the 1920s the belief began to circulate, for the first time at a popular level, that there were no longer any absolutes: of time and space, of good and evil, of knowledge, above all of value. Mistakenly, but perhaps inevitably, relativity became confused with relativism."[1] No one was more disturbed by that confusion than Einstein. In a letter to a colleague, he wrote, "You believe in a God who plays dice, and I in complete law and order in a world which objectively exists."[2]

Even as Einstein's theory was changing people's views of time and space, an Austrian physician named Sigmund Freud was altering their ideas about human behavior. His work conveyed the sense that the world was not what it seemed to be. Many came to believe the "senses, whose empirical perceptions shaped our ideas of time and distance, right and wrong, law and justice, and the nature of man's behavior in society were not to be trusted."[3] In such uncertain times, people often look for simple solutions to complex problems.

Although Germany was a unique place in the 1920s, the questions the German people faced then are similar to those confronting people today: Should all citizens be equal? How can a democracy maintain order without destroying freedom? Their decisions affected nations around the world, including our own.

READING 1

The Impact of Total War

War was a powerful engine for the enforcement of conformity . . . .

When the war began in the summer of 1914, crowds gathered to cheer the news in each of the great capitals of Europe. Young men, in particular, responded with great enthusiasm. The war gave them a sense of purpose, a focus many had never known before. The same was often true of young women. Historian Claudia Koonz's account of the way the war affected many young German women is also true of women in the other warring nations.

> War pulled women out of their families and into public life, giving them a stake in the nation that most had not previously felt. In 1914, women organized across political and religious divisions to knit, nurse, collect scrap material, and donate to charity. After 1916, as German generals realized the war would not end soon, the government recruited women to take the soldiers' places at strategically vital jobs. Overnight, it seemed, women were not only permitted but begged to mine coal, deliver the mail, drive trucks and trams, keep account books, and work in heavy industry—as well as continuing to roll bandages, nurse veterans, and perform charitable work. Suddenly a system that, until 1908, had made it illegal for women even to attend gatherings at which politics might be discussed and barred women from earning university degrees, told women the nation's very survival depended upon their taking up jobs previously done by men.[4]

But as the fighting dragged on, enthusiasm waned. This was no glorious war but a slaughter. The death toll was staggering. In all, the war claimed the lives of about thirteen million soldiers—over twice the number killed in all of the major wars fought between 1790 and 1914. In one battle in July, 1916 at Somme in France, Britain had over 60,000 casualties. That same year, Germany lost about 400,000 soldiers and France nearly half of its army in the battle of Verdun. By the end of the war, France alone had lost 1.2 million soldiers. Winston Churchill, who later served as Britain's prime minister, said of the casualties:

> All the horrors of all the ages were brought together, and not only armies but whole populations were thrust into the midst of them. The mighty educated States involved conceived—not without reason—that their very existence was at stake. Neither peoples nor rulers drew the line at any deed which they thought could help them win. Germany, having let Hell loose, kept well in the van of terror; but she was followed step by step by the desperate and ultimately avenging nations she had assailed. Every outrage against humanity or international law was repaid by reprisals—often of a greater scale and of longer duration. No truce or parley mitigated the strife of the armies. The wounded died between the lines: the dead mouldered into the soil. Merchant ships and neutral ships and hospital ships were sunk on the seas and all on board left to their fate, or killed as they swam. Every effort was made to starve whole nations into submission without regard to age or sex. Cities and monuments were smashed by artillery. Bombs from the air were cast down indiscriminately. Poison gas in many forms stifled or seared the soldiers. Liquid fire was projected upon their bodies. Men fell from the air in flames, or were smothered often slowly in the dark recesses of the sea. The fighting strength of armies was limited only by the manhood of their countries. Europe and large parts of Asia and Africa became one vast battlefield on which after years of struggle not armies but nations broke and ran. When all was over, Torture and Cannibalism were the only expedients that the civilized, scientific, Christian States had been able to deny themselves: and they were of doubtful utility.[5]

Historian George Mosse reflected on the hatred the war unleashed:

> Hatred of the enemy had been expressed in poetry and prose ever since the beginning of modern warfare in the age of the French Revolution. . . . But as a rule such questions as "Why do we hate the French?"—asked, for example, by Prussians during the German Wars of Liberation in 1813—were answered in a manner which focused upon the present war and did not cast aspersions upon French history or traditions, or indeed upon the entire French nation. . . . During the First World War, in contrast, inspired by a sense of universal mission, each side dehumanized the enemy and called for his unconditional surrender. . . .
>
> The enemy was transformed into the anti-type, symbolizing the reversal of all the values which society held dear. The stereotyping was

identical to that of those who differed from the norms of society and seemed to menace its very existence: Jews, Gypsies, and sexual deviants. . . . War was a powerful engine for the enforcement of conformity, a fact which strengthened the stereotype not only of the foreign enemy, but also of those within the borders who were regarded as a threat to the stability of the nation and who disturbed the image society liked to have of itself. . . .

At the beginning of the war Emperor Wilhelm II had proclaimed that all differences between classes and religions had vanished, that he knew only Germans. But already by 1915 there were fewer Jewish officers in the army than at the beginning of the war. More sensational action followed when on October 11, 1916, the Imperial War Minister ordered statistics to be compiled to find out how many Jews served at the front, how many served behind the front, and how many did not serve at all. What this meant for young Jews fighting side by side with their comrades in the trenches may well be imagined. This so-called Jew count was the result of anti-Semitic agitation which had begun in earnest a year earlier, and as the results of the count were never published, the suspicion that Jews were shirkers remained.[6]

Germany was not alone in turning against the "other." Other nations did the same. The most extreme example was the Armenian Genocide (Chapter 2, Reading 14). But there were incidents in every nation, including the United States, Britain, and Russia.

CONNECTIONS

How do nations unite in time of war? How was that task different during World War I? What role do women play? What are the risks in uniting people against a common enemy?

Churchill argues that there were no limits to what the "civilized states" did during World War I. Define the word *reprisal*. How are reprisals used to put down resistance? Are there limits to what soldiers may do to the enemy in time of war? Why were they not observed in this war?

It has been said that "hatred begins in the heart and not in the head. In so many instances we do not hate people because of a particular deed, but rather do we find that deed ugly because we hate them." How does the quotation apply to times of war?

Just before the United States entered the war, Woodrow Wilson warned, "Once lead this people into war and they'll forget there ever was such a thing as tolerance . . . . A nation cannot put its strength into a war and keep its head level; it has never been done." How do Churchill's comments support that view? How do Mosse's?

Mosse writes that "war was a powerful engine for the enforcement of conformity." How does war promote conformity? How does it strengthen stereotypes?

Every nation limited freedom during the war. Some suspended elections. Others curbed freedom of speech and the press. Why do you think that democracy is often one of the first casualties of war?

In Germany, many young Jews joined the army as a way of showing their patriotism. Yet no matter how many medals they won or acts of courage they performed, they continued to be regarded as "shirkers" and "traitors." Why was the myth stronger than the truth? Research the military experiences of African Americans in the United States during World War I. How were their experiences similar to those of German Jews? What differences seem most striking?

➤In his documentary, *The Arming of the Earth*, Bill Moyers discusses the ways World War I revolutionized modern warfare. The American effort in the war is portrayed in the film *Goodbye Billy*. Both films are available from the Facing History Resource Center.

READING 2

War and Revolution in Russia

*I*n a world weary of war and no longer certain of right and wrong, revolutions shook one nation after another. The first took place in Russia in 1917. Within months, a group known as the Bolsheviks had taken over the country. Their leader was Vladimir Ilyich Ulianov, better known as V. I. Lenin. His slogan of "Peace, Bread, and Land" had great appeal for a tired, hungry people.

In many ways, Russia was an old-fashioned country fighting a modern war. In battle after battle, Russian soldiers faced a well-equipped German army with little more than courage. They lacked guns, ammunition, and, by 1917, even warm clothes and food. Life on the homefront was not much better. A revolution began one morning in February, when the women of St. Petersburg went out to buy food and found the shops empty. As the angry shoppers gathered in the street, more and more people joined them. Suddenly, rioting began. When Czar Nicholas II sent troops to restore order, his soldiers mutinied. That is, they joined the rioters instead of obeying their commanders. Within days, the demonstrators had toppled the czar.

The years immediately after the war were marked by political and economic turmoil almost everywhere in the world. Many people were quick to look for someone to blame for the violence. Increasingly they labeled anyone who called for change a *Communist* or a *Bolshevik*.

Russia was now ruled by a temporary government committed to fighting the war, keeping order, and organizing a new, democratic political system for the nation. The government did not last long. By November the Bolsheviks were in control. They gave Russia a new name—the Union of Soviet Socialist Republics (USSR)—and a new kind of government. That government was based on the ideas of Karl Marx, a German thinker who lived from 1818 to 1883.

Marx saw all of history as a struggle between workers and property owners. That struggle, he believed, would end only when the public owned all land and other property. The people would hold that property—not as individuals but as members of a group. Only then would everyone be equal. Because of his belief in common, or shared, ownership of land and other resources, the system Marx envisioned was known as *communism*. Lenin agreed with most of Marx's ideas. But unlike Marx, Lenin was convinced that the workers could not bring about a revolution on their own. He maintained that a few strong leaders were needed to guide events. Those leaders would establish a dictatorship of the proletariat—the workers—because they alone knew what was best for the people. A dictatorship is a government led by a few individuals with absolute control over a nation.

As head of the new USSR, Lenin signed a treaty with Germany at Brest-Litovsk in the spring of 1918. That treaty not only ended Russia's involvement in the war but also turned over to Germany a third of Russia's farmland, most of its coal mines, and about half of its industries. Many Russians opposed the treaty, but with the Russian army in disarray, Lenin was in no position to bargain. Still, he considered the agreement a temporary setback. He insisted that a revolution, similar to Russia's, would soon sweep Europe and end all treaties, including the one with Germany. Such beliefs convinced Russia's former allies that Lenin was a dangerous man. He confirmed their fears, when he called on workers everywhere to end the war. To the dismay of many leaders, there were signs that a number of people were taking his suggestion seriously. In 1918, the war-weary German Reichstag supported a peace resolution. War weariness also affected Britain and France and it reached almost epidemic proportions in the trenches. There were serious mutinies on both sides.

Yet the fighting did not end immediately. Germany, now victorious in the east, transferred thousands of soldiers from its eastern front to battlefields in the west. There they faced a new opponent, the United States. In April 1917, President Woodrow Wilson had announced that his country was entering the war "to make the world safe for democracy." By June, American troops were arriving in France at the rate of 250,000 a month. By the fall of 1918, the Americans were helping the French and the British push the Germans farther and farther back. By November 1, they had broken through the center of the German line. It was now only a matter of days until the war was over.

The word *communist* has different meanings in different countries. Since 1918, however, it has most often been used to describe those who favor the kind of political and economic system that existed in Russia until 1991. Those who want both economic equality and a democratic political system are usually known as *social democrats* or *democratic socialists*. Communists and social democrats have often had difficulty getting along. Why do you think this is so?

The years immediately after the war were marked by political and economic turmoil almost everywhere in the world. Many people were quick to look for someone to blame for the violence. Increasingly they labeled anyone who called for change a *Communist* or a *Bolshevik*. To stop the threat of a "worldwide Communist revolution," Russia's former allies helped Lenin's enemies in the bloody civil war that divided Russia in 1919. Why do you think people were so fearful of communism and the Communists? How was this fear used to unite people against a common enemy?

What might lead a soldier to refuse to obey orders? Why do you think mutinies are rare? Write a working definition of the word *mutiny*. Add to your definition after you complete the next reading.

Write a working definition of the word *dictatorship*. Is a dictatorship of the proletariat an authoritarian government?

READING 3

War and Revolution in Germany

*R*ussia was not the only country threatened by revolution during the war. By the fall of 1918, Germany was also in danger. But, unlike Russia's rulers, Germany's leaders were not caught by surprise. They knew that there would be upheaval unless they found a way to maintain control of the nation. As a result, events there followed a different course.

By early September, the nation's top military leaders were aware that Germany would soon be defeated. The generals therefore reluctantly asked the kaiser to seek a peace agreement and Wilhelm II reluctantly agreed. His chancellor, Prince Max of Baden, secretly informed the Americans that Germany wanted to end the war. The generals, the kaiser, and the prince all worked behind closed doors. Not a word of the approaching defeat appeared in print. The German people had no idea that they were about to lose the war. They believed what they were told and official announcements remained optimistic. By November, that faith was beginning to shatter. German sailors stationed in Kiel mutinied rather than carry out what they considered a "suicidal" attack on the British navy. At the same time, Communists in Berlin and a number of other large cities began to openly plot a revolution.

In the belief that the Americans would be more sympathetic to a democratic government than a monarchy, the generals asked the Social Democrats to form a republic. Friedrich Ebert, the party's leader, shared the generals' feelings about the need for order. A saddlemaker by trade with little formal education, Ebert considered himself a reformer not a rabble-rouser. He and other Social Democrats respected authority and tried to avoid drastic changes. They were more than willing to promise that the new government would preserve German traditions and allow the nation's army officers, bureaucrats, judges, and teachers to keep their jobs. Like other discussions, these took place in secret.

The German people knew nothing until November 9—the day the kaiser fled to the Netherlands and the Social Democrats declared Germany a republic. That same day, the nation's new leaders learned that the Allies expected Germany to give up its armaments, including its navy, and evacuate all troops west of the Rhine River. If the Germans did not accept those terms within seventy-two hours, the Allies threatened to invade the nation.

Germany's new leaders turned to the military for advice. When Matthias Erzberger of the Catholic Center party met with Paul von Hindenburg, the commander of the German Armed Forces, the general tearfully urged him to do his patriotic duty. He and the other military leaders convinced the civilians that they had to accept the truce. German soldiers could not hold out much longer. So early on the morning of November 11, 1918, three representatives of the new republic traveled to France to sign an armistice agreement. They made the trip alone. The generals chose not to attend the ceremony.

As soon as the agreement was signed, people in many countries rejoiced, but there were no celebrations in Germany. People there were in a state of shock. How could they *possibly* have lost the war? Many were convinced that the loss had to be the work of traitors and cowards. Erzberger, who had long opposed the war, was an early target for their anger. He and the other signers were later characterized as the "November criminals" who had "stabbed Germany in the back." The charge was unfair, but the generals who knew the truth did not set the record straight. Indeed, they encouraged the belief that civilians had double-crossed the army.

Within just forty-eight hours, Germany was turned upside down. The stunned nation lost its monarch, its empire, and the war itself. To make matters worse, there was now fighting in the streets of many German cities, as the Communists tried to bring about a revolution. Berlin was so unsettled that the nation's new leaders met in the city of Weimar—which is why the new government became known as the Weimar Republic.

Despite the upheavals, work began on a constitution within days of the armistice. It was completed that winter. The document created a democracy with power divided among three branches of government. Of the three, only the judicial branch was appointed. The other two were elected by the people. In choosing a president, German voters selected among several candidates. But in electing members of the Reichstag, they cast their ballots for a particular party rather than a particular candidate. As long as a party got 1 percent of the vote, it was entitled to one deputy in parliament. The more votes a party received, the more deputies it was entitled to. For example, if the Social Democrats received 36 percent of the vote, they would be allowed 36 percent of the seats in the Reichstag. But party officials, rather than the voters, decided exactly who those representatives would be.

The party with a majority in the Reichstag chose the nation's chancellor, or prime minister. If no single party held a majority, two or more could band together to form a government. Almost any controversy could break up such a coalition. Whenever that happened, the government fell and a new election was held. In less than fourteen years, the Weimar Republic had twenty different governments.

The new constitution carefully protected individual freedom—including the rights of minorities. A total of fifty-six articles spelled out the "basic rights and obligations" of the German people. For the first time, they were guaranteed freedom of speech and press, although some censorship was permitted to combat "obscene and indecent literature, as well as for the protection of youth at public plays and spectacles." The constitution also guarded religious freedom. And, it gave women the right to vote and hold office. Indeed Germany was the first industrialized nation to allow women an equal say in government.

Yet there were signs that the people who framed the constitution were uneasy about democracy. Lawmakers did not replace old statutes, even though some limited freedoms promised in the constitution. For example, laws that discriminated against gays and "Gypsies" (the name Germans gave to two ethnic groups known as the Sinti and Roma) remained. And Article 48 of the document allowed the president to suspend the Reichstag in times of national emergency. Still, the Reichstag could regain power simply by calling for a new election.

Germany's new constitution, like all constitutions, was based on a series of compromises. No group got everything it wanted, but everyone got something—even those with no faith in democracy. One German later recalled his father's response to the new government: "Well, at least it should make the Americans happy; I understand they do that kind of thing all the time. The French also change their governments regularly . . . but the kings always come back and bring order. This nonsense won't last long . . . but perhaps we'll get a more advantageous peace. After all, our generals will see to it that Ebert and his fellow proletarians don't sign any dishonorable treaty, and things can't get much worse than they are now."[7]

Germany's new constitution, like all constitutions, was based on a series of compromises. No group got everything it wanted, but everyone got something—even those with no faith in democracy.

In January of 1919, almost every eligible voter went to the polls and most voted for parties that supported the republic. After that election—and once the results of the Treaty of Versailles became known—parties that favored democracy did not do nearly as well. They won less than half of the vote in every other election.

CONNECTIONS

Kaiser Wilhelm, Prince Max of Baden, the generals, and the Social Democrats all worked behind closed doors. How significant was their decision to keep the news of the approaching defeat from the public? Did the people have a right to know?

Why do you think the generals chose to remain silent when republican leaders were accused of "stabbing Germany in the back"? How did their silence threaten the traditions and values they were trying to preserve? How did it turn a lie into something that generations of German students learned as an "historical fact"?

Add to your working definition of the word *revolution*. Did Germany experience a revolution in 1918?

Starting a new government in a nation that has just lost a war is not an easy task. Compare the difficulties faced by the Weimar Republic in 1919 with those faced by the United States in 1787. What advantages did the United States have? What disadvantages? What advantages and disadvantages did Germany have?

Suppose you were asked to develop a government for a new nation. What kind of government would you establish? Would it be democratic? Rather than spell out every detail of your plan, explain the principles upon which it would be based. How would you educate people to support that government?

Who could be a citizen of Germany in 1919? What rights did German citizens have? What responsibilities? Find out how citizenship was defined in the United States in 1919. Who belonged and who did not? What parallels do you see? What differences seem most striking?

How important was the decision of Ebert and other Social Democrats to allow army officers, bureaucrats, judges, and teachers to keep their jobs? All had served the nation faithfully under the kaiser. Were they likely to be as loyal to a republic?

Review the identity chart you made in Chapter 1. Suppose you had lived through this period in history, not as an American but as a German. Record in your journal, how someone with your identity might have responded to the chaos in Germany at the end of the war, to the surrender, and to the new constitution.

The Treaty of Versailles

When the United States declared war on Germany in April 1917, President Woodrow Wilson vowed that this would truly be "the war to end all wars." He argued that the war would have been fought in vain if the world returned to the way it was in 1914. The President revealed his goals in a 1918 speech. In it, he listed fourteen points essential to achieving lasting peace. In his view, the most important was the final one. It called for a "league of nations," where nations would resolve differences around a table rather than on a battlefield.

Wilson based his proposals on a single principle: "It is the principle of justice to all peoples and nationalities, and their right to live on equal terms of liberty and safety with one another, whether they be strong or weak. Unless this principle be made its foundation, no part of the structure of international justice can stand."

Wilson also believed that frustrated nationalism had caused the war. Thus he reasoned that if each ethnic group in Europe had its own land and government, there would be less chance of another war. He called the idea *self-determination.* As a result, the Austro-Hungarian, German, Ottoman, and Russian empires all disappeared. In Europe, each was divided into independent nations. The victors did not even consider applying that principle to the rest of the world. When the Japanese asked that a statement opposing racial discrimination be written into the treaty, the idea was rejected. When a young Vietnamese nationalist known as Ho Chi Minh asked to address the allies, the victors refused to let him speak. Europe's map might be redrawn but not the maps of Asia or Africa. Both continents would continue to be ruled by Europeans.

Many Europeans were more interested in punishing the Germans than in preventing another world war. After all, the United States had been at war for just one year. Its European allies had been fighting for over four years. David Lloyd George of Britain demanded that Germany pay for the trouble it had caused; Vittorio Orlando of Italy insisted on a share of Germany's colonial empire. And France's Georges Clemenceau required not only the return of the provinces of Alsace and Lorraine but also assurances that his nation would be safe from future German aggression. Therefore the treaty contained the following articles:

80. Germany will respect the independence of Austria.

81. Germany recognizes the complete independence of Czechoslovakia.

87. Germany recognizes the complete independence of Poland.

119. Germany surrenders all her rights and titles over her overseas countries.

I am convinced that if this peace is not made on the highest principles of justice, it will be swept away by the peoples of the world in less than a generation.

159. The German military forces shall be demobilized and reduced not to exceed 100,000 men.

181. The German navy must not exceed 6 battleships, 6 light cruisers, 12 destroyers, and 12 torpedo boats. No submarines are to be included.

198. The Armed Forces of Germany must not include any military or naval air forces.

231. Germany and her Allies accept the responsibility for causing all the loss and damage to the Allied Powers.

233. Germany will pay for all damages done to the civilian population and property of the Allied Governments. [The figure was later set at $33 billion].

428. To guarantee the execution of the Treaty, the German territory situated to the west of the Rhine River will be occupied by Allied troops for fifteen years.

431. The occupation forces will be withdrawn as soon as Germany complies with the Treaty.

Not surprisingly, Germans felt betrayed by the treaty. One German newspaper, *Deutsche Zeitung*, denounced it with these words. "In the place where, in the glorious year of 1871, the German Empire in all its glory had its origin, today German honor is being carried to its grave. Do not forget it! The German people will, with unceasing labor, press forward to reconquer the place among the nations to which it is entitled. Then will come vengeance for the shame of 1919."[8] That view was widely shared. Even German Communists opposed the agreement. A number of non-German observers and some historians also considered the treaty too harsh. Others noted that it was not nearly as vindictive as the one Germany forced on Russia just a year earlier.

When Wilson arrived in Paris, he was cheered. By the time the Treaty of Versailles was completed in May of 1919, his popularity had dimmed not only abroad but also at home. Many Americans felt that Europe's problems were not their concern. They preferred isolation to a continuing involvement in world affairs. So, despite Wilson's pleas, the United States did not join the League of Nations. The League also began its work without Germany and the USSR. Both were viewed as "outlaw" nations. As a result, the League was an international peacekeeper that failed to include three key nations.

CONNECTIONS

What does the word *vindictive* mean? Was the Treaty of Versailles vindictive? The Treaty of Brest-Litovsk?

Before the war ended, Woodrow Wilson said, "I am convinced that if this peace is not made on the highest principles of justice, it will be swept away by the peoples of the world in less than a generation." What is a "just peace"? Why is it difficult to hold on to? What aspects of society work against peace? Why was it so hard to make peace in 1919? To keep the peace? What would it take to achieve a lasting peace today?

In small groups, evaluate the fairness of the Treaty of Versailles. What criteria did your group use to make its evaluation? What criteria did the victors use? The Germans? What similarities do you notice? What differences seem most striking?

Reading 3 described how Erzberger and the other signers of the armistice agreement came to be characterized as the "November criminals" who "stabbed Germany in the back." How do you think the terms of the treaty affected that view? How does a nation experience shame?

A democratic leader once said that it is impossible to lead if no one is following. What do you think he was saying about leadership in a democracy? Suppose leaders had put aside their political differences and worked out a treaty based on Wilson's Fourteen Points. Would their people have accepted such a treaty?

Woodrow Wilson believed that the war was caused by "frustrated nationalism." He maintained that the best way to reduce the chances of another war was through "self-determination." Wilson's Secretary of State, Robert Lansing, feared "self-determination" would have the opposite effect. In a letter to Wilson, he asked, "Will it not breed discontent, disorder and rebellion? The phrase is simply loaded with dynamite. It will raise hopes which can never be realized. It will, I fear, cost thousands of lives. What a calamity that the phrase was ever uttered! What misery it will cause!" What is *frustrated nationalism*? *Self-determination*? Was the former the cause of World War I? Was the latter a way to prevent another war? Support your opinion with evidence from current events.

Study a map of Europe before and after World War I. List the differences between the two maps. How do you account for differences? To what extent is *self-determination* reflected in your list of differences?

The fighting in the Balkans in 1992 prompted columnist A. M. Rosenthal to write, "Bosnians, Serbs, Croats, Albanians, Macedonians, Muslim or Christian, come out of a world where for centuries loyalties were built on the importance of separateness. The separate clan, tribe, family and village gave protection. The histories and fantasies of the individual group gave meaning and texture to life. The separateness created fear of others, which was intensified when the outsider was too close, a neighbor. Leaders used the fears to build their own power—feudal dukes once, now onetime Communist bosses like President Slobodan Milosevic of Serbia are building new power on old separations."[9] Are his comments true of world leaders after World War I? Are they true of other leaders in today's world? What is he suggesting is the proper role of a leader? Do you agree?

➤Professor Henry Friedlander argues that the Germans were more disturbed about losing the war than they were about the terms of the Treaty of Versailles. This argument is developed in his videotaped lecture, "The Rise of Nazism," available from the Facing History Resource Center and summarized in *Elements of Time*, page 341.

READING 5

Anger and Humiliation

Hitler wanted to create a "movement." He had no intention of being "one of the nameless millions who live and die by the whim of chance."

Ten years after the war, Erich Maria Remarque wrote a novel about his experiences as a soldier in the German army. The book, *All Quiet on the Western Front*, became an international best-seller. Soldiers all over the world identified with the hero's experiences and feelings. One of the most quoted parts of the novel takes place as Paul, the hero of the book, anticipates the end of the war. "All that meets me, all that floods over me are but feelings—greed of life, love of home, yearning of the blood, intoxication of deliverance. But no aims. Had we returned home in 1916, out of the suffering and the strength of our experiences we might have unleashed a storm. Now if we go back we will be weary, broken, burnt out, rootless, and without hope. We will not be able to find our way any more."

Soon after writing those words, Paul is killed, "on a day that was so quiet and still on the whole front, the army report confined itself to the single sentence: 'All quiet on the Western Front.'"Although Paul never returned home, Remarque and other German soldiers did. Some were indeed burned out. Others returned home angry and bitter—not with the war itself but with the surrender and the treaty that followed it. Johann Herbert was among them. His son later said of him:

> He had lost a leg on the battlefront, and he refused to try to use a wooden leg. Instead he rolled around the house in his wheelchair and stormed at the "bureaucrats and bloodsuckers" who had brought Germany into disgrace. He described the leaders of the civilian government as traitors, to whom we owed no loyalty or allegiance. When I brought home the black, red, and gold flag of the new republic (the old flag had been black, white, and red), he ripped it up, spit on it, slapped me in the face and told me never to bring that rag into the house again.[10]

Other veterans shared Herbert's anger. Some joined paramilitary groups like the Freikorps (Free Corps). These groups attempted not only to crush revolution at home but also to protect the nation's borders from the

Poles and the Bolsheviks. Members were recruited by former army officers who ran ads that read, "What's the use of studies, and what's the good of business or a profession? Enemies within and beyond are burning down our house. Help us, in the spirit of comradeship and loyalty, to restore our power of national defense."

Adolf Hitler was among those veterans who struggled to find a place for themselves in 1919. When the fighting began, Hitler was as enthusiastic about the war as most of the men of his generation. In *Mein Kampf*, his autobiography, he wrote that when he and the others in his unit returned from their first battle "even our step had changed. Seventeen-year-old boys now looked like men." The war gave those young men a sense of purpose and a way of distinguishing themselves.

Hitler, in particular, wanted to distinguish himself. Born in 1889 in a small Austrian town, he was one of six children, four of whom died in childhood. His father died when he was fourteen and he lost his mother a few years later. By then Hitler had left school with little more than an eighth-grade education and dreams of becoming an artist.

In 1907, Hitler moved to Vienna in hopes of winning a place at the Academy of Fine Arts. His failure to do so shattered his early views of the world. So did his mother's death. He was also bewildered by life in a large sophisticated city that was home to people of many nationalities. In 1913, he moved to Munich, Germany, probably to escape a military service that would have required that he fight in a multinational army. In *Mein Kampf*, he noted that the longer he lived in Vienna "the more my hatred grew for the foreign mixture of peoples which had begun to corrode the old site of German culture." Munich was, in his view, a more "German" city.

When the war began, Hitler was a drifter struggling to find his place in the world. When the war was over, that struggle continued but now it had a focus. In his autobiography, he recalls, "In the days that followed [the surrender] my own fate became known to me . . . . I resolved to go into politics." He was not alone. In the 1920s, many angry veterans joined political parties and clubs that plotted the takeover of the government. In fact, the army hired Hitler to spy on one of those groups, the German Workers' party. Instead, he became a member.

What attracted him to that particular party? His autobiography explains, "This ridiculous little makeshift [band] with its handful of members, seemed to offer one distinct advantage: it had not yet frozen into organization. Thus there were unlimited opportunities for individual activity." He set out to transform the group into something more than a political party in the ordinary sense. He wanted to create a "movement." He had no intention of being "one of the nameless millions who live and die by the whim of chance." He vowed to control his own destiny and the destiny of Germany.

By February 1920, the tiny party had a new name and a 25-point program. The new name was the National Socialist German Workers' Party

(Nationalsozialistische Deutsche Arbeiter Partei—NSDAP or Nazi, for short). And the party's new program demanded the following:

1. A union of all Germans to form a great Germany on the basis of the right to self-determination of peoples.
2. Abolition of the Treaty of Versailles.
3. Land and territory (colonies) for our surplus population.
4. German blood as a requirement for German citizenship. No Jew can be a member of the nation.
5. Non-citizens can live in Germany only as foreigners, subject to the law of aliens.
6. Only citizens can vote or hold public office.
7. The state ensures that every citizen live decently and earn his livelihood. If it is impossible to provide food for the whole population, then aliens must be expelled.
8. No further immigration of non-Germans. Any non-German who entered Germany after August 2, 1914, shall leave immediately.
9. A thorough reconstruction of our national system of education. The science of citizenship shall be taught from the beginning.
10. All newspapers must be published in the German language by German citizens and owners.

The program did not make headlines. The party was just one of many small political groups. Yet by 1921, Hitler was attracting thousands of new members. One early member of the Nazi party and the S.A., its private army, recalled the effect Hitler had on him.

> We, oldtime National Socialists, did not join the S.A. for reasons of self-interest. Our feelings led us to Hitler. There was a tremendous surge in our hearts, a something that said: "Hitler, you are our man. You speak as a soldier of the front and as a man; you know the grind, you have yourself been a working man. You have lain in the mud, even as we—no big shot, but an unknown soldier. You have given your whole being, all your warm heart, to German manhood, for the well-being of Germany rather than your personal advancement or self-seeking. For your innermost being will not let you do otherwise." No one who has ever looked Hitler in the eye and heard him speak can ever break away from him.[11]

CONNECTIONS

Make an identity chart for a member of the Freikorps. For Paul, the hero of Remarque's book. For Hitler. How are the three alike? What differences are most striking? How would Paul respond to the Nazi party?

American film makers created a movie based on *All Quiet on the Western Front*. German historian Golo Mann, then a student, recalled the way the

Nazis responded to the opening of the film in Berlin: "A few minutes after the showing began, grenades exploded against the screen, stink bombs were tossed, sneezing powder was spread around, and white mice were released. The film had to be stopped." Why do you think the Nazis attacked the film? What didn't they want people to see?

Some documents have to be studied carefully. The Nazi program is one of those documents. Divide into groups and focus on two or three points. As you study them, consider these questions:

- What is the aim of this particular point? What key phrases provide clues to its meaning?
- To whom will this particular point appeal? Why?
- If the word *American* were substituted for the term *German*, would your opinion of any point change? Which point or points?
- Do you think that any of these ideas would be acceptable to people today? If so, which one or ones?

To many people in the 1920s, the Nazi platform did not seem to be the work of an extremist group. What parts of the document may have seemed most reasonable?

Notice the first two points in the Nazi platform. If the Nazis were so critical of the Treaty of Versailles and Wilson, why did they invoke Wilson's "self determination of peoples"?

Is it possible to accept the good parts of the Nazi program and overlook the bad parts? What are the advantages of doing so? The risks?

Germans were not the only ones to join extremist groups in the early twentieth century. In 1915, the Ku Klux Klan was revived in the United States. It boasted that its purpose was to "uphold Americanism, advance Protestant Christianity, and eternally maintain white supremacy." Members were inspired by a movie called *The Birth of a Nation*. The movie glorified the Klan's activities during Reconstruction. Unlike the original Klan, however, the new group was not just anti-black but also anti-immigrant, antisemitic, and anti-Catholic. By the early 1920s, the Klan had nearly five million members

and controlled a number of state governments. Research the Klan's goals. Which were similar to those of the Nazis? What differences between the two groups seem most striking?

Research the platforms of American political parties in the 1920s. What parallels do you see between those platforms and the one the Nazis created? What difference is most striking?

Hitler wanted to create a "movement." He did not want be "one of the nameless millions who live and die by the whim of chance." What does this suggest about the man? Was he a *visionary*? If so, what was his vision and how do you think he would get others to accept it? Was he *dogmatic*? That is, did he believe that he alone had the truth? If so, what was the dogma he preached?

See *Elements of Time*, pages 39-40, for a summary of Sol Gittleman's video-taped talk, "The Weimar Era, 1919-1933." He discusses the ideas that influenced Nazi attitudes toward gender roles, politics, and art.

READING 6

Voices in the Dark

The vocabulary of political battle, the desire to utterly destroy the political enemy, and the way in which adversaries were pictured, all seemed to continue the First World War against a set of different, internal foes.

George Mosse writes, "To many all over Europe it seemed as if the First World War had never ended but was being continued during the interwar years. The vocabulary of political battle, the desire to utterly destroy the political enemy, and the way in which adversaries were pictured, all seemed to continue the First World War against a set of different, internal foes."[12] On a train ride just after the war, Henry Buxbaum, a veteran from Friedburg—a small town in the German state of Hesse—discovered that he had become the "enemy":

> The train was pitch-dark. The lights were out, nothing uncommon after the war when the German railroads were in utter disrepair and very few things functioned orderly . . . . That night, we were seven or eight people in the dark, fourth-class compartment, sitting in utter silence till one of the men started the usual refrain: "Those God-damned Jews, they are at the root of all our troubles." Quickly, some of the others joined in. I couldn't see them and had no idea who they were, but from their voices they sounded like younger men. They sang the same litany over and over again, blaming the Jews for everything that had gone wrong with Germany and for anything else wrong in this world. It went on and on, a cacophony of obscenities, becoming

more and more vicious and at the same time more unbearable with each new sentence echoing in my ears. Finally, I couldn't stand it any longer. I knew very well that to start up with them would get me into trouble, and that to answer them wasn't exactly the height of wisdom, but I couldn't help it. . . . I was burning with rage and told them exactly what I thought of them and their vicious talk. I began naturally with the announcement: "Well, I am a Jew and etc., etc." That was the signal they needed. Now they really went after me, threatening me physically. I didn't hold my tongue as the argument went back and forth. They began jostling me till one of them next to me and near the door, probably more encouraged by the darkness than by his own valor, suggested: "Let's throw the Jew out of the train." Now, I didn't dare ignore this signal, and from then on kept quiet. I knew that silence for the moment was better than falling under the wheels of a moving train. One of the men in our compartment, more vicious in his attacks than the others, got off the train with me in Friedburg. When I saw him under the dim light of the platform, I recognized in him a fellow I knew well from our soccer club. . . . I would never have suspected this man of harboring such rabid, antisemitic feelings.[13]

CONNECTIONS

Suppose the lights had not gone out. Would the conversation in the compartment have been the same?

If you had been on the train, do you think you would have said or done anything? Have you or someone you know ever had a similar experience? How did you feel? How did you respond?

In times of economic upheaval, political unrest, or social stress, people often feel powerless and angry. How do some leaders turn those feelings against "outsiders" or "strangers"?

In Chapter 1, a number of individuals said that what they learned as children stayed with them all of their lives. How do negative feelings about "others" turn into acts of hatred and violence in times of crisis? What is the relationship between tolerance and fear? Between humiliation and hatred?

His teachers were more interested in producing "mental machines" than in educating human beings.

What Did You Learn at School Today?

*T*he war did not alter every part of German life. The nation's schools changed very little, if at all. Albert Einstein, a student in Germany before the war, claimed that his teachers were more interested in producing "mental machines" than in educating human beings. The experiences of Albert Speer, who later became a high-ranking Nazi official, suggest that the leaders of the republic held similar views. Speer recalled that "In spite of the Revolution, which had brought us the Weimar Republic, it was still impressed upon us that the distribution of power in society and the traditional authorities were part of the God-given order of things. We remained largely untouched by the currents stirring everywhere in the early twenties. In school, there would be no criticism of courses or subject matter, let alone the ruling powers of the state. . . . It never occurred to us to doubt the order of things."[14] A German named Klaus, who was a little younger than Speer, had a similar experience:

> We were taught history as a series of facts. We had to learn dates, names, places of battles. Periods during which Germany won wars were emphasized. Periods during which Germany lost wars were sloughed over. We heard very little about World War I, except that the Versailles peace treaty was a disgrace, which someday, in some vague way, would be rectified. In my school, one of the best in Berlin, there were three courses in Greek and Roman history, four in medieval history, and not one in government. If we tried to relate ideas we got from literature or history to current events, our teachers changed the subject.
>
> I really don't believe that anyone was deliberately trying to evade politics. Those teachers really seemed to think that what went on in the Greek and Roman Empire was more important than what was happening on the streets of Berlin and Munich. They considered any attempt to bring up current political questions a distraction . . . because we hadn't done our homework.
>
> And there was always a great deal of homework in a school like mine, which prepared students for the university. At the end of our senior year, we were expected to take a detailed and exceedingly tough exam called the Abitur. How we did on the exam could determine our whole future. Again, the Abitur concentrated on our knowledge of facts, not on interpretation or on the expression of personal ideas. Looking back on it now, it also didn't seem to measure our ability to reason clearly. . .to draw conclusions, to interpret ideas.[15]

As Klaus reflected on his adolescence, he noted the emphasis on group activities rather than individual action.

I liked to wander in the woods around Berlin. So my mother enrolled me in a hiking club. I pointed out tactfully that this was not what I had in mind. Marching around the countryside, singing sentimental German folk songs with twenty other boys, was not my idea of fun. I liked to stroll around by myself . . . enjoying the quiet and the scenery. My mother somehow gave me to understand that this was unmasculine . . . and what's more, un-German.

There was a great deal of control over my life and that of my friends . . . from the school and from parents. But somehow we all felt that this was necessary, so that we could get through that Abitur, get into a good university . . . and be free. We lived for the future. We had to think very little, take almost no initiative, our days were charted out for us. It seems strange that with bloody street fights almost every weekend, groups of brown-shirted men singing aggressive songs on Saturday mornings as they marched to their training grounds, political assassinations on the front pages of the papers regularly, we never felt threatened, never afraid of anything but failure in school.[16]

Even when the "currents stirring everywhere" could not be ignored, teachers tried to do so. For example, in 1923, France occupied the Ruhr to force Germany to make reparations payments. Among the soldiers sent to enforce the Treaty of Versailles were men from French colonies in Africa. A teacher said of them:

Day after day I had to suffer the sight of French black troops marching from the one-time garrison city of Diez to their training place at Altendiez . . . . I taught the children under my care never so much as to look at these black fighters. If, by chance, they happened to pass by the school during recess, teachers and pupils would turn their backs and remain standing like pillars of salt. The German-speaking [French] officers and non-coms well understood this mute protest of German youth and its teachers, and not infrequently gave vent to their anger in the foulest language.[17]

CONNECTIONS

Speer speaks of learning the "God-given order of things." What does the phrase mean? How important is it to learn? Have you learned it?

The emphasis in German education was on the wars that Germany won rather than on the ones it lost. The failure to discuss World War I was an important omission. What schools choose *not* to teach is often as important as what they do teach. How did the failure to teach World War I distort German history? Betray German students?

Every school teaches attitudes and values as well as facts and skills. What attitudes and values were Klaus's teachers conveying when they tried to control what students learned? When they refused to discuss current events? What values are reflected in the emphasis on the *Abitur*, the exam that controlled so much of Klaus's life? What values did the children learn the day they were instructed to turn their backs on African soldiers?

Compare and contrast education in the United States today with education in the Weimar Republic. What values did German children learn in the 1920s? How well did their schools prepare them for life in a democracy? What values are stressed in American schools, including your own? How well prepared are you and your classmates for life in a democracy? (To find out more about education in your community, interview your parents, teachers, and principal. You may also wish to review the goals and objectives for the various courses that make up the curriculum at your school.) As an alternative project, review social studies textbooks used in American schools in the 1920s. What were American students learning? Compare and contrast their education to that of German students.

When Albert Einstein became a teacher, he encouraged his students to reflect, ask questions, and criticize ideas. Why is thinking essential to a scientist? How important is it to a citizen? For what reasons? Record your ideas so that you can refer to them later.

READING 8

Order and Law

*I*n German classrooms, teachers encouraged their students to value obedience and respect authority. Judges played a similar role in the nation's courtrooms. Unlike judges in the United States, German judges did not consider themselves responsible for upholding the nation's constitution. Instead they placed the need for order above the law. As one judge explained, just as the army protects Germany from enemies beyond the nation's borders, the courts must protect the nation within those borders.

That spirit was reflected in the way the judges handled two political upheavals. The first took place in the German state of Bavaria in April, 1919 when the Communists took over the state government. The revolution lasted about two weeks. Even before the army arrived to restore order, the emergency was over. Nevertheless, the troops, operating under martial—or military—law, executed over one thousand workers. And the national government charged the leaders of the revolt with high treason. One man was sentenced to death and over twenty-two hundred others received long prison terms.

On March 12, 1920, a second uprising occurred. This time a group of conservatives led by Wolfgang Kapp overthrew the national government and executed over two hundred people. The leaders of the Weimar Republic managed to regain control of the country only by appealing to people to "strike, stop working, strangle this military dictatorship, fight . . . for the preservation of the republic, forget all dissension! There is only one way to block the return of Wilhelm II: to cripple the country's economic life! Not a hand must move, not a single person must help the military dictatorship. General strike all along the line! Workers unite!"

To the surprise of many, Germans did unite and the strike was a stunning success. Within days, the putsch, or coup, was over and the republic restored. Most nations would have rounded up the leaders of the coup and tried them for treason. Yet the vast majority of those involved in this coup were never punished. Only a handful, including Kapp, were even arrested. He died in prison while awaiting trial. The court dropped charges against all but one of the others. Berlin's former chief of police was tried and found guilty but received the minimum sentence possible under the law. And he lost none of the privileges of citizenship, including the right to hold office.

The courts clearly did not consider all uprisings equal. The courts had other biases as well. In 1923, the German Supreme Court allowed the use of the term *Jew Republic* to describe the Weimar government on the grounds that "it can denote the new legal and social order in Germany which was brought about in significant measure by German and foreign Jews." At the same time, a worker who carried a sign saying "Workers, burst your chains!" was arrested for inciting class warfare. All speech was not equal either. Neither were all murders. Between 1919 and 1922, conservative groups were responsible for 354 political assassinations. Although 50 killers confessed to their crimes, over half were acquitted. The 24 found guilty spent an average of just four months in jail. Communist groups were responsible for 22 political assassinations during the same period. All of those cases went to trial and ten of the murderers were executed. The other 12 received an average prison term of fifteen years.

The judges had come to believe that "defense of the state" justified breaking the law. A German legal scholar was horrified at the idea that murder could be justified by a "national emergency." He wrote, "Such a decision does more than merely damage the legal order which judges are called upon to protect. This decision destroys it."[18] The Social Democrats agreed. In 1924, they warned that "administration of justice in this manner presents a danger to the republic, insofar as it enables subversive and monarchist organizations to amass weapons without giving that part of the population which supports democracy the possibility to defend itself or to insist on respect for the law."[19] The judges and the German people chose to ignore these warnings.

Unlike judges in the United States, German judges did not consider themselves responsible for upholding the nation's constitution. Instead they placed the need for order above the law.

CONNECTIONS

What did the scholar mean when he wrote that the decision to permit "defense of state" as justification for murder "destroys" the legal order that judges are called upon to protect? Do you agree? If judges in Weimar Germany were not responsible for upholding the Constitution, who was? People look to the courts to right wrongs. Where can they find justice if the courts refuse to protect their rights?

In *Elements of Time*, page 30, Henry Friedlander points out that there was minimal support for democracy in Weimar Germany. "Germans created a republic with a democratic constitution but no constituency." What evidence can you find in this reading to refute Friedlander's assessment? To affirm it?

Reread Abraham Lincoln's warnings about the real danger to democracies in Chapter 2, Reading 4. How do his remarks apply to the Weimar Republic? How do you think he would have responded to the two uprisings? To the trials of the men who led those uprisings?

Review the conversation between Carl Schurz and Otto von Bismarck in Chapter 2, Reading 6. Which man's view of democracy did German judges share in the 1920s? What do you think may be the consequences of that view?

German judges did not claim to be impartial. American judges, on the other hand, pride themselves on being impartial. But are they? Martha Minow, a legal scholar, argues that "impartiality is the guise that partiality takes to seal bias against exposure. It looks impartial to apply a rule denying unemployment benefits to anyone who cannot fulfill the work schedule, but it is not impartial if the work schedule was devised with one religious Sabbath, and not another in mind. The rule does not seem impartial to the employee who belongs to a minority religion. Until we try to imagine the point of view of someone unlike ourselves, we will not depart from our own partiality."[20] How difficult is it to view the world from someone else's perspective? Why does Minow believe it is the best way to be truly impartial?

In 1919, many Americans were also fearful that Communists or "Reds" would take over their country. They saw signs of the coming revolution in the more than three thousand strikes that took place in just one year's time. Although most were caused by postwar layoffs and wage cuts, many people were convinced that they were the work of Communist agents. When several bombings occurred—including one at the home of Attorney General A. Mitchell Palmer—they saw proof that a revolution had begun.

In fact, the bombings were the work of anarchists (people who want to destroy all government) rather than Communists. But many Americans were in no mood to see differences among anarchists, Communists, and other radicals. A number of communities and states passed laws limiting the right of radicals to express their ideas. The federal government also took action. Palmer organized raids on various labor unions and radical organizations. In December, he shipped to Russia 249 immigrants, of whom no more than a handful were Communists. In January 1920, his agents arrested over six thousand other immigrants suspected of radical activity. The arrests led many to conclude that all newcomers were dangerous and encouraged the passage of laws that restricted immigration. But a few Americans, including Assistant Secretary of State Louis Post, fought for the rights of the radicals. As a result of their efforts, most of those arrested were tried and acquitted. What does the "Red Scare" suggest about the way Americans regarded order and respect for authority? The way they regarded freedom?

What motivates censors? Molly Ivins, an American newspaper columnist and author, believes it is fear. To explain, she recounts the story of two boys so frightened by a chicken snake in the henhouse, they lit out simultaneously "doing considerable damage to themselves and the henhouse door." When one of the boys was reminded that chicken snakes are harmless, he replied, "Yes, Ma'am, but some things can scare you so much that you'll hurt yourself." Ivins writes, "In this country we get so scared of something terrible—of communists or illegal aliens or pornography or crime—that we decide the only way to protect ourselves is to cut back on our freedom . . . . Well now, isn't that the funniest idea—that if we were less free we would be safer?"[21] How do her comments apply to judges in Weimar Germany? To the United States today?

READING 9

Criticizing Society

Despite government efforts to silence criticism, many individuals spoke out. Others voiced their discontent through their art. Every work of art reflects the artist's values and beliefs. In the 1920s, a number of German artists created pictures that challenged authority or forced viewers to see their world as it really was—not as they wanted it to be. Among them was George Grosz. In 1924, the year he created the Berlin street scene shown on page 134, a German judge considered his work so disturbing that he found the artist guilty of "attacks on public morality" and fined him six thousand marks. It was not the first time Grosz was brought to court for criticizing German society nor would it be the last.

Every work of art reflects the artist's values and beliefs. In the 1920s, a number of German artists created pictures that challenged authority or forced viewers to see their world as it really was—not as they wanted it to be.

Three artists view the streets of Berlin: Bruno Voigt (top left), George Grosz (top right), and Albert Birkle (bottom).

CONNECTIONS

Freedom of expression is critical to a democratic society. People express ideas in pictures as well as words. In what other ways do individuals criticize their society? Research the First Amendment to the U.S. Constitution. How does it protect the rights of individuals to express their views? When have those rights been threatened?

Study Albert Birkle's *Street Scene, Berlin*. What is he saying about life in the city? About the people who make up that city? A critic has said of the people in Birkle's painting, "They grasp at emptiness, and reach out in the surrounding space, with eyes bereft of hope."[22] How do you see the Berliners in his painting?

Look carefully at Grosz's *Street Scene, Berlin*. What is he saying about life in the city? About the people who make up that city? How is his view similar to Birkle's? What difference seems most striking?

Both Grosz and Birkle created their street scenes in the 1920s. Bruno Voigt created his in 1932 when such paintings were no longer popular. Voigt deliberately invoked the past in his work to make a point about the present. Why do you think he drew heavy lines around the man seated in the foreground? Why do you think Voigt saw his work as a weapon in the fight against the Nazis?

READING 10

Inflation Batters the Weimar Republic

Overshadowing the violence and discontent in the early days of the Weimar Republic was a period of incredible inflation. Inflation is a time when the value of money decreases and/or general prices increase sharply. During the war, the German government printed money freely to pay for soldiers, guns, and ammunition. After the fighting ended, there was more money in circulation than there were things to buy. The result was inflation. To make matters worse, the French occupied the Ruhr in 1923, when Germany failed to make reparation payments. The Germans, in turn, responded to the occupation with a general strike. During that strike, they produced nothing. So the few goods available became even more valuable. Prices skyrocketed and the German mark purchased less and less.

In times of trouble, people often look for easy answers. Their fears and suspicions of those they regard as *the other* also increase.

Date	Marks	US Dollars
1918	4.2	1
1921	75	1
1922	400	1
Jan. 1923	7,000	1
Jul. 1923	160,000	1
Aug. 1923	1,000,000	1
Nov. 1, 1923	1,300,000,000	1
Nov. 15, 1923	1,300,000,000,000	1
Nov. 16, 1923	4,200,000,000,000	1

People who had saved their money in banks or were living on pensions or disability checks found themselves bankrupt. Those with jobs found that their salary increases could not possibly keep up with the almost instantaneous rise in prices. Artist George Grosz described what shopping was like in those days.

> Lingering at the [shop] window was a luxury because shopping had to be done immediately. Even an additional minute meant an increase in price. One had to buy quickly because a rabbit, for example, might cost two million marks more by the time it took to walk into the store. A few million marks meant nothing, really. It was just that it meant more lugging. The packages of money needed to buy the smallest item had long since become too heavy for trouser pockets. They weighed many pounds. . . . People had to start carting their money around in wagons and knapsacks. I used a knapsack.[23]

Under the leadership of Gustav Stresemann, a conservative politician who supported the republic, the government eventually brought inflation under control. But it took time and many people could not forget that the government had allowed it to happen. One German expressed their feelings when he wrote:

> Of course all the little people who had small savings were wiped out. But the big factories and banking houses and multimillionaires didn't seem to be affected at all. They went right on piling up their millions. Those big holdings were protected somehow from loss. But the mass of the people were completely broke. And we asked ourselves, "How can that happen? How is it that the government can't control an inflation which wipes out the life savings of the mass of people but the big capitalists can come through the whole thing unscathed." We who lived through it never got an answer that meant anything. But after that, even those people who used to save didn't trust money anymore, or the government. We decided to have a high-ho time whenever we had any spare money, which wasn't often.[24]

CONNECTIONS

In times of trouble, people often look for easy answers. Their fears and suspicions of those they regard as "the other" also increase. In the United States, during periods of high unemployment, there is often a corresponding rise in anti-immigrant legislation, hate crimes, and discrimination. The same has been true of nations in Europe both long ago and today. How do you account for such attitudes? How do they threaten minorities? Democracy itself?

Numbers can tell a story. What story do the numbers provided in this reading tell? Do they lead you to any conclusions? Numbers do not tell the whole story. What do the eyewitness accounts suggest about how inflation affected the way people saw themselves and their government? Who was hurt most by this kind of inflation?

It has been said that "any system can stand in fair weather; it is tested when the wind blows." How do economic crises test democracy? How do such crises encourage people to place their faith in leaders who offer simple solutions to complex problems? Find out how people in Russia and other former Communist nations are responding to similar crises today. How are their responses similar to those of Germans in the 1920s? What are the key differences?

READING 11

A Revolt in a Beer Hall

On the night of November 8, 1923, at the height of the inflation, Adolf Hitler and a band of armed supporters dramatically burst into a Munich beer hall. Hitler fired a shot at the ceiling and then declared that President Ebert and the national government had been deposed. The local police quickly put down the uprising. Two days later, Hitler was arrested and brought to trial.

Throughout the court proceedings, Hitler and his followers openly showed their contempt for the Weimar Republic by calling it a "Jew government." Yet the judge ruled that the defendants were "guided in their actions by a purely patriotic spirit and the noblest of selfless intentions." Therefore he refused to deprive them of their privileges as citizens. Instead, he gave them the minimum sentence possible under the law—five years in prison.

Hitler was not a German citizen. As an alien convicted of plotting against the government, he should have been deported. Indeed, the law required his deportation, but the judge chose not to follow the law. He explained, "In the case of a man whose thoughts and feelings are as

German as Hitler's, the court is of the opinion that the intent and purpose of the law have no application." Hitler and his comrades served just nine months of their prison term. The rest was suspended.

During his time in prison, Hitler and an associate, Rudolf Hess, worked on a book describing Hitler's life, his beliefs, and his plans for the future. Most of his ideas were based on antisemitic literature he read before the war, lessons he learned in the trenches, and observations made in the years that followed. British historian A. J. P. Taylor once called those ideas "a distorting mirror" of European thought. He saw Hitler as someone who took ideas that were widely held and carried them to an extreme.

The book entitled *Mein Kampf* or "My Struggle" was published in 1925. It maintained that a struggle among the races is the catalyst of history. A *catalyst* makes things happen. In Hitler's view, different races have different roles to play in society. Because he believed that the "Aryan" race was superior to all others, he insisted that "Aryan" Germany had the right to incorporate all of Eastern Europe into a new empire that would provide the nation with needed *Lebensraum*, or living space. The conquest of Eastern Europe was desirable because it would also be a victory over those who then controlled much of the region—the Communists. Hitler regarded the Communists as enemies of the German people. He repeatedly connected them to the Jews, yet another enemy, by claiming that the Jews were behind the teachings of the Communist party. "Jewish Bolshevism" became the phrase he used to link the two groups.

The Jews, according to Hitler, were everywhere, controlled everything, and acted so secretly that few could detect their influence. As proof of his claims, he often referred to the *Protocols of the Elders of Zion*. The document was supposedly a plan to take over the world that had been prepared by an international body of Jewish "elders." It was in fact a known forgery prepared by the Russian secret police in the 1890s to incite hatred against Jews. But Hitler was not interested in facts. In the 1920s, no more than a half million Jews lived in a country of about sixty million people. Yet Hitler's comments made it seem as if Germany were home to millions of Jews who controlled the entire nation. The charge was absurd; but repeating it again and again had an impact on those who heard it.

The idea that Germans of the Jewish faith were different from and inferior to Germans of the Christian faith was central to Hitler's charges. He often emphasized physical differences between Jews and non-Jews to strengthen his arguments. The blond haired, blue-eyed "Aryans," concluded Hitler, were superior to the dark-haired, swarthy Jews. These claims were false, but Hitler believed that if a lie was told often enough, people would come to believe it.

In *Mein Kampf*, Hitler offered a hierarchy of groups. At the bottom were not only Jews but also "Gypsies" and Africans. He claimed, for example, that those who thought that blacks were equal had been tricked: "From time to time illustrated papers bring it to the attention of the German people that some place or other a Negro has for the first time become a lawyer, teacher, even a pastor, in fact a heroic tenor, or something of the sort . . . . It doesn't dawn on this brainless world that this is positively a sin against all reason; that it is criminal lunacy to keep on drilling a [subhuman] until people think they have made a lawyer out of him, while millions of members of the highest race must remain in entirely unworthy positions. The fox is always a fox, the goose a goose, the tiger a tiger, etc."

Hitler often referred to the "good old days" in his speeches. The days he referred to were a mythical time when a community of "Aryans" lived peacefully together. He called upon the German *Volk* to restore that community by removing inferior races and eliminating the class hatred preached by the Communists. A supporter named Anna described the effects such a speech had on an audience in 1923.

> You cannot imagine how silent it becomes as soon as this man speaks; it is as if all of the thousand listeners are no longer able to breathe. When he angrily condemns the deeds of those who have ruled our people since the revolution and those who now prevent him and his followers from settling accounts with those November bigwigs, cheers ring through the hall for minutes on end. There is no silence until he waves his hands repeatedly to indicate that he wants to continue speaking . . . . Adolf Hitler is so firmly convinced of the correctness of his nationalistic views that he automatically communicates this conviction to his listeners. God grant that, as trailbreaker to better times, he will be able to gather many more racial comrades under the Swastika. After all, every class is represented. Workers and lower-ranking civil servants, officers and storm troopers, students and old pensioners—all sit together, and all are in agreement with the great concept embodied in the person of Adolf Hitler. It is often said that where eleven Germans come together, ten political parties are represented. Here, however, I have never heard anyone say that Hitler should do this, or that he should have done that. Sometimes it almost seems to me as if Hitler used a magic charm in order to win the unconditional confidence of old and young alike.[25]

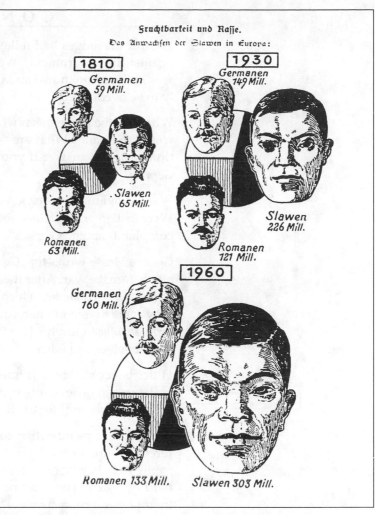

The Nazis played on fears that Germans would one day be outnumbered by "inferior peoples."

What if the judges had followed the law and deported Hitler for plotting against the government? Would people have protested the decision? Or was Hitler so unknown and unimportant at the time that his case was likely to be overlooked?

What did the judge mean when he said that Hitler's thoughts and feelings were "German"? What are "German thoughts and feelings"? Is the question easier to answer if you substitute the word *American* for the word *German*?

Were individual Jews or Jews as a group the subject of Hitler's complaints? Were Hitler's complaints about Africans specific or general? What of his complaints about "Gypsies"? Could any of these complaints be proven?

George Mosse writes that Germans used the word *subhuman* only occasionally before the war. After the war, they used it far more often. He also notes that the word *fanatic*, which had a negative connotation before the war, now came to "signify heroism and the willingness to fight." What does the term *subhuman* imply? How does the language we use affect the way we see ourselves and others?

Hitler believed that if you tell a lie big enough and often enough, people will come to believe it is true. What instances from your experiences support that assertion? Refute it?

What are the pictures that come into your mind when you hear about different groups in the United States today? Where do these images come from? Are they stereotypes or generalizations? What is the difference? In hard times, can you imagine neighbor turning against neighbor because of their physical characteristics?

The word *charisma* is defined as a quality attributed to those who have an exceptional ability to win the devotion of large numbers of people. What qualities made Hitler a charismatic leader? Anna speaks of the clarity of Hitler's viewpoint. How did that clarity contribute to his ability to attract followers? How did the fact that he seemed so sure of himself affect his audiences? Did Hitler's ideas on "race" contribute to his charisma? What leaders today do people consider charismatic? Do these leaders express their ideas clearly? Are they self-confident?

Anna offers one view of Hitler. Another German, Erika Mann, offers a very different view. She saw Hitler as uneducated, unathletic, weak, and uncourageous. In his analysis of *Mein Kampf*, George Sabine describes the man as "neither a scholar nor a theorist but a practical psychologist and an organizer." Compare and contrast the three descriptions. What do they say about the man? About each observer?

In the early 1990s, Serbia's leaders justified a brutal war with talk of the need to build a "Greater Serbia" through "ethnic cleansing." A prize-winning Yugoslavian novelist, Ivo Andric, referred to those Serbs as people "who easily make up fables and spread them quickly." In those fables, "reality is strangely and inextricably mixed and interwoven with legend." To what other groups today might his remarks also apply? To what other leaders? To what extent do his comments apply to Germans who joined extremist groups in the 1920s? To the leaders of those groups?

Henry Ford of the Ford Motor Company brought the *Protocols of the Elders of Zion* to the United States. Between 1920 and 1927, his newspaper, the *Dearborn Independent*, translated the document into English and printed it along with a series of articles accusing the Jews of using communism, banking, unions, gambling, even jazz music to weaken the American people and their culture. The entire series of articles was later published as a book, which sold over a half million copies in the United States and was translated into sixteen languages, including German. Hitler read the book and quoted it often. As a result of a law suit, Ford publicly apologized for spreading a lie. But the damage was already done. How difficult is it to "undo" a lie? Why do some people find it easier to believe an outrageous lie than a simple truth?

➤The documentary *Mein Kampf* uses footage from dozens of different sources to portray Hitler's life and consider the ideas he advocated. Portions of the documentary will be quite useful at various times in a study of the Nazi era. The film is available from the Facing History Resource Center.

Professor Paul Bookbinder maintains that Hitler's views of Jews were not uncommon in the 1920s. Therefore his antisemitic outbursts drew considerable support to the movement. See *Elements of Time*, page 42.

READING 12

Creating the Enemy

*I*n times of stress and uncertainty, it is all too easy to blame *them* for society's problems. People respond favorably because such attacks tap old prejudices and offer easy answers to complex problems. But was there any truth to the claims Hitler and other antisemites made? Did the Jews control Germany? Historian Donald L. Niewyk studied German census data in search of answers to those questions. He found that Jews

The very intensity with which the Jews were attacked in times of political uncertainty revealed how deep and irrational anti-Semitism was.

accounted for no more than 3.5 percent of all positions in trade, commerce, banking, law, and medicine, hardly enough to control a nation. He learned that although a few were very wealthy, the vast majority were not. He notes:

> In the twelve years between 1912 and 1924, the proportion of Berlin Jews with taxable incomes of more than 5,000 marks fell from 10.6 percent to 5.8 percent, while during the same period the number of Jews with annual taxable incomes under 1,200 marks rose from 73.3 percent to 83.6 percent of the city's Jewish population. Jews who lived on fixed incomes from savings or investments were ruined during the inflation. By the end of 1923, the Berlin Jewish Community had established nineteen soup kitchens, seven shelters, and an employment information and placement office for the destitute Jews of the city. Other big-city communities did the same.[26]

Niewyk points out that even during the "good years" of 1924-1929, the rate of unemployment in the Jewish community was high. The people who suffered most were Jews from Eastern Europe who settled in Germany before and just after the war to escape persecution and upheavals in the countries of their birth. They were subject to "chronic unemployment, sporadic official harassment, and the resentment of both Jewish and non-Jewish Germans." They had little opportunity to improve their conditions or protect their rights by becoming citizens. Conservative state governments made it almost impossible for them to become German citizens.

Historian Victoria Barnett places the number of Jews in Germany slightly higher—at 1 1/2 percent, mainly because she includes Christians of Jewish descent. But she, too, finds that Jews were far less influential than most people assumed. "Although many Germans blamed the uncertainties of the Weimar years on too much Jewish influence in the government, for example, only 4 of the 250 government ministers during the entire Weimar Republic were Jewish. Yet, in April 1933, Berlin church leader Otto Dibelius wrote, 'In the last 15 years in Germany, the influence of Judaism has strengthened extraordinarily. The number of Jewish judges, Jewish politicians, Jewish civil servants in influential positions has grown noticeably. The voice of the people is turning against this.'"[27]

The growing antisemitism had a profound effect on the way German Jews saw themselves and others. They had taken pride in being German and saw their nationality as an integral part of their identity. Now antisemitism forced many Jews, including Sigmund Freud, to reassess their identity. In 1926, the Austrian native told an interviewer, "My language is German. My culture, my attainments are German. I considered myself German intellectually, until I noticed the growth of anti-Semitic prejudice in Germany and German Austria. Since that time, I prefer to call myself a Jew." It was a particularly telling comment from a man who did not believe in God or organized religion.

Arnold Schoenberg, a world-famous composer, took an even stronger stand. In 1923, Wassily Kandinsky, a famous artist, invited him to join the faculty at the Bauhaus School of Design in Weimar. The composer was told that Jews were not normally welcome at the Bauhaus, but an exception would be made in his case. He angrily replied:

> [When] I walk along the street and each person looks at me to see whether I'm a Jew or a Christian, I can't very well tell each of them that I'm the one that Kandinsky and some others make an exception of, although of course that man Hitler is not of their opinion. And then even this benevolent view of me wouldn't be much use to me even if I were, like blind beggars, to write it around my neck for everyone to read . . . .
>
> I ask: Why do people say that the Jews are like what their black-marketeers are like? Do people also say that the Aryans are like their worst elements? Why is an Aryan judged by Goethe, Schopenhauer and so forth? Why don't people say the Jews are like Mahler, Altenberg, Schoenberg and many others?

Schoenberg then asked Kandinsky how he dared to "'reject me as a Jew.' Did I ever offer myself to you? Do you think that someone like myself lets himself be rejected! Do you think that a man who knows his own value grants anyone the right to criticize even his most trivial qualities? Who might it be, anyway, who could have such a right?"

Schoenberg ended his letter by warning, "But what is antisemitism to lead to if not to acts of violence? Is it so difficult to imagine that? You are perhaps satisfied with depriving Jews of their civil rights. Then certainly Einstein, Mahler, I, and many others will have been got rid of. But one thing is certain: they will not be able to exterminate those much tougher elements thanks to whose endurance Jewry has maintained itself unaided against the whole of mankind for twenty centuries."[28]

CONNECTIONS

Review the journal entries you made while reading Chapter 1. What do they suggest about why people look for scapegoats?

Statistics reveal that less than 1 percent of Germany's population was of Jewish descent. In other parts of Europe the percentage ranged from 10-11 percent in Poland to less than 1/2 percent in such countries as Sweden, Denmark, Italy, and Yugoslavia. Although a few were rich, most barely eked out a living. Yet throughout Europe, people saw Jews as a powerful and dangerous people. What did Chapter 1 suggest about the power of myths and misinformation? How does this reading confirm that view? What does it suggest about the power of a lie that is told again and again? About the vulnerability of minorities in times of stress?

Victoria Barnett argues, "The very intensity with which the Jews were attacked in times of political uncertainty revealed how deep and irrational anti-Semitism was."[29] What does she mean by that statement? Do you agree?

Draw an identity chart for Sigmund Freud. Why did he consider himself a Jew? Make a similar chart for Arnold Schoenberg. Does he believe that society has the right to define his identity?

Individuals today respond to racism much the way they did in the 1920s. An African American teenager recently wrote a poem called "Will They Ever Learn?" How would Schoenberg respond to the questions it raises? How would you respond?

> As I look down, on this world of mine,
> Several questions cross my mind.
> Why do they stare when I walk through the hall?
> Why do they think I can run with a ball?
> Why do they think I swear all the time?
> Why do they think I'll resort to crime?
> Why do they think I like to fight?
> Is it because I'm dark, not light?
> I hear them talk behind my back
> About my skin because it's black,
> Too black to be friendly, too black to be smart.
> Don't they know it breaks my heart
> To hear them tease without my concern.
> I wonder if they'll ever learn?[30]

How does being an "outsider" affect one's self-esteem? The way one sees himself or herself?

What does Schoenberg mean when he writes, "But what is antisemitism to lead to if not to acts of violence?" How would you answer the question? How are racism and violence linked? Record your answers in your journal so that you can refer to them later.

READING 13

Beyond the Stereotypes

James Luther Adams, a graduate of the Harvard Divinity School, traveled to Germany in 1927 to study at the University of Heidelberg. While visiting Nuremberg, he attended a Nazi rally. He later recalled:

> [Perhaps] I went there because I had read the Nazis were having a
> big rally and it was said that about 150,000 youth came for this

particular rally in Nuremberg and it was claimed that none of them rode for one step in order to show German vigor and show that they were genuine Germans—*echt Deutsch*. Each youth was to walk from whatever part of Germany he lived to Nuremberg for this conference and there was a rally and a parade that lasted about three or four hours. It was on a Sunday and singing Nazi songs and carrying banners and the crowds were very dense and here I was standing right in the front as these Nazis were marching by. These youth goose-stepping and I asked a couple of people standing with me, knowing what the answer should be. I asked, "Well what's the meaning of the swastika?" And these fellows gave me a typical Nazi answer about superiority of the German race and the necessity to purify Germany of Jewish blood and [in] the course of the conversation I asked them where are they [the Jews] going to go? "Well, we will put them out. They can find out where they're going to go."

The conversation became a little more intense and we were beginning to raise our voices. At this moment I was seized from behind. I, being a callow theological student, was inadequate for the situation. I couldn't get away. A fellow had seized me by both elbows from behind and pulled me out. I tried to get away and nobody paid any attention to me and I couldn't get away from him. He pushed me through that dense crowd and down the street into a side street and from there up into a dead-end alley marching me all the way. Nobody was interested in stopping him or anything and we got up to the end of the dead-end alley . . . and I didn't know, of course, what was going to happen to me. Was he going to beat me up because of what I had been saying and he wheeled me around and shouted at me in German, "You damn fool, don't you know that in Germany today you keep your mouth shut or you'll get your head bashed in." Well, I thought that was the next item on the agenda from his point of view and then he changed mood and smiled and he said, "You know what I have done. I've saved you from getting beaten up. They were not going to continue arguing with you. You were going to be lying flat on the pavement and I saw that coming and I grabbed you."

"Well," I said, "thank you very much. Why did you do that?"

"Well," he said, "I was in the General Merchant Marines and I've been in New York City several times and while the ship was there got acquainted with New Yorkers. I never, never in my life (I'm just an ordinary sailor) had such wonderful hospitality and you know what came to my mind—think of that—I watched you getting in trouble. I said look at all the hospitality I received from Americans and I never paid them back. I'm doing it today. I'm inviting you home to Sunday dinner and I want you to see what a typical Sunday dinner is."

So I went with him to a tenement house where some of the banisters were out of repair and so on and he was an unemployed anti-Nazi worker, a member of a trade union which was anti-Nazi, and we climbed four flights to get to his barren tenement . . . . An unemployed worker in a dilapidated tenement house and there was his wife and three children and we had Sunday dinner together and he gave me the first bottom line description of Nazi philosophy.[31]

CONNECTIONS

Did Adams's story surprise you? What did you think was going to happen when he was picked up and carried away? Why do you think an anti-Nazi attended a Nazi rally? Did it take courage for him to go?

What does Adams's story tell you about the political climate in Germany in the late 1920s? How significant is this story?

➤A videotaped interview with James Luther Adams is available from the Facing History Resource Center. In it, he recalls his experiences as a theology student in Germany during the late 1920s and early 1930s. Adams was amazed to learn that many theologians supported Hitler. What aspects of Hitler's philosophy might appeal to a religious leader?

READING 14

Hard Times Return

Historians note a decrease in tolerance and an increase in the number of hate groups during periods of depression and other forms of economic instability.

*B*y 1928, Germany had recovered from the war and business was booming, partly because German leaders had persuaded the Allies to lower reparations payments. Furthermore, Germany was no longer considered an "outlaw" nation. It was now a welcomed member of the League of Nations. As a result, fewer Germans seemed interested in Hitler's ideas. In the 1928 elections, the Nazis received only about 2 percent of the vote. Other conservative parties, like the People's Party, did far better. So did the Communists (KPD).

Then in 1929, a worldwide depression began. A *depression* is a time when economic activity slows as more and more businesses decrease production and lay off workers. Germany felt the effects of the depression almost immediately. Until 1929, loans from the United States helped fuel German recovery, but now hard-hit American banks began to call in those loans. As a result, many large German companies were forced to close their doors. Like leaders everywhere, those in Germany looked for ways to end the depression. And like other leaders in 1929, they failed. The chancellor of the Weimar Republic in 1929 was Hermann Mueller, a Social Democrat. By 1930, he and his party (SPD) were in trouble.

Number of Seats Political Parties Held in the Reichstag		
Party	1928	1930
SPD	153	143
Center	62	68
KPD	54	77
Nazi	12	107
People's	45	30

Heinrich Bruening of the Catholic Center party replaced Mueller as chancellor, but he, too, failed to solve the economic problems. Even though he suspended the Constitution by invoking Article 48, Bruening could not end the depression. Only the most extreme political parties seemed to have clear solutions to the crisis. The Communists won votes by blaming everything on wealthy industrialists. To end the depression, they argued, Germany had to replace the present system with a government like the one in Russia. The Nazis, on the other hand, blamed the Jews, Communists, liberals, and pacifists. And they, too, won support. Many saw the Nazis as an attractive alternative to democracy and communism. Among them were wealthy industrialists alarmed by the growth of the Communist party. They liked the Nazis' message; it was patriotic, upbeat, and energetic.

In 1932, Hitler ran for president against a Communist candidate and Hindenburg, the incumbent president. In order to do so, Hitler finally became a German citizen. The election was a spirited one, in which 84 percent of all eligible voters cast ballots. Those voters had to decide which party offered the best solution to the nation's problems. The decision was not an easy one. An observer noted that as voters went to the polls, each saw the war behind him, "in front of him social ruin, to his left he is being pulled by the Communists, to his right by the Nationalists, and all around him there is not a trace of honesty and rationality, and all his good instincts are being distorted into hatred." To appreciate those choices, compare the platforms of the Social Democratic party (SPD) and the Communist Party (KPD) with that of the Nazis (Reading 5).

Social Democratic Party Platform

We are committed to maintaining the Republic and a policy that will allow Germany to take its rightful place among the free governments of Europe.

1. We will support the present German Republic so that freedom, democracy, and justice will live in the hearts of our German countrymen.

2. We will honor all of Germany's obligations, political and financial, in order that Germany's honor and respect will not be decreased in the eyes of the world.

3. We plan to create more jobs by undertaking an extensive program of public works.

4. We will provide unemployment compensation for up to six months.

5. We will cut government expenditures to lower taxes.

6. We believe in the right of those who disagree with the party to speak and write on those issues without interference.

Communist Party Platform

We are committed to the overthrow of the presently existing, oppressive Republic and all of its economic and social institutions. We favor:

1. The abolition of private property.

2. The establishment of land reform programs, so that the government can take over the land and distribute it for the common good.

3. Government ownership of all industrial productive forces, so that they can be run for the benefit of the people rather than the capitalists.

4. A foreign policy that regards the Soviet Union as an ally against capitalism.

To the German people: The cause of your misery is the fact that French, British, and American capitalists are exploiting German workers to get rich themselves. Germans, unite to get rid of this terrible burden.

Which of these parties—SPD, KPD, or Nazi—would be most likely to appeal to the following German citizens?[32]

Hermann Struts

Hermann Struts, a lieutenant in the German army, fought bravely during the war. He comes from a long line of army officers and is himself a graduate of the German military academy. Struts has always taken pride in the army's able defense of the nation and its strong leadership.

Yet Struts is bitter about the fact that he has not had a promotion in over ten years. Few soldiers have, mainly because the German army was so drastically reduced by the Treaty of Versailles. In the old army, Struts would have been at least a captain by now and possibly a major. The treaty, he argues, has done irreparable harm not only to Germany's honor but also to his own honor as a soldier. He feels that if the civilian government had refused to sign the treaty and allowed the army to fight, both he and Germany would be better off.

Otto Hauptmann

Otto Hauptmann works in a factory in Berlin. Although his trade union has actively worked for better conditions and higher wages, it has not made many gains. Hauptmann blames their lack of success on the 1923 inflation and the current depression. He believes that the union would be more successful if the economy were more stable. Still, it is the union that has kept him employed. At a time when many of his friends have been laid off, his union persuaded the owners of his factory to keep men with seniority. In factories with weaker unions, managers kept only the young, claiming they are more productive.

Hauptmann worries about some of the ideas his fellow workers have expressed recently. They argue that when the owners are forced to cut back production, they take it out on the workers. So the only way to end the depression is to let the workers control the factories and the government. Hauptmann disagrees. He thinks that the workers do get fair treatment as long as they have a strong union. Moreover, he believes that managing the factories and government should be left to those who understand these complicated jobs.

Erich von Ronheim

Erich von Ronheim, the head of a Frankfurt textile factory, is very concerned about the depression. Sales are down and so are profits. If only Germany had not been treated so ruthlessly at Versailles, he argues, the nation would be far better off. Instead the government has had to impose heavy taxes to pay reparations to its former enemies. As a result, Germans are overtaxed with little money to spend on textiles and other consumer goods. The worldwide depression has made matters worse by eliminating possible foreign markets for German products. Even if the depression were over, Ronheim does not think taxes would come down because of reparation payments.

Ronheim considers the Communists a serious threat to Germany. He fears that if they set up a government like the one in the Soviet Union, capitalists like him would receive no mercy from the workers. He also thinks that Germany would become subservient to its old enemy, Russia.

Karl Schmidt

Karl Schmidt is an unemployed worker who lives in the rich steel-producing Ruhr Valley. Like so many men in the Ruhr, he lost his job because of the depression. Yet Schmidt notes that the owners of the steel mills still live in big houses and drive expensive cars. Why are they protected from the depression while their former employees suffer? Although the government does provide unemployment compensation, the money is barely enough to support Schmidt, his wife, and their two children. Yet the government claims that it cannot afford to continue even these payments much longer.

Schmidt feels that the government would be in a stronger position to help people if it cut off all reparations. But he also knows that if the government did so, the French might occupy the Ruhr Valley just as they did in 1923. What is needed is a government that is responsive to the workers—perhaps even one that is run by the workers, as some of his friends maintain. And he is convinced that Germany needs a government strong enough to stop reparation payments.

Wilhelm Schultz

Wilhelm Schultz works with his father on the family farm in East Prussia. The treaty has had a profound effect on Schultz and his family. The treaty turned part of East Prussia over to Poland. So even though his uncle lives just a few miles away, his home is now in Poland rather than Germany. Schultz's grandfather lives in Danzig. It is now a free state under the control of the League of Nations and it cannot be reached without traveling through Poland. As a result, the family cannot visit the grandfather without a passport and other official documents. That does not seem right to Schultz. As a child, he was taught to admire Germany's heroes, some of whom fought the Poles. So he is dismayed that his government signed a treaty that has subjected many Germans, including his uncle, to Polish rule. He is also bothered by greed and corruption he sees in government leaders. This is not the way Prussians should act.

Schultz also worries about the Communists. Neither he nor his father want a system that would eliminate private property. Both are proud to own their own land and anyone who wants to take it away is the enemy.

Elisabeth von Kohler

Elisabeth von Kohler, a prominent attorney who attended the University of Bonn, has a strong sense of German tradition. She believes that her people's contributions to Western civilization have been ignored. Kohler would like to see the republic lead a democratic Europe. She disapproves of the methods the Weimar Republic often uses to repress extremist parties. Her sense of justice is even more outraged by the way the Allies, particularly France, view Germany. She would like to prove to the world that the Germans are indeed a great race. She is proud to be an attorney and a German woman in the Weimar Republic.

Gerda Muenchen

Gerda Muenchen is the owner of a small Munich grocery store started by her parents. For years, her parents saved to send her to the university. But Muenchen chose not to go and the money stayed in the bank. In 1923, she had planned to use the money to pay for her children's education. But that year inflation hit Germany. Just before her older daughter was to leave for the university, the bank informed the family that its savings were worthless. This was a blow to Muenchen, but even more of a blow to her daughter, whose future hung in the balance.

Muenchen does not think she will ever regain her savings. With so many people out of work, sales are down sharply. And Muenchen's small grocery is having a tough time competing with the large chain stores. They can offer far lower prices. She and her children question a system that has made life so difficult for hardworking people.

CONNECTIONS

Was the Weimar Republic a success in 1928? If so, by whose standards? How do people measure the success of a nation? Of its government?

What does it mean to have one's "good instincts distorted into hatred"? How does that happen?

Write a working definition of *depression.* Historians note a decrease in tolerance and an increase in the number of hate groups during periods of depression and other forms of economic instability. How do you account for the decrease in tolerance? The rise in the number of hate groups? Are their observations as true today as they were in the past?

What was the significance of suspending Article 48?

Why did the Nazi message appeal to the industrialists? Why did many of them fear Communism? How do your answers help explain why people often look for simple answers to complex problems? Why they find ambiguity frightening? Record your ideas in your journal so that you can refer to them later.

Divide into small groups with each focusing on one of the individuals described in this reading. Before deciding how the individual that your group was assigned is likely to vote, compare the Nazi plan (Reading 5) with the two party platforms outlined in this reading. Be sure to justify your choices by identifying particular grievances and explaining how each party would redress those grievances. Think, too, about other factors that might persuade a voter to choose one party over another. What effect might such emotions as fear or pride have on the decision to support one party over another?

➤*Friedrich* is a novel about two young boys—one Christian and the other Jewish—who came of age in Germany during the early 1930s. What does it reveal about how neighbor can come to turn against neighbor? Multiple copies of the book are available from the Facing History Resource Center.

READING 15

Hitler in Power

*I*n July 1932, Paul von Hindenburg at the age of eight-four was re-elected president. He promptly chose a new chancellor, because the country was still operating under Article 48 of the German constitution. Hindenburg named Franz von Papen, a close friend, to the post. Papen ran the country for the rest of the year. When he, too, failed to end the depression, yet another of Hindenburg's friends, General Kurt von Schleicher, took over. He too was unable to bring about a recovery.

Schleicher, Papen, and Hindenburg's other advisers were all conservatives who represented wealthy landowners, industrialists, and other powerful people. They had little popular support. So in January of 1933, they decided to make a deal with Hitler. *He* had the popularity they lacked and *they* had the power he needed. They also agreed on a number of points, including opposition to Communism, hostility to the republic, and the need for *Lebensraum*.

Hindenburg's advisers convinced themselves that they could control Hitler. They also believed that he would be less "wild" once he was in power. And they were certain that he too would fail to end the depression. And *when* he failed, *they* would step in to save the nation. Surprisingly, many Communists also supported the move. Unlike the conservatives, *they* did not expect Hitler to become more responsible. Instead they believed he would ruin Germany—a good thing from their point of view. Then the real revolution could begin and they would be able to take over. Hitler fooled them all.

C O N N E C T I O N S

The chart below shows the results of elections to the Reichstag between 1928 and November 1932. Which parties gained the most seats? Why? How do you think the individuals introduced in Reading 15 reacted to Hitler's rise to power?

Party	1928	1930	July 1932	Nov. 1932
SPD	153	143	133	121
Center	62	68	75	70
KPD	54	77	89	100
Nazi	12	107	230	196
People's	45	30	7	11

Why do you think many people underestimated Hitler? Why do you think they failed to see him as a threat?

➤Christopher Isherwood's *The Berlin Stories* show German life in the last days of the Weimar Republic.

NOTES

1 Paul Johnson, *Modern Times: The World from the Twenties to the Eighties* (Harper & Row, 1983), 4.

2 Ibid.

3 Ibid.

4 Claudia Koonz, *Mothers in the Fatherland* (St. Martin's Press, 1987), 25.

5 Paul Johnson, *Modern Times*, 13-14.

6 George Mosse, *Fallen Soldiers* (Oxford University Press, 1990), 173-175.

7 Ellen Switzer, *How Democracy Failed* (Atheneum, 1977), 12.

8 Quoted in *Modern Germany* by Koppel Pinson (Macmillan, 1954), 398.

9 A. M. Rosenthal, Copyright © 1992 by The New York Times Company.

10 Ellen Switzer, *How Democracy Failed*, 20.

11 Theodore Abel, *Why Hitler Came into Power*, 132.

12 George Mosse, *Fallen Soldiers*, 160.

13 Henry Buxbaum, "Recollections." In *Jewish Life in Germany; Memoirs from Three Centuries*, ed. Monika Richarz; trans. Stella P. and Sidney Rosenfeld, (Indiana University Press, 1991), 303-304.

14 Albert Speer, *Spandau* (Macmillan, 1976).

15 Ellen Switzer, *How Democracy Failed*, 62-63.

16 Ibid.

17 Theodore Abel, *Why Hitler Came into Power*, 47-48.

18 Ingo Muller, *Hitler's Justice, The Courts of the Third Reich*, trans. Deborah Lucas Schneider, (Harvard University Press, 1991), 23.

19 Ibid., 22-23.

20 Martha Minow, *Making All the Difference*, 376.

21 Quoted in *The Sex Panic: Women, Censorship and "Pornography"* (National Coalition Against Censorship, 1993), 20-21.

22 Quoted in Reinhold Heller, *Art in Germany, 1909-1936: From Expressionism to Resistance* (Prestel, 1991), 163.

23 George Grosz, *A Little Yes and a Big NO*, trans. L. S. Dorin (Dial, 1946), 63.

24 Quoted in Ralph Knight, *A Very Ordinary Life*, 64.

25 Quoted in *Hitler: Great Lives Observed*, ed. George H. Stein (Prentice-Hall, 1968), 97-98.

26 Donald L. Niewyk, *The Jews in Weimar Germany* (Louisiana State University Press, 1980), 18.

27 Victoria Barnett, *For the Soul of the People* (Oxford University Press, 1992), 124.

28 Quoted in Frederic V. Grunfeld, *Prophets Without Honour, A Background to Freud, Kafka, Einstein and Their World* (Holt, 1979), 175-176.

29 Victoria Barnett, *For the Soul of the People*, 124.

30 Myron Magcanas, Whilliker, CA.

31 James Luther Adams, interview, *No Authority But From God*, vol. 1 (video), James Luther Adams Foundation.

32 The case studies that follow are composites based on real individuals in Germany in 1932.

4. The Nazis Take Power

Anyone who interprets National Socialism as merely a political movement knows almost nothing about it. It is more than a religion. It is the determination to create the new man.

ADOLF HITLER

OVERVIEW

Within weeks of taking office, Adolf Hitler was altering German life. Within a year, Joseph Goebbels, one of his top aides, could boast:

> The revolution that we have made is a total revolution. It encompasses every aspect of public life from the bottom up. . . .We have replaced individuality with collective racial consciousness and the individual with the community. . . .We must develop the organizations in which every individual's entire life will be regulated by the Volk community, as represented by the Party. There is no longer arbitrary will. There are no longer any free realms in which the individual belongs to himself. . . . The time of personal happiness is over.[1]

How did Hitler do it? How did he destroy the Weimar Republic and replace it with a totalitarian government—one that controls every part of a person's life? Many people have pointed out that he did not destroy democracy all at once. Instead, he moved gradually, with one seemingly small compromise leading to another and yet another. By the time many were aware of the danger, they were isolated and alone. This chapter details those steps. It also explores why few Germans protested the loss of their freedom and many even applauded the changes the Nazis brought to the nation. Historian Fritz Stern offers one answer. "The great appeal of National Socialism—and perhaps of every totalitarian dictatorship in this century—was the promise of absolute authority. Here was clarity, simplicity." To achieve that clarity, the German people gave up "what for so long they had taken for granted: the formal rule of law, a free press, freedom of expression, and the elementary protection of habeas corpus."[2]

British historian A. J. P. Taylor answers the question by focusing on a unique quality in Adolf Hitler: "the gift of translating commonplace thoughts into action. He took seriously what was to others mere talk. The driving force in him was a terrifying literalism. Writers had been running down democracy for half a century. It took Hitler to create a totalitarian dictatorship. . . . Again, there was nothing new in anti-semitism. . . . Everything which Hitler did against the Jews followed logically from the racial doctrines in which most Germans vaguely believed. It was the same with foreign policy. . . . Hitler took [the Germans] at their word. He made the Germans live up to their professions, or down to them—much to their regret."[3]

Other scholars note that upon taking office, Hitler stirred up a whirlwind of promises and demands, terrorizing opponents and dividing the German people. There was, as one man recalled, "no time to think . . . . The dictatorship, and the whole process of its coming into being, was above all diverting. It provided an excuse not to think for people who did not want to think anyway."[4] Hannah Arendt, a scholar who left Germany in the 1930s, spent years reflecting on totalitarian regimes. She concluded, "Of all the forms of political organization that do not permit freedom, only totalitarianism consciously seeks to crowd out the ability to think. Man cannot be silenced, he can only be crowded into not speaking. Under all other conditions, even within the racing noise of our time, thinking is possible."[5]

READING 1

The Democrat and the Dictator

*I*n the early 1930s, a severe depression threatened nations around the world. As unemployment mounted, a number of people came to believe that it was not just their leaders that had failed but government itself. Virtually every election around the world brought to power new leaders. Many of them, like Adolf Hitler, were enemies of democracy.

Three years before Hitler came to power, he publicly declared, "We National Socialists have never claimed to be representatives of a democratic point of view, we have openly declared that we would deploy democratic means only to attain power, and after our assumption of power we would deny our enemies all those means which are allowed to us while in opposition . . . . For us, parliament is not an end in itself but a means to an end." Few chose to take Hitler at his word. Many preferred to "overlook and excuse what was ominous and radically evil in National Socialism. They clutched at the pseudo-religious aspect of it, the promise of salvation held out so cleverly and on so many levels."[6]

We National Socialists have never claimed to be representatives of a democratic point of view . . . . For us, parliament is not an end in itself but a means to an end.

Bernt Engelmann was only twelve years old on January 30, 1933—the day Hitler became chancellor of Germany—but he never forgot the events of that day. He heard the news at noon. That evening when he and his parents gathered around the radio, they heard the voice of a new announcer.

> It was entirely different from the ones I was familiar with: no longer calm and objective, but full of a fanatic fervor . . . . Many years later, when the Third Reich was a thing of the past, I dug around in the archives of the Cologne broadcasting station and found the very text read by the announcer that evening of January 30. As I perused it, I felt the same amazement and disgust that had filled me as a twelve-year-old boy.
>
> There it was, in black and white, and the announcer had spoken the text as an overwhelmed eyewitness might describe the finish of the Monaco Grand Prix auto race:
>
> "A procession of thousands of blazing torches is streaming up Wilhelmstrasse . . . . They have marched through the Brandenburg Gate, the brown columns of the SA, victors in a long and arduous struggle, a struggle that claimed many victims. The banners glow blood-red, and against a white ground bristles the swastika, symbol of the rising sun! A glorious, an inspiring sight!

"And now—yes, it is! At this moment we hear from the south the thud of marching feet. It is the divisions of the Stahlhelm. The crowd listens with bated breath, the torches sway . . . . Everywhere torches, torches, torches, and cheering people! A hundred thousand voices shout joyously, 'Sieg Heil! Heil Hitler!' into the night!

And there, at his window, high above the cheering throngs and the sea of flaming torches stands Reich President von Hindenburg, the venerable field marshal . . . . He stands erect, stirred to the depths by the moment. And next door in the Reich Chancellery, the Fuehrer—yes, it is the Fuehrer! There he stands with his ministers, Adolf Hitler. . . the unknown soldier of the World War, the unyielding warrior, the standard-bearer of freedom. . . !"[7]

Melita Maschmann, then fifteen years old, was one of thousands of Germans who attended the parade. She later said, "Some of the uncanny feeling of that night remains with me even today. The crashing tread of the feet, the sombre pomp of the red and black flags, the flickering light from the torches on the faces and the songs with melodies that were at once aggressive and sentimental."[8]

The next day, Hitler told the German people:

[The] new national government will consider it its first and supreme duty to restore our nation's unity of will and spirit. It will safeguard and defend the foundations on which the strength of our nation rests. It will firmly protect Christianity, the basis of our entire morality; it will safeguard the family, the nucleus of our body politic and our state. It will, beyond estates and classes, make our people aware again of its national and political unity, and the duties that evolve therefrom. It wants to base the education of Germany's youth on a reverence for our great past, on pride in our old traditions. It will thus declare war on spiritual, political, and cultural nihilism. Germany must not and will not become prey to anarchic Communism.

In place of turbulent instincts, the government will once again make national discipline our guide. In so doing, it will consider with great care all institutions which are the true guarantors of the strength and power of our nation.

Max von der Gruen listened to that speech with family and friends.

On February 1, Hitler proclaimed his new government officially in power. He did not do so before the Reichstag, the elected Parliament, but over the radio. The meaning was clear enough. Now everyone knew that Hitler no longer needed a parliament.

Were the people clearly aware of his contempt for the parliament? I doubt it. In any case, my family considered it quite proper that Hitler had ceased to address "that crowd," i.e. the deputies of the Reichstag, and turned directly to the people. My grandmother regarded this procedure as a great step forward.[9]

On March 4, 1933—just a month after Hitler took office—Franklin Delano Roosevelt became president of the United States in an election marked by doubt and uncertainty. As reporter Thomas L. Stokes noted, "People were voting more 'agin' than for."

As anxious Americans gathered around their radios on Inauguration Day, Roosevelt reassured them. "This great Nation will endure as it has endured, will revive and will prosper. So, first of all, let me assert my firm belief that the only thing we have to fear is fear itself—nameless, unreasoning, unjustified terror which paralyzes needed efforts to convert retreat into advance. . . .We do not distrust the future of essential democracy. The people of the United States have not failed. In their need they have registered a mandate that they want direct, vigorous action. . . . They have made me the present instrument of their wishes. In the spirit of the gift I take it."

Stokes said of the president's first weeks in office, "Roosevelt could have become a dictator in 1933. He did not . . . . His first job was to do something, and do it quickly to save the nation's banking structure . . . . This he could have accomplished in one bold stroke by taking over the banks at the time and nationalizing them. But he did not take this way, though he was urged to do so. Instead he turned the banks back to their owners and operators and tried to realize his ends by the slow process of reform of the system through law."[10]

> So, first of all, let me assert my firm belief that the only thing we have to fear is fear itself—nameless, unreasoning, unjustified terror which paralyzes needed efforts to convert retreat into advance. . . . We do not distrust the future of essential democracy.

CONNECTIONS

Even though Fritz Stern was not quite seven years old in 1933, he, like Bernt Engelmann, never forgot the things he saw and heard the day Hitler took office. How do you account for the fact that most Germans never forgot the events of that day? Stern has called it the "beginning of my political education." What lessons do you think he learned that day and in the days that followed about the relationship between leaders and their followers? About the role of citizens in a democracy?

➤What kind of spell does a parade cast—particularly one held at night and lit by torches? What happens to the individual in the crowd? Why do you think parades and rallies have this effect? How did Hitler use it to his advantage? Walter Bieringer, an American businessman, witnessed the torchlight parade described in the reading. His reminiscences, available from the Facing History Resource Center, are summarized in *Elements of Time*, pages 72-73. Other accounts of the day can be found in two video montages *Childhood Experiences of German Jews* (*Elements of Time*, page 136) and *Friedrich* (*Elements of Time*, pages 157-159).

What did Hitler mean when he vowed that his new national government would "protect Christianity"? Jesus taught his followers to "love thy neighbor as thy self." How is it possible, then, for someone to protect Christianity by turning neighbor against neighbor?

Hitler vowed to declare war on "spiritual, political, and cultural nihilism." *Nihilism* is usually defined as the systematic denial of the reality of experience and the rejection of all value or meaning attributed to it. Whose "spiritual, political, and cultural" experiences did Hitler want acknowledged? Whose experiences did he wish to deny? How did he use language to hide meaning? To divert attention from his goals? How can listeners become more alert to the way some speakers use language to hide meaning?

The day after Hitler took office, newspaper editors around the world commented on the event. The *New York Times* printed an editorial entitled "The Tamed Hitler." Although it recognized the lawlessness of Hitler's past, it was hopeful about the future. The editors wrote, "Always, we may look for some such transformation when a radical or demagogue fights his way into responsible office." They argued that "the more violent parts of his alleged program" would be softened or abandoned. In your experience, do people change when they are given a responsible position? How likely was it that Hitler would change? Why do you think many chose to believe he had changed? What would they have had to do if they did not believe in his "transformation"?

What did Roosevelt mean when he said, "the only thing we have to fear is fear itself—nameless, unreasoning, unjustified terror?" How did Hitler use that fear?

Compare the themes of Hitler's February 1 proclamation with Roosevelt's inaugural address. What values were reflected in each man's speech? In each leader's approach to change?

In the 1930s, the invention of the radio brought world leaders closer to the people than ever before. For the first time, citizens could hear world leaders for themselves. Bill Moyers, a television journalist, can still recall the voices of Hitler and Roosevelt. In an interview with Margot Stern Strom, the executive director of Facing History, he noted, "I could sense even though no one said anything about it, this demonic fury that drove [Hitler]—this blind passion and this mesmerizing madness that had come over him, over his followers, and over much of Germany. Then, in listening to Franklin Roosevelt, I would hear that broadminded, magnanimous, and somewhat paternalistic individual who, although reared in circumstances of affluence and privilege, was still in touch with the deeper values of society." Moyers went on to note, "The human voice carried with it its own revelation about character and personality."[11] Today we can see as well as hear world leaders. How telling is that view? What can you learn about a person from the sound of his or her voice? From the way he or she appears on television?

➤ Bill Moyers's television documentary, *The Democrat and the Dictator*, compares and contrasts the way Hitler and Roosevelt attacked the problems of their respective nations. How was the United States able to preserve its democracy at a time when Germany could not? Moyers' documentary and his interview with Margot Stern Strom are both available from the Facing History Resource Center.

Threats to Democracy

As the worldwide depression deepened in the 1930s, some people turned to communism. Others were attracted to fascism—a political system that seemed to offer an alternative to both democracy and communism. Fascists opposed democracy, because it is "too slow" and divides a nation against itself. Democrats, they insisted, put selfish individual interests before the needs of the state. Fascists, on the other hand, place their faith in a strong, charismatic leader who expresses the will of the nation and satisfies the desires of the masses.

Benito Mussolini, a former socialist, established the first fascist government in Italy in 1922. It served as a model for Germany's. In both systems, the leader's or *Fuehrer's* word was law. He was not dependent on a legislature, courts, or voters. Whenever he changed his mind, public policy changed. According to Hitler, a *Fuehrer* is a leader "in whose name everything is done, who is said to be 'responsible' for all, but whose acts can nowhere be called into question," because "he is the genius or the hero conceived as the man of pure race."

Such a leader is not an emperor nor an aloof dictator. He knows what is going on around him. Again, in Hitler's words, he is a "practical psychologist and an organizer—a psychologist in order that he may master the methods by which he can gain the largest number of passive adherents, and an organizer in order that he may build up a compact body of followers to consolidate his gain." Among those followers are an elite group of advisors who are the "racially fittest" and who have been formed from "the struggle for power which is characteristic of nature."

This glorification of the nation's leader is based on the belief that people are "capable neither of heroism nor intelligence." They are "swayed only by gross and violent feelings like hatred, fanaticisms, and hysteria." So the "simplest arguments" must be "repeated again and again." They must be "fanatically one-sided and with unscrupulous disregard for truth, impartiality, or fair play."

Both Mussolini and Hitler maintained that only a few people were intelligent enough to rise in the world and that those men had the obligation to rule. Decision making was too important to be left to the people. It required a "man of the people" who could control the people. They, in turn, would give him unquestioning obedience.

Fascism was not solely a German or Italian aberration, nor a historical phenomenon confined to the 1930s and '40s. It recurs "wherever the immune system of a society is weakened by economic decline and political exhaustion, whenever democratic politicians try to fend off a challenge from the far right by acceding to the political mythology of racial or cultural purification.

Many people found fascism appealing in the 1930s. There were fascist groups not only in Italy and Germany but also in England, France, and the United States. Zabedi Barbi, a social psychologist, argues that many people were attracted to fascism because it "promised to solve the problems and give the people purpose and power." Other experts trace the rise of fascism to economics. They note that fascists were often brought to power by the rich and powerful people who saw democracy as a threat to their prestige, wealth, and influence. Still others, like Fritz Stern, believe the attraction lay in the clarity and simplicity of the solutions fascists offered.

CONNECTIONS

Draw a diagram showing how power is divided in a democracy. Who holds power? What role do the people play? What part do laws play? Draw a diagram showing the division of power in a fascist state. Where does power lie? What role do people play? What part do laws play? How well does either diagram square with reality?

Was the society described by Kurt Vonnegut in "Harrison Bergeron" (Chapter 2, Reading 1) a fascist society?

Reread the views of Carl Schurz and Otto von Bismarck (Chapter 2, Reading 6). Which of Hitler's ideas might each find attractive? Which would he disapprove of? Would either man be likely to join the Nazis?

In the early 1900s, people used words like *man* and *mankind* in two ways. Sometimes these terms referred to all of humankind, women as well as men. At other times, they referred only to men. When Hitler speaks of a fascist leader as "the man of pure race" or "the man of the people," in which sense was he using the word *man*? How was he linking racism with leadership? Research Mussolini's ideas about race and leadership. How were they similar to Hitler's? What differences seem most striking?

Hitler claimed that the people are "capable neither of heroism or intelligence." He insisted that they are "swayed only by gross and violent feelings like hatred, fanaticisms, and hysteria." How did the parade and the speech described in Reading 1 build on these beliefs?

In 1993, many people were surprised by the rise of fascism in the former Soviet Union. Editorial writer Alan Berger does not believe it should have been a surprise. In his view, "fascism was not solely a German or Italian aberration, nor a historical phenomenon confined to the 1930s and '40s." It can recur "wherever the immune system of a society is weakened by economic decline and political exhaustion, whenever democratic politicians try to fend off a challenge from the far right by acceding to the political mythology of racial or cultural purification."[12] According to Berger, why are people attracted to fascism? How do you explain the appeal of fascism? Record your ideas in your journal so that you can refer to them as you continue reading.

What is the best way to combat fascism? Journalist I. F. Stone believed that it is by keeping alive "the tradition of freedom; it must be freshly taught, explained, and fought for in every generation." He went on to say that a "society in which men are not free to speak their minds is not a good society no matter what material benefits it may offer the few or the many. The only absolute value I would affirm is freedom of the mind. Without it there cannot be social justice which is our duty toward others."[13] Compare his views to those of Hannah Arendt in the overview. What connection do they both see between thinking and social justice? Why do they see that link as critical to fighting fascism?

READING 3

Targeting the Communists

*F*rom the start, Hitler sought and found opportunities to abolish civil rights. The first came less than a month after he took office. A fire broke out in the building where the Reichstag met. Hitler rushed to the scene and amid the smoke and confusion, he vowed to punish those responsible. It did not take him long to decide who they were. That night, he screamed, "Now we'll show them! Anyone who stands in our way will be mown down! The German people have been soft too long. Every Communist official must be shot. All Communist deputies must be hanged this very night. All friends of the Communists must be locked up. And that goes for the Social Democrats . . . as well!"

Hitler immediately ordered the arrest of leaders of the Communist party, Communist labor unions, and anyone with ties to the Communists. Within days, Nazi storm troopers dragged off to prison camps four thousand Communists and other radicals. The rest went into hiding. Among them was Wolfgang Roth, a young artist who had nothing to do with the fire. But as a radical, he was under suspicion. He later recalled the days he and a friend spent "underground."

> Meta and I lived in different parts of the city from night to night. We hardly trusted anyone, often not even good friends, for in the meanwhile they could have become Nazi informers. Daily existence had become dangerous for us, and we never knew whether we would live to see the next night, the next day as free people . . . . The illegal groups consisted mostly of four to five people, who often hardly knew one another. Some of these cells were busted, since informers were

Anyone who stands in our way will be mown down! The German people have been soft too long. Every Communist official must be shot. All Communist deputies must be hanged this very night. All friends of the Communists must be locked up. And that goes for the Social Democrats. . . as well!

hanging around everywhere. We met in coffeehouses, pretended to be playing chess, without even knowing how. But this made it possible to meet and talk with one another.[14]

The police later picked up Roth for questioning. He was released only when officers from his old neighborhood vouched for him. His friends were not as fortunate. A number of them were murdered. Were they to blame for the fire? Hitler did not bother to find out. He saw an opportunity to get rid of his opponents and he took it.

The day after the fire, the chancellor issued two decrees. The titles—"For the Defense of Nation and State" and "To Combat Treason against the German Nation and Treasonable Activities"—reveal exactly how Hitler planned to use the fire to achieve his goals. He suspended, until further notice, those parts of the constitution that dealt with personal freedom. The government now had the right to censor mail, listen to private telephone conversations, and read telegrams. It could also search homes and confiscate property.

Although Germans no longer had the civil rights their constitution guaranteed, they still had the right to vote. And elections were held on March 5 as previously scheduled. Although the Nazis got 44 percent of the vote, they did not have a majority in the Reichstag. And even though they had singled out the Communists as "enemies of the state," the Communist party received about 12 percent of the vote, thus entitling it to 81 deputies in the Reichstag. But those representatives were never able to claim their seats. If they appeared in public, they faced arrest. Other opposition parties also held their own. The Social Democrats captured 119 seats and the Catholic Center party increased its representation from 70 to 73. On the other hand, the People's party and other conservative groups did poorly.

The election results did not stop Hitler. He continued to carry out his plans for the nation as if the election had not occurred. On March 11, he made Joseph Goebbels head of a new department in the government, the Ministry of Public Enlightenment and Propaganda. It was, in Hitler's view, a critical step in building a fascist state. Goebbels and his deputies would tell people whom to hate and why. Less than two weeks later, on March 23, the government announced the opening of the nation's first concentration camp at Dachau. The first inmates were two hundred Communists.

That same day, the Reichstag overwhelmingly approved, by a vote of 441 to 94, a bill entitled "Law for Terminating the Suffering of People and Nation." Also known as the Enabling Act, it was short and to the point. It "enabled" Hitler to punish anyone he considered an enemy of the state. The act also stated that "laws passed by the government may deviate from the Constitution." Only the Social Democrats voted against the law. Other deputies that opposed Hitler were on the run. With the new law in place, the Nazis began their slow but systematic destruction of democracy.

CONNECTIONS

Helen Fein, the author of *Accounting for Genocide,* has argued that the effects of singling out a group cannot be overestimated. She writes that in every case of genocide, "the victims have previously been defined as outside the universe of obligation of the dominant group." What does she mean by the "universe of obligation"? Who is a part of yours?

Imagine the police arresting four thousand people in a large city in a matter of days. How many people probably heard the police arrive at one building after another? Watched as four thousand men and women were herded into police vehicles? Noticed the unexplained absence of co-workers, neighbors, or friends? Why didn't anyone speak out? How do you think the fact that the storm troopers came for the Communists affected the way individuals responded? Did Germans consider Communists part of their "universe of obligation"?

The decrees proclaimed in February suspended the parts of the constitution that protected individual rights. The government could now read mail, listen to all calls, and search homes without warning. Why would Hitler call decrees that suspended personal freedom "For the Defense of Nation and State" and "To Combat Treason against the German Nation and Treasonable Activities"? Why would he call a statute that allows him to punish anyone he considers an enemy without a trial the "Law for Terminating the Suffering of People and Nation"? How is he using language to mask his goals? What was the atmosphere in the Reichstag when these laws were passed? How did that help Hitler?

In Chapter 3 Molly Ivins was quoted as saying that it is the "funniest idea" that "if we are less free we could be safer." How do her comments apply to the German people in February of 1933? Did they really believe that they were safer now that they were less free? Were they safer?

Why did the Reichstag agree to pass the Enabling Act? Why did people accept it? What were the consequences of their decision in the short run? In the long run?

Roth noted that "We hardly trusted anyone, often not even good friends, for in the meanwhile they could have become Nazi informers." What does that suggest about the way the Nazis won obedience?

What does it take to create a dictatorship out of a democracy? What are the steps? Record your answer in your journal.

Review the identity chart you created in Chapter 1. Imagine that you, with your particular strengths and weaknesses, associations and background, were transported to Germany in 1933. How do you like to think you would have responded to the events of the day? What would you know for sure about Hitler and the Nazis in March? What would not be as clear? Whom might you trust? What policies might you support? Oppose? Be sure to include your feelings as well as your stand on the issues. Are you scared? Uncertain? Confident? Record your comments in your journal.

READING 4

Targeting the Jews

*T*o bring about his revolution, Hitler had to isolate and then eliminate his opponents. Once the Communists were outside the protection of the law, he turned his attention to the Jews. He ordered Nazi leaders to "bring up the Jewish question again and again and again, unceasingly. Every emotional aversion, however slight, must be exploited ruthlessly. As a basic rule among the education professions the Jewish questions should be discussed from the standpoints of the findings of the science of race, of higher ethics, etc. While among members of the labouring classes one must seize on the purely emotional; the emotional aversion to Jews is to be heightened by all possible means."

As part of its campaign, the government announced a one-day boycott of Jewish businesses. On Saturday, April 1, Germans were to refuse to shop or do business at any company owned by Jews. Julius Streicher, the man in charge of the boycott and the publisher of the antisemitic *Der Stuermer*, created the lie that would be repeated constantly, just as Hitler instructed.

> The same Jew who plunged the German people into the blood-letting of the World War, and who committed on it the crime of the November Revolution (Weimar) is now engaged in stabbing Germany, recovering from its shame and misery, in the back . . . . The Jew is again engaged in poisoning public opinion. World Jewry is engaged again in slandering the German people . . . . At 10 A. M. Sat., 1 April, the defensive action of the German people against the Jewish world criminal will begin. A defensive fight begins, such as never has been dared before throughout the centuries.[15]

Although the boycott was not as successful as the Nazis had hoped, it offered many Jews a frightening glimpse into the future. Edwin Landau described the boycott in his hometown in West Prussia.

> In the morning hours the Nazi guards began to place themselves in front of the Jewish shops and factories, and every shopper was warned not to buy from the Jews. In front of our business, also, two young Nazis posted themselves and prevented customers from entering. To me the whole thing was inconceivable. It would not sink in that something like that could even be possible in the twentieth century, for

To me the whole thing was inconceivable. It would not sink in that something like that could even be possible in the twentieth century, for such things had happened, at most, in the Middle Ages. And yet it was the bitter truth that outside, in front of the door, there stood two boys in brown shirts, Hitler's executives.

such things had happened, at most, in the Middle Ages. And yet it was the bitter truth that outside, in front of the door, there stood two boys in brown shirts, Hitler's executives.

And for this nation we young Jews had once stood in the trenches in cold and rain, and spilled our blood to protect the land from the enemy. Was there no comrade any more from those days who was sickened by these goings-on? One saw them pass by on the street, among them quite a few for whom one had done a good turn. They had a smile on their face that betrayed their malicious pleasure. . . .

I took my war decorations, put them on, went into the street, and visited Jewish shops, where at first I was also stopped. But I was seething inside, and most of all I would have liked to shout my hatred into the faces of these barbarians. Hatred, hatred—when had it become part of me?—It was only a few hours ago that a change had occurred within me. This land and this people that until now I had loved and treasured had suddenly become my enemy. So I was not a German anymore, or I was no longer supposed to be one. That, of course, cannot be settled in a few hours. But one thing I felt immediately: I was ashamed that I had once belonged to this people. I was ashamed about the trust that I had given to so many who now revealed themselves as my enemies. Suddenly the street, too, seemed alien to me; indeed, the whole town had become alien to me. Words do not exist to describe the feelings that I experienced in those hours. Having arrived at home, I approached the one guard whom I knew and who also knew me, and I said to him: "When you were still in your diapers I was already fighting out there for this country." He answered: "You should not reproach me for my youth, sir. . . I've been ordered to stand here." I looked at his young face and thought, he's right. Poor, misguided young people![16]

C O N N E C T I O N S

What lies does Streicher tell in his speech? To what emotions did his speech appeal? Why did he use the word *defensive* to describe the action he would like Germans to take?

The night before the boycott, Joseph Goebbels, the newly appointed Minister of Public Enlightenment and Propaganda, gave a speech in which he referred to the Jews of Germany as "guests." He told his audience, "If they believe they can misuse our hospitality they are sadly mistaken." What is Goebbels implying about German citizens of Jewish descent? About their right to live in Germany?

Write a working definition of the word *boycott*. Research its use in American history. For example, how did the colonists use boycotts to express their disapproval of British taxes in the 1770s? How did civil rights workers use boycotts to express their disapproval of a particular company's racist policies in the 1950s and 1960s? How was the boycott of Jewish businesses similar to these boycotts? What differences seem most striking?

Make an identity chart for Edwin Landau before and after the boycott. How did the way he viewed himself change? How do you account for the change? Why did he think such a boycott was possible only in the Middle Ages? What was different about life in the twentieth century—the people or their government?

What choices were open to "Aryan" Germans when the Nazis announced the boycott? What choices were open to German Jews? How may what happened to the Communists have affected those decisions? What were the short-term consequences of each option? What do you think the long-term consequences may be? Did most Germans in 1933 regard Jews as part of their "universe of obligation"?

The boycott was voluntary. Although "Aryans" who entered a shop owned by Jews were harassed, no one was punished for doing so. Do you think Germans who chose to buy from Jewish merchants knew they would not be punished? Was it fear of punishment that kept other Germans from entering Jewish shops?

Hilda G., a young Jew living in rural Germany in 1933, recalls that the boycott suddenly turned her German neighbors against their Jewish neighbors. Peter Gay, a Jew who then lived in Berlin, remembers little antisemitism at the time of the boycott. (Their testimonies appear on the video *Childhood Experiences of German Jews* available from the Facing History Resource Center.) Why do you think Jews in rural communities were isolated more quickly than those in large urban areas?

READING 5

Legalizing Racism

The boycott set the stage for yet another step in carrying out Hitler's "racial" policies. People were whispering about those plans long before they were made public. President Paul von Hindenburg was among those who heard rumors of anti-Jewish legislation. On April 4, he asked Hitler to exempt Jewish veterans, their fathers, and sons from the new laws. Over one hundred thousand Jews had served in the German army during World War I and twelve thousand had died in the line of duty. About thirty-five thousand had been awarded medals. Mindful of that record, the president noted, "If they were worthy to fight and bleed for

Germany, then they should also be considered worthy to continue serving the fatherland in their professions."

Hitler responded to Hindenburg's letter with praise for his "noble motives." He promised to incorporate the president's suggestions into laws under consideration. But he did not back down from his position. Instead he reminded the president of why the laws were needed:

> The first is the glaring wrong created by the incredible discrimination against the German element that supports the state. For there are a whole number of intellectual professions today—medicine and the law, for instance—where in several places in Germany, in Berlin and elsewhere, the Jews hold up to 80 percent and more of all positions. At the same time, hundreds of thousands of German intellectuals, including countless war veterans, subsist on unemployment insurance, or are being ruined by finding themselves in some entirely subordinate position.
>
> The second is the great shock to the authority of the state which is being caused by the fact that an entirely alien body, which has never really become one with the German people, and whose talent is primarily a business talent, is pushing its way into government positions and providing the mustard seed of a kind of corruption of whose extent people to this day are not even approximately aware. One of the major reasons why the old Prussian state was such a clean one was that the Jews were granted only a very limited access to the civil service. The officer corps kept itself almost entirely pure.[17]

On April 7, a new law known as the "Law for the Restoration of the Professional Civil Service" went into effect. It removed non-Aryans from their jobs in order to "restore" the civil service to "true Germans." The only Jews to keep their positions were Jewish veterans, their fathers, and their sons. Another law, proclaimed the same day, dismissed Jewish prosecuting attorneys. Before the month was over, Jewish doctors who worked within the National Health System also lost their jobs. At about the same time, the government sharply limited the number of Jews who could attend a public high school or teach in one. As a result of these decrees, 20 percent of all German Jews lost their jobs. In the months that followed, the laws were expanded to include more and more people. By the end of the year, one-third of all Jews in Germany did not earn enough money to pay taxes. The new laws marked the beginning of the economic isolation of German Jews.

CONNECTIONS

The exchange of letters between Hindenburg and Hitler in April 1933 offers insights into political attitudes of the two German leaders. What prompted Hindenburg to write? Who was within his "universe of obligation"? How did Hitler respond? What was the tone of his letter?

Hitler described the Jews as an "alien body" and the German officer corps as "pure." What was he implying about the Jews? The people he called "Germans"? Was either view based on reality ?

Was Hitler right? Were most doctors and lawyers Jews? In 1933, a census revealed that 16.2 percent of the nation's lawyers were Jews, 10.8 percent of its doctors, and 2.7 percent of its judges. Some historians say that the truth is less important in understanding the past than what people think is true. What do they mean by that statement? Do you agree? Would Hitler have agreed?

How is Hitler's use of the word *restore* similar to Streicher's use of the word *defensive* in Reading 4?

What does it mean to be "economically isolated"? How does economic isolation turn the victims into "marginal people"?

➤ *Elements of Time* contains summaries of interviews with Walter Bieringer, an American businessman (page 72), and Peter Gay, a young Jew from Berlin (pages 100 and 136). The two recall what life was like for Jews in Germany just after Hitler came to power. Gay noted that many assimilated German Jews, especially those who were veterans of World War I, did not feel threatened by the Nazis because they thought of themselves as Germans rather than as Jews.

READING 6

Dismantling Democracy

German Jews were not the only ones affected by the "Law for the Restoration of the Professional Civil Service." The government could now dismiss any civil servant who was politically undesirable or who would not "support the national state at all times and without reservation." Indeed the government no longer needed a reason to dismiss a worker. It could now do so without cause.

The law had other effects as well. Judges were no longer expected to be impartial. Instead they were to approach a case with "a healthy prejudice" and "make value judgements which correspond to the National Socialist legal order and the will of political leadership." The message was clear: "In the everyday practice of law, genuine National Socialism is certainly best represented where the idea of the Fuehrer is silently but loyally followed."

Bernhard Rust, the new minister of education, argued that "it is less important that a professor make discoveries than that he train his assistants in the proper view of the world." Other officials agreed. Hans Schemm, the

In the everyday practice of law, genuine National Socialism is certainly best represented where the idea of the Fuehrer is silently but loyally followed.

Bavarian minister of culture, declared that the value of study lay not in a dedication to truth but in an adherence to "the spirit of the National Socialist revolution." Civil servants had to accept the new rules or lose their positions. Very few resigned. Horst Krueger's description of his father's response was typical of many bureaucrats.

> All his life he left home for the ministry at 8:23 A. M., traveling second class. At home, he read the old-line newspaper and the local daily, never joined the party, never knew anything about Auschwitz, never subscribed to the *Voelkischer Beobachter*, the Nazi party organ— but for twenty minutes, until the train pulled into Friedrichstrasse Station, he held it up before his face so that others might recognize his loyalty to the new people's state. At Friedrichstrasse he left the paper behind . . . .
>
> All his life he came home at 4:21 P. M., always on the same train, always in the same second-class compartment, if possible always at the same corner window, always holding a briefcase full of work in his right hand, with his left showing his monthly commutation ticket—he never jumped off the moving train. He had achieved his goal; he was a German civil servant. And no matter whether the government was headed by Noske or Ebert, Scheidemann or Bruening, Papen or Hitler, he was obligated to faith and loyalty. His office was his world. [18]

CONNECTIONS

What is the purpose of laws? How did the Nazis use laws to limit free speech? To disenfranchise people? Who supported their efforts?

Notice that yet another of Hitler's key advisors explains that truth is not the goal of the National Socialist revolution. What was the goal? Why do you think "truth" was the first victim of the revolution?

Create an identity chart for Horst Krueger's father. Why was he able to work for people who supported democracy as well as those who opposed it? To whom was he loyal? How was he like the bureaucrats described in *"the bear that wasn't"* (Chapter 1, Reading 1)? What differences seem most striking? Do such people exist today?

Turning Neighbor Against Neighbor

An aide to Hitler once expressed the new government's attitude toward its opponents. "The government will brutally beat down all who oppose it. We do not say an eye for an eye, a tooth for a tooth. No, he who knocks out one of our eyes will get his head chopped off, and he who knocks out one of our teeth will get his jaw bashed in."

According to Rudolf Diels, the chief of the political department of the Berlin police, that attitude could clearly be seen on city streets. "Every SA man was 'on the heels of the enemy'; each knew what he had to do. [The storm troopers] cleaned up the districts. . . . Not only Communists but anyone who had ever expressed himself against Hitler's movement was in danger." Some were confined to concentration camps like the one at Dachau. Others found themselves in "private prisons" that Diels described as "hellish torture."[19]

Although the storm troopers operated outside the law, they encountered very little opposition. Indeed, many openly supported their efforts. In a short story, Christopher Isherwood, a British writer, described the way the Germans he met responded to the Nazis.

> They smiled approvingly at these youngsters in their big, swaggering boots who were going to upset the Treaty of Versailles. They were pleased because it would soon be summer, because Hitler had promised to protect the small tradesmen, because their newspapers told them that the good times were coming. They were suddenly proud of being blond. And they thrilled with a furtive, sensual pleasure, like schoolboys, because the Jews, their business rivals, and the Marxists, a vaguely defined minority of people who didn't concern them, had been satisfactorily found guilty of the defeat and the inflation and were going to catch it.[20]

By April 26, the Nazis felt confident enough to take their campaign of terror and intimidation once step further. They created a special bureaucracy that would be responsible for all executive actions against their political enemies. Under the leadership of Hermann Goering, the Gestapo (an acronym created by the initial letters of *Geheime Staatspolizei*, or Secret State Police) was authorized to "protect public safety and order" by using methods that ranged from interrogation to consigning individuals to "private prisons" and later to concentration camps. According to historians Michael Burleigh and Wolfgang Wippermann, neither practice was "based upon judicial decisions or subject to judicial review."[21]

The government will brutally beat down all who oppose it. We do not say an eye for an eye, a tooth for a tooth. No, he who knocks out one of our eyes will get his head chopped off, and he who knocks out one of our teeth will get his jaw bashed in.

How did the Nazis use the language of warfare to describe their political enemies? To create an atmosphere of terror and intimidation?

Earlier you were asked to consider what it takes to create a dictatorship out of a democracy. What are the steps? How important was this one? How does Isherwood's account explain why many people chose to remain silent? How do you explain it?

Fritz Stern and other historians argue that Hitler was "ever anxious about the reaction to him at home and abroad." But in the first few months of Hitler's rule there was very little active opposition. And at every point he was emboldened by "silence, acquiescence, or support."[22] What other choices did ordinary people have in the spring of 1933? What could they have done? What might have been the short-term consequences of their actions? The long-term consequences?

READING 8

Taking Over the Universities

*E*ven as the Gestapo was organizing its program of terror and intimidation, one group after another was pledging its support to National Socialism. That process could most clearly be seen in the nation's universities, which had always boasted of their autonomy. Peter Drucker, an Austrian economist, was then a lecturer at Frankfurt University. Fearful of Hitler's plans for Germany, he was prepared to leave the country but hoped that it would not be necessary to do so. An incident convinced him otherwise.

> What made me decide to leave right away, several weeks after Hitler had come to power, was the first Nazi-led faculty meeting at the university. Frankfurt was the first university the Nazis tackled, precisely because it was the most self-confidently liberal of major German universities, with a faculty that prided itself on its allegiance to scholarship, freedom of conscience and democracy. The Nazis therefore knew that control of Frankfurt University would mean control of German academia. And so did everyone at the university.
>
> Above all, Frankfurt had a science faculty distinguished both by its scholarship and by its liberal convictions; and outstanding among the Frankfurt scientists was a biochemist-physiologist of Nobel-Prize caliber and impeccable liberal credentials. When the appointment of a Nazi commissar for Frankfurt was announced (around February 25 of

When Hitler arrived in 1933, the tradition of scholarship in Germany was destroyed, almost overnight. . . . Europe was no longer hospitable to the imagination—and not just the scientific imagination. A whole conception of culture was in retreat: the conception that human knowledge is personal and responsible, an unending adventure at the edge of uncertainty.

that year) and every teacher and graduate assistant at the university was summoned to a faculty meeting to hear this new master, everybody knew that a trial of strength was at hand. I had never before attended a faculty meeting, but I did attend this one.

The new Nazi commissar wasted no time on the amenities. He immediately announced that Jews would be forbidden to enter university premises and would be dismissed without salary on March 15; this was something no one had thought possible despite the Nazis' loud anti-Semitism. Then he launched into a tirade of abuse, filth, and four-letter words such as had been heard rarely even in the barracks and never before in academia. He pointed his finger at one department chairman after another and said, "You either do what I tell you or we'll put you into a concentration camp." There was silence when he finished; everybody waited for the distinguished biochemist-physiologist. The great liberal got up, cleared his throat, and said, "Very interesting, Mr. Commissar, and in some respects very illuminating: but one point I didn't get too clearly. Will there be more money for research in physiology?"

The meeting broke up shortly thereafter with the commissar assuring the scholars that indeed there would be plenty of money for "racially pure science." A few of the professors had the courage to walk out with their Jewish colleagues, but most kept a safe distance from these men who only a few hours earlier had been their close friends. I went out sick unto death—and I knew that I was going to leave Germany within forty-eight hours.[23]

Other professors chose a different course. Martin Heidegger, a noted philosopher whose thoughts on freedom inspired students like Hannah Arendt, now told his students and colleagues that Germany's soul needed fresh air to breathe and National Socialism would provide it. He argued that freedom of inquiry and free expression were negative and selfish ideas. Instead he encouraged his students to live up to their obligations to the national community in both "thought and deed."

CONNECTIONS

What does Drucker suggest about the way the Nazis won control over his university? About the way the Nazis were likely to take over other parts of German life? A liberal is one who favors individual freedom and tolerates differences. Why do you think the Nazis chose to take over the most liberal university first?

Max Planck, a German physicist, asked Hitler to let Jewish scientists keep their jobs. Hitler replied, "If the dismissal of Jewish scientists means the annihilation of contemporary German science, then we shall do without science for a few years." What does Hitler's response suggest about his priorities? What does Planck's question suggest about his?

Students often look to their teachers to set an example. Heidegger provided one kind of example. Max Planck and a few of his colleagues offered another when they arranged a memorial service for Fritz Haber, a "non-Aryan" chemist who died in exile. Despite the efforts of the Ministry of Education to keep professors from attending, many chose to pay their respects to a former colleague. Planck summed up their position. "Haber remained loyal to us; we will remain loyal to him." How did Heidegger define loyalty? How did Planck define it? What kind of example did each man set for his students? For the nation?

Fritz Stern writes, "We must not forget . . . that in the first weeks of the new regime the possibility of cautious criticism still existed without the price of martyrdom. It was a period in which the National Socialists themselves were still uncertain, in which the new wielders of power attacked Communists, Social Democrats, and prominent Jews with massive violence but were cautious and experimental in their dealings with 'respectable' people."[24] He goes on to note that even though a few individuals and groups did protest, most did not. How do you account for their failure to do so? What part did obedience play in their responses? The need to conform? Fear? Racism? Career aspirations?

Scholars share research and ideas by publishing their findings in books and journals and speaking at international meetings. By the summer of 1933, a few American and British scholars feared that academic freedom in Germany was being subordinated to "political and other considerations ulterior if not irrelevant to true scientific research and scholarship." They then had to decide whether to cut ties to their German counterparts. They chose not to do so. What may have motivated them? Were they right?

➤Jacob Bronowski said, "When Hitler arrived in 1933, the tradition of scholarship in Germany was destroyed, almost overnight. . . . Europe was no longer hospitable to the imagination—and not just the scientific imagination. A whole conception of culture was in retreat: the conception that human knowledge is personal and responsible, an unending adventure at the edge of uncertainty."[25] Drucker was one of many scholars who left Germany in 1933. The others included Albert Einstein, Sigmund Freud, Max Born, and Leo Szilard. How did their leaving affect German scholarship? German society? Bronowski discusses the shift from a search for truth to blind obedience in "From Knowledge to Certainty," a part of a series of documentaries entitled *The Ascent of Man*. Individual programs as well as the series as a whole are available from the Facing History Resource Center.

READING 9

Changes at School

Ellen Switzer, a student in Nazi Germany, later recalled how a classmate named Ruth responded to attempts at isolating the Jews.

Her most appealing qualities were her total sincerity and her willingness to share whatever she had with a classmate in need. If the school was cold . . . Ruth would always lend you her sweater; she insisted that the cold air made her feel more alive. If you forgot your lunch, Ruth shared hers; she was not very hungry that day. Out of the same generosity that prompted her to share her clothing and her food, she also shared her ideas. Ruth was a dedicated Nazi.

She always had a large number of pamphlets, booklets, newsletters and other materials in her book bag, along with her school supplies. If one wanted to discuss clothes or one's problem with a teacher or a parent with Ruth, she was always willing to do so. But somehow, the discussion tended to turn political. . . . "Here, take this booklet, it will explain what I'm talking about," she would often say, pressing in our hands yet another piece of literature, which often seemed surprisingly relevant to the problem we have been discussing. . . .

Some of us, especially those of us who were called "non-Aryan" (and therefore, thoroughly evil) in Ruth's booklets, often asked her how she could possibly have friends who were Jews or who had a Jewish background, when everything she read and distributed seemed to breathe hate against us and our ancestors. "Of course, they don't mean you," she would explain earnestly. "You are a good German. It's those other Jews, pacifists, socialists and liberals who betrayed Germany that Hitler wants to remove from influence." . . .

When Hitler actually came to power and the word went out that students of Jewish background were to be isolated, that "Aryan" Germans were no longer to associate with "non-Aryans" (i.e., those who were either Jewish or who had one Jewish ancestor, even though they themselves were Christians), Ruth actually came around and apologized to those of us to whom she was no longer able to talk. "The whole thing may be a misunderstanding," she explained, "Maybe it will all be straightened out later. But meanwhile, Hitler must know what he is doing, and I'll follow orders." Not only did she no longer speak to the suddenly ostracized group of classmates, she carefully noted down anybody who did, and reported them.[26]

How is it possible for a person to be as kind as Ruth and still be a Nazi? What does her story suggest about those who found the Nazis' teachings so attractive? What did Ruth mean when she said "Of course, they don't mean you"? Have you ever said or heard a similar remark when the stereotype of the group doesn't fit an individual within the group?

After the war, in talking to the headmistress of her school about Ruth, Switzer learned that Ruth had served as a nurse in a concentration camp where "so-called experiments were carried out on helpless inmates." The headmistress said of Ruth: "She was not really a bad person, she was what I call an ideologue. Once she had come to believe in an idea—no matter how perverted, illogical and evil—she couldn't let go. She's now in prison and she's probably still sure that what she believed was right." Do you agree with that assessment? A guide to teaching *How Democracy Failed* by Ellen Switzer is available from the Facing History Resource Center.

➤See *Childhood Memories*, available from the Facing History Resource Center, for Carl H.'s description of the power of Nazi racial theories. A summary appears in *Elements of Time*, pages 56-63 and 217-220.

R E A D I N G   1 0

Teaching a Lesson

By late spring, some Germans were openly turning on their neighbors. American journalist Quentin Reynolds reported a disturbing incident that took place in the "new" Germany:

> It happened when Bill and Martha Dodd, the son and daughter of our Ambassador, invited me to drive to Austria with them to attend the Salzburg music festival. We stopped in Nuremberg to spend the night. I had been there once before and knew it as a town that went to sleep early. When we arrived at our hotel on the Koenigstrasse about midnight, and found the street filled with an excited, happy crowd, we wondered if we had stumbled into a toymakers' festival.
>
> "Is there going to be a parade?" I asked the hotel clerk as we registered.
>
> He was a pleasant fellow, and he laughed until the tips of his mustache quivered. Then he said, "It will be a kind of parade. They are teaching someone a lesson."
>
> Martha and Bill and I walked out and joined the crowd. Everyone was keyed up, laughing, talking . . . .

We began to hear music, loud and brassy. The people around me pressed to the curb, laughing in anticipation. We could hear the roar of the crowd three blocks away, a laughing roar that swelled toward us with the music.

The band, I now saw, was one of Storm Troopers, not doll makers. Preceded by torchlights and swastika banners, it marched past. Behind it came two six-foot troopers, half supporting, half dragging a human figure. I could not at first tell if it was a man or a woman. Its head had been clipped bald, and face and head had been coated with white powder. Even though the figure wore a skirt, it might have been a man dressed as a clown. The crowd around me roared at the spectacle of this figure being dragged along. And then, as the SA men suddenly lifted it to its full height, we could read the placard hung around its neck: I wanted to live with a Jew.

I still could not be sure if it was a man or a woman, and the people around me were too busy laughing to hear my questions. After the figure had passed, I was propelled into the street with the crowd. A two-decker bus lumbered up and got stalled in the crush, the driver good-naturedly holding up his hands in surrender. Faces poked from the windows of the bus. On the upper deck people laughed and pointed. The SA men lifted their toy so that they could see it better.

Then someone got the idea of marching the thing into the lobby of our hotel. In it went, followed by part of the crowd. In the street the band played on. By now I had learned that the thing was a girl, and that her name was Anna Rath. The troopers brought her to the street again, and the mob surged forward, toward the next hotel.

Then, suddenly, everyone seemed a little tired of the fun. It was getting late. There were toys to be made tomorrow. The band began to play the Horst Wessel song. Up and down the Koenigstrasse perhaps five thousand people stood at attention, with right arm thrust out, their voices massed. Then the party was over. The banners and the band and the marchers disappeared down the street.

In the bar attached to our hotel, after the late drinkers had left, the Dodds and I asked the bartender about Anna Rath. He whispered her story and the part played in it by Herr S. "You have heard of Herr S., whose home is here?" he asked.

We nodded. He was speaking of Julius Streicher, Hitler's circus master of anti-Semitism. In Berlin it was said that Jews and other undesirables were tortured in the basement of the police building, near the Tomb of the Unknown Soldier. If so, their cries did not reach the street. In Nuremberg, the astute Streicher gave the people the entertainment they wanted.

Anna Rath, we learned, had made the mistake of attempting to marry her Jewish fiance after the ban on Aryan-Jewish marriages.

I went up to my room and telephoned Hawley in Berlin. The Nazis had all along been denying the atrocities that were occasionally reported abroad, but here was concrete evidence. No other correspondent had witnessed any atrocities. Hawley agreed that I had a big story but doubted that it would be allowed to go out on the wire. He recommended that I mail it. Further, he suggested that I should leave out mention of the Dodds, so as not to involve the Ambassador.

Writing the story, I found myself trembling. The grotesque white face of Anna Rath haunted me. In the morning, I posted the story to Barry Faris.

We drove on, then, and had our week in Austria. Among the messages waiting for me when I returned to Berlin was a cable from Barry saying that my story had received a big play. There was also a request for me to report immediately to the office of Ernst Hanfstaengl [Known as Putzi, he was a Harvard-educated Nazi].

Putzi, not to my surprise, was furious. "There isn't one damned word of truth in your story!" he shouted at me. "I've talked with our people in Nuremberg and they say nothing of the sort happened there."

This was a moment to enjoy. I grinned at Putzi. "You're dead right," I said. "I just wanted to impress my New York office so I faked that story from beginning to end."

Putzi began raving the way he played the piano—loud. I stopped him with the announcement that I had watched the affair in the company of two unimpeachable witnesses. When I told him their names, Putzi looked stricken. He slumped into his chair and clutched his head, grumbling that I should not have led him on. When I asked if he wouldn't like to telephone the Dodds and confirm it, he said it would not be necessary.

A few days later, Dr. Goebbels held a press conference. It drew at least forty reporters. Goebbels, who could be very disarming when he wanted to make the effort, himself brought up the question of atrocities against the Jews, saying that they were only isolated examples of behavior by irresponsible individuals.

In the front row of reporters I saw Norman Ebbutt, the head of the *London Times'* Berlin bureau, a mild-mannered man but relentless at follow-ups. "But Herr Minister," I heard him say, "you must surely have heard of the Aryan girl, Anna Rath, who was paraded through Nuremberg just for wanting to marry a Jew?"

Goebbels smiled. "I know that the Hearst Press and your paper, among others, has been interested in that story. Let me explain how such a thing might occasionally happen. All during the twelve years of the Weimar Republic our people were virtually in jail. Now our party is in charge and they are free again. When a man has been in jail for twelve years and he is suddenly freed, in his joy he may do something irrational, perhaps even brutal. Is that not a possibility in your country also?"

"If it should happen," Ebbutt said calmly, "we would throw the man right back in jail."

> Goebbels' face clouded. Then he smiled again and asked, "Are there any more questions?"
>
> That was the end of the press conference, but not quite the end of the Anna Rath story. Norman Ebbutt gave me that when he told me that one of his men had gone to Nuremberg and found her confined in a hospital for the insane.[27]

CONNECTIONS

What does Quentin Reynolds's story suggest about life in Nazi Germany? How would you describe the people who went to the parade? Why do you think that there was so much laughter?

According to the hotel manager, a lesson was taught. What was that lesson? At whom was it aimed: the victims or the bystanders?

Could the incident Reynolds describes happen here?

Photographs of carnivals held in Germany between 1934 and 1938 are reprinted in *Elements of Time*, pages 146-147. Compare those images. What similarities do you see in the way Jews are portrayed in the four photos? What differences seem most striking? Is there a connection between the way Jews are depicted at the various carnivals and the escalation of antisemitic measures?

READING 11

Killing Ideas

*B*y May, the Nazis were burning books. The first book burning took place on May 6, 1933. Students from the Berlin School of Physical Education demolished the Institute of Sexual Science, one of the first scholarly groups to study homosexuality, ceremonially hung a bust of the institute's founder, and then burned twelve thousand books as they sang the nation's anthem. Four days later, the Nazi German Students' Association set up more bonfires, this time to burn books written by Jews and other "undesirables." At one gathering, Joseph Goebbels told a cheering crowd, "The soul of the German people can again express itself. Those flames not only illuminate the final end of an old era; they light up a new!" Lilian T. Mowrer, an American who lived in Germany, described what happened next:

The books we were reading—whether by Thomas Mann, Bernard Shaw, Stefan Zweig, Werner Bergengruen, or Paul Claudel—like modern art—turned into bills of indictment against society. They made us confront National Socialism. They mobilized our defiance.

I held my breath while he hurled the first volume into the flames: it was like burning something alive. Then students followed with whole armfuls of books, while schoolboys screamed into the microphone their condemnation of this and that author, and as each name was mentioned the crowd booed and hissed. You felt Goebbels's venom behind their denunciations. Children of fourteen mouthing abuse of Heine! Erich Remarque's *All Quiet On The Western Front* received the greatest condemnation. . . it would never do for such an unheroic description of war to dishearten soldiers of the Third Reich.[28]

Of all the events that took place in Germany in the spring of 1933, the book burnings made the greatest impression abroad. Helen Keller, an American writer, sent the organizers of the event a letter. "History has taught you nothing if you think you can kill ideas. Tyrants have tried to do that often before, and the ideas have risen up in their might and destroyed them. You can burn my books and the books of the best minds in Europe, but the ideas in them have seeped through a million channels and will continue to quicken other minds."[29]

Others quoted the words of the great German poet, Heinrich Heine, whose family was Jewish. Referring to book burnings in the nineteenth century, the poet had said: "Where they burn books, they will soon burn people." Yet even those who quoted Heine could not truly believe that anyone would go that far.

CONNECTIONS

Why do you think the Nazis began the book burnings by casting books about gays into the flames? What other books were cast into the fire? Why were they singled out? Who made the decision?

Lilian T. Mowrer recalled that "the burning of books affected me more deeply than anything else. I could not have been more shocked by the sight of martyrs at the stake, for although torturing people was revolting enough, regimentation of the individual was ultimately more sinister and the Nazis were beginning to apply their racial theory with ruthless efficiency." For her full account of the event, see the packet on *Kristallnacht* available from the Facing History Resource Center. Why do you think she responded to the book burnings with such emotion? How do you account for Helen Keller's response? How do you think you would have responded?

In what respects is a book burning like a rally or a parade? What differences seem most striking? How do individuals make decisions at such events? How do you think the atmosphere that surrounds a book burning affects what is written? What is published?

Compare the book burnings in 1933 with the one in 1813 (Chapter 2, Reading 5). What similarities seem most striking? How do you account for differences?

Inge Scholl provides a different perspective on the book burnings. Although she, her brother, and her sister were attracted to the Nazis, they continued to read and exchange forbidden books:

> The books we were reading—whether by Thomas Mann, Bernard Shaw, Stefan Zweig, Werner Bergengruen, or Paul Claudel—like modern art—turned into bills of indictment against society. They made us confront National Socialism. They mobilized our defiance.
>
> These books, however, were not gifts from heaven—they came from the hands of young friends. . . . They came to grasp that experience arises not from what you read, but from what you do. Books could stimulate, could impart an insight, could light a candle. But all of this would be relevant to your own life, your true self, only when you put into practice what you had determined was right.[30]

In most authoritarian regimes, books are smuggled in and out of the country. Is reading a revolutionary act? Were Hitler and other authoritarian rulers right to believe that books are dangerous?

Ludwig L. Lenz, a physician who worked at the Institute of Sexual Science, raised a number of questions about the first book burning.

> [Our] Institute was used by all classes of the population and members of every political party. . . .We thus had a great many Nazis under treatment at the Institute. There was, for instance, a lady from Potsdam who, in referring to Dr. Hirschfeld [Magnus Hirschfeld, the director of the Institute] invariably said "Dr. Kirschfeld." When I drew her attention to this mistake, she replied blushing and glancing at the swastika on her breast: "Oh, Doctor, if you don't mind I should rather say 'Dr. Kirschfeld,' it sounds more Aryan."
>
> Why was it then, since we were completely non-party, that our purely scientific Institute was the first victim which fell to the new regime? "Fell" is, perhaps, an understatement for it was totally destroyed; the books from the big library, my irreplaceable documents, all the pictures and files, everything, in fact, that was not nailed down or a permanent fixture was dragged outside and burned. What explanation is there for the fact that the trade union buildings of the socialists, the communist clubs, and the synagogues were only destroyed at a much later date and never so thoroughly as our [peaceful] Institute? Whence this hatred, and what was even more strange, this haste and thoroughness?[31]

Lenz believed it was because "we knew too much." He insists that many Nazi leaders consulted the Institute for help or were known to doctors there through their victims. An historian argues that "if the Institute did indeed keep tens of thousands of confessions and biographical letters, does it make sense to assume that they were all thrown into the fire? Is it not rather more likely that they were saved for use by the Gestapo? Indeed, is it not possible that the entire event was staged to deceive, and that the apparent destruction of the Institute was really a cover operation to retrieve Hirschfeld's case histories and other incriminating evidence against prominent Nazis and their opponents?"[32] What do you think? Was the Institute targeted because it was associated with homosexual activity? Because the doctors knew too much? Or to acquire evidence that could be used against opponents?

READING 12

Whenever Two or Three Are Gathered

The desire to live one's life as best one can, to do one's own work and raise one's own children, is not a contemptible emotion. And to understand the ordinary Berliner in 1933, one can only try to imagine what one might do in a similar situation.

Throughout the spring and early summer of 1933, the Nazis terrorized one group after another in Germany. By May, they had eliminated the nation's trade unions. Workers now had to join a new organization called the Nazi Labor Front. It was to integrate workers, many of whom had supported the Social Democrats or the Communists, into the Nazi state. Then in June, Hitler outlawed the Social Democratic party. By mid-July, the Nazi party was the only political party in a country where the Reichstag no longer passed laws and the constitution no longer protected civil rights. These changes did not take place behind closed doors. They were loudly proclaimed and celebrated.

Other organizations were also brought into line. Not even special interest groups—glee clubs, soccer teams, historical societies, and so on—were allowed to function independently. As historian William Sheridan Allen put it, "Whenever two or three were gathered, the *Fuehrer* would also be present." Not everyone accepted the changes. Over twenty-seven thousand people went to prison. Thousands of others, including sixty-three thousand Jews, left the country by 1934. But most of the nation's sixty million people stayed and adapted to life in the "new Germany."

CONNECTIONS

Write a working definition of *totalitarianism*. You may wish to include a picture of a totalitarian government as part of your definition. Does totalitarianism mean that whenever two or three are gathered, the *Fuehrer* is also present? Why do you think the Nazis tried to turn every get-together into a "Nazi gathering"?

What kinds of resistance were needed in the summer of 1933? What might have been the consequences of such resistance?

In *Before the Deluge,* Otto Friedrich notes that "the desire to live one's life as best one can, to do one's own work and raise one's own children, is not a contemptible emotion. And to understand the ordinary Berliner in 1933, one can only try to imagine what one might do in a similar situation." How do you think you might have responded?

Make a timeline of Nazi laws. Think about which laws were announced first and why. How did the order in which the laws were announced set the stage for those which followed? Then reread the plan the Nazis issued in 1920 (Chapter 3, Reading 5). Which parts had been put into effect by 1933? What do you think will happen next?

How does the First Amendment to the United States Constitution protect the right of Americans to form clubs, political groups, unions, and other associations? To find out, consult *Choosing to Participate* (particularly Chapters 2 through 4) and other books that discuss the right to associate in a free society.

READING 13

Breeding the New German "Race"

*I*n July of 1933, the Nazis moved against yet another group. They announced the "Law for the Prevention of Hereditary Diseased Offspring." It permitted the government to sterilize anyone who suffered from such "genetically determined" illnesses as feeble-mindedness, schizophrenia, manic-depressive illness, genetic epilepsy, Huntington's Chorea, genetic blindness, deafness, and some forms of alcoholism. The purpose of the law was "to have at all times a sufficient number of genetically sound families with many children of high racial value. At the core of the idea of a healthy race is the notion of breeding. Future upholders of the law must be clear about the breeding aims of the German people."

The law was an attempt to create a racially pure society of "Aryans" by isolating and eliminating Germans the Nazis considered inferior. As Hitler stated in *Mein Kampf,* "Everything we admire on this earth today—science and art, technology and inventions—is only the creative product of a few peoples and originally perhaps <u>one</u> race (the Aryans). On them depends the existence of this whole culture. If they perish, the beauty of this earth will sink into the grave with them." To accomplish that goal, the Nazis planned to sterilize women "tainted" by the blood of an inferior race. That is, they planned to make it impossible for the daughters of mixed marriages—marriages between "Aryans" and Jews, Africans, or "Gypsies"—to have children. The Nazis also wanted to sterilize "Aryan" women who had disabilities or deformities. The idea was not a new one. A 1929 work of "scientific racism" stated that "the number of degenerate individuals born depends mainly on the number of degenerate women capable of procreation. Thus the sterilization of degenerate women is, for reasons of racial hygiene, more important than the sterilization of men."

The Germans modeled their new sterilization laws after similar laws in the United States. Between 1907 and 1930, twenty-nine states passed compulsory sterilization laws and about eleven thousand people were sterilized. Many states also had laws that banned marriages between whites and blacks, Native Americans, and Asians. Both sets of laws were prompted by a desire to eliminate "strains that are a burden to the nation or to themselves, and to raise the standard of humanity by the suppression of the progeny of the defective classes." The Nazis now took that goal much further than the Americans ever did.

Gregor Ziemer, an American educator, observed the results of the law when he toured a German hospital where sterilizations took place. A guide informed him that the patients were "the mentally sick, women with low resistance, women who had proved through other births that their offsprings were not strong. They were women suffering from defects . . . some were sterilized because they were political enemies of the State." He was told, "We are even eradicating color-blindedness in the Third Reich . . . . We must not have soldiers who are color-blind. It is transmitted only by women." When Ziemer asked who made the decision, the guide boasted: "We have courts. It is all done very legally, rest assured. We have law and order."[33]

To enforce the law, the Nazis created a Department for Gene and Race Care and "genetic health courts." There doctors and lawyers worked together to decide who would be sterilized. The individual had no say in the decision. Between 1933 and 1939, about 320,000 German women, some as young as fourteen, were sterilized under the law. By 1945, the number may have grown to as many as three million.

The Nazis, like the Americans, regarded sterilization as "negative eugenics." They also encouraged what they called "positive eugenics"— breeding a superior race. Heinrich Himmler, as head of the SS, was particularly concerned about the "racial quality" of his men. Each recruit was carefully screened. He had to prove that his family was "Aryan" dating back to at least 1750. In addition, Himmler and "the chiefs of the race offices inspected photographs of every applicant to make sure his face bore no sign of taint, such as 'orientally' prominent cheekbones, 'mongolian slit eyes, dark curly hair, legs too short in relation to the body, a body too long in relation to the arms, a bespectacled Jewish intellectual look.'" They were seeking "genuine descendents of the Indo-European tribes that had emigrated from Jutland (Denmark) and been settled in Germany since the third century B.C. These were to be the stock from which the new Teutonic race was to be bred and the SS to be recruited." Not only did every member of the SS have to pass the test but so did his prospective bride.

Eugenics is not a panacea that will cure human ills, it is rather a dangerous sword that may turn its edge against those who rely on its strength.

CONNECTIONS

After studying fascism, Irving Horowitz concluded, "The precondition for mass extermination was engineered dehumanization: the conversion of citizens into aliens." What evidence of that process of dehumanization can you find in this reading? Write a working definition of the word *dehumanize* in your journal.

How do you think old prejudices about the disabled and "less worthy races" affected the way people responded to the new law? How do you think the fact that the law was the work of doctors and professors affected the way people responded to it? Did those doctors and professors betray the German people?

Nazi officials often maintained that National Socialism was "nothing but applied biology." What aspects of biology were being applied? For what purpose?

What is "negative eugenics"? How does it differ from "positive eugenics"? How important is that difference?

Between 1907 and 1930, about 11,000 people in the United States were sterilized; about 53,000 by 1964. Germany had no sterilization law before 1933. Yet in just six years about 320,000 people were sterilized and in twelve years the number may have reached as high as three million. How do you account for the differences in numbers? How do you account for the fact that the United States was the first to practice "negative eugenics"?

In 1927, the U.S. Supreme Court upheld the decision of the lower courts to permit the sterilization of Carrie Buck, an eighteen-year-old white woman. Noting that she, her mother, and her child were all "feebleminded," the court ruled sterilization of "mental defectives" promoted the health of the patient and the "welfare of society." Compare the language used in this case with the language the Nazis used to justify their sterilization laws. What similarities do you notice? What differences seem most striking?

On his visit to a German hospital, Ziemer was told, "We have courts. It is all done very legally, rest assured. We have law and order." What right did victims have to protest? To whom could they protest? The Bill of Rights, the first ten amendments to the United States Constitution, protects the rights of all Americans. Yet, even with that protection, thousands of Americans were sterilized. What do these incidents say about why many perceive minorities as "vulnerable"?

Franz Boas, a professor of anthropology at Columbia University, argued in 1916, "Eugenics is not a panacea that will cure human ills, it is rather a dangerous sword that may turn its edge against those who rely on its strength." Why do you think he viewed eugenics as a "dangerous sword"? Where does the danger lie?

➤Robert Lifton discussed the way Nazi doctors responded to sterilization measures in a panel on medical ethics at the First Facing History Conference. For a summary of his presentation, see *Elements of Time*, page 376. A videotape of the event is available from the Facing History Resource Center.

READING 14

"One Nation! One God! One Reich! One Church!"

*A*s the Nazis increased their control over the German people, they targeted the nation's religious groups. National Socialism would have no competition. Among the first religious groups to be singled out were the nation's Catholics. They made up about one-third of the population. As a minority in a country with a Protestant majority, Catholics had always felt vulnerable to accusations that they were not "true Germans" because they "took orders from Rome." Over the years, they had protected their rights by organizing and supporting the Catholic Center party. Now Catholics, individually and as a group, had to decide whether to support the Nazis.

As early as 1931, a number of bishops warned Catholics that "what the National Socialists describe as Christianity is not the Christianity of Christ." Others urged a boycott of Nazi activities. But by the spring of 1933, such attitudes were changing. Some Catholic leaders now seemed to admire Hitler's call to "overcome the un-Germanic spirit." Others continued to oppose the regime but urged caution. That July, Hitler and Pope Pius XI signed a concordat. Historian Fritz Stern said of that agreement:

> On the face of it, the Vatican had scored a great triumph. No government under Weimar had been willing to sign such a concordat, which would recognize the principal rights of the church—rights that presumably would render it immune from the kind of persecution it had suffered [in the past]. By the terms of the concordat the church renounced all political activities and in turn the state guaranteed the right to free worship, to circulate pastoral epistles, to maintain Catholic schools and property. The Vatican had reason to be satisfied: Catholic rights had been put on a new basis and at the same time a regime had been strengthened that seemed to correspond to the Vatican's sense that Mussolini and Hitler were indispensable bulwarks against Bolshevism.
>
> Hitler had even more reason to be satisfied. The concordat was his first international agreement, and it vastly enhanced his respectability in Germany and abroad. A great moral authority had trusted his word.

> But did the Vatican . . . really believe that National Socialism would abide by the concordat, was there really much likelihood that the regime would leave untouched a rival organization with its own dogmas and with such sweeping power over education?[34]

Ten days after the agreement was signed, the Nazis set out to destroy the Catholic Youth League. In the months that followed, a number of Catholic leaders were arrested and several murdered. Yet the pope did not openly criticize the Nazis until 1937. By then it was too late. Roman Catholic opposition was limited to isolated individuals who could easily be removed from their positions.

Catholics were united into one church. Germany's forty-five million Protestants were not. They differed not only in their religious practices but also in their political views. A few openly opposed the Nazis, while others saw themselves as neutral. Still others actively supported fascism, even going so far as to call themselves "storm troopers of Jesus Christ." Hitler's encouragement of these "German Christians" led to conflicts with a number of Protestant ministers.

The first conflict arose when Hitler urged that Germany's 28 regional Protestant churches be united into one Reich church. Many church leaders supported the idea but did not approve of the man Hitler wanted to head the united church. The ministers preferred Friedrich von Bodelschwingh, the director of a large institution that served the mentally ill and the disabled. Hitler and the "German Christians" favored Ludwig Mueller, a little known pastor and a long-time member of the Nazi party. When Mueller was defeated, the Ministry of Culture ordered the firing, suspension, or arrest of a number of pastors. Soon after, Bodelschwingh was forced to resign.

A new election was held in July 1933. This time the Nazis took no chances. When Protestants entered their church to elect representatives to a regional synod, or church assembly, they found themselves face to face with SA members wearing sandwich boards that bore the names of "German Christian" candidates. The intimidation worked. "German Christians" won two-thirds of the vote in regional assemblies, thus paving the way for Mueller's election.

By January of 1934, Mueller was vowing to purge Christianity of all Jewish influence and foster the growth of the "German Christian movement." He claimed that "the eternal God created for our nation a law that is peculiar to its own kind. It took shape in the Leader Adolf Hitler, and in the National Socialist state created by him. This law speaks to us from the history of our people. . . . It is loyalty to this law which demands of us the battle for honor and freedom. . . . One Nation! One God! One Reich! One Church!"

To a number of Protestants, Mueller's words were blasphemy. They were also alarmed by the state's growing involvement in church matters. It now required that churches ban all Christians of Jewish descent. In protest,

Dietrich Bonhoeffer, Martin Niemoeller and other ministers started the Confessing Church. It taught that Jewish Christians had an "inviolable" right to remain in the church.

Soon after the group was formed, Niemoeller and three other leaders met with Hitler and his top aides. Hermann Goering, the head of the Gestapo, opened the meeting by revealing the details of a telephone conversation that Niemoeller had had earlier that day. He then divulged the contents of the Gestapo's files on all four ministers and their associates. The religious leaders responded by reaffirming their support for Hitler's domestic and foreign policies. They asked only for the right to dissent on religious matters. Furious, Hitler screamed, "You are traitors to the *Volk*. Enemies of the Fatherland and destroyers of Germany!"

Hertha von Klewitz, Niemoeller's daughter, later said that Hitler's outburst should have led to open resistance, but it did not. Although 7,000 of the nation's 16,500 clergymen openly supported the Confessing Church, they limited their opposition to defending Protestant teachings against Nazi influence. Klewitz noted sadly, "It was a church resistance and not political."

Only one group of Christians firmly opposed Hitler from the start. Members of the Jehovah's Witnesses refused to cooperate in any way with the new regime. Even after the Gestapo destroyed their national headquarters and the sect itself was outlawed, they refused to compromise their beliefs by even saying "Heil Hitler." Nearly half of the group's members ended up in concentration camps. Yet those same beliefs that fostered such firm opposition to the Nazis did not permit them to even vote during the years of the Weimar Republic. Their opposition was limited to witnessing for their faith.

CONNECTIONS

A *concordat* is a formal agreement or pact. It comes from a Latin word meaning "harmony." What did the Catholic Church hope to gain from the concordat it signed with Germany? What did Hitler hope to gain? What compromises did the pope make? What compromises did Hitler make? The Church kept its side of the bargain. What did the Church do when Hitler broke his promises? What other options did it have? What were the short-term consequences of those options? The long-term consequences?

From the start, Hitler saw the Confessing Church as a political threat even though its members promised to support his domestic and foreign policies. Kurt Scharf, a pastor in the Confessing Church, later explained why: "When a group within a totalitarian system resists on one single point, then they have come into political opposition to the total demands of such a system."[35] What is Scharf trying to say about the separation of church and state in totalitarian regimes? Do you agree? How might history have been altered if ministers in the Confessing Church had understood totalitarianism better in 1933?

As a Jehovah's Witness, Elizabeth Dopazo's father described his position this way, "We have already pledged allegiance to God, we cannot pledge allegiance to a mortal man, and certainly not someone like Hitler!" Many Americans agreed. Yet a few years later, they were troubled when a group of young Jehovah's Witnesses in the United States refused to pledge allegiance to the American flag. What are the similarities in the two cases? The differences?

➤ Additional information about Elizabeth Dopazo and her father can be found in Chapter 5, Reading 8 and *Elements of Time*, pages 220-227. A video of one of her talks is also available from the Facing History Resource Center.

READING 15

No Time to Think

Milton Mayer, an American college professor, wanted to find out how ordinary people reacted to Hitler's policies and philosophy. Seven years after the war, he interviewed German men from a cross-section of society. One of them, a college professor, told Mayer how he responded.

So Much Activity

[My] Middle High German was my life. It was all I cared about. I was a scholar, a specialist. Then, suddenly, I was plunged into all the new activity, as the university was drawn into the new situation; meetings, conferences, interviews, ceremonies, and, above all, papers to be filled out, reports, bibliographies, lists, questionnaires. And on top of that were demands in the community, the things in which one had to, was "expected to" participate that had not been there or had not been important before. It was all rigamarole, of course, but it consumed all one's energies, coming on top of the work one really wanted to do. You can see how easy it was, then, not to think about fundamental things. One had no time.

Too Busy to Think

. . . The dictatorship, and the whole process of its coming into being, was above all diverting. It provided an excuse not to think for people who did not want to think anyway. I do not speak of your "little men," your baker and so on; I speak of my colleagues and myself, learned men, mind you. Most of us did not want to think about

If the last and worst act of the whole regime had come immediately after the first and smallest, thousands, yes millions, would have been sufficiently shocked. . . . But of course this isn't the way it happens. In between come all the hundreds of little steps, some of them imperceptible, each of them preparing you not to be shocked by the next.

fundamental things and never had. There was no need to. Nazism gave us some dreadful, fundamental things to think about—we were decent people—and kept us so busy with continuous changes and "crises" and so fascinated, yes, fascinated, by the machinations of the "national enemies," without and within, that we had no time to think about these dreadful things that were growing, little by little, all around us. Unconsciously, I suppose we were grateful. Who wants to think?

Waiting to React

One doesn't see exactly where or how to move. Believe me, this is true. Each act, each occasion, is worse than the last, but only a little worse. You wait for the next and the next. You wait for one great shocking occasion, thinking that others, when such a shock comes, will join with you in resisting somehow. You don't want to act, or even talk alone; you don't want to "go out of your way to make trouble." Why not?—Well, you are not in the habit of doing it. And it is not just fear, fear of standing alone, that restrains you; it is also genuine uncertainty.

Uncertainty

Uncertainty is a very important factor, and, instead of decreasing as time goes on, it grows. Outside, in the streets, in the general community, "everyone" is happy. One hears no protest, and certainly sees none. You know, in France or Italy there would be slogans against the government painted on walls and fences; in Germany, outside the great cities, perhaps, there is not even this. In the university community, in your own community, you speak privately to your colleagues, some of whom certainly feel as you do; but what do they say? They say, "It's not so bad" or "You're seeing things" or "You're an alarmist."

And you are an alarmist. You are saying that this must lead to this, and you can't prove it. These are the beginnings; yes; but how do you know for sure when you don't know the end, and how do you know, or even surmise, the end? On the one hand, your enemies, the law, the regime, the Party, intimidate you. On the other, your colleagues pooh-pooh you as pessimistic or even neurotic. You are left with your close friends, who are, naturally, people who have always thought as you have.

But your friends are fewer now. Some have drifted off somewhere or submerged themselves in their work. You no longer see as many as you did at meetings or gatherings. Informal groups become smaller; attendance drops off in little organizations, and the organizations themselves wither. Now, in small gatherings of your older friends, you feel that you are talking to yourselves, that you are isolated from the reality of things. This weakens your confidence still further and serves as a further deterrent to—to what? It is clearer all the time that, if you are going to do anything, you must make an occasion to do it, and then you are obviously a troublemaker. So you wait, and you wait.

Small Steps

But the one great shocking occasion, when tens or hundreds of thousands will join with you, never comes. That's the difficulty. If the last and worst act of the whole regime had come immediately after the first and smallest, thousands, yes millions, would have been sufficiently shocked—if, let us say, the gassing of the Jews in '43 had come immediately after the "German Firm" stickers on the windows of non-Jewish shops in '33. But of course this isn't the way it happens. In between come all the hundreds of little steps, some of them imperceptible, each of them preparing you not to be shocked by the next. Step C is not so much worse than Step B, and, if you did not make a stand at Step B, why should you at Step C? And so on to Step D.

Too Late

And one day, too late, your principles, if you were ever sensible of them, all rush in upon you. The burden of self deception has grown too heavy, and some minor incident, in my case my little boy, hardly more than a baby, saying "Jew swine," collapses it all at once, and you see that everything, everything, has changed and changed completely under your nose. The world you live in—your nation, your people—is not the world you were born in at all. The forms are all there, all untouched, all reassuring, the houses, the shops, the jobs, the mealtimes, the visits, the concerts, the cinema, the holidays. But the spirit, which you never noticed because you made the lifelong mistake of identifying it with the forms, is changed. Now you live in a world of hate and fear, and the people who hate and fear do not even know it themselves; when everyone is transformed, no one is transformed. Now you live in a system which rules without responsibility even to God. The system itself could not have intended this in the beginning, but in order to sustain itself it was compelled to go all the way.

Living with New Morals

You have gone almost all the way yourself. Life is a continuing process, a flow, not a succession of acts and events at all. It has flowed to a new level, carrying you with it, without any effort on your part. On this new level you live, you have been living more comfortably every day, with new morals, new principles. You have accepted things you would not have accepted five years ago, a year ago, things that your father, even in Germany, could not have imagined.

Suddenly it all comes down, all at once. You see what you are, what you have done, or, more accurately, what you haven't done (for that was all that was required of most of us: that we do nothing). You remember those early meetings of your department in the university when, if one had stood, others would have stood, perhaps, but no one stood. A small matter, a matter of hiring this man or that, and you hired this one rather than that. You remember everything now, and your heart breaks. Too late. You are compromised beyond repair.[36]

> Suddenly it all comes down, all at once. You see what you are, what you have done, or, more accurately, what you haven't done (for that was all that was required of most of us: that we do nothing.)

Why did the professor obey? What factors led to his decision? How did he evaluate that decision nearly twenty years later? How do you evaluate it? Why does he emphasize the small steps he took? How do each of those small steps make it easier to take no action at all?

Draw an identity chart for the professor. What aspects of his identity may have influenced the decisions he made in 1933? How do you think life in a world dominated by fear affected the choices he made?

Reread Peter Drucker's decision (Reading 8). Compare it to those described in this reading. Does an individual have the responsibility to take a stand? When? Under what circumstances?

How might "thinking" have made a difference in the professor's decisions? At what point did the state take on so much power or the person give up so much power that human qualities were suppressed in the name of patriotism? Is it possible to think too much? Can thinking too much paralyze one's responses?

READING 16

A Refusal to Compromise

*I*n 1933, Helene Jacobs was a high-school student and one of the few Germans to refuse to make even the smallest compromise with the new government. She later recalled:

> I had begun to study during that time. You received an obligatory book which you had to sign; I didn't do it. At the technical high school where I last studied, I couldn't take any exam. But I didn't want to get involved in that. It was so obvious to me that [the Third Reich] wouldn't last. I thought, I'll just wait that long and then I'll continue. As a result, I didn't have any steady position. I worked for very little money for a Jewish attorney, and wasn't a member of any organization. Anywhere it said, "For Aryans only," I said, "What's that? There's no such thing." I kept myself away from such requirements.
>
> The point that aroused me from the beginning was that we as a people had to show our unwillingness in some fashion, not just when the crimes began, but before, when it started, with this so-called "Aryan" ancestry. They distributed questionnaires and you had to say whether you had "Aryan" ancestors. Everyone filled them out. I said, "We can't go along with this; it's not legal. We must do something against this and throw the questionnaires away."

> But today—the other people my age, they behaved totally differently at that time. Most of them built their careers then. When I said, "I'm not going to have anything to do with this," I isolated myself.[37]

CONNECTIONS

Why do you think Helene Jacobs was willing to isolate herself? Why were so few others willing to take the kind of stand she did? Why do people feel a need to belong to something?

Compare Jacobs's stand with those described in Readings 8 and 15. What similarities do you see? What differences are most striking?

➤The novel *Friedrich* by Hans Peter Richter describes how the antisemitic laws that went into effect between 1933 and 1939 severed the friendship of a German boy and his Jewish friend, Friedrich. An accompanying videotape, also entitled *Friedrich*, includes the video testimonies of survivors who recall incidents similar to those described in the novel. The video and class sets of the novel are available from the Facing History Resource Center.

READING 17

Eliminating Opposition

Hitler was determined to put down all opposition, even opposition within his own party. His main critic among fellow Nazis was Ernst Roehm, the leader of the SA—the Nazi storm troopers. Roehm and a few of his supporters felt that Hitler was not doing enough to promote socialism. They were also suspicious of his relationship with powerful industrialists and generals.

By June of 1934, Hitler was convinced that Roehm and the SA had outlived their usefulness. Too many Germans regarded the stormtroopers as thugs. So it was time to take action. In doing so, Hitler had the backing of military leaders who resented the fact that the army was limited to a hundred thousand men by the Treaty of Versailles while the SA's membership was as least four times that number. Industrialists supported the move as well. They did not approve of Roehm's socialist leanings or the violence they associated with the SA. They were also bothered by the fact that he was gay—a disgraceful practice in their view.

On June 30, Hitler ordered the SS and the regular army to eliminate all opposition within the party. During what was later called the "Night of the Long Knives," they murdered over two hundred SA leaders, including

Unpleasantnesses, of course there were unpleasantnesses; but such things, if talked about at all, must be seen in perspective. There were so many more positive aspects of the regime to chat about.

Roehm. They also killed Kurt von Schleicher and his wife. Neither was connected to Roehm or the SA. Schleicher, a friend of Hindenburg, was chancellor before Hitler took over in 1933.

Most people did not know about the events of June 30 until days later. The news came out only when Hitler's cabinet declared the purge "legal" retroactively. The papers then reported that Hindenburg had "congratulated the Fuehrer and the Reich Chancellor" on his "courageous personal intervention." Two weeks later, on July 13, Hitler justified the murders: "If anyone reproaches me and asks why I did not resort to the regular courts of justice, then all I can say to him is this: in this hour I was responsible for the fate of the German people, and thereby I became the supreme Justiciar of the German people. . . . And everyone must know for all future time that if he raises his hand to strike the State, then certain death is his lot."

According to Hannah Arendt, the massacre was misunderstood within Germany and without. She wrote that instead of realizing that the country was being run by "a gang of criminals," "many Germans believed that the purge of the SA represented Hitler's wish to halt the arbitrary terror of the SA in the streets and to restore a measure of legality to the country." Christabel Bielenberg, a British woman who became a German citizen shortly after her marriage, agreed. She was out of the country on June 30. When she returned a few weeks later, she found growing support for Hitler.

> It was considered that . . . with the murder of Roehm and the eclipse of his storm troopers (although the manner in which it had been carried out had not been exactly savoury), the Revolution had to all intents and purposes become respectable. Once everything distasteful had been neatly swept under the carpet, there was something almost touching about the anxious childlike pleasure with which so many tried to share in what they seemed to hope was a newly discovered respectability. Unpleasantnesses, of course there were unpleasantnesses; but such things, if talked about at all, must be seen in perspective. There were so many more positive aspects of the regime to chat about.[38]

CONNECTIONS

What does it mean that Hitler's actions were "legal retroactively"? How was he using language to obscure his actions? He justified the Night of the Long Knives by saying, "If anyone reproaches me and asks why I did not resort to the regular courts of justice, then all I can say to him is this: in this hour I was responsible for the fate of the German people, and thereby I became the supreme Justiciar of the German people." *Justiciar* was a word used in the Middle Ages to describe the leader responsible for justice in a country. What is Hitler saying about his relationship to the law? Is he the defender of justice? The guardian of the nation's laws? Or does he see himself as above the law?

Review your identity chart. How do you like to think you would have responded to the events of the Night of Long Knives? Record your responses in your journal.

How do you account for the fact that the massacre turned Hitler's regime from "a gang of criminals running the country" to "a newly discovered respectability"?

Many Germans believed that you had to overlook the bad in the new Nazi regime to get the good. How is that idea reflected in their response to the Night of the Long Knives?

Would the Night of the Long Knives have been possible in February 1933? What earlier events prepared the nation to accept Hitler's version of what happened that night? Earlier you were asked, "What does it take to create a dictatorship out of a democracy?" Review your answer. How important was the Night of the Long Knives to the process?

READING 18

Isolating Gays

After the Night of the Long Knives, the Nazis increased their attacks on gay men. Many Germans applauded the move. Hitler began by enforcing and then later strengthening a law passed at the turn of the century. It defined a homosexual act as "indecent" behavior that diminishes "the health of the state." During the Weimar Republic, the government did not pay much attention to the law. When Hitler took over, that policy changed. A man who lived near Hamburg recalled:

We lived like animals in a wild game park, always sensing the hunters.

> With one blow a wave of arrests of homosexuals began in our town. One of the first to be arrested was my friend, with whom I had had a relationship since I was 23. One day people from the Gestapo came to his house and took him away. It was pointless to enquire where he might be. If anyone did that, they ran the risk of being similarly detained, because he knew them, and therefore they were also suspect. Following his arrest, his home was searched by Gestapo agents. Books were taken away, note- and address books were confiscated, questions were asked among the neighbours . . . . The address books were the worst. All those who figured in them, or had anything to do with him were arrested and summoned by the Gestapo. Me, too. For a whole year I was summoned by the Gestapo and interrogated at least once every fourteen days or three weeks . . . . After

four weeks my friend was released from investigative custody. The fascists could not prove anything against him either. However the effects of his arrest were terrifying. Hair shorn off, totally confused, he was no longer what he was before . . . . We had to be very careful with all contacts. I had to break off all relations with my friend. We passed each other by on the street, because we did not want to put ourselves in danger. . . . We lived like animals in a wild game park, always sensing the hunters.[39]

CONNECTIONS

The gay men described in this reading were "Aryans." Yet they were not a part of the German people's "universe of obligation."

What does the German mean when he says "We lived like animals in a wild game park, always sensing the hunters"? What other Germans lived in similar ways?

What insights does the reading offer concerning the way the Nazis used fear to paralyze bystanders? The way they dehumanized those they isolated and arrested?

Many gays, like other enemies of the state, were sent to concentration camps. There inmates were defined by a cloth triangle sewn onto their clothing. Homosexuals wore pink triangles, criminals green, political prisoners red, Jehovah's Witnesses purple, immigrants blue, anti-socials black, and Gypsies brown triangles. Jews wore two yellow triangles arranged to form a Star of David. Why do you think the Nazis separated prisoners in this way?

Pledging Allegiance

When Paul von Hindenburg died on August 2, 1934, Hitler combined the positions of chancellor and president. He was now the Fuehrer and Reich Chancellor, the Head of State, and the Chief of Armed Forces. In the past, German soldiers had taken this oath: "I swear loyalty to the Constitution and vow that I will protect the German nation and its lawful establishments as a brave soldier at any time and will be obedient to the President and my superiors." Now Hitler created a new oath. "I swear by God this sacred oath, that I will render unconditional obedience to Adolf Hitler, the Fuehrer of the German Reich and people, Supreme Commander of the Armed Forces, and will be ready as a brave soldier to risk my life at any time for this oath."

In his book, *The Rise and Fall of the Third Reich*, William Shirer said the new oath "enabled an even greater number of officers to excuse themselves from any personal responsibility for the unspeakable crimes which they carried out on the orders of the Supreme Commander whose true nature they had seen for themselves. . . . One of the appalling aberrations of the German officer corps from this point on rose out of this conflict of 'honor'—a word . . . often on their lips . . . . Later and often by honoring their oath they dishonored themselves as human beings and trod in the mud the moral code of their corps."[40]

> The new oath "enabled an even greater number of officers to excuse themselves from any personal responsibility for the unspeakable crimes which they carried out on the orders of the Supreme Commander whose true nature they had seen for themselves."

Summarize the two oaths. What is the main difference between the two? How significant is that difference? What are the implications of swearing an oath to an individual leader rather than to a nation?

What oaths do people take today? For what reasons? Have you ever taken an oath? Did it make you feel part of something larger than yourself? Did it make you tell the truth? Make you keep your word?

Which comes first—one's military duty or one's moral duty? Can an oath excuse one from personal responsibility?

R E A D I N G   2 0

Do You Take the Oath?

Soldiers were not the only ones required to take the new oath. A German recalled the day he was asked to pledge loyalty to the regime.

> I was employed in a defense plant (a war plant, of course, but they were always called defense plants). That was the year of the National Defense Law, the law of "total conscription." Under the law I was required to take the oath of fidelity. I said I would not; I opposed it in conscience. I was given twenty-four hours to "think it over." In those twenty-four hours I lost the world . . . .
>
> You see, refusal would have meant the loss of my job, of course, not prison or anything like that. (Later on, the penalty was worse, but this was only 1935.) But losing my job would have meant that I could not get another. Wherever I went I should be asked why I left the job I had, and when I said why, I should certainly have been refused employment. Nobody would hire a "Bolshevik." Of course, I was not a Bolshevik, but you understand what I mean.
>
> I tried not to think of myself or my family. We might have got out of the country, in any case, and I could have got a job in industry or education somewhere else.
>
> What I tried to think of was the people to whom I might be of some help later on, if things got worse (as I believed they would). I had a wide friendship in scientific and academic circles, including many Jews, and "Aryans," too, who might be in trouble. If I took the oath and held my job, I might be of help, somehow, as things went on. If I refused to take the oath, I would certainly be useless to my friends, even if I remained in the country. I myself would be in their situation.
>
> The next day, after "thinking it over," I said I would take the oath with the mental reservation, that, by the words with which the oath

began, "*Ich schwoere bei Gott*," "I swear by God," I understood that no human being and no government had the right to override my conscience. My mental reservations did not interest the official who administered the oath. He said, "Do you take the oath?" and I took it. That day the world was lost, and it was I who lost it.

First of all, there is the problem of the lesser evil. Taking the oath was not so evil as being unable to help my friends later on would have been. But the evil of the oath was certain and immediate, and the helping of my friends was in the future and therefore uncertain. I had to commit a positive evil there and then, in the hope of a possible good later on. The good outweighed the evil; but the good was only a hope, the evil a fact. . . . The hope might not have been realized—either for reasons beyond my control or because I became afraid later on or even because I was afraid all the time and was simply fooling myself when I took the oath in the first place.

But that is not the important point. The problem of the lesser evil we all know about; in Germany we took Hindenburg as less evil than Hitler, and in the end, we got them both. But that is not why I say that Americans cannot understand. No, the important point is—how many innocent people were killed by the Nazis, would you say?. . . Shall we say, just to be safe, that three million innocent people were killed all together?. . . And how many innocent lives would you like to say I saved?. . . Perhaps five, or ten, one doesn't know. But shall we say a hundred, or a thousand, just to be safe?. . . And it would be better to have saved all three million, instead of only a hundred, or a thousand? There, then, is my point. If I had refused to take the oath of fidelity, I would have saved all three million. . . .

There I was, in 1935, a perfect example of the kind of person who, with all his advantages in birth, in education, and in position, rules (or might easily rule) in any country. If I had refused to take the oath in 1935, it would have meant that thousands and thousands like me, all over Germany, were refusing to take it. Their refusal would have heartened millions. Thus the regime would have been overthrown, or, indeed, would never have come to power in the first place. The fact that I was not prepared to resist, in 1935, meant that all the thousands, hundreds of thousands, like me in Germany were also unprepared, and each one of these hundreds of thousands was, like me, a man of great influence or of great potential influence. Thus the world was lost. . . .

These hundred lives I saved—or a thousand or ten as you will— what do they represent? A little something out of the whole terrible evil, when, if my faith had been strong enough in 1935, I could have prevented the whole evil. . . . My faith, I did not believe that I could "remove mountains." The day I said, "No," I had faith. In the process of "thinking it over," in the next twenty-four hours, my faith failed me. So, in the next ten years, I was able to remove only anthills, not mountains.

The fact that I was not prepared to resist, in 1935, meant that all the thousands, hundreds of thousands, like me in Germany were also unprepared, and each one of these hundreds of thousands was, like me, a man of great influence or of great potential influence. Thus the world was lost.

> My education did not help me, and I had a broader and better education than most men have had or ever will have. All it did, in the end, was to enable me to rationalize my failure of faith more easily than I might have done if I had been ignorant. And so it was, I think, among educated men generally, in that time in Germany. Their resistance was no greater than other men's.[41]

Not everyone was willing to take the oath. Among those who refused was Ricarda Huch, a poet and writer. She resigned from the prestigious Prussian Academy of Arts with this letter.

> That a German should feel German, I should take almost for granted. But there are different opinions about what is German and how German-ness is to be expressed. What the present regime prescribes as national sentiment, is not my German-ness. The centralization, the compulsion, the brutal methods, the defamation of people who think differently, the boastful self-praise I regard as un-German and unhealthy. Possessing a philosophy that varies so radically from that prescribed by the state I find it impossible to remain one of its academicians. You say that the declaration submitted to me by the Academy would not hinder me in the free expression of my opinion. Apart from the fact that "loyal collaboration in the national cultural tasks assigned in accordance with the Academy's statutes and in the light of the changed historical circumstances" requires an agreement with the government's programme that I do not feel, I would find no journal or newspaper that would print an oppositional view. Therefore, the right to express one's opinions freely remains mired in theory. . . . I herewith declare my resignation from the Academy.[42]

Huch sent the letter but could not publicize her stand by publishing it. She lived in Germany throughout the Nazi era as a silent dissenter in "internal exile."

CONNECTIONS

What did the man mean when he said his education failed him? That "no human being and no government had the right to override my conscience?" Did he have a conscience—that is, did he know right from wrong? If so, did his conscience also fail him? Milton Mayer wrote that there was a time in Nazi Germany when teachers could have made different decisions. Why was the decision of most teachers to take and obey the new oath to Hitler a crucial step toward totalitarianism?

What is the "problem of the lesser evil"? Find examples of it in this reading and in other readings in this chapter. Look for examples in your own experience.

Compare the decisions described in this reading with those detailed in earlier readings. What issues influenced each decision? What values and beliefs? The man quoted in this reading states, "I had to commit a positive evil there and then, in the hope of a possible good later on." Do you agree? Is it possible to distinguish among evils? Who today face similar dilemmas? How are those dilemmas resolved?

What is "silent dissenter"? "Internal exile?" How meaningful is either?

R E A D I N G 2 1

Defining a Jew

The Nazis passed forty-two anti-Jewish measures in 1933 and nineteen more in 1934. Each was designed to protect "Aryan blood" from contamination with "Jewish blood." Then in 1935, Hitler announced three new laws at the party rally in Nuremberg. The first two stripped Jews of citizenship. The third law isolated them from other Germans.

> Realizing that the purity of the German blood is the prerequisite for the continued existence of the German people, and animated by the firm resolve to secure the German nation for all future times, the Reichstag has unanimously passed the following law. . .
>
> 1. Marriages between Jews and citizens of German or kindred blood are hereby forbidden. Marriages performed despite this ban are void, even if, to contravene the law, they are performed abroad. Suits for annulment can be brought only by the district attorney.
>
> 2. Extramarital intercourse between Jews and citizens of German or kindred blood is forbidden.
>
> 3. Jews are not permitted to employ female citizens of German or kindred blood under 45 years of age as domestic help.

The law raised a question that had not yet been resolved: Who is a Jew? On November 14, the Nazis answered that question by defining a Jew as a person with two Jewish parents or three Jewish grandparents. The children of intermarriage were considered Jewish if they practiced the Jewish religion or were married to a Jew. They were also Jews if one parent was a practicing Jew. A child of intermarriage who was not Jewish according to these criteria was considered a Jewish *Mischling*—a person of "mixed race." By isolating Jews from other Germans and forbidding any mixing of races, the Nazis hoped that the problems of defining a *Mischling* would eventually disappear.

The Nazis passed over four hundred additional laws between 1933 and 1945. Being a Jew was no longer a matter of self-definition or self-

Being a Jew was no longer a matter of self-definition or self-identification. Now a person was considered a Jew because of what his or her grandparents had chosen to believe. Who you were no longer depended upon you.

identification. Now a person was considered a Jew because of what his or her grandparents had chosen to believe. Who you were no longer depended upon you. After noting that by 1935, "at least a quarter of the Jews who remained had been deprived of their professional livelihood by boycott, decree, or local pressure," historian Martin Gilbert noted:

> More than ten thousand public health and social workers had been driven out of their posts, four thousand lawyers were without the right to practise, two thousand doctors had been expelled from hospitals and clinics, two thousand actors, singers and musicians had been driven from their orchestras, clubs and cafes. A further twelve hundred editors and journalists had been dismissed, as had eight hundred university professors and lecturers, and eight hundred elementary and secondary school teachers.
>
> The search for Jews, and for converted Jews, to be driven out of their jobs was continuous. On 5 September 1935 the SS newspaper published the names of eight half-Jews and converted Jews, all of the Evangelical-Lutheran faith, who had been "dismissed without notice" and deprived of any further opportunity "of acting as organists in Christian churches." From these dismissals, the newspaper commented, "It can be seen that the Reich Chamber of Music is taking steps to protect the church from pernicious influence."[43]

CONNECTIONS

Most Christians in Germany supported the Nuremberg laws. Dietrich Goldschmidt, a Jew who converted to Christianity and later joined the Confessing Church, suggests why.

> The guilt of the Christians and church rests in the fact that the commandment to love your neighbor was interpreted or taken to mean one looked after the Christian brothers and sisters—those who had been baptized. That means that when Christians came into conflict with the state or with the police, the church or the parish took care of them as long as it had to do with the church . . . . When a Christian attended to politics, that was no longer something with which the church concerned itself. . . . In this sense, the responsibility for society, the responsibility for the Jews, Social Democrats, communists, gypsies, atheists, the responsibility for all these was not a responsibility of the church.[44]

Define *neighbor*. What responsibility do you have to your neighbors?

Being a Jew was no longer a matter of self-definition or self-identification. What does it mean to lose the right to define yourself? How was the dilemma confronting Germans of Jewish descent in 1935 similar to that of the Bear in *the bear that wasn't* (Chapter 1, Reading 1)? How did it differ?

In the United States in the years after the Civil War, many states isolated or segregated African Americans from other Americans. Each tried to define a "Negro" or African American according to the "race" of his or her parents, grandparents, and great-grandparents. Those laws were still in effect when Germany was struggling to define who was a Jew. And those laws remained on the books in some states until the 1980s, despite the efforts of African Americans to overturn them. Research segregation laws passed in the United States in the late 1800s and early 1900s. How was their definition of an African American similar to the Nazis' definition of a Jew? What differences seem most striking?

READING 22

The People Respond

Marta Appel, like many Germans of the Jewish faith, found that the Nuremberg Laws affected even old friendships. For years, she had been getting together once a month with women from her old high school. In 1935, she stopped attending, mainly because she did not want to embarrass her non-Jewish friends.

> One day on the street, I met one of my old teachers, and with tears in her eyes she . . . tried to convince me that [the women] were still my friends, and tried to take away my doubts. I decided to go to the next meeting. It was a hard decision and I had not slept the night before. I was afraid for my gentile friends. For nothing in the world did I wish to bring them trouble by my attendance, and I was also afraid for myself. I knew I would watch them, noticing the slightest expression of embarrassment in their eyes when I came. I knew they could not deceive me; I would be aware of every change in their voices. Would they be afraid to talk to me?
>
> It was not necessary for me to read their eyes or listen to the changes in their voices. The empty table in the little alcove that had always been reserved for us spoke the clearest language. It was even unnecessary for the waiter to come and say that a lady phoned that morning not to reserve the table thereafter. I could not blame them. Why should they risk losing a position only to prove to me that we still had friends in Germany?[45]

Suppose you were one of Appel's school friends. What do you like to think you would have done? Might you have attended the lunch in 1933? In 1935? What might the consequences of attending have been in 1933? In 1935? Of not attending? Suppose you were in Marta Appel's position. Do you like to think you would have gone to lunch?

How were the decisions Appel's friends made similar to one Milton Mayer described in Reading 15? What differences seem most striking?

Franklin Roosevelt told Americans in the 1930s that the only thing they had to fear was "fear itself." Does it take courage to face one's fears and do the right thing? What was the right thing in 1933? In 1935? When did it take more courage to do right?

READING 23

"The Hangman"

1.
Into our town the Hangman came,
Smelling of gold and blood and flame—
And he paced our bricks with a diffident air
And built his frame on the courthouse square.

The scaffold stood by the courthouse side,
Only as wide as the door was wide;
A frame as tall, or little more,
Than the capping sill of the courthouse door.

And we wondered, whenever we had the time,
Who the criminal, what the crime,
That Hangman judged with the yellow twist
Of knotted hemp in his busy fist.

And innocent though we were, with dread
We passed those eyes of buckshot lead;
Till one cried: "Hangman, who is he
For whom you raise the gallows-tree?"

Then a twinkle grew in the buckshot eye,
And he gave us a riddle instead of reply:
"He who serves me best," said he,
"Shall earn the rope on the gallows-tree."

And he stepped down, and laid his hand
On a man who came from another land.
And we breathed again, for another's grief
At the Hangman's hand was our relief.

And the gallows-frame on the courthouse lawn
By tomorrow's sun would be struck and gone.
So we gave him way, and no one spoke,
Out of respect for his hangman's cloak.
2.
The next day's sun looked mildly down
On roof and street in our quiet town
And, stark and black in the morning air,
The gallows-tree on the courthouse square.

And the Hangman stood at his usual stand
With the yellow hemp in his busy hand;
With his buckshot eye and his jaw like a pike
And his air so knowing and businesslike.

And we cried: "Hangman, have you not done,
Yesterday, with the alien one?"
Then we fell silent, and stood amazed:
"Oh, not for him was the gallows raised. . ."

He laughed a laugh as he looked at us:
". . .Did you think I'd gone to all this fuss
To hang one man? That's a thing I do
To stretch the rope when the rope is new."

Then one cried "Murderer!" One cried "Shame!"
And into our midst the Hangman came
To that man's place. "Do you hold," said he,
"With him that's meant for the gallows-tree?"

And he laid his hand on that one's arm,
And we shrank back in quick alarm,
And we gave him way, and no one spoke
Out of fear of his hangman's cloak.

That night we saw with dread surprise
The Hangman's scaffold had grown in size.
Fed by the blood beneath the chute
The gallows-tree had taken root;

Now as wide, or a little more,
Than the steps that led to the courthouse door,
As tall as the writing, or nearly as tall,
Halfway up on the courthouse wall.
3.
The third he took—and we had all heard tell––
Was a usurer and infidel. And:
"What," said the Hangman, "have you to do
With the gallows-bound, and he a Jew?"

And we cried out: "Is this one he
Who has served you well and faithfully?"
The Hangman smiled: "It's a clever scheme
To try the strength of the gallows-beam."

The fourth man's dark, accusing song
Had scratched out comfort hard and long;
And "What concern," he gave us back,
"Have you for the doomed—the doomed and black?"

The fifth. The sixth. And we cried again:
"Hangman, Hangman, is this the man?"
"It's a trick," he said, "that we hangmen know
For easing the trap when the trap springs slow."

And so we ceased and asked no more,
As the Hangman tallied his bloody score;
And sun by sun, and night by night,
The gallows grew to monstrous height.

The wings of the scaffold opened wide
Till they covered the square from side to side;
And the monster cross-beam, looking down,
Cast its shadow across the town.
4.
Then through the town the Hangman came
And called in the empty streets my name.
And I looked at the gallows soaring tall
And thought: "There is no one left at all
For hanging, and so he calls to me
To help him pull down the gallows-tree."
And I went out with right good hope
To the Hangman's tree and the Hangman's rope.

He smiled at me as I came down
To the courthouse square through the silent town,
And supple and stretched in his busy hand
Was the yellow twist of the hempen strand.

And he whistled his tune as he tried the trap
And it sprang down with a ready snap —
And then with a smile of awful command
He laid his hand upon my hand.

"You tricked me, Hangman!" I shouted then,
"That your scaffold was built for other men. . .
And I no henchman of yours," I cried.
"You lied to me, Hangman, foully lied!"

Then a twinkle grew in the buckshot eye:
"Lied to you? Tricked you?" he said, "Not I
For I answered straight and I told you true:
The scaffold was raised for none but you.

"For who has served me more faithfully
Than you with your coward's hope?" said he,
"And where are the others that might have stood
Side by your side in the common good?"

"Dead," I whispered; and amiably,
"Murdered," the Hangman corrected me;
"First the alien, then the Jew. . .
I did no more than you let me do."

Beneath the beam that blocked the sky,
None had stood so alone as I—
And the Hangman strapped me, and no voice there
Cried "Stay!" for me in the empty square.[46]

CONNECTIONS

What choices were open to the townspeople when the Hangman arrived? By the time he had finished his work in the town? Was there a way to stop the Hangman? If so, how? If not, why not?

How does the poem relate to Germany in the 1930s? To society today?

In 1933, Martin Niemoeller, a leader of the Confessing Church, voted for the Nazi party. By 1938, he was in a concentration camp. After the war, he is believed to have said, "In Germany, the Nazis came for the Communists, and I didn't speak up because I wasn't a Communist. Then they came for the Jews, and I didn't speak up because I wasn't a Jew. Then they came for the trade unionists, and I didn't speak up because I wasn't a trade unionist. Then they came for the Catholics, and I didn't speak up because I was a Protestant. Then they came for me, and by that time there was no one left to speak for me." How is the point Niemoeller makes similar to the one Maurice Ogden makes in "The Hangman"?

What is the meaning of the Hangman's riddle: ""He who serves me best," said he, "shall earn the rope on the gallows-tree"?

➤ "The Hangman" is also available on video from the Facing History Resource Center. Teachers who have used the film have indicated a need to show it several times to allow their students time to identify the various symbols and reflect on their meaning. After seeing it, think about why the filmmaker turned the animated people into paper dolls. Why did the shadow grow on the courthouse wall? Why did the gallows-tree take root?

A student who watched the film wrote, "The Hangman was to me strange. The 'hidden message' of this is harder to find than any other movie or section we have seen so far. I understand, now that instead of standing as a bystander all the time, I should voice my opinion before it is worthless." Another noted, "I guess most people would be like the man who stood by and watched the townspeople being hung. I mean who would really have the guts to stand up and say "stop". . . especially if you got no support from the crowd. I don't think I could." Which opinion is closest to your own?

NOTES

[1] Joseph Goebbels, *The Early Goebbels Diaries*, ed. H. Heiber (London, 1962).

[2] Fritz Stern, *Dreams and Delusions* (A. Knopf, Inc., 1987), 152.

[3] A. J. P. Taylor, *The Origins of the Second World War* (Atheneum, 1961), 71.

[4] Milton Mayer, *They Thought They Were Free: The Germans 1933-45* (University of Chicago Press, 1955), 167. Copyright © 1955 by the University of Chicago Press. Reprinted by permission.

[5] Quoted in Leon Botstein, "Hannah Arendt: The Jewish Question," *New Republic*, 21 October, 1978, 34.

[6] Fritz Stern, *Dreams and Delusions*, 152.

[7] Bernt Engelmann, *In Hitler's Germany* (Schocken, 1988), 21-22.

[8] Melita Maschmann, *Account Rendered* (Abelard-Schuman, 1965), 10–13.

[9] Max von der Gruen, *Howl with the Wolves; Growing Up in Nazi Germany*, trans. Jan Van Heurk (William Morrow, 1980).

[10] Thomas L. Stokes, *Chip Off My Shoulder* (Princeton University Press, 1940), 310.

[11] Margot Stern Strom, "An Interterview with Bill Moyers," *Facing History and Ourselves News*, Fall 1986.

[12] Alan Berger, "Zhirnovsky's Fascism Is Not an Isolated Phenomenon," *Boston Globe*, 19 December, 1993.

[13] I. F. Stone, "Izzy on Izzy," *New York Times Magazine*, 22 January, 1978.

[14] Wolfgang Roth, "It All Depends on the Lighting." In *Jewish Life in Germany*, ed. Monika Richarz, 321.

[15] Quoted in Nora Levin, *The Holocaust* (Schocken, 1973), 46.

[16] Edwin Landau, "My Life before and after Hitler." In *Jewish Life in Germany*, ed. Monika Richarz, 310-312.

[17] Quoted in Joachim Remak, *The Nazi Years: A Documentary History* (Prentice-Hall, 1969), 147.

[18] Horst Krueger, *A Crack in the Wall*, (Fromm International Publishing Corp., 1982), 19-20.

[19] Quoted in *Nazism: A History in Documents and Eyewitness Accounts, 1919-1945*, vol. 1, ed. J. Noakes and G. Pridham (Schocken, 1983, 1984), 147.

[20] Christopher Isherwood, *The Berlin Stories* (New Directions, 1945), 179.

21 Michael Burleigh and Wolfgang Wippermann, *The Racial State* (Cambridge University Press, 1991), 60.

22 Fritz Stern, *Dreams and Delusions*, 169.

23 Reprinted by permission from Peter F. Drucker, *Adventures of a Bystander.* Tramaction Publishers, 1994. Copyright Peter F. Drucker, 1978, 1991, 1994; first published in 1978.

24 Fritz Stern, *Dreams and Delusions*, 169.

25 FromTHE ASCENT OF MAN by Jacob Bronowski, 367. Copyright © 1973 by J. Bronowski. By permission of Little, Brown and Company.

26 Ellen Switzer, *How Democracy Failed*, 89-91.

27 Quentin Reynolds, *A London Diary* (Random House, 1941).

28 Quoted in *Witness to the Holocaust,* ed. Azriel Eisenberg, (Pilgrim Press, 1981), 79-82.

29 Quoted in Guy Stern, "Nazi Book Burning and the American Response" (unpublished paper, Wayne State University, 1989).

30 Quoted in Hermann Vinke, *The Short Life of Sophie Scholl* (Harper & Row, 1980), 61.

31 Quoted in Erwin J. Haeberle, "Swastika, Pink Triangle, and Yellow Star: The Destruction of Sexology and the Persecution of Homosexuals in Nazi Germany," *The Journal of Sex Research*, August 1981, 270-287.

32 Ibid.

33 Gregor Zeimer, *Education for Death: the Making of the Nazi* (Oxford University Press, 1941), 19.

34 Fritz Stern, *Dreams and Delusions*, 188.

35 Quoted in Victoria Barnett, *For the Soul of the People*, 63.

36 Milton Mayer, *They Thought They Were Free*, 177-181.

37 Victoria Barnett, *For the Soul of the People*, 31-32.

38 Christabel Bielenberg, *Christabel* (Penguin, 1989), 27-28.

39 Quoted in M. Burleigh and W. Wippermann *The Racial State*, 194.

40 William Shirer, *The Rise and Fall of the Third Reich* (Simon & Schuster, 1960), 227.

41 Milton Mayer, *They Thought They Were Free*, 177-181.

42 Quoted in Joachim Remak *The Nazi Years*, 162.

43 Martin Gilbert, *The Holocaust* (Holt, 1985), 47.

44 Victoria Barnett, *For the Soul of the People*, 133.

45 Marta Appel, "Memoirs." In *Jewish Life in Germany,* ed. Monika Richarz, 353.

46 Maurice Ogden, "The Hangman," Regina Publications.

5. Conformity and Obedience

When you think of the long and gloomy history of man, you find more hideous crimes have been committed in the name of obedience than have ever been committed in the name of rebellion.

C. P. SNOW

OVERVIEW

Chapter 4 considered *how* Germany became a totalitarian state. This chapter looks at *why* the German people allowed it to happen. Chapters 1 and 2 offered insights into the importance we, as individuals, place on our membership in various groups. This chapter shows how the Nazis took advantage of that yearning to belong. It describes, in Fritz Stern's words, how they used the "twin instruments of propaganda and terror" to coerce and cajole a people into giving up their freedom. A character in George Orwell's *1984*, a novel that details life in a state much like Nazi Germany, offers another view of the process.

> Already we are breaking down the habits of thought which have survived from before the Revolution. We have cut the links between child and parent, and between man and man, and between man and woman. No one dares trust a wife or a child or a friend any longer. . . . There will be no loyalty, except loyalty toward the Party. There will be no love, except the love of Big Brother. There will be no laughter, except the laugh of triumph over a defeated enemy. There will be no art, no literature, no science. When we are omnipotent we shall have no more need of science. There will be no distinction between beauty and ugliness. There will be no curiosity, no employment of the process of life. All competing pleasures will be destroyed. But always . . . there will be the intoxication of power, constantly increasing and constantly growing subtler. Always, at every moment, there will be the thrill of victory, the sensation of trampling on an enemy who is helpless. If you want a picture of the future, imagine a boot stamping on a human face—forever.

Others argue that the process of transforming a democratic society into a totalitarian one was not quite so simple. They note that "life is almost always more complicated than we think. Behind the gleaming ranks of those who seem totalitarian robots stand men and women, various and diverse, complex and complicated, some brave, some cowardly, some brainwashed, some violently idiosyncratic, and all of them very human."[1]

READING 1

A Matter of Obedience?

*I*n her study of totalitarian regimes, Hannah Arendt wondered, "How do average, even admirable, people become dehumanized by the critical circumstances pressing in on them?" In the 1960s, Stanley Milgram, a professor at Yale University, decided to find out by recruiting college students to take part in what he called "a study of the effects of punishment on learning." In Milgram's words, "The point of the experiment is to see how far a person will proceed in a concrete and measurable situation in which he is ordered to inflict increasing pain on a protesting victim. . . . At what point will the subject refuse to obey the experimenter?"[2]

Working with pairs, Milgram designated one volunteer as "teacher" and the other as "learner." As the "teacher" watched, the "learner" was strapped into a chair with an electrode attached to each wrist. The "learner" was then told to memorize word pairs for a test and warned that wrong answers would result in electric shocks. The "learner" was, in fact, a member of Milgram's team. The real focus of the experiment was the "teacher." Each was taken to a separate room and seated before a "shock generator" with switches ranging from 15 volts labeled "slight shock" to 450 volts labeled "danger—severe shock." Each "teacher" was told to administer a "shock" for each wrong answer. The shock was to increase by fifteen volts every time the "learner" responded incorrectly. The volunteer received a practice shock before the test began to get an idea of the pain involved.

Before the experiment began, Milgram hypothesized that most volunteers would refuse to give electric shocks of more than 150 volts. A group of psychologists and psychiatrists predicted that less than one-tenth of 1 percent of the volunteers would administer all 450 volts. To everyone's amazement, 65 percent gave the full 450 volts!

Later Milgram tried to isolate the factors that encouraged obedience by varying parts of the experiment. In one variation, he repeated the test in a less academic setting. Obedience dropped to nearly 48 percent, still a very high number. In another variation, the volunteers received instructions by telephone rather than in person. Without an authority figure in the room, only 21 percent continued to the end. Milgram also noted that when no one in authority was present, some volunteers reacted to the "pain" of the "learner" by repeating a relatively low level shock rather than increasing voltage as instructed—an innovative compromise in Milgram's view.

In a third version of the test, each volunteer was surrounded by authority figures who argued over whether to continue the experiment. In this variation, no "teacher" continued until the end. In yet another variation, it appeared as if three "teachers" were giving shocks at the same time. Two, however, worked for Milgram. When they "quit," only 10 percent of the real volunteers continued.

The distance between the volunteer and the "learner" also made a difference. Only 40 percent of the "teachers" obeyed when the "learner" was in the same room. Obedience dropped to 30 percent when volunteers had to place the "learner's" hand on a metal plate to give the shock. On the other hand, when they had a lesser role in the experiment, 92 percent "went all the way." Gender had little effect on the outcome of the experiment. Men and women responded in very similar ways. Women did, however, show more signs of conflict over whether to obey. Philip Zimbardo, a psychologist at Stanford University, said of the experiments:

> The question to ask of Milgram's research is not why the majority of normal, average subjects behave in evil (felonious) ways, but what did the disobeying minority do after they refused to continue to shock the poor soul, who was so obviously in pain? Did they intervene, go to his aid, did they denounce the researcher, protest to higher authorities, etc.? No, even their disobedience was within the framework of "acceptability," they stayed in their seats, "in their assigned place," politely, psychologically demurred, and they waited to be dismissed by the authority. Using other measures of obedience in addition to "going all the way" on the shock generator, obedience to authority in Milgram's research was total.[3]

Zimbardo observed similar behavior in an experiment he supervised in 1971. He chose twenty-four young men—"mature, emotionally stable, normal, intelligent college students"—from seventy applicants. These men were arbitrarily designated as "guards" or "prisoners" in a simulated prison. The "guards" met to organize the prison and set up rules. Zimbardo reported what happened next.

> At the end of only six days we had to close down our mock prison because what we saw was frightening. It was no longer apparent to most of the subjects (or to us) where reality ended and their roles began. The majority had indeed become prisoners or guards, no longer able to clearly differentiate between role playing and self. There were dramatic changes in virtually every aspect of their behavior, thinking and feeling. In less than a week the experience of imprisonment undid (temporarily) a lifetime of learning; human values were suspended, self-concepts were challenged and the ugliest, most base, pathological

The question to ask of Milgram's research is not why the majority of normal, average subjects behave in evil (felonious) ways, but what did the disobeying minority do after they refused to continue to shock the poor soul, who was so obviously in pain? Did they intervene, go to his aid, did they renounce the researcher, protest to higher authorities, etc.?

side of human nature surfaced. We were horrified because we saw some boys (guards) treat others as if they were despicable animals, taking pleasure in cruelty, while other boys (prisoners) became servile, dehumanized robots who thought only of escape, of their own individual survival and of their mounting hatred for the guards.[4]

CONNECTIONS

Milgram has defined *obedience* as "the psychological mechanism that links individual action to political purpose." How do you define the word? What is *blind obedience*? How does it differ from other forms of obedience? What is the difference between *obedience* and *conformity*?

What encourages obedience? Is it fear of punishment? A desire to please? A need to go along with the group? A belief in authority? Record your ideas in your journal so that you can refer to them later.

➤*Obedience*, a documentary describing the Milgram experiment, is available from the Facing History Resource Center. After watching the film, discuss the following questions.

- As students watch the film, some laugh. How do you account for that laughter? Is it because something was funny or was there another reason? Those who study human behavior say that laughter can be a way of relieving tension, showing embarrassment, or expressing relief that someone else is "on the spot." Which explanation is most appropriate in this case?
- How did the volunteers act as they administered the shocks? What did they say? What pressures were placed on them as the experiment continued? How did they decide whether to stop?
- Did you identify with any of the volunteers you observed in *Obedience*?

Zimbardo said that he "called off the [prison] experiment not because of the horror I saw out there in the prison yard, but because of the horror of realizing that I could have easily traded places with the most brutal guard or become the weakest prisoner full of hatred at being so powerless that I could not eat, sleep or go to the toilet without permission of the authorities."[5] How would you like to think you would react?

A student who took part in an experiment set up by Zimbardo on deafness-induced paranoia expressed a dilemma posed by experiments like those of Milgram and Zimbardo. "I agree with the people who say it's not right to deceive human beings; it's not right to treat people as if they were mice. But I agree with Professor Zimbardo that he couldn't do his work on deafness and paranoia without deceiving his subjects, because if they knew what was going on, they wouldn't react the same as if they didn't. I can see both sides. That's my dilemma, and I don't think there's any simple answer to it, only complicated ones."[6] What is your position on "research through deception"? Should scientists be allowed to carry out such experiments?

Sociologists Herbert Kelman and V. Lee Hamilton related Milgram's experiments to events during the Vietnam War. They characterized incidents like the My Lai massacre in which an American armed forces unit destroyed a hamlet and killed hundreds of women and children as a "crime of obedience." What does that phrase mean to you? Can obedience be a crime? If so, give an example you have seen or read about. If not, explain why obedience can never be a crime.

➤ *The Wave,* an award-winning film, re-creates Ron Jones's classroom "experiment," the Third Wave. It raises important questions about conformity, peer pressure, and loyalty. Both the video and a transcript are available from the Facing History Resource Center. A teacher said of her students' responses, "They were spellbound. Most felt they would have joined the Third Wave; they used phrases like 'the power of belonging' and we discussed the vulnerability in us that makes us want to be part of a group, especially if it's elite." As you watch the film or read the transcript, think about the way you responded.

- What did it teach you about yourself? About why many people are attracted to a particular leader or want desperately to be part of a particular group?

- How might you have felt if you had been a student in Jones's class? Did he have a right to manipulate students to "teach them a lesson"? Would your answer be different if students had known in advance they were taking part in an "experiment"?

Some teachers use simulations to engage students "emotionally" or simulate affective experiences and learning. Unless a simulation includes a cognitive component, however, it has little or no learning value. It may even leave some students with the impression that they now "know what it was like" to have been a victim of the Nazis. That is just not true. Keep in mind that simulations also tend to oversimplify events and leave students with an inaccurate picture of the past. In addition, a number of simulations reinforce stereotypes; build on students' fears or insecurities; encourage ridicule; or violate the trust between student and teacher.

A Substitute for Religion

The Nazis offered Germans a philosophy—a way of looking at the world. It was a philosophy that allowed for no uncertainty or doubt. And for some, it became a substitute for religion. That was exactly what Hitler intended. "That is the most stupendous thing, that our movement should create for the broad, searching and erring masses a new belief upon which they can have absolute confidence and build, that they not be forsaken in this world of confusion, that they find again at least in some place a position where their hearts can rest easy."

"Beginning with the primer," Hitler wrote in *Mein Kampf*, "every theater, every movie, every advertisement must be subjected to the service of one great mission." That is why Nazi rallies resembled religious gatherings. It is also why young children were taught the following "Confession of Faith."

> I believe in the German mother who gave me birth.
>
> I believe in the German peasant who breaks the sod for his people.
>
> I believe in the German worker who performs work for his people.
>
> I believe in the dead who gave their lives for their people.
>
> For my god is my people.
>
> I believe in Germany!

The Nazis created holidays to celebrate their new faith. January 30 marked the day Hitler became chancellor and April 20 his birthday. Days set aside for party rallies at Nuremberg were also holidays. So was November 9, the anniversary of the attempted coup in the Munich beer hall. It was known as the Day of the Martyrs of the Movement.

March 21 became the Day of National Revival. Hitler observed the first celebration of the holiday in 1933. In a church in Potsdam, he told the German people that their days of despair were over; a glorious future was about to unfold. William Sheridan Allen wrote of the way people celebrated the day in a town he called "Thalburg." Although the town is not real, the events Allen described actually took place.

> In Thalburg all public offices were closed for the day. Shops closed early and also during the period from eleven thirty in the morning until one in the afternoon, in order to hear the ceremony over the radio. Radio sets were brought into the schools where the children listened to the events in Potsdam and had the explanation given to them by their teachers that "a new epoch in German history was beginning." Then they were given a holiday for the rest of the day. All houses and public

buildings were to bedeck themselves with swastika flags. After dark came a torchlight parade which wound through the whole of Thalburg. Participating were the various Nazi and Nationalist paramilitary units, all the sports clubs in Thalburg, all the various veterans' and patriotic societies, all the schools, and such miscellaneous groups as the Artisans' Training Club, the clerks and mail carriers from the post office, and the Volunteer Fire Department. Led by the town band, the SA band, and the SA fife-and-drum corps, the parade finally came to a halt in the city park, where [the local leader of the Nazi party] gave a speech in which he praised the new unity of Germany: "The individual is nothing; the Volk is everything. Once we unite internally, then we shall defeat the external foe. Then it will be 'Germany above all in the world.'" Upon this cue the crowd sang *Deutchland ueber Alles* and then dispersed.[7]

The rally itself took place in the evening, in keeping with Hitler's warning to party officials: "Never try to convert a crowd to your point of view in the morning sun. Instead dim lights are useful—especially the evening when people are tired, their powers of resistance are low, and their 'complete emotional capitulation' is easy to achieve." To heighten those emotions, the Nazis often played the music of Richard Wagner, a nineteenth-century composer who was both an antisemite and a strong German nationalist. His operas, which are based on German legends and myths, show the German people as Hitler wanted them shown—as mighty, inspiring, energetic, and patriotic.

In 1934, William Shirer, then a young reporter, saw Adolf Hitler for the first time at the largest of the annual rallies. He wrote in his diary:

> Like a Roman emperor Hitler rode into this medieval town [Nuremberg] at sundown, past solid phalanxes of wildly cheering Germans who packed the narrow streets. . . . Tens of thousands of Swastika flags blot out the Gothic beauties of the place, the facades of the old houses, the gabled roofs. The streets, hardly wider than alleys, are a sea of brown and black uniforms. . . .
>
> About ten o'clock tonight I got caught in a mob of ten thousand hysterics who jammed the moat in front of Hitler's hotel, shouting: "We want our Fuehrer." I was a little shocked at the faces, especially those of the women, when Hitler finally appeared on the balcony for a moment. . . . They looked up at him as if he were a Messiah, their faces transformed into something positively inhuman.[8]

The next day, Shirer wrote:

> I'm beginning to comprehend, I think, some of the reasons for Hitler's astounding success. Borrowing a chapter from the Roman Church, he is restoring pageantry and colour and mysticism to the drab lives of twentieth-century Germans. The morning's opening meeting in the huge Luitpold Hall on the outskirts of Nuremberg was more than a

No trick was overlooked: the advantage of oratory over written argument; the effects of lighting, atmosphere, symbols, and the crowd; the advantage of meetings held at night when the power to resist suggestions is low. Leadership works by skillful use of suggestion, of collective hypnosis, of subconscious motivation.

colorful show; it had something of the mysticism and religious fervor of an Easter or a Christmas Mass in a great Gothic cathedral.

The hall was a sea of brightly colored flags. Even Hitler's arrival was made dramatic. The band stopped playing. There was a hush over the thirty thousand people packed in the hall. Then the band struck up the "Badenweiler March," a very catchy tune and used only, I'm told, when Hitler makes his big entries. Hitler appeared in the back of the auditorium and followed by his aides, [Hermann] Goering, [Joseph] Goebbels, [Rudolf] Hess and [Heinrich] Himmler, and the others, he strode slowly down the wide center aisle while thirty thousand hands raised in salute. It is a ritual, the old-timers say, which is always followed.[9]

At another rally—one for party officials—an observer wrote:

> As Adolf Hitler is entering the Zeppelin Field, 150 floodlights of the Air Force blaze up. They are distributed around the entire square, and cut into the night, erecting a canopy of light in the midst of darkness. For a moment, all is deathly quiet. The surprise still is too great. Nothing like it has ever been seen before. The wide field resembles a powerful Gothic cathedral made of light. Bluish-violet shine the floodlights, and between their cone of light hangs the dark cloth of night. One hundred and forty thousand people—for it must be that many who are assembled here—cannot tear their eyes away from the sight. Are we dreaming, or is it real? Is it possible to imagine a thing like that? A cathedral of light? They do not have much time to pursue such thoughts, for a new spectacle is awaiting them. It is perhaps even more beautiful and compelling for those whose senses can embrace it.
>
> . . .Twenty-five thousand flags, that means 25,000 local, district, and factory groups from all over the nation. . . . Every one of these flag bearers is ready to give his life in the defense of every one of these pieces of cloth. There is not one among them to whom this flag is not the final command and the highest obligation.[10]

Even those who did not attend the rallies were caught up in the spirit they evoked. Horst Krueger lived in Eichkamp, a Berlin suburb. People there were skeptical of Hitler at first, but many quickly changed their minds.

> Suddenly over this tiny green oasis of the nonpolitical, the storm of the wide world had broken, not a storm of politics, but a springtime storm, a storm of German rejuvenation. Who wouldn't want to trim his sails for it?
>
> The black, white, and red flags of Imperial Germany, which the citizens of Eichkamp had always displayed in preference to the black-red-gold ones of the republic, were now joined by Nazi flags, many small and some large, often homemade, with a black swastika on a white ground; in their hurry, some people had sewn the swastika on backwards, but their good intentions were evident just the same.

Suddenly one was a somebody, part of a better class of people, on a higher level—a German.

Krueger notes that "the citizens of Eichkamp were eager to give themselves over to intoxication and rapture. They were weaponless. Suddenly one was a somebody, part of a better class of people, on a higher level—a German. Consecration permeated the German nation."[11]

CONNECTIONS

What is a *philosophy*? A *dogma*? Why would Hitler want his followers to regard Nazi ideas not just as a philosophy but as dogma?

Compare the prayer the Nazis wanted children to recite with a traditional prayer. What parallels do you notice? What differences seem most striking? How do you account for those differences? What role do religious leaders play in society? Why do you think Hitler wanted to assume that role?

How did Shirer regard the rally? What did he mean when he called it a *ritual*? What is a ritual? How do rituals unite people? Encourage conformity? Create a sense of tradition?

In *Mein Kampf*, Hitler explained the meaning of the symbols on the Nazi flag. "In *red* we see the social idea of the movement, in *white* the nationalist idea, in the *swastika* the vision of the struggle for the victory of the Aryan man." The colors on that flag—white, black, and red—were identical to those on the flag of Imperial Germany. Why do you think Hitler used the same colors? How powerful is a flag as the symbol of a nation? What messages does it convey to those who carry it? To those who find themselves in "a sea of brightly colored flags"? How did the Nazis use the flag to build loyalty? To make people feel that they were part of a great movement?

What does Krueger mean when he says, "Suddenly one was a somebody, part of a better class of people, on a higher level—a German"? How important is it to be "somebody"?

Ingmar Bergman, the Swedish filmmaker, was an exchange student in Germany in 1934. During his stay in the country, he lived with a minister and his family. He later recalled attending a Nazi rally in Weimar and listening to Sunday sermons based on *Mein Kampf*. By the time he returned to Sweden he was a "little pro-German fanatic." Only later did he learn what Nazism really meant. At the time, he was caught up in the intoxicating spirit of Nazi rallies and the clarity of its teachings. What do you think attracted the young Swede to the Nazis? Why do you think he later felt "shame and humiliation" whenever he recalled that attraction?

George Sabine describes Hitler as a leader who "manipulates the people as an artist molds clay." He notes, "No trick was overlooked: the advantage of oratory over written argument; the effects of lighting, atmosphere, symbols, and the crowd; the advantage of meetings held at night when the power to resist suggestions is low. Leadership works by skillful use of suggestion, of collective hypnosis, of subconscious motivation."[12] What evidence can you find in this reading to support Sabine's conclusion? How does his analysis help explain why Bergmann experienced shame and humiliation when he recalled his attraction to the Nazis?

➤Two videotapes document Nazi rallies. *Swastika* is a compilation of Nazi film footage put together by the British after World War II. *The Triumph of the Will*, a documentary of the 1934 Nuremberg rally, is the work of Leni Riefenstahl, a German filmmaker who sympathized with the Nazis. Both are available from the Facing History Resource Center. Riefenstahl once said, "The object of propaganda has little to do with truth. Its object is to make people lose their judgment."

In watching either film, it is important not to get caught up in the feelings it is designed to evoke. Begin by describing exactly what you observed without interpretation or judgment. Then analyze the film. What message does it convey? Who is sending that message? Who is it for? How did the director make the film attractive to that group? What emotions does he or she try to evoke? How are symbols and visual images used to arouse those emotions?

➤Even Jews living in Germany were sometimes caught up in the excitement of National Socialism. In the novel *Friedrich,* a young Jewish boy accompanies a non-Jewish friend to a meeting of Hitler Youth. He tells the friend, "You know, I saw you all marching through town with your flag and singing. I think it's really great. I'd love to take part, but Father won't let me join the *Jungvolk.*" For a similar incident, see the story of Janet B. in *Elements of Time*, pages 157-160. Her testimony can also be seen in the video montage *Friedrich,* available from the Facing History Resource Center.

Hans and Sophie Scholl were among those who became enamored with the Nazi movement in 1933. Their older sister, Inge, recalled, "For the first time politics entered our lives.… We heard a great deal of talk about Fatherland, comradeship, community of the *Volk*, and love of homeland." For more, see *Elements of Time*, pages 158-159.

READING 3

Propaganda

The Nazis used propaganda to sway the people of Eichkamp and other cities and towns. As Minister of Public Enlightenment and Propaganda, Joseph Goebbels was responsible for creating it. His job was to make sure that every form of expression—from music to textbooks and even sermons—trumpeted the same message.

In his diary, Goebbels wrote, "That propaganda is good which leads to success, and that is bad which fails to achieve the desired result, however intelligent it is, for it is not propaganda's task to be intelligent; its task is to lead to success. Therefore, no one can say your propaganda is too rough, too mean; these are not criteria by which it may be characterized. It ought not be decent nor ought it be gentle or soft or humble; it ought to lead to success. . . . Never mind whether propaganda is at a well-bred level; what matters is that it achieves its purpose." To achieve that purpose, Hitler insisted that "it must be limited to a very few points and must harp on these in slogans until the last member of the public understands what you want him to understand by your slogan. As soon as you sacrifice this slogan and try to be many-sided, the effect will piddle away."

Hitler and Goebbels did not invent propaganda. The word itself was coined by the Catholic Church to describe its efforts to counter Protestant teachings in the 1600s. Over the years, almost every nation has used propaganda to unite its people in wartime. Both sides spread propaganda during World War I, for example. Hitler and Goebbels employed it in very similar ways. They, too, wanted to counter the teachings of their opponents, shape public opinion, and build loyalty. But in doing so, they took the idea to new extremes.

Goebbels left nothing to chance. He controlled every word heard over the radio or read in a newspaper or magazine. And that control went well beyond censorship. He issued daily instructions on what to say and how to say it. Max von der Gruen said of those changes:

> All the activities of everyday life were given a military orientation. This military aura extended even into the realm of language. Henceforth one heard only:
> instead of "employment office"—"labor mobilization". . .
> instead of "worker"—"soldier of labor"
> instead of "work"—"service to Fuehrer and folk". . .
> instead of "factory meeting"—"factory roll call". . .
> instead of "production"—"the production battle."
> It is easy to understand that if, for whatever reasons, these words are hammered into a person's brain every day, they soon become a part of his language, and he does not necessarily stop and think about where they came from and why they were coined in the first place.[13]

The power to label ideas, events, groups, and individuals was central to Nazi efforts. Such labels made it clear who were the heroes and who were the enemies. In the process, the Nazis defined themselves as the guardians of the "true" Germany and the custodians of the nation's glorious past.

CONNECTIONS

Give an example of propaganda. Then compare your example with others in your class. What do they have in common? Use your answer to define *propaganda*. How do dictionaries define the word? What is the difference between persuasion in advertising and propaganda?

George Orwell has written that, "If thought corrupts language, language can also corrupt thought." What is he saying about the way propagandists use language?

Euphemisms are inoffensive terms used in place of more explicit language. In Germany, euphemisms disguised events, dehumanized Jews and other "enemies of the state," and diffused responsibility for specific actions. Thus the Nazis spoke of "cleanups," rather than "murders." They did not throw enemies into jail but took them into "protective custody." What is the difference? List current examples of euphemisms. How is each used? What do they have in common? Why do people use these euphemisms?

Government leaders today do not speak of propaganda but of "managing public opinion" or "putting the right spin on events." Are those terms euphemisms? If so, why do people need euphemisms for propaganda? If not, how do they differ from propaganda?

In 1989, Vaclav Havel led a nonviolent revolution in Czechoslovakia that replaced a communist regime with a democratic government. As a result of his experiences with totalitarianism, Havel argues:

> No word—at least in the rather metaphorical sense I am employing the word "word" here—comprises only the meaning assigned to it by an etymological dictionary. The meaning of every word also reflects the person who utters it, the situation in which it is uttered, and the reason for its utterance. The selfsame word can, at one moment, radiate great hopes; at another, it can emit lethal rays. The selfsame word can be true at one moment and false the next, at one moment illuminating, at another, deceptive.[14]

Havel therefore urged that people "listen carefully to the words of the powerful, to be watchful of them, to forewarn of their danger, and to proclaim their dire implications or the evil they might invoke." What words have been both illuminating and deceptive? How do leaders transform words that radiate hope into "lethal rays"?

According to poet Stephen Vincent Benet, "There are certain words, our own and others, we're used to—words we've used, heard, inherited, stuck away in the back drawer, in the locked trunk, at the back of the quiet mind." Do you have such words? What images do they evoke? How are they used in propaganda?

➤Bill Moyers has said of the power of propaganda, "In George Orwell's novel, *1984,* Big Brother, the totalitarian state, banishes history to the memory hole, . . . the shredding machine which eliminates all thoughts which are inconvenient to the state and so rids history of the facts of the past that disappear down the memory hole. The ministry of truth, propagandists, have the job every morning of rewriting history, rewriting reality." From what you know of Nazi propaganda, how well does Moyers' explanation apply to the Nazi state? To nations today? Moyers's ideas about propaganda and its effects on memory are taken from an interview conducted by Margot Stern Strom. The complete interview is available on video from the Facing History Resource Center. A summary of his presentation also appears in *Elements of Time*, pages 367-368.

Sybil Milton, senior historian and chief researcher at the U.S. Holocaust Memorial Museum, discusses the power of both positive and negative images in Nazi propaganda in a presentation summarized in *Elements of Time*, pages 368-370.

READING 4

Propaganda and Sports

*I*n 1936, the Olympics took place in Germany. The international event gave the Nazis a chance to show the world the power of the "new Germany." In the past, Germany was not considered a strong contender in the Olympics. Now German athletes won medal after medal, as German newspapers boasted that the nation was breeding a superior race. Yet the most outstanding athlete at the Olympics that year was not a German but an American. Max von der Gruen, who was ten years old that summer, later recalled,

> Although it was drummed into our heads every day that anything or anyone non-German was completely worthless, a black man became our idol: the American Jesse Owens, winner of four Olympic medals. In the playing field we used to play at being Jesse Owens; whoever could jump the farthest or run the fastest or throw some object the greatest distance became Jesse Owens.
>
> When our teachers heard us, they forbade us to play such games, but they never replied to our question of how a black man, a member of an "inferior" race, could manage to be such a consummate athlete.[15]

Marion Freyer Wolff was also ten years old that summer. As a Jew living in Berlin, her memories are bittersweet:

> In August 1936, the free world honored Hitler by allowing the Olympic Games to be held in Berlin. Hitler was so eager to have them in Germany that he was willing to make some minor compromises: stores and restaurants removed their We Don't Serve Jews signs for the duration of the event, and Jewish athletes participated in the games. Three Jewish women, representing Hungary, Germany, and Austria, won medals in fencing and received them from the hand of Hitler himself! . . .

The success of the Jewish athletes received no notice in the German press, but nobody could hide the fact that Jesse Owens, the black American sprinter, had earned four gold medals. I wondered how Hitler, who fancied himself a member of the super race, must have felt when he met this "inferior" non-Aryan again and again in the winner's circle. To the Jewish kids of Berlin, Jesse Owens became an instant idol and morale booster.[16]

How did Hitler respond? When urged to congratulate Owens in the interest of good sportsmanship, the Fuehrer shouted. "Do you really think that I will allow myself to be photographed shaking hands with a Negro"? Most visitors paid no attention to the slur. They focused instead on what Von der Gruen called "the sugar-coated facade of the Third Reich." Among those visitors was David Lloyd George, a former British prime minister who had negotiated the Treaty of Versailles. After meeting with Hitler, he wrote:

Whatever one may think of his methods—and they are certainly not those of a parliamentary country—there can be no doubt that he has achieved a marvellous transformation in the spirit of the people, in their attitude towards each other, and in their social and economic outlook. . . .

It is true that public criticism of the Government is forbidden in every form. That does not mean that criticism is absent. I have heard the speeches of prominent Nazi orators freely condemned.

But not a word of criticism or disapproval have I heard of Hitler.

He is as immune from criticism as a king in a monarchical country. He is something more. He is the George Washington of Germany—the man who won for his country independence from her oppressors.[17]

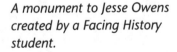

A monument to Jesse Owens created by a Facing History student.

CONNECTIONS

Some Americans wanted the United States to boycott the Olympics to show disapproval of Hitler's tactics. Others argued that sometimes you must overlook the bad to get to the good. That argument won many people over. As a result, the United States participated in the games. Based on your own experiences, does overlooking the bad help you get to the good? How does the argument allow one to avoid taking a stand? To duck his or her responsibility for "the bad"?

What connection do you see between the way German children viewed Owens and Hitler's refusal to congratulate him?

What did Lloyd George see when he visited Germany? What did he fail to see? Why do you think he was not bothered by the lack of democracy?

What was the function of sports in Nazi Germany? What role do sports play in the United States today?

For a discussion of the importance of sports in Nazi society, see the portrait of Peter Gay in *Elements of Time*, page 100.

READING 5

Art and Propaganda

*P*ropagandists have long know that "a picture is worth a thousand words." Therefore Hitler was determined that all works of art would reflect the ideals of National Socialism. He began by imprisoning or exiling what he called "degenerate" artists. Then he enlisted a corps of "obedient artists" willing to immortalize on canvas the fantasy world he described in his speeches and writings. In 1937, the Nazis sponsored three exhibits that reflected their views on art and artists.

The first, which opened in Munich in July, 1937, was a showing of nearly nine hundred paintings and sculptures of "true German art." The Nazis defined "true German art" as art that glorified the German countryside, the glories of the past, Aryan children, and animals. Such art was, of course, the work of "true German artists." All other artists and their work were considered "decadent" or "degenerate." According to historian Sybil Milton, "degenerate art" included "all works produced by Jewish artists; works with Jewish themes; works with pacifist subjects and art that did not glorify war; works with socialist or Marxist themes and works by other political enemies; works and objects with ugly faces and distorted figures; all expressionist works; all abstract art; and works that any Nazi bureaucrats found objectionable."[18]

Propagandists have long known that "a picture is worth a thousand words."

The Nazis also exhibited "degenerate art." That show was held in Munich too. To create the exhibit, a commission selected the 650 most "depraved" works of art from 16,000 paintings, drawings, prints, and sculptures confiscated from 32 German museums. Among the artists they singled out were George Grosz, Kaethe Kollwitz, and Wassily Kandinsky. The Nazis then grouped the art into such categories as "Insults to German Womanhood" and "Nature as Seen by Sick Minds." Next to each work , they hung a caption complaining about the price of the painting, its "Jewish-Bolshevik" leanings (actually only six of the 112 artists featured were Jewish), or its depiction of "cretins," "idiots," and "cripples." Over a four-year period, about three million people saw the exhibit in thirteen cities. When the show was over, about half of the art was destroyed. The rest was hidden in vaults.

The third exhibit, called *Der Ewige Jude* (The Eternal Jew), featured art that showed Jews as communists, swindlers, and sex-fiends. The Nazis used it to "teach" antisemitism. It, too, was well-attended. Over 150,000 people saw the exhibit in just three days. The art included in the show later found its way into a variety of publications, including children's books.

CONNECTIONS

Is "a picture worth a thousand words"? What can pictures do that words cannot do? Which makes a stronger impression on you?

The word *degenerate* means "evil" or "corrupt"; the word *decadent*, "decaying" or "rotting." Why do you think Hitler used these adjectives to describe art he considered "unGerman"?

➤An important lesson on propaganda is available from the Facing History Resource Center. In examining the propaganda piece included in that lesson or the one on this page:

- Look at the image and describe it exactly as you see it. Reserve judgment.
- Notice how the artist uses color, shape, space, and perspective to communicate a message. Look, too, for the way the artist uses symbols. What emotion is the artist trying to evoke?
- What is the message? To whom is it directed? Is it a single message? Or do others in your class interpret the work in other ways? Finally, make your own judgment about the poster.

Keep in mind that art is never objective; art is always subjective. It forces a viewer to adjust his or her perception in order to make a decision about the value and meaning of a particular work of art.

After World War II, the nations that defeated Germany had to decide what to do with art that glorified the Nazis. What would you have done?

Why did the Nazis find the works of art they considered "degenerate" so threatening? How were their attempts to destroy that art similar to the book burnings of 1933? What differences seem most striking? For a more detailed discussion of "degenerate" art, see the articles by Sybil Milton and David Joselit in *Elements of Time*, pages 368-372.

In 1991, the Los Angeles County Museum of Art displayed 175 works of art that were a part of Hitler's original exhibit of "degenerate art." The catalog for that exhibit is available from the Facing History Resource Center. Since then, other museums have shown the exhibit as well.

READING 6

Using Film as Propaganda

The Nazis were quick to see a potential for propaganda in a new form of art: film. It allowed them to combine visuals and words in ways that would have been impossible a few years earlier. Every movie made in Nazi Germany had a political function, even comedies. In each, Jews were always portrayed as villains or fools. The most inflammatory antisemitic films were *The Rothschilds*, *Jud Suess*, and *Der Ewige Jude* (The Eternal Jew). Goebbels even issued special instructions on how these movies were to be described. *The Rothschilds* and *Jud Suess*, for example, were to be treated as "faithful reenactments" of historical events. Therefore one publication referred to *The Rothschilds* as an historical account of the way Jews profited from England's victory over Napoleon "while nations are bleeding on the battlefield." Napoleon's defeat was a "victory won by gold, a Rothschild victory, a victory for the Star of David."

A brochure sent out by the information office stated, "Clean-shaven and dressed like a gentleman, the Jew Suess Oppenheimer contrives to be appointed Finance Minister to the Duke of Wuerttemberg. . . Matching one another in treachery, the court Jew and Minister Suess Oppenheimer and his secretary outbid one another in tricks and intrigue to bleed the people of Wuerttemberg. . . The Jew Suess Oppenheimer violates the beautiful Dorothea Sturm, an outrageous act which confirms the extent of his guilt . . . . Jew, hands off German women!"

In the beginning we create the enemy. We *think* others to death and then invent the battle-axe or the ballistic missiles with which to actually kill them. Propaganda precedes technology.

Although both films completely distorted historical events, German film critics praised their accuracy. One reporter admired *Jud Suess* for its "complete avoidance of bias," and said "its clear demonstration of a previous attempt in miniature to subjugate a country foreshadowed the later aspirations towards domination of the whole globe."

Although the third film, *Der Ewige Jude*, was hailed as a documentary, the narration made such outrageous accusations against the Jews that it was omitted from the version shown abroad. Officials feared the tone might damage the film's "credibility." Marion Pritchard, then a graduate student in the Netherlands, said of the film:

> At that time there were still Jewish students in the school and the faculty was partly Jewish. We went to see this movie and sat and made smart remarks all the way through and laughed at it because it was so outrageous. And yet when we came out of the movie, one of my Gentile friends said to me, "I wish I hadn't seen it. I know that it was all ridiculous and propaganda, but for the first time in my life I have a sense of them and us—Jews and Gentiles. I'm going to do everything I can to help them, but I wish I didn't have this feeling."[19]

CONNECTIONS

Most people regard unity as a positive idea, but, as an American diplomat once warned, unity can also be "organized hatred." How do his words apply to Hitler's efforts to build unity? To Hitler's focus on a common enemy? How do they explain why he once said that "if the Jew did not exist, we should invent him"? After the war, a minister who lived in Nazi Germany said of antisemitism, "It was already there. It's not at all the case that Herr Goebbels invented all of it; rather, the entire ideology and also the rhetoric were there. [The Nazis] had only to take it and carry it to the logical conclusion."[20] What is he suggesting about why some propaganda is more effective than other propaganda?

Hitler once wrote, "If you tell a lie big enough and long enough, people will believe you." How did he apply that principle to movies made during the Third Reich? Why did he have to be careful that the lie not be too big or too outrageous?

What did Marion Pritchard's friend mean when she said, "I know that it was all ridiculous and propaganda, but for the first time in my life I have a sense of them and us—Jews and Gentiles"? How do you explain her statement?

➤"In the beginning we create the enemy," writes Sam Keen. "We *think* others to death and then invent the battle-axe or the ballistic missiles with which to actually kill them. Propaganda precedes technology." Based on your reading thus far, how did this process unfold in Nazi Germany? What examples can you find in current events? Sam Keen's book, *Faces of the Enemy*, and the video by the same name, explore both questions in great detail and demonstrate that images of the enemy are remarkably similar in cultures around the world. Both the book and the video are available from the Facing History Resource Center.

➤➤Bill Moyers interviewed Fritz Hippler, the producer of *Der Ewige Jude*, fifty years after he made the film. Moyers later said that he was "struck by the cold realization that [Hippler] thought the only mistake Hitler had made was to lose the war. Here he was in 1981, sitting there in the reconstructed Germany of our times, regretting only that he, Hippler, and Adolf Hitler had been on the losing side." *The Propaganda Battle*, a video that contains the complete interview with Hippler, is available from the Facing History Resource Center. The video also includes an interview with Frank Capra who made propaganda films for the United States during World War II.

Bohdan Wytwycky writes, "One of the effects of prejudice directed at whole categories of people is that it robs these people of their humanity. Made stereotypes of evil, stupidity and social disease, the victims are forced to travel the first leg of the journey to subhuman status. Made a depository of inferior or socially pathological traits, they receive a rude shove down the slippery slope to total dehumanization."[21] How was that process evident in the way the Nazis used films to stereotype Jews?

➤➤How does the media shape our views of ourselves and others? African Americans make up about twelve percent of the population of the United States but represent only about three percent of the positive images projected by advertising. The images not only affect how they are seen but also how they view themselves. The video *Color Adjustments* documents the way African Americans are portrayed on television. You may wish to collect news stories, advertisements, and editorials that refer to African Americans or to another minority group—Arab Americans, Japanese Americans, Native Americans, or Puerto Ricans. How often was the group portrayed in a positive manner? In a negative way? After reporting your findings to the class, discuss how the media shapes our views of ourselves and others.

➤➤A video, *The World Is a Dangerous Place: Images of the Enemy on Children's Television*, is available from the Facing History Resource Center. What does it suggest about the power of images today? What can we do to protect ourselves from being manipulated by propaganda? What techniques would you recommend?

School for Barbarians

Hitler believed he was on the side of history. He claimed that "When an opponent declares, 'I will not come over to your side,' I calmly say, 'Your child belongs to us already. You will pass on. Your descendants, however, now stand in the new camp. In a short time they will know nothing else but this new community.'" In Hitler's mind, young Germans were the key. In speech after speech, he declared:

> We older ones are used up. Yes, we are old already. . . .We are cowardly and sentimental. . . . But my magnificent youngsters? Are there finer ones anywhere in the world? Look at these young men and boys? What material! With them I can make a new world. . . .
>
> A violently active, dominating, intrepid, brutal youth—that is what I am after. Youth must be all those things. It must be indifferent to pain. There must be no weakness or tenderness in it. I want to see once more in its eyes the gleam of pride and independence of the beast of prey. . . . I intend to have an athletic youth—that is the first and the chief thing. . . . I will have no intellectual training. Knowledge is ruin to my young men.

By 1939, about 90 percent of the "Aryan" children in Germany belonged to Nazi youth groups. They started at the age of six. At ten, boys were initiated into the *Jungvolk* and at fourteen promoted to the Hitler Youth or HJ (for Hitler Jugend). Girls belonged to the Jungmaedel and then the BDM (the *Bund Deutscher Maedel* or the League of German Girls). In such groups, said Hitler, "These young people will learn nothing else but how to think German and act German. . . . And they will never be free again, not in their whole lives."

Erika Mann, a German who opposed the Nazis, wrote a book called *School for Barbarians*. It explained to Americans how the Nazis tried to carry out Hitler's ideas.

> Every child says "Heil Hitler!" from 50 to 150 times a day, immeasurably more often than the old neutral greetings. The formula is required by law; if you meet a friend on the way to school, you say it; study periods are opened and closed with '"Heil Hitler!"; "Heil Hitler!" says the postman, the street-car conductor, the girl who sells you notebooks at the stationery store; and if your parents' first words when you come home to lunch are not "Heil Hitler!" they have been guilty of a punishable offense, and can be denounced. "Heil Hitler!" they shout, in the Jungvolk and Hitler Youth. "Heil Hitler!" cry the girls in the League of German Girls. Your evening prayers must close with "Heil Hitler!" if you take your devotions seriously.

When an opponent declares, "I will not come over to your side," I calmly say, "Your child belongs to us already. . . .You will pass on. Your descendants, however, now stand in the new camp. In a short time they will know nothing else but this new community."

Officially—when you say hello to your superiors in school or in a group—the words are accompanied by the act of throwing the right arm high; but an unofficial greeting among equals requires only a comparatively lax lifting of the forearm, with the fingers closed and pointing forward. This Hitler greeting, this "German" greeting, repeated countless times from morning to bedtime, stamps the whole day.

"Heil" really means salvation, and used to be applied to relations between man and his God; one would speak of ewiges Heil (eternal salvation), and the adjective "holy" derives from the noun. But now there is the new usage. . . .

You leave the house in the morning, "Heil Hitler" on your lips; and on the stairs of your apartment house you meet the Blockwart. A person of great importance and some danger, the Blockwart has been installed by the government as a Nazi guardian. He controls the block, reporting on it regularly, checking up on the behavior of its residents. It's worth it to face right about, military style, and to give him the "big" Hitler salute, with the right arm as high as it will go. All the way down the street, the flags are waving, every window colored with red banners, and the black swastika in the middle of each. You don't stop to ask why; it's bound to be some national event. Not a week passes without an occasion on which families are given one reason or another to hang out the swastika. Only the Jews are excepted under the strict regulation. Jews are not Germans, they do not belong to the "Nation," they can have no "national events."

You meet the uniforms on the way to school: the black [uniformed] S.S. men, the men of the Volunteer Labor Service, and the Reichswehr soldiers. And if some of the streets are closed, you know that an official is driving through town. Nobody has ever told you that the high officials of other countries pass without the precautions of closed streets.

H.J. DEUTSCHE ARBEITER JUGEND

And here, where a building is going up, the workmen are gone— probably because of the "national event." But the sign is on the scaffolding. "We have our Fuehrer to thank that we are working here today. Heil Hitler!" The familiar sign, seen everywhere with men at work, on roads, barracks, sport fields. What does it mean to you? Do you think of a world outside, with workers who need not thank a Fuhrer for their jobs? Certainly not—what you have, imprinted on your mind, is the sentence, deep and accepted as an old melody.

There are more placards as you continue past hotels, restaurants, indoor swimming pools, to school. They read "No Jews allowed;" "Jews not desired here;" "Not for Jews." And what do you feel? Agreement? Pleasure? Disgust? Opposition? You don't feel any of these. You don't feel anything, you've seen these placards for almost five years. This is a habit, it is all perfectly natural, of course Jews aren't allowed here. Five years in the life of a child of nine—that's his life, after four years of infancy, his whole personal, conscious existence.

Through the Nazi street walks the Nazi child. There is nothing to disturb him, nothing to attract his attention or criticism. The stands sell Nazi papers almost exclusively; all German papers are Nazi; foreign papers are forbidden, if they do not please the men at the top. The child won't be surprised at their huge headlines: "UNHEARD-OF ACTS OF VIOLENCE AGAINST GERMANY IN CZECHOSLOVAKIA!" "JEWISH GANGSTERS RULE AMERICA!" "THE COMMUNIST TERROR IN SPAIN SUPPORTED BY THE POPE!" "150 MORE PRIESTS UNMASKED AS SEXUAL CRIMINALS!"

"That's how it is in the world," the child thinks. "What luck we're in, to have a Fuehrer. He'll tell the whole bunch—Czechs, Jews, Americans, Communists and priests—where to get off!"

There are no doubts, no suspicion at the coarse and hysterical tone of the dispatches, no hint that they may be inexact or false. No, these things are part of the everyday world of the Nazis, like the Blockwart, the swastika, the signs reading "No Jews allowed." They add up to an atmosphere that is torture, a fuming poison for a free-born human being.

The German child breathes this air. There is no other condition wherever Nazis are in power; and here in Germany they do rule everywhere, and their supremacy over the German child, as he learns and eats, marches, grows up, breathes, is complete.[22]

CONNECTIONS

Hitler demanded that the nation produce a "violently active, dominating, intrepid, brutal youth." What part did the schools play in carrying out that goal? What part did youth groups play? The media? Society as a whole? How do your answers explain why Erika Mann called her book *School for*

Barbarians? What type of society would graduates of a "school for barbarians" create?

Hitler described his ideal youth. What is the ideal in American society? Do you know of anyone who fits either ideal?

Why do you think Hitler referred to German youth as "my young men"? Why didn't he mention young women?

What does Hitler mean when he says that after joining a Nazi youth group, young Germans "will never be free again, not in their whole lives"? What characteristics did the youth groups foster in young people? For example, why did members wear uniforms and arm bands? Have a special salute? Take part in rallies and parades?

Write a working definition of the word *indoctrinate*. How does it differ from the word *educate*? How did Hitler indoctrinate young Germans? Why did he focus his efforts on them rather than their parents?

Compare Hitler's view of education with traditional views of education in Germany (Chapter 3, Reading 7). What parallels do you notice? What differences seem most striking? How difficult would it be for a teacher in a traditional German school to teach in a Nazi school?

Describe the messages a child would hear in Nazi Germany. How would those messages affect the way he or she viewed the world? How does such an atmosphere turn hatred into a habit?

What did Erika Mann mean when she said that after a time the child did not feel anything? Does hearing the same message over and over again affect you in the same way? Is Mann's book propaganda?

➤*The Klan Youth Corps,* a CBS News Special Report produced in 1982, documents the efforts of the Ku Klux Klan to recruit young people. The video is available from the Facing History Resource Center. Today the Klan has competition from various neo-Nazi groups. Morris Dees, the founder of the Southern Poverty Law Center, says of young people attracted to such groups, "Psychologists say that these young haters generally come from deeply troubled, dysfunctional families and are fundamentally damaged long before they swing their first baseball bat at someone or plant their first pipe bomb. Vulnerable but streetwise youngsters, who are looking for an excuse to fight, they are easy prey for older white supremacist leaders, who cynically offer a sense of family and purpose—along with a hate-filled ideology."[23] Compare members of neo-Nazi groups with members of the Klan Youth Corps and Hitler Youth. What traits do they share? What differences seem most striking?

Morris Dees and the Southern Poverty Law Center are described in Chapter 11, Reading 2. See also *Choosing to Participate,* pages 205-212.

Belonging

Alfons Heck, like many of his classmates, was eager to join Hitler Youth. He later recalled:

> Far from being forced to enter the ranks of the Jungvolk, I could barely contain my impatience and was, in fact, accepted before I was quite 10. It seemed like an exciting life, free from parental supervision, filled with "duties" that seemed sheer pleasure. Precision marching was something one could endure for hiking, camping, war games in the field, and a constant emphasis on sports. . . . To a degree, our pre-war activities resembled those of the Boy Scouts, with much more emphasis on discipline and political indoctrination. There were the paraphernalia and the symbols, the pomp and the mysticism, very close in feeling to religious rituals. One of the first significant demands was the so-called Mutprobe: "test of courage," which was usually administered after a six-month period of probation. The members of my Schar, a platoon-like unit of about 40-50 boys, were required to dive off the three-meter board—about 10 feet high—head first in the town's swimming pool. There were some stinging belly flops, but the pain was worth it when our Fahnleinfuehrer, the 15-year-old leader of our Fahnlein (literally "little flag"), a company-like unit of about 160 boys, handed us the coveted dagger with its inscription Blood and Honor. From that moment on we were fully accepted.[24]

Not everyone in Nazi Germany was accepted. When Elizabeth Dopazo and her brother were very young, their parents were sent to concentration camps because of their religious beliefs; they were Jehovah's Witnesses. Elizabeth and her brother went to live with their grandparents. She recalls:

> I had met my grandparents once before. It was very difficult for my brother and me. I was seven at this point and he was six, and we spoke a dialect much as if Southern children would come up here and people made fun of them because of how they look and sound and what their parents stand for. My grandparents were Jehovah's Witnesses too, but not as strong. They stopped going to meetings when we came because they felt they would be arrested too and then what would happen to us? So they kept a very low profile.
>
> We had to quickly change our way of speaking so maybe we wouldn't be so noticeable. In school right away it started, you see. We had to raise our right arm and say "Heil Hitler" and all that sort of thing and then we didn't do it a few times. A few times was all right. You can drop a handkerchief, you can do a little something, but quickly

they look and they say, "Ah, you're different and you're new in the school." So you're watched a little more closely. You might get one or two children who'd tell on you but it was rare. The teacher would bring you to the front of the class and say "Why don't you say Heil Hitler"? and you were shaking already because you knew, unlike other children, if you told them the real reason there'd be trouble. For us to say "Heil Hitler" and praise a person would be against our belief. We shouldn't, because we had already pledged our allegiance to God and that's it. So, we could stand and be respectful to the government, but we were not to participate in any adulation for political figures.

We didn't want to offend God. We thought we could die, but that doesn't mean much, but if we offend God then we lose out altogether. That much we knew, but then we didn't want to explain why because we were afraid that by the time we got home our grandparents wouldn't be there and we would be put in an institution, so we used to make little excuses but you can't do that every day. So in no time at all we also said it, because we were just too afraid.

My brother and I talked about all these things at home after school. We had a little attic we used to go in and discuss what would be best. We grew up very fast. We never really had a childhood. . . .

Later, around age twelve or thirteen, we joined the Hitler Youth, which we actually didn't want to do, but the Gestapo came to my grandparents' house, just like you've seen it in the movies with the long leather coats on and they stood at the front door and they were saying, "Your grandchildren have to join the Hitler Youth and if they don't by Thursday we will take stronger measures." After they'd left we told our grandparents we'll join tomorrow, even if we hate all that stuff. They agreed we'd better do it and we very quickly donned those uniforms. . . .

As time went on, my brother, when he was thirteen or fourteen, sort of was swayed. You know, you have to believe in something. He wanted to be a German officer and said our father had been wrong all along and that we went to the dogs for our father's beliefs. He died for his ideals and where are we? He was very angry. I was too, but not as much. I was torn between what would be the good thing to do and what would not.

In fact, just before the war ended, we were afraid my brother would denounce—that he would go to the authorities and say that my family is against the regime and I don't want anything to do with them anymore; I want to join the army and I don't want my family hindering me in getting ahead because they've done that enough as it is. We were not allowed to go to higher education because we were a detriment to others. So you can imagine how he felt when the war finished. He was all disillusioned and shattered.[25]

If belonging was difficult for Elizabeth Dopazo and her brother, it was impossible for Frank, one of two Jewish children in a school in Breslau. He too still recalls his school days.

> People started to pick on me, "a dirty Jew," and all this kind of thing. And we started to fight. In the break time there was always one of us fighting. There was my friend, and he was one class above me, he fought in every break. . . . I started to fight, too, because they insulted me too much or they started to fight, whatever it was.
>
> We were very isolated, and one order came out after another. . . . [One] order says all Jews must greet with the German greeting. The German greeting was "Heil Hitler" and raising your hand. Then the next order came out, and it says the Jews are not allowed to greet people with the "Heil Hitler" signal. Okay, so, in Germany you had to greet every teacher. When you see a teacher on the street, you had to respect them and you had to greet him—you had to bow down. . . .
>
> Now we were in an impossible situation because we went up the stairs, and we saw one teacher, and we said "Heil Hitler." And he turned around. "Aren't you a Jew? You're not allowed to greet me with Heil Hitler." But if I didn't greet him at all, then the next teacher would say "Aren't you supposed to greet [me with] Heil Hitler"? And this was always accompanied with a punishment . . . . Not all of them but some of them, the teachers that knew me and would pick on me—they'd punish me, put me in a corner, or humiliate me in one way or another . . . .
>
> You had to raise your hand and salute when the flag passed and Jews weren't allowed to do it. . . . If you don't salute, you immediately were recognized as a Jew, and you really were left to the mercy of the people who saw you, what they would do with you. They could perfectly well kill you on the street and, you know, nobody really would say anything because there was no such thing as a court and, after all, it was only a Jew. So we were. . . we knew that we were in constant danger, that if we would stick out, that if we would do anything, we were at the mercy of people. There was nobody to complain to. You couldn't complain to the Jews. You couldn't complain to any courts. You couldn't complain to the police.[26]

CONNECTIONS

How important is it to you to "look right"? To "act right"? Fit in? How do you feel when you don't belong? How does it affect your self-esteem? When in a child's development is he or she most vulnerable to issues related to "in" and "out" group behavior? Are adolescents more or less vulnerable than young children?

The Nazis created a world in which young people were "free" from parental supervision. Why would such a world be particularly appealing to adolescents? What problems did that world create for children like Elizabeth who wanted to belong but also wanted to remain true to her family's values and beliefs? Do young people today ever find themselves in similar situations? If so, how do they cope?

What situation did Frank face in school? On the street? Was there any place where he was safe? Did Frank have to accept Hitler's definition of a Jew? Explain your answers.

➤More memories of school days in Nazi Germany can be found in the video montage *Childhood Experiences of German Jews*, available at the Facing History Resource Center. A description of those reminiscences appears in *Elements of Time*, pages 135-153. A video entitled *Confessions of a Hitler Youth* recounts Alfons Heck's experiences in Nazi Germany. It, too, is available from the Resource Center.

READING 9

Models of Obedience

Hede von Nagel now lives in California but grew up in Nazi Germany. She writes of her childhood:

> As my parents' second daughter, I was a great disappointment to my father, who wanted to produce sons for the Fuehrer and the nation—and, because he was of the nobility, to carry on the family name.
>
> He was furious that, unlike my fair-haired older sister, who looked so Nordic, I had been cursed with auburn hair and dark brown eyes. Then came a third child, this time a male, but he was a dark-eyed redhead—another letdown for my patriotic father. Only when another son was born and proved to be the very model of a tow-headed, blue-eyed Aryan was my father satisfied. "At last," he said, "the child I wanted."
>
> Our parents taught us to raise our arms and say "Heil Hitler" before we said "Mama." This type of indoctrination was universal. Children experienced it in kindergarten, at home—everywhere. We grew up believing that Hitler was a supergod, and Germany an anointed nation. We were taught our German superiority in everything. Country, race, science, art, music, history, literature.
>
> At the same time, our parents and teachers trained my sister and me to be the unquestioning helpmates of men; as individuals, we had no right to our own opinion, no right to speak up. We were to be models of obedience, work and toughness, ever eschewing complaints, creativity or artistic pursuits.

The worst fate was to be laughed at and publicly humiliated—grim possibilities that served the Nazis as a major educational technique.

Indeed, it would have been dangerous for us to show any initiative or spontaneity, nor would it have befitted a German girl to favor feminine dresses, ruffles or makeup.

As for gentleness or sweetness or tearfulness, these were forbidden traits, and any display of them would have made us outcasts. The worst fate was to be laughed at and publicly humiliated—grim possibilities that served the Nazis as a major educational technique.

The books we read were full of stories glorifying Hitler. In them, the bad guy was usually a Jew. I had never known a Jew personally, and so the Jews I read about were personifications of the devil—too evil to be real.[27]

A former member of Hitler Youth has similar memories.

[It's] especially easy to manipulate children at that age. . . . If you can drill the notion into their heads, you are from a tribe, a race that is especially valuable. And then you tell them something about the Germanic tribes, their loyalty, their battles, how Germanic women let themselves be hitched up to carts to fight against the Romans. You, you're a child of this race, a people that dealt the Romans a destructive blow in the year 9 A.D., all that sort of thing. Then there were the songs. . . ."What we swear is written in the stars, he who directs the stars will hear our voice". . . "Before the foreigner robs you of your crown, O Germany, we would prefer to fall side by side." Or "The flag is dearer than death." Death was nothing. The flag, the people—they were everything. You are nothing, your people everything. Yes, that's how children were brought up, that's how you can manipulate a child.[28]

Alfons Heck is not as certain it was just propaganda.

Traditionally, the German people were subservient to authority and respected their rulers as exalted father figures who could be relied on to look after them. A major reason why the Weimar Republic, despite its liberal constitution, did not catch on with many Germans, was the widespread impression that no one seemed to be firmly in charge. Hitler used that yearning for a leader brilliantly. From our very first day in the Jungvolk, we accepted it as a natural law—especially since it was merely an extension of what we had learned in school— that a leader's orders must be obeyed unconditionally, even if they appeared harsh, punitive or unsound. It was the only way to avoid chaos. This chain of command started at the very bottom and ended with Hitler.

I still recall with wonder that [our leader] once marched all 160 of us in his Fahnlein into an ice-cold river in November because our singing had displeased him. We cursed him bitterly under our breath, but not one of us refused. That would have been the unthinkable crime of disobeying a "direct order." During the war, such a refusal could be used—and frequently was—to put the offender before a firing squad.[29]

How did each of the Germans quoted in this reading believe they acquired their attitudes and values? How do you think you acquired yours? Compare your upbringing to theirs. What differences seem most striking?

Why is it important that a child be taught to obey? At what point does obedience become dangerous? What is the difference between obedience and conformity? How do you address the issue of "blind obedience"? Examine the process of your thinking.

Just as it was a status symbol for German parents to have a blonde-haired child, it was a stigma to have a disabled child. What value do parents today and society in general place on a child's gender? His or her appearance?

➤ An interview with Robert Spaethling, a former member of Hitler Youth and now a professor at the University of Massachusetts in Boston, is available from the Facing History Resource Center. See also Carl's excerpt in *Childhood Memories*.

READING 10

The Birthday Party

*E*rika Mann described what happened when the parents of a 12-year-old boy organized a birthday party.

> They gave him a birthday party, with ordinary, normal, "civilian" presents: a paintbox, a picture puzzle, a shining new bicycle—and lit twelve candles on his birthday cake. How they looked forward to that party! And it went off like a political conference. Six boys had been invited, and five of them came right on time.
>
> "Who's missing"? the mother asked.
>
> "Can't you see"? said the boy, "HE's missing—Fritzekarl!"
>
> "What a pity!" she answered. That it should be just Fritzekarl. Two years older than her son, he was the leader in the Jungvolk, and his presence at the party was of great importance. If he did not appear, it was a sign of disfavor; the whole thing would be spoiled.
>
> The boys, in their Hitler Youth uniforms, stood around the birthday table, not knowing quite what to do with the toys. The bicycle pleased all of them, with its bell (which they took turns ringing) and its rubber tires, which were so hard to get nowadays, and which the father had finally been able to obtain after using all of his contacts in the Party, paying a high cash price, and emphasizing the fact that this was a wheel for a boy, a Jungvolk boy, and not for a girl who would never go

to war. Now it stood there, complete with instructions and a copy of the German Cyclist, saying, "Boys on bicycles must try to remember the names of towns, rivers, mountains and lakes as well as the material and type of architecture of bridges, etc. They may be able to make use of this knowledge for the good of the Fatherland."

The bell rang, and the son dashed to the front door. A sharp voice came through, crying "Heil Hitler!" and the five boys at the table turned on their heels as the answer came in a voice already breaking, "Heil Hitler!" Their superior officer was received with the "German salute," five hands raised, great composure, solemn faces. Solemnly, Fritzekarl gave the host his birthday present—a framed photograph of the Leader of the Reich Youth, Baldur von Schirach, with a facsimile autograph. The son clicked his heels as he received it.

"I wish to speak to your father," Fritzekarl said curtly.

The mother answered in her friendly voice, "My husband is not free just now—he's upstairs working."

Fritzekarl attempted to keep the note of military command in his shrill young voice. "Just the same, madam, I should prefer to speak to your husband for a moment. . . . In the interest of your son."

His manner was correct, in spite of his tone. He bowed slightly to the mother as he finished his masterful little speech.

"Fourteen years old!" she thought, "but the mechanism of power backs him up, and he knows it."

The son was blushing violently. "For goodness' sake call him!" he said, stepping toward his mother.

The father came down at once.

"Heil Hitler!" cried Fritzekarl.

"Heil Hitler!" repeated the man. "What can I do for you, Lieutenant"?

"Pardon me," says Fritzekarl, who doesn't get the joke, and retains his martial stare, "but your son was absent from our last practice exercises. . . ."

"Yes, I know," the father interrupts at this point, "he had a cold."

"It was at your suggestion that he absented himself," Fritzekarl continues, his voice breaking and going hoarse over the phrase, "You wrote me some sort of excuse, to say that he was staying home at your wish."

The father puts his weight first on one foot and then on the other. "As a matter of fact, it is my wish that he stay home when he has such a severe cold."

"Oh, I didn't have such a bad cold at all," the son breaks in. He is leaning on the handlebars of the bicycle that his father had to fight for. "I could have gone, perfectly well."

The man looks at his son, a long look of surprise and pain and the resignation he has learned. "Well," he says, and moves toward the door.

But Fritzekarl stops him. "A moment, please," he insists, but politely. "Your son was in school on that day and the following day. So he cannot have been really ill. Let me call your attention to the fact that he should have been present at practice and that it is my duty to report the absence!"

"Oh, please—" the boy was speaking for his father, quickly, bargaining "—don't do that, please? It won't ever happen again—will it, father? —really, never again!"

The father wanted to protest; he felt the despairing look of his wife, the outrage and embarrassment of the scene. "How dare you speak to me like that!" was what he was repeating in his mind. But he knew the consequences of such an argument, for himself, and for his son. Even if he could convince the Nazi authorities of his own part, and Fritzekarl's rudeness, his son would still have to face the Jungvolk, paying for his father's moment of "courage." And so he only said, hesitatingly and stiffly, "No—it certainly will never happen again!"

"I thank you," replied the fourteen-year-old superior of the treasonable son. The father was dismissed.

He cannot air his resentment; he has to expect eavesdroppers and spies everywhere. His wife tells their son everything—not out of malice, but in the mistaken hope of reclaiming him this way. And the new maid is a person to be feared. She listens at doors, reads everything that's lying around the house, and she happens to be having an affair with a Blockwart; he could destroy a family single-handed. The boy would hardly denounce his own father, the man reflects, but if he repeats some remark to the maid, she will run to her Blockwart, the Gestapo (Secret State Police) will have it right away, and the doom will begin to move on them. Or, if they decide to dismiss the maid, her vengeance hanging over their heads may be even worse.[30]

CONNECTIONS

After reading this story, a boy said that "this is like a world upside down—the children have the power." Do you agree? Did the children really have power? If so, what was the source of their power?

The boy's mother hoped to reclaim her son. How was he lost? The father wanted to protest but feared the consequences. What were the consequences? What did he mean when he said his son would have to pay for the father's "courage"?

Today people speak of family values. What are they? How do they relate to life in Nazi Germany?

➤Walter K., the only Jewish boy in a German classroom in 1935, lamented that when he was treated unfairly by his teacher, there was "no one to complain to." Because his teacher was a Nazi, neither his parents nor the principal could be of help. Have you ever felt helpless? Unable to secure assistance from the adults in your life? How did you feel? How did you cope? For more about Walter's experiences, see *Elements of Time*, pages 234-238, and the video *Childhood Memories* available from the Facing History Resource Center. Also available is the video *Blood and Honor*, which offers another view of Hitler Youth.

READING 11

A Matter of Loyalty

*H*ans Scholl, like Fritzekarl, was a group leader in Hitler Youth. His sister described how he became disillusioned with the movement.

Hans had assembled a collection of folk songs, and his young charges loved to listen to him singing, accompanying himself on his guitar. He knew not only the songs of the Hitler Youth but also the folk songs of many peoples and many lands. How magically a Russian or Norwegian song sounded with its dark and dragging melancholy. What did it not tell us of the soul of those people and their homeland!

But some time later a peculiar change took place in Hans; he was no longer the same. Something disturbing had entered his life. It could not be the remonstrances of his father—no, because to them he simply played deaf. It was something else. His songs were forbidden, the leader had told him. And when he had laughed at this, they threatened him with disciplinary action. Why should he not be permitted to sing these beautiful songs? Only because they had been created by other peoples? He could not understand it, and this depressed him, and his usual carefree spirit began to wane.

At this particular time he was given a very special assignment. He was to carry the flag of his troop to the party's national rally at Nuremberg. He was overjoyed. But when he returned we hardly dared trust our eyes. He looked tired, and on his face lay a great disappointment. We did not expect an explanation, but gradually we learned that the youth movement which had been held up to him as an ideal image was in reality something totally different from what he had imagined the Hitler Youth to be. There drill and uniformity had been extended into every sphere of personal life. But he had always believed that every boy should develop his own special talents. Thus through his imagination, his ingenuity, his unique personality, each member could have enriched the group. But in Nuremberg everything had been done according to the same mold. There had been talk, day and night, about loyalty. But what was the keystone of all loyalty if not to be true to oneself? My God! There was a mighty upheaval taking place in Hans.

One day he came home with another prohibition. One of the leaders had taken away a book by his most beloved writer, *Stellar Hours of Mankind* by Stefan Zweig. It was forbidden, he was told. Why? There had been no answer. He heard something similar about another German writer whom he liked very much. This one had been forced to escape from Germany because he had been engaged in spreading pacifist ideas.

Ultimately it came to an open break.

Some time before, Hans had been promoted to standard-bearer. He and his boys had sewn themselves a magnificent flag with a mythical beast in the center. The flag was something very special. It had been dedicated to the Fuehrer himself. The boys had taken an oath on the flag because it was the symbol of their fellowship. But one evening, as they stood with their flag in formation for inspection by a higher leader, something unheard-of happened. The visiting leader suddenly ordered the tiny standard-bearer, a frolicsome twelve-year-old lad, to give up the flag. "You don't need a special flag. Just keep the one that has been prescribed for all." Hans was deeply disturbed. Since when? Didn't the troop leader know what this special flag meant to its standard-bearer? Wasn't it more than just a piece of cloth that could be changed at one's pleasure?

Once more the leader ordered the boy to give up the flag. He stood quiet and motionless. Hans knew what was going on in the little fellow's mind and that he would not obey. When the high leader in a threatening voice ordered the little fellow for the third time, Hans saw the flag waver slightly. He could no longer control himself. He stepped out of line and slapped the visiting leader's face. From then on he was no longer the standard-bearer.[31]

CONNECTIONS

Compare Hans to Fritzekarl (Reading 10). How would Fritzekarl respond to Hans's question, "But what was the keystone of all loyalty if not to be true to oneself"? What led Hans to ask such a question? What led to his "break" with Hitler Youth?

What events would disturb a Nazi youth enough to make him or her change? How would he or she hear other points of view? Find enough courage to overcome peer pressure? Is it fair to expect a child to know enough to change?

Review the reading describing Milgram's experiment (Reading 1). How does it help explain why the standard bearer refused to obey?

Propaganda and Education

*I*n *Education for Death,* American educator Gregor Ziemer described schooling in Nazi Germany. As part of his research, he studied curriculum materials used in German schools. He noted:

> A teacher is not spoken of as a teacher (*Lehrer*) but an *Erzieher*. The word suggests an iron disciplinarian who does not instruct but commands, and whose orders are backed up with force if necessary.
>
> Matters of the spirit are frankly and energetically belittled. Physical education, education for action, is alone worthy of the Nazi teacher's attention. All else can be dismissed as non-essential.
>
> Nazi education transcends old-fashioned pedagogy. Education in Hitler schools is not the result of a gradual evolution, but of revolution. It stems from political conflict and political victory.
>
> The Nazi schools are no place for weaklings. All children must, of course, finish the primary school before they are ten; but after that schools are proving-grounds for the Party. Those who betray any weakness of body or have not the capacities for absolute obedience and submission must be expelled.
>
> "Students who are unable to produce required results or who betray any weakness, are to be kept out of the secondary schools," states the iron Minister to his iron-minded teachers on page one of his iron-clad manual.
>
> The regime draws a sharp distinction between girls, inherently weak, and boys, natural exponents of Strength. Boys and girls have nothing in common. Their aims, their purposes in life, are fundamentally different. Boys will become soldiers; girls will become breeders. Co-educational schools are manifestations of decadent democracies and hence are taboo.
>
> [Dr. Bernhard Rust, the Nazi Minister of Education,] decrees that in Nazi schools the norm is physical education. After that, German, biology, science, mathematics, and history for the boys; eugenics and home economics for the girls. Other subjects are permissible if they are taught to promote Nazi ideals. Spiritual education is definitely unimportant.[32]

CONNECTIONS

Who would be attracted to the kind of education Rust described?

Every culture defines the roles men and women are expected to play in society. How were those roles defined in traditional German society? In Nazi society? How were those ideas reflected in German schools? Interview people who grew up in the United States in the 1930s and 1940s to find out how those roles were defined in American culture. Research the ways those ideas were reflected in American schools. What remnants of those ideas can still be found in the schools?

How would you describe American education today? What do your parents and teachers expect you to learn? What kind of person do they want you to become? Compare your own views of American education with those of your classmates. How hard is it to reach a consensus?

➤James Clavell's "The Children's Story" describes a teacher who wins over an elementary-school class in less than thirty minutes. The story raises questions about education, indoctrination, and citizenship. Copies are available from the Facing History Resource Center. A packet of materials that compares "Aryan" women with women from groups the Nazis deemed "unworthy of life" is also available.

READING 13

Racial Instruction

Soon after Hitler took power, a new course was added to the curriculum in every German school. The Nazi Minister of Education outlined the objectives of the course:

1. Give pupils an insight into the relationship, causes and effects of all basic facts having to do with the science of heredity and race.

2. Impress the pupils with the importance of the science of heredity and race for the future of the nation and the purposes of the government.

3. Awaken in the pupils a sense of responsibility toward the nation, as represented by both its ancestry and its posterity; imbue the pupils with pride in the fact that the German people are the most important exponent of the Nordic race, and to influence them in favor of complete (Nordification) of the German people.

   This is to be accomplished early enough so that no child shall leave school without a conviction of the necessity of pure blood.

As homework for the new "race science" classes, students were to:

> Collect from illustrated magazines, newspapers, etc., pictures of great scholars, statesmen, artists and others who distinguish themselves by their special accomplishments (for example, in economic life, politics, sports). Determine the preponderant race and admixture, according to physical characteristics. Repeat this exercise with the pictures of great men of all nations and times. . . .
>
> Observe the Jew: his way of walking, his bearing, gestures, and movements when talking.

Racial instruction was not limited to a single course. It was included in all classes, even arithmetic. One book entitled *Germany's Fall and Rise— Illustrations Taken from Arithmetic Instruction in the Higher Grades of Elementary School,* asks, "The Jews are aliens in Germany—In 1933 there were 66,060,000 inhabitants of the German Reich, of whom 499,682 were Jews. What is the percentage of aliens"?

CONNECTIONS

What do the assignments described in the reading have in common? What were teachers trying to teach their students? How effective do you think such assignments were?

After World War II, American composers, Richard Rogers and Oscar Hammerstein, wrote a song about prejudice and hate. According to that song, children have to be taught how to hate and they must learn before they are seven or eight. Do you agree? Would Hitler agree?

➤Frank S., a Jewish boy in a German school during the Nazi era, recalls the humiliating lessons of "race science." He can still remember being hauled to the front of the class to demonstrate his "Jewish features." Carl, an Aryan schoolboy whose father belonged to the Nazi party, also remembers those days. He tells of the time a professor from the Office of Racial Research at the University of Wuerzburg visited his third-grade class. "We were given a lecture on what an Aryan was supposed to be, and sent into the village to find and describe a local Aryan." What impact do you think such lessons had on both Jewish and non-Jewish students? For the testimonies of Frank, Carl, and other students in Nazi Germany, see excerpts 1-5 in the video montage *Childhood Memories,* available from the Facing History Resource Center and described in *Elements of Time,* pages 207-238.

Although American students did not take a course called "race science" in the 1930s and 1940s, similar ideas were a part of their education as well. After all, many attended schools that were segregated by "race," read science textbooks that claimed that the "Negro race" was inferior to the "white race," and studied history from books that described the Indians as "savages." A history book written in 1946 and used in elementary schools after World War II ends with the following paragraph:

The people who came to the New World were the heirs of all the past. They brought with them many of the customs and ways of doing things they had known in their Old World homes. To that new land they carried the precious heritage of freedom and justice which their ancestors had struggled for centuries to achieve. And in that new land was to be written a wonderful new chapter in the story of man's effort to make the world a better and happier place to live in. Out of the society which the people of Europe created in the New World developed the United States and the other American nations—nations of free people.[33]

According to the book, who built the United States and other nations in the Americas? What do the authors imply about Native Americans? African Americans? Asian Americans?

READING 14

Schools for Girls

German girls attended school until the age of fourteen. Although they went to school Monday through Saturday, they had no textbooks and no homework. Their education was minimal except in matters relating to childbirth. After a visit to a girls' school, Gregor Ziemer wrote:

According to the teacher there was no such thing as a problem of morals in Hitler's Germany. The Fuehrer wanted every woman, every girl to bear children—soldiers. She herself was willing to have a child, even though she was not married. The State would rear and educate it.

"All of us women can now enjoy the rich emotional and spiritual experiences of having a baby by a healthy young man without the restricting ties of the old-fashioned institutions of marriage," were her words.

Hitler and his school authorities urge BDM girls to have babies. But they do not permit the girls to be educated in the same schools with boys. Girls do not require the same sort of education that is essential for boys. The schools for boys teach military science, military geography, military ideology, Hitler worship; those for the girls prepare the proper mental set in the future mates of Hitler's soldiers.

One of Minister Rust's officials, a Herr Geheimrat Becker, discussed the problem of co-education with me. He knew something about American schools. It was his contention that the system of trying to put women on the same plane with men, even in matters of the mind, was a waste of time. He admitted there were women who could think as well as men—in their field. But the German schools had one aim: every course, every class had to contribute in some way to Hitler's ideology. He pointed out that the boys who learned about chemistry of war . . . should not be bothered with the presence of girls in their classes. Girls had a definite purpose. In moments of recreation boys needed girls. . . .

Every girl, he said, must learn the duties of a mother before she is sixteen, so she can have children. Why should girls bother with higher mathematics, or art, or drama, or literature? They could have babies without that sort of knowledge. . . .

Becker reminded me that Hitler devotes thirty pages of *Mein Kampf* to the education of boys. Besides, he mentions the subject frequently. Seven lines he grants to the girls. And that just about indicated the relative importance of the two, Becker said.[34]

CONNECTIONS

What were girls supposed to learn? Why? How did their education differ from the education boys received? Why did it differ? What are the legacies of this type of thinking?

Many people in the early 1900s believed that gender determines what one can and cannot do. What roles were women expected to play in Nazi Germany? In the Weimar Republic? In the United States in the 1920s and 1930s? What roles do they play today? What similarities do you notice? What differences seem most striking? Compare and contrast beliefs that gender determines behavior and aptitude with beliefs concerning "race" and religion.

What do you think would happen to a girl who demanded more than a minimal education? How would her situation be similar to that of Harrison Bergeron (Chapter 2, Reading 1)? How would it differ?

READING 15

A Lesson in Current Events

Gregor Ziemer visited a geography class in one school. He wrote of that class:

The teacher was talking about Germany's deserved place in world affairs. He ascribed her recent swift rise to the Fuehrer's doctrine of race purity. Not every country could boast of a pure race. Czechoslovakia, for instance, was nothing but a few remnants of a race formerly under German rule, mixed with Slavs, Jews, and Galicians. The Poles were no race. But there were other countries that were fast going downhill because of racial sins. He asked his boys to name some.

They mentioned Russia, England, France. The teacher was not satisfied.

"Well, which country has always called itself the 'melting pot' of all other nations? Jungens, that you must know."

Then came the chorus, "Amerika.". . .

The teacher launched into a devastating diatribe that made short shrift of the United States, that country which had joined the last war just to make money. He worked himself into an emotional fervor.

He explained how during the centuries there had been many men and women who could not get along in Europe. Most of them were criminals and crooks, reprobates and renegades. They were the undesirables. Whenever they tangled with the law in Germany, or any other European country, they got on a boat and went to the United States. There they married each other. And now the children—well, any German boy with intelligence could see what the result would be. These children, in turn, mingled with Jews and Negroes. The citizens of the United States were sinking lower and lower.

But he wasn't through.

'There are many other weaknesses as a result of this lack of racial purity," he continued. "Their government is corrupt. They have a low type of government, a democracy. What is a democracy"?

I wrote down a few of the answers:

"A democracy is a government by rich Jews."

"A democracy is a form of government in which people waste much time."

"A democracy is a government in which there is no real leadership."

"A democracy is a government that will be defeated by the Fuehrer."

"*Das sowieso*," the teacher grinned. "That in any case." He expressed the conviction that the democratic form of government could not last long in a world where National Socialism was fast getting the upper hand. Democracies had too many flaws.

"Look at the United States," he said. "It is the richest country in the world. It has almost all the gold in the world. But it also has the largest number of unemployed of any country. Look at some of these pictures."

He had pictures, cut from German illustrated weeklies, purporting to depict starving men along sidewalks and wharves in American cities.

Moreover, the United States was abusing its minorities. The American Indian was almost exterminated; the Negro was lynched on the nearest tree.

The lot of the laboring man was especially unenviable. He reminded the boys of the benefits their fathers were deriving from the labor front, the Nazi Arbeitsfront, which provided pensions, free vacations, trips to the Mediterranean. But in America capital and labor were engaged in an eternal struggle. As a result there were innumerable strikes.

The boys, most of them nine years old, did not know what strikes were. There had not been any in Germany since 1933. The teacher explained, and used more pictures, allegedly of American strikes.

The reactions were written clearly on the faces of the listening boys. A country where such things could be need not be respected, much less feared.

The teacher had one parting shot. "And the leader of the United States? Who is he"?

"Roosevelt," somebody said.

The teacher's voice got mysterious. "Roosevelt he calls himself. But his real name is Rosenfeldt. What does that show you"?

"He's a Jew," shouted the class.

A bell rang. The boys were dismissed.[35]

CONNECTIONS

What did the teacher say about the United States? Which statements were true? Which were false? What did he emphasize? What message was he giving his students?

What is the difference between education and indoctrination? Was the instructor teaching his students or indoctrinating them?

Roosevelt was not Jewish. Did the teacher actually say he was? Find other examples of false statements or faulty logic in his lesson.

The Nazis used this cartoon for propaganda. How does it portray the United States? Why would the Nazis want Germans to see Americans in this way? How does the teacher quoted in this reading promote that view?

READING 16

Rebels Without a Cause

Not all young people accepted the Nazis' ideas. By the late 1930s, a number of teenagers were questioning the system Hitler created. Among them were members of the Edelweiss Pirates—a loose collection of independent gangs in western Germany. Those gangs included the Roving Dudes of Essen, the Kittelbach Pirates of Oberhausen and Duesseldorf (after a river north of Duesseldorf), and the Navajo Wild Boys of Cologne. These groups would get together from time to time for weekend trips. Members would pitch tents in the forest, sing, talk, and "bash" Hitler Youth patrols.

A Nazi official in Duesseldorf said of the gangs:

> Re: "Edelweiss Pirates". The said youths are throwing their weight around again. I have been told that gatherings of young people have become more conspicuous than ever [in a local park]. . . . These adolescents, aged between 12 and 17, hang around into the late evening with musical instruments and young females. Since this riff-raff is in large part outside the Hitler Youth and adopts a hostile attitude towards the organization, they represent a danger to other young people. It has recently been established that members of the armed forces too are to be found among these young people and they, owing to their membership in the Wehrmacht, exhibit particularly arrogant behaviour. There is a suspicion that it is these youths who have covered the walls of the pedestrian subway on the Altenbergstrasse with slogans "Down with Hitler." "The [Military High Command] is lying," "Medals for Murder," "Down with Nazi Brutality" etc. However often these inscriptions are removed, within a few days new ones reappear on the walls.[36]

In Duesseldorf, the Gestapo arrested 739 teenagers who belonged to twenty-eight different groups in December of 1942. In Cologne, the Nazis publicly hung the leaders of the Cologne Edelweiss Pirates in 1944. Yet young people continued to join these gangs.

Not everyone who rebelled joined a gang. Some defined themselves in terms of their favorite music. They called themselves the *Swing-Jugend* or "swing youth." Historian Detlev J. K. Peukert says of them:

> The swing youth were not anti-fascist in a political sense—their behaviour was indeed emphatically anti-political—both Nazi slogans and traditional nationalism were of profound indifference to them. They sought their counter-identity in what they saw as the "slovenly" culture of . . .England and America. They accepted Jews and "half-Jews" into their groups—another outrage for the Nazis—and gave ovations to visiting bands from Belgium and Holland.

> The very disgust shown by the authors of the Nazi reports and their dramatisation of events indicate that Nazi officialdom felt attacked at the heart of its concept of itself and of the state. This is the only way, too, to explain the reaction of Heinrich Himmler, who wanted to put the "ringleaders" of the swing movement into concentration camps for at least two or three years of beatings, punitive drill and forced labor.[37]

The kind of behavior that led Himmler to advocate concentration camps is described in a report. It is an account of a 1940 swing festival attended by five to six hundred teenagers in Hamburg.

> The dance music was all English and American. Only swing dancing and jitterbugging took place. At the entrance to the hall stood a notice on which the words "Swing prohibited" had been altered to "Swing requested." Without exception the participants accompanied the dances and songs by singing the English lyrics. Indeed, throughout the evening they attempted to speak only English; and some tables even French.
>
> The dancers made an appalling sight. None of the couples danced normally; there was only swing of the worst sort. Sometimes two boys danced with one girl; sometimes several couples formed a circle, linking arms and jumping, slapping hands, even rubbing the backs of their heads together; and then, bent double, with the top half of the body hanging loosely down, long hair flopping into the face, they dragged themselves round practically on their knees. When the band played a rumba, the dancers went into wild ecstasy. They all leaped around and mumbled the chorus in English. The band played wilder and wilder numbers; none of the players was sitting any longer, they all "jitterbugged" on the stage like wild animals. [38]

CONNECTIONS

Why do you think German teenagers were attracted to gangs? To the swing youth? What need did these groups fill that Hitler Youth failed to provide?

Reread Reading 1. What insights does Milgram's experiment offer into the behavior of the two groups?

What similarities do you see between the groups described in this reading and teen groups in your community? What is the main difference?

What do the two groups suggest about the success of Nazi propaganda? About its failures?

NOTES

[1] Harrison E. Salisburg, Forward to *Mischling, Second Degree: My Childhood in Nazi Germany* by Ilse Koehn (Greenwillow, 1977), viii-ix.

[2] Stanley Milgram, *Obedience to Authority* (Harper & Row, 1974), 3-4.

[3] Philip Zimbardo, "The Pathology of Imprisonment," *Societies,* April, 1972, 109.

[4] Ibid.

[5] Ibid.

[6] Quoted in "Research through Deception" by Morton Hunt, *New York Times Magazine.*

[7] William Sheridan Allen, *The Nazi Seizure of Power* (Quadrangle Books, 1965), 199.

[8] William Shirer, *Berlin Diary* (Alfred Knopf, 1940), 17-18.

[9] Ibid., 18-19.

[10] Quoted in *The Nazi Years; A Documentary History*, ed. Joachim Remark, 79.

[11] Horst Krueger, *A Crack in the Wall*, trans. Ruth Hein (Fromm International Publishing Corp.,1982), 15-16.

[12] George Sabine, *History of Political Theory*, 3rd Edition (Holt, Rinehart & Winston, 1965), 904.

[13] Max von der Gruen *Howl Like the Wolves.*

[14] Vaclav Havel, "Words on Words," *New York Review of Books*, 18 January 1990, 5.

[15] Max von der Gruen, *Howl Like the Wolves.*

[16] Marion Freyer Wolff, *The Shrinking Circle: Memories of Nazi Berlin, 1933-1939* (UAHC, 1989), 21.

[17] David Lloyd George, "I Talked to Hitler," *London Daily Express,* 17 November, 1936.

[18] Sybil Milton, "Social Responsibility of the Artist," Facing History and Ourselves Foundation. (videotape)

[19] Quoted in *Courage to Care*, ed. Carol Rittner and Sondra Myers, (New York University Press, 1986), 28.

[20] Victoria Barnett, *For the Soul of the People*, 123.

[21] Bohdan Wytwycky, *The Other Holocaust: Many Circles of Hell* (The Novak Report, 1980), 83.

[22] Erika Mann, *School for Barbarians* (Modern Age, 1938).

[23] Morris Dees, Interview by Curtis White, *The Boston Globe,* 17 June, 1993.

[24] Alfons Heck, *Diary of a Hitler Youth.*

[25] Elizabeth Dopazo, "Reminiscences," unpublished interview, 1981, Facing History and Ourselves Foundation.

[26] From *Childhood Experiences of German Jews* Facing History and Ourselves Foundation (video)

[27] Mede von Nagel, "The Nazi Legacy—Fearful Silence for Their Children," *Boston Globe,* 23 October, 1977.

[28] Quoted in Dan Bar-On, *Legacy of Silence* (Harvard University Press, 1989), 216.

[29] Alfons Heck, *Diary of a Hitler Youth.*

[30] Erika Mann, *School for Barbarians* (Modern Age, 1938).

[31] Inge Scholl, *Students Against Tyranny*, trans. Arthur R. Schultz, (Wesleyan University Press, 1970), 7-10.

[32] Gregor Ziemer, *Education for Death*, 15-16.

[33] Gertrude Hartman, *Builders of the Old World*, 2nd ed. (D.C. Heath, 1946, 1959), 447.

[34] Gregor Ziemer, *Education for Death*, 128-129.

[35] Ibid., 68-69.

[36] Adapted from Detlev J. K. Peukert, *Inside Nazi Germany* (Yale University Press, 1987), 161.

[37] Ibid., 168.

[38] Ibid., 166.

6. Escalating Violence

And what was said long ago is true: Nations are made not of oak and rock but of men, and, as the men are, so will the nations be.

MILTON MAYER

OVERVIEW

*I*n Chapter 2, we saw that every individual and every nation has a "universe of obligation"—a circle of persons "toward whom obligations are owed, to whom rules apply and whose injuries call for [amends] by the community." Each, however, defines that universe just a little differently. Chapter 6 focuses on the way individuals and nations defined their "universes of obligation" in the late 1930s and the consequences of those definitions.

Hitler made no secret of his racist views or his plans to build a "Greater Germany." As early as 1928, he spelled them out in *Mein Kampf*. It was all there—the antisemitism, the militarism, and the demands for *Lebensraum*, or living space in the East. Throughout the 1930s, he advanced those plans step by step. When one action against an individual or a nation encountered little or no opposition, he carried the next step a little further. This chapter highlights the steps he took between 1936 and 1940 and explores the following questions: Why didn't the German people stop Hitler when he threatened minorities at home? When he turned on neighboring countries? Why didn't world leaders take a stand?

The chapter also considers what it meant to be outside a "universe of obligation." To be, in Richard Rubenstein's words, "superfluous." As he puts it, "Men without political rights are superfluous men. They have lost all right to life and human dignity. Political rights are neither God-given, autonomous nor self-validating. The Germans understood that no person has any rights unless they are guaranteed by an organized community with the power to defend such rights."[1] His words were as true of nations as they were of individuals.

READING 1

Hitler's "Saturday Surprises"

*I*n foreign policy, as in domestic policy, Hitler acted on his belief that "every road . . . is expedient." As early as 1933, he realized that he could set the terms of international affairs by complaining about the terms of the Treaty of Versailles. This allowed him to portray himself as a patriot who wanted only justice for his country. In October, he used the treaty to explain Germany's withdrawal from the League of Nations. There was, in fact, no link between the two events. The treaty did not force Germany to join the League. German leaders chose to do so years after the treaty was signed. Yet no one challenged Hitler's stand.

Although most world leaders were aware that the treaty had nothing to do with Germany's decision to join the League of Nations nor with the decision to withdraw, they chose to remain silent. They knew that the treaty held Germany responsible for the war even though it was not the only nation at fault. So Hitler's comments made some feel a little guilty. Others feared that challenging Hitler might lead to war and almost everyone wanted to avoid another war. There were, of course, other reasons no one spoke out. Many admired Hitler's stand against communism. They, too, saw the Russians as the "enemy." Although few shared Hitler's belief in a Jewish conspiracy at work everywhere in the world, many considered Jews "different," perhaps even dangerous. There were, of course, world leaders who disagreed with Hitler's views, but few believed that he would go to war to achieve his goals. As a result, Hitler found that he could make outrageous demands without fear of a confrontation.

On March 8, 1935, Hitler sprang the first of his "Saturday surprises" on the world. Like the others, it took place on a weekend when British leaders retreated to their country homes. In the name of "defense," Hitler announced that he was rebuilding the German air force, reinstating the draft, and rearming the nation. He assured the world these were purely "defensive" measures. In a speech to the Reichstag, he contended that "the principal effect of every war is to destroy the flower of the nation.

There were, of course, world leaders who disagreed with Hitler's views, but few believed that he would go to war to achieve his goals. As a result, Hitler found that he could make outrageous demands without fear of a confrontation.

Germany needs peace and desires peace." He vowed that "the German government is ready to agree to any limitation which leads to abolition of the heaviest arms, especially suited for aggression, such as the heaviest artillery and the heaviest tanks." And he warned that "whoever lights the torch of war in Europe can wish for nothing but chaos."

The speech was praised both at home and abroad. When journalist William Shirer, one of Hitler's early critics, reread his diary forty-five years later, he was astonished to discover that he, like so many others, "left the Reichstag that evening convinced that Hitler, despite all my reservations about him, really wanted peace and had made the West, at least, a serious offer. I had been derisive of the Germans for swallowing Hitler's propaganda. I should have included myself."

The second "Saturday surprise" took place on March 7, 1936. That day German soldiers marched into the Rhineland as German fighter planes roared overhead. The Treaty of Versailles had set aside the Rhineland, a strip of land thirty-one miles wide, as a buffer between Germany and both France and Belgium. Although it was officially part of Germany, the nation could not keep troops there or fortify the area. Now Hitler simply ignored that agreement.

German generals opposed the move into the Rhineland. They feared that the French would defeat their half-trained, inadequately equipped army within hours. But Hitler was so confident that the French would not intervene that he promised to retreat if they even tried to stop the invasion. Fredric Zeller recalls what happened next:

Everybody seemed to hunch up and hold their breath. But nothing happened. Nothing. France and England did nothing. The press was jubilant. There was euphoria in the streets. Strangers smiled at each other, comrades in arms. Even anti-Nazis, friends of my parents, now said Hitler was doing some good things for Germany.

"Germany has been on her knees too long," we heard them say, wagging a finger. "And look at unemployment . . . he's certainly doing something about that."

My parents didn't reply. I heard them say later, "He's clearing up unemployment. . . yes, but how? The *Reichsarbeitsdienst*—Universal Labor Service conscription—hard labor with practically no pay. Military service call-up for millions. Armament production. Don't people see where it's all going? Do they really want another war? Are our last good Christian friends turning into Nazis too?"

And then Father mentioned a Jewish businessman in Spandau who said that Hitler was really doing good things for Germany.

"'He's making us strong,' Herbert said. 'He'd be all right if only he didn't have this thing about the Jews.'"

Father caught me following the conversation, saw my eyes widen at his saying—making "us" strong—and smiled:

"Yes. . . the man said 'us.'"[2]

Why didn't the French challenge Hitler? They did not want another war. Too many people in France still remembered the battles of World War I where thousands died to gain a mile or two of territory. The French were also reluctant to act without British support. Geoffrey Dawson, the editor of the *Times*, reflected the views of most people in Britain when he asked, "What has it got to do with us? It's none of our business, is it? It's their own back-garden they are walking into."

Winston Churchill, then a member of Britain's Parliament, was among the few to disagree. He argued, "The violation of the Rhineland is serious from the point of view of the menace to which it exposes Holland, Belgium, and France. It is also serious from the fact that when it is fortified . . . it will be a barrier across Germany's front door, which leaves her free to sally out eastward and southward by the back door."[3] For years, Churchill, like most Europeans, had regarded Joseph Stalin, the head of the Soviet Union, as the most dangerous leader in Europe. By 1936, he considered Hitler a greater threat.

Most people, however, preferred to believe that Hitler was sincere when he called the invasion of the Rhineland a "purely defensive" move. They applauded when he declared, "We have no territorial demands to make in Europe!" And they took heart from his vow that "Germany will never break the peace." Many believed him because they feared that if Hitler were overthrown, the Communists would take over Germany. In their view, a communist Germany would be a more serious threat to world peace than a fascist Germany.

Others simply wanted to avoid another world war. In Britain, thousands of college students pledged that they would never go to war—no matter what the circumstances. In 1935, the United States Congress passed the first in a series of neutrality laws. These laws stated that the United States would do more than just stay out of all "foreign wars." The nation would not make loans, sell arms, or provide any other assistance to warring nations.

CONNECTIONS

By 1936, William Shirer had become more skeptical of Hitler's words. The evening he filed a news story describing Hitler's announcement of the invasion of the Rhineland and his latest peace proposal, he wrote in his diary, "The [peace] proposal is a pure fraud, and if I had any guts, or American journalism had any, I would have said so in my dispatch. But I am not supposed to be 'editorial.'"[4] What is a reporter's responsibility to his or her readers? Is it to describe events? Or to make judgments about those events?

How did Hitler use such words as *peace* and *defense*? Were they euphemisms?

What did Hitler assume about human behavior? About the foreign policy objectives of other nations? What did the leaders of other nations assume about his objectives? How accurate were these assumptions? Record your answers so that you can refer to them later.

Why were Fredric Zeller and his parents surprised at the reaction of the businessman who was Jewish to the invasion? What does his reaction suggest about the willingness of people to overlook the bad in order to attain the good? What was the businessman willing to overlook? What did he hope to gain?

What assumptions did the United States Congress make when it passed the neutrality laws? What do those laws suggest about the way members of Congress defined the nation's "universe of obligation"?

When should one nation get involved in a crisis in another country? How do leaders decide? What say does the average American have? How can he or she influence government policy? Such questions are still being debated as Americans struggle to define the nation's role in the affairs of such countries as Somalia, Bosnia, and Haiti. Investigate the arguments of those who support intervention and those who oppose it. Evaluate each argument. Is the reasoning logical? Is it moral? Then compare the arguments to those made in response to Hitler's actions in the 1930s. What similarities do you notice? What differences are most striking?

Taking Austria

*H*itler had a clear objective that guided his dealings with other nations. "We National Socialists must hold unflinchingly to our aim in foreign policy, namely, to secure for the German people the land and soil to which they are entitled on this earth." Hitler argued that some of that land would come from territories lost in World War I, most of which lay to the east. "Russia and her vassal border states" also lay to the east of Germany and Hitler was eager to claim those lands as well. After all, the Russians were not only Communists but also Slavs, a people he regarded as "subhuman." In his view, they, like other "subhumans," were a clear threat to the racial purity of the German people.

In the fall of 1936, Hitler allied with Italy. The agreement had a number of consequences. It gave Mussolini German support for his invasion of Ethiopia. It also opened the way for the *Anschluss*, or union of Germany and Austria. Now Mussolini sided with Germany. By 1938, Hitler was ready to make his move. On February 12, he summoned Austrian Prime Minister Kurt von Schuschnigg to a secret meeting that consisted of eleven hours of insults and threats. At one point, the Fuehrer flew into a rage and screamed that Austria must become a part of "Greater Germany." When Schuschnigg disagreed, Hitler gave him three days to change his mind. The Austrian leader used the time to organize a national election so that the people of Austria could decide the matter for themselves.

Before the voting could take place, the Fuehrer announced that unless Schuschnigg and the Austrian president resigned, he would invade to "restore order in a chaotic country." Schuschnigg responded in a radio address. "I declare before the world that the reports launched in Germany concerning disorders by the workers, the shedding of streams of blood, and the creation of a situation beyond the control of the Austrian government are lies from Λ to Z."

The reports were indeed false. Yet when German troops entered Austria on March 11, no one came to the nation's defense. When the Nazis called for a vote on the *Anschluss* a few weeks after the invasion, 99.7 percent of Austria's voters expressed approval. Most outsiders felt that Austria was not worth fighting over. Once again, Winston Churchill disagreed. Comparing Germany to "a boa constrictor" that has "devoured a goat or a deer," he warned that Czechoslovakia would be next. Most people dismissed his remarks as "war-mongering."

Hitler believed that every road was expedient, including lying.

Hitler believed that every road was expedient, including lying. What power did that position give him over other world leaders?

What point was Churchill making when he compared Germany to a boa constrictor? Who is the "deer"?

Schuschnigg later said of his meeting with Hitler that the Fuehrer might as well be "speaking Hindustani"; he was "a man from another world." Do you think he really lost control or were the insults and threats part of a strategy?

In Chapter 4 (Reading 15), a professor interviewed by Milton Mayer described the small, seemingly unimportant compromises he made that led to larger ones later. Was the *Anschluss* a small step that might lead to a larger compromise later? How can individuals and national leaders know which compromises are significant and which are not? Historian William Manchester writes that Churchill had a "moral compass" that guided his responses to Hitler's actions. What is a "moral compass"? To what extent does it guide leaders today? How does it guide you?

R E A D I N G 3

Stateless People

Can a state, without upsetting the basis of our civilisation, and indeed, of all civilisation, arbitrarily withdraw nationality from a whole class of its citizens, thereby making them stateless persons whom no country is compelled to receive on its territory?

*I*n *Mein Kampf*, Adolf Hitler argued that "the race question not only furnishes the key to world history, but also to world culture." He went on to say, "There is absolutely no other revolution but a racial revolution. There is no economic, no political, no social revolution. There is only the struggle of the lower races against the dominant, higher races." As Hitler expanded eastward, he applied these ideas of race to the peoples he now ruled. Austria's two hundred thousand Jews were the first to discover what that meant.

Within weeks of the *Anschluss*, observers were reporting hundreds of antisemitic incidents throughout the nation. Some noted the sharp increase in suicides, as thousands of Jews tried desperately to emigrate only to find stumbling blocks wherever they turned. Their difficulty in leaving "Greater Germany" could not be blamed on the Nazis. The Nazis were more than eager to see the Jews go as long as they left their money and possessions behind. Indeed in just six months, Adolf Eichmann, a young SS officer who made himself an expert on the "Jewish question," had pushed 50,000 Jews out of Austria. The problem lay with other nations. They had no interest in accepting thousands of penniless Jewish refugees.

Shortly after the *Anschluss*, United States President Franklin Roosevelt called for an international conference to discuss the growing refugee crisis. In July 1938, delegates from thirty-two nations met in Evian, France. There, each representative expressed sorrow over the growing number of "refugees" and "deportees," boasted of his nation's traditional hospitality, and lamented its inability to do more in the "present situation." The British noted that many refugees wanted to go to Palestine, which was under British rule. They would like to admit them, but in view of the ongoing conflict between Jews and Arabs, it was not a practical solution. The French claimed that their country had already done more than its fair share. The Americans noted that Congress would have to approve any change in immigration. The delegates spoke in general terms and few referred to refugees as *Jews*.

Only one representative addressed the real issue. M. J. M. Yepes of Colombia told the delegates that there were two central questions. One was a question of fact that each nation had to answer for itself: "How many refugees would it admit?" The other question involved a matter of principle: "Can a state, without upsetting the basis of our civilisation, and indeed, of all civilisation, arbitrarily withdraw nationality from a whole class of its citizens, thereby making them stateless persons whom no country is compelled to receive on its territory?"

Yepes went on to say that as long as the central problem was not decided, the work of the conference would not be lasting and a dangerous example would be set—an example that in his view would make the world "uninhabitable." Most delegates did not want to deal with either issue.

As the Jewish observer from Palestine, Golda Meir, who later became prime minister of Israel, was not allowed to speak. She later wrote, "I don't think that anyone who didn't live through it can understand what I felt at Evian—a mixture of sorrow, rage, frustration, and horror. I wanted to get up and scream at them, 'Don't you know that these so-called numbers are human beings, people who may spend the rest of their lives in concentration camps, or wandering around the world like lepers if you don't let them in?' Of course, I didn't know then that not concentration camps but death camps awaited the refugees whom no one wanted."[5]

Only the Dominican Republic agreed to accept Jewish immigrants. The nation's leader, Rafael Trujillo Molina, hoped that Jews would marry local inhabitants and "lighten" the race. He also believed that Jews were good at making money and would therefore be an asset to his country. He granted visas to one thousand Jews who were to live in Sosua, a special community established for them. After the conference, Hitler concluded, "Nobody wants these criminals."

Men without political rights are superfluous men. They have lost all right to life and human dignity. Political rights are neither God-given, autonomous, nor self-validating. The Germans understood that no person has any rights unless they are guaranteed by an organized community with the power to defend such rights.

CONNECTIONS

What is a *political refugee*? How do nations today regard such individuals? What does your answer suggest about the way they define their "universe of obligation?" *Elements of Time*, pages 138-152, discusses the impact that a narrow definition had on German Jews.

Compare the way the nations that attended the Evian Conference defined their "universe of obligation" with more modern definitions. What similarities do you notice? What differences seem most striking?

The Dominican Republic based its immigration policies on racist beliefs. It was not alone. In the early 1900s, many Americans also supported an immigration policy based on "racial" considerations. A psychology professor at Princeton University maintained: "According to all evidence available, then, American intelligence is declining, and will proceed with an accelerating rate as the racial admixture becomes more and more extensive." He proposed that "legal steps" be taken "which would insure a continuously progressive upward evolution." Among those steps? "Immigration should not only be restrictive but highly selective."[6] Other Americans agreed and in the 1920s, Congress passed a series of immigration laws that limited the number of European immigrants to 150,000 and virtually cut off immigration from Asia and Africa. How did Hitler take advantage of the attitudes and beliefs that shaped those laws?

In the late 1800s, Emma Lazarus wrote these words:

> Give me your tired, your poor;
> Your huddled masses yearning to breathe free;
> The wretched refuse of your teeming shore;
> Send these, the homeless, tempest-tossed to me;
> I lift my lamp beside the golden door.

What is the poet saying about the United States? Why do you think the poem is carved on the base of the Statue of Liberty? How widespread were such beliefs in the 1920s and 1930s? How widespread are they today? Investigate attitudes toward refugees today. What values and beliefs are reflected in debates over the arrival of "boat people" from Haiti? Vietnam? China?

Germany was not the only nation to turn some of its citizens into "stateless" people. In the 1920s, the Soviet government deprived about 1.5 million Russians of their citizenship rights. Most were opponents of the new Communist regime. In the years that followed, the number of stateless people grew. Some, like the Russians, lost citizenship when they lost a civil war within their country. Others became stateless because they were a hated or feared minority. Richard Rubenstein calls these men, women, and children "outlaws."

> [They were not] outlaws because of any crime they had committed, but because their status had been altered by their country's civil service or police bureaucracy. They had been deprived of all political status by bureaucratic definition. As such, they had become superfluous men. . . . What made [them] superfluous was no lack of ability, intelligence, or potential social usefulness. There were gifted physicians, lawyers, scholars, and technicians among them. Nevertheless, in most instances no established political community had any use for the legitimate employment of their gifts. This was especially true of the Jewish refugees, but they were by no means alone.[7]

The overview to this chapter quoted Rubenstein as saying, "Men without political rights are superfluous men. They have lost all right to life and human dignity. Political rights are neither God-given, autonomous nor self-validating. The Germans understood that no person has any rights unless they are guaranteed by an organized community with the power to defend such rights." How does this reading support his argument? What current events support Rubenstein's position? What events call it into question?

➤The film *Sosua* contains footage from newsreels that show the early days of the Jewish colony in the Dominican Republic. It also explores what happened to those who came to Sosua and its status today. Walter Bieringer discusses the results of the Evian Conference in a videotaped interview, discussed in *Elements of Time*, pages 72-73. Both videos are available from the Facing History Resource Center. So is a videotape of a lecture by Henry Feingold, author of *Politics of Rescue.* He argues that the failure of world leaders to respond to the plight of the Jews is a negative legacy of the modern nation state. He warns of the dangers of similar failures to respond to threats from dictators in recent times. His lecture is summarized in *Elements of Time*, pages 360-361.

READING 4

Appeasing Hitler

J ust as Jews had no one to come to their aid, nations also found themselves isolated and alone as Hitler threatened their freedom. Austria was the first to fall. Hitler then turned his attention to Czechoslovakia, much as Churchill had predicted. About three million German-speakers lived in western Czechoslovakia in an area known as Sudetenland. In 1938, with secret funding from the Nazis, many of those Germans agitated for "a return to the Reich." By summer, Hitler was openly supporting those demands. Fearful, the Czechs turned to their allies for help. France and Russia were among the nations that had promised to protect the country's independence.

You were given the choice between war and dishonour. You chose dishonour and you will have war.

As tensions mounted, Prime Minister Neville Chamberlain of Britain decided to defuse the situation by appeasing the Germans. That is, he called for concessions to avoid a war. Chamberlain even made a dramatic flight to Germany to confer with Hitler. Not long after his arrival, he confided in a letter to his sister Ida, "I had established a certain confidence, which was my aim, and on my side, in spite of the hardness and ruthlessness I thought I saw in his face, I got the impression that here was a man who could be relied upon when he had given his word."

Yet over the next few weeks, Chamberlain was unable to find a compromise Hitler would accept. Hitler remained firm in his demand for the Sudetenland. And the Czechs were equally firm in their refusal to give up the territory. Then, at what seemed to be the last minute, Benito Mussolini of Italy invited German, French, and British leaders to a meeting in Munich, Germany, to resolve the crisis. There the four nations agreed to give Hitler the Sudetenland. He, in turn, promised that it would be his last territorial demand.

The agreement infuriated the Czechs. And it worried at least one of the leaders who negotiated the pact. When Edouard Daladier, the prime minister of France, returned from Munich, he fully expected to be jeered for his failure to stand up to the Germans. Instead, the French gave him a hero's welcome. He shook his head and muttered that those who rejoiced at the pact were fools.

Chamberlain was also hailed. Thousands of admiring Germans lined the streets of Munich to cheer the British leader as he traveled to the airport. When he landed in London, another crowd of well-wishers gathered to hear him promise that the agreement would bring "peace for our time." He added that it would be a "peace with honor." Critics were less optimistic. Still most believed that he had preserved the peace for at least a few years. Only Winston Churchill disagreed. He told Chamberlain, "You were given the choice between war and dishonour. You chose dishonour and you will have war."

Although Russia was not invited to the meeting, Joseph Stalin was willing to send troops to help the Czechs. But Poland and Romania would not allow those troops to march through their territory. They feared that doing so might draw them into another war. As a result, Czechoslovakia stood alone.

CONNECTIONS

Winston Churchill defined an *appeaser* as "one who feeds a crocodile—hoping that it will eat him last." Do you agree? Or is it one who overlooks the bad in order to attain the good—in this case, peace? Reread "The Hangman" (Chapter 4, Reading 23). Were the townspeople appeasers?

How were the methods Hitler used to take Czechoslovakia similar to those used to acquire Austria? What differences seem most striking?

Study a map of Europe in 1938. After the Germans took Austria and the Sudetenland, which countries had the most cause for concern?

Research newspapers or news magazines published in the fall of 1938. How did each publication report the Munich agreement? What do the letters to the editor suggest about the way ordinary people viewed the event? Then research newspapers or news magazines published in the fall of 1994. How did each publication react to the crises in what was Yugoslavia? What do the letters to the editor suggest about the way ordinary people viewed the situation? What similarities do you notice between the two crises? What differences seem most striking?

READING 5

The Night of the Pogrom

At Evian, the delegate from Colombia raised a fundamental question, "Can a state, without upsetting the basis of our civilisation, and indeed, of all civilisation, arbitrarily withdraw nationality from a whole class of its citizens, thereby making them stateless persons whom no country is compelled to receive on its territory"? It was a question that went unanswered that July. By November, the failure to answer it would lead to yet another crisis.

Throughout 1938, Hitler and his top officials accelerated their campaign against his primary enemy, the Jews. The first step was the mandatory "Aryanization" of Jewish businesses. Up until then, it was voluntary. But now the Nazis required that all Jewish-owned companies be sold to "Aryans," usually at a fraction of their value. Then in June, the Nazis rounded up Jews "previously convicted" of crimes to remove the "criminal element" from the population. Although many were guilty of nothing more than a traffic violation, about five hundred men described as "antisocial" were sent to a concentration camp at Buchenwald, a town near Weimar, Germany.

In August, a new law required that all Jews have a "Jewish first name" by January 1, 1939. If the name chosen was not on a list of approved "Jewish first names," the Nazis would add "Israel" to the man's name and "Sarah" to the woman's. In September, the government announced that Jewish lawyers could no longer practice their profession. A month later, at the request of Switzerland, which was bombarded by Jews trying to leave Germany, the Nazis began to mark the passport of every Jew with the letter J. The Nazis then turned their attention to Jews who were not German citizens. Their first target was Russian Jews.

After the Nazis expelled every Jew who held a Russian passport, the Polish government feared that Jews with Polish passports would be next. To keep them from returning to Poland, the nation required that they secure a special stamp for their passports. The order affected about seventy thousand Jews living in Germany. Although few wanted to return to Poland, they needed passports to emigrate to any other nation. Yet when they tried to get the required stamp, Polish officials turned them away.

The crisis came to a head when the Polish government announced that October 31 was the last day it would issue stamps. On October 26, the Nazis responded by expelling all Polish Jews. When Poland refused to accept them, thousands of men, women, and children ended up in refugee camps near the German-Polish border. Among them were the parents of seventeen-year-old Herschel Grynszpan.

Grynszpan was living in France at the time. Angry and frustrated by his inability to help his family, he marched into the German Embassy in Paris on November 7 and shot a Nazi official. When the man died two days later, the Germans decided to avenge his death. The night of November 9-10 came to be known as *Kristallnacht* ("Night of the Broken Glass") outside Germany and as the Night of the Pogrom within the nation. That night the Nazis looted and then destroyed thousands of Jewish homes and businesses in every part of the country. They set fire to 191 synagogues, killed over ninety Jews, and sent thirty thousand others to concentration camps.

Joseph Goebbels, Hitler's minister of propaganda, held a press conference the next day. He told reporters that *Kristallnacht* was not a government action but a "spontaneous" expression of German dissatisfaction with the Jews. "It is an intolerable state of affairs that within our borders and for all these years hundreds of thousands of Jews still control whole streets of shops, populate our recreation spots and, as foreign apartment owners, pocket the money of German tenants, while their racial comrades abroad agitate for war against Germany and gun down German officials." Two days later, the government fined the Jewish community one billion marks for "property damaged in the rioting."

Frederic Morton, a writer whose family fled from Vienna shortly after *Kristallnacht*, never forgot that night.

> The day began with a thudding through my pillow. Jolts waked me. Then, like an alarm clock, the doorbell rang. It was six in the morning. My father, my mother, my little brother and I all met in the foyer, all in our robes. We did not know yet exactly what. But we knew. We were Jews in Vienna in 1938. Everything in our lives, including our beds, stood on a cliff.
>
> My father opened the door on Frau Eckel, the janitress.
>
> "They are down there. . .they are throwing things." She turned away. Went on with her morning sweep. Her broom trembled.
>
> We looked down into the courtyard. Pink-cheeked storm troopers chatted and whistled. Chopped-up furniture flew through the window.

The troopers fielded the pieces sportively, piled them into heaps. One hummed something from "The Merry Widow."

"Franz! Run somewhere!" my mother said to my father.

By that time we'd gone to the window facing the street. At the house entrance two storm troopers lit cigarettes for each other. Their comrades were smashing the synagogue on the floor below us, tossing out a debris of Torahs and pews.

"Oh, my God!" my mother said.

Something overwhelming wanted to melt down my eyes. I couldn't let it. All this might not be real as long as real tears did not touch my face. A crazy last-resort bargain with fate.

"All right," my father said. "Meanwhile we get dressed."

Meanwhile meant until they come up here. No other Jews lived in the building. It had no back door. But as long as I could keep my tears down, I could keep them down. While they were destroying down there, they would not come up here. As long as the shaking of the floor continued, the axe blows, the sledgehammer thuds, we might live.

I had gym for my first class. I laced on my sneakers. I knew I never would see school that morning. I didn't care that I knew. I only cared not to cry. I tried to pour my entire mind into the lacing of my sneakers.

We met in the living room. We saw each other dressed with a normality made grotesque by the crashing of the perdition downstairs. It stopped. The shaking and the thudding stopped. Silence. A different sound. Heavy, booted steps ascending. I relaced my sneakers.

My father had put on his hat. "Everybody come close to me," he said. "My two sons, you put your hands on top of your heads."

We put our hands on top of our heads, as hats. My father put his arms around all our shoulders, my mother's, my brother's, mine.

"Shema Yisroel," my father said. "Repeat after me: *Shema Yisroel Adonoy Elohenu Adonoy Ehod. . . .*" ["Hear, O Israel: the Lord our God, the Lord is One. . . ."]

The doorbell rang. Once. Ever since the Anschluss, we'd rung our doorbell twice in quick succession to signal that this was a harmless ringing, not the dreaded one. Now the dreaded ring had come.

"Hansi, you go," my father said.

"No!" my mother said.

"Hansi is the only one they might not hurt on sight," my father said. "Hansi, go."

My brother, a tiny blond eight-year-old, an Aryan-looking doll, went.

A minute later he returned. Behind him towered some 10 storm troopers with heavy pickaxes. They were young and bright-faced with excitement. Ten bridegrooms on their wedding day. One had freckles. How could a freckle-faced man kill us? The freckles kept me from crying.

"House search," the leader said. "Don't move."

We all stood against the wall, except my father. He placed himself, hat still on, a foot in front of us.

They yanked out every drawer in every one of our chests and cupboards, and tossed each in the air. They let the cutlery jangle across the floor, the clothes scatter, and stepped over the mess to fling the next drawer. Their exuberance was amazing. Amazing, that none of them raised an axe to split our skulls.

"We might be back," the leader said. On the way out he threw our mother-of-pearl ashtray over his shoulder, like confetti. We did not speak or move or breathe until we heard their boots against the pavement.

"I am going to the office," my father said. "Breitel might help."

Breitel, the Reich commissar in my father's costume-jewelry factory, was a "good" Nazi. Once he'd said we should come to him if there was trouble. My father left. My mother was crying, with relief, with terror; she cradled against herself my little stunned brother. I turned away from her. I swore I would do something other than cry.

I began to pick up clothes, when the doorbell rang again. It was my father.

"I have two minutes."

"What?" my mother said. But she knew. His eyes had become glass.

"There was another crew waiting for me downstairs. They gave me two minutes."

Now I broke down. Now my father was the only one not crying. His eyes were blue glass, relentlessly dry. His kiss felt stubbly. He had not shaved this morning. After one more embrace with my mother he marched to the door, turned on his heel, called out.

"Fritz!"

I went to him, sobbing.

"Stop!"

I couldn't stop.

Harshly his hands came down on my shoulders.

"If I don't come back—avenge me!"

He was gone. The fury of his fingers stung. It burned into my skin a sense of continuity against all odds. I stopped.

Four months later he rang our doorbell twice, skull shaven, skeletal, released from Dachau, somehow alive.

Forty years later, today, he is practicing the tango with my mother in Miami Beach. My little brother Hansi is chairman of the political science department at Queens College. I am a writer in America with an American family. We are atypically lucky. But to this day we all ring our American doorbells twice.[8]

CONNECTIONS

The Germans call *Kristallnacht* the "Night of the Pogrom." A *pogrom* is a government-organized or inspired massacre of a minority group, particularly of Jews. It is a Russian word that literally means "riot" or "destruction." Over one hundred years ago, the nobles of St. Petersburg demanded that the "people's wrath" be vented against the Jews. The peasants in the nearby town of Elizanetgrad responded with the first pogrom in modern times. A Russian writer has described the subsequent murders, rapes, and looting as the "unending torture" of a religious and ethnic minority. Was *Kristallnacht* a pogrom? What evidence suggests it was planned? That the murder of the Nazi official was an excuse for a riot, not its cause?

At the time of the first pogrom, the Russian government blamed the Jews for the violence. Whom did the Germans blame? Are victims ever to blame for violence committed against them?

Morton was an eyewitness to the events of *Kristallnacht*. How does his account differ from the official view? What insights does he offer as to why many Jews saw *Kristallnacht* as a turning point?

Edwin Landau (Chapter 4, Reading 4) said of the Nazis' boycott of Jewish businesses in 1933, "To me the whole thing was inconceivable. It would not sink in that something like that could even be possible in the twentieth century, for such things had happened, at most, in the Middle Ages." How do you think someone like Landau would have responded to this new outrage? Would he have been as shocked in 1938 as he was in 1933? Trace the steps that led to *Kristallnacht*. How did each prepare the public for state-sanctioned violence against a minority within the nation? What attitudes and values allowed people to remain silent when their neighbors were deprived of citizenship?

➤What is the significance of the name *Kristallnacht?* How does the name cloud the fact that it was more a night of broken lives than of broken glass?

➤Peter Gay, a Jewish teenager in Berlin during the 1930s, reflects on the way *Kristallnacht* differed from earlier events that targeted Jews in *Elements of Time*, pages 103-105. Joan B. in the video montage *Friedrich* describes how it altered life for her family and contributed to the death of her parents. The video is available from the Facing History Resource Center. A study guide on *Kristallnacht* is also available.

Taking a Stand

German Jews saw *Kristallnacht* as a turning point. So did many "Aryan" Germans. They also made important choices that night and in the days that followed. Dan Bar-On, an Israeli psychologist, describes the decision one family made:

For the space of a second I was clearly aware that something terrible had happened there. Something frighteningly brutal. But almost at once I switched over to accepting what had happened as over and done with, and avoiding critical reflection.

> It was the autumn of 1938. Andre was twelve years old and lived with his parents in a small town in northern Germany. One evening he came home from his youth movement meeting.
>
> "Daddy," he said to his father, "we were told at the meeting that tomorrow we are supposed to throw stones at the Jewish shops in town. Should I take part?"
>
> His father looked at him. "What do you think?"
>
> "I don't know. I have nothing against the Jews—I hardly know them—but everyone is going to throw stones. So what should I do?"
>
> Their conversation proceeded, the son presenting questions to his father, the father turning the questions back to his son.
>
> "I understand," said Andre. "You want me to make up my own mind. I'm going for a walk. I'll let you know what I've decided when I come back."
>
> When Andre returned a short while later, he approached his parents, who were sitting at the table.
>
> "I've made up my mind, but my decision involves you too."
>
> "What is it?"
>
> "I've decided not to throw stones at the Jewish shops. But tomorrow everyone will say, 'Andre, the son of X, did not take part, he refused to throw stones!' They will turn against you. What are you going to do?"
>
> His father's sigh was one of relief tinged with pride. "While you were out, your mother and I discussed this question. We decided that if you made up your mind to throw stones, we would have to live with your decision, since we had let you decide, after all. But if you decided not to throw stones, we would leave Germany immediately."
>
> And that is what they did. The following day, Andre's family left Germany.[9]

Other Germans made other choices. Some protested by resigning their membership in the Nazi party—though many made it clear that they were not objecting to antisemitism but to mob violence. Others sent anonymous letters of protest to foreign embassies. Still others quietly brought Jewish families food and other necessities to replace items that had been destroyed. Neighbors told one Jewish woman that helping her was a way to "show the Jews that the German people had no part in this—it is only Goebbels and his gang."

Most Germans, however, responded much the way Melita Maschmann did. She lived in a small suburb of Berlin and knew nothing of *Kristallnacht* until the next morning. As she picked her way through the broken glass on her way to work, she asked a policeman what had happened. After he explained, she recalls:

> I went on my way shaking my head. For the space of a second I was clearly aware that something terrible had happened there. Something frighteningly brutal. But almost at once I switched over to accepting what had happened as over and done with, and avoiding critical reflection. I said to myself: the Jews are the enemies of the New Germany. Last night they had a taste of what this means. . . . With these or similar thoughts, I constructed for myself a justification of the pogrom. But in any case, I forced the memory of it out of my consciousness as quickly as possible. As the years went by, I grew better and better at switching off quickly in this manner on similar occasions.[10]

Maschmann was not alone in rationalizing the events of that night. Dietrich Goldschmidt, a minister in the Confessing Church, explains that for most Germans "the persecution of the Jews, this escalating persecution of the Jews, and the 9th of November—in a sense, that was only one event, next to very many gratifying ones. Here the famous stories of all the things Hitler did come in: 'He got rid of unemployment, he built the Autobahn, the people started doing well again, he restored our national pride again. One has to weigh that against the other things.'"[11]

C O N N E C T I O N S

Each of the individuals quoted in this reading reached a decision as a result of the events of *Kristallnacht*. How did each make his or her decision? What values and beliefs shaped the choice each made?

What were the short-term consequences of each choice described in the reading? The long-term consequences? For example, what do you think happened to non-Jews who resigned from the Nazi party? Tried to emigrate? Protested? What does each decision tell you about the person's "universe of obligation"? How were the choices open to each individual different from the ones he or she could have made in 1933? In 1935?

What did Melita Maschmann mean when she says "I constructed for myself a justification of the pogrom"? Why did she find it necessary to do so? What did she mean when she says as the years went by, she grew better and better "at forcing the memory of events like the pogrom out of my consciousness as quickly as possible"?

Evaluate Goldschmidt's explanation of why public outrage did not last long. Did the good outweigh the "other things"?

➤ *Now. . . After All These Years*, offers a glimpse of *Kristallnacht* by combining interviews of current citizens of Rhina, a small town in Germany, with those of the town's former citizens. The video, which is available from the Facing History Resource Center, raises questions about how one's perspective affects one's view of an event.

READING 7

World Responses

Newspapers around the world reported *Kristallnacht*. The story filed by Otto D. Tolischus of the *New York Times* was typical of many.

There are times when the mere instincts of humanity make silence impossible.

> A wave of destruction, looting and incendiaries unparalleled in Germany since the Thirty Years War and in Europe generally since the Bolshevist revolution, swept over Greater Germany today as National Socialist cohorts took vengeance on Jewish shops, offices and synagogues for the murder by a young Polish Jew of Ernst vom Rath, third secretary of the German Embassy in Paris.
>
> Beginning systematically in the early morning hours in almost every town and city in the country, the wrecking, looting and burning continued all day. Huge but mostly silent crowds looked on and the police confined themselves to regulating traffic and making wholesale arrests of Jews "for their own protection."
>
> All day the main shopping districts as well as the side streets of Berlin and innumerable other places resounded to the shattering of shop windows falling to the pavement, the dull thuds of furniture and fittings being pounded to pieces and clamor of fire brigades rushing to burning shops and synagogues. Although shop fires were quickly extinguished, synagogue fires were merely kept from spreading to adjoining buildings.[12]

People everywhere were outraged. As the Archbishop of Canterbury, Cosmo Gordon Lang, wrote in a letter to the editor of the *Times*, "There are times when the mere instincts of humanity make silence impossible." Thousands of Americans agreed. They showed their outrage at huge rallies held in support of German Jews. In reporting these events to Berlin, the German ambassador expressed a fear that these protests might jeopardize the Munich agreement.

The Bangor Daily News

BANGOR, ME., FRIDAY, NOVEMBER 11, 1938   FIVE CENTS

Anti-Jew Violence Sweeps Germany

GOP Makes Gain Of 81 Seats In House   Outbreak Due To Paris Shooting

Position To Block Roosevelt

Leaders Prepare to Serve Ultimatum Warning President — Veer to Right or Face Stalemate in Congress

New Dealers Defection Is Not Result of President's... — Leaders Predict Broad Revision

Beloved Soldier Poet's Last Photo

Mobs Burn and Pillage In Widespread Day of Vengeance

Final Answer to Jewry to be Given In New Drastic Law, Says Goebbles as He Calls Halt In Demonstration

By LOUIS P. LOCHNER

BERLIN, Nov. 10—(AP)—The greatest wave of anti-Jewish violence since Adolf Hitler came to power in 1933 swept Nazi Germany today and Jews were the...

Although *Kristallnacht* strained the policy of appeasement, it did not end it. When members of Britain's Parliament pressed Neville Chamberlain to condemn the pogrom, he simply verified that newspaper reports were "substantially correct." He also acknowledged "deep and widespread sympathy" for those who were made "to suffer so severely" for the "senseless crime committed in Paris."

Similar attitudes in France led the editor of a newspaper called *La Lumière* to warn, "In the past, when we protested against massacres in Ethiopia, China, Spain, we were told, 'Silence! You are warmongering.' When we protested against the mutilation of Czechoslovakia, we were told, 'Keep quiet! You are a war party.' Today, when we protest against the contemptible persecution of defenseless Jews and their wives and children, we are told, 'Be silent! France is afraid.'"[13]

The only world leader to take a stand was Franklin D. Roosevelt. He did so only after a number of individuals and groups had urged him to speak out. On November 15, six days after *Kristallnacht*, he opened a press conference by stating, "The news of the last few days from Germany has deeply shocked public opinion in the United States. Such news from any part of the world would produce a similar profound reaction among American people in every part of the nation. I myself could scarcely believe that such things could occur in a twentieth-century civilization." Although he announced that the United States was withdrawing its ambassador to Germany, he did not offer to help the thousands of Jews now trying desperately to leave the Third Reich.

He that would make his own liberty secure, must guard even his enemy from oppression, for if he violates this duty, he establishes a precedent that will reach to himself.

Few Americans criticized Roosevelt's stand. According to a poll taken at the time, 57 percent of all Americans approved the recall. But 72 percent did not want more Jewish refugees in the United States and over half opposed aid to refugees who wished to settle elsewhere.

CONNECTIONS

➤What did the Archbishop of Canterbury mean when he said, "There are times when the mere instincts of humanity make silence impossible"? What are those "instincts"? Do all humans have them? At what times is silence impossible? How do such times affect government responses today? Individual reactions? An ABC special about Bosnia, available from the Facing History Resource Center, explains why a few State Department officials resigned in protest of the failure of the United States government to take meaningful action to stop the killings in the Balkans.

In 1776, Thomas Paine said, "He that would make his own liberty secure, must guard even his enemy from oppression, for if he violates this duty, he establishes a precedent that will reach to himself." How did he define his "universe of obligation"? Which of the following shared that definition: the archbishop, Chamberlain, the editor of *La Lumière*, or Roosevelt?

What does the poll suggest about the way many Americans defined their "universe of obligation"? About the limits of people's outrage?

Compare the way people responded to *Kristallnacht* in Germany with responses abroad. What similarities do you notice? What differences seem most striking?

What was the editor of *La Lumiere* trying to tell people? How is his message similar to the one found in"The Hangman" (Chapter 4, Reading 23)? What is the key difference?

READING 8

The Narrowing Circle

German leaders also reacted to *Kristallnacht* and the public outcry that followed. On November 10, Propaganda Minister Joseph Goebbels called a press conference "to remove certain misunderstandings that appear to have found their way into reports sent abroad." He warned that if Jews continued to spread "exaggerations of yesterday's happening, of the kind contained in the accounts and leading articles of the American press, then they would defeat their own ends, and they would be digging the graves of the Jews in Germany."

Most government officials, however, were opposed to *Kristallnacht* and other "undisciplined individual actions." Indeed, the Night of the Pogrom was the last occasion when Jews had to fear street violence in Germany. After *Kristallnacht,* writes Richard Rubenstein, "the hoodlums were banished and the bureaucrats took over." In the weeks that followed, key Nazi officials, led by Heinrich Himmler, saw to it that measures against the Jews were strictly "legal." On November 15, the bureaucracy excluded all Jewish children from state schools. By December 6, Jews could no longer walk or drive in certain parts of every major city. Jews who lived in those areas had to have a police permit to go home. Jews were advised to move and perhaps even exchange residences with "Aryans" who lived in "Jewish sections of town."

At about the same time, the government announced that Jews could no longer attend German universities. A few days later, Himmler prohibited them from owning or even driving a car. Jews were also banned from theaters, movie houses, concert halls, sports arenas, parks, and swimming pools. The Gestapo even went door to door confiscating radios owned by Jewish families.

> The Night of the Pogrom was the last occasion when Jews had to fear street violence in Germany. After Kristallnacht, "the hoodlums were banished and the bureaucrats took over."

C O N N E C T I O N S

A number of Jews who lived in Germany during those years spoke of a "narrowing circle." What do you think they meant? Picture what your world would be like if you could no longer attend school, shop at the mall, see a movie, play ball in the park, or even watch TV.

How significant was the decision to banish the "hoodlums" and let the bureaucrats take over? How was it like the actions the Nazis took after the Night of the Long Knives (Chapter 4, Reading 17)? How did it differ? How do you think the outcry over the events of *Kristallnacht* affected the decision? Was *Kristallnacht* a turning point for the Nazis?

Shortly after *Kristallnacht*, the Nazis released the film *Der Ewige Jude* (Chapter 5, Reading 6). How might the two events be linked?

➤ The novel *Friedrich* by Hans Peter Richter describes the effects of *Kristallnacht* on two German families, one Christian and the other Jewish. Classroom sets of the books are available from the Facing History Resource Center.

Death Threats and Broken Promises

On January 30, 1939, six years after he became chancellor of Germany, Hitler told the Reichstag that other nations were hypocritical in their complaints that Germany mistreated the Jews.

> In accordance with their own declarations they cannot find a single reason to excuse themselves for refusing to receive this most valuable race in their own countries. Nor can I see a reason why the members of this race should be imposed upon the German nation, while in the States, which are so enthusiastic about these "splendid people," their settlement should suddenly be refused with every imaginable excuse. I think that the sooner this problem is solved the better; for Europe cannot settle down until the Jewish question is cleared up. . . .
>
> One thing I should like to say on this day which may be memorable for others as well as for us Germans: In the course of my life I have very often been a prophet, and have usually been ridiculed for it. During the time of my struggle for power it was in the first instance the Jewish race which only received my prophecies with laughter when I said that I would one day take over the leadership of the State, and with it that of the whole nation, and that I would then among many other things settle the Jewish problem. Their laughter was uproarious, but I think that for some time now they have been laughing on the other side of their face. Today I will once more be a prophet: If the international Jewish financiers in and outside Europe should succeed in plunging the nations once more into a world war, then the result will not be the bolshevization of the earth, and thus the victory of Jewry, but the annihilation of the Jewish race in Europe!

Less than two months later, Hitler took over all of Czechoslovakia. "Peace in our time" had lasted just six months. World leaders were remarkably silent. Neville Chamberlain spoke out only when Hitler threatened Poland. He vowed that Britain would come to the nation's aid in case of attack. France made a similar promise. Although the United States was an ocean away, Roosevelt was also concerned. He asked Mussolini and Hitler to promise they would not attack 30 specific countries. William Shirer described Hitler's response:

> He claimed he had asked the nations which Roosevelt thought threatened whether they so considered themselves and "in all cases the reply was negative." States like Syria, he said, he could not ask because "they are at present not in possession of their freedom, but are occupied and consequently deprived of their rights by the military

agents of democratic countries." And "the fact has obviously escaped Mr. Roosevelt's notice that Palestine is at present occupied not by German troops but by the English." And so on in this sarcastic manner, from which with a masterly touch—Hitler was a superb actor today— he drew every last drop of irony. America champions the conference method of settling disputes? he asked. But was it not the first nation to shrink from participation in the League [of Nations]? "It was not until many years later that I resolved to follow the example of America and likewise leave the largest conference in the world."[14]

In the end, Hitler gave "an assurance of the kind desired by Mr. Roosevelt" and concluded the session by demanding the return of the city of Danzig and part of Poland. Once again, Hitler vowed that it would be his last territorial claim in Europe.

CONNECTIONS

What is Hitler's solution to the "Jewish question"? Was he offering it as an idea or as a policy? How did he expect other nations to respond?

Were Hitler's charges true? Were his arguments believable? If so, whom would they convince? How did he use history to make his case? How did he distort the past? Do you think his response to the questions Roosevelt raised was sincere or was he acting?

READING 10

The Failure to Help

By 1939, more and more Jews were obsessed by the need for "papers." They needed official passports to leave Germany, Austria, and other countries now under Nazi rule. They also needed written documents to enter another country. Among the Jews caught up in the search for the "right papers" were the 937 men, women, and children who boarded the ship, the *St. Louis,* on May 14. Each had paid $150—a huge sum of money in 1939—for permission to land in Cuba. For only a few was the island their final destination. Most were on a waiting list for entry to the United States.

As the *St. Louis* neared Cuba, President Federico Laredo Bru suddenly canceled the landing permits of the Jewish passengers. As they and various international Jewish groups tried to change his mind, the ship's captain was optimistic. He reasoned that most of his passengers would eventually be allowed to enter the United States. Therefore, even if the situation in Cuba deteriorated, the American government would quickly resolve the matter by accepting them a little sooner. His passengers were less hopeful. Two tried to commit suicide. To prevent other attempts, the crew lowered lifeboats and lit the waters around the ship. When the captain heard rumors of a mass suicide pact, he added special patrols.

When news of the first suicide attempt (the second one was kept secret) reached the United States, many Americans demanded that their government accept the passengers. Others sent Bru telegrams of protest, but he refused to reconsider his stand. As a result, the ship left Cuban waters on June 2 with all but 30 passengers still on board. The 30 were non-Jews or Jews with special visas. Unsure of where to take the remaining passengers, the captain marked time while negotiations continued. When they ended on June 7 without a settlement, he was forced to return to Germany. As the ship recrossed the Atlantic, the desperate passengers cabled Neville Chamberlain: "Beg to be saved by being granted asylum in England or at least disembarkation at Southampton as return to Hamburg impossible and acts of desperation would be unavoidable."

The Nazis turned the incident into propaganda. They claimed that it demonstrated that the Jews were universally disliked and distrusted. On June 10, Belgium responded with an announcement that it would accept two hundred passengers. Two days later, the Netherlands promised to take 194. Britain and France took in the rest. The United States remained silent. Furious at the role the United States government played in the crisis, a resident of Richmond, Virginia, wrote to a local paper:

> [The] press reported that the ship came close enough to Miami for the refugees to see the lights of the city. The press also reported that the U.S. Coast Guard, under instructions from Washington, followed the ship. . .to prevent any people landing on our shores. And during the days when this horrible tragedy was being enacted right at our doors, our government in Washington made no effort to relieve the desperate situation of these people, but on the contrary gave orders that they be kept out of the country. . . . The failure to take any steps whatever to assist these distressed, persecuted Jews in their hour of extremity was one of the most disgraceful things which has happened in American history and leaves a stain and brand of shame upon the record of our nation.[15]

In the 1930s Americans were more concerned with unemployment at home than with stateless Jews in Europe. Although many were willing to accept a few famous writers, artists, and scientists who happened to be Jewish, they were less willing to let in thousands of ordinary Jews. A 1939 poll helps explain why. Over 5,000 people were asked with which of the following statements they agreed:

> In the United States the Jews have the same standing as any other people and they should be treated in all ways exactly like all other Americans.

By 1939, more and more Jews were obsessed by the need for papers. They needed official passports to leave Germany, Austria, and other countries now under Nazi rule. They also needed written documents to enter another country.

Jews are in some way distinct from other Americans but they make respected and useful citizens so long as they do not try to mingle socially where they are not wanted.

Jews have somewhat different business methods and, therefore, measures should be taken to prevent Jews from getting too much power in the business world.

We should make it a policy to deport Jews from this country to some new homeland as fast as it can be done without inhumanity.

Although 39 percent agreed with the first statement, 53 percent regarded Jews as different from "real Americans." About 32 percent wanted to restrict their "business methods" and about 10 percent favored their deportation. Eight percent had no opinion. Other polls resulted in similar findings. Few Americans were violently antisemitic, but many felt that Jews had to be kept in their "place."[16]

Enforcement of the nation's immigration laws reflected these views. The United States could legally admit as many as 26,000 German immigrants each year. Yet in 1934, the State Department allowed only about 5,000 to enter the nation. Approximately 6,000 were permitted to enter in 1935 and less than 11,000 in 1936.

Then in February 1939, Senator Robert Wagner of New York and Representative Edith Nourse Rogers of Massachusetts sponsored a bill that would bypass the immigration laws and temporarily admit 20,000 Jewish children who would stay in the country only until it was safe for them to return home. As most were too young to work, they would not take away jobs from Americans. Furthermore, their stay would not cost taxpayers a penny. Various Jewish groups had agreed to assume financial responsibility for the children.

Yet the bill encountered strong opposition. Why, opponents asked, were Christian children from Poland or Chinese children (Japan invaded China in 1933) not included? Others made openly antisemitic remarks. One warned "that twenty thousand children would soon grow into twenty thousand ugly adults." The bill was never passed.

CONNECTIONS

The *St. Louis* was not the only boat to be turned away from the United States in the late 1930s. What do such incidents suggest about the nation's "universe of obligation"?

How would you respond to the letter written to the Virginia newspaper? How do you think a government official would respond?

What does the controversy over the Rogers Bill suggest about antisemitism in the United States? About anti-immigrant feeling? In 1993, a poll similar to the one taken in 1939 revealed that 60 percent regarded immigration as a "bad thing for this country." About 62 percent believed that immigrants take the jobs of U.S. workers. Compare the two polls.

Over fifty years after the *St. Louis* incident, boatloads of refugees from Haiti, Vietnam, and China sought asylum in the United States and once again government officials turned them away. The officials claimed that the only refugees allowed to enter the nation were those whose lives would be in danger if they were returned to their homeland. Check newspapers and magazines written in the early 1990s to find out how Americans responded to that policy. How did memories of the *St. Louis* affect their reaction?

➤ The Fortunoff Video Archive for Holocaust Testimonies at Yale University has created *Flight From Destiny*, a video montage that deals with the voyage of the *St. Louis*. The video is described in detail in *Elements Of Time*, pages 189-197 and is available from the Facing History Resource Center. Also available is a PBS special on American attitudes during those years. In addition, a study guide is available for use with a video of Lianne Rief Lehrer and documents that detail what happened to some passengers on the *St. Louis*. Walter K.'s memories of the *St. Louis* are summarized in *Elements of Time*, pages 234-236.

READING 11

Enemies become Allies

*B*y the summer of 1939, war in Europe seemed inevitable. As people braced themselves, many wondered how the Soviet Union would respond. In the mid-1930s, Joseph Stalin had shifted from a policy of opposition to all capitalist nations to one that targeted fascist regimes. Still, no one could be sure what Stalin or Hitler would do.

On August 23, 1939, the two dictators shocked the world by announcing a nonaggression pact. They also secretly agreed to divide Poland. In addition, Hitler promised Stalin a free hand in Finland, Estonia, Latvia, Lithuania, and Bessarabia—areas that had been part of the Russian Empire before World War I. Although the treaty did not alter the long-range policies of either leader, it did startle people in both Russia and Germany. Max von der Gruen was thirteen years old when the treaty was signed.

> I can remember the day the pact was signed as if it were yesterday. Probably the reason this agreement caused such a sensation and stirred up so many people was that ever since 1933 it had been drummed into the heads of the Germans that they were waging a life-and-death struggle against the forces of Bolshevism. But now the Nazis had made a pact with the Russians. People did not understand this; they were rattled, and suddenly began to have doubts about the Fuehrer.

That evening von der Gruen attended a meeting of Hitler Youth. The boys asked their squad leader to explain why Hitler had formed an alliance with his archenemy Stalin. Von der Gruen recalled:

> The squad leader ... said that the explanation was really quite simple: To be sure, Hitler had always been against Bolshevism, but only against the Bolshevism in the German Reich, not that in the Soviet Union; therefore, the pact was logical, understandable, and even long overdue. ...
>
> And yet people continued to feel uneasy. On those rare occasions when one of us children dared to ask questions, our teachers did not know what to reply. They used to repeat the things that were said over the radio, which Goebbels controlled. The Fuehrer, they said, must know what he was doing, and thus he had a right to make a pact with the devil himself if he wanted to. Our history teacher actually said this to us.[17]

CONNECTIONS

Why were Germans so uncomfortable with the alliance with the Soviet Union? What does their discomfort suggest about the strengths and weaknesses of German propaganda?

For over twenty years, Germans were taught to regard the Bolsheviks as their enemies. Now they were told otherwise. How do enemy nations become allies? How does the average citizen come to view a former enemy as a friend? What part does propaganda play in the creation of enemies? In the process of turning those same enemies into allies? How can years spent learning to hate a particular group be unlearned?

READING 12

Those Considered Unworthy to Live

As Hitler consolidated his power at home and abroad, he moved against yet another enemy. This enemy consisted of the weakest Germans—the people he called "useless eaters." They included epileptics, alcoholics, people with birth defects, hearing losses, mental illnesses, and personality disorders as well as those who were visually impaired, had developmental lags, or even suffered from certain orthopedic problems. In his view, these people were "marginal human beings" who had to make a case for their own survival at a time when the nation was preparing for war.

The first to be eliminated were too young to speak on their own behalf. In the fall of 1938, the parents of a severely disabled infant petitioned Hitler for the right to kill the child. He granted the petition and saw in the request an opportunity to encourage what he called "mercy killings" or "euthanasia." According to his chief medical officer, "the Fuhrer was of the opinion that such a program could be put into effect more smoothly and rapidly in time of war, and that in the general upheaval of war, the open resistance anticipated from the church would not play the part that it might in other circumstances."

The following spring, Hitler set up a committee of physicians to prepare for the murder of disabled and "retarded" children. Known as the "Reich Committee for the Scientific Treatment of Severe Hereditary and Congenital Diseases," the group was told to keep its mission secret. Then just two weeks before the invasion of Poland, members asked doctors and midwives to fill out a questionnaire for every child with a deformity or disability. The focus was on children under the age of three. The committee claimed it was using the data "to clarify certain scientific questions." In fact, the information was used to determine which children would be allowed to live.

The committee used the questionnaires to make its decisions. Members did not personally examine the children, consult with other physicians, or speak to the families involved. Once the decision was made, the committee told the child's parents only that their baby was being placed in a special hospital to "improve" treatment. There death came quickly. After the war, a doctor involved in the program told Robert Jay Lifton, "According to the thinking of that time, in the case of children killing seemed somehow justifiable . . . whereas in the case of the adult mentally ill, that was definitely murder."[18]

The doctor went on to describe how nurses were ordered to give the children sedatives that were harmless in small amounts but deadly in large doses. The doctor noted, "And with these sedatives . . . the child sleeps. If one does not know what is going on, he [the child] is sleeping. One really has to be let in on it to know that . . . that he really is being killed and not sedated." Lifton added:

> While Dr. F. admitted that one might wonder about a child, "Why is he sleeping so much?" he insisted (quite erroneously) that one could ignore that inner question because "the death rate of [those killed] wasn't much above the regular death rate with such children." He stressed the absence of either a direct command ("If I get the order to kill. . . I don't know but I [think I] would refuse. . . but certainly there was no such order . . . for us") or of manifest homicide ("I mean if you had directed a nurse to go from bed to bed shooting these children . . . that would not have worked.") As a result, "there was no killing, strictly speaking. . . . People felt this is not murder, it is a putting-to-sleep."[19]

The program was later expanded to include not only young children but also teenagers and adults. One "euthanasia expert" justified the murders by arguing, "The idea is unbearable to me that the best, the flower of our youth, must lose its life at the front, in order that feebleminded and asocial elements can have a secure existence in the asylum." Another

If you had directed a nurse to go from bed to bed shooting these children. . . that would not have worked. As a result, "there was no killing, strictly speaking. . . . People felt this is not murder, it is a putting-to-sleep."

suggested that a doctor's duty is to rescue the "fit" for the future by weeding out the "unfit" in the present.

In some places, doctors used mobile gas vans to carry out the killings. By June 1940, the vans were being replaced with "showers" that sprayed gas. Between 1939 and 1941 at least seventy thousand persons were killed. A number of experts place the figure higher, claiming that at least two hundred fifty thousand were murdered.

CONNECTIONS

What is "mercy killing"? "Euthanasia"? Was either the goal of the Nazi program? Who decided who would live and who would die? Does it matter who makes that decision?

A poster widely distributed in Nazi Germany stated: "Everyday, a cripple or blind person costs 5-6 [Reichsmarks], a mentally ill person 4, a criminal 3.50. A worker has 3-4 [Reichsmarks] a day to spend on his family." To what prejudices does the poster appeal? How does it justify killings without ever mentioning them?

What distinction does the doctor Lifton interviewed make between murder and "putting to sleep"? Between the killing of young children and adults? How do the euphemisms make the killing easier? Help the perpetrators rationalize their actions?

A Nazi eugenics manual referred to doctors as "alert biological soldiers." What did the name mean? How would you define a doctor?

A bureaucracy developed to implement the new policies. It included not only doctors, nurses, and other medical personnel but also administrators, secretaries, and file clerks. They saw to it that the policy was "properly" carried out. What choices did these men and women make as they did their jobs? How do you account for the fact that they never mutinied or rebelled? Who was part of their "universe of obligation"? Who was not?

How did the name "Reich Committee for the Scientific Treatment of Severe Hereditary and Congenital Diseases" cloud the real work of the group? Why did the Nazis choose to mask its real task?

➤In the 1930s, a number of states in the United States had laws that called for the sterilization of individuals with certain disabilities. And some physicians openly discussed "euthanasia" as a way of dealing with the "unfit." Yet no state ever permitted the practice. Why were Americans willing to go only so far and no further? Additional information on the eugenics movement in the United States can be found on the video *Medicine at the Crossroads*, available from the Facing History Resource Center. The Resource Center also has a packet of materials that provides insights into the legacy of eugenics on American society, including its educational system.

How do Americans today view children with disabilities? Adults with the same disabilities? What prejudices does each group encounter? How do those attitudes make individuals with disabilities a potential target for discrimination and isolation?

READING 13

Opposition to "Euthanasia"

Government officials went to great lengths to keep the euthanasia program secret. Unlike other Nazi policies, this one was not loudly proclaimed. There were, however, too many people involved in the murders to keep the truth from coming out. From the start, families, religious leaders, and hospital personnel were suspicious of the government. When they raised awkward questions, the government either denied any wrongdoing or refused to answer questions because of the need for secrecy in wartime.

As rumors mounted, a few people demanded answers. Among them were Friedrich von Bodelschwingh and Paul-Gerhard Braune. The two men were ministers in the Confessing Church (Chapter 4, Reading 14) and heads of institutions that served disabled adults. Once they realized how the questionnaires were being used, they refused to fill out forms, voiced objections with key Nazi officials, and stalled as long as possible to keep their patients from being taken away.

Fearful that a public stand might jeopardize his patients, each man worked behind the scenes. Braune, however, sent top government officials a long report with detailed evidence of the murders. In it, he asked, "How far does one want to go with the extermination of so-called lives unworthy of life? The mass actions up to now have shown that many people have been taken who were in large part clear and of sane mind. Where does the limit lie? Who is abnormal, anti-social, who is hopelessly ill?. . . It is a dangerous venture to abandon the integrity of the person without any legal foundation. . . . Will it not endanger the ethics of the entire population, when human life counts for so little?"[20]

A month later, Braune was imprisoned for "sabotaging measures of the regime in an irresponsible manner." His fellow pastors in the Confessing Church gave him little support. Most wanted more proof before they took a stand. The few who did speak out lived in villages and small towns. They had no way of being heard beyond their community.

Then in May 1941, the Reich Committee for the Scientific Treatment of Severe Hereditary and Congenital Diseases began sending its questionnaires to homes for the elderly. A few months later, Clemens Graf von

> It is a dangerous venture to abandon the integrity of the person without any legal foundation. . . . Will it not endanger the ethics of the entire population, when human life counts for so little?

Galen, the Catholic bishop of Muenster, asked his congregation, "Do you or I have the right to live only as long as we are productive?" If so, he argued, "Then someone has only to order a secret decree that the measures tried out on the mentally ill be extended to other 'nonproductive' people, that it can be used on those incurably ill with a lung disease, on those weakened by aging, on those disabled at work, on severely wounded soldiers. Then not a one of us is sure anymore of his life."[21]

The sermon was secretly reproduced and distributed throughout Germany. Three weeks later, Hitler signed an order officially ending the program. In fact, it did not end. It continued secretly throughout the war and may have claimed one hundred thousand more lives.

CONNECTIONS

What does the phrase "unworthy of life" mean? What are the consequences of believing that some are "unworthy of life"?

How did the Nazis answer the questions raised in Braune's report? The questions the bishop raised? How did the German people answer them in 1939? How would you respond?

Braune asked,"Will it not endanger the ethics of the entire population, when human life counts for so little"? How would you answer? Was the question asked publicly? Was it asked when the Nazis took the first steps against dissenters, Communists, and Jews? When is it too late to speak out?

Although most Nazi activities against the "other" were loudly proclaimed, the "euthanasia" program was kept secret. Why do you think the Nazis chose to do so?

How do you account for the fact that few Germans protested "euthanasia" even though it was directed against "Aryan" Germans as well as Jews and other minorities?

➤*Ambulance*, an eight-minute silent video, is a dramatization showing a group of children and their adult caretaker about to board a mobile gas van. As the four Nazi soldiers prepare the van, the teacher remains calm in order to keep the children from feeling any panic. The children are playing blind man's bluff and other children's games as they unknowingly await their death. The film then follows the careers of the doctors responsible for these deaths. The video is available from the Facing History Resource Center.

Do you or I have the right to live only as long as we are productive?

Targeting the "Gypsies"

*A*s the Nazis prepared for war, they also moved against the people they called "Gypsies." At first, the Nazis were content to enforce existing laws against the Sinti and Roma. In time, however, they amended laws that singled out other groups to include the "Gypsies." Among those laws was a 1933 act calling for the sterilization of "mental defectives," a 1934 law allowing the deportation of "undesirable aliens," and the 1935 Nuremberg Laws aimed at the Jews. The Nazis also added a new law entitled the "Fight against the Gypsy Menace." Its authors stated: "Experience gained in the fight against the Gypsy menace and the knowledge derived from race-biological research have shown that the proper method of attacking the Gypsy problem seems to be to treat it as a matter of race."

Under the new law, the Sinti and the Roma were required to register with the police. They were then issued special papers indicating their racial identity. The next step was deportation. Some were shipped to ghettos, while others were sent to a special camp just for "Gypsies." Still others were herded off to concentration camps such as Buchenwald, Dachau, and Ravensbrueck. One man, then a boy known as Bubili, recalled the day the SS arrived for his family.

> [On the morning of] June 26, 1939 (I can never forget the date), SS and Austrian police surrounded the wagons at daybreak. My aunt tried to signal me to leave. She sang as loudly as she could in our Romani language. "Bubili, run." But when one is young, one sleeps so well. When I did not wake up, she sang louder, "Run, run, the police are here. The Deathheads have come."
>
> I grabbed my pants and started to jump out the door. A waiting SS man seized me. "You," he said, pushing me down the hill, "join the others."
>
> "I'll help my uncle take the horses out of the stall so the horses can pull the wagon to the police station," I said.
>
> "No," the SS man said. "Leave them in the stable. You'll pull the wagon yourself."
>
> My uncle had only one leg. My aunt and I and two others harnessed ourselves to the wagon. Just outside the city, I tried to dart away. But the SS man grabbed me. In the courtyard of the police station, so many Sinti were there already that we stood there together like herrings crammed in a barrel.
>
> While the police were registering the men, my aunt whispered, "Bubili, hide beneath my petticoat." Our women wore three and four skirts that touched the ground. I was very thin and agile and could easily have hidden.

At first, the Nazis were content to enforce existing laws against the Sinti and Roma. In time, however, they amended laws that singled out other groups to include the "Gypsies."

"I can't. Uncle has only one foot. I have to help him."

The next day, the Germans forced all the young men to climb into busses and trucks. I was the only young boy among 1,035 men. The women and children were released to go home. Where was my father?

My father had been picked up in an earlier raid on Brueck an der Mur. At the railroad station, he found out that my uncle and I had been taken. He asked the Germans to let us travel in the same boxcar. Two days later, June 28, the train stopped just outside the gates of Dachau. We waited, locked in the airless boxcar for about three quarters of an hour. Then we heard a shout as thirty or forty young SS men unlocked the bolts and threw open the doors. "Austrian pigheads," they screamed. "Out, out. Run, you Congo niggers, run." Their whips fell on us, killing two men as we ran toward the gates of Dachau.

"Line up. Faces to the sun." The whole square was filled with prisoners in striped uniforms. Many of them wore yellow stars on their shirts. The others had different colored triangles on their uniforms.

We stood on the assembly place, the sun beating down on us from early morning until three in the afternoon. If someone dropped, we were not allowed to pick him up. Then an SS man with a whip drove us into a building.

"Sit down," the guard said. He held a board with my name and number 3 4016 across my chest. The photographer snapped my picture. With his foot, the photographer pushed a lever that punched a nail into my rear. Like a trained monkey, I jumped through the small window leading to the property room. Why couldn't they just tell us to get up instead of punching us with a nail?

In the property room, the guards shouted at us, 'Take off all your clothes. Put everything else in the two baskets—your jewelry, your papers, your money." We stood there naked as the guards led us toward the showers. It was after the shower I lost my hair. I wondered what more could the Nazis do to us?

The prisoners in charge of the clothing laughed as they threw it at us. If you were tall, you got striped pants that were too short. If you were short, you got striped pants that were too long. I would not look any more ridiculous. I "found" thread and shortened my pants.

The shoes were even worse. Only the kapos, the prisoners in charge of other prisoners, and the block "elders" had leather shoes. The rest of us were thrown wooden clogs. The wooden shoes hurt and bruised my feet. I had to figure out how to get a pair of leather shoes. It was summer, and we were taken out to help the farmers bring in crops. At the risk of my life, I smuggled potatoes in my shirt into camp. The big commodity was schnapps (whiskey). By bartering, I got Schnaps, which someone had stolen from the SS. The Schnaps I traded for leather shoes.[22]

Nazi officials were divided on the fate of the Roma and the Sinti once they were in the camps. Some advocated sterilization to render the "Gypsies" "biologically harmless." Others favored annihilation.

CONNECTIONS

How were the techniques used to isolate the Sinti and Roma similar to those used to isolate Jews? What differences seem most striking?

What does it mean to render a people "biologically harmless"? What does the phrase suggest about the way the Nazis viewed the "Gypsies"? Why do you think the Nazis referred to them as "Congo niggers"?

In 1956, the West German Federal Supreme Court decided that "until May of 1943 most deportations of Gypsies were carried out for military or 'crime-preventing' reasons, not on racial grounds." As a result, only token restitution has been granted to the "Gypsies" by the German government (about $3 for each day spent in a death camp). In 1992, young Germans attacked the "Gypsies." The government responded by deporting the Sinti and the Roma. What stereotypes are inherent in the court ruling? In the deportations?

➤ In the video *Triumph of Memory*, non-Jewish prisoners testify to the treatment of the Sinti and Roma. The video is available from the Facing History Resource Center, as is an article entitled "The Other Victims: Non-Jews Persecuted and Murdered by the Nazis."

READING 15

Targeting Poland

On August 31, 1939, the Nazis took a group of prisoners from a concentration camp to Gleiwitz, a town on the Polish border. After being dressed in Polish army uniforms, the prisoners were killed. The next morning, the German army and the SS marched into Poland. They claimed that they were retaliating for a Polish "attack on Gleiwitz."

It is the Fuhrer's and Goring's intention to destroy and exterminate the Polish nation.

Max von der Gruen's grandparents had one of the few radios in their small village in Germany. That evening, relatives and neighbors gathered to listen to Hitler declare war on Poland.

> No one cheered at the end of the speech, not even my aunt who had always cheered for Hitler; no one cried "Heil!" or turned somersaults with joy. Perturbation was written on everyone's face. No one spoke, and even the neighbors who had come to listen with us said nothing.

My grandfather wept. I could scarcely believe that I was seeing this old, worn-out man crying. No one asked him why he was crying. They were distressed because all of them knew what he had gone through during World War I. He had often told me about it.

No one displayed any enthusiasm. Not in school, not on the streets, not in the shops, not even among the Hitler Youth. No one dared to look anyone else in the face for fear that he might be asked what he thought about the war.

Of course, not everyone felt this way. A few of the boys in my class—we were thirteen years old—regretted that they were not older, for then they could have volunteered to join the Army; meanwhile, I consoled myself with the thought that the war would be over by the time I got out of school. . . .

Three days after Hitler attacked Poland, Great Britain and France declared war on Germany. . . .

People who in the past had been opposed to Hitler were now reluctantly forced to acknowledge that he was a great general and statesman. After all, he had defeated Poland in only 18 days.[23]

Immediately after the invasion, Germany's Quartermaster General, Colonel Eduard Wagner noted in his diary, "It is the Fuehrer's and Goering's intention to destroy and exterminate the Polish nation. More than that cannot even be hinted at in writing." Jacob Birnbaum, a Jew who lived in the town of Piotrkow, quickly discovered what those secret plans meant to the Jews of Poland.

Whenever one pulls the trigger in order to rectify history's mistake, one lies.

The next day, Saturday, September 2, at 8:30 in the morning, Piotrkow was heavily bombed, resulting in many casualties. The heavy bombing continued through the following day, destroying a number of public buildings, including the city hall, police headquarters, the State Bank, the post office, and the city's water system. On Tuesday, September 5, at 4:00 in the afternoon, German ground troops entered Piotrkow and conquered the city after two hours of street fighting. That same day they set out on a search for Jews in the almost deserted city, found twenty, among them Rabbi Yechiel Meir Fromnitsky, and shot them in cold blood. Thus it began.

The next day, September 6, the Germans set fire to a few streets in the Jewish quarter and shot Jews trying to escape from their burning homes. . . . Both individually and in groups the Germans invaded the Jewish community and stole virtually everything they feasibly could—clothes, linen, furs, carpets, valuable books. They often invited the Poles on the streets to take part in the looting, after which they would fire bullets into the air in order to give the impression that they were driving away the Polish "thieves." These scenes were photographed by the Germans to demonstrate for all that they were protecting Jewish property from Polish criminals.

Jews, many of them elderly, were kidnapped and sent to forced labor camps where they were tortured and beaten—often to the point of loss of consciousness. These kidnappings took place during the days preceding Rosh Hashanah, as well as on the holy day itself. Jewish men hid themselves in cellars, attics, and elsewhere, yet most were caught. The worst fate was that of the Jews sent to the SS Precinct. The main objective of the work there was torture, not productivity. Jews were forced, for instance, to do "gymnastics" while being beaten and subjected to various other forms of humiliation. . . .

One common insult suffered by the Jews during the early days under the new regime was their being chased away or beaten as they tried to wait in line for food together with other citizens. All Jews who attempted to resist were gunned down immediately.

During the holy days of Rosh Hashanah, as Jews hurriedly gathered to pray in the synagogues and private homes, still more torture was inflicted upon them. Several German officers entered the Great Synagogue stirring up much confusion among the worshipping Jews, many of whom attempted to escape. Twenty-nine worshippers were beaten brutally and taken away to prison, among them the lay leader of the congregation. The news of this event spread rapidly through the city, causing a great deal of fright, consternation, and anxiety. There were no worshippers in the synagogue on the second day of Rosh Hashanah.

Two days before Yom Kippur, German officers and troopers entered the shut synagogue, broke up the furnishings, and completely demolished the beautifully ornamented eastern wall.[24]

CONNECTIONS

Hitler believed that if a lie were outrageous enough, people would believe it. How does the incident that led to war reflect that belief?

How do you account for reactions in Max von der Gruen's village to news of the invasion?

In 1933, the Nazis isolated the Communists. Then they turned against gays, Jews, and "Gypsies." By 1939, they were targeting the disabled. Now they labeled an entire nation as "unfit" and "subhuman." How did each step in the process prepare for the next one? How did the notion that some groups are "subhuman" or "unworthy of life" make opposition more difficult? Where was the opposition?

What does Jacob Birnbaum's description of the events in Piotrkow tell you about Nazi policy in Poland?

In the 1990s, Serbs, Croats, and Bosnians fought for land and power in what was once Yugoslavia. Joseph Brodsky, a Nobel-Prize-winning poet, wrote of that conflict:

> What's happening now in the Balkans is very simple: It is a bloodbath. Terms such as "Serbs," "Croats," "Bosnians" mean absolutely nothing. Any other combination of vowels and consonants will amount to the same thing: killing people. Neither religious distinctions—Orthodox, Catholic, Muslim—nor ethnic ones are of any consequence. The former are forfeited with the first murder (for "Thou shalt not kill" pertains at least to any version of the Christian creed); as for the latter, all these people are what we in our parts define as Caucasian.
>
> Evocations of history here are bare nonsense. Whenever one pulls the trigger in order to rectify history's mistake, one lies. For history makes no mistakes, since it has no purpose. One always pulls the trigger out of self-interest and quotes history to avoid responsibility or pangs of conscience. No man possesses sufficient retrospective ability to justify his deeds—murder especially—in extemporaneous categories, least of all a head of state.[25]

How do Brodsky's comments apply to events in Europe in the 1930s? To violence in other parts of the world today?

READING 16

Conquests in the East

*A*fter the surrender of Poland in the fall of 1939, the Nazis quickly incorporated western Poland and parts of central and southern Poland into Germany and renamed the territory Warthegau. Hitler called the rest of the country "the General Government of Poland" and placed it under the rule of Hans Frank, one of his chief advisors. To "Aryanize" Warthegau, the Nazis deported millions of Poles as well as all Jews and "Gypsies" to the General Government.

From the start, the Nazis made their plans clear: "Poles who have failed to understand that they are the conquered and we are conquerors and who act against . . . regulations, expose themselves to the most severe punishment." According to those regulations, Poles were required to "leave the pavement free" for their conquerors; they had to serve Germans and German Poles first in every shop; and they were to tip their hats to "important personalities of State, Party and armed forces" but were not allowed to say "Heil Hitler!"

Educated Poles were subject to arbitrary arrest. In early November, 1939, the Nazis shipped 167 professors at Cracow University to Sachsenhausen, a concentration camp outside Berlin. Later that week, they arrested a thousand Polish intellectuals. In December, Hitler issued a special decree, allowing anyone considered a threat to German security to "vanish without a trace into the night and fog."

Six months later, in May 1940, Heinrich Himmler plotted the future of Polish children. "For the non-German population of the East, there must be no higher school than the fourth grade of elementary school. The sole goal of this schooling is to teach them simple arithmetic, nothing above the number 500; writing one's name; and the doctrine that it is divine law to obey the Germans. . . . I do not think that reading is desirable." Only "racially valuable" children—Polish children with "Aryan" features and backgrounds—were exempt. To turn them into true "Aryans," the Nazis kidnapped an estimated two hundred thousand children and shipped them to Germany. There the boys were trained as soldiers and the girls prepared for motherhood.

Even before Warsaw fell to the Nazis, Reinhard Heydrich, the Chief of the Reich Central Security Office, called a meeting in Berlin of the leaders of several SS units known as the *Einsatzgruppen*. At the meeting, Heydrich distinguished between "the final aim (which will require extended periods of time)" and "the stages leading to the fulfillment of this final aim (which will be carried out in short periods)." He began by ordering the concentration of the Jews from the countryside into large cities. Jewish communities with less than five hundred persons were to be dissolved and those living there transferred to the nearest "concentration center."

By the end of 1939, every Jew had to wear a "yellow star." Jews were also subject to a curfew that kept them off the streets between 9:00 P.M. and 5:00 A.M. Failing to abide by these or any one of the other laws the Nazis imposed could mean ten years in prison. The Nazis established nearly 400 ghettoes and 437 forced labor camps in occupied Poland. Within months, they had reenacted six years of step-by-step measures in Germany. Although Polish Jews had long lived with antisemitism, they were in no way prepared for the Nazis.

Warsaw, with over 350,000 Jews, had the largest Jewish population in Europe. Even though the Nazis did not set up a ghetto there until the fall of 1940, a reign of terror began almost immediately. In December 1939, Chaim Kaplan, the principal of a Warsaw Hebrew school, recorded in his diary two stories from the city of Lodz, a major center of Jewish life. The first concerned a group of girls.

> These girls were compelled to clean a latrine—to remove the excrement and clean it. But they received no utensils. To their question: "With what?" the Nazis replied: "With your blouses." The girls removed their blouses and cleaned the excrement with them. When the job was done they received their reward: the Nazis wrapped their faces

in the blouses, filthy with the remains of the excrement, and laughed uproariously. And all this because "Jewish England" is fighting against the Fuehrer with the help of the Juden.

The second story focused on a rabbi forced to spit on the Torah, the Five Books of Moses.

In fear of his life, he complied and desecrated that which is holy to him and to his people. After a short while he had no more saliva, his mouth was dry. To the Nazi's question, why did he stop spitting, the rabbi replied that his mouth was dry. Then the son of the "superior race" began to spit into the rabbi's open mouth, and the rabbi continued to spit on the Torah.[26]

These incidents not only shocked Kaplan. They also bothered some Germans. When one medical officer complained that some soldiers were disturbed by such cruelty, Hitler "took note of it calmly enough at first, but then began another long tirade of abuse at the 'childish ideas' prevalent in the army's leadership; you cannot fight wars with the methods of the Salvation Army."

A few generals also complained. Foremost among them was Johannes Blaskowitz, the commander-in-chief of the Eastern Territories. He was particularly concerned about the effects of these incidents on his men. In his view, they resulted in "tremendous brutalization and moral depravity which is spreading rapidly among precious German manpower like an epidemic." And he warned, "If high-ranking SS and police officials demand and openly praise acts of violence and brutality, before long people who commit acts of violence will predominate alone."[27] Hans Frank responded by threatening to dismiss Blaskowitz. In the end, Blaskowitz kept his job and later went on to head the German army in the Netherlands. What of the policies he protested? They continued. The Nazis had no intention of abandoning them.

CONNECTIONS

Are all enemies equal? Compare the way the Nazis regarded Jewish and Gentile Poles. What similarities do you see? What differences seem most striking? Does what happens to one group eventually happen to all groups in a society?

What do the stories Kaplan recounted in his diary tell you about life in Warsaw? Why do you think he included them in his diary?

Do you agree with Blaskowitz that incidents of violence lead to "tremendous brutalization and moral depravity"?

What conclusions can you draw from Blaskowitz's protest? What does it suggest about his "universe of obligation"? What conclusions can you draw from the fact that he did not lose his job despite his protests?

Why did it take the Germans six years to isolate German Jews but only a few weeks to isolate Polish Jews? What does your answer suggest about the Germans' "universe of obligation"?

➤Krysta S., a Polish schoolgirl who studied in secret throughout the war, describes how the Nazis tried to curtail education in her country in the video montage *Childhood Memories*, available from the Facing History Resource Center and summarized in *Elements of Time*, pages 228-233.

READING 17

A Return to the Ghettoes

*B*y the summer of 1941, Jews throughout Eastern Europe had been forced into ghettoes. Just two weeks before the Jewish section of Warsaw was closed off, Chaim Kaplan wrote in his diary, "A Jewish ghetto in the traditional sense is inconceivable. Many churches and government buildings are in the heart of the ghetto. They cannot be eliminated, they fulfill necessary functions. Besides that, it is impossible to cut off the trolley routes going from one end of the city to the other through the ghetto. . . . To differentiate citizens of one country according to race, and erect partitions between them, is a sick pathological idea." Two days later, Kaplan noted, "The face of Warsaw was changed so that no one who knows it would recognize it. People from outside do not enter now, but if a miracle were to take place and one of its inhabitants who fled returned to the city, he would say, 'Can this be Warsaw?' "28

Before long a brick wall nine feet high encircled the Warsaw ghetto. Although public utilities still linked it to the outside world, in almost every other way the inhabitants were isolated. Within its walls about 33 percent of the city's population lived on less than 3 percent of the land. The Nazis rationed enough food for only twenty percent of the ghetto's inhabitants. As a result, nearly one-fifth ultimately died of "natural causes"—hunger and disease.

Still, many Jews felt the ghetto offered them some measure of protection. They believed that they would be safe "as long as we are among Jews." The Nazis encouraged that delusion by creating a *Judenrat* or "Council of Jewish Elders" in each ghetto. The *Judenrat* gave Jews the impression that they had some measure of authority over their own community. In fact, they had none. Shmuel Zygelboim, a member of the Warsaw *Judenrat*, wrote:

The face of Warsaw was changed so that no one who knows it would recognize it. People from outside do not enter now, but if a miracle were to take place and one of its inhabitants who fled returned to the city, he would say, "Can this be Warsaw?"

> [About] 50 Gestapo men under the command of an officer entered the hall. All carried pistols or whips. . . . Finally, in a threatening, harsh voice the officer uttered: "Jews, you listen to me, and listen carefully! The commandant has ordered that all Jews of Warsaw must leave their present homes and move to the streets that have been designated for the ghetto, not later than Tuesday. To assure that the order is strictly carried out, all 24 alternates will be taken hostages. With their heads they are responsible for the exact execution of the order. You, the members of the Judenrat, are also responsible with your heads. We are not taking you away now simply because somebody must remain here to take care of the execution of the order." The 24 Jews, present only by accident, were then surrounded by the Gestapo men. Orders were shouted:
>
> "About face, forward march" and they marched out. Outside, in the street, trucks were waiting and the Jews were carried away.[29]

Terror became a part of daily life. After watching the Nazis toss a three-year-old into the snow, Emanuel Ringelblum wrote, "Its mother jumped off the wagon and tried to save the child. The guard threatened her with a revolver. The mother insisted that life was worthless for her without her child. Then the Germans threatened to shoot all the Jews in the wagon. The mother arrived in Warsaw, and here went out of her mind."[30]

CONNECTIONS

Richard Rubenstein writes:

> According to [historian Raul] Hilberg, the measure that gave the civil service bureaucrats least difficulty in exterminating their victims was the imposition of a starvation diet. In a bureaucratically controlled society where every individual's ration can be strictly determined, starvation is the ideal instrument of 'clean' violence. A few numbers are manipulated on paper in an office hundreds of miles away . . . and millions can be condemned to a prolonged and painful death. In addition, both the death rate and the desired level of vitality of the inmates can easily be regulated by the same bureaucrats. As starvation proceeds, the victim's appearance is so drastically altered that by the time death finally releases him, he hardly seems like a human being worth saving.[31]

How were the distinctions the bureaucrats made between starvation and other forms of murder similar to those German physicians made between murdering patients and "putting them to sleep"? What differences seem most striking?

Heinz Jost, a German soldier, spent a rare day off (it was, in fact, his birthday) taking pictures in the Warsaw Ghetto. The 129 photographs have been arranged in an exhibit called *A Day in the Warsaw Ghetto*. In an article about the exhibit, *Newsweek* reported that "at his birthday dinner that evening, Jost found he had no appetite. In his letters home during the rest of the war, he made no mention of what he'd seen." How do you account for his response? How is it similar to the way many Germans responded to *Kristallnacht?*

➤To create the B.B.C. video, The *Warsaw Ghetto*, the producers used Nazi newsreels and "documentaries." The result is a powerful film that offers vivid proof of what happens when one group considers another "subhuman." Historian Lucy Dawidowicz, however, expressed concern at this use of images shot as propaganda. Do you agree?

> Nowadays we live in an era of photomania, where photographs are regarded as the magic key to unlock the doors of the past, which only the more effortful study of history had previously been able to open. Nowadays people regard pictures as the essence of truth, forgetting that, like written documents, pictures too can lie, can distort the truth. Even more effectively than written documents, the camera falsifies objective reality because it creates its own illusion of reality.
>
> Too often pictures have been made to serve the uses of propaganda. Selective photography, posed or staged subject matter, technical tricks of the trade which bring into existence nonexistent subjects—these are the standard ways the camera is made to lie. Too often the camera serves ends that contribute neither to the truth of art nor to the truth of history.[32]

READING 18

A Return to Tradition?

In categorizing Jews as outsiders, Hitler was giving new life to those old prejudices.

Many Jews in Europe saw Nazi rules and regulations as a "return to the Middle Ages." During the Middle Ages, the Church enacted a series of laws that isolated Jews from their Christian neighbors (Chapter 1, Reading 14). In *A Boy of Old Prague*, Sulamith Ish-Kishor describes the effects of those laws on a young Christian in 1556. Tomas grew up accepting all that he had heard about the people of the ghetto until the day his master sent the frightened boy to work for a Jew.

> I held back heavy as a dummy, while Paul and Girard pushed and dragged me to the gate. They whistled three times, and the watchman came slowly out of his cottage beside the [Ghetto] wall. He was a Christian, and I thought he looked at me with a mocking wink. As we passed through those terrible gates into the abode of the accursed, I

remembered all the dreadful tales of witchcraft and black magic I had heard told of the Jews. One night came back to me, when we boys sat together over the kitchen fire, eating nuts and apples and telling terrible stories about the Jews: a Jew had cut himself up in pieces, and put himself into a flask, and had become immortal; another had made himself invisible with the herb Andromeda when the Devil came for his soul; another had turned the sun red with the stone called heliotrope, and another had cut off his shadow and given it to his master the Devil in a cave; another had brought on a terrible storm by means of a copper basin. I thought I saw the Archdemon himself grinning over the walls; I made one prayer to the Virgin Mary, and fainted. . . .

The tall, gloomy houses were solid black and terrifying in the night; their gabled tops seemed to waver and mock at me, and here and there a lighted window stared like the eye of a devil. I wondered weakly how anyone could have the cruelty to do what my lord was doing to a Christian soul.

At last we came through the muddy streets, as crooked and close as an eagle's claws, to a high, narrow house, bolted and dark. A black cat gliding between my legs nearly upset my balance again, so weak was I with terror. . . .

"Here's the boy my lord has promised you," scowled Girard. "Mind you don't cut his heart out and bake it for Satan's supper. . . ."

The old Jew pushed open a door into a large, warm room. There was an Eastern carpet on the floor, and several couches around the walls. A fire roared in the grate. The Jew left me alone for a while, and I crept nearer the fire, and looked around the room.

There was a low table, from which the chairs had been hastily pushed back; on it was a board painted with red and black squares, with funny little wooden figures tumbling out of a box beside it. These, I thought, must be puppets which the Jews had made, in order to prick them and cause the death of the Christians whom they represented. On the floor, face upward, lay a painted rag doll.

I looked up, and nearly fell backward into the fire. The Jew was approaching me with a large knife in his hand! Now I knew why I had been bought! It would soon be the Passover festival, when the Jews kill Christians in order to drink their blood! My scalp pricked, my blood felt thick and dry, my heart beat loud and fast, and I saw nothing for a moment.

The Jew stood before me, waiting.

"You want to sleep all tied up like an animal?" he exclaimed sourly. Getting behind me he began sawing away at the rope that bound my hands together. The small of my back contracted painfully, in expectation of the sharp, penetrating dig of the knife. I stood stiff, saying more prayers in that moment than ever before in my life. But nothing happened to me; the rope fell from my hands, and he motioned me to the table on which he had placed a large piece of black bread and several slices of meat. So I saw that I was not to be slaughtered at present.

In time, Tomas learned that Jews were not demons but people much like himself. If he had not been sent to work among them, however, he would have never known. In categorizing Jews as outsiders, Hitler was giving new life to those old prejudices. Historian Raul Hilberg revealed the connection between past and present when he compared Nazi laws with those enacted during the Middle Ages.

CHURCH LAW	NAZI LAW
1. Prohibition of intermarriage and sexual intercourse between Christians and Jews—Synod of Elvira, A.D. 306	1. Law for the Protection of German Blood and Honor—Sept. 15, 1935
2. Jews and Christians not permitted to eat together—Synod of Elvira, 306	2. Jews barred from dining cars—Dec. 30, 1939
3. Jews not allowed to hold public office—Synod of Clermont, 535	3. Law for the Re-establishment of the Professional Civil Service —April 7, 1933
4. Jews not allowed to employ Christian servants or possess Christian slaves—3rd Synod of Orleans, 538	4. Law for the Protection of German Blood and Honor—Sept. 15, 1935
5. Jews not permitted in the streets during Passion Week—3rd Synod of Orleans, 538	5. Decree authorizing local authorities to bar Jews from streets on certain days—Dec. 3, 1938
6. Burning of the Talmud and other books—12th Synod of Toledo, 691	6. Book burnings in Germany—1933
7. Christians not permitted to patronize Jewish doctors—Trulanic Synod, 692	7. Decree of July 25, 1938
8. Christians not permitted to live in Jewish homes—Synod of Narbonne, 1050	8. Directive by Goring providing for concentration of Jews in houses—December 28, 1938
9. Jews obliged to pay taxes for support of the Church to the same extent as Christians—Synod of Gerona, 1078	9. Jews must pay special income tax in lieu of donations to the Party imposed on Nazis—Dec. 24, 1940
10. Jews not permitted to be plaintiffs or witnesses against Christians in the Courts—3rd Lateran Council, 1179	10. Jews not permitted to institute civil suits—Sept. 9, 1942
11. The marking of Jewish clothes with a badge—4th Lateran Council, 1215	11. Decree of Sept. 1, 1941
12. Construction of new synagogues prohibited—Council of Oxford, 1222	12. Destruction of synagogues in entire Reich—Nov. 10, 1938
13. Christians not permitted to attend Jewish ceremonies —Synod of Vienna, 1267	13. Friendly relations with Jews prohibited—Oct. 24, 1941
14. Compulsory ghetto—Synod of Breslau, 1267	14. Order by Heydrich—Sept. 21, 1939
15. Christians not permitted to sell or rent real estate to Jews, Synod of Ofen, 1279	15. Decree providing for compulsory sale of Jewish real estate —Dec. 3, 1938
16. Adoption by a Christian of the Jewish religion or return by a baptized Jew to the Jewish religion defined as a heresy—Synod of Mainz, 1310	16. Adoption of Jewish religion by a Christian places him or her in jeopardy of being treated as a Jew—6/26/42
17. Jews not permitted to obtain academic degrees—Council of Basel, 1434.	17. Laws against Overcrowding of German Schools and Universities— April 25, 1933 [33]

CONNECTIONS

Like most people of his day, Tomas could not read or write. Where then did he learn to hate? How did he learn whom to fear? Whom to hate?

At one point in the story, Tomas fears that the Jew is planning to kill him and then drink his blood. That notion resulted from stories that linked Jews with the demons who were widely believed to murder Christian children for religious purposes. Tomas's terror shows the power of these stories. How do such stories incite hatred and violence? What do they suggest about the way fear blurs one's vision? The way stereotypes distort the truth?

How do dictionaries define the word *myth*? What is the connection between myth and misinformation? To what extent were Tomas's views of Jews based on myths? How does isolation foster myths? How did the fact that those myths were rooted in tradition affect their power? Are people more likely to obey a new idea or an old one?

Write a working definition for the word *ghetto*. Compare the ghettoes of the sixteenth century with those the Nazis built in the twentieth century. In what respects are they similar? What differences seem most striking?

How did the Nazis give life to old prejudices? Do leaders today do the same thing?

Lydia Gasman-Csato was fifteen when the Nazis took over Romania. She later described the humiliation of the new rules as being as "bad as dying. Humiliation. Lack of dignity. . . . I consider human dignity to be as important as food and as breathing, and that is what I was deprived of." Compare her response to Frederick Douglass's view of slavery (Chapter 2, Reading 3). What similarities seem most striking?

READING 19

Conquests in the West

*I*n the spring of 1940, the Nazis turned their attention to the West. In April, they conquered Denmark and Norway. Early in May, they overran Belgium, the Netherlands, and Luxembourg. By June 22, France had fallen. Hitler now controlled all of Western Europe except Britain. While the British fought on alone, many conquered nations formed governments-in-exile in London. Each prepared for the day its people would be free again.

Nazi victories led to a change in leadership in Britain. Winston Churchill became prime minister in May 1940. Upon taking office, he vowed to "wage war, by sea, land or air, with all our might and with all the

In 1933 a French premier ought to have said. . . "The new Reich Chancellor is the man who wrote Mein Kampf, which says this and that. This man cannot be tolerated in our vicinity. Either he disappears or we march!" But they didn't do it. They let us alone.

strength God can give us; to wage war against a monstrous tyranny, never surpassed in the dark, lamentable catalogue of human crime. That is our policy. You ask, what is our aim? I can answer in one word: It is victory, victory at all costs, victory in spite of all terror, victory however long and hard the road may be; for without victory there is no survival."

Churchill spoke in one of the worst moments in the war. The Nazis and their allies now controlled almost all of Europe. Only Spain, Portugal, Switzerland, and Sweden were still neutral. Germany's successes encouraged allies and would-be allies both in Europe and in Asia. In the Middle East, the Grand Mufti of Jerusalem, a Muslim leader, saw in those successes an opportunity.

> Germany and Italy recognize the illegality of the "Jewish Home in Palestine." They accord to Palestine and to other Arab countries the right to solve the problem of the Jewish elements in Palestine and other Arab countries in accordance with the interest of the Arabs, and by the same method that the question is now being settled in the Axis countries. Under this agreement no Jewish immigration into the Arab countries should be permitted.[34]

In most conquered nations, the Nazis established a new government. In some places, it was a military government, in others, it was headed by civilians, and in still others, by the SS. Occasionally, it was a complicated mixture of all three. France was divided among three different governments. Alsace and Lorraine, the provinces Germany lost in World War I, were restored to the "Fatherland." A German military commander governed northern France and the area along the Atlantic coast. Henri Philippe Petain, a hero of World War I, and Pierre Laval, a French politician, were in charge of the rest of the nation. After the two agreed to work with the Nazis, they were allowed to set up a government in the town of Vichy.

Antisemitism was official policy in every conquered nation. Although Jews legally had the same rights as other citizens, they quickly found themselves separated from their neighbors. One of the first laws passed by the Vichy government declared that Jews were inferior and were therefore barred from employment in government, the military, education, or the media. The number of Jewish doctors and lawyers was also limited. The only exceptions were veterans with distinguished combat records.

When French Jews were ordered to register at local police stations, many protested. Among them was Marc Haguenau, who later died fighting to free France from the Nazi rule. "I count in my family too many generations of French Israelites, who have lived under all regimes—monarchies, empires, republics—not to be capable of judging in a completely French spirit what a backward step this is for our country, as regards the respect for all spiritual values in which I was raised, and to which I remain attached. I would have considered it contrary to my dignity not to make this brief and useless declaration."[35]

Democracies don't like to listen to bad news. Democracies don't want to think about bad possibilities in the future. Democracies don't want their comfort or profits interfered with. Democracies may or may not win out in the long term. It is entirely possible that until now they have merely been lucky.

Marion Pritchard, then a student, recalled the way the Germans also separated the Jews from "Aryans" in the Netherlands.

> Gradually the Germans instituted and carried out the necessary steps to isolate and deport every Jew in the country. They did it in so many seemingly small steps, that it was very difficult to decide when and where to take a stand. One of the early, highly significant measures was the Aryan Attestation: all civil servants had to sign a form stating whether they were Aryans or not. Hindsight is easy; at the time only a few enlightened people recognized the danger and refused to sign. Then followed the other measures: Jews had to live in certain designated areas of the towns they lived in, and the curfew was stricter for them than for the general population. Jews over the age of six had to wear yellow stars on their clothing; Jewish children could not go to school with gentile children; Jews could not practice their professions, use public transportation, hire a taxicab, shop in gentile stores, or go to the beach, the park, the movies, concerts, or museums. The Jewish Committee was instructed by the Germans to publish a daily newspaper in which all these measures were announced, the regular Dutch press was not allowed to print anything about Jewish affairs.[36]

When the Germans tried to deport four hundred Jews in February 1941, Gentiles in the Netherlands decided to take a stand. Miep van Santan Gies, who later hid Anne Frank and her family recalled:

> In order to show the full measure of indignity, we Dutch felt about the treatment of Jewish people, we called a general strike for February 25. We wanted our Jews to know that we had great concern for what was happening to them.
>
> On February 25 all hell broke loose! All transport and industry ground to a halt. At the forefront of the strike were our dockworkers, and all other workers followed suit. Before the German occupation, Holland had had a great many different parties and political groups. Now, suddenly, we were all one: anti-German.
>
> The February strike lasted for three marvelous days. I heard that the morale of Dutch Jews rose tremendously; everyone felt the solidarity the strike inspired. Dangerous, yes, but wonderful to be doing something against our oppressors. But after three days the Nazis reasserted themselves with brutal reprisals.[37]

After the Nazis ended the strike, they shipped the Jews to death camps. Then mass deportations began. By 1941, Hitler had achieved most of his foreign policy goals. Just a year earlier, Joseph Goebbels reflected on his methods in a secret meeting with German journalists:

> Up to now we have succeeded in leaving the enemy in the dark concerning Germany's real goals, just as before 1932 our domestic foes never saw where we were going or that our oath of legality was just a

We wanted to come to power legally, but we did not use power legally.

trick. We wanted to come to power legally, but we did not use power legally. . . . They could have suppressed us. They could have arrested a couple of us in 1925 and that would have been that, the end. No they let us through the danger zone. That's exactly how it was in foreign policy too. . . . In 1933 a French premier ought to have said (and if I had been the French premier I would have said it): "The new Reich Chancellor is the man who wrote *Mein Kampf*, which says this and that. This man cannot be tolerated in our vicinity. Either he disappears or we march!" But they didn't do it. They let us alone and let us slip through the risky zone, and we were able to sail around all dangerous reefs. *And when we were done, and well armed, better than they, then they started the war!*

CONNECTIONS

How did Nazi policy in Western Europe differ from policy in Eastern Europe? How do you account for those differences?

Make an identity chart for Marc Haguenau. What does he mean when he says, "I would have considered it contrary to my dignity not to make this brief and useless declaration"?

What did the Dutch response to antisemitism demonstrate? What does it suggest about the choices people had in other conquered nations?

Why didn't the French premier or anyone else, for that matter, stop the Nazis?

Columnist William Pfaff compared world problems in the 1990s with those in the 1930s:

In the 1930s there certainly was no popular clamor for the democracies to block Hitler from remilitarizing the Rhineland, or annexing Austria, or partitioning Czechoslovakia. Chamberlain and Daladier were the popular politicians, calm and reasonable men who refused to take risks over distant issues and improbable dangers. The public turned to Churchill and de Gaulle only after all the combinations of appeasement (and collaboration) had been tried and had failed.

So there is nothing new in what is happening. But it does reiterate a lesson. Governments that are passively dependent upon public opinion, as democracies are as a general rule, are incapable of dealing with long-term threats requiring the sacrifice of lives, or even the serious risk of lost lives, even when a reasoned case can be made that this will save lives in the long run. . . . .

The fact is that democracies compete badly with despotisms. Democracies don't like sacrifices, or the politicians who demand them. Democracies are no good at looking after their security interests when a gun is not pointed at their heads. Democracies don't like to listen to bad news. Democracies don't want to think about bad possibilities in the future. Democracies don't want their comfort or profits interfered with. Democracies may or may not win out in the long term. It is entirely possible that until now they have merely been lucky.[38]

How are Pfaff's warnings similar to the ones Lincoln made in 1838? What differences seem most striking? What are the responsibilities of democratic leaders? Is it to follow public opinion or to stand up for things they believe are right? What are the responsibilities of a citizen?

READING 20

The Invasion of Russia

For Hitler, World War II was more than a series of battles between rival armies. It was also a "racial" war against those he regarded as "inferior," "subhuman," or simply "unworthy of life." He told his officers, "I know that the necessity of making war in such a manner is beyond the comprehension of you generals, but I cannot and will not change my orders, and I insist that they be carried out with unquestioning and unconditional obedience." That demand for obedience would be stretched farther and farther.

On June 22, 1941, Hitler ordered the invasion of Russia to destroy once and for all the "Jewish-Bolshevik menace." As the German army advanced into what was then the Soviet Union, four SS units known as the *Einsatzgruppen* followed close behind. Each had its own territory: *A* served in the north, *B* along the central Russian front, *C* in the northern Ukraine, and *D* in the southern Ukraine, the Caucasus, and Crimea. Each had orders to murder anyone the Nazis considered an "enemy of the state." There were murders before the invasion. But now, the killings became more systematic, deliberate, and routine. On July 31, Hermann Goering gave the following order to Reinhard Heydrich, Chief of the Security Police:

> I hereby charge you with making all necessary preparations with regard to organizational and financial matters for bringing about a complete solution of the Jewish question in the German sphere of influence in Europe.
>
> Wherever other governmental agencies are involved, these are to cooperate with you.
>
> I charge you furthermore to send me, before long, an overall plan concerning the organizational, factual, and financial measures necessary for the execution of the desired solution of the Jewish question.[39]

Goering used code words to protect the secrecy of the operation. On October 10, 1941, the commander in chief on the eastern front spoke more bluntly to his troops.

For Hitler, World War II was more than a series of battles between rival armies. It was also a "racial" war against those he regarded as "inferior," "subhuman," or simply "unworthy of life."

NORWAY
82 years

ESTONIA
600 years

DENMARK
311 years

LATVIA
400 years

HOLLAND
800 years

MEMEL
269 years

LITHUANIA
600 years

BELGIUM
700 years

WHITE RUSSIA
550 years

DANZIG
400 years

Włodawa

GERMANY
1,612 years

UKRAINE
816 years

POLAND
800 years

LUXEMBOURG
647 years

CZECHOSLOVAKIA
1,000 years

CRIMEA
1,900 years

SAAR
312 years

AUSTRIA
1,030 years

HUNGARY
1,900 years

FRANCE
1,930 years

ITALY
2,100 years

RUMANIA
1,800 years

YUGOSLAVIA
1,000 years

BULGARIA
1,900 years

GREECE
2,233 years

RHODES
2,000 years

miles 300
kilometres 400

The essential aim of the campaign against the Jewish-Bolshevist system is the complete crushing of its means of power and the extermination of Asiatic influence in the European cultural region.

This poses tasks for the troops which go beyond the one-sided routine of conventional soldiering. In the Eastern region, the soldier is not merely a fighter according to the rules of the art of war, but also the bearer of an inexorable national idea and the avenger of all bestialities inflicted upon the German people and its racial kin.

Therefore, the soldier must have full understanding for the necessity of a severe but just atonement on Jewish subhumanity. An additional aim is to nip in the bud any revolts in the rear of the army, which, as experience proves, have always been instigated by Jews. . . .

Apart from any political consideration of the future, the soldier has to fulfill two tasks:

1. The total annihilation of the false Bolshevist doctrine, of the Soviet State, and of its armed forces;

2. The pitiless extermination of alien treachery and cruelty, and thus the protection of the lives of the German forces in Russia.

Only in this way will we do justice to our historic task of liberating the German people, once and for all, from the Asiatic-Jewish peril.[40]

Russian Jews had no idea that they were in danger. According to German intelligence reports, they were "remarkably ill-informed." "They do not know how Jews are treated in Germany, or for that matter, in Warsaw, which after all is not so far away." By the end of 1941, they were only too aware of the danger. By then, the Germans had murdered over seven hundred thousand Jews. They also killed thousands of Ukrainians, "Gypsies," Poles, and other "enemies."

Prejudice and racism are in fact the cornerstones of dehumanization.

CONNECTIONS

Why did the Germans camouflage their activities and plans? How did they use language to do so?

Why do you think the general referred to his victims as members of the "Jewish subhumanity"? Is a "subhuman" entitled to the same respect as a "fellow human"? The Jews were not the only people the Germans regarded as "subhuman"? Who else did they dehumanize?

Although some consider dehumanization the "extreme end of a scale which also includes prejudice and racism," Bohdan Wytwycky has argued that is a "dangerously misleading" view. He maintains that "prejudice and racism are in fact the cornerstones of dehumanization." He warns, "The possibility of mass atrocities appears to be so remote that we are unlikely to pay serious attention to the budding of poisonous attitudes. However, given a sudden and traumatic shift in social conditions, dehumanization can easily develop its own deadly momentum if the ground is fertile."[41] How does this reading support Wytwycky's view? How does his warning apply to events in the news today?

READING 21

The United States Enters the War

As 1941 drew to a close, the Nazis reevaluated their plans. They had expected Russian soldiers to turn against their Communist leaders. Instead they fought bravely in battle after battle. The same was true of the Russian people. Instead of rebelling against the Communists, they fiercely protected their homeland. The people of Leningrad held out against the Germans for nearly two and one-half years. And in the end, it was the Germans who withdrew. As the war dragged on, the Nazis found themselves waging a land war against the Soviets in the east and mainly an air war against the British in the west.

Then on December 8, 1941, the United States declared war on Japan. The day before, the Japanese had bombed Pearl Harbor, the United States naval station in Hawaii. Japan and Germany were allies. So on the morning of December 9, the Japanese ambassador to Germany asked for Hitler's support against the United States. Some of the Fuehrer's advisors argued that the Japanese had provoked the Americans by bombing Pearl Harbor. So Germany was not obligated to support Japan. Hitler, however, was not looking for a way to avoid a fight. On December 11, he declared war on the United States. In doing so, he united three powerful nations—Britain, the Soviet Union, and the United States—against Germany. Although the three did not always agree, they were united in their determination to win the war.

CONNECTIONS

A mystery of the war is why Hitler chose to declare war on the United States. How do you account for his decision? You may want to do some research before you offer an opinion. For example, you may want to find out whether there were strategic advantages in expanding the war. Or you might want to investigate the military strength of the United States in 1941. Did Hitler have reason to believe that the United States was too weak to be a threat?

➤Historian Steve Cohen discusses the significance of the events of 1941 in his presentation, "1941: Turning Point in World War II," described in *Elements of Time*, pages 345-346. A videotape of the talk is available from the Facing History Resource Center.

READING 22

"They were trying to escape," said the wolves, "and, as you know, this is no world for escapists."

Blame the Rabbits

James Thurber, an American humorist and social critic, is the author of a fable in which the animals behave like people.

Within the memory of the youngest child there was a family of rabbits who lived near a pack of wolves. The wolves announced that they did not like the way the rabbits were living. (The wolves were crazy about the way they themselves were living, because it was the only way to live.) One night several wolves were killed in an earthquake and this was blamed on the rabbits, for it is well known that rabbits pound on the ground with their hind legs and cause earthquakes. On another night one of the wolves was killed by a bolt of lightning and this was also blamed on the rabbits, for it is well known that lettuce-eaters cause lightning. The wolves threatened to civilize the rabbits if they didn't behave, and the rabbits decided to run away to a desert island. But the other animals, who lived at a great distance, shamed them, saying, "You must stay where you are and be brave. This is no world for escapists. If the wolves attack you, we will come to your aid, in all probability." So the rabbits continued to live near the wolves and one day there was a terrible flood which drowned a great many wolves. This was blamed on the rabbits, for it is well known that carrot-nibblers with long ears cause floods. The wolves descended on the rabbits, for their own good, and imprisoned them in a dark cave, for their own protection.

When nothing was heard about the rabbits for some weeks, the other animals demanded to know what had happened to them. The wolves replied that the rabbits had been eaten and since they had been eaten the affair was a purely internal matter. But the other animals warned that they might possibly unite against the wolves unless some reason was given for the destruction of the rabbits. So the wolves gave them one. "They were trying to escape," said the wolves, "and, as you know, this is no world for escapists."

Moral: Run, don't walk, to the nearest desert island.[42]

CONNECTIONS

Explain the moral of the fable. To whom does it apply? Why? How does the moral apply to what you have read so far in the Resource Book? What other morals might you add? For what reasons?

NOTES

[1] Richard Rubenstein, *The Cunning of History* (Harper & Row, 1975), 33.

[2] Fredric Zeller, *When Time Ran Out: Coming of Age in the Third Reich* (The Permanent Press, 1989), 82-83.

[3] Quoted in William Manchester. *The Last Lion: Winston Spencer Churchill Alone; 1932-1940* (Little, Brown, 1988), 189.

[4] William Shirer, *Berlin Diary*, 51.

[5] Golda Meir, *My Life* (G.P. Putnam's Sons, 1975), 158.

[6] Carl C. Brigham, *A Study of American Intelligence* (1923), 210.

[7] Richard Rubenstein, *The Cunning of History*, 15.

[8] Frederic Morton, "Kristallnacht," *New York Times*, 10 November 1978, Op-Ed page). Copyright © 1978 by The New York Times Company. Reprinted by permission.

[9] Dan Bar-On, *Legacy of Silence*, 1.

[10] Melita Maschmann, *Account Rendered*, 56-57.

[11] Quoted in Victoria Barnett, *For the Soul of the People*, 142.

[12] Otto D. Tolischus, "The Pogrom," *New York Times*, 19 November, 1938. Copyright © 1938 by The New York Times Company. Reprinted by permission.

[13] Quoted in Anthony Read and David Fisher, *Kristallnacht; The Unleashing of the Holocaust* (Peter Bedrick Books, 1989), 155.

[14] William Shirer, *Berlin Diary*, 166.

[15] Quoted in Arthur Morse, *While Six Million Died* (Overlook Press, 1985), 280.

[16] Charles Stember (ed.), *Jews in the Mind of America* (1966), 120-125.

[17] Max von der Gruen, *Howl Like the Wolves*.

[18] Robert Jay Lifton, *Nazi Doctors*. Copyright © 1986 by Robert Jay Lifton. Reprinted by permission of Basic Books, a division of Harper Collins, Publishers, Inc.

[19] Ibid.

[20] Quoted in Victoria Barnett, *For the Soul of the People*, 110-111.

[21] Ibid., 117.

[22] Quoted in Ina Friedman, *The Other Victims* (Houghton Mifflin, 1990), 10-12.

[23] Max von der Gruen, *Howl Like the Wolves*.

[24] Jacob Birnbaum, "Account of the Piotrkow Ghetto," unpublished document. Available from the Facing History Resource Center.

[25] Joseph Brodsky, "Blood, Lies and the Trigger of History," *New York Times*, 4 August 1993, Op-Ed page. Copyright © 1993 by The New York Times Company. Reprinted by permission.

[26] Chaim Kaplan, *Scroll of Agony: The Warsaw Diary of Chaim Kaplan* (Macmillan, 1965). Reprinted by permission.

[27] Quoted in *The Good Old Days*, ed. Ernst Klee, et al., trans. Deborah Burnstone (The Free Press, 1991), 5.

[28] Chaim Kaplan, *Scroll of Agony*.

[29] From *The Zygelboim Book*, compiled by J. S. Herz, quoted in Nora Levin *The Holocaust Years* (Krieger Publishers, 1990), 203.

[30] Quoted in Martin Gilbert, *The Second World War*, (Henry Holt, 1989), 152.

[31] Richard Rubenstein, *The Cunning of History*, 25-26.

[32] Lucy Dawidowicz, "Visualizing the Warsaw Ghetto," *Mainstream*.

[33] Adapted from Raul Hilberg, *The Destruction of the European Jews* (Holmes & Meier, 1985), 11-12.

[34] Quoted in "During WWII, Grand Mufti Plotted to Do Away with All Jews in the Mideast," *Response: The Wisenthal Center World Report*, Fall 1991, 2-3.

[35] Quoted in Leon Poliakov, *Harvest of Hate* (Greenwood Press, 1951), 54.

[36] Quoted in *The Courage to Care*, 28-29.

[37] Miep Gies with Alison Leslie Gold, *Anne Frank Remembered: The Story of the Women Who Helped Hide the Frank Family*, (Simon & Schuster, 1987), 68.

[38] William Pfaff, "The Complacent Democracies." Copyright © 1993 Los Angeles Times Syndicate.

[39] Quoted in Nora Levin, *The Holocaust Years*, 234.

[40] Quoted in *The Holocaust Reader*, ed. Lucy Dawidowicz (Berman House, 1976), 70-71.

[41] Bohdan Wytwycky, *The Other Holocaust*, 82-83.

[42] James Thurber, "The Rabbits Who Caused all the Trouble" in *Thurber Carnival* (Dell Books, 1962).

7. The Holocaust

*The more we come to know about the Holocaust,
how it came about, how it was carried out, etc., the greater the
possibility that we will become sensitized to inhumanity
and suffering whenever they occur.*

EVA FLEISCHNER

OVERVIEW

Chapter 7 focuses on the deliberate murder of one third of all the Jews in the world. The Nazis singled out children, women, and men for destruction *solely* because of their ancestry. Winston Churchill called that act "a crime without a name." In the years that followed people have given that crime various names. In the United States, it is referred to as the Holocaust, a word people have been using since ancient times. "The word *'holocaust'* means complete destruction by burning; all matter is totally *consumed* by the flames," writes Paul Bookbinder. "Although the word is of Greek origin, it has become synonymous with the destruction of European Jews by the Germans during the Second World War. The crematoria of Auschwitz brought the word 'holocaust' to mind, and in its sound the enormity of the horror of those days was confirmed."[1]

Over the years, Auschwitz has become a symbol of the Holocaust. It represents the thousands of camps in which millions of Europeans died. Israel Gutman, the Director of the Center for Holocaust Research at Yad Vashem in Israel, estimates that about 85 to 90 percent of all those murdered at Auschwitz were Jews. Among the others were Russian prisoners of war and "Gypsies." Most were selected for immediate death. The rest were kept alive for slave labor. Surviving one selection was no guarantee that one would survive the next. Nothing in one's previous existence prepared an individual for Auschwitz. Primo Levi, a Holocaust survivor, wrote that soon after arriving there, "we became aware that our language lacks words to express this offence, the demolition of a man. In a moment, with almost prophetic intuition, the reality was revealed to us: we had reached the bottom. It is not possible to sink lower than this; no human condition is more miserable than this, nor could it conceivably be so."[2]

Neither our vocabulary nor our standards for behavior can adequately imagine this history. In reading or hearing the accounts of survivors, Professor Lawrence Langer notes, "one is plunged into a world of moral turmoil that may silence judgment . . . but cannot completely paralyze action, if one still wishes to remain alive. . . . As one wavers between the 'dreadful' and the 'impossible,' one begins to glimpse a deeper level of reality in the death camps, where moral choice as we know it was superfluous and inmates were left with the futile task of redefining decency in an atmosphere that could not support it."[3] Facing that history is extraordinarily difficult, but it is necessary for one simple reason: The Holocaust *happened*. That in itself is a fact that we can neither erase nor evade. Many students use their journals to reflect on what they read and view. As one student wrote, "This history is grim and it can build up inside and make you feel ugly and hopeless. At times I did. My journal was a confidant that no person could have been because it was always there."

READING 1

"Sanitary" Language

The Nazis used various euphemisms to refer to the killing of Jews, "Gypsies," and others they considered "unworthy of life."

German Word	Literal Meaning	Real Meaning
Ausgemerzt	exterminated (pest)	murdered
Liquidiert	liquidated	murdered
Erledigt	finished (off)	murdered
Aktionen	actions	missions to seek out Jews and others and kill them
Sonderaktionen	special actions	special killing missions
Sonderbehandlung	special treatment	the death process in camp
Saeuberung	cleansing; purge	sent through the death process
Ausschaltung	elimination	murder of Jews and others
Aussiedlung	evacuation	murder
Umsiedlung	resettlement	murder
Exekutivmassnahme	executive measure	order for murder
Entsprechend behandelt	treated appropriately	murdered
Loesung der Judenfrage	solution of the Jewish question	murder of Jewish people
Judenfrei gemacht	made free of Jews	all Jews in an area killed
Spezialeinrichtungen	special installations	gas chambers and crematoria
Badeanstalten	bath installations	gas chambers
Leichenkeller	corpse cellar	crematorium
Endloesung	the Final Solution	the decision to commit genocide

There is something odious about playing the numbers game. Every single human life is precious, as the rabbis of old remind us. But we can attain universality only through particularity; there are no short cuts.

CONNECTIONS

Compare the literal meaning of each word with its actual meaning. What differences seem most striking? What effect do euphemisms have on a listener or reader? On the speaker or writer? On perpetrators?

Euphemisms are used to distance oneself from an event, deny it, camouflage it, or trivialize it. How do these euphemisms reflect those aims? How do they differ from others you have encountered?

Euphemisms masked not only the Holocaust itself but also the way people viewed individual deaths. Eva Fleischner, a Catholic theologian and educator, has said of the emphasis people place on the number of Jews that were murdered:

> There is something odious about playing the numbers game. Every single human life is precious, as the rabbis of old remind us. But we can attain universality only through particularity; there are no short cuts. The more we come to know about the Holocaust, how it came about, how it was carried out, etc., the greater the possibility that we will become sensitized to inhumanity and suffering whenever they occur. If we take shortcuts we are in danger of losing all distinctions, of what Yosef Yerushalmi calls the "debasement of our vocabulary." We may soon, then, have simply one more word which for a short time was a new and powerful symbol, but which quickly became empty of meaning.[4]

How do we "attain universality" through "particularity"? How does "their" history become "our" history? Why are there no shortcuts? Many African Americans have labeled their experiences with slavery and dehumanization a "holocaust." Is the word *holocaust* ever a useful metaphor for other events? What power do words have to shape our views of the past?

READING 2

A War within a War

The war against the Jews took place within the context of the larger war. Otto Ohlendorf, the leader of *Einsatzgruppe* D, said his troops would "enter a village or a city [in occupied Soviet territory] and order the prominent Jewish citizens to call together all Jews for the purpose of resettlement. They were requested to hand over their valuables to the leader of the unit and shortly before execution to surrender their outer clothing. The men, women, and children were led to a place of execution which in most cases was located next to a more deeply excavated anti-tank ditch. Then they were shot, kneeling or standing, and the corpses thrown into the ditch."[5] Leslie Gordon, one of eleven thousand forced laborers at Kamenets Podolsk, recalls:

I was taken to a group of young men, about twenty-five or thirty young men. We were first given food and then we were given shovels and other tools and were taken about two or three kilometres out of the town beyond the hills.

We had been taken up there and they told us to start digging ditches. We believed that this was for the tanks, that perhaps the Russians were coming back, and the size of the ditches had almost convinced us that this is what was going to be.

We finished one of the trenches at about late evening, I don't know the time. The size of that trench was about twenty metres long on both sides and about five metres wide and about two to two-and-a-half metres deep. That night we were sent to our place to sleep. Before going to sleep they gave us some food.

Next day we started to dig another trench until about late forenoon when we saw two cars coming to the place. Stepping out were very high ranking SS officers, about six or seven of them. They were talking to our commanders and to our guards. We could not hear what they were saying but they pointed to our trenches we had dug.

Shortly after this we saw the people coming up also with shovels and different tools in their hands and they had been ordered to lay down their tools.

These people they ordered to take off all their clothes, they were put in order, and then they were all naked. They were sent to these ditches and SS men, some of them drunk, some of them sober, and some of them photographing, it seems, these people numbering about three hundred to four hundred, I don't know the exact number, were all executed and most of them only got hurt and got buried alive. Quicklime was brought there too, four or five trucks of quicklime.

Firstly, after the shooting we were ordered to put some earth back on the bodies, some of them were still crying for help. We put the earth back on the bodies and then the trucks were emptied of the quicklime.

I am talking about people who are all Jews, no exception. There were some Christians who were trying to hide some Jews and they were hanged.[6]

In larger cities, the Nazis could not kill everyone at once. Instead they collected hundreds at a time for "resettlement in the East." Abba Kovner, a young Lithuanian Jew, said of one such roundup in Vilna:

People were taken out of their flats, some carrying a few of their possessions, some without any possessions, out of all the courtyards, out of all the flats, they were driven out with cruel beatings. I don't know whether out of wisdom or instinct or momentary weakness I found myself in a stairway, in a dark recess there and I stood there. Out of a small window I saw what was happening in that narrow street.

Until one o'clock A.M., past midnight, this operation was still in progress. During those hours, at midnight I saw from the other

Ask any survivor; he will tell you, he who has not lived the event will never know it. And he who went through it will not reveal it, not really, not entirely. Between his memory and his reflection there is a wall—and it cannot be pierced.

courtyard on the other side of the street, it was 39 Ostrashun Street, a woman was dragged by the hair by two soldiers, a woman who was holding something in her arms. One of them directed a beam of light into her face, the other one dragged her by her hair and threw her on the pavement.

Then the infant fell out of her arms. One of the two, the one with the flashlight, I believe, took the infant, raised him into the air, grabbed him by the leg. The woman crawled on the earth, took hold of his boot and pleaded for mercy. But the soldier took the boy and hit him with his head against the wall, once, twice, smashed him against the wall.[7]

The *Einsatzgruppe* then trucked the victims to open pits where they were slaughtered. Those who remained in the ghetto had no way of knowing what had happened. While some suspected the worst, most hoped for the best. A few British spies did manage to learn the truth, however. In August of 1941, Winston Churchill shared that information with the British people. In a radio address, he reported that "whole districts are being exterminated. Scores of thousands—literally scores of thousands—of executions in cold blood are being perpetrated by the German police-troops upon the Russian patriots who defend their native soil. " He did not specifically refer to the slaughter of Jews but Churchill did note that "we are in the presence of a crime without a name."

CONNECTIONS

Professor Lawrence Langer pushes the reader to make distinctions between memoirs by survivors that help one cope and those writings that encourage confrontation with the Holocaust experience. Do the memories included in this reading help the reader cope with the Holocaust? Or do they encourage the reader to confront the Holocaust experience?

Langer believes that the literature of the Holocaust is not a history of survival but of mass extermination, and that makes knowing impossible. Elie Wiesel agrees. "Ask any survivor; he will tell you, he who has not lived the event will never know it. And he who went through it will not reveal it, not really, not entirely. Between his memory and his reflection there is a wall— and it cannot be pierced."[8] What is the wall to which Wiesel refers? Why can't it be pierced?

So far in this book, the emphasis has been on choice and decision-making. But now, the victims are faced with what Lawrence Langer refers to as "choiceless choices." In *Versions of Survival*, he describes these as decisions made in the "absence of humanly significant alternatives—that is, alternatives enabling an individual to make a decision, act on it, and accept the consequences, all within a framework that supports personal integrity and self-esteem." What distinguishes a "choiceless choice" from other decisions? Why does Langer believe that normal standards for judging behavior will not apply to all of the "choices" of victims?

Some teachers use simulation games to engage students emotionally or stimulate affective experiences and learning. Such games tend to oversimplify an event or series of events. To imply, for example, that students can "experience the existence of a person victim to the Holocaust" is unfair. It is also unfair to even try to re-create the feelings of participants in this history without carefully preparing students for the experience by helping them view the world from other perspectives. It may be helpful to keep in mind the comments of the boy at Auschwitz who wrote: "If heaven was full of paper and the oceans full of ink—I could not express my pain."

READING 3

Reserve Police Battalion 101

Who were the perpetrators? What kind of person massacres civilians? Slaughters old people? Murders babies? To find answers to such questions, historian Christopher Browning studied interrogations made in the 1960s and early 1970s of 210 men in Reserve Police Battalion 101. The battalion was originally formed from the German equivalent of city policemen and county sheriffs. After 1939, it and other Order Police battalions also served as occupation forces in conquered territory. Battalion 101 was assigned to the district of Lublin in Poland.

Like the National Guard in the United States, battalions were organized regionally. Most of the soldiers in Battalion 101 came from working and lower-middle-class neighborhoods in Hamburg, Germany. They were older than the men who fought in the front lines. The average age was thirty-nine, with over half between thirty-seven and forty-two. Most were not well-educated. The majority had left school by the age of fifteen. Very few were Nazis and none was openly antisemitic. Major Wilhelm Trapp, a 53-year-old career police officer who rose through the ranks, headed the battalion. He became a Nazi in 1932, but he was not a member of the SS , although his two captains were.

The unit's first killing mission took place on July 13, 1942. Browning used interrogations to piece together the events of that day.

> Just as daylight was breaking, the men arrived at the village [of Jozefow] and assembled in a half-circle around Major Trapp, who proceeded to give a short speech. With choking voice and tears in his

A few who admitted that they had been given the choice and yet failed to opt out were quite blunt. One said that he had not wanted to be considered a coward by his comrades. Another—more aware of what truly required courage—said quite simply: "I was cowardly."

eyes, he visibly fought to control himself as he informed his men that they had received orders to perform a very unpleasant task. These orders were not to his liking, but they came from above. It might perhaps make their task easier, he told the men, if they remembered that in Germany bombs were falling on the women and children. Two witnesses claimed that Trapp also mentioned that the Jews of this village had supported the partisans. Another witness recalled Trapp's mentioning that the Jews had instigated the boycott against Germany. Trapp then explained to the men that the Jews in Jozefow would have to be rounded up, whereupon the young males were to be selected out for labor and the others shot.

Trapp then made an extraordinary offer to his battalion: if any of the older men among them did not feel up to the task that lay before him, he could step out. Trapp paused, and after some moments, one man stepped forward. The captain of 3rd company, enraged that one of his men had broken ranks, began to berate the man. The major told the captain to hold his tongue. Then ten or twelve other men stepped forward as well. They turned in their rifles and were told to await a further assignment from the major.

Trapp then summoned the company commanders and gave them their respective assignments. Two platoons of 3rd company were to surround the village; the men were explicitly ordered to shoot anyone trying to escape. The remaining men were to round up the Jews and take them to the market place. Those too sick or frail to walk to the market place, as well as infants and anyone offering resistance or attempting to hide, were to be shot on the spot. Thereafter, a few men of 1st company were to accompany the work Jews selected at the market place, while the rest were to proceed to the forest to form the firing squads. The Jews were to be loaded onto battalion trucks by 2nd company and shuttled from the market place to the forest.

Having given the company commanders their respective assignments, Trapp spent the rest of the day in town, mostly in a schoolroom converted into his headquarters but also at the homes of the Polish mayor and the local priest. Witnesses who saw him at various times during the day described him as bitterly complaining about the orders he had been given and "weeping like a child." He nevertheless affirmed that "orders were orders" and had to be carried out. Not a single witness recalled seeing him at the shooting site, a fact that was not lost on the men, who felt some anger about it. Trapp's driver remembers him saying later, "If this Jewish business is ever avenged on earth, then have mercy on us Germans."[9]

In describing the massacre, Browning notes, "While the men of Reserve Battalion 101 were apparently willing to shoot those Jews too weak or sick to move, they still shied for the most part from shooting infants, despite their orders. No officer intervened, though subsequently one officer warned his men that in the future they would have to be more energetic."

As the killing continued, several more soldiers asked to be relieved of their duties. Some officers reassigned anyone who asked, while others pressed their men to continue despite reservations. By midday, the men were being offered bottles of vodka to "refresh" them. As the day continued, a number of soldiers broke down. Yet the majority continued to the end. After the massacre ended, the battalion was transferred to the north part of the district and the various platoons were divided up, each stationed in a different town. All of the platoons took part in at least one more shooting action. Most found that these subsequent murders were easier to perform. Browning therefore sees that first massacre as an important dividing line.

> Even twenty-five years later they could not hide the horror of endlessly shooting Jews at point-blank range. In contrast, however, they spoke of surrounding ghettos and watching [Polish "volunteers"] brutally drive the Jews onto the death trains with considerable detachment and a near-total absence of any sense of participation or responsibility. Such actions they routinely dismissed with a standard refrain: "I was only in the police cordon there." The shock treatment of Jozefow had created an effective and desensitized unit of ghetto-clearers and, when the occasion required, outright murderers. After Jozefow nothing else seemed so terrible.[10]

In reaching conclusions from the interviews, Browning focuses on the choices open to the men he studied. He writes:

> Most simply denied that they had any choice. Faced with the testimony of others, they did not contest that Trapp had made the offer but repeatedly claimed that they had not heard that part of his speech or could not remember it. A few who admitted that they had been given the choice and yet failed to opt out were quite blunt. One said that he had not wanted to be considered a coward by his comrades. Another—more aware of what truly required courage—said quite simply: "I was cowardly." A few others also made the attempt to confront the question of choice but failed to find the words. It was a different time and place, as if they had been on another political planet, and the political vocabulary and values of the 1960s were helpless to explain the situation in which they found themselves in 1942. As one man admitted, it was not until years later that he began to consider that what he had done had not been right. He had not given it a thought at the time.[11]

As one man admitted, it was not until years later that he began to consider that what he had done had not been right. He had not given it a thought at the time.

The men who did not take part were more specific about their motives. Some attributed their refusal to their age or the fact that they were not "career men." Only one mentioned ties to Jews as a reason for not participating. Browning therefore notes:

> What remains virtually unexamined by the interrogators and unmentioned by the policemen was the role of anti-Semitism. Did they not speak of it because anti-Semitism had not been a motivating factor? Or were they unwilling and unable to confront this issue even after twenty-five years, because it had been all too important, all too pervasive? One is tempted to wonder if the silence speaks louder than words, but in the end—the silence is still silence, and the question remains unanswered.
>
> Was the incident at Jozefow typical? Certainly not. I know of no other case in which a commander so openly invited and sanctioned the nonparticipation of his men in a killing action. But in the end the important fact is not that the experience of Reserve Battalion 101 was untypical, but rather that Trapp's extraordinary offer did not matter. Like any other unit, Reserve Police Battalion 101 killed the Jews they had been told to kill.[12]

CONNECTIONS

What part did peer pressure play in the massacre? What part did opportunism play? Antisemitism? What other factors may have influenced participation? Compare the massacre to others you have read about. What differences seem most striking?

The officers described in the reading were concerned for their own psychological well-being and that of their men. Yet they showed no concern for their victims. What does this suggest about their sense of morality—of right and wrong?

What does Browning mean when he writes, "After Jozefow, nothing else seemed so terrible"?

What insights does Stanley Milgram's research (Chapter 5, Reading 1) offer in understanding the massacre at Jozefow? In Chapter 5, Philip Zimbardo was quoted as saying: "The question to ask of Milgram's research is not why the majority of normal, average subjects behave in evil (felonious) ways, but what did the disobeying minority do after they refused to continue to shock the poor soul, who was so obviously in pain?" How do his comments apply to the soldiers who refused to take part in the killing? To Major Trapp?

Browning writes of the men who took part in the murders, "A few who admitted that they had been given the choice and yet failed to opt out were quite blunt. One said that he had not wanted to be considered a coward by his comrades. Another—more aware of what truly required courage—said quite simply: 'I was cowardly.'" Write a working definition of the word *coward*.

➤The film *Genocide*, available from the Facing History Resource Center, shows Heinrich Himmler visiting a pit during an *Einsatzgruppen* action. As he bent forward to see what was happening, he "had the deserved good fortune to be splattered with brains." According to witnesses, he was more shaken by the damage to his uniform than by the murders. How do you account for his response?

READING 4

Mechanizing Death

On December 7, 1941—the same day the Japanese bombed Pearl Harbor—the Nazis transported seven hundred Jews from Kolo, a village in Poland, to the nearby town of Chelmno. There, groups of eighty were herded into vans previously used in the Nazis' "euthanasia program." By the end of the day, all seven hundred were dead.

Six weeks later, in January, 1942, the Nazis ordered the 1,600 Jews in the Polish town of Izbica Kujawska to assemble in the town square. Suspicious of the order, the community's *Judenrat* (or Jewish Council) urged people to flee to nearby forests. Hundreds took their advice. In retaliation, the Nazis shot members of the *Judenrat*. Then they shipped every Jew they could round up to Chelmno. One of them, Yakov Grojanowski, recalled:

> We didn't have to wait long before the next lorry (bus) arrived with fresh victims. It was specially constructed. It looked like a normal large lorry, in grey paint with two hermetically closed rear doors. The inner walls were of steel metal. There weren't any seats. The floor was covered by a wooden grating, as in public baths, with straw mats on top. Between the driver's cab and the rear part were two peepholes. With a [flashlight] one could observe through these peepholes if the victims were already dead.
>
> Under the wooden grating were two tubes about fifteen centimetres thick which came out of the cab. The tubes had small openings from which gas poured out. The gas generator was in the cab, where the same driver sat all the time. He wore a uniform of the SS death's head units and was about forty years old. There were two such vans.
>
> When the lorries approached we had to stand at a distance of five metres from the ditch. The leader of the guard detail was a high-ranking SS man, an absolute sadist and murderer.

He ordered that eight men were to open the doors of the lorry. The smell of gas that met us was overpowering. The victims were gypsies from Lodz. Strewn about the van were all their belongings: accordions, violins, bedding, watches and other valuables.

After the doors had been open for five minutes orders were screamed at us, "Here! You Jews! Get in there and turn everything out!" The Jews scurried into the van and dragged the corpses away.

The work didn't progress quickly enough. The SS leader fetched his whip and screamed, "The devil, I'll give you a hand straight away!" He hit out in all directions on people's heads, ears and so on, till they collapsed. Three of the eight who couldn't get up again were shot on the spot.

When the others saw this they clambered back on their feet and continued the work with their last reserves of energy. The corpses were thrown one on top of another, like rubbish on a heap. We got hold of them by the feet and the hair. At the edge of the ditch stood two men who threw in the bodies. In the ditch stood an additional two men who packed them in head to feet, facing downwards.[13]

When Grojanowski learned that everyone in his family had been killed, he made an important decision. He told an interviewer:

On Monday the 19th January we again boarded the bus in the morning. I let all the others get on in front of me and was the last one aboard. The gendarme sat in front. On this day no SS men rode behind us. To my right was a window which could be opened easily. During the ride I opened the window. When fresh cold air streamed in I caught fright and quickly shut the window again. My comrades, among them Monik Halter in particular, encouraged me, however.

After I made a decision I softly asked my comrades to stand up so the draught of cold air shouldn't reach the gendarmes. I quickly pulled the windowpane out of its frame, pushed my legs out and turned round. I held on to the door with my hand and pressed my feet against the hinges. I told my colleagues they should put the windowpane back immediately after I had jumped. I then jumped at once.

When I hit the ground I rolled for a bit and scraped the skin off my hands. The only thing that mattered to me was not to break a leg. I would hardly have minded breaking an arm. The main thing was that I could walk in order to get to the next Jewish settlement. I turned round to see if they had noticed anything on the bus but it continued its journey.

I lost no time but ran as fast as I could across fields and woods. After an hour I stood before the farm of a Polish peasant. I went inside and greeted him in the Polish manner: "Blessed be Jesus Christ." While I warmed myself I asked cautiously about the distance to Chelmno. It was only 3 kilometres. I also received a piece of bread which I put in my pocket. As I was about to go the peasant asked me if I was a Jew—

which I absolutely denied. I asked him why he suspected me, and he told me they were gassing Jews and Gypsies at Chelmno. I took my leave with the Polish greeting and went away.[14]

On his way to Warsaw, Grojanowski stopped in Grabow where he told the rabbi his story. The rabbi, in turn, wrote to friends in Lodz. But the news came too late to save the Jews of Grabow. They were gassed at Chelmno shortly after the letter was written.

After establishing the first mechanized death camp at Chelmno, the Nazis built three more along rail lines near the former border between Poland and Germany: Belzec, Treblinka, and Sobibor. The only workers in these camps were those who disposed of the corpses. Many of them were previously employed at "euthanasia centers." There are few written accounts of the four death camps. Only two people survived Belzec and three came through Chelmno alive. Fewer than forty people lived through Treblinka, while sixty-four survived Sobibor.

CONNECTIONS

In his letter to his friends in Lodz, Jacob Schulmann, the rabbi of Grabow, wrote, "Do not think that this is being written by a madman. Alas, it is the tragic, horrible truth." Why are those who bring terrible news often dismissed as "mad"?

➤ For background on understanding oral testimonies, see Lawrence Langer's essays in *Elements of Time*, pages 291-316. See also the video, *Imagining the Unimaginable,* available from the Facing History Resource Center and described in *Elements of Time*, pages 180-189.

READING 5

Blueprint for the "Final Solution"

*I*n January 1942, representatives from the SS, the SS Race and Settlement Office, the SD, the *Einsatzgruppen*, the Party Chancellery, the Interior Ministry, the Office of the Four-Year Plan, the Justice Ministry, the Office of the Governor General of Poland, the Foreign Office, and the Reich Chancellery met in the Berlin suburb of Wannsee. They had come together to discuss the "Final Solution of the Jewish Question." It was an official meeting. So minutes were taken and distributed to those who could not attend.

The conference did not mark the start of the Holocaust. Jews were being killed long before the meeting. It was significant, mainly because it turned the "final solution" over to the bureaucrats.

At the beginning of the meeting the Chief of Security Police and the SD, SS Obergruppenfuehrer [Reinhard] Heydrich, announced his appointment by the Reich Marshal [Hermann Goering], as Plenipotentiary for the Preparation of the Final Solution of the European Jewish Question, and pointed out that this conference had been called to clear up fundamental questions. The Reich Marshal's request to have a draft sent to him on the organizational, functional, and material concerns on the final solution of the European Jewish question necessitates prior joint consideration by all central agencies directly concerned with these questions, with a view to keeping policy lines parallel. . . .

In the course of the practical implementation of the final solution, Europe is to be combed from west to east. The Reich area, including the Protectorate of Bohemia and Moravia, will have to be handled in advance, if only because of the housing problem and other socio-political necessities.

The evacuated Jews will be brought, group by group, into so-called transit ghettos, to be transported from there farther to the east.[15]

The murder of Jews would now be carried out in a systematic way. It would be done according to "rules and regulations."

Heydrich argued that there were more than eleven million European Jews if strict racial definitions were applied. The participants then established a complicated set of rules to determine who was and who was not a Jew. The conference did not mark the start of the Holocaust. Jews were being killed long before the meeting. It was significant, mainly because it turned the "final solution" over to the bureaucrats. The murder of Jews would now be carried out in a systematic way. It would be done according to "rules and regulations."

CONNECTIONS

Note the language used in the minutes of the Wannsee Conference. How do you account for the way the task is described?

➤ The notes taken at the Wannsee Conference, only a small portion of which are included in this reading, are the basis for a feature-length film called *The Wannsee Conference*. The film, available from the Facing History Resource Center, shows how murder can be discussed without ever using the word.

Historical events do not follow a neat timeline. For the most part, mass shootings ended after the Wannsee Conference. But ghettoes were enlarged in some places, even as others were destroyed and their inhabitants shipped to death camps.

READING 6

Obeying Orders

The Wannsee Conference made the "Final Solution" a matter of bureaucratic policy. It was now up to the clerks, administrators, guards, and other employees to enforce it. After the war, journalist Bernt Engelmann listened as a friend described one of those administrators, his cousin Klaus-Guenter. According to Engelmann's friend, Klaus-Guenter later claimed, "I didn't harm a hair on anyone's head and none of us believed in that racial nonsense anyway. We were just little cogs in a huge machine—important cogs, true, but on the whole we did nothing different from any general staff officer."

Engelmann's friend went on to say, "Imagine he showed me an old-fashioned gold cigarette case shortly before his chauffeur came for him. 'The woman to whom this belonged was someone I got an exit visa for—it almost cost me my life,' he told me. 'You see, we weren't monsters.' I looked at the cover, which had the words engraved, 'In memory of Lieutenant Helmut Lilienfeld,' or something like that, and then his date of birth, his regiment, and the day on which he fell 'for his beloved Fatherland.' . . ." When Engelmann expressed surprise that Klaus-Guenter kept the case, his friend replied:

> No—I'm convinced that Klaus-Guenter thinks of himself as not only competent and hardworking, but even decent and kindhearted. I suppose that's why he always has the cigarette case on him—as a piece of evidence, so to speak. After all, he didn't save the woman's life because of the gold cigarette case. He could have simply kept it and shipped her off to Auschwitz. No, there were other reasons: first of all, this was not an anonymous victim, but a living human being standing before him. Somehow the woman had managed to get in to see him. And then she showed him the cigarette case that had belonged to her dead husband, to prove that she was a war widow. Then he helped her, and he kept the case only to have a memento of his own decency. . . .
>
> Types like my cousin can cold-bloodedly murder tens of thousands from their desks, issuing orders on official stationery in standard memorandum form; and they take great pride in their efficiency. But don't think for a moment Klaus-Guenter would have been capable of beating an old man unconscious and dragging him onto the streetcar tracks, or attacking women and children and driving them into the streets. . . . [Yet none] of it would have taken place if it hadn't been ordered from "on high," if there hadn't been experts, most of them with university educations, organizing everything so that the "operation" could be carried out with split-second timing. . . .They sat

[None] of it would have taken place if it hadn't been ordered from "on high," if there hadn't been experts, most of them with university educations, . . . They sat in their offices and dealt with issues of "political necessity." They dictated telegraph messages and signed lists and special orders.

in their offices and dealt with issues of "political necessity." They dictated telegraph messages and signed lists and special orders—like Klaus-Guenter.

Engelmann agreed, adding "And girls like my cousin Gudrun, from solid middle-class families, assisted them. They sat there with their chic hairdos and pretty white blouses and typed neat lists of the victims—an important service for *Fuehrer*, *Volk*, and *Vaterland*."[16]

C O N N E C T I O N S

Draw an identity chart for Klaus-Guenter. What did he mean when he said "I didn't harm a hair on anyone's head"? Was he lying? Rationalizing? Or did he truly believe he was innocent? How could he and his co-workers send Jews to their deaths and yet argue that "none of us believed in that racial nonsense anyway"? Why do you think he needed "a memento of his own decency"?

Is there a difference between murdering "tens of thousands from their desks" and "shooting Jews at point-blank range" as the men of Reserve Police Battalion 101 did? Compare Klaus-Guenter with the men described in Reading 4. How are they alike? What differences seem most striking? Review Milgram's experiment (Chapter 5, Reading 1). How does proximity to the victim affect participation? How does the source of the order? For example, are people more obedient to orders if they come from someone who seems to be in authority?

The Germans used the best data-processing device available to help them identify and ultimately deport Jews and other victims. The German-made and American-engineered machine was the forerunner of today's computer. Herman Hollerith, the inventor, developed the device to help the U.S. government with the 1890 census. He later founded his own company, known today as International Business Machines (IBM). An almost wholly German owned subsidiary manufactured the machines needed to compile deportation lists, prepare concentration camp records, and identify conscript laborers. How did those machines help people like Klaus-Guenter preserve the illusion that they had nothing to do with the murders? Did the fault lie in the technology or the way it was used?

Compare Gudrun's role to that of her bosses. How is her role similar to theirs? What differences seem most striking? Is she as responsible as they are?

READING 7

The "Final Solution" Accelerates

At the time the first death camp opened, most Polish Jews lived in ghettoes. There they desperately struggled to survive and keep their culture alive. Yet by the spring of 1942, one-fourth of all Jews who would be killed by the Nazis had already died. Just eleven months later—by February, 1943—three-fourths were dead. In 1961, a survivor named Rivka Yosselevscka testified about that eleven-month period. She painfully focused on events in Zagordski, a Polish town that was home to five hundred Jewish families on a Sabbath day in August 1942.

> I remember that day very well. Jews were not allowed to go to pray, yet they would risk their lives and go into a cellar in the ghetto. . . the only Jews left in the ghetto would endanger their very lives to go into the cellar to pray—very early, before dawn. On that night, there was too much commotion in the ghetto. There was always noise in the ghetto. Germans would be coming in and leaving the ghetto during all hours of the night. But the commotion and noise on that night was not customary, and we felt something in the air.
>
> . . . We saw that the place was full of Germans. They surrounded the ghetto. We went down and asked—there were some of the police that we knew—and we asked what was going on. Why so many Germans in the ghetto? . . .
>
> [The policemen] told us that there was a partisan woman trying to get into the ghetto and mix with us. A group of partisans, and if they succeed in mixing amongst us, they hope not to be caught. [The partisans were men and women who engaged in guerilla warfare against the Germans.] This was not true. Our Father came up from the cellar, after his prayer. He could not speak to us. He only wished us "a good month." This was the first day of the month. I remember very well—this was the first day of the month of Elul—the month of prayer before the Jewish New Year. We were told to leave the houses—to take with us only the children. We were always used to leave the ghetto at short order, because very often they would take us all out for a roll-call. Then we would all appear. But we felt and realized that this was not an ordinary roll-call, but something very special. As if the Angel of Death was in charge. The place was swarming with Germans. Some four to five Germans to every Jew.[17]

According to Yosselevscka, the Germans "began saying that he who wishes to save his life could do so with money, jewels and valuable things. This would be ransom, and he would be spared. Thus we were held until

The Nazi purpose was to obliterate the victim, not merely punish or defeat him: to nullify his spirit, grind up his bones, disperse his ashes, until he literally vanished from the face of the earth.

the late afternoon, before evening came." But she noted, "We had nothing to hand over. They already took all we had before."

Toward sunrise, "[The] children screamed. They wanted food, water. This was not the first time. But we took nothing with us. We had no food and no water, and we did not know the reason. The children were hungry and thirsty. We were held this way for 24 hours while they were searching the houses all the time—searching for valuables."

While the Nazis searched, a large truck arrived to take the Jews away. Before loading the truck, the Germans made sure that everyone was accounted for. Yosselevscka explained that she and others who could not be fit on the truck were forced to run after it.

I had my daughter in my arms and ran after the truck. There were mothers who had two or three children and held them in their arms—running after the truck. We ran all the way. There were those who fell—we were not allowed to help them rise. They were shot—right there—wherever they fell. All my family was amongst them. When we all reached the destination, the people from the truck were already down and they were undressed—all lined up. All my family was there—undressed, lined up. The people from the truck, those who arrived before us.

Q: Where was that?

A: This was some three kilometres from our village—to the place. There was a kind of hillock. At the foot of this little hill, there was a dugout. We were ordered to stand at the top of the hillock and the four devils shot us—each one of us separately.

Q: Now these four—to what German unit did they belong?

A: They were SS men—the four of them. They were armed to the teeth. They were real messengers of the Devil and the Angel of Death.

Q: Please go on—what did you see?

A: When I came up to the place—we saw people naked lined up. But we were still hoping that this was only torture. Maybe there is Hope—hope of living. One could not leave the line, but I wished to see—what are they doing on the hillock? Is there anyone down below? I turned my head and saw that some three or four rows were already killed—on the ground. There were some twelve people amongst the dead. I also want to mention that my child said while we were lined up in the Ghetto, she said, "Mother, why did you make me wear the Shabbat dress; we are being taken to be shot;" and when we stood near the dugout, near the grave, she said, "Mother, why are we waiting, let us run!" Some of the young people tried to run, but they were caught immediately, and they were shot right there. It was difficult to hold on to the children. We took all children not just ours, and we carried—we were anxious to get it all over—the suffering of the children was difficult; we all trudged along to come nearer to the place and to come nearer to the end of the torture of the children. The children were taking leave of their parents and parents of their elder people. . . .

We were driven; we were already undressed; the clothes were removed and taken away; our father did not want to undress; he remained in his underwear. We were driven up to the grave, this shallow. . . .

Attorney-General: And these garments were torn off his body, weren't they?

A: When it came to our turn, our father was beaten. We prayed, we begged with my father to undress, but he would not undress, he wanted to keep his underclothes. He did not want to stand naked.

Q: And then they tore them off?

A: Then they tore off the clothing off the old man and he was shot. I saw it with my own eyes. And then they took my mother, and she said, let us go before her; but they caught mother and shot her too; and then there was my grandmother, my father's mother, standing there; she was eighty years old and she had two children in her arms. And then there was my father's sister. She also had children in her arms and she was shot on the spot with the babies in her arms.

Q: And finally it was your turn.

A: And finally my turn came. There was my younger sister, and she wanted to leave; she prayed with the Germans; she asked to run, naked; she went up to the Germans with one of her friends; they were embracing each other; and she asked to be spared, standing there naked. He looked into her eyes and shot the two of them. They fell together in their embrace, the two young girls, my sister and her young friend. Then my second sister was shot and then my turn did come.

Q: Were you asked anything?

A: We turned towards the grave and then he turned around and asked "Whom shall I shoot first?" We were already facing the grave. The German asked "Who do you want me to shoot first?" I did not answer. I felt him take the child from my arms. The child cried out and was shot immediately. And then he aimed at me. First he held on to my hair and turned my head around; I stayed standing; I heard a shot, but I continued to stand and then he turned my head again and he aimed the revolver at me and ordered me to watch and then turned my head around and shot at me. Then I fell to the ground into the pit amongst the bodies; but I felt nothing. The moment I did feel I felt a sort of heaviness and then I thought maybe I am not alive any more, but I feel something after I died. I thought I was dead, that this was the feeling which comes after death. Then I felt that I was choking; people falling over me. I tried to move and felt that I was alive and that I could rise. I was strangling. I heard the shots and I was praying for another bullet to put an end to my suffering, but I continued to move about. I felt that

I was choking, strangling, but I tried to save myself, to find some air to breathe, and then I felt that I was climbing towards the top of the grave above the bodies. I rose, and I felt bodies pulling at me with their hands, biting at my legs, pulling me down, down. And yet with my last strength I came up on top of the grave, and when I did I did not know the place, so many bodies were lying all over, dead people; I wanted to see the end of this stretch of dead bodies but I could not. It was impossible. They were lying, all dying; suffering; not all of them dead, but in their last sufferings; naked; shot, but not dead. Children crying "Mother," "Father;" I could not stand on my feet.

Presiding Judge: Were the Germans still around?

A: No, the Germans were gone. There was nobody there. No one standing up.

Attorney-General: And you were undressed and covered with blood?

A: I was naked, covered with blood, dirty from the other bodies, with the excrement from other bodies which was poured onto me.

Q: What did you have in your head?

A: When I was shot I was wounded in the head.

Q: Was it in the back of the head?

A: I have a scar to this day from the shot by the Germans; and yet, somehow I did come out of the grave. This was something I thought I would never live to recount. I was searching among the dead for my little girl, and I cried for her—Merkele was her name—Merkele! There were children crying "Mother!" "Father!"—but they were all smeared with blood and one could not recognize the children. I cried for my daughter. From afar I saw two women standing. I went up to them. They did not know me, I did not know them, and then I said who I was, and then they said, "So you survived." And there was another woman crying "Pull me out from amongst the corpses, I am alive, help!" We were thinking how could we escape from the place. The cries of the woman, "Help, pull out from the corpses!" We pulled her out. Her name was Mikla Rosenberg. We removed the corpses and the dying people who held onto her and continued to bite. She asked us to take her out, to free her, but we did not have the strength.

Attorney-General: It is very difficult to relate, I am sure, it is difficult to listen to, but we must proceed. Please tell us now: after that you hid?

A: And thus we were there all night, fighting for our lives, listening to the cries and the screams and all of a sudden we saw Germans, mounted Germans. We did not notice them coming in because of the screamings and the shoutings from the bodies around us.

Q: And then they rounded up the children and the others who had got out of the pit and shot them again?

A: The Germans ordered that all the corpses be heaped together into one big heap and with shovels they were heaped together, all the corpses, amongst them many still alive, children running about the place. I saw them. I saw the children. They were running after me, hanging onto me. Then I sat down in the field and remained sitting with the children around me. The children who got up from the heap of corpses.

Q: Then the Germans came again and rounded up the children?

A: Then Germans came and were going around the place. We were ordered to collect all the children, but they did not approach me, and I sat there watching how they collected the children. They gave a few shots and the children were dead. They did not need many shots. The children were almost dead, and this Rosenberg woman pleaded with the Germans to be spared, but they shot her.

Attorney-General: Mrs. Yosselevscka, after they left the place, you went right next to the grave, didn't you?

A: They all left—the Germans and the non-Jews from around the place. They removed the machine guns and they took the trucks. I saw that they all left, and the four of us, we went onto the grave, praying to fall into the grave, even alive, envying those who were dead already and thinking what to do now. I was praying for death to come. I was praying for the grave to be opened and to swallow me alive. Blood was spurting from the grave in many places, like a well of water, and whenever I pass a spring now, I remember the blood which spurted from the ground, from that grave. I was digging with my fingernails, trying to join the dead in that grave. I dug with my fingernails, but the grave would not open. I did not have enough strength. I cried out to my mother, to my father, "Why did they not kill me? What was my sin? I have no one to go to. I saw them all being killed. Why was I spared? Why was I not killed?"

And I remained there, stretched out on the grave, three days and three nights.[18]

CONNECTIONS

According to Lawrence Langer, our usual vocabulary is inadequate when applied to the Holocaust.

All survivor accounts, and all narratives about survivors and their experience, are limited by a number of inescapable restrictions. . . . They must depend on a vocabulary that finds little resonance in the universe of the death camps: "suffocation in the gas chamber" grates harshly against more consoling descriptions like "salvation through suffering" or "tragic insight." But some writers on the Holocaust find it so difficult to absorb this abrasive contradiction that instead of altering our perception of moral reality, they try to adapt the fact of extermination to ideas of suffering and heroism."[19]

Langer goes on to say:

> Many students of the Holocaust seem dismayed by how easily that event undermined men's sense of their physical and spiritual worth. The Nazi purpose was to obliterate the victim, not merely punish or defeat him: to nullify his spirit, grind up his bones, disperse his ashes, until he literally vanished from the face of the earth. Although the full purpose miscarried, the attempt is still very much alive to the human imagination, which must now rebuild a sense of worth in a universe that was willing to see so many perish for nothing. But let us be honest about the implications of this process. Words can be used to strip the facade from atrocity, or to masquerade a dignified image of the humiliated self.[20]

READING 8

The Jewish Councils

*I*n every ghetto, members of the *Judenrat* convinced themselves that there *was* a path to survival *if* they could only find it. The notes of their meetings reveal their agonized efforts to find the *right* solution. In Bialystok, for example, the minutes of August 15, 1942 read as follows:

> [Engineer Ephraim] Barash takes the floor for a report.
>
> The most important events in the ghetto lately have been the visits to our enterprises, and generally to the ghetto. They are important for our fate, our being or nonbeing hangs on these visits, says Eng. Barash. . .
>
> The opinions which we heard both from them and their escorts prove that our way—to make the ghetto useful to the authorities—is the correct one.
>
> The scope of the enterprises is unbelievable. They employ 1,700 persons. In knitwear the number of women at work has doubled. The new factories which we had planned to set in operation—of barrels and horseshoes—are already long at work. . . .
>
> About our fate? Everyone would gladly hear our opinions. In the ghetto people often spread different false rumors. That comes no doubt from the great fear which seizes the populace, and sometimes they may possibly be circulated with malice aforethought; perhaps someone wants to create panic among the Jews. Eng. Barash asserts that the rumors [presumably about imminent deportations] are complete and utter lies.

What is Bialystok's situation? I am convinced that our path is the only correct one. True, there have been such signals before, that the Bialystok ghetto is too large, too many Jews are here. This view is expressed especially by the new faces, just arrived, but the regularly stationed Germans here are for the ghetto, the local authorities appreciate us. And as long as there is no general decree from above, no peril awaits us.[21]

At another meeting, on October 11, Barash argued that people would be safe if they were useful to the Nazis. At the end of that meeting, Rabbi Rosenman closed the meeting with these words:

You have heard reports about the situation, mainly from Eng. Barash, and at the end I want to add: We always entreat and pray: "Stop the mouths of our enemies and detractors." But we ourselves, by our own behavior, open their mouths. We must conduct ourselves rightly, so they should not say that Jews are a gang of liars, parasites, loafers; we must prove that we are fit to work and honest people, and thereby we will be saved.[22]

Work did not save the Jews of Bialystok just as it failed to save those in other ghettoes. Why did people continue to believe that there was a way out of the madness? The story of Adam Czerniakow, the head of the *Judenrat* in the Warsaw Ghetto, offers some clues. In July, 1942, he heard rumors that deportations would soon begin. But Nazi officials assured him that only the unemployed would be affected. When the rumors persisted, he asked again and was again told that workers would be safe. Yet, just two days later, the Nazis came to him with a demand that six thousand Jews be deported from the ghetto each day. Czerniakow wrote in his diary, "When I asked for the number of days per week in which the operation would be carried out, the number was seven days a week." He concluded, "There is nothing left for me but to die." He committed suicide later that same day.

Soon after Czerniakow's death, Jan Karski, a Gentile member of the Polish resistance, visited the Warsaw ghetto. Jan Karski was smuggled in just before he left the country so that he could tell the world what was happening to the Jews of Poland. He said of the ghetto:

It was not a world. This was not humanity. Streets full, full. Apparently all of them lived in the street, exchanging what was the most important, everybody offering something to sell—three onions, two onions, some cookies. Selling. Begging each other. Crying and hungry. Those horrible children—some children running by themselves or with their mothers sitting. It wasn't humanity. It was . . . some hell. Now in this part of the ghetto, the central ghetto, there were German officers. If the Gestapo released somebody, the Gestapo officers had to pass through the ghetto to get out of it. There were also Germans, German traffic. Now the Germans in uniform, they were

In every ghetto, members of the *Judenrat* convinced themselves that there *was* a path to survival *if* they could only find it. The notes of their meetings reveal their agonized efforts to find the *right* solution.

walking. . . silence! Everybody frozen until they passed. No movement, no begging, nothing. Germans. . . contempt. This is apparent that they are subhuman. They are not human. . . .

But I reported what I saw. It was not a world. It was not a part of humanity. I was not part of it. I did not belong there. I never saw such things, I never. . . nobody wrote about this kind of reality. I never saw any theater, I never saw any movie. . . this was not the world. I was told that these were human beings—they didn't look like human beings. Then we left. [The man who brought me to the ghetto] embraced me then. "Good luck, good luck." I never saw him again.[23]

CONNECTIONS

Study the minutes of the meetings in Bialystok. Was Barash's reasoning logical? To disagree, what would you have had to believe?

In his memoir, *Night*, Elie Wiesel wrote that in the ghetto neither German nor Jew ruled. What does he mean? What evidence can you find to support his statement in this reading? In other readings?

➤Y. Rudashevski, a young Jew in the Vilna Ghetto, wrote on December 13, 1942, "Today the ghetto celebrated the circulation of the 100,000th book in the ghetto library. . . . Hundreds of people read in the ghetto. The reading of books in the ghetto is the greatest pleasure to me. The book unites us with the future, the book unites us with the world." Samuel Bak, now an internationally-known artist, held his first art exhibition at the age of nine in the Vilna Ghetto. How do you account for such efforts to not only preserve but enrich Jewish culture amid the death and destruction of ghetto life? For additional information about Samuel Bak and his family, see *Elements of Time*, pages 4-10. Slides of his boyhood work are available from the Resource Center. One of his paintings appears on the cover of this book.

➤How did Jan Karski describe the inhabitants of the Warsaw Ghetto? How did he account for what he saw? A video-taped interview with Karski is available from the Facing History Resource Center. (A summary of that interview can be found in *Elements of Time*, page 64.) The film, *Shoah*, is also available. It is the work of Claude Lanzmann, who conducted 350 hours of interviews over a period of eleven years in fourteen nations. Although the video is too long for classroom use, many teachers use sections of the documentary in their classrooms.

Emptying the Ghettoes

Members of every *Judenrat* had to decide who in their community would be "resettled in the east." It was the most painful choice each would ever make. Before carrying out a deportation order, Chaim Rumkowski, the head of Lodz *Judenrat,* told his fellow Jews, "Yesterday I received an order to send over 20,000 Jews out of the ghetto. 'If you don't do it, we will.' And the question arose, 'Should we do it or leave it to others?' Even more important is the question of not how many will we lose but of how many can we save?" He then urged that the sick be sacrificed to save the healthy. But no one was willing to make such choices. So when the *Judenrat* did not supply enough Jews for deportation, the SS and the German police did the job for them. The same was true in other ghettoes.

One of the most haunting deportations involved Henryk Goldsmit, a Warsaw physician and one of the most respected men in Poland. Known to Jews and Christians alike as Janusz Korczak, Goldsmit offered advice on child-rearing over the radio before the war. He also ran an orphanage in what became the Warsaw Ghetto. Once the war began, Goldsmit tried desperately to protect his young charges. Only his diary revealed the depths of his despair. In June, 1942 , he noted that "the day began with the weighing of the children. The month of May showed a marked decline. The earlier months of this year were not too bad, and even May isn't yet all that alarming. But we still have two months or more before the harvest. . . . The children look dreamy. Only their outer skin looks normal. Underneath lurks fatigue, discouragement, anger, mutiny, mistrust, resentment, longing. The seriousness of their diaries hurts."

When the Nazis ordered Goldsmit and his children deported, a number of Polish Gentiles offered to hide him. He refused, choosing instead to remain with his orphans. One observer wrote:

> It was an unbearably hot day. I put the children from the home at the far end of the square, near the wall. I thought that I might manage to save them that way at least until the afternoon, and possibly until the next day. I suggested to Korczak that he come with me to the ghetto officials and ask them to intervene. He refused, because he didn't want to leave the children for even a minute. They began loading the train. I stood by the column of ghetto police who were putting people in the boxcars and watched with my heart in my mouth in the hope that my stratagem would succeed. But they kept packing them in and there was still room left. Urged on by whips, more and more people were jammed into the cars. Suddenly Schmerling—the sadistic ghetto police officer whom the Germans had put in charge of the Umschlagplatz—

I'll never forget the sight to the end of my life. It wasn't just entering a boxcar—it was a silent but organized protest against the murderers, a march like which no human eye had ever seen before.

commanded that the children be brought to the cars. Korczak went at their head. I'll never forget the sight to the end of my life. It wasn't just entering a boxcar—it was a silent but organized protest against the murderers, a march like which no human eye had ever seen before. The children went four-by-four. Korczak went first with his head held high, leading a child with each hand. The second group was led by Stefa Wilczynska [Korczak's assistant]. They went to their death with a look full of contempt for their assassins. When the ghetto policemen saw Korczak, they snapped to attention and saluted. "Who is that man?" asked the Germans. I couldn't control myself any longer, but I hid the flood of tears that ran down my cheeks with my hands. I sobbed and sobbed at our helplessness in the face of such murder.[24]

CONNECTIONS

What options did the members of each *Judenrat* think were open to them? For example, Rumkowski believed that he had "to cut off limbs to save the body." What were the "limbs"? The "body"? What were the likely results if Rumkowski and others refused to cooperate with the Nazis? What were the results if they agreed to go along?

Why were observers so moved by deportation of Goldsmit and the orphans? Why did the observer describe the event as "a silent but organized protest against the murderers, a march like which no human eye had ever seen before"? In what sense was it a protest? Record your thoughts in your journal.

➤Roman Vishniac's book *The Life That Disappeared* contains photographs of Jewish life in Eastern Europe, just before the Nazi invasion of Poland. Vishniac's pictures "constitute the last pictorial record of a unique world that vanished only one year later." They also offer an interesting contrast to *The Camera of My Family*, a visual record of a German Jewish family that was wiped out in the Holocaust. The two sets of materials counter the image of the Jews found in *The Warsaw Ghetto*, a documentary made by the BBC from Nazi films and photographs. (See Connections in Chapter 6, Reading 17 for Lucy Dawidowicz's concerns about showing propaganda films.)

Deception, Terror, and Resistance

Resistance was complicated by a variety of factors. Some victims were unable to believe what lay ahead. They were easily deceived by the slivers of hope the Nazis offered their victims. Sometimes it was the possibility of a ghetto run entirely by Jews; at others it was the hope of resettlement in the east. Often people were willing to believe on the strength of little more than the need to buy a railroad ticket. Surely people being shipped to their deaths would not have to buy a ticket!

The Nazis also used fear and intimidation to prevent resistance. Anyone who challenged them could expect immediate retaliation. In May, 1942, for example, two Czech resistance fighters parachuted into their country from a British plane and assassinated Reinhard Heydrich. The Nazis executed not only the two soldiers but also five other members of the Czech resistance. Then, claiming that Lidice had served as a base for Heydrich's killers, the Nazis murdered every male in the town and set fire to every building. When the fire burned out, they dynamited the ruins and leveled the rubble. Czechs were not the only ones to pay. The day Heydrich died, the Nazis executed 158 Jews in Berlin and shipped three thousand others from Theresienstadt, a concentration camp in Czechoslovakia, to death camps farther east.

Resistance was also complicated by the way many non-Jews regarded Jews. In 1944, Isabella Leitner was a teenager living in Kisvarda, an Hungarian town of about 20,000. She recalls her last day.

> On Monday morning, May 29, 1944, the ghetto was evacuated. Jews, thousands upon thousands of Jews—every shape and form, every age, with every ailment, those whose Aryan blood was not Aryan enough, those who had changed their religion oh, so long ago—dragged themselves down the main street toward the railroad station for what the Germans called "deportation." Upon their backs, bundles and backpacks—the compulsory "50 kilos of your best clothing and food" (which the Germans could later confiscate in one simple operation).
>
> And the Hungarian townspeople, the gentiles—they were there too. They stood lining the streets, many of them smiling, some hiding their smiles. Not a tear. Not a good-bye. They were the good people, the happy people. They were the Aryans.
>
> "We are rid of them, those smelly Jews," their faces read. "The town is ours!"
>
> Main Street, Hungary.[25]

Leitner later wondered, "You could have thrown a morsel of sadness our way but you didn't. Why?" Similar scenes were repeated throughout

The question is not why all the Jews did not fight, but how so many of them did. Tormented, beaten, starved, where did they find the strength—spiritual and physical—to resist?

Europe. Yet Jews in every part of Europe fought back. Even in places where resistance seemed impossible, it occurred. In the Vilna ghetto, where the Nazis had been killing Jews since the fall of 1941, Abba Kovner issued this call in January 1942:

> Let us not be led like sheep to the slaughter!
> Jewish youth!
> In a time of unparalleled national misfortune we appeal to you!
> We do not yet have the words to express the whole tragic struggle which transpires before our eyes. Our language has no words to probe the depths to which our life has fallen. . . .
> Let us defend ourselves during a deportation!
> For several months now, day and night, thousands and tens of thousands have been torn away from our midst, men, the aged, women, and children, led away like cattle—and we, the remainder, are numbed. The illusion still lives within us that they are still alive somewhere, in an undisclosed concentration camp, in a ghetto.
> You believe and hope to see your mother, your father, your brother who was seized and has disappeared.
> In the face of the next day which arrives with the horror of deportation and murder, the hour has struck to dispel the illusion: There is no way out of the ghetto, except the way to death!
> No illusion greater than that our dear ones are alive.
> No illusion more harmful than that. It deadens our feelings, shatters our national unity in the moments before death.
> Before our eyes they led away our mother, our father, our sisters—enough!
> We will not go!
> Comrades! Uphold this awareness and impart to your families, to the remnants of the Jerusalem of Lithuania.
> —Do not surrender into the hands of the kidnappers!
> —Do not hand over any other Jews!
> —If you are caught, you have nothing to lose!
> —Let us defend ourselves, and not go!
> Better to fall with honor in the ghetto than to be led like sheep to Ponary![26]

To succeed, the Jews of Vilna needed weapons. Yet their efforts to secure arms were repeatedly blocked. Many gentile resistance groups refused to help them, arguing that the Jews had a different agenda. Resistance also required an organization and a people united in the belief that there was no other alternative. Jews could not agree on much. They were divided politically, economically, and religiously. Still, the Jews of Vilna were eventually able to put aside these differences and work together. So did Jews in Warsaw, Kovno, Bialystok, Bedzin-Sosnowiec, Cracow, and eleven other cities.

Elie Wiesel has observed, "The question is not why all the Jews did not fight, but how so many of them did. Tormented, beaten, starved, where did they find the strength—spiritual and physical—to resist?" How might Kovner answer Wiesel's question? How would you answer it?

In Reading 9, a witness saw the march of the orphans as testimony to the human spirit. Here Kovner likens a similar march to "sheep being led to slaughter." Which view comes closest to your own?

Because of Nazi reprisals, anyone who resisted put others at risk. Does one have the right to endanger others in this way?

In France and other western nations, many Jews joined non-Jews in the Resistance—the fight to free their country from the Nazis. In the East, resistance groups were often reluctant to accept Jews. How do you account for the difference? How do you think the Germans took advantage of the difference?

R E A D I N G   1 1

The Uprising in the Warsaw Ghetto

When the Nazis began to deport Jews from Warsaw in the summer of 1942, many Jews there called for open resistance. That fall, some of them organized the ZOB (its initials in Yiddish stand for the Jewish Fighting Organization). When the Nazis began a new round of deportations in January, 1943, the ZOB struck back. Surprised by the move, the Nazis stopped deportations for a time, but the Jews had no reason to rejoice. It was only a matter of time until they began again.

On April 19, 1943, the first day of the Jewish holiday of Passover, General Juergen Stroop arrived in Warsaw. He came prepared to wipe out all opposition by the following day, Hitler's birthday. Stroop had 2,100 soldiers with 13 heavy machine guns, 69 hand-held machine guns, 135 submachine guns, several howitzers, and 1,358 rifles. The 1,200 Jewish resisters had 2 submachine guns and 17 rifles. A week later, Stroop reported to his superiors in Berlin:

> The resistance put up by the Jews and bandits could be broken only by relentlessly using all our force and energy by day and night. On 23 April 1943 the Reichsfuehrer SS issued through the higher SS and Police Fuehrer East at Cracow his order to complete the combing out of the Warsaw Ghetto with the greatest severity and relentless tenacity. I therefore decided to destroy the entire Jewish residential area by setting every block on fire, including the blocks of residential buildings

Some have called resistance a choice Jews made about how to die rather than about how to live. Others argue that resistance is more about the will to live and the power of hope than it is about death.

near the armament works. One concern after the other was systematically evacuated and subsequently destroyed by fire. The Jews then emerged from their hiding places and dug-outs in almost every case. Not infrequently, the Jews stayed in the burning buildings until, because of the heat and the fear of being burned alive they preferred to jump down from the upper stories after having thrown mattresses and other upholstered articles into the street from the burning buildings. With their bones broken, they still tried to crawl across the street into blocks of buildings which had not yet been set on fire or were only partly in flames. Often Jews changed their hiding places during the night, by moving into the ruins of burnt-out buildings, taking refuge there until they were found by our patrols. Their stay in the sewers also ceased to be pleasant after the first week. Frequently from the street, we could hear loud voices coming through the sewer shafts.[27]

Simha Rottem, a survivor, later told filmmaker Claude Lanzmann:

During the first three days of fighting, the Jews had the upper hand. The Germans retreated at once to the ghetto entrance, carrying dozens of wounded with them. From then on, their onslaught came entirely from the outside, through air attack and artillery. We couldn't resist the bombing, especially their method of setting fire to the ghetto. The whole ghetto was ablaze. All life vanished from the streets and houses. We hid in the cellars and bunkers. From there we made our sorties. We went out at night. The Germans were in the ghetto mostly by day, leaving at night. They were afraid to enter the ghetto at night. . . .

I don't think the human tongue can describe the horror we went through in the ghetto. In the streets, if you can call them that, for nothing was left of the streets, we had to step over heaps of corpses. There was no room to get around them. Besides fighting the Germans, we fought hunger and thirst. We had no contact with the outside world; we were completely isolated, cut off from the world. We were in such a state that we could no longer understand the very meaning of why we went on fighting. We thought of attempting a breakout to the Aryan part of Warsaw, outside the ghetto.

Just before May 1 Sigmund and I were sent to try to contact Antek [second-in-command of the Jewish Combat Organization, whose real name was Itzhak Zuckermann] in Aryan Warsaw. We found a tunnel under Bonifraternska Street that led out into Aryan Warsaw. Early in the morning we suddenly emerged into a street in broad daylight. Imagine us on that sunny May 1, stunned to find ourselves in the street, among normal people. We'd come from another planet. People immediately jumped on us, because we certainly looked exhausted, skinny, in rags. Around the ghetto there were always suspicious Poles who grabbed Jews. By a miracle, we escaped them. In Aryan Warsaw, life went on as naturally and normally as before. The cafes operated

> normally, the restaurants, buses, streetcars, and movies were open. The ghetto was an isolated island amid normal life.[28]

The Jews managed to hold out for nearly a month. When the Nazis finally put down the uprising on May 16, they destroyed the ghetto and killed many of the rebels. Others took their own lives before the Nazis could reach them. Only a few managed to escape through the sewers that lay beneath the ghetto to join other Polish resistance fighters.

CONNECTIONS

Some have called resistance a choice Jews made about how to die rather than about how to live. Others argue that resistance is more about the will to live and the power of hope than it is about death. Which view is closest to your own?

Compare Rottem's description of the uprising in the Warsaw Ghetto with Stroop's. What differences are most striking?

➤ "I was very immature, a very sheltered little girl. And when the world war came I grew up overnight. I really did," recalls Helen K., a survivor of the Warsaw Ghetto Uprising and Majdanck. What do you think she means when she says that she grew up overnight? Helen's experiences as a teenager in the Warsaw Ghetto are available on videotape from the Facing History Resource Center and are described in *Elements of Time*, pages 35-39.

➤ Jan Karski, the Polish courier who visited the Warsaw Ghetto, recalls how difficult it was for Jews to escape from the ghetto, because the Poles refused to help them. A videotape of Karski's testimony is available from the Facing History Resource Center and is summarized in *Elements of Time*, pages 64-65.

READING 12

In Hiding

*H*istorian Deborah Dwork believes that uprisings like the one in the Warsaw Ghetto were "spectacular, awe-inspiring, and monumentally courageous." Yet in her mind there were other forms of courage and resistance in the ghettoes that were equally spectacular. What were they?

> The policy, for example, of Czerniakow in Warsaw and Gens in Vilna to educate, feed, and protect children out of proportion to their ghettos' resources was another way in which Jews opposed the press of Nazism and held fast to their principles and responsibilities. The activities of Jewish networks throughout Nazi-occupied Europe to save

the children is also too frequently forgotten. And, most poignant, the decisions taken by the children's parents on behalf of their daughters and sons is an overwhelmingly painful form of courage and resistance. It cannot be stressed too fervently that it was the parents who took the first step and the most terrifying step in the protection of their children, as it was they who had to determine whether it was best to send them into hiding, to try to smuggle them out of the country, or to keep them at their side.[29]

Among those who went into hiding was the Frank family in the Netherlands. Otto and Edith Frank chose to "disappear" with their two daughters soon after Margot, their eldest child, received a deportation notice. In the summer of 1942, Otto Frank led the family into a hiding place in his business. His youngest daughter, thirteen-year-old Anne, called it the "Secret Annex" in her diary. The Franks were later joined by the van Pels family and later still by a dentist, Dr. Pfeffer. (In the diary, the van Pelses became the van Daans and Pfeffer became Dussel.) The eight remained hidden for twenty-five months. In her diary, Anne poured out her feelings to Kitty, an imaginary friend:

> As you can easily imagine we often ask ourselves here despairingly: "What, oh, what is the use of the war, why can't people live peacefully together, why all this destruction?" The question is very understandable, but no one has found a satisfactory answer to it so far, yes, why do they still make more gigantic planes in England, still heavier bombs and then prefabricated houses for reconstruction? Why are millions spent daily on the war and not a penny on medical services, artists or on poor people? Why do some people have to starve while there are surpluses rotting in other parts of the world? Oh, why are people so crazy? I don't believe the big men, the politicians and the capitalists alone are responsible for the war, oh no, the little man is just as guilty, otherwise the people of the world would have risen in revolt long ago! There's in people an urge simply to destroy, an urge to kill, to murder and rage and until all mankind without exception undergoes a great change wars will be waged, everything that has been built, cultivated and grown will be cut down and disfigured to begin all over after that![30]

Anne and the others stayed alive with the help of four former employees of Otto Frank: Miep Gies (born Hermine Santrouschitz), Victor Kugler, Johannes Kleiman, and Elli Voskuijl.

> They have pulled us through up till now and we hope they will bring us safely to dry land. Otherwise, they will have to share the same fate as the many others who are being searched for. Never have we heard one word of the burden which we certainly must be to them, never has one of them complained of all the trouble we give. They all come upstairs every day, talk to the men about business and politics, to the women about food and wartime difficulties, and about newspapers and books with the

"The policy, for example, of Czerniakow in Warsaw and Gens in Vilna to educate, feed, and protect children out of proportion to their ghettos' resources was another way in which Jews opposed the press of Nazism and held fast to their principles and responsibilities.

children. They put on the brightest possible faces, bring flowers and presents for birthdays and bank holidays, are always ready to help and do all they can. That is something we must never forget; although others may show heroism in the war or against the Germans, our helpers display heroism in their cheerfulness and affection.[31]

For those who sheltered Jews, finding a safe hiding place was only a part of the problem. Food was rationed during the war. So rescuers had to find extra ration books or buy supplies on the "black market." Illness posed a special risk. Miep Gies later wrote that by the winter of 1943, "all Jews in Amsterdam were gone. About the only way a Jew was seen now was floating face down in a canal. Jews were thrown there by the very people who had hidden them, for one of the worst situations that could arise for us helpers was if someone in hiding died. What to do with the body? It was a terrible dilemma, as a Jew could not properly be buried."[32]

Anne followed the course of both wars: the one between the Nazis and the Allied troops *and* the one against the Jews. Some events gave her nightmares. Others offered hope. On July 15, 1944, she wrote.

That's the difficulty in these times: ideals, dreams, and cherished hopes rise within us, only to meet the horrible truth and be shattered. It's really a wonder that I haven't dropped all my ideals, because they seem so absurd and impossible to carry out. Yet I keep them, because in spite of everything I still believe that people are really good at heart. I simply can't build up my hopes on a foundation consisting of confusion, misery and death. I see the world gradually being turned into a wilderness, I hear the ever approaching thunder, which will destroy us too, I can feel the sufferings of millions and yet, if I look up into the heavens, I think that it will all come right, that this cruelty too will end, and that peace and tranquillity will return again.

In the meantime, I must uphold my ideals, for perhaps the time will come when I shall be able to carry them out.[33]

Three weeks later, on the morning of August 4, 1944, the Nazis marched into the "Secret Annex" and captured everyone. Only Miep Gies, a native of Vienna, was not arrested—possibly because the officer in charge was also Viennese. All eight Jews were shipped to death camps. Only Otto Frank survived. When he returned to Amsterdam after the war, Miep Gies gave him some papers found after the arrests. Anne's diary was among them.

The Franks were not the only ones to go into hiding. In the Netherlands alone, twenty-five thousand people tried to find a safe place. Most hid alone and few stayed in one place longer than a few weeks. Max Gosschalk recalls:

I came from a safe home. I had to understand so many things which I could not understand. You had left all your safety, all your security. You had to grow up in a week; it's not possible. But you felt so insecure. If you took something with you it was always fear; fear of being caught, fear of being tortured, fear of betraying other people.

> Those are three of the worst. You never got any love from anyone. As a young person, I've been in the houses of wonderful people. And I never could trust them because today I was there—how long? One week, two weeks, nobody ever said anything. Then suddenly, something new. Never a chance of getting attached to someone.[34]

CONNECTIONS

How does historian Deborah Dwork define *courage*? *Resistance*? How does she expand our understanding of both words?

Why do you think Anne Frank has become a symbol of the millions of men, women, and children who died in the Holocaust?

What did Frank mean when she differentiated between the "big men" and the "little men"? Do you agree?

A man hidden as a boy describes the experience as "all of a sudden a way of life without life." What is he saying about the experience? Would Anne Frank agree? Max Gosschalk?

➤Paul D., then a child in Moldava, recalled his first memory of the horror of deportation. "We [my family and I] went into hiding and I remember we were in the attic of a gentile friend of the family. And I saw through a little crack in a window Jews being herded toward the railroad station." Paul was only five years old at the time. His story and that of Menachem S. appear in the video montage *Childhood Memories* available from the Facing History Resource Center.

➤Rachel G., a Jewish girl from Belgium, recalls the day her father took her into hiding with a priest. "My mother could not take me to those people. . . Of course, I couldn't understand. My mother crying and only my father could take and explain to me, 'Don't forget, you're a Jewish little girl and we're going to see you again. But you must do that, you must go away. We are doing this for your best.'" How could this action be for Rachel's best since she and her parents were so unhappy and desperate? For Rachel's story and others, see the video montage *Stories of Separation* available from the Facing History Resource Center and described in *Elements of Time*, pages 198-206.

➤The film *So Many Miracles* explores the experiences of Jews hidden in Poland; *Weapons of the Spirit* examines how several thousand Jewish children were hidden among Christians in the French town of Le Chambon. Both films are available from the Facing History Resource Center with accompanying study guides.

➤The Facing History Resource Center has a study guide to accompany the exhibition "Anne Frank in the World, 1929-1945." Also available from the center are videos about the Frank Family—*Dear Kitty, Just a Diary*, and an interview with Otto Frank from the film *Avenue of the Just*. A videotaped lecture entitled "The World of Anne Frank: Historical Background" by Paul Bookbinder is also available.

READING 13

The "Model" Concentration Camp

At the Wannsee Conference in January, 1942, SS Chief of Security Reinhard Heydrich had discussed the idea of creating a "privileged camp." It would be a propaganda tool to deceive Jews about the dangers of deportation and fool the world about what was really happening to the Jews. The Nazis chose Theresienstadt, a prison camp forty miles north of Prague, Czechoslovakia, for the purpose. The Nazis promoted it as a "model" camp where elderly Jews, much decorated veterans of World War I, and prominent individuals whose murder might raise awkward questions could live and work in "comfortable circumstances." The inmates included a number of famous poets, painters, musicians, composers, and scholars.

German officials often referred to the camp as Theresienbad. (*Bad* is the German word for *spa*.) They claimed that it was a "paradise ghetto" and forced inmates to create propaganda that supported that image. In real life, Terezinstadt was no paradise. Peter Fischel, a fifteen-year-old who died at Auschwitz, wrote of the camp.

> We have gotten used to getting up at 7 o'clock in the morning, standing in a long line at midday, and at 7 o'clock in the evening, holding a plate into which they pour some hot water tasting a trifle salty, or perhaps with a suggestion of coffee, or to get a small portion of potatoes. We have got used to sleeping without beds, to greeting any person wearing a uniform, to keeping off the footpaths. We have got used to have our faces slapped for no reason whatsoever, to getting hit, and to killings. We have got used to seeing people wallowing in their own excrement, to seeing coffins full of dead people, to seeing the sick lying in filth and stench and to seeing the doctors powerless.[35]

In the summer of 1943, the Nazis allowed a committee from the German Red Cross to tour the camp for the first time. The group's refusal to speak about their visit did not serve the Nazis' purpose, however. So in 1944, they invited the Danish Red Cross, the Danish foreign minister, and the International Red Cross to inspect the camp. This time, the Nazis were prepared. Before the visitors arrived, they ordered the prisoners to pave streets, repair housing, build a playground, and even plant twelve hundred rosebushes. The Nazis also deported seventy-five hundred young men and women to Auschwitz to make the camp seem less crowded and to substantiate their claim that it was a ghetto for old people. The visitors were suitably impressed.

Flushed with their success, the Nazis decided to create a "documentary-style" film about Terezinstadt in the summer of 1944. Kurt Gerron, an inmate who had been a well-known actor and director, was put in charge of the filming of *The Fuehrer Gives a City to the Jews*. But he was not allowed to edit the film or even view the developed footage. Two weeks after the movie was completed, he and other participants were sent to Auschwitz. Gerron was gassed soon after his arrival.

During World War II, over 150,000 Jews passed through Terezinstadt. About 33,000 died there from malnutrition, disease, and overwork. Many of the rest were shipped to death camps. Fewer than 16 percent survived. After the war, some Germans claimed that all they knew of the concentration camps was what they had heard about Theresienstadt.

CONNECTIONS

Why did the Nazis create a "model" concentration camp? Why did they want outsiders to see it? How important was it to deceive the Red Cross? Why?

➤The Facing History Resource Center has an educational packet on Terezinstadt which includes slides of art prepared for Nazi propaganda as well as art prepared secretly to document camp life. The packet also includes video interviews with survivors of the camp. Of particular interest is the testimony of Helga, a young artist who tried to paint what she saw— not what she thought she saw or wanted to see.

READING 14

Auschwitz

Within months of the invasion of the Soviet Union, Heinrich Himmler, who oversaw the "Final Solution," transformed what had been a camp for Polish political prisoners into a larger version of a camp in Poland called Majdanek. Auschwitz, known in Polish as Oswiecim, was chosen because even though it was on a major rail line, it was far enough from the battlefields that there was little danger of bombing. Rudolf Hoess, the commandant of Auschwitz, later described the role the camp played in the "Final Solution."

> The extermination procedure in Auschwitz took place as follows: Jews selected for gassing were taken as quietly as possible to the crematoriums, the men being separated from the women, in the undressing rooms, prisoners of the Special Detachment, detailed for this purpose, would tell them in their own language that they were going to be bathed and deloused, that they must leave their clothes neatly together and above all remember where they had put them, so that they would be able to find them again quickly after the delousing. The prisoners of the Special Detachment had the greatest interest in seeing that the operation proceeded smoothly and quickly. After undressing, the Jews went into the gas chambers, which were furnished with showers and water pipes and gave a realistic impression of a bathhouse.
>
> The women went in first with their children, followed by the men who were always the fewer in number. This part of the operation nearly always went smoothly, for the prisoners of the Special Detachment would calm those who betrayed any anxiety or who perhaps had some inkling of their fate. As an additional precaution these prisoners of the Special Detachment and an SS man always remained in the chamber until the last moment.
>
> The door would now be quickly screwed up and the gas immediately discharged by the waiting disinfectors through vents in the ceilings of the gas chambers, down a shaft that led to the floor. This insured the rapid distribution of the gas. It could be observed through the peephole in the door that those who were standing nearest to the induction vents were killed at once. It can be said that about one-third died straight away. The remainder staggered about and began to scream and struggle for air. The screaming, however, soon changed to the death rattle and in a few minutes all lay still. After twenty minutes at the latest no movement could be discerned. The time required for the gas to have effect varied according to the weather, and depended on

whether it was damp or dry, cold or warm. It also depended on the quality of the gas, which was never exactly the same, and on the composition of the transports which might contain a high proportion of healthy Jews, or old and sick, or children. The victims became unconscious after a few minutes, according to their distance from the intake shaft. Those who screamed and those who were old or sick or weak, or the small children, died quicker than those who were healthy or young.

Every prisoner was labeled. Badges became part of one's identity.

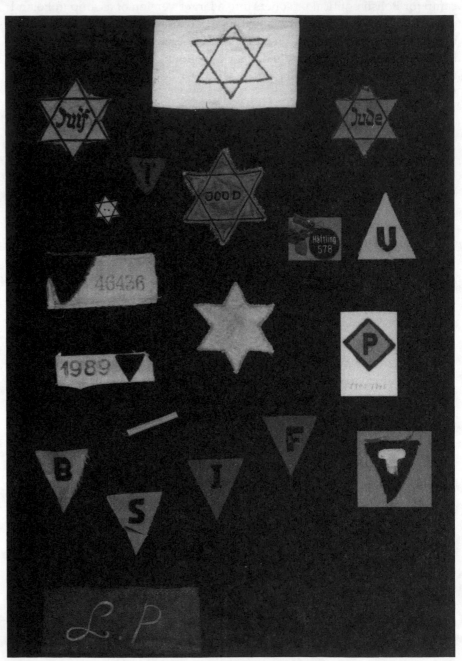

The door was opened half an hour after the induction of the gas, and the ventilation switched on. Work was immediately begun on removing the corpses. There was no noticeable change in the bodies and no sign of convulsions or discoloration. Only after the bodies had been left lying for some time, that is to say after several hours, did the usual death stains appear in the places where they had lain. . . .

The special detachment now set about removing the gold teeth and cutting the hair from the women. After this, the bodies were taken up by the elevator and laid in front of the ovens, which had meanwhile been stoked up. Depending on the size of the bodies, up to three corpses could be put into one oven retort at the same time. The time required for cremation also depended on this, but on an average it took twenty minutes.

During the period when the fires were kept burning continuously, without a break, the ashes fell through the grates and were constantly removed and crushed to powder. The ashes were taken in trucks to the Vistula, where they immediately drifted away and dissolved.[36]

Himmler later ordered the original camp enlarged so that it could contain thirty thousand people (Auschwitz I). He also established a second camp in nearby Birkenau, which was to hold one hundred thousand prisoners-of-war (Auschwitz II). And he called for the construction of a labor camp to provide workers for a factory run by I. G. Farben, one of Germany's leading industrial firms (Auschwitz III). By the summer of 1942, Auschwitz had grown beyond Himmler's original plans. Rita Kesselman recalled her first view of the camp:

For three days and three nights, we were taken. Destination unknown. Trains were stopping in villages and train stations, in cities. We were screaming through the windows, "Water, water." We were hungry. The pail in the corner filled up very quickly. And then people went on the floor. The stink, the smell, in the cattle car was terrible. People were changing positions. One was standing up, and one was sitting down. I was alone. I didn't have my parents to cuddle up with. I was sitting there by myself.

After three days and three nights, we arrived in a big field. And that was Auschwitz. Auschwitz was a city, and Birkenau was a suburb. In Birkenau went on all the killing, gassing, and burning the people. There were four crematoriums in Birkenau. When I came into Auschwitz, the trains didn't go to Birkenau. They came into Auschwitz. And we were made, the people that were selected. . . , they made us come off the train. In front of us, SS men with guns and dogs. And on trucks, more SS men with guns, watching us.

And we saw people in striped clothes, helping the people coming off the train. At the time, we didn't know who they were. They were like mutes. They didn't talk. They weren't allowed to talk. They were Jews, most of them, that helped the people come off the train. They were prisoners that had to help the Germans.

We were told to separate the men from the women. On the side were empty trucks waiting. The women and children were told to go on the trucks. And older people. And then, from the younger people were selected, people to go to the right and to the left. At the time, we did not know that the people who were selected to go to the right, would live and the rest would die. About one hundred people were picked from the women to go to work. And we envied the others, because we thought that they would go on the trucks. And after three nights being exhausted and hungry, we had to walk.

It was smoggy and raining. We walked for miles, and as we came closer, we saw like a camp with barbed wires. A band was playing at the gate. And the SS men were watching the camp from towers. A band of women played at the gate. They brought us inside. There were barracks— twenty-five barracks. They put us in an empty barrack on the floor. And we waited all night, not knowing what is going to happen to us.

In the morning, the SS came, women and men SS, and they took us to another barracks. It was a bathhouse. We were made to undress, leave the clothes on one side, and they took us to the other side. Every person was given a tattoo. My number was thirty thousand seven hundred seventy-five. . . .

Our hair was shaved and we were given striped clothes and wooden shoes. And that was our uniform for the two years I was in Auschwitz. I never bathed. I never saw water. I never had water to drink.[37]

Primo Levi, an Italian Jew who fought in a resistance unit in Italy, was deported to Auschwitz in 1944. He recalled his first days there:

Then for the first time we became aware that our language lacks words to express this offence, the demolition of a man. In a moment, with almost prophetic intuition, the reality was revealed to us: we had reached the bottom. It is not possible to sink lower than this; no human condition is more miserable than this, nor could it conceivably be so. Nothing belongs to us any more; they have taken away our clothes, our shoes, even our hair; if we speak, they will not listen to us, and if they listen, they will not understand. They will even take away our name: and if we want to keep it, we will have to find ourselves the strength to do so, to manage somehow so that behind the name something of us, of us as we were, remains.

We know that we will have difficulty in being understood, and this is as it should be. But consider what value, what meaning is enclosed even in the smallest of our daily habits, in the hundred possessions which even the poorest beggar owns: a handkerchief, an old letter, the photo of a cherished person. These things are part of us, almost like limbs of our body; nor is it conceivable that we can be deprived of them in our world, for we immediately find others to substitute the old ones, other objects which are ours in their personification and evocation of our memories.

Imagine now a man who is deprived of everyone he loves, and at the same time of his house, his habits, his clothes, in short, of everything he possesses: he will be a hollow man, reduced to suffering and needs, forgetful of dignity and restraint, for he who loses all often easily loses himself. He will be a man whose life or death can be lightly decided with no sense of human affinity, in the most fortunate of cases, on the basis of a pure judgement of utility. It is in this way that one can understand the double sense of the term "extermination camp," and it is now clear what we seek to express with the phrase: "to lie on the bottom."

Halftling: I have learnt that I am Halftling. My number is 174517; we have been baptized, we will carry the tattoo on our left arm until we die.

The operation was slightly painful and extraordinarily rapid; they placed us all in a row, and one by one, according to the alphabetical order of our names, we filed past a skillful official, armed with a sort of pointed tool with a very short needle. It seems that this is the real, true initiation: only by "showing one's number" can one get bread and soup. Several days passed, and not a few cuffs and punches, before we became used to showing our number promptly enough not to disorder the daily operation of food-distribution; weeks and months were needed to learn its sound in the German language. And for many days, while the habits of freedom still led me to look for the time on my wristwatch, my new name ironically appeared instead, a number tattooed in bluish characters under the skin.[38]

> And for many days, while the habits of freedom still led me to look for the time on my wristwatch, my new name ironically appeared instead, as numbers tattooed in bluish characters under the skin.

One day, Levi broke off an icicle that hung outside a window. A guard immediately took it away from him. Levi knew enough German to ask why. The guard replied, "There is no why here."

CONNECTIONS

In describing "improvements" to the camp, Hoess noted that the first cremations took place in the open and then explained why a change was needed.

> During bad weather or when a strong wind was blowing, the stench of burning flesh was carried for many miles and caused the whole neighborhood to talk about the burning of Jews, despite official counterpropaganda. It is true that all members of the SS detailed for the extermination were bound to the strictest secrecy over the whole operation, but, as later SS legal proceedings showed, this was not always observed. Even the most severe punishment was not able to stop their love of gossip.[39]

What is missing from his discussion? Where is the moral point of view? Hoess's complete description of the killing procedures at Auschwitz are available from the Facing History Resource Center.

What did Levi mean when he said that "our language lacks words to express this offence"? What did the guard mean when he told Levi, "There is no why here"? How are the two comments related?

Levi said of the language used to describe life in the camps:

> Just as our hunger is not that feeling of missing a meal, so our way of being cold has need of a new word. We say "hunger," we say "tiredness," "fear," "pain," we say "winter" and they are different things. They are free words, created and used by free men who lived in comfort and suffering in their homes. If the [camps] had lasted longer, a new, harsh language would have been born; and only this language could express what it means to toil the whole day in the wind with the temperature below freezing, and wearing only a shirt, underpants, cloth jacket and trousers, and in one's body nothing but weakness, hunger and knowledge of the end drawing nearer.[40]

Richard Rubenstein, author of *The Cunning of History*, sees Auschwitz as the "arch-creation of the Nazi genius." He writes: "The death-camp system became a society of total domination only when healthy inmates were kept alive and forced to become slaves rather than killed outright." Novelist William Styron explained further:

> There was ultimately systematized not only mass murder on a scale never known before but mass slavery on a level of bestial cruelty. This was a form of bondage in which the victim was forced to work for a carefully calculated period (usually no more than three months) and then through methods of deprivation calculated with equal care, allowed to die. As Rubenstein points out, only in a situation where human bodies were endlessly replaceable could such a form of slavery attempt to be efficient—but the Nazis, who aspired to be among the century's leading efficiency experts, had no cause for concern on this count, supplied as they were with all the Jews of Europe, besides thousands of Poles, Russian prisoners of war, and others. These became victims of bureaucratic *modernization* of slavery. And although the concept was not entirely unique in the long chronicle of bondage (for a period in the West Indies the British, with a glut of manpower, had no qualms about working slaves to death), certainly no slaveholders had on such a scale and with such absolute ruthlessness made use of human life according to its simple *expendability*. [It] is this factor of expendability, an expendability which in turn derives from modern attitudes toward the stateless, the uprooted and rootless, the disadvantaged and dispossessed—which provides still another essential key to unlocking the incomprehensible dungeon of Auschwitz. The matter of surplus population which Rubenstein touches upon again and again haunts this book like the shadow of a thundercloud.[41]

JEWS MURDERED BETWEEN 1 SEPTEMBER 1939 AND 8 MAY 1945: AN ESTIMATE

FINLAND
11

NORWAY
728

ESTONIA
1,000

DENMARK
77

LATVIA
80,000

MEMEL
8,000

LITHUANIA
135,000

HOLLAND
106,000

WHITE
RUSSIA

WESTERN
RUSSIA

BELGIUM
24,387

SOVIET
UNION
1,000,000

FREE CITY
OF DANZIG
1,000

GERMANY
160,000

POLAND
3,000,000

VOLHYNIA

LUXEMBOURG
700

CZECHOSLOVAKIA
217,000

RUTHENIA
60,000

GALICIA

PODOLIA

UKRAINE

BUKOVINA
124,632

BESSARABIA
200,000

FRANCE
83,000

AUSTRIA
65,000

HUNGARY
200,000

NORTHERN
TRANSYLVANIA
105,000

CRIMEA

RUMANIA
40,000

Black
Sea

ITALY
8,000

YUGOSLAVIA
60,000

7,122
4,221

MACE-
DONIA

THRACE

ALBANIA
200

KOS
120

RHODES
1,700

GREECE
65,000

CRETE
260

North
Sea

Baltic
Sea

Adriatic
Sea

Aegean
Sea

Mediterranean
Sea

furthest German advance

miles
0   300
kilometres
0   400

The map above shows the approximate numbers of Jews the Nazis
murdered. Where were the numbers highest?

➤ *Elements of Time* includes the stories of a number of survivors. See the
stories of Sonia Weitz, Rena Finder, Edith P., and Zezette Larsen (pages 10-
34 and 250-257). Helen K. describes life at Majdanek on pages 35-39. See
also the testimony of Renee Scott, a non-Jewish prisoner in Ravensbrueck
and Mauthausen. In addition, see Jan Karski's observations of Belzec
(pages 66-68). Videos of these testimonies are available from the Facing
History Resource Center.

"Hell Has No Bottom"

Charlotte Delbo, a French woman shipped to Auschwitz for distributing anti-Nazi propaganda, recalled:

> The projectors light the barbed wire strung between high white poles. Encircled by light, the camp lies in darkness and in this black abyss nothing can be distinguished
> nothing except darker shapes swaying
> ghostlike upon the ice.
> The roll-call siren has emptied the barracks. By swaying clusters, the women have all stumbled out, clinging to each other so as not to fall.
> And when one does fall, the whole cluster reels and falls and gets back up, falls again and rises, and in spite of it all moves on.
> Without a word.
> There is only the screaming of the furies who want the barracks to empty faster, want the reeling shades to move faster from the barracks to the space where the roll is called.
> In the darkness, for the beams of the projectors do not reach the spaces between the barracks. They light only the gate and the barbed wire enclosure so that the sentinels up in the watchtowers may spot those trying to escape and shoot
> as if one could escape
> as if one could cut through the fence of high-tension live barbed wire
> as if. . .[42]

Alexander Donat, a prisoner at Majdanek, said of daily routines:

> Beating and being beaten was taken for granted at Majdanek, and was an integral part of the system. Everyone could beat an inmate and the more experienced inmates never questioned why. They knew that they were beaten merely because they happened to run into someone who wanted to beat them. In most cases, the beating did not even involve personal anger or hatred; the authorities hated their victims as a group because when you wrong people for no reason, sooner or later you must come to hate them. It is difficult for man to endure the idea he is a beast and maltreats another human being, without cause; therefore, he eventually discovers justification for his behavior and imputes the fault to his victim. Thus, beating was part of the system. Thus, also, the victim was expected to take his licks standing rigidly at attention. Attempts to avoid blows, to cover one's face or head, were

treated as additional offenses. Some made the mistake of smiling stupidly as if they understood the "joke" being played on them, as if they appreciated the authorities' "sense of humor," which served only to irritate the beaters further. Worst of all were the beatings undertaken for sheer distraction, for there the morbid imagination of the executioners knew no bounds. Some derived their greatest pleasure from refined torture and were delighted by the professional approval of their colleagues. Some were motivated by sadistic curiosity: they wanted to see how a man suffers and dies.[43]

Donat, a survivor of the Warsaw Ghetto, was almost relieved to be sent to Majdanek. He thought that he had reached bottom. After a few days in the camp, he decided that "Hell has no bottom."

CONNECTIONS

➤Zezette Larsen, who was in her early teens when she was imprisoned at Auschwitz, says of herself, "I worked like hell to be as inconspicuous as possible. . . . I think that I was probably trying to survive. . . . I was ripped apart from my parents and I'm sure I was traumatized. . . . I was probably completely traumatized." Based on your readings, in what other ways did victims cope? Zezette Larsen's testimony is found in the video montage *Childhood Memories* and is summarized in *Elements of Time*, pages 250-251.

READING 16

"Choiceless Choices"

Nothing in one's previous existence prepared an individual for the camps. Although some were luckier than others, no inmate had any control over his or her life. Primo Levi often thought about the pressures individuals faced in the camps. He reflected on those who became *kapos*— prisoners in charge of other inmates. He also wondered about another group of prisoners.

With this duly vague definition, "Special Squad," the SS referred to the group of prisoners entrusted with running the crematoria. It was their task to maintain order among the new arrivals (often completely unaware of the destiny awaiting them) who were to be sent into the gas chambers, to extract the corpses from the chambers, to pull gold teeth from jaws, to cut women's hair, to sort and classify clothes, shoes, and the contents of the luggage, to transport the bodies to the crematoria and oversee the operation of the ovens, to extract and eliminate the ashes. The Special Squad in Auschwitz numbered, depending on the moment, from seven hundred to one thousand active members.

These Special Squads did not escape everyone else's fate. On the contrary, the SS exerted the greatest diligence to prevent any man who had been part of it from surviving and telling. Twelve squads succeeded each other in Auschwitz, each remaining operative for a few months, whereupon it was suppressed, each time with a different trick to head off possible resistance. As its initiation, the next squad burnt the corpses of its predecessors.[44]

Levi concluded that people in Special Squads were not collaborators but victims. They were not making choices in a world where individuals can choose among various options. Lawrence Langer agrees. He argues that behavior in the camps "cannot be viewed through the same lens we used to view normal human behavior since the rules of law and morality and the choices available for human decisions were not permitted in these camps for extermination. As important as it is to point out situations of dignity and morality which reinforce our notions of normal behavior, it is all the more important here to try to convey the 'unimaginable,' where surviving in extremity meant an existence that had no relation to our system of time and space and where physical survival under these conditions resulted in 'choiceless choices!'"[45]

As important as it is to point out situations of dignity and morality . . . , it is all the more important here to try to convey the "unimaginable," where surviving in extremity meant an existence that had no relation to our system of time and space and where physical survival under these conditions resulted in "choiceless choices!"

CONNECTIONS

What is a "choiceless choice"? Is it a choice?

➤Elie Wiesel's memoir *Night* relates what Auschwitz was like for him and his father. Accounts of incidents similar to those described in *Night* can also be found in *Elements of Time*, pages 15-35, along with suggestions for related reading. The video *Challenge of Memory*, available from the Facing History Resource Center, can be used to accompany a reading of *Night*. Each incident in the film highlights a complex moral issue that prisoners dealt with on a daily basis. See *Elements of Time*, pages 291-316 for additional comments and observations by Lawrence Langer.

A Commandant's View

*I*n an interview with journalist Gitta Sereny after his arrest in Brazil in 1971 and subsequent trial, Franz Stangl, the commandant of the death camp at Sobibor and later at Treblinka, responded to questions.

"You've been telling me about your routines," I said to him. "But how did you feel? Was there anything you enjoyed, you felt good about?"

A. "It was interesting to me to find out who was cheating," he said. "As I told you, I didn't care who it was; my professional ethos was that if something wrong was going on, it had to be found out. That was my profession; I enjoyed it. It fulfilled me. And yes, I was ambitious about that; I won't deny that."

"Would it be true to say that you got used to the liquidations?"

A. He thought for a moment. "To tell the truth," he then said, slowly and thoughtfully, "one did become used to it."

"In days? Weeks? Months?"

A. "Months. It was months before I could look one of them in the eye. I repressed it all by trying to create a special place: gardens, new barracks, new kitchens, new everything; barbers, tailors, shoemakers, carpenters. There were hundreds of ways to take one's mind off it; I used them all."

"Even so, if you felt that strongly, there had to be times, perhaps at night, in the dark, when you couldn't avoid thinking about it?"

A. "In the end, the only way to deal with it was to drink. I took a large glass of brandy to bed with me each night and I drank."

"I think you are evading my question."

A. "No, I don't mean to; of course, thoughts came. But I forced them away. I made myself concentrate on work, work and again work."

"Would it be true to say that you finally felt they weren't really human beings?"

A. "When I was on a trip once, years later in Brazil," he said, his face deeply concentrated, and obviously reliving the experience, "my train stopped next to a slaughterhouse. The cattle in the pens, hearing the noise of the train, trotted up to the fence and stared at the train. They were very close to my window, one crowding the other, looking at me through that fence. I thought then, 'Look at this; this reminds me of Poland; that's just how the people looked, trustingly, just before they went into the tins. . .'"

"Cargo," he said tonelessly. "They were cargo."

"You said tins," I interrupted. "What do you mean?" But he went on without hearing, or answering me.

A. ". . . I couldn't eat tinned meat after that. Those big eyes. . . which looked at me. . . not knowing that in no time at all they'd all be dead." He paused. His face was drawn. At this moment he looked old and worn and real.

"So you didn't feel they were human beings?"

A. "Cargo," he said tonelessly. "They were cargo." He raised and dropped his hand in a gesture of despair. Both our voices had dropped. It was one of the few times in those weeks of talks that he made no effort to cloak his despair, and his hopeless grief allowed a moment of sympathy.

"When do you think you began to think of them as cargo? The way you spoke earlier, of the day when you first came to Treblinka, the horror you felt seeing the dead bodies everywhere—they weren't 'cargo' to you then, were they?"

A. "I think it started the day I first saw the Totenlager [death camp] in Treblinka. I remember [Christian] Wirth [the man who set up the death camps] standing there, next to the pits full of blue-black corpses. It had nothing to do with humanity—it couldn't have; it was a mass—a mass of rotting flesh. Wirth said, 'What shall we do with this garbage?' I think unconsciously that started me thinking of them as cargo."

"There were so many children, did they ever make you think of your children, of how you would feel in the position of those parents?"

A. "No," he said slowly, "I can't say I ever thought that way." He paused. "You see," he then continued, still speaking with this extreme seriousness and obviously intent on finding a new truth within himself, "I rarely saw them as individuals. It was always a huge mass. I sometimes stood on the wall and saw them in the tube. But—how can I explain it—they were naked, packed together, running, being driven with whips like. . . " the sentence trailed off.

. . . "Could you not have changed that?" I asked. "In your position, could you not have stopped the nakedness, the whips, the horror of the cattle pens?"

A. "No, no, no. This was the system. Wirth had invented it. It worked. And because it worked, it was irreversible."[46]

[The system] worked. And because it worked, it was irreversible.

CONNECTIONS

How did Stangl view his role in the death camps? How much power did he think he had?

Elie Wiesel has described the process in which the Nazis reduced a person to a prisoner; the prisoner to a number; and the number to an ash, which was itself dispersed. To what extent does Stangl's account explain that process?

In thinking about ways of preventing another Holocaust, what can be learned from the words of perpetrators like Stangl?

READING 18

Rationalizing Genocide

*T*he Nazis set out to make Europe *Judenfrei* ("free of Jews"). The work was not done by machines but by real people—each with his or her own weaknesses, prejudices, values, and beliefs. In a speech to SS officers in the fall of 1943, Heinrich Himmler acknowledged those factors.

> I also want to make reference before you here, in complete frankness, to a really grave matter. Among ourselves, this once, it shall be uttered quite frankly; but in public we will never speak of it. Just as we did not hesitate on June 30, 1934, to do our duty as ordered, to stand up against the wall comrades who had transgressed, and shoot them, so we have never talked about this and never will. It was the fact which I am glad to say is a matter of course to us that made us never discuss it among ourselves, never talk about it. Each of us shuddered, and yet each one knew that he would do it again if it were ordered and if it were necessary.
>
> I am referring to the evacuation of the Jews, the annihilation of the Jewish people. This is one of those things that are easily said. "The Jewish people is going to be annihilated," says every party member. "Sure, it's in our program, elimination of the Jews, annihilation—we'll take care of it." And then they all come trudging, 80 million worthy Germans, and each one has his one decent Jew. Sure, the others are swine, but this one is an A-1 Jew. Of all those who talk this way, not one has seen it happen, not one has been through it. Most of you must know what it means to see a hundred corpses lie side by side, or five hundred, or a thousand. To have stuck this out and—excepting cases of human weakness—to have kept our integrity, that is what has made us hard. In our history, this is an unwritten and never-to-be-written page of glory, for we know how difficult we would have made it for ourselves if today—amid the bombing raids, the hardships and the deprivations of war—we still had the Jews in every city as secret saboteurs, agitators, and demagogues. If the Jews were still ensconced in the body of the German nation, we probably would have reached the 1916-1917 stage by now.

Among ourselves, this once, it shall be uttered quite frankly; but in public we will never speak of it.

The wealth they had we have taken from them. I have issued a strict order, carried out by SS-Obergruppenfuehrer Pohl, that this wealth in its entirety is to be turned over to the Reich as matter of course. We have taken none of it for ourselves. Individuals who transgress will be punished in accordance with an order I issued at the beginning, threatening that whoever takes so much as a mark of it for himself is a dead man. A number of SS men—not very many—have transgressed, and they will die, without mercy. We had the moral right, we had the duty toward our people, to kill this people which wanted to kill us. But we do not have the right to enrich ourselves with so much as a fur, a watch, a mark, or a cigarette or anything else. Having exterminated a germ, we do not want, in the end, to be infected by the germ, and die of it. I will not stand by and let even a small rotten spot develop or take hold. Wherever it may form, we together will cauterize. All in all, however, we can say that we have carried out this heaviest of our tasks in a spirit of love for our people. And our inward being, our soul, our character has not suffered injury from it.[47]

CONNECTIONS

To what events was Himmler referring, when he told SS officers, "Among ourselves, this once, it shall be uttered quite frankly; but in public we will never speak of it"? Why was it to be kept a secret?

To what event in 1934 does Himmler refer? How does he link it to the annihilation of the Jewish people?

What does it mean that "each one has his one decent Jew"?

What does Himmler mean when he says, "We had the moral right, we had the duty toward our people, to kill this people which wanted to kill us." How is it a way of justifying his orders? Of rationalizing them? Why did he need to justify? To rationalize?

Consider the choices the victimizers had in the following situation:

Prominent guests from Berlin were present at the inauguration of the first crematorium in March 1943. The "program" consisted of the gassing and burning of 8,000 Cracow Jews. The guests, both officers and civilians, were extremely satisfied with the results and the special peephole fitted into the door of the gas chamber was in constant use. They were lavish with their praise of this newly erected installation.[48]

It should be remembered that German companies and technical engineers competed for contracts from the government to design the gas chambers and crematoriums.

Resistance in the Death Camps

*I*n the death camps, resistance was far more difficult than in the ghettoes. Yet even there individuals fought back and a handful even managed to escape. These were last-ditch efforts by men and women who had nothing left to lose. The rebellion in Treblinka began in August 1943 in the camp's repair shop where inmates duplicated the key to the camp armory. The plan was to take the weapons stored there, kill as many guards as possible, and then escape into the forest. All seven hundred Jews in the camp took part. Stanislaw Kon described what happened after a pistol shot signaled the start of the revolt.

> Exactly at four in the afternoon, emissaries are sent to the groups with the order to come immediately to the garage to receive weapons. Rodak from Plock is in charge of distributing them. Everyone who comes to receive a weapon is obliged to state the password: "Death!" To which comes the answer: "Life!" "Death-life," "Death-life"—the ardent messages are repeated in quick succession and hands are stretched out to grasp the longed-for rifles, pistols, and hand grenades. At the same time, the chief murderers in the camp are being attacked. Telephone contact is immediately cut off. The guard towers are set alight with petrol. Captain Zelomir attacks two SS guards with an axe and breaks through to us. He takes over command. By the garage stands a German armored car whose engine Rodak has immobilized in good time. Now the car serves him as shelter, from which he fires at the Germans. His shots fell Sturmfuehrer Kurt Meidlar and several of Hitler's hounds. The armory is captured by force by Sodovitz's group. The weapons are divided up among the comrades. We have two hundred armed men. The remainder attack the Germans with axes, spades, and pickaxes. The crematoria are set alight. The false railway station with its signs "Bialystok-Volkowisk," "Ticket Office," "Cashier," "Waiting Room," etc. burns. The Max Bull barracks also burn. The flames and the echoes of the shots summon Germans from all around. SS men and gendarmes from Kosov, soldiers from the nearby airfield, and even a special SS unit from Warsaw arrive. The order is given to destroy and to breach the siege to the nearest forest. Most of our warriors fall, but Germans fall as well. Few of us are left.[49]

About 150 prisoners escaped. The rest were murdered but not before they killed sixteen guards. By the end of September, Treblinka was closed. An armed revolt at Sobibor took place two weeks later. The Security Police sent the following report to Berlin:

On October 14, 1943, at about 5:00 P.M., a revolt of Jews in the SS camp Sobibor, twenty-five miles north of Cholm. They overpowered the guards, seized the armory, and, after an exchange of shots with the camp garrison, fled in unknown directions. Nine SS men murdered, one SS man missing, two foreign guards shot to death.

Approximately 300 Jews escaped. The remainder were shot to death or are now in camp. Military police and armed forces were notified immediately and took over security of the camp at about 1:00 A.M. The area south and southwest of Sobibor is now being searched by police and armed forces.[50]

The SS tracked down most of the prisoners. Local residents turned over others to the Nazis. Only a few individuals reached resistance groups. Some were turned away because they were Jews. No more than a few dozen were able to find groups willing to accept them. As in Treblinka, the Nazis closed the camp after the revolt.

A revolt also occurred in Auschwitz-Birkenau in October of 1944. There the Special Squad organized the break-out by working with Jewish women employed in an ammunitions factory at Auschwitz. The women smuggled explosives into the death camp so that the inmates could blow up a crematorium and kill the guards. The odds were against the revolt from the start. The few who managed to escape were immediately captured and then executed.

CONNECTIONS

Evaluate the importance of the revolts in the death camps.

Sonia Schreiber Weitz spent her adolescence in concentration camps. She and a sister were the only survivors in a large family. She recalls:

One . . . day, I sneaked into my father's barracks on the other side of the barbed wire fence. While I was there, I met a boy who was about my age—14 or 15. The boy was playing a harmonica, an offense punishable by death. My father and I listened to the music and my father said to me, "You and I never had a chance to dance together". . . and so we danced. It is such a precious image, a bizarre and beautiful gift.[51]

Why would Sonia Weitz, her father, and the young harmonica player risk death for a few moments of pleasure? Why does Weitz call those moments "a bizarre and beautiful gift"? Were they also an act of resistance? Sonia Weitz's book, *I Promised I Would Tell*, is a blend of reminiscences and poetry. It is available from the Facing History Resource Center.

➤Max Bork, a slave laborer at Dora-Nordhausen, recalls ordering fellow prisoners to urinate on electrical wires so that the denotations would not function. Reprisals were severe. Everyone involved except Bork was killed. What did the prisoners gain from such resistance? For Bork's story see *Elements of Time*, page 124. See also Helen K.'s description of the effort of prisoners to blow up the crematoria at Auschwitz in October, 1944. See the summary of her testimony in *Elements of Time*, pages 35-39. A video portrait is available from the Facing History Resource Center. For additional information on resistance in the camps and Nazi reprisals, see *Elements of Time*, pages 124-125. Renee Scott, a young French resister, was captured and sent to Ravensbrueck and other camps. Her video portrait is also available from the Resource Center. Information on women in the resistance and the camps can be found in *Elements of Time*, pages 40-45.

READING 20

Is This a Person?

Less than a year after the war ended, Primo Levi wrote a poem called "The Shema." In Hebrew, the word means to hear or listen.

You who live secure
In your warm houses,
Who return at evening to find
Hot food and friendly faces:
    Consider whether this is a man,
    Who labors in the mud
    Who knows no peace
    Who fights for a crust of bread
    Who dies at a yes or a no.
    Consider whether this is a woman,
    Without hair or name
    With no more strength to remember
    Eyes empty and womb cold
    As a frog in winter.
Consider that this has been:
I commend these words to you.
Engrave them on your hearts
When you are in your house, when you
walk on your way,
When you go to bed, when you rise.
Repeat them to your children.
Or may your house crumble,
Disease render you powerless,
Your offspring avert their faces from you.[52]

CONNECTIONS

The word *shema* means "to hear." It also refers to the opening words of a prayer that religious Jews recite three times a day: "Hear O' Israel. The Lord is our God. The Lord is one." Jews are commanded to keep those words in their hearts and teach them to their children. Levi paraphrases parts of the prayer.

What does Levi want kept in the hearts of his readers? Why do you think he calls his poem "The Shema"?

In *The Drowned and the Saved*, Primo Levi points out how difficult escape and rebellion were. He also speaks of his frustration in explaining those difficulties to young people who ask, "Why did you not escape? Why did you not rebel?" In response he writes:

> For everyone else, the pariahs of the Nazi universe (among whom must be included Gypsies and Soviet prisoners, both military and civilian, who racially were considered not much superior to the Jews), the situation was quite different. For them escape was quite different and extremely dangerous; besides being demoralized, they had been weakened by hunger and maltreatment; they were and knew they were considered less than beasts of burden. . . .
>
> The particular (but numerically imposing) case of the Jews was the most tragic. Even admitting that they managed to get across the barbed wire barrier and electrical grill, elude the patrols, the surveillance of the sentinels armed with machine guns in the guard towers, the dogs trained for man hunts: In what direction could they flee? To whom could they turn for shelter? They were outside the world, men and women made of air. They no longer had a country.[53]

How would you answer the questions, "Why did they not escape? Why did they not rebel?" How does Levi's account help you understand the realities of the camp and its relationship to the outside world? Would prisoners have had more opportunities to escape if the outside world was more hospitable? For a more complete excerpt from Levi's remarks on resistance, see "Beyond Judgment" in *Elements of Time*, pages 316-327. Also compare Levi's discussion of hostility in the outside world with Jan Karski's video testimony, available from the Facing History Resource Center.

NOTES

[1] Paul Bookbinder, "An Historical Inquiry into the Background Causes of the Holocaust." Paper presented at session on the Historical Roots of Antisemitism, 25 July, 1991, Facing History and Ourselves Summer Institute, Chicago.

[2] Primo Levi, *Survival in Auschwitz*, trans. S. Woolf, (Collier Books, 1993), 26-27.

[3] Lawrence Langer, *Versions of Survival; The Holocaust and the Human Spirit* (State University of New York Press, 1982), 74.

[4] Eva Fleischner, ed. *Auschwitz: Beginning of a New Era?* (KTAV Publishing House, 1977), 288-289.

[5] Quoted in Lucy Dawidowicz, *The War Against the Jews*, 170.

[6] Quoted in Martin Gilbert, *The Holocaust*, 187-188.

[7] Quoted in *A Holocaust Reader*, ed. Lucy Dawidowicz, 334-335.

[8] Elie Wiesel, "Art and Culture After the Holocaust," in *Auschwitz: Beginning of a New Era?*, ed. Eva Fleischner, 405.

[9] Christopher R. Browning, "One Day in Jozefow: Initiation to Mass Murder" in *The Path to Genocide: Essays on Launching the Final Solution* (Cambridge University Press, 1992), 174-175.

[10] Ibid., 179.

[11] Ibid., 181-182.

[12] Ibid., 183.

[13] Quoted in Martin Gilbert, *The Holocaust*, 227-229.

[14] Ibid.

[15] Minutes of Wannsee Conference, 20 January, 1942. NG-2586-G. *Trials of War Criminals before the Nuremberg Military Tribunals*, XIII, Washington, D.C., 1952, 210-211, 218-219.

[16] Bernt Engelmann, *In Hitler's Germany*, 127-128.

[17] Testimony, session 30, 8 May, 1961, uncorrected English transcription, in *Documents of Destruction*, Raul Hilberg, ed. (Quadrangle Books, 1971), 59-62.

[18] Ibid.

[19] Lawrence Langer, *Versions of Survival*, 8.

[20] Ibid., 10.

[21] Quoted in *A Holocaust Reader*, ed. Lucy Dawidowicz, 280.

[22] Ibid., 287.

[23] Quoted in Claude Lanzmann, *Shoah: An Oral History of the Holocaust* (Pantheon, 1985), 172-175.

[24] Quoted in *The Holocaust Years*, ed. Nora Levin, 272-273.

[25] Excerpt from pages 3-4 of *Fragments of Isabella: A Memoir of Auschwitz* by Isabella Leitner, edited and with an Epilogue by Irving A. Leitner. (Thomas Y. Crowell, Publishers) copyright © 1978 by Isabella Leitner and Irving A. Leitner. Reprinted by permission.

[26] Quoted in *A Holocaust Reader*, ed. Lucy Dawidowicz, 334-335.

[27] Quoted in *The Holocaust Years*, ed. Nora Levin, 259-260.

[28] Quoted in Claude Lanzmann, *Shoah*, 197-198.

[29] Deborah Dwork, *Children with a Star* (Yale University Press, 1991), 255.

[30] *The Diary of Anne Frank* (Pocket Books, 1952), 201.

[31] Ibid., 131-132.

[32] Miep Gies, *Anne Frank Remembered*, 166-167.

[33] *The Diary of Anne Frank*, 237.

[34] Quoted in Deborah Dwork, *Children with a Star*, 79-80.

[35] Quoted in *I Never saw Another Butterfly: Children's Drawings and Poems from Terezin Concentration Camp* (Shocken, 1978), 14.

[36] Rudolf Hoess, *Commandant of Auschwitz* (World Publishers, 1959), 222-223.

[37] "Rita Kesselman at South Boston High School," transcript of a videotape (Facing History and Ourselves, 1987).

[38] Primo Levi, *Survival in Auschwitz*, 26-27.

[39] Rudolf Hoess, *Commandant of Auschwitz*, 217.

[40] Primo Levi, *Survival in Auschwitz*, 123.

[41] William Styron, Introduction to *The Cunning of History*, x-xi.

[42] Charlotte Delbo, *Days and Memory*, trans. Rosette Lamont (The Marlboro Press, 1990), 9.

[43] Alexander Donat, *The Holocaust Kingdom* (Holt, 1963), 177-178.

[44] Primo Levi, *The Drowned and the Saved*, trans. Raymond Rosenthal (Summit, 1988), 50-51.

[45] Lawrence Langer, *Versions of Survival*.

[46] Gitta Sereny, *Into That Darkness* (Pan Books, 1977), 200-202.

[47] Quoted in *A Holocaust Reader*, ed. Lucy Dawidowicz, 132-133.

[48] Quoted in *A Holocaust Reader*, ed. Lucy Dawidowicz, 119.

[49] Quoted in Leni Yahil, *The Holocaust* (Oxford University Press, 1990), 484.

[50] Quoted in Raul Hilberg, *Documents of Destruction*, 223.

[51] Sonia Weitz, *I Promised I Would Tell* (Facing History and Ourselves, 1993), 34.

[52] Primo Levi, "The Shema" in *Collected Poems*, trans. Ruth Feldman and Brian Swann (Faber & Faber, 1988), 9-10.

[53] Primo Levi, *The Drowned and the Saved*.

8. Bystanders and Rescuers

The world is too dangerous to live in—not because of the people who do evil, but because of the people who sit and let it happen.

ALBERT EINSTEIN

OVERVIEW

Chapter 7 focused on the victims of the Holocaust and the perpetrators. Chapter 8 considers the choices open to everyone else once the Holocaust began. "Most contemporaries of the Jewish catastrophe were neither perpetrators nor victims," writes Raul Hilberg. "Many people, however, saw or heard something of the event. Those of them who lived in Adolf Hitler's Europe would have described themselves, with few exceptions, as bystanders. They were not 'involved,' not willing to hurt the victims and not wishing to be hurt by the perpetrators." Hilberg says of these bystanders, "The Dutch were worried about their bicycles, the French about shortages, the Ukrainians about food, the Germans about air raids. All of these people thought of themselves as victims, be it of war, or oppression, or 'fate.'"[1]

Were they "victims of fate"? Or did they still have choices? Albert Camus, a French writer who joined the resistance, believed that individuals can always make a difference.

I know that the great tragedies of history often fascinate men with approaching horror. Paralyzed, they cannot make up their minds to do anything but wait. So they wait, and one day the Gorgon monster devours them. But I should like to convince you that the spell can be broken, that there is an illusion of impotence, that strength of heart, intelligence and courage are enough to stop fate and sometimes reverse it.[2]

And Cynthia Ozick warns, "When a whole population takes on the status of bystander, the victims are without allies; the criminals, unchecked, are strengthened; and only then do we need to speak of heroes. When a field is filled from end to end with sheep, a stag stands out. When a continent is filled from end to end with the compliant, we learn what heroism is."[3]

READING 1

What Did People Know?

Holocaust survivor Primo Levi was often asked, "Did the Germans know what was happening?" He replied with a question of his own. "How is it possible that the extermination of millions of human beings could have been carried out in the heart of Europe without anyone's knowledge?" He concluded:

> In spite of the varied possibilities for information, most Germans didn't know because they didn't want to know. Because, indeed, they wanted not to know. It is certainly true that State terrorism is a very strong weapon, very difficult to resist. But it is also true that the German people, as a whole, did not even try to resist. In Hitler's Germany a particular code was widespread: those who knew did not talk; those who did not know did not ask questions; those who did ask questions received no answers. In this way the typical German citizen won and defended his ignorance, which seemed to him sufficient justification of his adherence to Nazism. Shutting his mouth, his eyes and his ears, he built for himself the illusion of not knowing, hence not being an accomplice to the things taking place in front of his very door.[4]

In *The Destruction of European Jews*, Raul Hilberg proved that many had the opportunity to know about the killings:

> Organizing the transportation of victims from all over Europe to the concentration camps involved a countless number of railroad employees and clerical workers who had to work the trains and maintain the records. National Railroad tickets were marked for a one-way trip. Currency exchange at the borders had to be handled.

In Hitler's Germany a particular code was widespread: those who knew did not talk; those who did not know did not ask questions; those who did ask questions received no answers. In this way the typical German citizen won and defended his ignorance, which seemed to him sufficient justification of his adherence to Nazism.

Finance ministers of Germany moved to seize the pensions of victims from banks, yet the banks requested proof of death. Many building contracts and patents for ovens and gas chambers were required. . . .

The railroads were an independent corporation which was fully aware of the consequences of its decisions.

The civilian railroad workers involved in operating rails to Auschwitz were simply performing their daily tasks. These were individual people making individual decisions. They were not ordered or even assigned.

Orders from the SS to the railroads were not even stamped "secret" because that would admit guilt of something abnormal in the bureaucracy. The many clerical workers who handled these orders were fully aware of the purpose of Auschwitz.[5]

For the film *Shoah*, Claude Lanzmann interviewed Walter Stier, the person responsible for "special trains."

What's the difference between a special and a regular train?

A regular train may be used by anyone who purchases a ticket. Say from Krakow to Warsaw. Or from Krakow to Lemberg. A special train has to be ordered. The train is specially put together and people pay group fares. . .

. . . but why were there more special trains during the war than before or after?

I see what you're getting at. You're referring to the so-called resettlement trains.

"Resettlement." That's it.

That's what they were called. Those trains were ordered by the Ministry of Transport of the Reich. You needed an order from the Ministry. . .

But mostly, at that time, who was being "resettled"?

No. We didn't know that. Only when we were fleeing from Warsaw ourselves, did we learn that they could have been Jews, or criminals, or similar people.

Jews, criminals?

Criminals. All kinds.

Special trains for criminals?

No, that was just an expression. You couldn't talk about that. Unless you were tired of life, it was best not to mention that.

But you knew that the trains to Treblinka or Auschwitz were—

Of course we knew. I was the last district; without me these trains couldn't reach their destination. For instance, a train that started in Essen had to go through the districts of Wuppertal, Hannover, Magdeburg, Berlin, Frankfurt/Oder, Posen, Warsaw, etcetera. So I had to. . .

Did you know that Treblinka meant extermination?

Of course not!

You didn't know?

Good God, no! How could we know? I never went to Treblinka. I stayed in Krakow, in Warsaw, glued to my desk.

You were a. . .

I was strictly a bureaucrat![6]

Hilberg told Lanzmann how the "special trains" were financed.

. . . Jews were going to be shipped to Treblinka, were going to be shipped to Auschwitz, Sobibor or any other destination so long as the railroads were paid by the track kilometer, so many pfennigs per mile. The rate was the same throughout the war. With children under ten going at half-fare and children under four going free. Payment had to be made for only one way. The guards, of course, had to have return fare paid for them because they were going back to their place of origin.

Excuse me, the children under four who were shipped to the extermination camps, the children under four. . .

. . . went free.

They had the privilege to be gassed freely?

Yes, transport was free. In addition to that, because the person who had to pay, the agency that had to pay, was the agency that ordered the train—and that happened to have been the Gestapo, Eichmann's office—because of the financial problem which that office had in making payment, the Reichsbahn agreed on group fares. The Jews were being shipped in much the same way that any excursion group would be granted a special fare if there were enough people traveling. The minimum was four hundred, a kind of charter fare. Four hundred minimum. So even if there were fewer than four hundred, it would pay to say there were four hundred and in that way get the half-fare for adults as well. And that was the basic principle. Now of course if there were exceptional filth in the cars, which might be the case, if there was damage to the equipment, which might be the case because the transports took so long and because five to ten percent of the prisoners died en route. Then there might be an additional bill for that damage. But in principle, so long as payment was being made, transports were being shipped. . . . *Mitteleuropaeisches Reisebuero* (The Middle European Travel Agency) would handle some of these transactions—the billing procedure, the ticketing procedure—or if a smaller transport was involved, the SS would. . .

It was the same bureau that was dealing with any kind of normal passenger?

Absolutely. Just the official travel bureau. *Mitteleuropaeisches Reisebuero* would ship people to the gas chambers or they will ship vacationers to their favorite resort, and that was basically the same office and the same operation, the same procedure, the same billing.

No difference?

No difference whatsoever. As a matter of course, everybody would do that job as if it were the most normal thing to do. . . .

This was a self-financing principle. The SS or the military would confiscate Jewish property and with the proceeds, especially from bank deposits, would pay for transports.

You mean that the Jews themselves had to pay for their death?

You have to remember one basic principle. There was no budget for destruction. So that is the reason confiscated property had to be used in order to make the payments.[7]

CONNECTIONS

What did Levi mean when he wrote that "those who knew did not talk; those who did not know did not ask questions; those who did ask questions received no answers"? According to Levi, how did that attitude allow "the typical German citizen" to win and defend "his ignorance, which seemed to him sufficient justification of his adherence to Nazism"? How does someone "win and defend" ignorance? Why would anyone wish to do so?

Suppose officials like Stier had acknowledged what they knew. Would they have had to act on that knowledge? If so, what could they have done? If not, how might they have justified their failure to stop the killings? Record your ideas so that you can refer to them later.

➤The interviews with Stier and Hilberg can be seen in the film *Shoah*. The video is available from the Facing History Resource Center.

READING 2

Is Knowledge Enough?

During the war, Jan Karski, a courier for the Polish Resistance, tried to alert people to the mass murder of European Jews. After the war, he explained how he came to be a messenger. He was approached by representatives of two Jewish organizations. Karski later recalled:

Both men were in despair. They were fully aware that the deportations from the Warsaw ghetto as well as from other ghettos in Poland would lead to the extermination of the Jewish people. They knew that the Jews were being transported to extermination camps (those were their exact words) although they did not know the details of the operation. They both stressed that unless dramatic, extraordinary measures were immediately put into effect, the entire Jewish people would perish. . . . When the two learned that my mission covered meetings not only with the Polish authorities in London but also with the highest circles of the Allied governments, they asked me to transmit a number of specific demands. [8]

The two men also insisted that Karski see with his own eyes at least part of what he heard from them:

> They understood as well as I that in my future talks with Western statesmen I would be much more convincing if my report was backed by eyewitness testimony. The extermination of the Jews was without precedent in the history of mankind. No one was prepared to grasp what was going on. It is not true, as sometimes has been written, that I was the first one to present to the West the whole truth of the fate of the Jews in occupied Poland. There were others. . . . The tragedy was that these testimonies were not believed. Not because of ill will, but simply because the facts were beyond human imagination.
>
> I experienced this myself. When I was in the United States and told [Supreme Court] Justice Felix Frankfurter the story of the Polish Jews, he said, at the end of our conversation, "I cannot believe you." We were with the Polish ambassador to the US, Jan Ciechanowski. Hearing the justice's comments, he was indignant. "Lieutenant Karski is on an official mission. My government's authority stands behind him. You cannot say to his face that he is lying." Frankfurter's answer was, "I am not saying that he is lying. I only said that I cannot believe him, and there is a difference."[9]

It is possible to live in a twilight between knowing and not knowing. It is possible to refuse full realization of facts because one feels unable to face the implications of these facts.

Among those who dismissed stories of German atrocities as war propaganda was W. A. Visser't Hooft, a Dutch theologian and the first secretary of the World Council of Churches. He changed his mind only after hearing an eyewitness's account.

> From that moment onward I had no longer any excuse for shutting my mind to information which could find no place in my view of the world and humanity. And this meant that I had to do something about it.
>
> Hitler's strength was that he did the unimaginable. . . . A considerable number of people in Germany, in occupied countries, in the allied and neutral countries heard stories about mass killings. But the information was ineffective because it seemed too improbable. Everyone who heard it for the first time asked whether this was not a typical piece of wildly exaggerated war-time propaganda.

Visser't Hooft believed that "people could find no place in their consciousness for such an unimaginable horror and that they did not have the imagination, together with the courage, to face it. It is possible to live in a twilight between knowing and not knowing. It is possible to refuse full realization of facts because one feels unable to face the implications of these facts."[10]

CONNECTIONS

Think about Frankfurter's statement. What is the difference between saying that someone is lying and saying that you cannot believe what he or she is saying? Why do you think he chose not to believe?

Historian Leni Yahil divides knowledge into three parts: receipt of information, acknowledgment of that information, and action based on the information. What are the differences? How important are those differences? What facts would have been hardest for a Dutch Protestant like Visser't Hooft to accept? For an American Jew of German descent like Frankfurter? What do you think you would have had the most difficulty acknowledging? Laws that set Jews and others apart as the "enemy"? The campaign of terror? The mass deportations? The concentration camps? The gas chambers?

How does Yahil's division of knowledge apply to the way people today respond to the murders in Bosnia? To mass starvation in Somalia? To catastrophes in other parts of the world? Do people *know*? Have they *acknowledged* the information? Have they *acted* on that knowledge?

Visser't Hooft speaks of "shutting my mind to information which could find no place in my view of the world and humanity." How does one shut one's mind? What does the statement suggest about Visser't Hooft's view of the world and humanity? What view would have allowed him to accept the information as soon as he heard rumors? What does it mean to say that something is "beyond our imaginations"? Does it takes courage to face the truth?

➤Lawrence Langer believes that an underlying reason for the failure of Westerners to respond to news of the Holocaust was the "passive notion of what we might call the imagination of disaster. Even with the evidence before our eyes, we hesitate to accept the worst. When the evidence is founded on unconfirmed rumor, we hesitate even more." From what you have learned so far, how do you account for the widespread failure to believe reports of mass murders? Why were those who reported the murders thought of as "mad"? The video montage, *Imagining the Unimaginable*, available from the Facing History Resource Center, explores the reasons so many people were unable to believe reports of mass murder. See also *Elements of Time*, pages 119-120, for an excerpt from Elie Wiesel's *Night* describing a "madman" who reported mass killings in Poland.

➤For more on Jan Karski's efforts to inform Americans about the death camps and ghettos, see *Elements of Time*, pages 64-71. A video interview with Karski is available from the Resource Center.

Walter Bieringer, an American businessman who visited Germany in the 1930s, organized the Boston Refugee Committee for German Jewish Refugees. He quickly discovered that eliciting help from Jewish and

Christian groups in the United States was more difficult than he expected, mainly because people refused to believe that the threat was as great as he said it was. One person told him, "You Jews exaggerate too much." For additional information on Bieringer's work, see *Elements of Time*, pages 72-79.

Bystanders at Mauthausen

Professor Ervin Staub believes that bystanders play a far more critical role in society than people realize.

> Bystanders, people who witness but are not directly affected by the actions of perpetrators, help shape society by their reactions. . . .
> Bystanders can exert powerful influences. They can define the meaning of events and move others toward empathy or indifference. They can promote values and norms of caring, or by their passivity of participation in the system, they can affirm the perpetrators.[11]

Events in Mauthausen, a small town ninety miles from Vienna, support Staub's argument. After Austria became part of the Third Reich, the Nazis built a labor camp for political prisoners there. As the camp's operations expanded, the Nazis took over buildings in a number of nearby villages. One of those buildings was Hartheim Castle. Until the Nazis closed it for remodeling in 1939, it was a home for children labeled as "retarded." In the 1980s, historian Gordon I. Horwitz asked townspeople about the castle's renovation. A man he identifies as Karl S. wrote to the chairman of a euthanasia trial held in 1969. That letter stated in part:

> [The] house of my parents was one of the few houses in Hartheim from which one could observe several occurrences. After Castle Hartheim was cleared of its inhabitants (around 180 to 200 patients) in the year 1939, mysterious renovations began which, to an outsider, however, one could hardly divine, since no [local] labor was used for it, and the approaches to the castle were hermetically sealed. Following completion of the renovations, we saw the first transports come and we could even recognize some of the earlier residents who showed joy at returning to their former home.

Karl watched the buses arrive from a window in his father's barn. He recalled that transports of two to three buses came as frequently as twice a day. Soon after they arrived, "enormous clouds of smoke streamed out of a certain chimney and spread a penetrating stench. This stench was so disgusting that sometimes when we returned home from work in the fields we couldn't hold down a single bite."[12]

Bystanders, people who witness but are not directly affected by the actions of perpetrators, help shape society by their reactions.

Sister Felicitas, a former employee, has similar memories:

> My brother Michael, who at the time was at home, came to me very quickly and confidentially informed me that in the castle the former patients were burned. The frightful facts which the people of the vicinity had to experience at first hand, and the terrible stench of the burning gases, robbed them of speech. The people suffered dreadfully from the stench. My own father collapsed unconscious several times, since in the night he had forgotten to seal up the windows completely tight.[13]

Horwitz notes, "It was not just the smoke and stench that drew the attention of bystanders. At times human remains littered parts of the vicinity. In the words of Sister Felicitas, 'when there was intense activity, it smoked day and night. Tufts of hair flew through the chimney onto the street. The remains of bones were stored on the east side of the castle and in ton trucks driven first to the Danube, later also to the Traun.'"[14]

As evidence of mass murders mounted, Christian Wirth, the director of the operation, met with local residents. He told them that his men were burning shoes and other "belongings." The strong smell? "A device had been installed in which old oil and oil by-products underwent a special treatment through distillation and chemical treatment in order to gain a water-clear, oily fluid from it which was of great importance to U-boats [German submarines]."

Wirth ended the meeting by threatening to send anyone who spread "absurd rumors of burning persons" to a concentration camp.[15] The townspeople took him at his word. They did not break their silence.

CONNECTIONS

Why do you think the townspeople chose to believe Wirth despite evidence that he was lying? If they had acknowledged the truth, what would they have had to do? Would they have agreed with Visser't Hooft (Reading 2) when he argued that it takes courage to face the truth?

Who was a part of the town's "universe of obligation"?

According to Staub, what choices do bystanders have? What choices did people in Mauthausen make? What were the consequences?

How do the people of Mauthausen support Albert Einstein's observation: "The world is too dangerous to live in—not because of the people who do evil, but because of the people who sit and let it happen"? What arguments might they offer in their own defense?

A concentration camp was located in Ravensbrueck, Germany. The townspeople knew about the camp; some local shopkeepers even used prisoners as slave labor. Yet very few people in the town expressed concern for the inmates until the war was over. Only then did local women aid prisoners dying of typhus. How do you account for efforts to help the sick prisoners only after the war had ended? Was it terror that kept people from helping earlier? Or is there another explanation?

➤Ervin Staub presented his study on the behavior of perpetrators, victims, bystanders, and rescuers at a Facing History Summer Institute. A video of his lecture is available from the Resource Center.

R E A D I N G   4

A Matter of Courage

*I*n time, rumors of the mass killings reached Berlin. There, too, people had to decide how to respond. Ruth Andreas-Friedrich, a journalist who belonged to a resistance group, wrote in her diary in 1944:

> "They are forced to dig their own graves," people whisper. "Their clothing, shoes, shirts are taken from them. They are sent naked to their deaths." The horror is so incredible that the imagination refuses to accept its reality. Something fails to click. Some conclusion is simply not drawn. Between knowledge in theory and practical application to individual cases. . . there is an unbridgeable gulf. . . . We don't permit our power of imagination to connect the two, even remotely. . . . Is it cowardice that lets us think this way? Maybe! But then such cowardice belongs to the primeval instincts of man. If we could visualize death, life as it exists would be impossible. One can imagine torture, horror, and suffering as little as death. . . . Such indifference alone makes continued existence possible. Realizations such as these are bitter, shameful and bitter.[16]

Herbert Mochalski, a German soldier who took part in the invasion of Poland and a pastor in the Confessing Church, told an interviewer after the war, "It's nonsense when a German soldier says. . . that he never saw anything, that the soldiers didn't know anything. It's all simply not true!" Haunted by what he had observed, he noted, "One saw it only driving by, you know. We sat on our trucks and saw it. . . so that we had no chance to learn what the SS was thinking. All right, we could, we should, have protested then, but how? We couldn't have changed anything. I mean, all that is no excuse. Indeed, we all failed in this respect, that things went that far at all, isn't that so? And that is the awful thing that weighs on all of us, up to today."[17]

The horror is so incredible that the imagination refuses to accept its reality. Something fails to click. Some conclusion is simply not drawn.

What did Ruth Andreas-Friedrich mean when she wrote, "Indifference alone makes continued existence possible"? According to Staub, what else does indifference make possible? How would Andreas-Friedrich respond to Camus' belief that individuals cannot only stop fate but sometimes reverse it?

Some victims and perpetrators speak openly of the choices they made. Bystanders are more reluctant to speak of their decisions. How do you account for the difference?

READING 5

From Bystanders to Resisters

What we wrote and said is believed by many others. They just don't dare to express themselves as we did.

A mong the few Germans to act on what they knew were Hans Scholl and his younger sister Sophie. In the spring of 1942, they and a friend, Christoph Probst, formed a small group known as the White Rose. In July, the group published a leaflet that boldly stated: "We want to inform you of the fact that since the conquest of Poland, 300,000 Jews in that country have been murdered in the most bestial manner. Here we see the most terrible crime against the dignity of man, a crime that has no analogy in human history. . . . Why do the German people react in such an apathetic way to these revolting and inhuman crimes?"

The following February, the Nazis arrested the Scholls and Probst and brought them to trial. The three freely admitted that they were responsible for the leaflets. Sophie Scholl told the judges, "Somebody, after all, had to make a start. What we wrote and said is also believed by many others. They just don't dare to express themselves as we did." She, her brother Hans, and Probst were found guilty and guillotined later that same day. Soon after their deaths, three other members—a university professor named Kurt Huber and two students, Alexander Schmorell and Willi Graf—were also tried, convicted, and beheaded.

Although the Nazis were able to destroy the White Rose, they could not stop their message from being heard. Helmuth von Moltke, a German aristocrat, smuggled copies to friends in neutral countries. They, in turn, sent them to the Allies who reproduced each leaflet and then dropped thousands of copies over German cities. The information in the leaflets came as no surprise to Moltke. As a lawyer who worked for the German Intelligence Service, he had been aware of the murders for some time.

After the invasion of the Soviet Union in 1941, Moltke wrote to his wife of "reports that in transports of prisoners or Jews only 20 percent arrive, that there is starvation in the prisoner-of-war camps, that typhoid and all the other deficiency epidemics have broken out, that our own people are breaking down from exhaustion. What will happen when the nation as a whole realizes that this war is lost, and lost differently from the last one? With a blood-guilt that cannot be atoned for in our lifetime and can never be forgotten, with an economy that is completely ruined? Will men arise capable of distilling contrition and penance from this punishment, and so, gradually, a new strength to live? Or will everything go under in chaos?"[18]

In September, in yet another letter, he observed.

> An officer reports that ammunition produced in violation of international law was found on Russians: dum-dum bullets. That they were such could be proved by the evidence of the Medical Officer, one Panning, who used the ammunition in a large-scale experimental execution of Jews. This produced the following results: such and such was the effect of the projectile when fired at the head, such when fired at the chest, such in abdominal shots, such when limbs were hit. The results were available in the form of a scientific study so that the violation of international law could be proved without a doubt. That surely is the height of bestiality and depravity and there is nothing one can do.[19]

What shall I say when I am asked, and what did you do during that time?

By late October, Moltke was asking, "How is one to bear the burden of complicity?. . . In France there are extensive shootings while I write. Certainly more than a thousand people are murdered in this way every day and another thousand German men are habituated to murder. And all this is child's play compared with what is happening in Poland and Russia. May I know this and yet sit at my table in my heated flat and have tea? Don't I thereby become guilty too? What shall I say when I am asked, and what did you do during that time?"[20]

Moltke sought an answer to that question by meeting secretly with a number of other prominent Germans at Kreisau, his country estate. There they considered ways of fighting the Nazis and building a new Germany after the war. By the summer of 1944, a few members of the Kreisau circle were ready to act, but not Moltke. He argued, "Let Hitler live. He and his party must bear responsibility to the end of the fatal destiny for which they have prepared the German people; only in this way can the National Socialist ideology be obliterated."

On July 20, a member of the group, Claus von Stauffenberg, placed a briefcase containing explosives under a massive table around which Hitler and his staff were meeting. The bomb exploded as planned, but the table blunted the damage. As a result, Hitler and other top officials survived the explosion. They promptly retaliated by executing nearly twelve thousand people, including Moltke who knew of the plan but did not take part in it. Before his execution in January, 1945, Moltke wrote his sons, ages six and three.

Throughout an entire life, even at school, I have fought against a spirit of narrowness and unfreedom, of arrogance and lack of respect for others, of intolerance and the absolute, the merciless consistency among the Germans, which found its expression in the National Socialist state. I exerted myself to help to overcome this spirit with its evil consequences, such as excessive nationalism, racial persecution, lack of faith, and materialism.[21]

C O N N E C T I O N S

Friederich Reck-Malleczewen, a staunch monarchist who fought in World War I, kept a journal from 1936 until his murder at Dachau in 1944. In March 1943, he wrote of the Scholls:

I never saw these two young people. In my rural isolation, I got only bits and pieces of what they were doing, but the significance of what I heard was such that I could hardly believe it. The Scholls are the first in Germany to have had the courage to witness for the truth. . . . On their gravestones let these words be carved, and let this entire people, which has lived in deepest degradation these last ten years, blush when it reads them: . . . . "He who knows how to die can never be enslaved." We will all of us, someday, have to make a pilgrimage to their graves, and stand before them, ashamed. [22]

Why do you think Reck-Malleczewen believes that it takes courage to "witness for the truth?" What does he mean when he says, "We will all of us, someday . . . stand before them, ashamed?" What is he suggesting about the responsibility of bystanders? Would Moltke agree?

Moltke wrote, "Certainly more than a thousand people are murdered in this way every day and another thousand German men are habituated to murder." Why do you think he looks at murder in terms of its effect on both the victim and the perpetrator? What does it mean to live in a society where thousands have been "habituated to murder"?

Moltke asked, "How is one to bear the burden of complicity?" What is *complicity*? Is his complicity a result of his knowledge of mass murders? Or of his failure to act on that knowledge?

On July 21, 1944, Reck-Malleczewen wrote:

And now the attempt to assassinate Hitler. . . . Ah, now, really, gentlemen, this is a little late. You made this monster, and as long as things were going well you gave him whatever he wanted. You turned Germany over to this archcriminal, you swore allegiance to him by every incredible oath he chose to put before you. . . .

> And now you are betraying him, as yesterday you betrayed the
> Republic, and as the day before yesterday, you betrayed the Monarchy.
> Oh, I don't doubt that if this coup had succeeded, we, and what
> remains of the material substance of this country, would have been
> saved. I am sorry, the whole of this nation is sorry, that you failed.[23]

What distinction does Reck-Malleczewen make between the actions of
the White Rose and those of Von Stauffenberg and his associates? How
important is that distinction? How would you assess the actions of the
Scholls and their friends? Of Moltke and Von Stauffenberg?

Compare the choices open to individuals like Hans and Sophie Scholl,
Moltke, and Von Stauffenberg in the 1920s and 1930s with those in the
1940s. What options were no longer possible? What choices were now
more risky? What do your answers suggest about the difficulties of taking
a stand at the eleventh hour?

READING 6

Protest at Rosenstrasse 2-4

There is evidence of only one successful protest in Germany against the
Nazis. According to historian Nathan Stoltzfus, it began on Saturday,
February 27, 1943.[24] It was the day the SS rounded up the last Jews in
Berlin—about ten thousand men, women, and children. Most were picked
up at work and herded onto waiting trucks. Others were kidnapped from
their homes or pulled off busy streets. It was not the city's first mass deportation, but this one was different from any other. This time, two thousand
Jews in intermarriages were among those targeted. The Nazis had excluded them from earlier deportations, but now they were to be treated like
other Jews.

When these "privileged" Jews did not return home as expected, their
"Aryan" relatives began to make phone calls. They quickly discovered that
their loved ones were being held at the administration building of the
Jewish community at Rosenstrasse 2-4. Within hours, relatives began to
gather there. Most were women. (A Jewish woman who married an
"Aryan" did not have to wear a yellow star, but a man did. So the only
females picked up in the raid were the daughters of mixed marriages.)

As the women arrived at Rosenstrasse 2-4, each loudly demanded to
know what crimes her husband and children had committed. When the
guards refused to let the women enter the building, the protesters vowed
to return until they were allowed to see their relatives. They kept their

word. In the days that followed, people blocks away could hear the women chanting. Charlotte Israel, one of the protesters, recalls:

> The situation in front of the collecting center came to a head [on March 5]. Without warning the guards began setting up machine guns. Then they directed them at the crowd and shouted: "If you don't go now, we'll shoot."
>
> Automatically the movement surged backward in that instant. But then for the first time we really hollered. Now we couldn't care less. We bellowed, "you murderers," and everything else that one can holler. Now they're going to shoot in any case, so now we'll yell too, we thought. We yelled "Murderer, Murderer, Murderer, Murderer." We didn't scream just once but again and again, until we lost our breath.
>
> Then I saw a man in the foreground open his mouth wide—as if to give a command. It was drowned out. I couldn't hear it. But then they cleared everything away. There was silence. Only an occasional swallow could be heard.

The next day, Joseph Goebbels ordered the release of all Jews married to "Aryans." Why? A man who worked for Goebbels later claimed the Jews were released "so that others didn't take a lesson from it, so that others didn't begin to do the same."

CONNECTIONS

Draw identity charts for the protestors in the Rosenstrasse. How do their charts differ from those of Germans not married to Jews? Who was a part of each group's "universe of obligation"?

In December 1943, Himmler ordered the deportation of all Jews in inter-marriages whose spouses had died or divorced them. The only exceptions were those who had children. Why do you think Himmler made those exceptions? What do they suggest about the importance the Nazis placed on public opinion?

While the crowds gathered at Rosenstrasse 2-4, eight thousand Jews who did not have "Aryan" relatives were shipped to death camps. No one spoke on their behalf. Why were the protesters silent when those Jews were sent to their deaths?

Fateful Decisions

*F*ew people in Nazi-occupied Europe were involved in resistance movements, protest marches, or plots to assassinate Hitler. Most tried to live as "normal" a life as possible at a time when life was far from normal. But as more and more relatives, friends, and strangers were herded off to camps, some were forced to make fateful choices.

Jolana Roth described the decision one man made. "My father's very best childhood friend fought in the war with him and was very close. He was a Christian. When they came to get us for the transport, when they came to get us, my father knew. He rushed to his friend and begged him to raise my ten-year-old brother, to save his life. On his knees, he begged him. The friend said No."[25]

In Germany, Christabel Bielenberg, an Englishwoman married to a German, was asked to save two lives.

> It happened early in 1943. . . . The actual date is immaterial. . . . "Submarines" they were called, those Jews who at that time removed their stars and went underground, surfacing here, there, or anywhere, they might hope to find refuge. They had no ration cards and, every week, Ilse Liedke [an acquaintance of Bielenberg's] went the rounds of her friends collecting spare food coupons, which were becoming more and more difficult to provide.
>
> She had a blonde woman with her that morning; rather extra blonde who, after shaking my hand, hesitated on the doorstep and seemed unwilling to come into the house. Ilse, too, seemed satisfied that her companion should stay outside and, after glancing at our telephone to see that it was not plugged in, she explained why. The woman was a Jewess. She had removed her star when the Gestapo had come hammering at the door of her flat, and she and her husband had clambered down the fire escape and had been living in attics and cellars ever since. A safe hairdresser had dyed her hair, and latterly, a priest had housed them in his attic. . . . Since yesterday the good Father had felt himself and his house to be under surveillance. Ilse explained that the priest had not asked his lodgers to leave, but they knew that the time had come and now they had no place to go. She added that the woman could pass as an Aryan, and would willingly take on any housework, any work at all in fact, which might be useful to me; but that her husband looked so unmistakably Jewish that he would have to live in the cellar and go out only at night.

Bielenberg was silent for a long time. Her husband, Peter, was in Norway on business and she was responsible for their two young sons.

Because she was born in England, two neighbors had had to vouch for her before her husband could leave the country. She decided to consult one of them before making a decision. She later wrote:

> I pushed through the gap in the hedge to Langbehn's garden and found Carl at home, luckily alone. Knowing that he and Puppi Sarre [an acquaintance] were looking after a houseful of Jews somewhere in Potsdam, I do not think I expected his reaction to my story. It was explosive. I had come to him for advice, well, his advice was quite definite. Under no circumstances whatsoever could I give refuge to the man, or to the woman. I did not know them, I was English, Peter was away, I had no idea what I had contemplated doing. Seeing that Nick [her oldest son] was going to school, it could not be long before I would be found out, and the punishment for giving refuge to Jews was concentration camp, plain and simple—not only for myself but for Peter. "But—" perhaps the expression on my face showed something of a deep and very painful horror which I could feel beginning to take root somewhere behind my ribs. . . . Where were they to go? Was I to be the one to send them on their way?
>
> All of a sudden I had rather a different Carl before me, different at least from the friend I had thought of before as a cheerful extrovert. He drew up a chair and, sitting astride it, took both of my hands in his. "Listen Chris," he said gently. "I know exactly the way you feel, do not think that I do not know. Why do you suppose I do the crazy things I do? Into the Prinz Albrechtstrasse, out of the Prinz Albrechtstrasse, pitting my wits against those SS bastards, saving the odd one here, the odd one there, but always wondering whether the next visit won't be my last, knowing all the time that single small acts of compassion are not the solution, they are stop-gaps which somehow have to be used if one wants to keep any sort of self-respect. . . . Believe me, it is the deeper issue, the elimination of the whole filthy regime which must occupy our minds day and night. Now you have come to a crossroads, a moment which must probably come to us all. You want to show your colours, well my dear you can't, because you are not a free agent. You have your children, and while Peter is away you are my responsibility. You are British and, in spite of that fact, Hans Oster too has vouched for you, and, believe me, Oster is playing a very big game indeed.. . . "
>
> As soon as I pushed through the hedge again and opened our gate to the road, letting it click back shut behind me, I sensed rather than saw some movement in the darkness about me. "What is your decision Gnaedige Frau?" The voice, when it came, was quite close to me and pitched very low—it must have belonged to a small man, for I was staring out over his head. "I can't," I said, and I had to hold on to the railings because the pain in my side had become so intense that I could hardly breathe, "at least—", did I hope to get rid of that pain by some sort of feeble compromise? "at least I can't for more than a night,

perhaps two." "Thank you," again just the voice—the little man could not have been much taller than the railings—thanking me, in heaven's name, for two miserable days of grace. I loathed myself utterly as I went back to the house to fetch the cellar key.[26]

CONNECTIONS

Is there a difference between rescuing someone you know and saving a stranger? Is there a difference between refusing to rescue someone you know and refusing to save a stranger?

How did Christabel Bielenberg define her "universe of obligation"? What were the consequences of that definition? How did they contribute to her feeling that "I loathed myself utterly?" What other options did she have? How were they different from the choices she could have made earlier?

READING 8

Goodness, like evil, often begins in small steps. Heroes evolve; they aren't born.

Choosing to Rescue

*I*n Germany, the government imprisoned anyone caught sheltering a Jew. In Poland, the penalty was death. Yet, about 2 percent of the Polish Christian population chose to hide Jews. They did so in a nation with a long history of antisemitism. After the war, sociologist Nechama Tec interviewed a number of the rescuers. One factory worker told her sadly that she had done very little during the war. She had saved only one Jew and she had rescued that person only by chance. As her story unfolded, Tec discovered that Stefa Dworek had gone to incredible lengths to save a stranger.

It all began in the summer of 1942, when Stefa's husband, Jerezy, brought home a young Jewish woman named Irena. A policeman involved in the Polish underground had asked him to hide her for a few days. The woman looked too "Jewish" to pass for a Christian. So the couple decided to keep her concealed in the one-room apartment they shared with their infant child. To shield her from unexpected visitors, the Dworeks pushed a freestanding wardrobe a few inches from the wall. The space between the wall and the wardrobe became the woman's hiding place.

A "few days" stretched to a week and the week, in turn, became a month and still the unexpected guest remained. The policeman was unable to find another hiding place for her. After several months, Jerezy Dworek demanded that Irena leave. His wife Stefa, however, insisted that the woman stay. The quarrel ended with Jerezy stomping out of the apartment and vowing to denounce both Irena and his wife. What did Stefa do?

> I called Laminski [the policeman]. . . [and] he went to talk to my husband. He told him, "Here is my pistol; if you will denounce them you will not live more than five minutes longer. The first bullet will go into your head." After that my husband stopped coming. . . . This ended my marriage. But Ryszard Laminski continued to come, helping us, warning us about danger. He never abandoned us.

Was Stefa aware of the danger to herself and her baby?

> Sure I knew. Everybody knew what could happen to someone who kept Jews. . . . Sometimes when it got dangerous, Irena herself would say, "I am such a burden to you, I will leave." But I said, "Listen, until now you were here and we succeeded, so maybe now all will succeed. How can you give yourself up?" I knew that I could not let her go. The longer she was there the closer we became.[27]

Then in 1944, the people of Warsaw rebelled against the Germans. As the fighting spread, it became too dangerous to stay in the apartment. So Irena bandaged her face and Stefa introduced her to neighbors as a cousin who had just arrived in the city. When the Germans finally put down the uprising, a new threat developed. Irena later described it to a commission:

> Before the end of the war there was a tragic moment. . . . We learned that the Germans were about to evacuate all civilians. My appearance on the streets even with my bandaged face could end tragically. Stefa decided to take a bold step which I will remember as long as I live. She gave me her baby to protect me. [The Germans did not evacuate mothers with young children.] As she was leaving me with her child, she told me that the child would save me and that after the war I would give him back to her. But in case of her death she was convinced that I would take good care of him. . . . Eventually we both stayed.[28]

What motivated Stefa Dworek? "I knew I could not let her go. What could I do? Even a dog you get used to and especially to a fine person like she was. I could not act any other way. . . . I would have helped anyone. It did not matter who she was. After all I did not know her at first, but I helped and could not send her away. I always try to help as best as I can."[29]

CONNECTIONS

How does the dictionary define the word *altruism*? What does the word mean to you? Was Stefa Dworek altruistic?

In his study of rescuers, Ervin Staub states, "Goodness, like evil, often begins in small steps. Heroes evolve; they aren't born. Very often the rescuers make only a small commitment at the start—to hide someone for a day or two. But once they had taken that step, they began to see themselves differently, as someone who helps. What starts as mere willingness becomes intense involvement."[30] Write a working definition of the word *hero*. Was Stefa Dworek a hero?

➤Nechama Tec and Ervin Staub discussed the sociology and motivations of rescuers at the Second Annual Facing History Conference. Both agreed that the decision to rescue Jews had little to do with the rescuer's religion, nationality, schooling, class, or ethnic heritage. Most rescuers were independent individuals who refused to follow the crowd. They also had a history of performing good deeds and did not perceive rescue work as anything out of the ordinary. How does Stefa Dworek fit their description? A video of their joint presentation is available at the Facing History Resource Center.

➤Both Tec and Staub benefitted from the help Christians gave Jews during the Holocaust. Nechama Tec relates her personal experiences in her memoir, *Dry Tears*. She also described those years to a group of Facing History students. A videotape of that talk is available from the Resource Center. See *Elements of Time*, pages 45-49 for a brief portrait of Tec. The book also contains a bibliography and study questions. Ervin Staub has explored ways of using information about rescuers to help students become more caring adults. The Resource Center also has video presentations of his talks at Facing History Summer Institutes.

Inge Deutschkorn, a Jew who was hidden along with her mother during the war, attributes her survival to German Socialists who created a network to help Jews. Members took unbelievable risks and even sacrificed their own ration cards to feed hidden Jews. Her story is recounted in *Outcast: A Jewish Girl in Wartime Berlin*, available from the Facing History Resource Center.

READING 9

Links in a Chain

Rescuers did not simply happen on opportunities for rescue; they actively created, sought, or recognized them where others did not.

*I*n their book *The Altruistic Personality*, Samuel and Pearl Oliner quote Johan, a Dutch teenager who rescued Jews. "My father said the world is one big chain. One little part breaks and the chain is broken and it won't work anymore." The Oliners went on to observe, "Rescuers did not simply happen on opportunities for rescue; they actively created, sought, or recognized them where others did not. Their participation was not determined by circumstances but their own personal qualities. Chance sometimes provided rescuers like Johan with an opportunity to help, but it was the values learned from their parents which prompted and sustained their involvement."[31]

The experiences of Marion Pritchard, a graduate student in 1940—the year the Germans invaded the Netherlands—confirms the Oliners' view that the decision to rescue was a conscious choice. One morning in 1942, as she was riding her bicycle to school, she passed a home for Jewish children. What she observed that day changed her life.

The Germans were loading the children, who ranged in age from babies to eight-year-olds, on trucks. They were upset, and crying. When they did not move fast enough the Nazis picked them up, by an arm, a leg, the hair, and threw them into the trucks. To watch grown men treat small children that way—I could not believe my eyes. I found myself literally crying with rage. Two women coming down the street tried to interfere physically. The Germans heaved them into the truck, too. I just sat there on my bicycle, and that was the moment I decided that if there was anything I could do to thwart such atrocities, I would do it.

Some of my friends had similar experiences, and about ten of us, including two Jewish students who decided they did not want to go into hiding, organized very informally for this purpose. We obtained Aryan identity cards for the Jewish students, who, of course, were taking more of a risk than we were. They knew many people who were looking to *onderduiken*, "disappear," as Anne Frank and her family were to do.

We located hiding places, helped people move there, provided food, clothing, and ration cards, and sometimes moral support and relief for the host families. We registered newborn Jewish babies as gentiles . . . and provided medical care when possible.[32]

The decision to rescue Jews had great consequences. Pritchard described what happened when she hid a man with three children.

The father, the two boys, and the baby girl moved in and we managed to survive the next two years, until the end of the war. Friends helped take up the floorboards, under the rug, and build a hiding place in case of raids. These did occur with increasing frequency, and one night we had a very narrow escape.

Four Germans, accompanied by a Dutch Nazi policeman came and searched the house. They did not find the hiding place, but they had learned from experience that sometimes it paid to go back to a house they had already searched, because by then the hidden Jews might have come out of the hiding place. The baby had started to cry, so I let the children out. Then the Dutch policeman came back alone. I had a small revolver that a friend had given me, but I had never planned to use it. I felt I had no choice except to kill him. I would do it again, under the same circumstances, but it still bothers me, and I still feel that there "should" have been another way. If anybody had really tried to find out how and where he disappeared, they could have, but the general attitude was that there was one less traitor to worry about. A local undertaker helped dispose of the body, he put it in a coffin with a legitimate body in it. I hope the dead man's family would have approved.

Was I scared? Of course the answer is "yes." Especially after I had been imprisoned and released. There were times that the fear got the

Somewhere in between was the majority, whose actions varied from the minimum decency of at least keeping quiet if they knew where Jews were hidden to finding a way to help them when they were asked.

better of me, and I did not do something that I could have. I would rationalize the inaction, feeling it might endanger others, or that I should not run a risk, because what would happen to the three children I was now responsible for, if something happened to me, but I knew when I was rationalizing.[33]

CONNECTIONS

In reflecting on her decision and the choices others made during the war, Pritchard is troubled by a "tendency to divide the general population during the war into the few 'good guys' and the large majority of 'bad guys.' That seems to me to be a dangerous oversimplification. . . . The point I want to make is that there were indeed some people who behaved criminally by betraying their Jewish neighbors and thereby sentenced them to death. There were some people who dedicated themselves to actively rescuing as many people as possible. Somewhere in between was the majority, whose actions varied from the minimum decency of at least keeping quiet if they knew where Jews were hidden to finding a way to help them when they were asked."[34]

Why do you think Pritchard sees the oversimplification as dangerous? Would Christabel Bielenberg and her neighbor agree? Do you agree?

Pritchard says of her own decision: "I think you have a responsibility to yourself to behave decently. We all have memories of times we should have done something and didn't. And it gets in the way of the rest of your life." She notes that she has always had "a strong conviction that we are our brothers' keepers. When you truly believe that, you have to behave that way in order to live with yourself." Whom does she include in her "universe of obligation"?

How was Pritchard's decision similar to that of Stefa Dworek? How did it differ? Was Pritchard altruistic?

The Oliners contrast Nazi resisters with rescuers.

> For most rescuers . . . helping Jews was an expression of ethical principles that extended to all of humanity and, while often reflecting concern with equity and justice, was predominantly rooted in care. While other feelings—such as hatred of Nazis, religion, and patriotism, or even deference to an accepted authority whose values the rescuer shared—influenced them, most rescuers explain their actions as responses to a challenge to their fundamental ethical principles. This sense that ethical principles were at stake distinguished rescuers from their compatriots who participated in resistance activities only. For these resisters, hatred of Nazis and patriots were most often considered sufficient reasons for their behaviors; for rescuers, however, such reasons were rarely sufficient.[35]

Was Pritchard a resister or a rescuer? What about Stefa Dworek? The Scholls? Moltke? Christabel Bielenberg and her neighbor?

➤The film *Avenue of the Just* tells the stories of ten rescuers, while *So Many Miracles* focuses on the Rubineks and the Polish family that saved them. Both videos are available from the Resource Center.

READING 10

The Courage of Le Chambon

*I*n a tiny mountain town in south-central France, people were also aware that Jews were being murdered and took action to save as many people as possible. The people of Le Chambon were Protestants in a country where most people are Catholic. They turned their community into a hiding place for Jews from all over Europe. Magda Trocme, the wife of the local minister, explained how it all began.

> Those of us who received the first Jews did what we thought had to be done—nothing more complicated. It was not decided from one day to the next what we would have to do. There were many people in the village who needed help. How could we refuse them? A person doesn't sit down and say I'm going to do this and this and that. We had no time to think. When a problem came, we had to solve it immediately. Sometimes people ask me, "How did you make a decision?" There was no decision to make. The issue was: Do you think we are all brothers or not? Do you think it is unjust to turn in the Jews or not? Then let us try to help!

When asked of the risks she faced, Magda Trocme replied:

> In the beginning, we did not realize the danger was so big. Later, we became accustomed to it, but you must remember that the danger was all over. The people who were in the cities had bombs coming down and houses coming in on their heads, and they were killed. Others were dying in the war, in battles. Other people were being persecuted, like those in Germany. It was a general danger, and we did not feel we were in much more danger than the others. And, you see, the danger was not what you might imagine.
>
> You might imagine that the people were fighting with weapons in the middle of the square, that you would have had to run away, that you would have to go into a little street and hide. The danger was not that kind at all. The danger was in having a government that, little by little, came into the hands of the Germans, with their laws, and the French people were supposed to obey those laws.[36]

Sometimes people ask me, "How did you make a decision?" There was no decision to make. The issue was: Do you think we are all brothers or not?

Early in the war, the police arrested Trocme's husband Andre and his assistant, Edouard Theis. Although they were later released, the Gestapo continued to monitor their activities. In the summer of 1943, the Gestapo forced Andre Trocme into hiding for ten months by offering a reward for his capture. Many knew his whereabouts but no one turned him in. When they were interviewed forty years later, the people of Le Chambon did not regard themselves as heroes. They did what they did, they said, because they believed that it had to be done. Almost everyone in the community of three thousand took part in the effort. Even the children were involved. When a Nazi official came to organize a Hitler Youth camp in the village, the students told him that they "make no distinction between Jews and non-Jews. It is contrary to Gospel teaching."

The people of Le Chambon drew support of people in other places. Church groups, both Protestant and Catholic, helped fund their efforts. So did Visser't Hooft's World Council of Churches (Reading 2). People in nearby towns also helped. For example, a group known as the Cimade led hundreds of Jews across the Alps to safety in Switzerland.

Pierre Sauvage, a Jew whose parents were hiding at the time he was born, believes that the villagers' courage must never be forgotten.

> If we do not learn how it is possible to act well even under the most trying circumstances, we will increasingly doubt our ability to act well even under less trying ones. If we remember solely the horror of the Holocaust, we will pass on no perspective from which meaningfully to confront and learn from that very horror. If we remember solely the horror of the Holocaust, it is we who will bear the responsibility for having created the most dangerous alibi of all: that it was beyond man's capacity to know and care. If Jews do not learn that the whole world did not stand idly by while we were slaughtered, we will undermine our ability to develop the friendships and alliances that we need and deserve. If Christians do not learn that even then there were practicing Christians, they will be deprived of inspiring and essential examples of the nature and requirements of their faith. If the hard and fast evidence of the possibility of good on earth is allowed to slip through our fingers and turn into dust, then future generations will have only dust to build on. If hope is allowed to seem an unrealistic response to the world, if we do not work towards developing confidence in our spiritual resources, we will be responsible for producing in due time a world devoid of humanity—literally.[37]

Magda Trocme also saw the rescuers as teaching a lesson. After the war, she told an interviewer, "When people read this story, I want them to know that I tried to open my door. I tried to tell people, 'Come in, come in.' In the end, I would like to say to people, 'Remember that in your life there will be lots of circumstances that will need a kind of courage, a kind of decision of your own, not about other people but about yourself. I would not say more.'"

If the hard and fast evidence of the possibility of good on earth is allowed to slip through our fingers and turn to dust, then future generations will have only dust to build on.

Not long after Andre Trocme and his family settled in Le Chambon, he wrote, "The humblest peasant home has its Bible and the father reads it every day. So these people, who do not read the papers but the scriptures, do not stand on the moving soil of opinion but on the rock of the Word of the Lord." How do his comments help explain why people there were willing to risk so much for strangers? Would the villagers have been as willing to take a stand if they lived among people who did not share their convictions?

As Protestants in a nation of Catholics, the people of Le Chambon knew what it was like to be an oppressed minority. How do you think that experience shaped their response to the plight of the Jews? Encouraged them to respond as a community?

Emile Durkheim, a French sociologist who lived in the early 1900s, believed that no society can survive unless its members are willing to make sacrifices for one another and their community. He argued that altruism is not a "sort of agreeable ornament to social life" but the basis of society. Would the people of Le Chambon agree? Do you agree?

Magda Trocme wrote, "We had no time to think. When a problem came, we had to solve it immediately. Sometimes people ask me, 'How did you make a decision?' There was no decision to make. The issue was: Do you think we are all brothers or not? Do you think it is unjust to turn in the Jews or not? Then let us try to help!" Compare her response with that of the professor Milton Mayer interviewed (Chapter 4, Reading 15). He, too, had no time to think, but his response was very different from Trocme's. How do you account for that difference?

Albert Camus was staying near Le Chambon when he wrote a novel called *The Plague*. Some think he was referring to the village and its people when the narrator states, "There always comes a time in history when the man who dares to say that two plus two equals four is punished with death. . . . And the issue is not a matter of what reward or punishment will be the outcome of that reasoning. The issue is simply whether or not two plus two equals four. For those of our townspeople who were then risking their lives, the decision they had to make was simply whether or not they were in the midst of a plague and whether or not it was necessary to struggle against it." Was the decision that simple for the people of Le Chambon?

What does Magda Trocme mean when she says the decision she and others made was not about other people but about oneself? What circumstances today require that kind of courage? For what reasons?

➤Sauvage's film about the villagers, *Weapons of the Spirit*, is available through the Facing History Resource Center. So is *The Courage to Care* and the book that accompanies the video. The film features the work of five rescuers in France, the Netherlands, and Poland. Among those included are Marion Pritchard and the Trocmes. The accompanying book includes many more rescuers from both Eastern and Western Europe.

What did you learn from the stories of rescuers? What do they teach us about human behavior? Elie Wiesel offers one answer in the preface to *The Courage to Care:* "Let us not forget, after all, that there is always a moment when the moral choice is made. Often because of one story or one book or one person, we are able to make a different choice, a choice for humanity, for life. And so we must know these good people who helped Jews during the Holocaust. We must learn from them, and in gratitude and hope, we must remember them."

After a visit to El Salvador in 1990, Rembert George Weakland, the archbishop of Milwaukee, commented on the life of Oscar Romero and other Catholic priests killed for trying to bring about change in El Salvador. "What set these people apart is that they stood for a kind of religion—a religious belief—that influences lives. Religion, for them, was not a case of obeying rules but of influencing lives—and that is a very threatening thing to those who want to keep order. But if religion doesn't influence lives why bother with it?"[38] How do his comments apply to Le Chambon?

R E A D I N G 1 1

The Mysterious Major

Many have wondered how the people of Le Chambon were able to keep so many Jews hidden for so long without Nazi retaliation. When Philip Hallie, a professor of philosophy, wrote a book about the town, he asked the townspeople that very question. Many attributed their safety to "le major." So did the Trocmes. They claimed he was responsible for the anonymous phone calls they received just before a raid.

Hallie discovered that the mysterious major was Julius Schmahling, the Nazi occupation governor of the Haute-Loire district which included Le Chambon. Although the Nazis replaced him in 1943, he stayed on as second-in-command until the war was over. According to Hallie, Schmahling was "no hero, no declared enemy of Nazism or of any other 'ism'—seen from a distance he was just one more dutiful member of the Nazi war machine. But seen up close, and seen from the point of view of the hundreds, possibly thousands of people he protected from the Gestapo and from his own vicious auxiliary troops in the Haute-Loire, he was a good man. He compromised with evil, and helped defenseless people as much as he could." Why did he choose to help when so many others looked the other way? Hallie cites two incidents in response to that question. The first took place when Schmahling was a young teacher.

He had prepared a dramatic lesson on the king of beasts, and full of it, and of himself, he walked into the classroom. As he spoke the first words, "The lions," he noticed a little boy in the back of the room who had been sitting dumbly on his wooden bench during the whole term. The boy was waving his hand in the air to catch his teacher's eye. The young teacher kept talking about the great beasts. In a few moments the boy jumped off his bench and called out "Herr Professor, Herr—" Schmahling looked at him in anger—he could not believe that this little dunce was going to interrupt his discourse on lions. Then the boy did something that really amazed the teacher. He called out, without permission, "Yesterday, yes, yesterday I saw a rabbit. Yesterday I really saw a rabbit."

Before the words were all out, Schmahling yelled out, "Sit down, you little jackass." The boy sat down and never said a word for the rest of the year.

In his old age, Schmahling looked back at that moment as the most decisive one in his whole life. Then, while he was crushing the boy with all the power of his German pedagogical authoritarianism, he was destroying something in himself in the very act of destroying the moment of sunlight in that little boy's life. When the class was over he vowed to himself that he would never do such a thing again to a human being. Teaching and living for him, he vowed, would from that moment forward involve making room for each of his students and each of the people he knew outside of the classroom to speak about the rabbits they had seen.

And he kept his vow. It was as simple as that—and as infinitely complex as keeping such a vow during the German occupation of France.

The other incident took place just after the war ended and Schmahling was brought to trial by the French Resistance.

As he rolled down the aisle with his sturdy body and in his slightly worn, green-gray, Wehrmacht officer's uniform, he was not a figure of distinction, and he seemed an easy target for all the hatred the French were feeling against the Germans.

But when he was halfway down the aisle everybody in the room, including the toughest chiefs of the Haute-Loire Resistance, stood up and turned to him. As he walked up the aisle, people whispered to him, "Major, do you need more food in jail? Do you need writing materials or books?" As he walked, he smiled, and shook his head gently.

When he came up to the head of the tribunal, the tough old French Resistance chief who was chairman of the [hearing] bowed to him (for he had stood up with all of the others) and made a little speech of gratitude to him on the part of all of the Frenchmen in the Haute-Loire.

Didn't they realize that decency needs no rewards, no recognition, that it is done out of the heart, now immediately, just in order to satisfy the heart now?

Later, in his diary, Schmahling described the meeting as *"fast peinlich,"* almost painful: he was glad for their praise and their affection, but didn't they realize decency is the normal thing to do? Didn't they realize that decency needs no rewards, no recognition, that it is done out of the heart, now, immediately, just in order to satisfy the heart now?[39]

CONNECTIONS

What did Schmahling mean when he said that in crushing the boy in his classroom, he was destroying something in himself? What was he destroying? How was it like what the Nazis were destroying in the people they ruled? In themselves?

"In studying [Schmahling] and in learning to admire him, I have learned much about respecting myself and others," Hallie wrote. "I learned that ethics is not simply a matter of good and evil, true north and true south. It is a matter of mixtures, like most of the other points on the compass, and like the lives of most of us. We are not all called upon to be perfect, but we can make a little, real difference in a mainly cold and indifferent world." Do you agree?

READING 12

Schindler's List

To say "yes" is to follow the mass, to do what is commonly expected. To say "no" is to deny the crowd, to be set apart, to reaffirm yourself.

Jerzy Kosinski, who spent his childhood hiding in Nazi-occupied Europe, writes in *The Devil Tree,* "Of all mammals only a human being can say 'no.' A cow cannot imagine itself apart from the herd. That's why one cow is like any other. To say 'yes' is to follow the mass, to do what is commonly expected. To say 'no' is to deny the crowd, to be set apart, to reaffirm yourself." Schmahling reaffirmed himself by refusing to compromise his principles and so became an unlikely hero. Oskar Schindler, a German who joined the Nazi party for business reasons, was an even more unlikely one.

Before the war, Schindler was known mainly for his interest in making a "fast buck" and his love of wine and women. During the war, he continued to look for easy money, chase after women, and carouse. Indeed he saw the war at first as a chance to indulge in all three. Soon after the invasion of Poland, he came to the city of Cracow in search of business opportunities. With equal doses of bribery and charm, he managed to convince the Nazis that he was the right man to take over a failed cookware factory outside the city. He then proceeded to make a fortune turning out mess kits for German soldiers. Schindler's profits were extraordinarily high because he used low-paid Jewish workers from the ghetto the Nazis established in the city.

There was little to distinguish Schindler from the other businessmen who cooperated with the Nazis, until the Germans began to evacuate the Cracow ghetto. He and a friend went horseback riding that day. From the hills that overlooked the city, they could see the entire operation. Thomas Keneally reconstructs what Schindler and his companion saw that day in a novel called *Schindler's List*.

> [SS teams with dogs] rampaged through the fetid apartments; as a symptom of their rush, a suitcase flew from a second-story window and split open on the sidewalk. And running before the dogs, the men and women and children who had hidden in attics or closets, inside drawerless dressers, the evaders of the first wave of search, jolted out onto the pavement, yelling and gasping in terror of the Doberman pinschers. Everything seemed speeded-up, difficult for the viewers on the hill to trace. Those who had emerged were shot where they stood on the sidewalk, flying out over the gutters at the impact of the bullets, gushing blood into the drains. A mother and a boy, perhaps eight, perhaps a scrawny ten, had retreated under the windowsill on the western side of Krakusa Street. Schindler felt an intolerable fear for them, a terror in his own blood which loosened his thighs from the saddle and threatened to unhorse him.

He *knew* they had no shame . . . . But worst of all, if there was no shame, it meant there was official sanction.

Through it all, Schindler focused on a toddler dressed in red who ambled down the street seemingly unaware of the danger. Keneally then tells of Schindler's attempt to digest the horrors he had witnessed:

> Their lack of shame, as men who had been born of women and had to write letters home (What did they put in them?), wasn't the worst aspect of what he had seen. He *knew* they had no shame, since the guard at the base of the column had not felt any need to stop the red child from seeing things. But worst of all, if there was no shame, it meant there was official sanction. No one could find refuge any more behind the idea of German culture, nor behind those pronouncements uttered by leaders to exempt anonymous men from stepping beyond their gardens, from looking out their office windows at the realities on the sidewalk. Oskar had seen in Krakusa Street a statement of his government's policy which could not be written off as a temporary aberration. The SS men were, Oskar believed, fulfilling there the orders of the leader, for otherwise their colleague at the rear of the column would not have let a child watch.
>
> Later in the day, after he had absorbed a ration of brandy, Oskar understood the proposition in its clearest terms. They permitted witnesses, such witnesses as the red toddler, because they believed the witnesses would perish too.[40]

Schindler could not forget what he saw that day. It led him to deal with the Nazis in a different way. This time Schindler was not concerned with making a profit. Indeed he now spent enormous sums of money to keep his workers safe. He began by turning his factory into an official subcamp of a newly constructed labor camp at Plazow. For a time, it was a haven for about five hundred Jews. Then in the fall of 1944, the Nazis ordered both camps closed and all workers shipped to Auschwitz. Schindler refused to let that happen. He put together a list of eleven hundred men, women, and children that he claimed as his workers. He then used his money and influence to transport those workers to a new factory he was building at Brinnlitz, Czechoslovakia. When the Jewish women who worked in his factory were transported to Auschwitz by mistake, he accomplished the impossible. He managed to get the women back by offering Nazi officials a fortune in bribes.

CONNECTIONS

Kosinski wrote, "To say 'no' is to deny the crowd, to be set apart, to reaffirm yourself." How does his comment apply to Schindler? To Marion Pritchard and other rescuers? To the Scholls?

Review your working definition of the word *hero*. What makes a person "heroic?" Does a hero possess certain qualities? Or is a hero defined by his or her actions? Was Schindler a hero?

According to Jewish tradition, "whoever saves one life saves the world entire." How does it apply to Schindler? To other rescuers?

After the war, Schindler's wife, Emilie, told a reporter that her husband had done nothing astounding before the war and had been unexceptional since. She went on to say he was fortunate that in that "short fierce era between 1939 and 1945 he had met people who summoned forth his deeper talents." Do you agree with her assessment? What do her remarks suggest about courage? About an individual's capacity to grow and change?

➤ The book *Schindler's List* by Thomas Keneally provides a detailed account of Schindler's efforts. Steven Spielberg's film of the same name is based on the book and provides a powerful perspective on the man and the time. The video and a study guide are available from the Facing History Resource Center. After viewing the film, Dorothy Rabinowitz wrote that it reminded her of other unlikely rescuers:

> I have in mind, namely Hitler's allies, the Italians, whose government ministries and army and highest political circles moved heaven and earth to see to it that not a single Jew was deported from Italy. They schemed, they plotted, they resorted to the wiliest of strategies and delaying efforts—including the invention of the most wonderfully complicated "census-taking" known to man—to ensure

that no Jews under their governance fell into German hands. . . . Not only would the Italian government—reflecting the popular attitude of the citizenry at large—resist deportation, its army and consuls undertook extraordinary efforts to rescue Jews in their zones of occupation. As an Axis partner, Italy's forces occupied a large sector of Greece, part of Yugoslavia, and eight sectors of southeastern France, including Nice.[41]

How do you account for the way Rabinowitz describes the stand the Italians took? In what sense was it like the one Schindler took? In what ways did it differ? You may wish to research the way other writers regard the position the Italians took.

➤Rena Finder was one of the individuals on "Schindler's List." Her testimony is available on video from the Facing History Resource Center and is described in *Elements of Time*, pages 25-29. A 15-minute vignette on Schindler, "The Making of a Hero," is also available.

R E A D I N G   1 3

A Nation United

Oskar Schindler responded to the plight of European Jews as an individual. In Le Chambon, people responded as a community. In Denmark, they responded as a nation. The Germans conquered Denmark in the spring of 1940. Although Hitler allowed the prewar government to stay in power and kept only a token military force in the nation, the Danes deeply resented the occupation of their country and some struck back with acts of sabotage, riots, and strikes. In the summer of 1943, the Nazis decided to retaliate. They limited the power of King Christian X, forced the Danish government to resign, and disbanded the Danish army. They also ordered the arrest of a number of Christian and Jewish leaders.

Leo Goldberger's father, the chief cantor at Copenhagen's Great Synagogue, was among those the Nazis planned to arrest. They arrived at the family's apartment before dawn one morning. Goldberger recalls what happened next:

> My father came into my brother's and my room and whispered that the Germans were outside and that he would not under any circumstances open the door. For me, this was the most terror-filled moment I had ever experienced. The insistent knocks of rifle butts. Fearing that they would break down the door any minute, I implored my father to open it, but he was determined not to. Then in the nick of time, we heard our upstairs neighbor's voice telling the German

The Danes were able to resist the cruel stupidity of Nazi anti-Semitism because this fundamental truth [thou shalt love thy neighbor as thyself] was important to them.

soldiers that we—the Goldbergers—were away for the summer, and that three o'clock in the morning was in any case no time to make such a racket![42]

Although the Germans posted a guard outside the building before they left, the family managed to escape. By the middle of September, the crisis seemed to be over and the family returned to Copenhagen. A few weeks later, the Goldbergers and other Jews in Denmark learned that the Germans were planning to round them all up for deportation. The news came from Georg Ferdinand Duckwitz, a German diplomat stationed in Norway. When he received secret orders to prepare four cargo ships for transporting Danish Jews, he passed on the information to leaders in the resistance. They, in turn, informed Copenhagen's Jewish community. The Jews were urged to hide and then prepare for evacuation to Sweden. Goldberger, who was just thirteen years old at the time, remembers:

Where to hide? Our first night was spent as guests of a wealthy Jewish family who lived in Bedbaek, on the coast some 35 miles away. To our chagrin the family took off for Sweden during the night without even telling us or their Jewish refugee maid. Apparently my father had been asked by our host whether he wanted to chip in for a boat to take us all to Sweden but had been forced to decline. He simply did not have that kind of money. Near panic but determined to "get tough" and to find a way somehow, my father took a train back to the city; he needed to borrow money, perhaps get an advance on his salary and to see about contacts for passage on a fishing boat. As luck would have it, on the train a woman whom he knew only slightly recognized him and inquired about his obviously agitated facial expression. He confided our plight. Without a moment's hesitation the lady promised to take care of everything. She would meet my father at the main railroad station with all the information about the arrangements within a few hours. It was the least she could do, she said, in return for my father's participation some years back in a benefit concert for her organization—"The Women's League for Peace and Freedom."

True to her word, she met my father later that day and indicated that all was arranged. The money would be forthcoming from a pastor, Henry Rasmussen. . . . The sum was a fairly large one—about 25,000 Danish crowns, 5,000 per person, a sum which was more than my father's annual salary. (Though it was ostensibly a loan, I should add that pastor Rasmussen refused repayment after the war.) The next step was to head for a certain address near the coast, less than an hour from Copenhagen. After hurriedly getting some things together from our apartment—-a few clothes, some treasured papers and family photos, and, in my case, [a] newly acquired police flashlight—we were off by taxi to our unknown hosts for the night and our uncertain destiny.

The following night we were standing, huddled in some low bushes along the beach near Dragur, an outskirt of Copenhagen's island of Amager. It was a bitter cold October night. My youngest brother, barely three years old, had been given a sleeping pill to keep him quiet. My brave and stoic little mother was clutching her bag with socks and stockings to be mended which she had taken along for reasons difficult to fathom rationally. We were anxiously and eagerly waiting for the promised light signal. As we were poised to move toward the signal, I could not help but wonder *why* this was happening. What had we ever done to be in hiding, escaping like criminals? Where would it all end? And why in God's name did the signal not appear? Then finally the lights flashed. We were off. Wading straight into the sea, we walked out some 100 feet through icy water, in water that reached up to my chest. My father carried my two small brothers on his arm. My mother held on to her bag of socks. And I clutched my precious flashlight. My older brother tried valiantly to carry the suitcases but finally had to drop them in the water. We were hauled aboard the boat, directed in whispers to lie concealed in the cargo area, there to stretch out covered by smelly canvases; in the event the German patrols were to inspect the boat, we would be passed over as fish. There seemed to have been some 20 other Jews aboard. As we proceeded out toward open sea my father chanted a muted prayer from the Psalms.

A few hours later, bright lights and the pastoral scenery of Skane along the coast outline of Sweden appeared. Wonderful, peaceful Sweden. A welcoming haven, never to be forgotten, where we remained until our return to Denmark at the end of the war in 1945.[43]

Hundreds of other fishing boats carried nearly every Jew in Denmark—7,220 men, women, and children—to safety. It was a community effort—organized and paid for by hundreds of private citizens—Jews and Christians alike. The money was used to pay fishermen to transport the Jews to Sweden. Although a few offered their boats for nothing, many could not afford to lose a day's pay. The money also went for bribes. It was no accident that all German patrol ships were docked for repairs the night of the rescue.

Not everyone managed to get out. Some were captured as they waited for a boat, while others were picked up at sea. But in the end, the Nazis were able to deport only 580 Jews. They were sent to Terezinstadt, the "model" concentration camp (Chapter 7, Reading 13). Still, no Dane was shipped to a death camp, in part because the Danish government constantly questioned the Nazis about their status.

> It was a community effort—organized and paid for by hundreds of private citizens—Jews and Christians alike.

Were the Danes rescuers or resisters? Was their aim to save the Jews or to express their opposition to Nazi rule?

Compare the way the Goldbergers' neighbors responded when the Nazis banged on the family's door to the way people in earlier readings responded when the Nazis came for Communists and later Jews. What similarities to do you see? What differences seem most striking?

Thomas Merton, a theologian, said of the Danes:

> The Danes were able to do what they did because they were able to make decisions that were based on clear convictions about which they all agreed and which were in accord with the inner truth of man's own rational nature, as well as in accordance with the fundamental law of God in the Old Testament as well as in the Gospel: thou shalt love thy neighbor as thyself. The Danes were able to resist the cruel stupidity of Nazi anti-Semitism because this fundamental truth was important to them. And because they were willing, in unanimous and concerted action to stake their lives on this truth. In a word, such action becomes possible where fundamental truths are taken seriously.[44]

What "fundamental truth" did the Danes take seriously? What difference did that make in the way they responded to the Nazis?

Albert Camus argued "that strength of heart, intelligence and courage are enough to stop fate and sometimes reverse it." How do the Danes support his belief? Could others have done what they did?

READING 14

The Role of the Protestant Churches

As a leader in Germany's Confessing Church watched the Gestapo round up Jews for deportation, he asked "Should we live on as if nothing had happened?" It was a question that many religious leaders asked during the Holocaust, but they did not all answer it in the same way. When leaders in the Danish church learned of plans to deport the Jews, they sent a letter to German officials. On Sunday, October 3, 1943, that letter was read from every pulpit in the nation.

> Wherever Jews are persecuted because of their religion or race it is the duty of the Christian Church to protest against such persecution, because it is in conflict with the sense of justice inherent in the Danish people and inseparable from our Danish Christian culture through

centuries. True to this spirit and according to the text of the Act of the Constitution all Danish citizens enjoy equal rights and responsibilities before the Law and full religious freedom. We understand religious freedom as the right to exercise our worship of God as our vocation and conscience bid us and in such a manner that race and religion per se can never justify that a person be deprived of his rights, freedom or property. Our different religious views notwithstanding, we shall fight for the cause that our Jewish brothers and sisters may preserve the same freedom which we ourselves evaluate more highly than life itself. With the leaders of the Danish Church there is a clear understanding of our duty to be law-abiding citizens who will not groundlessly rebel against the authorities, but at the same time our conscience bids us to assert the Law and protest against any violation of the Law. We shall therefore in any given event unequivocally adhere to the concept that we must obey God before we obey man.

The Danish ministers who wrote that letter were Lutherans. So were most German Protestants. Yet few German ministers took as strong a stand. The German Evangelical Church expressed concern only for the plight of Christian Jews sent to concentration camps. A church official asked Adolf Eichmann to allow them to hold church services. Eichmann refused, telling him "that a Jew was a Jew, whether baptized or not." The official claimed that Eichmann "could, however, assure me that the entire Jewish question here in [Germany] was only a transportation question." He and others in his church never again concerned themselves with the "Jewish question."

Ilse Harter, a leader in the Confessing Church, later commented:

> More people than one thinks gave practical help. Would that have been possible had the Confessing Church protested better? I don't know. On no account do I wish to excuse the Confessing Church. We all became guilty, even those of us who helped the Jewish people. We didn't scream it out, because we knew, indeed: If what we do becomes known, these people will go to their deaths in any case, just as our path would lead to the concentration camp. Whereas, when we help secretly, perhaps they will survive. But show me the person who can be at peace with that position.[45]

After the war, Dietrich Goldschmidt, a leader in the Confessing Church, offered another reason no one "screamed it out." He noted that "the idea that, from a Christian consciousness, one had to stand up for the Jews occurred to very few people. . . .The Jews were 'damned.' This teaching that the Jews had condemned Jesus, the teaching that God had indeed made a covenant with the Jews but that this covenant was void after the murder of Jesus, and that the Christians are the people of the new covenant—that pops up even today in the heads of pastors."[46]

Wherever Jews are persecuted because of their religion or race it is the duty of the Christian Church to protest against such persecution, because it is in conflict with the sense of justice inherent in the Danish people and inseparable from our Danish Christian culture through centuries.

Helmut Gollwitzer, another church leader, added:

> We, too, had to learn that we had grown up with these prejudices theologically. At first, we thought that the Jews deserved our human pity, and the Jewish Christians needed our brotherly solidarity. . . [that] we had to help the Jews in Germany because they were a threatened people.
>
> In the meantime, Karl Barth [a German theologian] had progressed further theologically. His basis for demanding that we help the Jews was that they are the people of God. That was a new basis for understanding the Bible, Judaism, and with that, for understanding anti-Semitism as well. The view that anti-Semitism was merely the antipathy of a majority against a minority had to be abolished.
>
> It became more complicated because Hitler killed the gypsies as well, but. . . if he hadn't waged this complete campaign against the Jews, he wouldn't have been able to treat the gypsies in the same way. The Jews are truly the key. That is the central point with the Jews, theologically and biblically: How do we go about unlearning this part of the Christian tradition? This remains one of the most provocative questions in German Christianity today.[47]

CONNECTIONS

How did leaders of the Danish church define their "universe of obligation"? How did leaders in the German Evangelical Church define theirs? The Confessing Church? What similarities do you notice? What differences?

Reread the letter the Danish ministers sent German officials. Why do you think they read it from the pulpit? How did they regard Jews? Freedom of religion? Their duty as "law abiding citizens"? What effect might a similar letter have had on German Christians?

What part does "patriotism" play in explaining differences in the way Danish church leaders responded to the Holocaust with the way German church leaders responded? How difficult is it to speak out against your own country in time of war?

Is Ilse Harter's explanation of why she did not "scream out" a rationalization? How is her explanation similar to those of Christabel Bielenberg (Reading 7)? Why is neither "at peace" with her position?

In describing the response of German Christians to the Holocaust, Dietrich Goldschmidt wrote, "Perhaps you know T. S. Eliot's 'Murder in the Cathedral'? There's a place where the archbishop comes from France, and the choir, the women of Canterbury don't want him: 'Yet we have gone on living, living and partly living. . . leave us and leave us be.' This phrase has stayed in my memory. Don't burden us with any knowledge, 'living and partly living, we want to get through.'"[48] What is Goldschmidt saying about the way most religious leaders responded to the question, "Should we live on as if nothing had happened?" To the larger question of "Are we our brothers' keepers?" What part did old myths and misinformation play in the way they responded? What part did fear play? Conformity? Obedience?

READING 15

The Role of the Catholic Church

Leaders in the Catholic Church were also silent as Jews were deported to death camps. On May 27, 1941, a week after the first round-up, Germaine Ribiere, a student in Paris, wrote in her diary:

> For the past two weeks the sky has become more and more overcast. The Church, the hierarchy, remain silent. They allow the truth to be profaned. Father Lallier [a priest in charge of the Catholic student movement in Paris] told me that there are more urgent things for us to worry about than the Jews. . . .
>
> The tide is rising, rising. I am afraid that one of these days, when we wake up, it will be too late and we shall all have become Nazis. I am afraid, because people are asleep. Those who should keep watch are the ones who put others to sleep. We must shout the truth no matter what the cost. But who will do it? I know that there are Christians who are willing to accept martyrdom if necessary; but they do not know what is happening. They wait for a voice, and the voice does not speak. We must pray that it will speak.
>
> France has betrayed her soul, and now Nazism is gaining the upper hand. All genuine values are dragged in the dust. We no longer have any honor. Petain has become the French Hitler. The great dance has begun and the world is blind. It is blind because it is afraid of death. The clergy remain passive. As in Austria, they accept what is happening. . . .[49]

It would be a year later, in August 1942, before Archbishop Jules-Gerard Saliege of Toulouse told Catholics: "That children, that women, that men, that fathers and mothers should be treated like a vile herd, that members of the same family should be separated from one another and sent to an unknown destination—this sad spectacle it was reserved for our times to see. . . . These Jews are men, these Jewesses are women; these aliens are men and women. You cannot do whatever you wish against these men, against these women, against these fathers and mothers. They are part of humankind. They are our brothers, as are so many others. No Christian can forget that."[50]

The tide is rising, rising. I am afraid that one of these days, when we wake up, it will be too late and we shall all have become Nazis. I am afraid, because people are asleep. Those who should keep watch are the ones who put others to sleep.

Why did it take so long for the archbishop and other leaders in the Catholic church to respond? In reviewing the Church's role during the Holocaust, some historians focus on Eugenio Pacelli who became Pope Pius XII in 1939. In 1920, he became the pope's ambassador to Germany; in 1929, he was elevated to cardinal. The following year, he became the Vatican's secretary of state. Like many people, Pacelli considered communism far more dangerous than fascism. Indeed he was convinced that Nazi Germany was a fortress in the fight against "godless" communism. He also believed that he had a duty to protect the Church in Germany from the Nazis. Those views led him to negotiate a concordat, or agreement, with Germany in July 1933. It was Hitler's first foreign policy success.

After he became pope, Pius encouraged efforts to rescue Jews who had converted to Christianity but not other Jews. Although the Vatican had detailed information about mass murders as early as the fall of 1941, Pius remained silent until the Christmas of 1942. Only then did he speak of the "hundreds of thousands who through no fault of their own, and solely because of their nation or race, have been condemned to death or progressive extinction." Although he was clearly speaking of the Jews, he never mentioned them by name.

Then in the fall of 1943, the Italians overthrew Mussolini. Almost immediately, Germany took control of Italy and began to deport Italian Jews. The Church responded by opening sanctuaries for "non-Aryans" in Vatican City. Yet Pius himself said nothing until the summer of 1944 when Admiral Miklos Horthy of Hungary began deporting Jews. A month after the deportations started, Pius cabled Horthy. "We have been requested from several sides to do everything possible to ensure that the sufferings which have had to be borne for so long by numerous unfortunate people in the bosom of this noble and chivalrous nation because of their nationality or racial origin shall not be prolonged and made worse. Our fatherly heart, in the service of a solicitous charity which embraces all mankind, cannot remain insensitive to these urgent wishes. Therefore I am turning personally to Your Excellency and I appeal to your noble feelings, in full confidence that Your Excellency will do everything in your power to spare so many unfortunate people further suffering."[51]

Father John Pawlikowski, Professor of Social Ethics at the Catholic Theological Union in Chicago and a member of the United States Holocaust Memorial Council, has studied the way the Catholic church and other religious groups responded to the Nazis. He concluded:

(1) an overwhelming majority of Christian clergy acquiesced in the destruction of European Jews;

(2) church leaders were unable to mount a successful effort against the Nazis. This bears serious reflection for the continuing struggles which the churches face in the contemporary world;

(3) the church's self-understanding and its own sufferings under the Nazis were far too isolated from the sufferings of non-Christians, Jews

in particular, to whom suffering meant death. Why did the churches raise the issue of Nazi murder of "baptized" Jews to the exclusion of the Jewish people at large?;

(4) the churches were far too connected with the dynamics of German society to really stand in judgment against it;

(5) the Jewish Question could not be adequately addressed because of the long-standing theological tradition of anti-Judaism in the churches. This tradition must be obliterated once and for all by the post-Holocaust Christian community;

(6) the churches, which will never regain the kind of control over society they once had, must reflect anew on how to combat totalitarian power. Where are their primary resources in such a context?; and, finally,

(7) the churches' fear of communism blinded them to all other forms of totalitarian oppression. Is there danger of repetition in our day?[52]

CONNECTIONS

What did Germaine Ribiere mean when she wrote that France betrayed its soul? How does a nation betray its soul?

As head of the Technical Disinfection Services of the Waffen SS, Kurt Gerstein delivered prussic acid and other poison gases to Belzec. He tried repeatedly to warn the nuncio, or papal ambassador to Germany, that the Nazis were murdering the Jews. After several unsuccessful efforts, he wrote:

> What action against Nazism could one demand of an ordinary citizen when the representative of Jesus on earth himself refused even to hear me, although tens of thousands of human beings were being murdered every day; and although to wait only a few hours seemed to me criminal? Even the Nuncio in Germany refused to be well-informed on this monstrous violation of the fundamental basis of the laws of Jesus: "Thou shalt love thy neighbor as thyself."[53]

How do you account for the nuncio's failure to acknowledge Gerstein's information? For his failure to act on that information?

In 1993, James Carroll, a newspaper columnist and a Roman Catholic, wrote, "In 1963, a play by Rolf Hochhuth, 'The Deputy,' savaged the Vatican, especially Eugenio Pacelli—Pope Pius XII—for its complicity. Most Catholics doggedly rejected that play's accusations, but when Pope John XXIII was asked not long before he died what to do about Hochhuth's play, he replied, 'Do? What can one do about the truth?'"[54] What options were open to the Church in 1933? In 1939? In 1941? What were the risks of each choice? Possible consequences?

➤Father John S. was a Jesuit seminarian in Hungarian-occupied Czechoslovakia at the time Jews were being deported to Auschwitz. He recalls looking through a hole in a fence and seeing a Nazi guard brutally attack a Jew. "I just didn't know what to do. At that time I was immobilized. . . . It was beyond my experience—I was totally unprepared." Father S.'s testimony is included in the video montage *Seeing* available from the Facing History Resource Center and described in *Elements of Time*, page xxix.

Professor Franklin Littel has studied the way churches and universities in the United States responded or failed to respond to the Holocaust. He found that many American religious leaders and academics were paralyzed in much the way their German counterparts were. A summary of a talk by Littel on the topic can be found in *Elements of Time*, pages 356-357.

READING 16

The Response of the Allies

Soon after the Nazi invasion of the Soviet Union in June 1941, rumors of mass murders began to circulate in the United States. To many, the stories were too incredible to be true. On the front page of its June 14, 1942 edition, the *Chicago Tribune* ran this headline:

HITLER GUARDS STAGE NEW POGROM, KILL 258
MASSACRED BY BERLIN GESTAPO IN "BOMB PLOT"
Families Herded for Deportation

The story that followed described the murder of 258 Berlin Jews on an obviously trumped-up charge. The Nazis were claiming that Jews planted bombs in Berlin at a time when their movements were restricted and they were subject to a strict curfew. The story came from "various trustworthy sources" in Berlin—sources with access to officials in the SS and the Propaganda Ministry.

On June 16, 1942, the same paper ran a story on page 6 under this headline: "25,000 LATVIAN JEWS VICTIMS OF NAZIS." The information for this story came from the Federation of Jewish Relief Organizations. Exactly two weeks later, also on page 6, readers encountered this headline: "One Million Jews Victims of Nazis." The World Jewish Congress was the source for this story.

Deborah Lipstadt, the author of *Beyond Belief: The American Press and the Coming of the Holocaust*, argues that the first story made the front page because "258" sounds authoritative. It is precise, unlike "about 260" or "over 250." On the other hand, a number like "25,000" is more "difficult" to accept and "one million" is simply "incredible."

Lipstadt notes that the larger numbers were harder to accept for another reason—they came from groups that represented the victims. Recalling atrocity stories during World War I that later proved to be false, publishers were cautious about claims of mass murder. So even though they printed the reports, they did not feature them and they carefully qualified claims. On November 26, 1942, the following appeared on page 16 of the *New York Times:*

> SLAIN POLISH JEWS PUT AT A MILLION
> One-third of Number in Whole Country Said to Have Been Put to Death by Nazis
> Nearly a third of Poland's Jewish population—1,000,000 persons—has perished in three years of German occupation, Dr. Ignacy Szwarcbart, Jewish member of the Polish National Council in London, told this correspondent today, amplifying Polish Government information on the new Nazi onslaught on the Jews.
> Plans outlined by Dr. Alfred Rosenberg—Germany's race theorist, who says that the Jewish problem of Europe will be solved when no Jews are left—are systematically carried out. The victims of executions by mass-murder and gassing are only part of the thousands dying through "the organized spreading of diseases and artificial creation of conditions in which children, elderly people and the sick cannot survive," as Dr. Szwarcbart described it.
> A million more persons, at least, are menaced by starvation and the lack of medical supplies. The Nazis make it plain that all Jews not wanted for military reasons must die. Poland is now a mass grave. Jews from all Europe are brought to the Warsaw ghetto and separated into two groups: the able-bodied young and the children, old and sick, who are dispatched eastward to meet sure death. Lublin, indeed, has two ghettoes, one for able workers, the other for the useless condemned to destruction.
> One hundred twenty thousand have been brought from Czechoslovakia and tens of thousands from Germany, Austria, Hungary, Holland, Belgium and France. The Lodz ghetto, containing many Jews from the West, has been completely closed for several weeks and no news has been allowed to penetrate through its walls. . . .
> Rabbi Stephen S. Wise, acting as chairman of a special conference of Jewish organizations, announced here yesterday that the organizations were convinced of the authenticity of a rumored Hitler order for the immediate extirpation of all Jews in German-controlled Europe. . . .
> These organizations, Rabbi Wise said, had authorized him to invite the aid of any Christian organization ready to speak out on behalf of the Jewish victims. They had also set Sunday, Dec. 13, as a day of mourning, to be observed by fasting and prayer by Jews "in all the lands where Jews are still free."

By the end of 1942, the CBS radio network had picked up the story. In a broadcast from London on December 13, Edward R. Murrow bluntly reported, "What is happening is this. Millions of human beings, most of them Jews, are being gathered up with ruthless efficiency and murdered. The phrase 'concentration camps' is obsolete, as out of date as economic sanctions or nonrecognition. It is now possible only to speak of extermination camps."

Four days later, the governments of the United States, Britain, and the Soviet Union issued joint declarations stating that "the German authorities, not content with denying to persons of Jewish race in all the territories over which their barbarous rule has been extended the most elementary human rights, are now carrying into effect Hitler's oft-repeated intention to exterminate the Jewish people in Europe."

The declaration contained very specific charges:

> Jews are being transported, in conditions of appalling horror and brutality, to Eastern Europe. In Poland, which has been made the principal Nazi slaughterhouse, the ghettos established by the German invaders are being systematically emptied of all Jews except a few highly skilled workers required for war industries. None of those taken away are ever heard of again. The able-bodied are slowly worked to death in labour camps. The infirm are left to die of exposure and starvation or are deliberately massacred in mass executions. The number of victims of these bloody cruelties is reckoned in many hundreds of thousands of entirely innocent men, women and children.

Thus, the Allies acknowledged the mass murders for the first time. Yet they continued to do nothing. Golda Meir, who later became prime minister of Israel, described Britain's response to her demands and those of other Jews in British-controlled Palestine:

> What was it that we demanded of the British and that they so stubbornly refused to give us? Today the answer seems incredible even to me. The truth is that all that [we] wanted from 1939 to 1945 was to take in as many Jews as could be saved from the Nazis. That was all. Just to be allowed to share the little we had with men, women, and children who were fortunate enough not to have been shot, gassed or buried alive by the very people to whose downfall the entire British Empire was in any case committed. . . .
>
> [Yet the] British remained adamant. They went on to fight like lions against the Germans, the Italians, and the Japanese, but they couldn't or wouldn't stand up to the Arabs at all—although much of the Arab world was openly pro-Nazi. . . .
>
> After all, what would have happened if the British had [allowed Jews to find refuge in Palestine]? A few Arab leaders might have made threatening speeches. Perhaps there would have been a protest march or two. Maybe there would even have been an additional act of pro-

The phrase "concentration camps" is obsolete, as out of date as economic sanctions or nonrecognition. It is now possible to speak only of extermination camps.

Nazi sabotage somewhere in the Middle East. And maybe it would have been too late to save most of the Jews of Europe anyway. But thousands more of the [millions murdered] might have survived. Thousands more of the ghetto fighters and Jewish partisans might have been armed. And the civilized world might then have been freed of the terrible accusation that not a finger was lifted to help the Jews in their torment.[55]

The United States took a stand similar to Britain's until January 1944—fourteen months after news of the mass murders reached the Allies and thirteen months after the Allied resolution. Then on January 13, 1944, Secretary of the Treasury Henry Morgenthau received a memo entitled, "Report to the Secretary on the Acquiescence of this Government in the Murder of Jews." It was prepared by a young Treasury Department lawyer, Josiah DuBois, and signed by his superior, Randolph Paul. The memo stated:

> One of the greatest crimes in history, the slaughter of the Jewish people in Europe, is continuing unabated.
>
> This Government has for a long time maintained that its policy is to work out programs to save those Jews of Europe who could be saved.
>
> I am convinced on the basis of the information which is available to me that certain officials in our State Department, which is charged with carrying out this policy, have been guilty not only of gross procrastination and willful failure to act, but even of willful attempts to prevent action from being taken to rescue Jews from Hitler.
>
> I fully recognize the graveness of this statement and I make it only after having most carefully weighed the shocking facts which have come to my attention during the last several months.
>
> Unless remedial steps of a drastic nature are taken, and taken immediately, I am certain that no effective action will be taken by this Government to prevent the complete extermination of the Jews in German controlled Europe, and that this Government will have to share for all time responsibility for this extermination.
>
> The tragic history of this Government's handling of this matter reveals that certain State Department officials are guilty of the following:
>
> (1) They have not only failed to use the Governmental machinery at their disposal to rescue Jews from Hitler, but have even gone so far as to use this Government machinery to prevent the rescue of these Jews.
>
> (2) They have not only failed to cooperate with private organizations in the efforts of these organizations to work out individual programs of their own, but have taken steps designed to prevent these programs from being put into effect.
>
> (3) They not only have failed to facilitate the obtaining of information concerning Hitler's plans to exterminate the Jews of Europe but in their

I am convinced on the basis of the information which is available to me that certain officials in our State department. . . have been guilty not only of gross procrastination and willful failure to act, but even of willful attempts to prevent action from being taken to rescue Jews from Hitler.

official capacity have gone so far as to surreptitiously attempt to stop the obtaining of information concerning the murder of the Jewish population of Europe.

(4) They have tried to cover up their guilt by:

(a) concealment and misrepresentation;

(b) the giving of false and misleading explanations for their failures to act and their attempts to prevent action; and

(c) the issuance of false and misleading statements concerning the "action" which they have taken to date.

Morgenthau, whose father served as ambassador to Turkey during the massacres of the Armenians in World War I, condensed the report and then sent it to the president with a few comments of his own. Within days of receiving it, the president set up the War Refugee Board, under Morgenthau's supervision. It saved about two hundred thousand Jews through diplomacy, bribery, and trickery. John Pehle, Jr., the man who headed the group, later remarked that "what we did was little enough. It was late. Little and late, I would say."

What we did was little enough. It was late. Little and late, I would say.

CONNECTIONS

Why would articles about the mass murders fail to make the front pages of newspapers around the world? How have newspapers, magazines, and television treated events in Bosnia? When do stories about "ethnic cleansing" make headlines? When are those stories reduced to a brief mention? How do you account for the change?

Compare the charges Golda Meir made with those in Morgenthau's memo. What could the United States have done? What could Britain have done? Could either have stopped fate or even reversed it?

When the United States failed to take an aggressive stand against "ethnic cleansing" in Bosnia in 1993, a number of state department officials resigned. What else can individuals do to express their outrage? To influence public policy?

One of the reasons often cited for the failure of Americans to respond to the Holocaust was inadequate coverage in the media. Another was widespread antisemitism in the United States in general and within the State Department in particular. "Indication that hostility toward Jews was reaching an ominous level," writes historian David Wyman, "came from a series of ten surveys conducted between 1938 and 1941." Based on those polls, he concludes that "as much as one third of the American population was prepared to approve an anti-Jewish movement, nearly the same proportion would have stood against such action, and the remainder would have been little concerned." For a discussion of how those attitudes affected the nation's immigration policies during and after the war, see *Elements of Time*, pages 77-79.

➤The Fifth Annual Facing History Conference focused on the responsibility of the media to inform citizens of human rights abuses and genocidal situations. A videotape of the panel on "Media and the Coverage of Injustice" is available from the Resource Center.

READING 17

Should Auschwitz Have Been Bombed?

By 1944, most European Jews were either dead or on the way to death camps. Only one large group was still alive: the Jews of Hungary. They were safe chiefly because Hungary was an ally of Germany rather than a conquered nation. As an ally, Hungary had its own anti-Jewish laws that defined the status of Jews and allowed the government to take their land with minimal compensation. The nation was not willing to go any further, however. Then in 1943, Hitler asked Miklos Horthy to grant Germany jurisdiction over Hungarian Jews. When Horthy refused, Hitler announced that Hungary was no longer an ally. The following year, he invaded the nation and established a new government. Soon after, the Nazis, under the leadership of Adolf Eichmann, began shipping twelve thousand Hungarian Jews a day to Auschwitz.

As word of the deportations reached the outside world, Jewish organizations appealed to the United States to bomb the railroad lines that led to Auschwitz or the camp itself. Assistant Secretary of War, John J. McCloy, asked the War Department to look into the matter. Two days later, on June 26, 1944, officials dismissed the idea as "impractical" because the bombing "could be executed only by diversion of considerable air support essential to the success of our forces now engaged in decisive operations." Yet, between July 7 and November 20, American planes dropped bombs near Auschwitz on ten different occasions. On August 20, 1,336 bombs were released just five miles from the gas chambers. On three occasions, American pilots hit industrial areas near the camp.

McCloy supported the War Department's recommendations. On August 14, 1944, he told the World Jewish Congress that *even* if bombing Auschwitz was possible, he would oppose it. The bombings, argued McCloy "might provoke even more vindictive action by the Germans." He and others in the government insisted that "we must constantly bear in mind the most effective relief which can be given victims of enemy persecution is to insure the speedy defeat of the Axis."

CONNECTIONS

➤What factors affected the American decision not to target Auschwitz for bombing? How do you evaluate the final decision? For more information on the decision, see the video *America and the Holocaust: Deceit and Indifference*, available from the Facing History Resource Center.

Why did the plight of the Hungarian Jews get more attention from the outside world than did the plight of Polish or Russian Jews?

READING 18

A Man with a Mission

What would have happened if, in 1943, neutral nations had offered protection to the Jews of Warsaw, if great powers had offered citizenship to the Jews of Paris and Amsterdam?"

*A*t a time when many insisted it was too late to alter the fate of Europe's Jews, a thirty-two-year-old Swedish businessman saved thousands from the death camps. Raoul Wallenberg came to Budapest in July, 1944, as an agent of the American War Refugee Board and the Swedish government. He was officially the secretary of the Swedish legation in Hungary with the authority to issue passports.

By the time Wallenberg got to Hungary, over 400,000 Jews had already been deported. Only about 250,000 remained. He tried to save those Jews by creating a new passport that placed the holder and his or her property "under the protection of the Swedish legation until such time as his emigration to Sweden could be arranged." Although he persuaded the Hungarian government to honor the passport, he was unable to get the Germans to do the same. When they refused to allow Jews to travel through Germany to Sweden, Wallenberg used the money he received from the American War Refugee Board to purchase or rent thirty-two buildings in Budapest. There he housed at least twenty thousand Jews awaiting "emigration" to Sweden.

Wallenberg inspired others to help as well. Per Anger, who worked as an attache in the Swedish embassy, described their efforts:

> Other foreign legations, too, the Swiss, Spanish, Portuguese, and the Papal Nuncio, got to work issuing identification papers of a similar sort. Ever since the German occupation began, the nuncio, Angelo Rotta, had been making energetic representations to the Hungarian government to help the Jews. . . . Rotta had to work alone, without any particular support from the Vatican.
>
> At the Swiss legation, Consul Charles Lutz carried on a tireless labor in the Jews' behalf. Once the Swiss had assumed the British interests in Hungary, they took care of conveying certificates to those Jews who had been granted entry to Palestine. True, this emigration

had. . . stopped altogether with the German occupation. However, this did not hinder Lutz from issuing papers or protective passports for a large number of fictional or actual holders of such certificates. The number approved by the Hungarian authorities rose to around 8,000 but in actuality the Swiss followed our example and took considerably more under their protection.

It is also well known how the Swiss, by taking over the interests of San Salvador at American request, succeeded in furnishing several thousand Jews with papers of citizenship in that Central American country. Actually, San Salvador had no citizens in Hungary, as the Americans were well aware. But what was involved was continually trying to find new ways to save human lives. [56]

According to Anger, the various foreign legations and the International Red Cross saved nearly fifty thousand Jews. The Swedes alone accounted for almost half of that number, chiefly through the efforts of Wallenberg. Whenever Jews were in danger, he would appear to distribute passports or offer help. Susan Tabon, one of the Hungarian Jews he saved, said of him:

He gave us the sense that we were still human beings. My mother and I were among thousands taken one night to stay at a brick factory outside Budapest. There was no food, no water, no sanitation facilities, no light. Then Wallenberg appeared and said he would try to return with passports, or "safety passes," as we called them, and would also try to get medical attention and sanitation facilities. Soon afterward, some doctors and nurses came from the Jewish Hospital.

The point about Wallenberg is that he came himself. He talked to us and showed us that one human being cared about what was happening to us.[57]

Wallenberg even managed to protect the seventy thousand Jews living in what the Nazis called the "sealed ghetto." When he heard that the Hungarian Nazis were planning to kill every Jew there, he demanded that the German commander prevent the murders. To the amazement of many people, the commander agreed. Wallenberg had convinced him that if the Jews died, Wallenberg would see to it that the commander was hung as soon as the Russians marched into the city.

Yet when the Soviet army liberated Budapest, it was Wallenberg who was in danger. The Russians immediately took him prisoner. No one knows exactly why they did so. Nor does anyone know what happened to him after January 17, 1945. Over the years, the Russians have insisted that he died in 1947. Yet some people claim to have seen him since then. In 1981, the United States honored Wallenberg for his courage and heroism by making him an honorary citizen. He was the second person to be so honored. Winston Churchill was the first.

In an introduction to Per Anger's book about Wallenberg, Elie Wiesel notes, "Sadly, tragically, Raoul Wallenberg belonged to a small minority. And his mission started late, much too late, at a time when, except for those in the Hungarian capital, there were no more Jews left to be saved. Why had he not been sent earlier? Why had other diplomats not been dispatched to other cities, on similar rescue operations? What would have happened if, in 1943, neutral nations had offered protection to the Jews of Warsaw, if great powers had offered citizenship to the Jews of Paris and Amsterdam?" How would you answer Wiesel's questions? Would such an effort have stopped fate or even reversed it?

Lars Berg, a member of the Swedish legation in Budapest, has offered one explanation of why the Russians took Wallenberg prisoner.

> For the Russians, with their understanding or, more accurately, their lack of understanding for human problems, it was completely inconceivable that Wallenberg, the Swede, had come down to Budapest to try and rescue Hungarian Jews. He must have come for some other reason.
>
> In those days I was naive enough to believe that they were only accusing us of being spies for the Germans. One couldn't have known then that the Russians regarded the Americans as enemies at least as deadly as the Germans. Yet when you think about the fact that Wallenberg did come to Budapest at President Roosevelt's personal request, and that the funds at his disposal originated from the War Refugee Board in Washington, then you can understand better why the Russians regarded Raoul in particular as an American spy. And in the eyes of the Russians that was considerably worse than working for the Germans![58]

For years, the Raoul Wallenberg Committee has been demanding that the Russians tell the world what happened to Wallenberg. How important is it to know his fate?

In Lithuania, Senpo Sugihara, the Japanese consul, provided visas to thirty-five hundred Jews. Those visas not only protected Jews from deportation but also allowed them to emigrate to Shanghai, China—then under Japanese rule. Sugihara stopped only when he was removed from his post at the request of the German government. How do you account for his willingness to take risks when others refused?

In March of 1993, the pupils of Class V13 in Bosnia and their teacher Borislav Trivunovic sent the following message to the world:

> We wait spring. . . War is here. We wait peace. . . Nobody hears us, we are in a corner of world. All year we hope. We are fearless and persisting. Our fathers earn 3-4 DEM (or 5 kg flour) for month, we

haven't water, electric, heating—we bear it, but we can't bear hate and evil. War is hate and evil.

Our teacher learn us about love, concord and righteousness. He told us about Anne Frank and her hiding and life. After this story we took Anne's Diary from school's library. We read her Diary and acknowledge that our youth is very similar. After fifty years' history repetition again in Bosnia—war, hate, killing, hiding displacements.

We are twelve years old and we can't influence on politics and war. . . . . but we want to say for all world that we want to continue our lives in freedom and peace. In our country is war and <u>WE WANT TO STOP THIS CRAZY WAR IN BOSNIA AND STOP ALL WARS ALL AROUND THE WORLD FOREVER!</u>

We wait spring. . . we wait peace like Anne Frank fifty years before. She didn't live to see peace, but we . . . ?

How can a letter like this one help sensitize people and make them do something in regard to the crisis in Bosnia?

➤A vignette featuring Wallenberg is part of a thirty-minute documentary, "The Making of a Hero" that aired on *Chronicle.* A video is available from the Facing History Resource Center. Also available is the video testimony of Vera Goodkin, a survivor from Hungary who benefitted from Wallenberg's efforts. She regards him as the ultimate example of an individual who made a difference.

➤In her autobiography *Choices,* actor Liv Ullman writes of a child with no choice:

I had to travel [to Somalia] beyond my profession and the people I loved and the events I had known [to see] an ultimate victim of war and indifference. . . . A little boy showed me that we are not all really good deep down, because he was sacrificed to our lack of compassion. And since then, this small child has been with me, and his thin little hand is still holding my finger. One small child whose short life was affected by those who did not even know of his existence. One small boy with no choice at all, because the choices were taken over his head and he was never a part of choice. One little boy affected by cold choice, or maybe lack of choice would very soon lie down to desert sand and die.[59]

What are ways individuals can help to bring more choices to children in places like Somalia and Bosnia? What roles in particular can American students play in this process? A video interview with Liv Ullman is available from the Facing History Resource Center.

As the War Ended

[On] this day in 1945, I was to discover what human suffering was all about. . . . I was going to be able to see clearly that, yes, I suffered and I was hurting because I was black in a white society, but I had also begun to understand that suffering is universal. It is not just relegated to me and mine; it touches us all.

As the war drew to a close in the winter of 1945, the Soviet army pushed westward. To avoid them, the Nazis closed Auschwitz and other death camps in the east and forced inmates to march to camps farther west. As a result, camps like Bergen-Belsen, Buchenwald, and Dachau were overrun with the dead and the dying. When Allied soldiers entered those camps, they saw things they would never forget. Lewis Weinstein, a lieutenant colonel in the U.S. army, later recalled:

On March 31, 1945, during my daily visit to the Situation Room with its War Maps in our Paris headquarters, as I studied the Order of Battle on the large scale Nazi Western Front, I noticed near the town of Gotha an "X" in red crayon with the words "Death Camp." It was the first time I had ever seen those two words on a map or in a report. A red arrow pointed to these words, and was marked "Fourth Armored Division."

Immediately there flashed through my mind, "Death camp, death camp? It can't be a cemetery. It must be a murder camp and the victims must be Jewish; a death camp to murder Jews."

Nazi murders of Jews had been in the news when I enlisted in 1942, and the number seven hundred thousand was the highest I had heard until the number two million seemed to emerge in 1944. I had heard that number on my arrival in London. When I questioned my acquaintances in G-2 (Intelligence) about Nazi murders of Jews, the only answer was "It's an exaggeration, war propaganda." In January 1945, my sources described the numbers of Jews murdered as in the range of two or three hundred thousand. When there was a report on the liberation of Auschwitz, they told me that the reported numbers of dead were "in the realm of fancy." Even the reported numbers were sufficiently horrifying. And the words "Final Solution" had always been described to me as "resettlement."

Within minutes after seeing the words "Death Camp," I talked to the Deputy Assistant Chief of Staff, G-2. He said that a million or perhaps two million Jews had been murdered at Auschwitz and that this information was "top secret.". . . The Intelligence Officer said that Ohrdruf was one of the smaller death camps, as compared with Auschwitz, Buchenwald or Dachau, but it would be the first to be liberated by the American Army. He showed me other locations in our Allied zones. He was sparing of details, almost embarrassed, and he seemed reluctant to talk. I listened but I heard little. I was almost in a state of shock.[60]

After seeing Ohrdruf, Weinstein asked General Dwight Eisenhower to visit. Eisenhower later wrote that "I have never felt able to describe my emotional reactions when I first came face to face with indisputable evidence of Nazi brutality and ruthless disregard of every shred of decency. Up to that time I had known about it only generally or through secondary sources. I am certain, however, that I have never at any other time experienced an equal sense of shock."[61]

Although Weinstein and Eisenhower had known the camps existed before they saw them, they were not ready for what they actually saw. Leon Bass, a young soldier, was even less prepared for his first view of Buchenwald.

> [On] this day in 1945, I was to discover what human suffering was all about. I was going to take off the blinders that caused me to have tunnel vision. I was going to be able to see clearly that, yes, I suffered and I was hurting because I was black in a white society, but I had also begun to understand that suffering is universal. It is not just relegated to me and mine; it touches us all.
>
> And so I walked through the gates of Buchenwald, and I saw the dead and the dying. I saw people who had been so brutalized and were so maltreated; they had been starved and beaten. They had been worked almost to death, not fed enough, no medical care. One man came up and his fingers were webbed together, all of his fingers together by sores and scabs. This was due to malnutrition, not eating the proper foods. There were others holding on to each other, trying to remain standing. They had on wooden shoes; they had on the pajama-type uniform; their heads had been shaved. Some had the tattoos with numbers on their arms. I saw this. I saw them with the wooden bowls. Some of them were standing waiting for food and hitting on the fence, this was wire fence, and making gutteral sounds; not words —just sounds.
>
> I said, "My God, what is this insanity that I have come to? What are these people here for? What have they done? What was their crime that would cause people to treat them like this?" You see, I wasn't prepared for this. I was only nineteen. I had no frame of reference to cope with the kind of thing that I was witnessing.
>
> As I stood there, looking, a young man came over who spoke English. He hadn't been there very long because he looked rather healthy. He came over and he started to tell us about how many hundreds of thousands had come through the camp, and how many had died there.
>
> And he had taken us around and showed us different places. He took us to a barracks, a place where they slept, and he said that usually fifty people would fit into these barracks, but they had jammed more than 150 in there. They had bunks going almost to the ceiling. . . .

Leon Bass tells his story to Facing History students.

The odor was so bad I backed up, but I looked at a bottom bunk and there I saw one man. He was too weak to get up; he could just barely turn his head. He was skin and bones. He looked like a skeleton; and his eyes were deep set. He didn't utter a sound; he just looked at me with those eyes, and they still haunt me today. I remember looking at him. I backed off the steps, joined my friend, and started to walk away when another of the inmates came up, he could barely move. . . .

After seeing all of that it was too traumatic; I was not fit for anything. I came out of there and I was not able to eat, I didn't talk, I just got back on the truck and went back to my tent. I never talked about this with my friends who were with me. It was so horrible you don't want to deal with it. You try to push it away, and this I was able to do.

The war ended; they broke up my unit. They sent me down to the Philippines for six months, but I didn't talk about what I had seen at Buchenwald. I came home in 1946, and I never told my parents. I went to college, met my wife, got married, had children, got a job—I still didn't talk about this. I pushed it away. But you can't push things away forever.[62]

Sonia Weitz wrote a poem describing the day she was freed.

Students at Boston English High School meet with Facing History Speaker Sonia Weitz.

Liberation Day (Mauthausen, May 5, 1945)

A black G.I. stood by the door
(I never saw a black before)
He'll set me free before I die,
I thought, he must be the Messiah.

A black Messiah came for me . . .
He stared with eyes that didn't see,
He never heard a single word
Which hung absurd upon my tongue.

And then he simply froze in place
The shock, the horror on his face,
He didn't weep, he didn't cry
But deep within his gentle eyes
. . . A flood of devastating pain,
his innocence forever slain.

For me, with yet another dawn
I found my black Messiah gone
and on we went our separate ways
For forty years without a trace.

But there's a special bond we share
Which has grown strong because we dare
To live, to hope, to smile . . . and yet
We vow NOT EVER TO FORGET.[63]

CONNECTIONS

How did Weinstein react when he saw the words *death camp* on a map? What did he know at the time? Why do you think he wanted Eisenhower to see the camp?

➤How did Sonia Weitz view the African American soldier who freed her? Why was his skin color significant to her? What does she mean when she says in the last stanza that they share a bond because they both "dare to live"? Classroom sets of Sonia Weitz's book *I Promised I Would Tell* are available from the Facing History Resource Center. The book contains her poems as well as her memories of the war years.

On April 15, 1945, the American journalist Edward R. Murrow reported his visit to Buchenwald to his radio audience: "Permit me to tell you what you would have seen and heard had you been with me on Thursday. It will not be pleasant listening. If you are at lunch or if you have no appetite to hear what Germans have done, now is a good time to switch off the radio, for I propose to tell you of Buchenwald." Why did Murrow feel it was important to give details? Was he being a responsible reporter in doing so? For additional information on liberation, see *Elements of Time*, pages 92-95.

➤Leon Bass's video testimony is available from the Facing History Resource Center and is described in *Elements of Time*, pages 82-90. For another account of liberation, see the portrait of Marcus Orr, an American soldier wounded while on reconnaissance at Dachau just before liberation, on pages 90-95. Also available from the Resource Center is Lewis Weinstein's article, "The Liberation of Nazi Death Camps by the American Army—1945: The Report of an Eyewitness."

➤The thirty-minute video *You Are Free* includes testimonies of Americans who witnessed the camps as well as survivors of those same camps. It provides an excellent overview of the confusing and troubling days that followed the end of the war. Leon Bass is among the witnesses featured in the documentary.

NOTES

1 Raul Hilberg, *Perpetrators, Victims, Bystanders: The Jewish Catastrophe 1933-1945* (HarperCollins, 1992), xi.

2 Albert Camus, *Notebooks*.

3 Cynthia Ozick, Prologue to *Rescuers: Portraits of Moral Courage in the Holocaust,* by Gay Block and Malka Drucker, (Holmes & Meier, 1992), xiii.

4 Primo Levi, *The Drowned and the Saved*.

5 Raul Hilberg, *The Documents of Destruction*, 148-149.

6 Claude Lanzmann, *Shoah*, 133, 134-135.

7 Ibid., 142-144.

8 Quoted in Macief Kozlowski, "The Mission That Failed: A Polish Courier Who Tried to Help the Jews" in *My Brother's Keeper? Recent Polish Debates on the Holocaust,* ed. Antony Polonsky (Routledge, 1990), 83.

9 Ibid., 87-88.

10 Quoted in Leni Vahil, *The Holocaust* (Oxford University Press, 1990), 545.

11 Ervin Staub, *The Roots of Evil: The Origins of Genocide and Other Group Violence* (Cambridge University Press, 1989), 86-87.

12 Gordon I. Horwitz, *In the Shadow of Death: Living Outside the Gates of Mauthausen* (The Free Press, 1990), 59.

13 Ibid., 60.

14 Ibid., 60-61.

15 Ibid., 61-62.

16 Ruth Andreas-Friedrich, *Berlin Underground*, trans. Barrows Mussey (Holt, 1947), 116-117.

17 Victoria Barnett, *For the Soul of the People*, 164.

18 Helmuth James von Moltke, *Letters to Freya, 1939-1945,* ed. and trans. Beate Ruhm von Oppen (Knopf, 1990), 155-156.

19 Helmuth James von Moltke, *Letters to Freya*, 160.

20 Helmuth James von Moltke, *Letters to Freya*, 175.

21 Quoted in *The Nazi Years*, ed. Joachim Remak, 170.

22 Friederich Reck-Malleczewen, *Diary of a Man in Despair*, trans. Paul Rubens, (Collier Books, 1970), 179-181.

23 Ibid., 195-196.

24 Based on information in Nathan Stoltzfus "Civil Disobedience and Mass Protest as Successful Resistance in Nazi Germany" (unpublished manuscript).

25 Claudia Koonz, *Mothers in the Fatherland*, 422-423.

26 Christabel Bielenberg, *Christabel*, 111-115.

27 Nechama Tec, *When Light Pierced the Darkness: Christian Rescue of Jews in Nazi-Occupied Poland* (Oxford University Press, 1986), 54.

28 Ibid., 55.

29 Ibid., 176.

30 Quoted in Daniel Goldman, "Is Altruism Inherited?" *Baltimore Jewish Times*, 12 April, 1985, 70.

31 Samuel and Pearl Oliner, *The Altruistic Personality: Rescuers of Jews in Nazi Europe,* (The Free Press, 1988), 142.

32 Marion Pritchard in *Courage to Care*, ed. C. Rittner and S. Myers, 29.

33 Ibid., 29-31.

34 Ibid., 32-33.

[35] Samuel and Pearl Oliner, *The Altruistic Personality*, 170.

[36] *Courage to Care*, ed. C. Rittner and S. Myers, 102.

[37] Ibid., 135.

[38] Ibid., 107.

[39] Philip Hallie, "Major Julius Schmahling" in *Courage to Care,* ed. C. Rittner and S. Myers, 112-113; 114-115.

[40] Thomas Keneally, *Schindler's List* (Simon & Schuster, 1982), 129-130.

[41] Dorothy Rabinowitz, "An Army of Schindlers from Italy," *Wall Street Journal*, 22 December, 1993.

[42] Leo Goldberger in *Courage to Care,* ed. C. Rittner and S. Myers, 92.

[43] Ibid. 93-95.

[44] Ibid.

[45] Victoria Barnett, *For the Soul of the People,* 153-154.

[46] Ibid., 128.

[47] Ibid., 132.

[48] Ibid., 154.

[49] Quoted in Eva Fleischner, "Can the Few Become the Many? Some Catholics in France Who Saved Jews during the Holocaust," (Montclair State College, unpublished paper), 3.

[50] Nora Levin, *The Holocaust: The Destruction of European Jewry, 1933-45* (Schocken, 1973), 435.

[51] John T. Pawlikowski, "The Vatican and the Holocaust: Unresolved Issues" (unpublished paper, Catholic Theological Union), 6-7.

[52] Ibid.

[53] Quoted in Pierre Joffroy, *A Spy for God: The Ordeal of Kurt Gerstein,* trans. Norman Denny (Harcourt Brace, 1969), 174.

[54] John Carroll, "The Pope Owes Israel a Confession," *Boston Globe* 23, November, 1993, op. ed.

[55] Golda Meir, *My Life,* 164.

[56] Per Anger, *With Raoul Wallenberg in Budapest,* trans. D. and M. Paul, (Holocaust Library, 1981), 58-59.

[57] Quoted in Harvey Rosenfeld, *Raoul Wallenberg* (Prometheus, 1982), 58.

[58] Quoted in Per Anger, *With Raoul Wallenberg in Budapest,* 161.

[59] Liv Ullman, *Choices* (Alfred Knopf, 1984), 104-105.

[60] Lewis Weinstein, "The Liberation of Nazi Death Camps by the American Army-1945," (unpublished paper, 1985).

[61] Dwight Eisenhower, *Crusade in Europe* (Doubleday, 1948), 408-409.

[62] Quoted in *Elements of Time* (Facing History and Ourselves, 1989), 83-84.

[63] Sonia Weitz, *Elements of Time,* 87.

9. Judgment

History, despite its wrenching pain,
Cannot be unlived, but if faced
With courage, need not be lived again.

MAYA ANGELOU

OVERVIEW

*I*n the spring of 1945, as the war finally came to an end, the world at last confronted the atrocities the Nazis had committed. Benjamin Ferencz, a young American lawyer assigned to investigate those atrocities, recalls:

> It was a grisly assignment. Among my duties, I had to dig up bodies of young American flyers who had parachuted or crashed, and were beaten to death by enraged German mobs or murdered by local Gestapo officials. This, however, was merely the initiation of horrors yet to come. It was not until I joined the American troops advancing toward German concentration camps that I realized the full extent of the Nazi terror. . . .
>
> It was often impossible to tell whether the skeleton-like inmates lying near-naked in the dust were dead or alive. Those who could walk had been whisked away by panic-stricken SS guards. Their flight was made visible only by the trail of dead bodies strewn along the road. The bedraggled prisoners who could not keep pace with the retreat were shot on the spot and left dead or dying. I helped to uncover many mass graves where innocent victims had been massacred.
>
> I had peered into hell.[1]

Alan Moorehead, a British journalist, had a similar reaction to his first glimpse of Bergen-Belsen that same spring. "With all one's soul, one felt: 'This is not war. Nor is it anything to do with here and now, with this one place at this one moment. This is timeless and all mankind is involved in it. This touches me and I am responsible. Why has it happened? How did we let it happen?'"

Earlier chapters considered how and why the Holocaust happened. Chapter 9 focuses on questions related to personal responsibility not only for the Holocaust but also for the war itself and the way that war was fought. It therefore raises such questions as:

- Should those who participated in the atrocities committed during the war be punished? If so, who ought be held accountable?

- Should those individuals be tried before a court of law? What is the purpose of a trial? Is it to punish evil-doing? Or is it to set a precedent for the future?

- Who should be tried? Are individuals responsible for their crimes if they have obeyed the laws of their nation? Or are there higher laws? If so, what are those laws?

- How does one determine punishment? Is everyone equally guilty? Or do some bear more responsibility than others? Can an entire nation be guilty?

Chapter 9 explores these questions by focusing on the international trials held after the war. John Fried, the Special Legal Consultant to the United States War Crimes Tribunals at Nuremberg, Germany, from 1947 to 1949, explained the purpose of those trials:

> The awesome, unprecedented nature of the Nazi war crimes demanded a response from the victorious Allies after World War II. That response, embodying the shock and outrage of mankind, was the Nuremberg Tribunals, in which the Nazi leadership was tried for its crimes.
>
> The Allied judges sought. . . to decide. . . if the Nazi civilian and military leaders had instigated a war of aggression and then pursued that war by unacceptable means and in violation of normal standards [and] to determine an individual's responsibility for crimes which could not be disputed. No one, that is, could deny the reality of Dachau and the mass slaughter of civilians; the question to be answered was: who was responsible?[2]

Between 1945 and 1950, the fate of 199 individuals was decided in thirteen separate trials held in Nuremberg. Those trials established important precedents that have become "part of the unwritten laws of nations in the years since." After 1950, similar trials for war crimes were held not only in Europe but also in Asia. Hannah Arendt attended one of those trials—the 1961 trial of Adolf Eichmann. She found that it raised important questions about good and evil. In her view, thinking is the urgent work of a species that is responsible for its own survival. She therefore wondered if the habit of "examining whatever comes to pass can be among the considerations that make men abstain from evil-doing or even actually condition them against it."[3]

READING 1

Dogma Makes Obedient Ghosts

This is the concentration camp and crematorium at Auschwitz. This is where people were turned into numbers. . . . And that was not done by gas. It was done by arrogance. It was done by dogma. It was done by ignorance. When people believe that they have absolute knowledge, with no test in reality, this is how they behave. This is what men do when they aspire to the knowledge of gods.

Until 1933, German scientists explored scientific questions from various perspectives. They were pioneers in the theory of tolerance. After 1933, German scientists, like most Germans, served the aims of National Socialism and dogma became a substitute for truth. In their eagerness to show their loyalty, scientists developed a technology for mass murder. There are those who blame that technology for the atrocities committed at Auschwitz and other death camps. In *The Ascent of Man*, scientist Jacob Bronowski disagreed. While bending over at a pond in Auschwitz, he posed the two parts to what he considered to be "the central dilemma of the twentieth century":

> One [part] is the belief that the end justifies the means. That push-button philosophy, that deliberate deafness to suffering, has become the monster in the war machine. The other is the betrayal of the human spirit: the assertion of dogma that closes the mind, and turns a nation, a civilisation, into a regiment of ghosts—obedient ghosts, or tortured ghosts.
>
> It is said that science will dehumanize people and turn them into numbers. That is false, tragically false. Look for yourself. This is the concentration camp and crematorium at Auschwitz. This is where people were turned into numbers. Into this pond were flushed the ashes of [over a million] people. And that was not done by gas. It was done by arrogance. It was done by dogma. It was done by ignorance. When people believe that they have absolute knowledge, with no test in reality, this is how they behave. This is what men do when they aspire to the knowledge of gods.
>
> Science is a very human form of knowledge. We are always at the brink of the known, we always feel forward for what is to be hoped. Every judgment in science stands on the edge of error, and is personal. Science is a tribute to what we can know although we are fallible. In the end the words were said by Oliver Cromwell: "I beseech you, in the bowels of Christ, think it possible you may be mistaken."

I owe it as a scientist to my friend Leo Szilard, I owe it as a human being to the many members of my family who died at Auschwitz, to stand here by the pond as a survivor and a witness. We have to cure ourselves of the itch for absolute knowledge and power. We have to close the distance between the push-button order and the human act. We have to touch people.[4]

CONNECTIONS

Define *dogma*. How does it close the mind, and turn individuals, groups, even a nation, into a "regiment of ghosts—obedient ghosts, or tortured ghosts"? What is an "obedient ghost"? Give an example of one you have personally encountered or read about.

 Leo Szilard was a scientist who fled Nazi Germany. In 1939, he urged that the United States build an atomic bomb but later tried unsuccessfully to prevent its use. Bronowski recalled that when someone said, in Szilard's presence, that "it was the tragedy of scientists that their discoveries were used for destruction," Szilard replied that "it is the tragedy of mankind." What point was Szilard trying to make? How did Bronowski support that point when he discussed the role of science at Auschwitz?

Some Nazis pictured themselves as "victims to the technological obsession of our times." Does that explain their behavior? Absolve them of responsibility for their acts?

Max Redeinreich insists that Nazi officials were not the only ones responsible for atrocities. Many of the nation's scholars, including its most famous scientists, were also to blame. According to Redeinrich, many German scholars were accomplices to the crimes. They provided the ideas and techniques that led to and justified the "unparalleled slaughter." What is the difference between a murderer and his or her accomplice? Are they equally responsible for the crime? Are they equally guilty?

Jerzy Kosinski was quoted in Chapter 8 as saying, "Of all mammals only a human being can say 'no.' . . .To say 'no' is to deny the crowd, to be set apart, to reaffirm yourself." Compare Kosinski's remarks with Bronowski's. What similarities do you see in the way the two men view human behavior? What differences seem most striking? What is your view? Does your behavior always reflect that view?

The Rules of War

The story of the Nuremberg tribunals offers a concrete instance in which an individual's responsibility for a terrible crime is examined before the world. Not an abstract debate, but a life and death matter for the defendants.

Toward the end of the war, as rumors of Nazi atrocities were confirmed, many people were convinced that the individuals responsible had to be tried before an international court. They wanted each to take personal responsibility for his or her actions. At first, the British resisted the idea. Winston Churchill argued that the Nazis ought to be summarily hung. Only after considerable pressure from the Russians and the Americans did he and other British officials change their stand.

Still, before a trial could take place, the Allies had to work out a number of issues. Trials decide questions of law. But what laws had the Germans broken? The Allies argued that the Germans had violated international law—a body of rules that has evolved out of centuries of encounters among the peoples of the world. Although some insist that "all's fair in love and war," most recognize that there are limits to what soldiers can do in wartime. During Europe's Middle Ages, for example, the rules of chivalry guided a knight's behavior in battle. Over the years, such rules were expanded and refined. In 1863, in the midst of the Civil War, the United States became one of the first nations in the world to give its soldiers a code "authorized by the laws and usages of war." Compiled by Frances Lieber, a legal expert, and based on "principles of justice, honor and humanity," the Lieber Code detailed how civilians, prisoners of war, and spies were to be treated. Later, other nations—including Germany, France, and Britain—prepared similar manuals. As new weapons were introduced, those manuals were updated and revised.

In the late 1800s and early 1900s, a number of international conferences furthered the idea that there are accepted rules of war. Delegates to a 1907 meeting in the Hague, in the Netherlands, focused on the rights of civilians and soldiers who have surrendered. They also set rules for the occupation of enemy territory. A series of conferences held in Geneva, Switzerland, established how prisoners-of-war were to be treated and called for the protection of the wounded.

Over the years, however, people have found it easier to establish rules in peacetime than to prosecute violators during or even after a war. For example, a commission established after World War I concluded that even though Germany's attack on Belgium was unprovoked, international law had not yet reached a point where German leaders could be tried for "aggression" or violations of the "laws of humanity." Still, the Treaty of Versailles held Kaiser Wilhelm II responsible for the attack and ordered that he stand trial. But that trial never took place. The treaty also called for the indictment of German soldiers accused of atrocities. But the German government refused to try them.

The various international laws set forth in military manuals and treaties dealt only with crimes committed as a part of a war. They did not address genocide—"the crime with no name." The first attempt to do so occurred in 1915, just after the massacre of the Armenians. In May of that year, the Allies formally accused Turkish leaders of a "crime against humanity and civilization." Although a new Turkish government agreed to bring the nation's former leaders to justice, it had to try them in absentia. The defendants had fled the country. Because they were not present for the trial, the proceedings did not command worldwide attention.

This time, the Allies were determined to punish anyone who violated international law. On January 13, 1942, representatives of nine Nazi-occupied nations signed a declaration vowing to hold accountable not only those who ordered "war crimes" but also those who participated in them. On October 20, 1943, the United Nations War Crimes Commission was established to carry out those aims. Less than two weeks later, the United States, Britain, and the Soviet Union issued a declaration reaffirming their commitment to those goals.

In October of 1945, at Nuremberg, an International Military Tribunal (IMT), created by Britain, France, the United States, and the Soviet Union, indicted 24 Nazis for one or more of the following crimes:

1. Conspiracy—Leaders, organizers, instigators, and accomplices in the formulation or execution of a common plan, or conspiracy to commit any of the following crimes are responsible for all acts performed by any persons in execution of such a plan;

2. Crimes Against Peace: namely, planning, preparation, initiation or waging of a war of aggression, or a war in violation of international treaties, agreements or assurances, or participation in a common plan or conspiracy for the accomplishment of any of the foregoing;

3. War Crimes: namely, violations of the laws or customs of war. Such violations shall include, but not be limited to, murder, ill-treatment or deportation to slave labor or for any other purpose of civilian population of or in occupied territory, murder or ill-treatment of prisoners of war or persons on the seas, killing of hostages, plunder of public or private property, wanton destruction of cities, towns or villages, or devastation not justified by military necessity;

4. Crimes Against Humanity: namely, murder, extermination, enslavement, deportation, and other inhumane acts committed against any civilian population, before or during the war; or persecutions on political, racial or religious grounds in execution of or in connection with any crime within the jurisdiction of the Tribunal, whether or not in violation of the domestic law of the country where perpetrated.

John Fried said of the trials that followed, "The story of the Nuremberg tribunals offers a concrete instance in which an individual's responsibility for a terrible crime is examined before the world. Not an abstract debate, but a life and death matter for the defendants, those age-old questions converged in the city of Nuremberg, and the standards established in that trial have become part of the unwritten law of nations in the years since."[5]

CONNECTIONS

Who should be judged? The individuals who gave orders? The people who carried out those orders? Those who allowed it to happen?

What is the purpose of a trial? Is it to punish the guilty? Avenge the victims? Warn those who might commit similar acts in the future?

In the overview to this chapter, Fried referred to the "unprecedented nature of the Nazi war crimes" that resulted in the "shock and outrage of mankind." What point was he trying to make? How does it explain why the Allies tried the Nazis for their *personal* conduct in the war? What responsibility do soldiers and government officials have for their actions in time of war?

In the 1200s, St. Thomas Aquinas defined a "just war" as one fought by a legitimate government for a just cause and with the intention of bringing about good. Was the battle waged by the Allies a "just war"?

Every nation has its own values and beliefs. Each also has accepted standards of behavior. How then can one nation judge the actions of another? Are there moral values that transcend obedience to the laws of a particular nation?

Why do you think the Allies looked to the past to justify its claims that Germany had violated international laws?

The Allies held the international war crimes trials in Nuremberg. What role did Nuremberg play in Nazi Germany? Why do you think the Allies decided to locate the trials there?

In 1945, the United States dropped atomic bombs on two Japanese cities, Hiroshima and Nagasaki. Research the bombings and decide whether they were "war crimes."

How important is it to establish rules of warfare? Does the knowledge that those rules cannot always be implemented affect your response?

➤As Hitler prepared for the "final solution of the Jewish question," he asked, "Who after all, speaks today of the annihilation of the Armenians?" What was he saying about international law? The "rules of war"? Professor Richard Hovannisian maintains that had the perpetrators of the Armenian Genocide been more vigorously prosecuted and punished for their crimes, the case might have served as a deterrent for the Holocaust. Do you agree? A video of Hovannisian's lecture is available from the Resource Center.

READING 3

"Humanity's Aspirations to Do Justice"

*T*he first Nuremberg trial began on November 20, 1945. The chief prose-cutor was Robert H. Jackson, a justice on the United States Supreme Court. He opened the trial with a speech.

The privilege of opening the first trial in history for crimes against the peace of the world imposes a grave responsibility. The wrongs which we seek to condemn and punish have been so calculated, so malignant, and so devastating, that civilization cannot tolerate their being ignored because it cannot survive their being repeated. That four great nations, flushed with victory and stung with injury, stay the hand of vengeance and voluntarily submit their captive enemies to the judgment of the law is one of the most significant tributes that Power ever has paid to Reason.

What these men stand for we will patiently and temperately disclose. We will give you undeniable proofs of incredible events. . . . They took from the German people all those dignities and freedoms that we hold natural and inalienable rights in every human being. The people were compensated by inflaming and gratifying hatreds toward those who were marked as "scapegoats." Against their opponents, including Jews, Catholics, and free labor, the Nazis directed such a campaign of arrogance, brutality and annihilation as the world has never witnessed since the pre-Christian ages. They excited the German ambition to be a "master race," which, of course, implies serfdom for others. They led their people on a mad gamble for domination. They diverted social energies and resources to the creation of what they thought to be an invincible war machine. They overran their neighbors. To sustain the "master race," in its war-making, they enslaved millions of human beings and brought them into Germany, where these helpless creatures now wander as displaced persons.

Jackson went on to say, "We must never forget that the record on which we judge these defendants today is the record on which history will judge us tomorrow. To pass these defendants a poisoned chalice is to put it to our own lips as well. We must summon such detachment and intellectual integrity that this trial will commend itself to posterity as fulfilling humanity's aspirations to do justice."

Only twenty-four Nazis were indicted and two of them never stood trial. Robert Ley, the head of the Nazi labor movement, committed suicide before the trial began. And the court ruled that Gustav Krupp, an industrialist, was too ill to be tried. Many other top Nazis leaders, including Hitler and Goebbels, killed themselves in the final days of the war. Others, like Adolf Eichmann, managed to disappear during the confusion that marked Germany's defeat. The defendants were the most prominent the Allies could find at the time.

Of the men actually brought to trial, five were military leaders and the rest were prominent government or party officials. Their trial was organized much the way criminal trials are organized in the United States. The defendants were made aware of all charges against them. Each was entitled to a lawyer and had the right to plead his own case, offering witnesses and evidence in his own behalf .

> We must never forget that the record on which we judge these defendants today is the record on which history will judge us tomorrow.

CONNECTIONS

Throughout the trial, the prosecution used the Nazis' own records as evidence. Jackson himself was amazed not only at the quantity of records available but also at the incredible detail in those records. He did not think "men would ever be so foolish as to put in writing some of the things the Germans did. The stupidity of it and the brutality of it would simply appall you." Focusing on the words of the perpetrators allows us to think about *why* they acted as they did. It also raises the question of how they persuaded others to participate. And it forces us to think about how similar acts of evil can be prevented. Based on what you have read so far in this book, how would you answer those questions? Record your responses in your journal so that you can refer to them as you continue reading the chapter.

Using Nazi documents as evidence had important consequences. One was the focus on conspiracy and crimes of aggression. Both were easier to prove from such evidence than "war crimes" or "crimes against humanity." Reread the explanation of the four charges to figure out why.

What does Jackson mean when he says, "We must never forget that the record on which we judge these defendants today is the record on which history will judge us tomorrow"?

➤The First Annual Facing History Conference, "The Impact of Nuremberg: Today and the Future," considered the legacy of the trials. Participants at the conference included a number of individuals who took part in the prosecution—Telford Taylor, Benjamin Ferencz, Walter Rockler, Drexel Sprecher, Richard Hovannisian, Elizabeth Holtzman, Gerald Stern, and Thomas Lambert. Also participating in the conference were Father Robert Drinan, Alan Dershowitz, Robert Lifton, and Irwin Cotler—individuals whose careers have focused on aspects of international law that were affirmed at Nuremberg. Videos of key sessions at the conference, including one that highlights the impact of the trials on medicine and international law, are available from the Facing History Resource Center. Those sessions are also described in *Elements of Time*, pages 375–376.

➤A twenty-minute film, *The Nuremberg Trials*, offers an overview of the International Military Tribunal. It includes footage from the trial. William Shirer, who narrates the film, stresses the role the United States played in the trial. The video is available from the Facing History Resource Center.

READING 4

Obedience to Orders

Throughout the trial, the defendants vehemently denied responsibility for crimes against humanity. They argued that wars have always been brutal and this war was much like any other. They also insisted that the victors were equally guilty. After all, in wartime, both sides commit "excesses." And they maintained that they were only obeying orders. General Alfred Jodl's attorney summarized that argument by telling the court, "It is true that without his generals Hitler could not have waged the wars. . . . If the generals do not do their job, there is no war. But one must add: if the infantryman does not, if his rifle does not fire. . . . there is no war. Is, therefore, the soldier, the gunsmith. . . guilty of complicity in the war? Does Henry Ford share in the responsibility for the thousands of accidents which his cars cause every year?"

The judges disagreed with that argument. Ruling that orders from a superior do not excuse a crime, they convicted all but three of the men on one or more of the charges. Of the twelve sentenced to die, one—Martin Bormann, Hitler's secretary—was tried in absentia and never captured. The leading defendant at the trial itself was Hermann Goering. According to the judges, he was "the moving force for aggressive war, second only to Hitler." He was also "the creator of the oppressive pogrom against the Jews and other races, at home and abroad." And it was he who "developed the Gestapo and created the first concentration camps." Apart from other anti-Jewish measures, "by decree of July 31, 1941, he directed [Heinrich] Himmler and [Reinhard] Heydrich to 'bring about a complete solution to the Jewish question in the German sphere of influence in Europe.'" His death sentence came as no surprise, but the court was never able to carry it out. He committed suicide first.

Jochaim von Ribbentrop, Hitler's foreign minister, was also found guilty of having "played an important part in Hitler's 'final solution' of the Jewish question." The judges cited his role in "deporting" Jews from occupied countries "to the East." They noted that it was he who informed Hungarian leaders on April 17, 1943, that the nation's Jews "must either be exterminated or taken to concentration camps."

Alfred Rosenberg, the author of one of the most widely read Nazi texts, *The Myth of the Twentieth Century*, was also hung. As the Reich Minister for the Occupied Eastern Territories, the court ruled, "his directives provided for the segregation of Jews, ultimately in ghettos. His subordinates engaged in mass killings of Jews. . . . In December, 1941, he made the suggestion to Hitler that in a case of shooting 100 hostages, Jews only be used."

Arthur von Seyss-Inquart, an Austrian, was also considered a top Nazi official. He served as an administrator in Czechoslovakia, deputy governor general in Poland and, more importantly, as Reich Commissioner in the Netherlands. In that position, the judges pointed out, he was responsible for "the mass deportation of almost 120,000 Jews to Auschwitz."

If the generals do not do their job, there is no war. But one must add: if the infantryman does not, if his rifle does not fire. . . . there is no war. Is, therefore, the soldier, the gunsmith. . . guilty of complicity in the war? Does Henry Ford share in the responsibility for the thousands of accidents which his cars cause every year?

CONNECTIONS

Hermann Goering, the leading defender of the Third Reich at Nuremberg, told a fellow defendant that "you must accept the fact that your life is lost. The only question left is whether you are willing to stand by me and die a martyr's death. You should not feel too sad; some day the German people will rise again and acknowledge us as heroes, and our bones will be moved to marble caskets, in a national shrine." How did the Allies hope to keep that from happening?

During the trial, von Ribbentrop argued, "I assure you, we are all appalled by all these persecutions and atrocities. It is simply not typically German! Can you imagine that I could kill anyone? Tell me honestly, do any of us look like murderers?" What does a murderer look like? Is someone who plans and then orders a murder as guilty as the person who pulls the trigger?

How would you respond to the questions Jodl's lawyer raised: "Is, therefore, the soldier, the gunsmith. . . guilty of complicity in the war? Does Henry Ford share in the responsibility for the thousands of accidents which his cars cause every year?"

Was the trial revenge or was it based on views similar to those expressed by John Fried? He wrote in his book on the Nuremberg trials, "Crimes against international law (and this applies, of course, to the Holocaust) are committed by men, not by abstract entities (such as states)."

After the Civil War, Captain Henry Wirz, commander of the Confederate prisoner-of-war camp at Andersonville, Georgia, was convicted of cruelties that resulted in the deaths of thousands of Union prisoners. Wirz argued that he was only obeying the orders of his commander. The evidence supported Wirz's claims. But the judges convicted him because he followed orders willingly rather than under duress. What is the difference? What were the judges saying about obedience as a defense for a criminal act? Do you agree?

<hr>

READING 5

A Man of Words

Among the twenty-two men who stood trial at Nuremberg was Julius Streicher, the publisher of *Der Stuermer*, an antisemitic newspaper with over six hundred thousand readers. Week after week, month after month, he described Jews as "vermin in need of extermination." In a typical article he ranted that the Jew was not a human being, but "a parasite, an enemy, an evil-doer, a disseminator of diseases which must be destroyed in the interest of mankind." In May of 1939 (four months before the war began and twenty-five months before the invasion of Russia), Streicher told his readers, "A punitive expedition must come against the Jews in Russia. . . the Jews in Russia must be killed. They must be exterminated root and branch."

In the early days of the war, as the Germans conquered more and more territory, Streicher intensified his efforts to incite persecution of the Jews. Between August 1941 and September 1944, he published twenty-four articles, twelve of which he wrote himself, demanding the extermination of the Jewish people. By 1943, the magazine was openly suggesting that a "Final Solution" was underway, despite an official policy to keep the mass murders a secret.

Streicher was not a government official. He did not set policy or carry out orders. His only weapons were his words. And he was punished for using those words to turn citizen against citizen.

At Nuremberg, the judges found Streicher guilty of "inciting of the population to abuse, maltreat and slay their fellow citizens. . . to stir up passion, hate, violence and destruction among the people themselves aims at breaking the moral backbone even of those the invader chooses to spare." They sentenced him to death because his "incitement to murder and extermination at the time when Jews in the East were being killed under the most horrible conditions clearly constitutes persecution on political and racial grounds. . . and (therefore) a Crime against Humanity."

CONNECTIONS

Streicher was not a government official. He did not set policy nor carry out orders. His only weapons were his words. And he was punished for using those words to turn citizen against citizen. Can words be used as weapons? Can they turn neighbor against neighbor? Should a person be held responsible for his or her words?

What did the judges mean when they found Streicher guilty of "breaking the moral backbone" of a nation? Does a nation have a moral backbone? By finding Streicher guilty, what message were the judges sending to others who would stir up hatred in similar ways? The power of Julius Streicher's publications to incite hatred against Jews and other non-Aryans is discussed in *Elements of Time*, pages 61-62, 163-164, and 368.

In the United States, the First Amendment to the Constitution protects freedom of speech and freedom of the press. Does that mean that individuals have the right to incite hatred? To publish symbols of hatred? To spread racism? After discussing your answers to these questions, find out how the United States courts have answered those same questions. Compare your opinion to theirs.

READING 6

Betraying the Children

Alfons Heck, a high-ranking member of Hitler Youth, (Chapter 5, Reading 8) recalled the effect the Nuremberg Trials had on him.

> I was captured on March the seventh, 1945, in my own hometown. During my captivity, I was forced to look at documentary footage of concentration camps and death camps. And it was the first time that I was shown the atrocities committed by our nation. We looked at this, and I said to my friends, "What do they take us for? This stuff is staged!" And one of us began to snicker, and our captors became so

incensed that they started yelling at us, "You Goddamned Nazi bastards! Do you think this is a comedy? This is what you have done!"

It was almost a year later before I was able to accept the veracity of the films that I had seen. And it occurred at the war crimes trials in Nuremberg in 1946. When I arrived in the city of Nuremberg, I was stunned by the total change in the Nuremberg I had seen at the Nazi Party Rally of 1938. While I listened on the loudspeakers outside, I heard the full evidence of the accusations directed at the 22 top Nazis who were on trial. One of them was my leader, the former leader of the Hitler Youth, Baldur von Schirach. He was the principal reason why I came to Nuremberg. I wanted to know what he had to say, in particular, in regard to the activities of the Hitler Youth. Von Schirach told the Court, "It was my guilt that I have trained youth for a man who became a murderer a million times over."

Baldur von Schirach received twenty years for crimes against humanity. That, in turn, implicated me too in the count of mass murder because I had served Hitler as fanatically as von Schirach. I had an overwhelming sense of betrayal in Nuremberg and I recognized that the man I had adored was, in fact, the biggest monster in human history. It's a devastating feeling if you follow it to its conclusion—that you are a part of the human race.

The experience of the Hitler Youth in Nazi Germany constitutes a massive case of child abuse. Out of millions of basically innocent children, Hitler and his regime succeeded in creating potential monsters.

Could it happen again today? Of course it can. Children are like empty vessels: you can fill them with good, you can fill them with evil; you can fill them with compassion. So the story of the Hitler Youth can be repeated because, despite Auschwitz, the world has not changed for the better all that much.[6]

"The experience of the Hitler Youth in Nazi Germany constitutes a massive case of child abuse. Out of millions of basically innocent children, Hitler and his regime succeeded in creating potential monsters. Could it happen again today? Of course it can.

CONNECTIONS

The word *veracity* means truth. How do you account for the fact that Heck refused to accept the veracity of films made in the concentration camps and death camps but did believe confessions of guilt by Schirach and other Nazi leaders?

Were Baldur von Schirach and other leaders of the Hitler Youth guilty of betraying the children they led? Were they guilty of "child abuse"? Does blaming them absolve Heck of responsibility?

What do Heck's remarks suggest about the value of the trial to the German people? Was it important for them to hear the events of the war in the perpetrators' own voices?

Heck believes that what happened to him could happen to others—that other young people could also be betrayed by their leaders. And he was right. In the 1970s in Cambodia, the Khmer Rouge also used propaganda to win over the young and help them commit genocide.

One survivor believes the Nuremberg Trials were premature. "While Europe was in turmoil at the close of the war, people were rebuilding their cities and their lives. This was not a time for theater, for staging; the judges were the jury then. Humanity never had a chance to attend." Would Heck agree? Do you agree?

➤Alfons Heck wrote a book about his experiences in Hitler Youth. He also made a film entitled *Heil Hitler: Confessions of a Nazi Youth*. It is available from the Facing History Resource Center. Do you think someone like Heck can be denazified ? For additional information on denazification, see *Elements of Time*, pages 56-60.

<hr>

READING 7

"We Were Not Supposed to Think"

After the first set of trials ended, the United States held twelve others at Nuremberg. These trials were authorized by multinational agreements and based on international law. Telford Taylor, who served in the United States Army Intelligence during the war and was transferred to Justice Jackson's staff during the first trials, supervised the new proceedings. He said of them, "The judgments of these subsequent trials added enormously to the body and the living reality of international penal law. No principle deserves to be called such unless men are willing to stake their consciences on its enforcement. That is the way law comes into being, and that is what was done at Nuremberg." Among those brought to trial were:

- 26 military leaders, including five field marshals;
- 56 high-ranking SS and other police officers, including leaders in the *Einsatzgruppen* and key officials in Heinrich Himmler's central office which supervised the concentration camps and the extermination program,
- 14 officials of other SS organizations that engaged in racial persecution.

The defendants did not deny the accusations against them. Often their own testimony was used to convict them. Otto Ohlendorf, the former Chief of one of the *Einsatzgruppen*, was sentenced to death for the murder of about ninety thousand Jews and "Gypsies" after admitting that he ordered his men to kill children as well as adults.

At the trial, Rudolf Hoess, the Commandant at Auschwitz, was asked if he had considered whether the Jews he murdered deserved such a fate. According to trial transcripts, he responded:

> Don't you see, we SS men were not supposed to think about these things: it never even occurred to us.—And besides, it was something already taken for granted that the Jews were to blame for everything. . . . We just never heard anything else. It was not just newspapers like *Der Stuermer* but it was everything we ever heard. Even our military and ideological training took for granted that we had to protect Germany from the Jews. . . . It only started to occur to me after the collapse that maybe it was not quite right, after I had heard what everybody was saying. . . .We were all so trained to obey orders without even thinking that the thought of disobeying an order would simply never have occurred to anybody and somebody else would have done just as well if I hadn't. . . . You can be sure that it was not always a pleasure to see those mountains of corpses and smell the continual burning.—But Himmler had ordered it and had even explained the necessity and I really never gave much thought to whether it was wrong. It just seemed a necessity.

We were all so trained to obey orders without even thinking that the thought of disobeying an order would simply never have occurred to anybody and somebody else would have done just as well if I hadn't.

CONNECTIONS

Why does Taylor argue that passing laws is not enough? What part does enforcement play in creating laws? Find examples in American history or your own experience that shows how enforcement helps to create laws.

How did the individuals charged at this new trial differ from those charged at the earlier Nuremberg trial? As the power of Nazi officials diminishes does their guilt also diminish?

According to the *superior order principle*, a person who commits a crime is not automatically excused by the fact that he obeyed a law, a decree, or an order from a superior. He is only excused if he did not have a *moral choice* to act differently. The Nuremberg judges did not define *moral choice* as requiring that one obey a criminal order at the cost of one's own life. Review Christopher Browning's description of the *Einsatzgruppen* in Chapter 7, Reading 3. How were the officers and their men initiated into violence? Did Ohlendorf have a moral choice? What about the other officers? The soldiers?

Review Hannah Arendt's comments on thinking in the overview to this chapter. How often does Hoess use some form of the word *think*? What is the relationship between thoughtlessness and evil-doing?

The Scientists of Annihilation

The Allies also indicted the scientists who made the Holocaust possible. Among them were physicians who performed "medical experiments" on concentration camp inmates as well as the engineers and technicians who helped create the technology of mass death. Leo Alexander, a psychiatrist who served as a consultant to the Secretary of War of the United States on duty with the Office of the Chief Counsel for War Crimes in Nuremberg, summarized his own findings.

> A large part of [German] research was devoted to the science of destroying and preventing life, for which I have proposed the term "ktenology," the science of killing. In the course of this ktenologic research, methods of mass killing and mass sterilization were investigated and developed for use against non-German peoples or Germans who were considered useless.
>
> Sterilization methods were widely investigated but proved impractical in experiments conducted in concentration camps. A rapid method developed for sterilization of females, which could be accomplished in the course of a regular health examination, was the intra-uterine injection of various chemicals. . . .The injections were extremely painful, and a number of women died in the course of the experiments. Professor Karl Clauberg reported that he had developed a method at the Auschwitz concentration camp by which he could sterilize 1000 women in one day.
>
> Another method of sterilization, or rather castration, was proposed by Viktor Brack especially for conquered populations. His idea was that x-ray machinery could be built into desks at which the people would have to sit, ostensibly to fill out a questionnaire requiring five minutes; they would be sterilized without being aware of it. This method failed because experiments carried out on 100 male prisoners [resulted in] severe x-ray burns . . . on all subjects. . . .
>
> The development of methods for rapid and inconspicuous individual execution was the objective of another large part of the ktenologic research. . . . Poisons were the subject of many of these experiments. A research team at the Buchenwald concentration camp, consisting of Drs. Joachim Mrugowsky, Erwin Ding-Schuler and Waldemar Hoven, developed the most widely used means of individual execution under the guise of medication treatment— namely, the intravenous injection of phenol or gasoline.[7]

It was left to the engineers, however, to develop the technology for mass death. When the Russians entered Auschwitz-Birkenau, they found records that detailed the construction of the crematoriums, complete with precise costs and calculations of the number of corpses each furnace could incinerate in a single day. The Russians captured four of the engineers who designed and built the furnaces for a company called Topf and Sons. Historian Gerald Fleming recently uncovered a transcript of their interrogation by the Russians. On March 5, 1946, Kurt Pruefer, one of the four, was asked:

How often and with what aim did you visit Auschwitz?

Answer. Five times. The first time [was] at the beginning of 1943, to receive the orders of the SS Command, where the "Kremas" were to be built. The second time [was] in spring 1943 to inspect the building site. The third time was in autumn 1943 to inspect a fault in the construction of a "Krema" chimney. The fourth time [was] at the beginning of 1944, to inspect the repaired chimney. The fifth time [was] in September-October 1944 when I visited Auschwitz in connection with the intended relocation [from Auschwitz] of the crematoriums, since the front was getting nearer. The crematoriums were not relocated, because there were not enough workers. . . .

Q. Did you see a gas chamber next to the crematorium?

A. Yes, I did see one next to the crematorium. Between the gas chamber and the crematorium there was a connecting structure.

Q. Did you know that in the gas chambers and the crematoriums there took place the liquidations of innocent human beings?

A. I have known since spring 1943 that innocent human beings were being liquidated in Auschwitz gas chambers and that their corpses were subsequently incinerated in the crematoriums. . . .

Q. Why was the brick lining of the muffles so quickly damaged?

A. The bricks were damaged after six months because the strain on the furnaces was colossal.

Q. What motivated you to continue with the building of the other crematoriums as senior engineer with Topf?

A. I had my contract with the Topf firm and I was aware of the fact that my work was of great importance for the national socialist state. I knew that if I refused to continue with this work, I would be liquidated by the Gestapo.

On March 7, the Russians also questioned Fritz Sander about the crematoriums. He expressed concern about the strain on the furnaces.

I decided to design and build a crematorium with a higher capacity. I completed this project . . . and I submitted [it] to a State Patent Commission in Berlin.

This "Krema" was to be built on the conveyor belt principle. That is to say, the corpses must be brought to the incineration furnaces without interruption. When the corpses are pushed into the furnaces, they fall onto a grate, then slide into the furnace and are incinerated. The corpses serve at the same time as fuel for the heating of the furnaces. . . .

Q. Although you knew about the mass liquidation of innocent human beings in crematoriums, you devoted yourself to designing and creating higher capacity incineration furnaces for crematoriums—and on your own initiative.

A. I was a German engineer and key member of the Topf works and I saw it as my duty to apply my specialist knowledge in this way in order to help Germany win the war, just as an aircraft construction engineer builds airplanes in wartime, which are also connected with the destruction of human beings. [Mr. Sander's design was never carried out.][8]

CONNECTIONS

Physicians are bound by the Hippocratic oath. It is a vow to help the sick and abstain from any act that may be harmful to the patient or that has an ulterior motive. The oath specifically prohibits the giving of deadly medicine or poison to anyone or suggesting that others give it. What responsibility does a physician have to his or her patients? To society?

To what extent were doctors and health-care professionals in the Third Reich guided by ideology rather than the interests of medicine and their patients? What aspects of their training may have led Nazi doctors and other health professionals to overemphasize techniques and medical technology at the expense of patient care?

The Americans also tried sixteen Nazi jurists, including an acting minister of justice, who drafted the special regulations that deprived many people of the basic rights of a fair trial, ordered their indefinite transfer to concentration camps, and ultimately deprived them of life. They also tried prosecutors who charged and judges who condemned individuals to death on trumped-up charges. The court declared that the judges hid the "murderer's knife" beneath their judicial robes. What did they mean? What is a judge's responsibility? How did the judge Alexander describes violate that responsibility?

Just a few years after the trials, American scientists and physicians secretly experimented on prisoners and mentally retarded children to discover the effects of radiation. Most Americans knew nothing of the tests until Energy Secretary Hazel O'Leary opened the records to the public in 1993. Use newspapers and magazines to research the story that reporters then discovered. Many have argued that the experiments violated people's trust by failing to get their consent. How would you judge those scientists and physicians?

➤The Facing History Resource Center has a copy of Jean-Claude Pressac's *Auschwitz—Techniques and Operation of the Gas Chambers*. It includes the actual plans for Auschwitz and a technical analysis of how the gas chambers and crematoria worked. Also available is a video of the panel on medical ethics at the First Annual Facing History Conference. Robert Lifton gave the main presentation with comments by Steven Chorover, La Vonne Veatch, and George Annas. In addition, the Resource Center has papers and photographs from the Doctors' Trial at Nuremberg, donated by Leo Alexander. The material includes comprehensive information on female victims of leg experiments at Ravensbrueck. Some of that information has been included in the educational packet, "Questions of Medical Ethics During the Holocaust." It contains eyewitness accounts of experiments conducted in the camps, testimonies, and an excerpt from Leo Alexander's 1949 article, "Medical Science under a Dictatorship."

READING 9

Less than Slaves

Albert Speer, Hitler's favorite architect, was among the twenty-two Nazi leaders tried at Nuremberg. He also served as minister for armaments and munitions. In that role he was responsible for all assignments to prisoner-of-war, work, and concentration camps. At the trial, Speer pictured himself as shortsighted, even deluded, and described his partnership with Hitler as a pact with the devil. He told the tribunal, "The trial is necessary. There is a common responsibility for such horrible crimes, even in an authoritarian system." He insisted, however, that he could not be held accountable for the death camps, because he was unaware of their existence.

Speer was sentenced to twenty years in prison for his role in the Third Reich. His testimony and government records later led to the indictment of a number of German executives, including the top officials at I. G. Farben Company. Their indictment stated in part:

> Farben, in complete defiance of all decency and human considerations, abused its slave workers by subjecting them, among other things, to excessively long, arduous, and exhausting work, utterly disregarding their health or physical condition. The sole criterion of the right to live or die was the production efficiency of said inmates. By virtue of inadequate rest, inadequate food (which was given to the

inmates while in bed at the barracks), and because of inadequate quarters (which consisted of a bed of polluted straw, shared by from two to four inmates), many died at their work or collapsed from serious illness there contracted. With the first signs of a decline in the production of any such workers, although caused by illness or exhaustion, such workers would be subjected to the well-known "Selektion." Selektion, in its simplest definition, meant that if, upon a cursory examination, it appeared that the inmate would not be restored within a few days to full productive capacity, he was considered expendable and was sent to the "Birkenau" camp at Auschwitz for the customary extermination. The meaning of Selektion and Birkenau was known to everyone at Auschwitz. . . .

The working conditions at the Farben Buna plant were so severe and unendurable that very often inmates were driven to suicide by either dashing through the guards and provoking death by rifle shot, or hurling themselves into the high tension electrically charged barbed wire fences. As a result of these conditions, the labor turnover in the Buna plant in one year amounted to at least 300 percent. Besides those who were exterminated and committed suicide, up to and sometimes over 100 persons died at their work every day from sheer exhaustion. All depletions occasioned by extermination and other means of death were balanced by replacement with new inmates. Thus, Farben secured a continuous supply of fresh inmates in order to maintain full production.

A man forced to work for Krupp Munitions testified, "We were not slaves but less than slaves. We were deprived of freedom and became a piece of property which our masters drove to work. But here all similarity with any known form of slavery ends. . . . The machinery had to be operated with care, oiled, greased, and allowed to rest; its life span was protected. We, on the other hand, were like a bit of sandpaper which, rubbed a few times becomes useless and is thrown away to be burned with the garbage."[9]

In his book *Less than Slaves,* Benjamin Ferencz, who served as an American prosecutor at Nuremberg, notes:

Well over half a million inmates were leased out by the SS to hundreds of German firms by the end of 1944. The workers included Germans who might have committed some minor infraction, Communists, Socialists, other political opponents of the Nazi regime, priests, Seventh Day Adventists, as well as homosexuals, 'asocials,' and common criminals. . . . As a class, there can be no doubt that the Jews suffered most of all, but in focusing on their claims, I have not wished to minimize the suffering of all the others. . . . Jews were regarded as contagious vermin by their Nazi oppressors, and were treated accordingly. They were given the most strenuous and most dangerous work. Jews who could not work were either dead or about to die.[10]

Ferencz points out that although some industrialists were tried and convicted, most were free within a few years and richer than ever. Although some survivors sued German companies, settlements were very small. And no firm ever acknowledged guilt.

CONNECTIONS

Albert Speer claimed that no industrialist was ever forced to use concentration camp labor and there is considerable evidence to support his statement. Why then did many choose to do so? Were they all guilty of war crimes? Crimes against humanity? Would your answers be different if they had been forced to use slave labor?

Compare the actions of officials at I. G. Farben and Krupp with those of Oskar Schindler (Chapter 8, Reading 12). If he could save the lives of his employees, why couldn't others do the same?

Speer is often viewed as the only Nazi at Nuremberg to admit his guilt. But did he admit guilt or just take responsibility? What is the difference between the two? In 1981, shortly after Speer's death, Mel London wrote a letter that appeared in the *New York Times*. It said in part:

> A few years back, I spent 10 days with Albert Speer in Heidelberg, producing a series of television interviews. During one interview, held on Speer's lawn, I began a question, "You were the only person at Nuremberg to admit his guilt. . . " and he stopped me with, "I did not admit guilt—I said I was responsible."
>
> For all these years, I have mulled over his answer, not sure where his legal and ethical culpability ended and his responsibility began. I have come to the conclusion that Speer was a clever survivor who knew exactly what he was doing when he was on trial at Nuremberg, and I also agree that he was never truly repentant about his role in the Third Reich. . . .
>
> He was a charming, though methodical man. He knew exactly what he was doing, and his answers had been well thought out during his 20 years in Spandau.[11]

In a film based on Speer's journals, the director had to add a character. The character was Speer's mother. Her role was to ask the moral questions. She served as a guide to what was good and what was evil. The director feared that without that character American audiences would find Speer so attractive that they would fail to notice the evil acts he committed.

➤Available from the Facing History Resource Center are a paper on the Nuremberg trials by Benjamin Ferencz and a video of a talk he gave at the First Annual conference.

Toward International Standards

*I*n 1945, the United States, Britain, the Soviet Union, and the recently liberated France divided Germany into four zones of occupation. Each nation held war-crimes trials in its zone. Together, Britain, France, and the United States convicted over five thousand Nazis and sentenced eight hundred to death. The Soviets held similar trials but did not release statistics. The Allies also extradited many Nazis to nations once occupied by Germany. The Poles and the Czechs, for instance, tried, convicted, and executed Rudolf Hoess, the commandant of Auschwitz; Arthur Greiser, the man who set up the first death camp at Chelmno; Juergen Stroop, the SS leader who liquidated the Warsaw Ghetto; and Kurt Daluege, the head of the German police. The Belgians convicted 75 Nazis; the Luxembourgers 68; the Dutch 204; the Danes and the Norwegians 80 each; and the Poles thousands.

Some nations in Nazi-occupied Europe also brought to trial leaders who collaborated with the Nazis. The Norwegians convicted Prime Minister Vidkun Quisling and the French Henri-Philippe Petain and Pierre Laval. The war-crimes trials also extended to Asia. U.S. General Douglas MacArthur created an international tribunal to bring key Japanese offenders to justice. A number of nations occupied by Japan during the war also held their own trials.

These trials reflected a heightened commitment to international standards of behavior in wartime. Known as the "Principles of International Law Recognized in the Charter of the Nuremberg Tribunal and in the Judgment of the Tribunal," they were affirmed unanimously by the first General Assembly of the United Nations.

Principle I

Any person who commits an act which constitutes a crime under international law is responsible therefore and liable to punishment.

Principle II

The fact that internal law does not impose a penalty for an act which constitutes a crime under international law does not relieve the person who committed the act from responsibility under international law.

Principle III

The fact that a person who committed an act which constitutes a crime under international law acted as Head of State or responsible government official does not relieve him from responsibility under international law.

Principle IV

The fact that a person acted pursuant to order of his Government or of a superior does not relieve him from responsibility under international law, provided a moral choice was in fact possible to him.

Principle V

Any person charged with a crime under international law has the right to a fair trial on the facts and law.

Principle VI

The crimes hereinafter set out are punishable as crimes under international law:

a. Crimes against peace:

(1) Planning, preparation, initiation or waging of a war of aggression or a war in violation of international treaties, agreements or assurances;

(2) Participation in a common plan or conspiracy for the accomplishment of any of the acts mentioned under (1).

b. War crimes:

Violations of the laws or customs of war which include, but are not limited to, murder, ill-treatment or deportation to slave-labor or for any other purpose of civilian population of or in occupied territory, murder or ill-treatment of prisoners of war or persons on the seas, killing of hostages, plunder of public or private property, wanton destruction of cities, towns, or villages, or devastation not justified by military necessity.

c. Crimes against humanity:

Murder, extermination, enslavement, deportation and other inhuman acts done against any civilian population, or persecutions on political, racial or religious grounds, when such acts are done or such persecutions are carried on in connection with any crime against peace or any war crime.

Principle VII

Complicity in the commission of a crime against peace, a war crime, or a crime against humanity as set forth in PRINCIPLE VI is a crime under international law.

CONNECTIONS

Why were people like Quisling (whose name has become synonymous with traitor), Petain, and Laval tried by their own courts rather than in an international tribunal? Do you think it was fair to do so?

How does Principle II help explain why the judges at Nuremberg did not regard obedience as a defense?

Reread Principle IV. When is it not possible for a perpetrator to make a moral choice?

When Jackson opened the Nuremberg trials by stating, "We must never forget that the record on which we judge these defendants today is the record on which history will judge us tomorrow," many in the courtroom looked at the two Soviet judges. After all, the Russians had invaded Poland in 1939 and Finland in 1940 and were widely believed to be responsible for the massacre of thousands of Polish officers in the Katyn Forest. They were also responsible for the murder of thousands of their own citizens in the 1930s as part of Stalin's efforts to consolidate his control over the nation. But by 1970, Telford Taylor could sadly write that "now the wheel has spun full circle, and the fingers of accusation are pointed not at others. . . but at ourselves. Worse yet, many of the pointing fingers are our own. Voices of the rich and poor and black and white, strident voices and scholarly voices, all speaking our own tongue, raise question of the legality under the Nuremberg principles of our military actions in Vietnam, and in Cambodia."[12]

Use a recent history book to research the Vietnam War to find out why Telford Taylor made the statement. In the early 1990s, they pointed toward Bosnia. A number of American and European leaders demanded that government leaders responsible for the nation's policy of "ethnic cleansing" stand trial. To whom do the "fingers of accusation" point today? As a research assignment, find current examples of abuses of power that have led individuals and nations to call for international trials.

Professor Henry Huttenbach of City College of New York wonders whether leaders have learned from the past. He writes:

> So far there are few signs that the training groups of those professions that participated in the genocide have taken radical steps to examine themselves in depth. Where is there a Medical School which asks graduates to swear the Hippocratic Oath in the light of the Mengele Syndrome [named for the notorious Nazi doctor who experimented on twins in the death camps]? Where is there a Law School mentioning the dangers of legalism as a path to genocide? What Schools of Business include in their curriculum a case study of I. G. Farben and its pursuit of profit all the way to Auschwitz? Is there a seminary that asks about the final implications of the martyrdom of the Jewish People? Do Schools of International Law and Diplomacy teach the merits of drafting anti-genocide [laws]? Not until a Holocaust conscious elite permeates western society will it be possible to speak of an historical encounter with the Holocaust.[13]

What evidence can you find in the news that leaders have not yet come to terms with the questions Huttenbach asks? Is he right to stress the importance of training the elite—a nation's leaders—or should every citizen in a society examine himself or herself "in depth?"

READING 11

"Making Good Again"

After the war, the Allies had to deal not only with questions of guilt and innocence but also with questions of restitution. What claims did the victims have on the perpetrators? On Germany itself?

The Allied Military Government in Germany tried to answer those questions by requiring that all property seized by the Nazis or transferred to them by force be returned to its rightful owners. If the rightful owner had died and left no heir, the property was to be used to aid survivors of Nazi persecution. Then in 1949, disagreements among the Allies led to the division of Germany. France, the United States, and Britain combined their zones into the Federal Republic of Germany (West Germany). The Soviet Union turned its zone of occupation into the German Democratic Republic (East Germany) at about the same time. Although both Germanies tried former Nazis for war crimes, only West Germany tried to make restitution for wrongs committed during the war.

In 1951, West Germany declared that "unspeakable crimes had been committed in the name of the German people which entails an obligation to make moral and material amends" and promised to make reparations to both the state of Israel and various Jewish organizations involved in the resettlement and rehabilitation of survivors. In 1953, West Germany also set up a special program to compensate all those who suffered injury or discrimination "because of their opposition to National Socialism or because of their race, creed, or ideology." The program is known in German as "*Wiedergutmachung*," which means "making good again."

To be eligible, an individual had to prove that he or she had been persecuted for racial, religious, or ideological reasons and suffered injuries that were not only disabling but also the direct result of persecution. These requirements excluded thousands who had suffered from Nazi brutality but could not meet the rigid burden of proof. It also excluded the 350,000 people who had undergone forced sterilization and families that lost loved ones as a result of the "euthanasia" program. Their applications were routinely turned down "because sterilization was not a form of persecution but was performed purely for medical reasons" and "the Law for the Prevention of Hereditary Diseases was not unconstitutional as such." Gays were denied compensation on similar grounds.

I hate the expression. What can one make good again? Absolutely nothing. One can pay damages.

The Sinti and Roma were also excluded. On January 7, 1956, a West German court ruled that the deportation of twenty-five hundred "Gypsies" from Hamburg, Bremen, Cologne, Duesseldorf, Stuttgart, and Frankfurt in May, 1940, was not a result of racial discrimination but a "security measure." Other rulings argued that "Gypsies" were not targeted because of race but because they were "work shy" or "asocial."

Dietrich Goldschmidt, a minister in the Confessing Church who was imprisoned at Dachau, said of *Wiedergutmachung*:

> I hate the expression. What can one make good again? Absolutely nothing. One can pay damages . . . .
>
> I find it a particular scandal that an entire group of special cases have not yet received damages. . . whether it's the Mengele twins [the twins on whom Josef Mengele experimented] or the socially persecuted, whether it's the gypsies or the Jews in Israel, who according to the regional principle, haven't received anything—the Polish Jews who were in Auschwitz or Theresienstadt receive no reparations. . . .
>
> One can best compare reparations for the war victims with the pensions of former career soldiers. The pensions of former career soldiers, including the SS increase very regularly, just as all pensions increase.[14]

A German who took part in the resistance and later worked in the reparations office confirmed Goldschmidt's charges. Helene Jacobs told an interviewer, "I stood fairly alone among my colleagues. I tried to do everything for the benefit of the persecuted. The tendency was more to reject all claims—that was also easier, according to the law, and they wanted to act only according to the law."[15]

Many of Jacobs' co-workers had served in the Third Reich. Soon after its establishment, West Germany passed a law guaranteeing employment to any member of the Nazi civil service who applied. The few who were ineligible often received generous pensions. For example, although Franz Schlegelberger, an undersecretary in the Nazis' ministry of justice, was sentenced to life in prison after the war, he won his freedom in 1951. Soon after, he was awarded a large pension and received back pay for time spent in prison. In *Hitler's Justice,* Ingo Mueller tells of a Nazi judge who "was named presiding judge of a board in Hamburg to hear the cases of war victims claiming damages; here he decided claims filed by the survivors of his own earlier trials, and by the relatives of those he had sentenced to death."

CONNECTIONS

The word *reparations* refers to the process of making amends. Why do you think it often involves a financial payment? Was West Germany right to make reparations? Can a nation be guilty of crimes? Can a nation be held responsible for the crimes its leaders commit?

What does *Wiedergutmachung* suggest about the difficulty of erasing Nazi influences in government? Should the government have refused to hire former Nazi officials?

After the United States declared war against Japan, 120,000 Japanese Americans who lived on the West Coast were shipped to detention camps. Many lost homes and businesses. Yet no Japanese American was ever found guilty of sabotage or treason. When Japanese Americans challenged the legality of the camps, the Supreme Court ruled in 1944 that it was a valid use of the nation's war powers. It would take forty years before the United States government agreed to make reparations. Why do you think it took so long? How was the American government's response to Japanese Americans similar to that of the German government's response to Jews, "Gypsies," and other victims of discrimination? What differences seem most striking?

READING 12

Levi Versus Mertens

*I*n earlier chapters, Raul Hilberg used the German railroad as an example of the "bureaucratic structure serving the extermination." He pointed out, "The civilian railroad workers involved in operating rails to Auschwitz were simply performing their daily tasks. These were individual people making individual decisions. They were not ordered or even assigned." Primo Levi, like many survivors of the Holocaust, wondered about "those individual people making individual decisions."

> It might be surprising that in the Camps one of the most frequent states of mind was curiosity. And yet, besides being frightened, humiliated, and desperate, we were curious: hungry for bread and also to understand. The world around us was upside down and so somebody must have turned it upside down, and for that reason he himself must have been upside down: one, a thousand, a million antihuman beings created to twist that which was straight, to befoul that which was clean. It was an unpermissible simplification, but at that time and in that place we were not capable of complex ideas.
>
> As regards the lords of evil, this curiosity, which is not limited to the Nazi chiefs, still lingers. Hundreds of books have come out on the psychology of Hitler, Stalin, Himmler, Goebbels, and I have read dozens of them and been left unsatisfied: but probably it is a matter here of the essential inadequacy of documentary evidence. It almost never has the power to give us the depths of a human being; for this purpose the dramatist or poet are more appropriate than the historian or psychologist.

He was an almost-me, another myself, turned upside down. . . . Potentially two colleagues: in fact we worked in the same factory, but I was inside the barbed wire and he outside.

Nevertheless, this search of mine has not been entirely fruitless: a strange, indeed provocative fate some years ago put me on the track of "someone on the other side," not certainly one of the greats of evil, perhaps not even a fully qualified villain, but nevertheless a specimen and a witness. A witness in spite of himself, who did not want to be one, but who has testified without wanting to, and perhaps even unknowingly. Those who bear witness by their behavior are the most valuable witnesses, because they are certainly truthful.

He was an almost-me, another myself, turned upside down. We were contemporaries, not dissimilar in education, perhaps not even in character. He, Mertens, was a young chemist, German and Catholic, and I a young chemist, Italian and Jewish. Potentially two colleagues: in fact we worked in the same factory, but I was inside the barbed wire and he outside. However, there were forty thousand of us employed in the Buna Works at Auschwitz. That the two of us, he an Oberingenieur and I a slave-chemist, ever met is improbable, and in any case no longer verifiable, nor did we ever see each other later on.

Whatever I know about him comes from letters of mutual friends. The world turns out to be laughably small at times, small enough to permit two chemists from different countries to find themselves linked by a chain of acquaintances who help to weave a network of exchanged information, which is a poor substitute for a direct encounter but still better than mutual ignorance. By such means I learned that Mertens had read my books about the Camp and, in all likelihood, others as well, because he was neither cynical nor insensitive. He tended to block out a certain segment of his past, but was intelligent enough to keep from lying to himself. He did not make himself a gift of lies, but blanks, lacunae.

The first report I have of him goes back to the end of 1941, a period of rethinking for all Germans still capable of reasoning and resisting propaganda. The victorious Japanese are overrunning all of Southeast Asia, the Germans are laying siege to Leningrad and are at the doors of Moscow, but the era of the blitzes is over, the collapse of Russia has not taken place. Instead, aerial bombings of the German cities have begun. Now the war involves everybody. In every family there is at least one man at the front, and no man at the front is sure any longer of the safety of his family: behind the house doors, warmongering rhetoric no longer carries much weight.

Mertens is a chemist in a metropolitan rubber factory, and the manager of the firm makes him a proposal that is almost an order: he will find career, and perhaps also political, advantages if he accepts an offer to transfer to the Buna Works at Auschwitz. It's a tranquil zone, far removed from the front and outside the range of the bombers. The work is the same, the salary better, and there will be no difficulty about housing: many Polish houses are empty. . . . Mertens talks it over with his colleagues. Most of them advise against it; one doesn't exchange the certain for the uncertain, and besides, the Buna Works are in an ugly, marshy, and unhealthy region. Unhealthy even historically, Upper Silesia is one of those corners of Europe that have changed masters too many times and are inhabited by mixed peoples, hostile to one another.

But no one has objections to the name Auschwitz: it is still an empty name that does not provoke echoes; one of the many Polish towns which have changed their names since the German occupation. Oswiecim has become Auschwitz, as if that is enough to change into German the Poles who have lived there for centuries. It is a small town like many others.

Mertens thinks about it; he is engaged and to set up a household in Germany, under the bombings, would be foolhardy. He asks for a short leave and goes to have a look. What he thought during this first survey is not known: the man went back, got married, spoke to no one, and left again for Auschwitz with wife and furniture to settle down there. His friends, those in fact who wrote the story for me, asked him to speak but he remains silent.

Nor did he speak the second time he was seen in Germany, in the summer of 1943, on vacation (because even in wartime in Nazi Germany, people went on vacation in August). Now the scenario has changed: Italian fascism, defeated on all fronts, has come apart and the Allies are pushing up the peninsula. The aerial battle against the British is lost and by now no corner of Germany is spared from pitiless Allied retaliation. Not only did the Russians not collapse but at Stalingrad they inflicted on the Germans and on Hitler himself, who directed the operations with the obstinacy of a madman, the most scathing defeat.

The Mertens couple are the objects of very guarded curiosity, because at this point despite all precautions Auschwitz is no longer an empty name. There have been rumors, imprecise but sinister: it must be put alongside Dachau and Buchenwald. It seems that it may even be worse. It is one of those places about which it is risky to ask questions, but after all, we're all intimate friends here, from way back; Mertens has come from the place, he surely must know something, and if he does he should say so.

But, while all the living-room conversations interweave, the women talking about evacuations and black market, the men about their work, and someone in a whisper tells the latest anti-Nazi joke, Mertens goes off by himself. In the next room there is a piano; he plays and drinks, returns to the living room now and again, only to pour himself another glass. By midnight he is drunk but his host has not lost sight of him; he drags him to the table and says to him loud and clear, "Now you're going to sit down here and tell us what the hell is happening down there, and why you have to get drunk instead of talking to us."

Mertens feels torn between intoxication, caution, and a certain need to confess. "Auschwitz is a Camp," he says, "actually a group of Camps, one is right next to the plant. There are men and women, filthy, ragged, they don't speak German. And they do the most exhausting work. We are not allowed to talk to them."

"Who says you can't?"

"Management. When we arrived we were told that they are dangerous, bandits and subversives."

"And you have never talked to them?" asks the host.

"No," Mertens replies, pouring himself another drink.

Here young Mrs. Mertens joins in: "I met a woman who cleaned the manager's house. All she said to me was 'Frau, Brot. . . Lady, bread'. . . but I. . . ."

Mertens mustn't have been all that drunk after all because he says brusquely to his wife: "Stop it!" and, turning to the others: "Would you mind changing the subject?"

I don't know much about Mertens's behavior after the collapse of Germany. I do know that he and his wife, like many other Germans of the eastern regions, fled before the Soviets down the interminable roads of defeat, covered with snow, rubble, and corpses, and that afterwards he went back to his profession of technician, but refusing all contacts and withdrawing more and more into himself.

He spoke a little more, many years after the end of the war, when there was no more Gestapo to frighten him. This time he was questioned by a "specialist," an ex-prisoner who today is a famous historian of the Camps, Hermann Langbein. In reply to precise questions, he said he had agreed to move to Auschwitz to prevent a Nazi from going in his place, that for fear of punishment he had never spoken to the prisoners, but had always tried to alleviate their working conditions; that at that time he knew nothing about the gas chambers because he had not asked anyone about anything. Didn't he realize that his obedience was a concrete help to the Hitler regime? Yes, today he did, but not at the time. It had never entered his mind.

I never tried to meet Mertens. I felt a complex reluctance, of which aversion was only one component. Years ago I wrote him a letter; I told him that if Hitler had risen to power, devastated Europe and brought Germany to ruin, it was because many good German citizens behaved the way he did, trying not to see and keeping silent about what they did see. Mertens never answered me, and he died a few years later.[16]

CONNECTIONS

Draw an identity chart for Mertens in 1942. What changes would you make in his chart after he spoke with Langbein? Draw a similar chart for Levi. What changes would you make in his chart after Auschwitz? Thirty years later? How do the various charts help explain why Levi claims that Mertens was "almost me"?

Was Mertens guilty? Was he responsible for war crimes? How did Levi judge Mertens's behavior? Do you agree with his assessment? What factors most influenced your judgments? Is a conscience a personal matter? Or is there an international conscience? What is the difference been responsibility and guilt? Should Mertens have been brought to trial?

READING 13

On Trial

In 1964, Horst Krueger, a German journalist, attended a trial held in Frankfurt. He arrived late because he could not find a parking place.

> As always happens when you arrive at a movie or play after it has started, I sat there a little perplexed and benumbed and could not find my place in the plot. So this is it, this is the famous Auschwitz trial, and I distinctly felt a little disappointment rising in me. I had thought it would be different, harsher, more dignified, more dramatic—the prosecution in tall chairs, and the accused on low benches. I remembered the Nuremberg trials. . . . Those proceedings had an element of stature and drama: Day of Judgment, nemesis, the tribunal and the verdict of history. Where was it here?
>
> I found myself seated in a medium-sized pleasantly middle-class hall in which a board of inquiry was clearly in session. The room was about a hundred and twenty yards long and forty yards wide, with walls paneled in wood all the way up to the ceiling—pale brown, cheap wood. Green draperies concealed a stage to the right, with a large relief map representing the camp of Auschwitz mounted next to it. Eight lamps reminiscent of the stiff modernism of the 1930s lit the high-ceilinged room. On the main wall hung the blue, red, and white coats of arms of the nation and the city.
>
> The hall, the solid administrative furniture—slightly clumsy benches and lighter, modern chairs—and even the faces of the judges seated under the coat of arms radiated solid middle-class spirit, respectable calm and paternalism. . . . The presiding officer was a short, stocky, round-headed gentlemen perhaps in his late fifties. He sat behind huge piles of documents, and sometimes he turned a page or two. To the right and left of him sat the other two judges, one of them young, the other very old; they too turned the pages of documents. A voice came over the loudspeaker.

Some chased after money and others attended the Auschwitz trials, some covered up and others uncovered. These were two sides of the same German coin. This Hitler, I thought, remains with us—all the days of our lives.

I looked around the hall for the defendants, but I could not find them. I looked for the witness stand, but I could not locate it. I had a good seat, I could see everything, but it all seemed so strange, so incomprehensible and confused. There were about a hundred and twenty or a hundred and thirty Germans in this chamber, citizens of our nation, Federal Republican Germans of the year 1964, and I could not tell who here actually were the accusers and who the accused.

Over the loudspeaker the voice, somewhat dusky and blurred, cut through the room. It must be the voice of the witness, and since I could not yet identify the roles being acted out here, I decided simply to listen. The voice said, "Birkenau was divided into three parts, BI, BII, and BIII." After a pause it continued. "And then there was the mysterious BIIb Division, a mystery in this hell, a segment of Auschwitz where women and children and men lived together, did not have their heads shaved. The children were given milk and had a nursery school." After another pause the voice added, "But the bitter end came for them as well. Six months after their arrival, the more than three thousand residents of BIIb were suddenly gassed."

A few moments later the voice rang from the loudspeaker again. "I will now describe my own arrival in Auschwitz. . . . Over the gate through which they marched us were written, Work Liberates. There was waltz music to the left, a band was practicing. It never occurred to us that we were going to be sent to hell. Everything looked so peaceful, so calm."

Krueger listened as an unseen witness told of how he was saved from the gas chamber only to become a doctor in a section of the camp. As the man spoke, Krueger wondered:

To have lived in Auschwitz for five years—to have survived Auschwitz—meant not only to have suffered for five years but also to have become accustomed to it, to have made one's peace with it, to have come to terms with it, with indifference, coldness, even one's own wickedness in the face of the misery of the lost.

Horrifying confirmation: man is the product of his environment. In the city of death, everyone becomes a supporting player. Whether you hand out bread or gas, you are a part of it. . . . An incomprehensible, raging will to survive must have ruled the man with the voice—I won't die, not me, I will survive. . . . To eat, to drink, to obey, to work, to participate, not to go under, to endure—endure in order to bear witness some day to what man did to man in this place. The time would come; it would take twenty years, it would be February 27, 1964, it would be in Frankfurt. . . . The hour of truth has arrived.

As the witness continued, Krueger was startled by a word he had not heard in years. The word was *Sanka*. As he struggled to recall where he had heard the term before, the voice said, "Most of them were hosed down with phenol in the Sankas." Suddenly Krueger remembered. *Sanka* was the word soldiers used to refer to an ambulance. Krueger himself drove one on the Eastern front.

> I drove my Sanka to the central field dressing station in Smolensk. I was simply following orders, like seventy million other Germans. All of us were simply following orders. But what would have happened if my travel orders had accidentally borne not the word Smolensk but that other word—the unknown, meaningless Auschwitz? How would it have been? Of course I would have taken my wounded there as well; of course—a soldier always does as he is ordered. I would have taken them to Auschwitz and perhaps I would have delivered them to the very prison doctor who was now bearing witness. One or two hundred wounded a day for the medical barracks in Auschwitz—that wasn't a lot.
>
> And then? What else would I have done? It could hardly have escaped my notice that the business there was not curing but killing. What would I have done?

As Krueger tried to decide what he would have done, someone opened a window as a streetcar rumbled by.

> The squeaking and humming of the streetcar mingled strangely with the voice from the loudspeaker, which now spoke of children who, because the gas was scarce, were thrown alive into the fire. "There is no other way to make our quota," the directive from above had read. And they wanted to make their quota—of course. I felt fear and horror rising in me. Outside the 18 Line was rolling past, and here, inside, the Day of Judgment was happening. And I—where was I? Where did I stand?
>
> I came as a stranger, a German journalist; all I wanted was to be a spectator. But as I followed the voice again, I felt that no one could remain a spectator here.

When the court recessed for a few minutes, Krueger saw a fellow reporter and asked him where the defendants were.

> My colleague looked at me in astonishment. He smiled ironically, put his hand to his mouth as if he were about to whisper, and answered, "Hey, man, can't you see? Right here, right next to you, back there. Those men in the armchairs, and those over there by the window, and the one at the checkroom counter. All over."
>
> Then, for the first time, I understood that all these amiable people in the chamber, whom I took to be journalists or lawyers or spectators, that they were the defendants, and that of course there was no way to tell them from the rest of us. . . . Like me, they had parked their cars outside the building. They come to the trial just like me. There was nothing to distinguish them.

I came as a stranger, a German journalist; all I wanted was to be a spectator. But as I followed the voice again, I felt that no one could remain a spectator here.

Krueger stared at the men in horror. He wrote:

> I was aghast to find that murderers look like this—so harmless, so amiable and fatherly. But then I realized that these goodnatured gentlemen were not the usual kind of murderers, not people who commit crimes of passion, who kill someone in a fit of temper or out of lust or desperation. All those are human motives. There are such things. But the men here are modern murderers, a breed unknown until now, the administrators and bureaucrats of mass death, the bookkeepers and button pushers and clerks of the machinery, technicians who operate without hatred or feeling. . . desk-chair murderers. Here a new style of crime became manifest: death as administrative action.

Krueger's colleague told him the defendants were all respected citizens. There was nothing to single them out as murderers. As the trial continued, Krueger concluded: "Hitler still ruled in the dark, underground: somehow he had made a crack in all of us. Some chased after money and others attended the Auschwitz trials, some covered up and others uncovered. These were two sides of the same German coin. This Hitler, I thought, remains with us—all the days of our lives."[17]

CONNECTIONS

Why was Krueger unable to tell the defendants from the spectators? Why did his inability shock him? Would it have shocked you? What does Krueger mean when he concludes, "I felt that no one could remain a spectator here."

Ten years after his book was published, Krueger wrote, "The value I assign to self-cleansing, to cleaning house, seems to me not to have changed in the course of my life. The message of the key sentence in this book, at the very end—'This Hitler, I think, remains with us—all the days of our lives'—still holds true." What is Krueger saying about himself and other Germans? About guilt and innocence? Do you agree?

Journalist Gitta Sereny was able to do what Krueger could not do. She interviewed one of the "bureaucrats of mass death," Franz Stangl—the commandant of Sobibor and Treblinka. She recorded that interview in her book, *Into That Darkness*. Chapter 7, Reading 17 contains excerpts from her interview. Do those excerpts answer Krueger's questions? Do they answer your own questions or do they raise new ones?

In "The Hangman at Home," American poet Carl Sandburg wonders how the hangman gets through his day. What does he think about? Is everything "easy for a hangman"?

What does the hangman think about
When he goes home at night from work?
When he sits down with his wife and
Children for a cup of coffee and a
Plate of ham and eggs, do they ask
Him if it was a good day's work
And everything went well or do they
Stay off some topics and talk about
The weather, baseball, politics
And the comic strips in the papers
And the movies? Do they look at his
Hands when he reaches for the coffee
Or the ham and eggs? If the little
Ones say, Daddy, play horse, here's
A rope—does he answer like a joke:
I seen enough rope for today?
Or does his face light up like a
Bonfire of joy and does he say:
It's a good and dandy world we live
In. And if a white face moon looks
In through a window where a baby girl
Sleeps and the moon-gleams mix with
Baby ears and baby hair—the hangman—
How does he act then? It must be easy
For him. Anything is easy for a hangman,
I guess.[18]

Franz Stangl said of his victims, "I rarely saw them as individuals. It was always a huge mass." How did that attitude help Stangl in his role as commandant? How was he like the hangman in Sandburg's poem? What differences seem most striking?

➤ Reread "The Hangman" by Maurice Ogden (Chapter 4, Reading 23) or replay the video. Was Stangl the hangman? Or was he one of the townspeople? Judge the hangman. Is he guilty? Is he responsible? What about the townspeople? Were they guilty? Were they responsible?

Justice Avoided

Many Nazi leaders disappeared at the end of the war. Some were aided by relatives and friends with international connections. Others were smuggled into the Middle East or South America by sympathetic priests. A few got help from former SS officers who formed an alumni group of sorts—*Organisation Der Ehemaligen SS-Angehoerigen* (Organization of Former SS Members). As the result of a novel by Frederick Forsyth, the group is better known by its initials—ODESSA.

For a few Nazis with special interests and abilities, help came from their former enemies. Even before the war ended, the Soviet Union and its former allies were at odds. Some Nazis saw an opportunity in the growing division among the Allies to barter their expertise for freedom. Both the United States and the Soviet Union were eager to recruit Nazi scientists. American officials were even willing to alter the files of Nazi medical researchers and physicists to help them gain admission to the United States. Among them were scientists who helped the United States develop its rocket science program. The Americans also recruited Siegfried Ruff, who conducted experiments at Dachau on human survival capabilities at high altitudes. And both the British and the Americans struck deals with Nazis who had expertise as spies and undercover agents. The director of the American Joint Intelligence Objectives Agency justified their employment on the ground that there was no need to continue "beating a dead Nazi horse."

CONNECTIONS

What role did the rivalry between the United States and the Soviet Union play in the process of bringing accused Nazis to justice? Why did it affect that process ?

Were the Allies right to recruit former Nazis? Why would Nazis work for a former enemy? How loyal would they be to their new employers?

By 1960, the war was over for 15 years. Was it time to stop "beating a dead Nazi horse"? Should there a statute of limitations on war crimes?

Eichmann in Jerusalem

Adolf Eichmann was an Austrian who moved to Germany in 1933 and quickly made himself the nation's leading "expert" on the "Jewish Question." By the time of the Wannsee Conference in 1942, he was the chief organizer of what became the "Final Solution." Much of his work, however, took place behind the scenes. As a result, the Allies knew little about him. Few people were even aware of what he looked like.

While the Allies were trying Goering and other top Nazis officials, Eichmann was hiding in a prisoner-of-war camp. When he learned that his name had emerged at the Nuremberg trial, he quickly left the camp. By the summer of 1950, he had settled in Argentina under the name "Ricardo Klement." He arrived there under a passport issued by the Vatican to "displaced persons." His wife and sons later joined him.

Long after other nations had lost interest in punishing the Nazis, Israel remained committed to finding every individual who had escaped judgment. Eichmann was one of the nation's main targets. A tip in 1957 led the Israelis to Argentina. In May of 1960, they kidnapped Eichmann and then smuggled him into Israel to stand trial. In February 1961, he was indicted on fifteen counts, including "crimes against the Jewish people," "crimes against humanity," "war crimes," and "membership in a hostile organization." At his trial, which began in April, Gideon Hausner, Israel's attorney general, called over one hundred witnesses and entered sixteen hundred documents into evidence. Eichmann's lawyer, Robert Servatius, did not dispute the facts of the Holocaust as presented by Hausner. Instead, he defended Eichmann as a loyal bureaucrat.

In reply to his attorney's questions about the Wannsee Conference (Chapter 7, Reading 5), Eichmann argued that the meeting proved his innocence. "I could, thanks to the Wannsee Conference, say to myself, declare myself. . . that I am not to blame, like Pontius Pilate who had washed his hands, I am innocent. For at that conference hard and fast rules were laid by the elite, the leadership, by the Popes of the Kingdom. And myself? I only had to obey!" At the end of the trial, Eichmann reaffirmed that belief, stating, "I am not the monster I am made out to be. I am the victim of a fallacy." The judges disagreed, finding him guilty on all counts. After an appeal failed, Eichmann was hung at midnight on May 31, 1962.

Hannah Arendt covered the trial as a journalist for the *New Yorker*, an American magazine. Although Eichmann's name had long been synonymous with evil, Arendt used the word *banal* to describe Eichmann and his deeds. She was trying to say that, in many ways, he was much as he was describing himself—a little man caught up in a big machine whose main

Arendt used the word *banal* to describe Eichmann and his deeds. She was trying to say that, in many ways, he was much as he was describing himself—a little man caught up in a big machine whose main crime was "thoughtlessness."

crime was "thoughtlessness." She was not suggesting that he was innocent. Instead she argued that the judges should have sentenced Eichmann
with these words.

> You told your story in terms of a hard-luck story, and, knowing the
> circumstances, we are, up to a point, willing to grant you that under
> more favorable circumstances it is highly unlikely that you would ever
> have come before us or before any other criminal court. Let us assume,
> for the sake of argument, that it was nothing more than misfortune that
> made you a willing instrument in the organization of mass murder;
> there still remains the fact that you have carried out, and therefore
> actively supported, a policy of mass murder. For politics is not like the
> nursery; in politics obedience and support are the same. And just as you
> supported and carried out a policy of not wanting to share the earth
> with the Jewish people and the people of a number of other nations—as
> though you and your superiors had any right to determine who should
> and who should not inhabit the world—we find that no one, that is, no
> member of the human race, can be expected to want to share the earth
> with you. This is the reason, and the only reason, you must hang.[19]

Arendt's observations sparked considerable controversy. They led to a
debate over good and evil, guilt and responsibility, and an individual's role
in society. Others argued that even though Eichmann might seem banal in
a Jerusalem courtroom 15 years after the war, the real Eichmann was the SS
officer who issued orders, created timetables, and made a string of decisions that determined the fate of millions. Julius Blum, a Hungarian Jew,
recalled that image of Eichmann in his testimony at the trial:

> In September 1944, something was in the air. The soldiers, the
> kapos (they were those in charge of the prisoners) were extremely
> strict, more strict than usual, and hygiene had to be immaculate.
> Everything had to be just so. Although the camp was always clean—
> the barracks were always immaculate, but these few days suddenly it
> became even more so. So naturally we suspected that something was
> going on. We figured that the only thing that could be happening was
> that we would be getting some high-falutin visitors. And we
> speculated that maybe Himmler himself was coming. Who knows?
> During the night before we left for work, they started building
> something in the middle of the square. You see, as you went in the
> camp to the right were the barracks. Then there was the washroom in
> an L shape and coming back was the kitchen and then the certain
> barracks where the elite used to live. So it was almost a square—a U
> shape. In the middle of the Lager, we had the Platz. They started
> building something, but we didn't know what they were building. We
> thought maybe it was a podium or something.
> So, we went to work as usual at 6:45 and rumors—Himmler's
> coming, Himmler's coming—and we're going to be visited. At two

[Although] Eichmann
might seem banal in a
Jerusalem courtroom 15
years after the war, the
real Eichmann was the SS
officer who issued orders,
created timetables, and
made a string of decisions
that determined the fate
of millions.

o'clock, for the first time in all those months, the whistle blows in the middle of the day. Never did that happen before. They told us to line up, we're going back to the camp. That never happened before—that we had to line up during the day. Usually we went to work at 7, we worked until 7. At 7:15 we lined up going back to the camp (Reverse for the night shift).

At 2 o'clock we line up, we're going back to camp. As we cross the gate, as we come to the gate, we notice in the tube five prisoners standing in a line. We had no idea. They take us to the Platz to the center of the square (usually they told us to break up because they counted us as we came in by the gate and they didn't have to count us again at the Platz until we were ready to go to sleep). This time, we lined up, and naturally, when we got to the Platz, we saw what they were building so early in the morning. They were building a gallows. So we start adding up. We saw the five guys, five gallows. So, obviously, you didn't have to be a genius to figure out what's going on. We tried to find out why—what happened to those guys. Nobody knew.

Later on, we found out that they were picked up. They were from the night shift and they were supposed to be sleeping, but, during the day, you were allowed to go to the bathroom if you had to. They went to the bathroom and they were going back to their room to the barracks, and they were picked out and put in the tube. And they spent the rest of the day in the tube waiting for the hanging.

So, after about a half hour waiting in front of the gallows, we see a group of officers—the camp commander, his cronies, and all his officers with him and a few high-ranking additional officers. Then suddenly, the grapevine started moving. "It's Eichmann, it's Eichmann, it's Eichmann." So we saw them walk in front of the gallows and sit in the chairs. They sat down and the five poor souls were brought from the tube. They line them up in front of the gallows. A German soldier put a noose around their neck, and they were standing there all waiting. No speeches. No reasons. Actually, it was in honor of the visitor who turned out to be Mr. Eichmann. It was in his honor to have a hanging party to please His Majesty. Naturally, I would have said some dignitaries would have been satisfied with a bouquet of flowers. He had to have a hanging party.

After a while the German soldier who put the noose around their necks and they were standing on five stools, he went by and kicked each stool out of there. They dangled and some of them urinated and they emptied themselves as they were dangling. It was the worst sight. I had seen dead people before, but this was the worst sight I've ever seen before or since. I saw these five men, innocent young fellows from Budapest. I knew them personally.

They [the Nazi officers] were carrying on a conversation among themselves and we were wondering what was going to happen next.

After a few minutes the officers stood up, and actually I could see Eichmann clapping his hands and stomping his foot like in joy. Like he had seen a beautiful performance of some sort. Laughing and joking among themselves. After a while, Eichmann and the camp officers, like inspection, started going in front of the prisoners. They were lined up, five deep.

As we were lined up, he goes by and he picked out one guy first. The first one in the line that he passed. Then he walks second and stands right in front of me. He looks in my eye, piercing my eye. I don't know what I was thinking, what doing. Suddenly, as he was reaching out to grab me. For some reason, I don't know what happened then. Many times I thought about that moment. I'm thinking about Abraham and that story in the Bible how the Angel passed his hand. I must say I felt the same thing. His hand was reaching toward me, and suddenly he reached behind me and grabbed the poor guy behind me and pulled him out by his collar. He was the second one. He picked three more and lined them up again on the gallows. Same thing again. The noose, the kicking, the chair, the hanging, the dangling, and they were taken away. The party was over.

At the end of his testimony, Blum was asked, "No announcement, no charges?" He replied, "No charges. No announcements. No reasons. Just for fun."

CONNECTIONS

What was Eichmann guilty of? Was he more or less guilty than the commander of the death camps?

The Eichmann trial was the first to make extensive use of the testimony of survivors. What do their words add that other evidence cannot provide?

Was Israel right to kidnap Eichmann and bring him to trial? Or should some other nation have assumed that responsibility? Would your answer change if no other country was willing to do so?

➤One of the most interesting features of the Eichmann Trial was that it examined the entire course of the Third Reich, from the rise of the Nazis and their consolidation of power to the planning and implementation of the Holocaust. The video *Witness to the Holocaust* presents that history through the testimonies of witnesses at the trial. The testimonies were taken from 170 hours of tape. The ninety-minute video is available from the Facing History Resource Center, as are excerpts from testimonies not included in the film.

➤The Facing History Resource Center has a twelve-minute segment originally shown on *60 Minutes*, "The Devil Is a Gentleman." It not only provides an introduction to Eichmann's entire career but also helps observers think about the meaning of *evil* and decide whether Eichmann fits that definition. Facing History's Fifth Annual Conference, "The Judgment of Adolf Eichmann: Evil, the Media & Society," focused on the impact of media coverage of the trial on public opinion. The sessions are described in *Elements of Time*, pages 381-382 and are also available on video from the Resource Center, as is a study guide that examines the way propaganda and opportunism influenced Eichmann's decisions.

➤A video presentation by John Loftus entitled *The Belarus Secret* shows how the United States helped hundreds of Nazi war criminals get into the United States and eventually obtain citizenship. Loftus believes that the "Cold War" against the Soviet Union led American officials to conspire with former Nazis. The video is available from the Facing History Resource Center and is summarized in *Elements of Time*, pages 364-365. A video entitled *Prosecuting Nazi War Criminals* made at the First Annual Facing History Conference offers a different view of the way American officials dealt with Nazi war criminals. Allan Ryan, Jr., the first director of the Office of Special Investigations, presented the principal paper. The video, which is available from the Resource Center, is described in *Elements of Time*, page 376.

READING 16

The United Nations and Genocide

As the horrors of the Third Reich unfolded, people everywhere resolved that such things must never be allowed to happen again. The United Nations was created partly in response to Nazi atrocities, as was the unanimous affirmation of the Nuremberg Principles, making "wars of aggression" and "crimes against humanity" punishable offenses.

During World War II, Raphael Lemkin, a lawyer, coined the term *genocide* to describe "crimes against humanity." It combined a Greek word *gens* meaning "a race or tribe" with the Latin *cide* meaning "to kill." Thus the word *genocide* refers to the deliberate destruction of a group of people. On December 9, 1948, the United Nations adopted the Genocide Convention which classified genocide as a crime under international law. It states in part:

> **Article I**
>
> The Contracting Parties confirm that genocide, whether committed in time of peace or in time of war, is a crime under international law which they undertake to prevent and punish.

The word *genocide* refers to the deliberate destruction of a group of people. On December 9, 1948, the United Nations adopted the Genocide Convention which classified genocide as a crime under international law.

Article II

In the present Convention, genocide means any of the following acts committed with intent to destroy, in whole or in part, a national, ethnical, racial or religious group, as such:

(a) Killing members of the group;

(b) Causing serious bodily or mental harm to members of the group;

(c) Deliberately inflicting on the group conditions of life calculated to bring about its physical destruction in whole or in part;

(d) Imposing measures intended to prevent births within the group;

(e) Forcibly transferring children of the group to another group.

Article III

The following acts shall be punishable:

(a) Genocide;

(b) Conspiracy to commit genocide;

(c) Direct and public incitement to commit genocide;

(d) Attempt to commit genocide;

(e) Complicity in genocide.

Article IV

Persons committing genocide or any of the other acts enumerated in article III shall be punished, whether they are constitutionally responsible rulers, public officials or private individuals.

The United Nations also created a permanent international criminal court to handle cases of genocide. In doing so, the organization was declaring its determination to protect individuals and groups against abuse by the state. Yet in the years that followed, no one has been tried for genocide despite repeated charges of the crime. In the 1960s, at least a half million East Timorese were slaughtered in Indonesia. In the 1970s, three million Bangladeshis and over a million Khmers in Cambodia were also victims of genocide, as were thousands of Native Americans living in the Amazon Valley in Brazil. In the 1980s, the Chinese were accused of genocide in Tibet. The same charge was leveled against the Serbs for their treatment of the Croats and the Muslims in the former Yugoslavia. The questions Senator George McGovern of South Dakota raised concerning mass murders in Cambodia might be asked of any these incidents: "How can or should the international community react in the face of the knowledge that a government is massacring its own people? Where do human rights supersede those of sovereignty? What lesson, if any, can be derived from the world's inaction over the murder of the Jews? How can we now meet the promise of 'never again' made in 1945?"

No nation came to the aid of Cambodians or other victims of genocide. Indeed the United States did not ratify the Genocide Convention until 1986 even though a number of Americans had helped draft the document. When it finally passed, Senator William Proxmire of Wisconsin, who had worked hard for its passage, told fellow senators, "This treaty has tremendous symbolic import. There's no question about it. . . .The first step we need to take is to adopt implementing legislation—making genocide a crime under U.S. law—which will complete the ratification process." The following year, Congress did complete the process by passing the Genocide Convention Implementation Act, also known as the Proxmire Act.

American participation has not made genocide easier to prosecute. Part of the difficulty stems from the definition of the term. Many have argued that it is too vague. Yet neither lawmakers nor scholars have been able to agree on a more precise definition. Helen Fein, an expert on the subject, offered this definition:

> Genocide is a series of purposeful actions by a perpetrator to destroy a collectivity through mass or selective murders of group members and suppressing the biological and social reproduction of the collectivity through the imposed proscription or restriction of reproduction of group members, increasing infant mortality, and breaking linkage between reproduction and socialization of children in the family or group of origin. The perpetrator may represent the state of the victim, another state, or another collectivity.[20]

Other scholars have tried shorter definitions. Frank Chalk and Kurt Jonassohn, who have also written on the subject, suggest that genocide is "a form of one-sided mass killing in which a state or other authority intends to destroy a group, as that group and membership in it are defined by the perpetrator." After studying other definitions and finding them lacking, Professor Henry Huttenbach concluded in 1988 that genocide could most profitably be defined as "any act that puts the very existence of a group in jeopardy."

CONNECTIONS

Length is the most obvious difference in the various definitions of the term *genocide*. What other differences seem most striking? How important is a precise definition? Can such a definition get in the way of our ability to identify and acknowledge inhumanity and suffering?

Some people claim that each of the following is an example of genocide:

- the destruction of the Native American population by various European colonial powers and later the United States;
- the enslavement of Africans in the United States;
- Iraq's treatment of the Kurds after the Gulf War;
- Serbia's policy of "ethnic cleansing" in what was once Yugoslavia;
- the anarchy in Somalia that has led to mass starvation.

Investigate one of these cases or an example cited in the reading and then decide whether it was a genocide. Present your findings to the class. Do your classmates agree with your assessment? What difficulties did you encounter in trying to reach a consensus on what constitutes genocide?

How would you answer the questions raised by Senator McGovern?

➤Arn Chorn, a survivor of the Cambodian Genocide, speaks to American youth of his experiences and traces similarities between his experiences and the Holocaust. A video of his presentation is available from the Facing History Resource Center and is described in *Elements of Time*, page 379.

➤Professor Eric Goldhagen argues that genocide existed long before the twentieth century. He maintains that unlike earlier genocides, genocide in the twentieth century is distinguished by ideologies that give perpetrators a belief system and a sense of purpose. A video of Goldhagen's lecture is available from the Facing History Resource Center and is described in *Elements of Time*, pages 347-348. Also available is *The History and Sociology of Genocide* by Frank Chalk and Kurt Jonassohn. It is an overview of modern genocides.

➤Professor Ervin Staub, author of *Roots of Evil*, examines the minds of the perpetrators of genocides in modern times by comparing their behavior with that of bystanders and rescuers. He uses four case studies: the Armenian Genocide, the Holocaust, the Cambodian Genocide, and the Argentinian murders. A video of Staub's presentation on genocide to a Facing History Summer Institute is available from the Resource Center.

➤The difficulty of defining *genocide* and making distinctions among the various manifestations of genocide was discussed at the Facing History symposium, "Teaching Genocide at the College Level." Videos are available from the Facing History Resource Center. Also available are the proceedings of the symposium, *Teaching Genocide on the College Level*, edited by Helen Fein and Joyce Freedman-Apsel.

Choices

*I*n 1991, Guido Calabresi, the dean of the Yale School of Law, gave a commencement address in which he told four stories involving choices made during World War II. The first focused on his father's decision to leave Italy.

His father's decision "to leave an enormously comfortable life for the life of an activist, of a revolutionary, of a hunted person" puzzled Calabresi, and when he finally asked about it, his father told him of being beaten and jailed for not applauding after a speech at his university given by the fascist minister of education.

"After that," his father said, "it was all over. I was an activist. I couldn't hide any longer. The decision had been made. It wasn't my choice, it had just happened."

"That non-choice," said Calabresi, "if it be that, changed his life totally—and fortunately mine, too." The second story involved a cousin who, in the middle of the war, because he was Jewish, went into hiding with a Catholic family. The cousin's family took assumed names so that they would not be recognized.

The captain in charge of some occupying German troops abused the cousin, thinking he was a draft dodger. The captain "behaved in every way appallingly," said Calabresi. He was "a dreadful man in every way."

One day, the German captain called to his cousin's four-year-old son, by the assumed family name. The boy "forgot the assumed name and didn't answer. . . so the captain went up to him and grabbed him and said, 'That isn't your name, is it?' And the little boy, shaking, said, 'No.' And he said, 'That isn't your name because you're Jewish.' And the little boy said, 'Yes,' and broke away and ran into the house.'"

The frightened family waited to be picked up and taken away. But nothing happened. They noticed that the German captain was a little nicer to the cousin, perhaps because he didn't think that he was there as a draft dodger, Calabresi speculated.

"Somehow, this dreadful man made a choice, a decision that he was not going to turn these people in," Calabresi said. "Somehow this dreadful, dreadful man could not do this one thing. . . He made a choice. . . and it was an extraordinary one."

The third tale involved a farmer on some lands of Calabresi's family in Italy. "It was well known," Calabresi recalled, "that this illiterate farmer had, at the risk of his life, hidden Allied servicemen who had been caught behind German lines and were escaping; Jews

A non-choice by a good person, a dramatically good choice by an evil person, a wonderful and troublesome choice by a person who didn't think it was a choice at all. And evil choices by people who are good.

who were escaping from the Nazis; [and]. . . when things had turned, he hid Germans who were running away. . .

"I thought that this was terrible—that he was somebody who didn't understand the difference between right and wrong; that he couldn't distinguish between hiding people who deserved to be hidden and criminals. I was a young twit, and already sounded like a lawyer. . . I asked him what he had done, why he didn't know the difference between right and wrong."

The farmer replied, "Politics, politics. I don't know about those things. I don't care about them. When they came here, when they were running away, each of them was in trouble. *Eran tutti figli di mamma*— they were each the child of some mother somewhere—*tiriam a campar*— we all struggle to live."

"There was something," Calabresi mused, "about that humanity, that decision to look after the individual who was in trouble, and to care about the person before him which represented an attitude, a point of view which explained why so few people were taken away in Italy during the Nazi time, why so many were saved. An awful lot of people didn't worry about law, didn't worry about politics, didn't worry about rules which told them to turn people in, but just looked at the individual in need, the mothers' and fathers' sons and daughters before them, and this led them to hide and protect that person at the risk of their own lives."

"My last story is the only one which deals with famous people," Calabresi said. "On our wedding trip, my wife and I were driving through the Vosges, in France. . . and we came to a town called Sainte-Marie-Aux-Mines [where] Private Eddie Slovak was shot during World War II."

In 1944 the war was going well when the Germans made a counter-offensive—the Battle of the Bulge. The Germans came rushing through, and a lot of Allied soldiers, youngsters, green troops, sent in "because everything was over," deserted. "The military," Calabresi said, "decided that an example was needed in order to steel up the troops. But the trouble was there were too many deserters. . . so they decided to take a double deserter. I'm not sure what a double deserter is, I guess it's somebody who deserted and got caught and got sent back and being scared out of his wits, deserted again."

Calabresi said that Gen. Eisenhower reportedly said: "Get me some psychologists. Have them examine these people. I want a loser."

"They came up with somebody, Eddie Slovak, who didn't seem to have family, who'd been unemployed, may even have been a petty thief, didn't seem to have anybody or anything going for him. And they shot him," Calabresi said.

Actually, Slovak had a wife and the story came out when she tried to get insurance and was unable to because her husband had been shot as a deserter, Calabresi noted.

"This was a terrible choice, an awful decision, made by somebody who. . . I'm sure was a very decent person," said Calabresi.

"I could name others, Hugo Black. . . Earl Warren . . . Franklin Roosevelt. . . the people who were as responsible in some ways as any for the exclusion of Japanese-Americans during the Second World War, for placing of these people in concentration camps. Appalling choice. Appalling choice. And yet the people who made those choices were decent people—Eisenhower, Black, Warren, Roosevelt.

"A non-choice by a good person, a dramatically good choice by an evil person, a wonderful and troublesome choice by a person who didn't think it was a choice at all. And evil choices by people who are good. What can I tell you about these stories?" asked Calabresi.

"Not much, not much. In one sense I'd much rather let them speak for themselves. I cannot, for instance, tell you what made some choose well and some not." . . .

"In one of these stories," he concluded, "a bad person, a very bad person, made a dramatically good choice. And we should remember that, both when we see someone whom we think of as bad, and equally so, when we think of ourselves as bad. We should remember that the capacity to do good. . . .unexpectedly to do something which is profoundly right, even if profoundly dangerous, is always there.

"But more important, some good people made catastrophically bad decisions. And it is on this that I would focus. It is not that we are wrong in viewing Eisenhower, or for that matter Black or Warren or Roosevelt, as good. . . .All of us, I and you, are as subject to being careless, uncaring. We will all thoughtlessly applaud at times we shouldn't. Or even dramatically at times, like Eisenhower, Black and the others, mislead ourselves into following what seem like good reasons—politically orthodox reasons. . . to a dreadful decision. . . .

"I would like to leave with you the ease, the simplicity, of making mistakes. Not to dishearten you—far from it—but in the hope that it will both make you more careful, more full of care of others in need, and more understanding of those who do wrong because they can be, they are, you and me. . . I emphasize this to remind you that the choices which reoccur, do make a difference. If not always or even often to the world, they will make a difference to the children of some mothers and fathers around us as we all struggle to live."[21]

CONNECTIONS

Why do you think Calabresi focused on World War II? How did you expect each story to end? Did any end the way you expected it to?

What conclusions did Calabresi reach about the types of people who reach certain decisions? Are his conclusions optimistic or pessimistic?

How does Calabresi use the word *good?* Is *good* the opposite of *evil?* For example, did the German captain who failed to betray the frightened family commit a good act or did he just fail to commit an evil one? What is the difference?

READING 18

Learning from the Past

*I*n 1989, the people of East Germany overthrew their Communist government. The following year, the two Germanies were reunited. After reunification, some Germans wanted to try four former East German border guards believed responsible for the death of a young man shot attempting to escape to West Germany. According to reporter Peter Schneider, the purpose of the trial was not to "take revenge on the culprits, or even to punish them. The goal is to establish a moral consensus: no one who has invoked orders or higher authority to trample on human rights should feel confident, now or in the future, that he will go unscathed. Even if he can't be legally punished for his deed, society will still hold him personally responsible."[22]

There was considerable opposition to the trial. Schneider notes:

> Almost everyone agrees that, if this is to happen at all, it should start with indictments against those who instigated and gave the orders. . . . But that's where unanimity ends. There is more at stake than this single trial. If the proceeding against the four soldiers ends in a valid legal decision, it will bring dozens of similar trials in its wake. . . . And naturally a legal investigation of the "second" German past couldn't stop with the shots at the wall. It would have to deal with the entire Stalinist terror apparatus. So this fundamentally unfortunate and possibly misguided trial has occasioned a debate on principles: does the legal system of the Federal Republic have the authority to pass judgment on crimes of the German Democratic Republic?[23]

CONNECTIONS

How would you answer the questions Schneider raises? How would you respond to his observations of the popular response to the trial?

> I think we Germans ought to take a particular interest in clearing up "administrative" crimes, by which I mean state-ordered crimes that civil servants executed out of blind obedience and careerism. If the

legal means won't serve, alternatives must be found. Anything—a public tribunal, a fact-finding commission of historians—is better than shoulder-shrugging and forgetfulness. And if people are talking amnesty, they need to get out on the table what they want to pardon.[24]

READING 19

Telling Right from Wrong

Underlying the trials and the discussions of what the Nazis did and did not do is an important question: If a government orders an individual to do something that, in normal circumstances, is illegal and, even more to the point, morally wrong, must the individual obey?

As she watched Eichmann's trial, Hannah Arendt observed: "Eichmann said he recognized that what he had participated in was perhaps one of the greatest crimes in history, but, he insisted, if he had not done so, his conscience would have bothered him at the time. His conscience and morality were working exactly in reverse. This reversal is precisely the moral collapse that took place in Europe."

Arendt concluded that the act of resistance was extraordinarily difficult during World War II. There were no acceptable role models. "Those few who were still able to tell right from wrong went really only by their own judgments, and they did so freely; there were no rules to be abided by, under which the particular cases with which they were confronted could be subsumed. They had to decide each instance as it arose, because no rules existed for the unprecedented."[25]

Simon Wiesenthal wrote a story called "The Sunflower" that raises many of the same questions. The jacket of the book in which it appears summarizes the tale.

A young Jew is taken from a death-camp to a makeshift army hospital. He is led to the bedside of a Nazi soldier whose head is completely swathed in bandages. The dying Nazi blindly extends his hand toward the Jew, and in a cracked whisper begins to speak. The Jew listens silently while the Nazi confesses to having participated in the burning alive of an entire village of Jews. The soldier, terrified of dying with this burden of guilt, begs absolution from the Jew. Having listened to the Nazi's story for several hours—torn between horror and compassion for the dying man—the Jew finally walks out of the room without speaking. Was his action right? Or moral?[26]

CONNECTIONS

How would you answer the questions Wiesenthal raises?

Wisenthal's tale is followed by the responses of theologians, philosophers, historians, and writers to the two questions. In his response to the questions, Hans Habe wrote:

> One of the worst crimes of the Nazi regime was that it made it so hard for us to forgive. It led us into the labyrinth of our souls. We must find our way out of the labyrinth—not for the murderers' sake but for our own. Neither love alone expressed in forgiveness, nor justice alone, exacting punishment, will lead us out of the maze. A demand for atonement and forgiveness is not self-contradictory; when a man has willfully extinguished the life of another, atonement is the prerequisite for forgiveness. Exercised with love and justice, atonement and forgiveness serve the same end: life without hatred. That is our goal: I see no other.[27]

Why does Habe believe that "We must find our way out of the labyrinth—not for the murderers' sake but for our own"? Do you agree?

Primo Levi argued that it was right to refuse to pardon the dying man because it was "the lesser evil: you could only have forgiven him by lying or inflicting upon yourself a terrible moral violence." Are there lesser and greater evils? What "moral violence" would the man have inflicted upon himself through forgiveness? How do you think Habe would respond?

When asked about forgiveness, Elie Wiesel replied, "No one asked for it." What is he saying about the perpetrators? About the bystanders?

NOTES

1 Benjamin Ferencz, *Planethood* (Vision Books, 1988), 14-16.

2 John Fried, *Trial at Nuremberg: Freedom and Responsibility* (National Project Center for Film and Humanities and the Research Foundation of the City University of New York, © 1973).

3 Hannah Arendt, *The Life of the Mind: Thinking,* (Harcourt, 1977), 5.

4 From pages 370 and 374 of *The Ascent of Man* by J. Bronowski, © 1973 by J. Bronowski. Reprinted by permission of Little, Brown and Company.

5 John Fried, *Trial at Nuremberg: Freedom and Responsibility.*

6 Alfons Heck, *A Child of Hitler,* (Renaissance House, 1985).

7 Leo Alexander, "Medical Science under Dictatorship," *New England Journal of Medicine,* 14 July 1949, 5.

8 Gerald Fleming, "Engineers of Death," *New York Times,* 18, July, 1993, op. ed. Copyright © 1993 by The New York Times Company. Reprinted by permission.

9 Quoted in Benjamin Ferencz, *Less Than Slaves,* (Harvard University Press, 1979), 191.

10 Ibid.

11 Mel London, "Letter to the Editor," *New York Times,* 3 September, 1981. Copyright © The New York Times Company. Reprinted by permission.

12 Telford Taylor, *Nuremberg and Vietnam: An American Tragedy,* (Quadrangle Books, 1970), 12.

13 Henry Huttenbach in *Holocaust and Genocide Studies,* vol. 3, 1988, 297.

14 Victoria Barnett, *For the Soul of the People,* 231.

15 Ibid., 232.

16 Primo Levi, "The Quiet City" in *Moments of Reprieve* (Summit Book, 1985), 99-105.

17 Horst Krueger, *A Crack in the Wall,* 199-232.

18 Carl Sandburg, "The Hangman at Home," in *Smoke & Steel* (Harcourt Brace, 1920).

19 Hannah Arendt, *Eichmann in Jerusalem* (Viking Press, 1963), 255-256.

20 Helen Fein, *Accounting for Genocide.*

21 Guido Calabresi, "Choices" *Williams Alumnus Review,* Summer, 1991, 18-22.

22 Peter Schneider, "Facing Germany's Newer Past," *New York Times,* 30 September, 1991. Copyright © 1991 by The New York Times Company. Reprinted by permission.

23 Ibid.

24 Ibid.

25 Hannah Arendt, *Eichmann in Jerusalem,* 2.

26 Simon Wiesenthal, *The Sunflower* (Schocken, 1976).

27 Ibid.

10. Historical Legacies

Only the spectators, who constitute the space of history (memory) in which all actions and works of art fall. . . can pass ultimate judgment on an event or action by the quality of their attention.

HANNAH ARENDT

OVERVIEW

"Anyone who closes his eyes to the past is blind to the present," said President Richard von Weizsaecker of West Germany in a speech that marked the fortieth anniversary of World War II. "Whoever refuses to remember the inhumanity is prone to new risks of infection." Chapter 10 looks at the power of our memories to shape the present. It looks too at why so many are reluctant to confront those memories. The first readings in the chapter explore the legacies of the Holocaust. The chapter then considers the effects of two other painful histories, that of the Armenians and of African Americans. The chapter ends with a discussion of the ways history is taught and memorialized.

The chapter also expands on an idea introduced in Chapter 2. Orlando Patterson noted that slaves were "not allowed freely to integrate the experience of their ancestors into their lives, to inform their understanding of social reality with inherited meanings of their natural forebears, or to anchor the living present in any conscious community of memory." He went on to describe their struggle to maintain their identity by preserving their heritage. In every society, a group's right to include its story in a nation's history and preserve its heritage is the power to shape generations to come. To deny that right is cultural genocide. A survivor of Dachau recalls:

> The SS guards took pleasure in telling us that we had no chance of coming out alive, a point they emphasized with particular relish by insisting that after the war the rest of the world would not believe what happened; there would be rumors, speculations, but no clear evidence, and people would conclude that evil on such a scale was just not possible."[1]

That survivor and others like him were determined to not only live but also remember and bear witness. Reverend Vartan Hartunian, who translated his father's memoirs of the Armenian Genocide, explained why when he wrote, "Any crime that is forgotten or forgiven is a crime that has been sanctioned and blessed. The surviving victims must proclaim the truth, must insist on due punishment and must do all in their power to prevent the powerful in their advance against corruption."[2]

Journalist Judith Miller agrees. "Knowing and remembering the evil in history and in each of us might not prevent a recurrence of genocide. But ignorance of history or the suppression of memory removes the surest defense we have, however inadequate, against such gigantic cruelty and indifference to it." Miller notes that "cultures suppress what they would like to forget in remarkably similar ways, even when the events themselves are strikingly different." One way people suppress "what they would like to forget" is to deny it ever happened. Another is to shift the blame to someone else. People also rationalize. A rationalization is a way of explaining behavior that is self-satisfying and even true as far as it goes but not the sole explanation or even the most important. People also suppress the past by suggesting the event was but one of many similar events. The process is known as relativism or what some call the "yes, but" syndrome. What then fosters memory? For Miller, it is fostered by anything that makes the past more real and less abstract. She believes abstraction "kills [memory] because it encourages distance and often indifference."[3]

READING 1

Survivors and Memory

After taking part in the Warsaw Ghetto uprising, Alexander Donat was sent to Majdanek, Auschwitz, and later Dachau. He writes, "I felt I was a witness to disaster and charged with the sacred mission of carrying the Ghetto's history through the flames and barbed wire until such time I could hurl it into the face of the world. It seemed to be that this mission would give me the strength to endure everything."[4]

Many survivors have shared his need to tell the world what happened. Rose Murra traces her obligation to conversations she had with her mother after her father, uncle, and brother were killed. For a time, she and her mother managed to elude the authorities. But each day was a test of survival. And in the end, they, like so many others, were herded onto cattle cars bound for Majdanek. Rose wanted to join the many young people who jumped off the train, but her mother begged her to stay. As the two huddled together, they spoke of what lay ahead.

I felt I was a witness to disaster and charged with the sacred mission of carrying the Ghetto's history through the flames and barbed wire until such time I could hurl it into the face of the world.

Rose Murra's family in 1938.

"Ma, listen we gonna go to a camp—I don't know they're gonna kill me. They're gonna kill you? Who gonna get killed first?"

"Listen don't cry over me—if I be killed—because that's the way of life—that's gonna be—don't cry—your little boy got killed—your husband—everybody died already—so what you think—we have to be the chosen ones—we don't have to be the chosen ones—we're gonna die too. So take it nice and easy. Death is not so bad. After death there's nothing to remember no more—so maybe death is the solution of it. I mean suffering—even more—look Ma—we went through typhus and hunger—the cold and the hiding—How much more can you take of this?"

So my mother said—"Okay my child, I was thinking—okay I would die—at least I want you to live. Somebody—somebody from the family should live and survive."

I said, "Listen—a lot of families are killed already—nobody left already from a family."

"In case you live through—don't ever forget to tell the story what your family went through."

I said, "If I come through—which I know I'm not, well, I tell, I tell." So that's what it is!

When we entered Majdanek—the young went to one side—the old to another side—I was going with my mother—we came closer to the soldier and he told my mother to go to this side—"You mean this side"—my mother said—"I'm still young. I can work."

The soldier said—"If you don't shut up your mother—I'm gonna beat you to death." And that's the last I saw of my mother—she just like disappeared."[5]

Isabella Leitner never forgot her mother's words either. On the train that took the family to Auschwitz, her mother told her children.

Stay alive, my darlings—all six of you. Out there, when it's all over, a world is waiting for you to give it all I gave you. Despite what you see here—and you are all young and impressionable—believe me, there is humanity out there, there is dignity. I will not share it with you, but it's there. And when this is over, you must add to it, because sometimes it is a little short, a little skimpy. With your lives, you can create other lives and nourish them. You can nourish your children's souls and minds, and teach them that man is capable of infinite glory. You must believe me. I cannot leave you with what you see here. I must leave you with what I see. My body is nearly dead, but my vision is throbbing with life—even here. I want you to live for the very life that is yours. And wherever I'll be, in some mysterious way, my love will overcome my death and will keep you alive. I love you.[6]

Isabella Leitner lived with those words for the rest of her life. In her memoirs, she tells why May is an especially difficult month.

May is such a "big" month. The first of May has overtones of political celebrations, and that is meaningful to me. In my teens, the first of May meant serenading under your window, a burst of spring, love, music, all sentimentally shouting hosannas in your body, masking the dread of reality.

May 1st is my sister's birthday. There is something special about being born on May 1st, and dear little Rachel is special. There is something special about being born any time in May—May 1st, May 28th. The scent of spring is delicious. It permeates the air. It sings the song of birth, of life. All is drenched in sun. The earth smiles. It is happy you are here.

The world ended in May. I was born in May. I died in May. We started the journey of ugliness on May 29th. We headed for Auschwitz. We arrived on May 31st.

The scent of spring wasn't delicious. The earth didn't smile. It shrieked in pain. The air was filled with the stench of death. Unnatural death. The smoke was thick. The sun couldn't crack through. The scent was the smell of burning flesh. The burning flesh was your mother.

I am condemned to walk the earth for all my days with the stench of burning flesh in my nostrils. My nostrils are damned. May is

I want to tell my mother that I kept her faith, that I lived because she wanted me to, that the strength she imbued me with is not for sale, that the god in man is worth living for, and I will make sure that I hand that down to those who come after me.

damned. May should be abolished. May hurts. There should be only eleven months in a year. May should be set aside for tears. For six million years, to cleanse the earth.

For more than twenty years I have walked zombie-like toward the end of May, deeply depressed, losing jobs, losing lovers, uncomprehending. And then June would come, and there would be new zeal, new life.

Now I am older, and I don't remember all the pain, and June hurts, and so does May. May laughs sometimes, and so does June, and now in May I bend down to smell the flowers, and for moments I don't recall the smell of burning flesh. That is not happiness, only relief, and relief is blessed. Now I want to reinstate the month of May. I want to reincarnate the month, reincarnate the dead. I want to tell my mother that I kept her faith, that I lived because she wanted me to, that the strength she imbued me with is not for sale, that the god in man is worth living for, and I will make sure that I hand that down to those who come after me.

I will tell them to make what is good in all of us their religion, as it was yours, Mother, and then you will always be alive and the housepainter will always be dead. And children someday will plant flowers in Auschwitz, where the sun couldn't crack through the smoke of burning flesh. Mother, I will keep you alive.[7]

CONNECTIONS

What did Rose Murra's mother mean when she told her daughter, "don't forget to tell the story"? Why was it important that it be told?

Does it matter what you remember? What did Isabella Leitner's mother want her children to remember? What was her legacy to them?

How does Isabella Leitner approach the past? How does her past define her present? Her plans for the future?

➤Edith P., a survivor, ends her testimony by expressing her sadness at the plight of the Cambodian people. "Why do we do nothing?" she asks. For more of Edith's story, see *Elements of Time*, pages 32-34. A video portrait is available from the Facing History Resource Center.

➤The video montage *Future Imperfect* describes the way Holocaust survivors have dealt with their memories in recent decades. The montage is available from the Facing History Resource Center and is described in *Elements of Time*, pages xxxi-xxxii.

Preserving Evidence of Evil

Many survivors like Alexander Donat, Rose Murra, and Isabella Leitner bear witness by telling their story. Others try to preserve the physical evidence of the Holocaust. That experience can be enormously painful. Journalist Timothy Ryback explains why:

In November of 1989, the United States Holocaust Memorial Museum in Washington, D.C., received from the State Museum of Auschwitz-Birkenau a shipment of artifacts for inclusion in the new museum's exhibitions tracing the history of the Holocaust. In addition to planks from an Auschwitz barracks, rubble from a crematorium, a pole from an electrified barbed-wire fence, and twenty empty cans of Zyklon B—the cyanide gas used in the extermination process—the shipment contained a large number of personal items, among them hairbrushes, mirrors, razors, toothbrushes, clothes hangers, shoe daubers, clogs, and suitcases. One box contained approximately twenty pounds of human hair.

"When we first received the hair, we regarded it as just another artifact for the museum," Jacek Nowakowski, who was in charge of acquiring objects for the exhibition, says, "but then, when the Content Committee met to discuss the best way to display it, it became clear that the members viewed human hair differently from other objects."

The Content Committee, which consisted of twenty scholars, Holocaust survivors, and museum officials, and which was responsible for deciding on the substance of the museum's exhibitions, devoted two emotional and highly charged meetings to the issue of displaying the hair, which was a jumble of braids, curls, and long strands shorn from women's heads. According to Nowakowski, these discussions were among the most sensitive deliberations of the entire project, which had been under way for more than ten years. "Hair is a highly personal matter," Nowakowski says. "It is not only a part of the human body; it is also a part of the human personality—part of one's identity. How you wear your hair tells a lot about you as a person. Hair is so simple—but it is so fundamental."

Many committee members felt strongly that the hair, which had been discovered in large bales when the Red Army liberated the concentration camp, in January of 1945, should be displayed in the museum. "The basic argument was that we were trying to make a convincing case against any possible Holocaust deniers," Jeshajahu Weinberg, the director of the Museum and the chairman of the Content Committee, explains. "It was not even so much for the present generation as it was for future generations. The hair was one piece of clear evidence." Other members vehemently opposed the idea of such a display. "The women survivors, in particular, objected to the presence of the hair in the exhibition," Weinberg says. "'For all I know, my mother's hair might be in there,' one of them said. 'I don't want my mother's hair on display.'" Weinberg, who initially had no objection to exhibiting the hair, was moved by the appeal, as was the rest of the committee. Eventually, the museum decided to install a wall-length photographic mural of the nearly two tons of human hair on exhibit at the Auschwitz Museum.

While the question of whether or not to display the hair of Holocaust victims has been settled at the Holocaust Museum, conservators and administrators at the Auschwitz Museum in Oswiecim, Poland, are grappling with a more practical problem: how to preserve the four thousand pounds of human hair on display in their museum.

This issue has recently risen to prominence with the initiation of a multi-million-dollar effort to preserve the ruins of the Auschwitz concentration-camp complex. As conservators from around the world confer on how best to save the remaining barracks, the barbed-wire fencing, the watchtowers, the ruins of the gas chambers, and the heaps of hair, they have to take a hard look at what it means to preserve a "relic."

Ever since Auschwitz was liberated, these remnants of human beings have stood as one of the most chilling symbols of the Holocaust. The Nazis did not just murder millions of men, women, and children but literally "harvested" their remains to drive Germany's industrial machine. In the early nineteen-forties, a brisk trade emerged between German death camps, such as Auschwitz, Majdanek, and Treblinka, and German felt and textile manufacturers who used the versatile fibre in the production of thread, rope, cloth, carpets, mattress stuffing, lining stiffeners for uniforms, socks for submarine crews, and felt insulators for the boots of railroad workers. . . .

In May 1945, just days after the German capitulation, Polish officials dispatched ten pounds of human hair found at Auschwitz to the Institute of Forensic Medicine at Cracow. Following a series of chemical tests, Jan Robel, the head of the institute, confirmed, in his final report, "the presence of traces of cyanide, particularly the poisonous compound bearing the name Zyklon." Such findings served as evidence in trials against Nazi war criminals, including Rudolf Hoess, the commandant at Auschwitz, who was sentenced to death on April 2, 1947, and was hanged fourteen days later beside the former crematorium of the *Stammlager*, the main Auschwitz camp.

Since then, the human hair has continued to bear witness: on the second floor of Block IV, a former Auschwitz barrack, it lies in heaps inside a row of large display cases. . . . Witold Smrek, the Auschwitz

There is nothing that speaks louder against the Nazi crimes than this hair. On the transport that I came on, all the women and children were taken from the train and immediately gassed. The hair, along with the combs and suitcases and shoes, is all that remains of them.

Museum's chief conservator, and other museum officials are currently deliberating on the fate of this display. "Some people are telling us that the exhibition is offensive, that it is in poor taste to have human hair on display like this,' Smrek told me recently. "[8]

Among those people is Adam Zak, the rector of the Jesuit College in Cracow. "Hair is part of a victim's body and, as such, it should be accorded the dignity due to it," he claims. "People say that you need the hair as evidence of the Nazi atrocities, but with the film footage and the shoes and the brushes, there is enough other evidence to prove that the Holocaust took place."

Ernest Michel, a Jewish survivor of Auschwitz, disagrees. "There is nothing that speaks louder against the Nazi crimes than this hair. On the transport that I came on, all the women and children were taken from the train and immediately gassed. The hair, along with the combs and suitcases and shoes, is all that remains of them. No matter how painful it may be to look at, it is all part of the story that I believe has to be told."

Smrek's main concern, however, is not whether to display the hair but how to preserve it. Years of storage in a room that has no temperature or humidity control has faded the hair and left it brittle. Some of it has already turned to dust. Smrek has sought advice from museums all over the world on the best way to preserve the remaining hair but so far has no answer. He says, "No one else has ever had this problem before."[9]

A mound of shoes bears witness at the U.S. Holocaust Memorial Museum.

CONNECTIONS

What is the purpose of a museum? Is it to preserve the relics of the past? Foster memory? Bear witness?

Why do exhibits that feature the hair of the victims arouse such debate? How important is hair to one's identity? To one's personality? How does hair differ from the mounds of suitcases on display in Holocaust museums? The piles of shoes and other personal items?

Ernest Michel, a Jewish survivor of Auschwitz, argues, "No matter how painful it may be to look at, it is all part of the story that I believe has to be told." Should a "bad" or painful history be remembered? Studied?

READING 3

Amnesia

Many survivors feel they have a duty to remember the Holocaust. Many bystanders and perpetrators, on the other hand, have chosen, consciously or unconsciously, to forget. Psychologist Daniel Goleman views such experiences not as isolated events but as the result of a lacuna or blind spot. He explains by focusing on the experiences of one of his students:

Questions that can't—or won't—be asked are a sure sign of a lacuna [an empty space or gap].

> Bini Reichel, born in 1946 in Germany, describes how, in the postwar years, "amnesia became a contagious national disease, affecting even postwar children. In this new world. . . there was no room for curious children and adolescents. We postponed our questions and finally abandoned them altogether." In her history books, the Nazi years were covered in ten to fifteen pages of careful condemnation. . . .
>
> In an attempt to break through this group amnesia, Reichel recently sought out and questioned some of the generation who had fought in the war. One question she asked of a former Nazi was why he had never discussed those years with his own children. His reply: "It was beyond discussion. Besides, they didn't ask."
>
> Questions that can't—or won't—be asked are a sure sign of a lacuna [an empty space or gap]. The creation of blind spots is a key of repressive regimes, allowing them to obliterate information that threatens their official line.[10]

CONNECTIONS

How did the survivors quoted in the previous readings recall the Holocaust? How did the German quoted in this reading recall it? In what respects are their memories similar? What differences are most striking? How do you account for those differences?

In what sense is the kind of "group amnesia" described in this reading contagious? What does Goleman suggest as a cause of that amnesia? As a possible cure? Do you agree?

What questions do you find it difficult to ask? Are they a sign of a blind spot or lacuna?

The Germans are not the only people reluctant to face their past. The French have also found it difficult to do so. In 1983, Klaus Barbie, the chief of the Gestapo in occupied Lyons and the man responsible for the murders of 4,342 members of the French resistance and 7,591 French Jews, was tried for crimes against humanity. Many people in France feared that his trial would open old wounds. As Barbie himself reminded the court, the war was long over. "I have forgotten," he said. "If they have not forgotten, it is their business. I have forgotten." Should he or they be allowed to forget? What happens to a history that is not confronted?

Barbie was found guilty and sentenced to life in prison. Yet many of the arguments he raised have persisted, partly because they offer people a way of avoiding responsibility for the past. In *One by One by One,* Judith Miller quotes Simone Veil, a Holocaust survivor and the former president of the European Parliament, as saying that Barbie and his lawyer tried "to show that every war-related death—the Nazi genocide, Hiroshima, Algeria, Vietnam, Cambodia, and the like—is the same. If everyone is guilty, then no one is guilty." Miller argues that the relativism and rationalization inherent in that tactic is one of "the most common, insidious, and hence problematic forms of the suppression of memory." Why?

READING 4

Family Legacies

*E*very event touches not only those who witnessed it but also their children and their children's children. Our identity is shaped, at least in part, by our family history. Indeed, our most treasured history is learned at home, the place where our most powerful memories reside. Nancy Sommers writes of her family and the legacy of the Holocaust:

> The sepia-toned photograph sits on a shelf in my study inviting me to find my face in the line-up of family members gathered for my grandparents' engagement. Here are the eight brothers and sisters of my grandfather's family, my grandmother's three sisters and my great-grandparents. They are gathered in the garden of my grandmother's home in Regensburg, Germany. It is autumn, 1920, and the photograph captures something of the safety, serenity, and joy these families knew in that place, in that time. All but one are dead now; yet I remain attached to the world through them, to their Germanic names I love, to my Grandmother's name, Irma, my middle name, to their laughter and their resilience, to my grandmother's lyrical, dreamy gaze and to my grandfather's exuberant confidence. . . .
>
> [That photograph and a few others] were the secret sustenance of my childhood. What had once been a large, capacious family living

The photographs spoke to me what my parents couldn't find the words to say about love and loss, about memory and desire. No single image told me the whole story, for a story is more than a snapshot, more than one moment in time. And yet these moments in time are what form the stuff of history.

close together in neighboring Bavarian towns now was either decimated or exiled to whatever safe havens they could find in Argentina, Israel, England, or New York. In Indiana, where my parents landed, we no longer had a garden, woods or mountains to hike. No family rituals to observe. Mine was a somber childhood, filled with silences about a history I felt I possessed and yet had never lived. In fact, for a long time I knew very little about what was called "the past" except the one story my mother repeatedly told about Albert Selz, her best friend's father, who in 1937 was shot in the head by the Nazis when he answered his front door. As if trying to justify the three locks on our front door in Terre Haute, my father always said that he would not answer if the Nazis came, as his father had done on Kristallnacht when they forcibly took my grandfather from their home and transported him to Buchenwald. Trying to absorb such enormous losses, my parents would attempt to convince themselves that maybe if they didn't talk about the past too much, it would go away. The photographs spoke to me what my parents couldn't find the words to say about love and loss, about memory and desire. No single image told me the whole story, for a story is more than a snapshot, more than one moment in time. And yet these moments in time are what form the stuff of history.[11]

Just as the Holocaust shaped Nancy Sommers' identity, it also shaped the identity of a man who grew up in West Germany just after World War II:

> We were ashamed of our country. We were told what happened—the marching—the books—the Sieg Heils and the beatings, the loud brutal and vulgar crowds—the people we loved being driven out—Albert Einstein, Thomas Mann, Brecht—their books, paintings and music scores burned. Other people we had never heard of—those nameless millions who so silently went to the camps where their voices were gassed forever silent. This was no country to be proud of. We were also pained, lonesome kids amid adults who could not, must not, ever be trusted. How could I trust my parents who, balancing me on their knees, sang *"Deutschland, Deutschland, ueber Alles"* with me? Who would have me call after a man in the street, a man I didn't even know, "Jew! Jew!" Who with my father—once a high-ranking officer—would tell me they'd never heard of any camps. And who, when I asked him about the 6 million Jews that had been put to death, insisted that it was 4.5 million—the figure I had quoted, he said, had been made up by the notoriously deceitful Jewish media—4.5 while my heart was counting—one and one and one. . . .[12]

Not every child wants to confront the past. In "I Dream in Good English Too," Donia Blumenfeld Clenman, a survivor of the Holocaust who now lives in Canada, writes of her children's reluctance to acknowledge her experiences.

How could I trust my parents who, balancing me on their knees, sang *"Deutschland, Deutschland, uber Alles"* with me? Who would have me call after a man in the street, a man I didn't even know, "Jew! Jew!"

Sometimes
I am a stranger to my family
for I bring Europe's ghosts
into the well-lit living room
of Canadian internationalism
and mobile,
passionately objective youth.

My scars are nicely healed,
and my concerns properly intellectual,
yellow with the stamp of legality
of naturalization papers
twenty years old.
Yet somehow,
the smoke of the past
darkens Heinz's clear consomme
and, though only a witness,
I spread fear
by my very presence,
a living fossil
at a table worshipping the "Now."

They love me deeply
and tenderly,
yet would exorcise a part of me,
dreading an eruption of memory
no matter how oblique
to force them
into captive partnership.

This is my past
not theirs,
their hostile glances shout.
We are all descendants of Adam.
Why bring Abraham
into happy Canadian homes?

I was no child on arrival
and yet, so well assimilated,
even my verses are native,
and I dream in good English too.
So I put on the ointment of reason
and tape heartbreak with Band-aids
and they are relieved,
and reassured,
to get back
their normal Canadian mother.[13]

CONNECTIONS

What does Nancy Sommers mean when she writes, "Mine was a somber childhood, filled with silences about a history I felt I possessed and yet had never lived"? What is she saying about the way she is linked to her family's history? About the power of the past to shape the present and the future?

Why do you think Sommers' parents tried to "convince themselves that maybe if they didn't talk about the past too much, it would go away"? Would Isabella Leitner agree?

For what reasons does the German man feel ashamed of his parents and his country? How did they betray his trust? Once you have betrayed someone's trust, can it ever be rebuilt?

Make an identity chart for Donia Clenman. Make a similar chart for her family. How are the charts similar? What difference seems most striking? How does that difference account for Clenman's view of her children: "They love me deeply and tenderly, yet would exorcise a part of me, dreading an eruption of memory no matter how oblique to force them into captive partnership"? What is the "captive partnership" her children fear? Why does she find it so difficult to be a "normal Canadian mother?"

In what respects are all three families described in this reading similar? What differences seem most striking? How do you account for them?

READING 5

Germans Confront the Past

As memories of World War II fade, individuals struggle to make meaning of their past. Just as no two individuals recall the past in the same way, no two people find the same meaning in that history. Victoria Barnett, the author of *For the Soul of the People*, contrasts the memories of the Jews and Protestants in Germany:

> For many conscientious Germans, the Holocaust became a symbol of political injustice and evil. For Jews, it was not just a symbol but a reality that lived on in the broken lives of the survivors and the new awareness, in every Jew, of what was possible . . . . To many Jews, the emphasis by some Germans on the Holocaust as a symbol of political evil in general seemed to diminish the full horror of what they had experienced. "Never again," said the Jews, and they meant one thing only. "Never again," said many Germans, and they meant different things: never again dictatorship, never again war. They meant taking clear political positions that symbolically represented anti-Nazism.

Observing the postwar discrimination that Turks and other guest workers suffered in West Germany, for example, some Germans drew the parallel that the "Turks are the Jews of today." The recognition of racism and discrimination in postwar Germany was important and necessary. The problem was that viewing the Jewish experience under Nazism in this symbolic fashion removed it from the larger context of the Holocaust and changed many Germans' perceptions of the Holocaust itself. It evaded the historical fact that anti-Semitism has existed in all kinds of political and economic systems—in other words, that it is not merely a political problem but has its roots in the dynamics of prejudice. . . .[14]

The difference in perspective Barnett describes could clearly be seen in the way individuals responded to an incident that occured in 1985, forty years after the war ended. Chancellor Helmut Kohl invited United States President Ronald Reagan to West Germany to mark the anniversary of the victory in Europe, V-E Day. As part of the event, there was to be a special ceremony in a military cemetery at Bitburg. When the plans were made public in the spring of 1985, Americans discovered that among those buried in the cemetery were 49 Waffen SS soldiers. (The Waffen SS was an elite military unit that had been involved in many atrocities during the war.) U.S. veterans' groups, various religious organizations, and Holocaust survivors all urged the president to cancel the trip. But Reagan refused to do so. Still, stunned by the criticism, the president added a visit to a concentration camp to his itinerary. Journalist Marvin Kalb paid a visit to Bitburg the next day.

> I visited the cemetery the morning after President Reagan and Chancellor Helmut Kohl placed wreaths of reconciliation in front of its chapel. For years, the cemetery had been largely ignored; now, it was an instant shrine, a focus of political debate. Small flower pots marked many flat graves, forty-nine of them honoring Waffen SS troops. By the end of my visit, many hundreds of Germans and occasional Americans from the nearby Air Force base paused before the wreaths. Some took pictures. Mothers hushed children. A religious air seemed to saturate the scene.
>
> But look and listen; all around there were the sights and sounds of the new Germany—and the old. Six feet to the left of the president's wreath stood an equally impressive one. Across its banner: "To the Waffen SS who fell at Leningrad." No more than a foot to the right of the Chancellor's was another wreath: "For the fallen comrades of the Waffen SS."
>
> These two wreaths had been placed in the chapel, out of sight, hours before the president arrived. They were restored to their original places of honor only hours after he left. In the ensuing tranquility, the Waffen SS could again be honored in the springtime sun.

"Never again," said the Jews, and they meant one thing only. "Never again," said many Germans, and they meant different things: never again dictatorship, never again war. They meant taking clear political positions that symbolically represented anti-Nazism.

A middle-aged visitor from Nuremberg said the Waffen SS were simply soldiers—young conscripts doing their duty. "Let them rest in peace. For us, a dead soldier is a dead soldier, not a hero."

A native of Bitburg, who looked to be in his twenties, expressed a view I was to hear with disturbing regularity. "We Germans and Americans have been cooperating very well"—and he lowered his voice—"until the Jews began to make trouble."

Another Bitburger zeroed in on Elie Wiesel [who had publicly objected to the visit]. "Imagine the nerve of a Jew lecturing President Reagan. I saw him on television, making trouble the way they all do."

An old woman complained that Mr. Reagan had spent only eight minutes at the cemetery. "You know why the visit had to be cut back? Because of the Jews." She stalked away to join a group of friends nodding in agreement.

A man with a cane stopped and said: "If they don't like it here, the Jews, let them go away. We were better off without them in Germany." There are only 28,000 left, he was reminded. "Too many," he replied.

The people of Bitburg are pleased that Mr. Reagan came to visit, that he didn't yield to pressure. But it's clear they resent their new notoriety—and equally clear whom they consider responsible for the unwelcome change: the Jews and the media. The Jews are seen as a group separate from Germans and Americans—an indigestible lump, a foreign body. The media are seen as intrusive and irresponsible and, somehow, controlled by the Jews.

So it went. A few days later, a Munich newspaper editor explained that anti-Semitism is an "anthropological phenomenon" in Germany. The controversy seems only to have uncorked the venom once again. There is a sad irony. Bitburgers consider themselves remarkably enlightened. In 1933, when Hitler won a critical election, this conservative Catholic town voted overwhelmingly against him.

Is Bitburg an aberration? It is impossible to judge and dangerous to generalize. But a number of leading West German politicians and professors—several close to Kohl—think anti-Semitism was on the rise even before Bitburg. "The Jews were getting too impertinent," one politician said, citing, among other things, their opposition to West German tank sales to Saudi Arabia. "We've listened to them much too long. It's enough."

The pursuit of reconciliation by way of Bitburg has been a failure. What should have been obvious from the beginning is that reconciliation is a long process—not a single photo opportunity, an event, a moment frozen in time. Bitburg, exposing clumsiness and poor political judgment in Bonn and Washington, in the process lifted the scab of dark corners of recent German history. There is a time to know when to leave well enough alone. As I entered the cemetery, I noticed a sign: "Please do not disturb the peace and rest of the dead." Too late.[15]

As I entered the cemetery, I noticed a sign: "Please do not disturb the peace and rest of the dead." Too late.

CONNECTIONS

How does Barnett summarize German Protestant perceptions of the Holocaust? Jewish perceptions? What is the key difference between the two perceptions? Why does Barnett view those differences as significant? What is she suggesting about the importance of confronting the past? About the dangers of refusing to do so?

In Reading 3, Daniel Goleman writes that the creation of a lacuna, or gap in memory, is important to repressive regimes. What does Barnett suggest about its uses in democratic societies? What does she consider the lacuna in modern-day Germany? How does Kalb's account support her view?

What is an *anthropological phenomenon*? Why did the Munich newspaper editor call antisemitism an "anthropological phenomenon"? Was he right to do so?

Kalb called his article, "'New' SS Wreaths, Old Anti-Semitism." What idea is he trying to express in the title? Do you agree?

➤ In 1981, Anja Elisabeth Rosmus, a young German student from the town of Passau, entered a contest sponsored by the president of West Germany. She chose to write about something she had learned in school—the way the people of her town had resisted the Nazis. She approached her topic with every confidence that the history she had learned was correct. Yet her efforts to document that history were repeatedly blocked. The local librarian refused to give her access to town records. So did city officials. Rosmus seemed to stir up old memories and old hatreds as she tried to uncover the truth. In the end, she discovered the people of Passau had not resisted the Nazis at all. Indeed many had enthusiastically supported Hitler.

An interview with Rosmus that originally aired on *60 Minutes* is available from the Facing History Resource Center. Also available is the film *The Nasty Girl*, a fictionalized version of her story. The producer of the film, noting that "old habits die hard," told an interviewer, "People blame one or two guilty individuals or a guilty group for everything that transpired. Then they distance themselves from that person or group, cutting them off and isolating them as the source of the problem."[16] What evidence can you find in Kalb's account of that process? What evidence can you find in other readings? In your own confrontrations with the past?

Accepting Responsibility

Many individuals feel an obligation to confront their past. Nations also feel obliged to face their history. Richard von Weizsaecker, the president of West Germany, attempted to do so on the fortieth anniversary of V-E Day. He said in part:

> May 8 is a day of remembrance. Remembering means recalling an occurrence honestly and undistortedly so that it becomes a part of our very beings. This places high demands on our truthfulness.
>
> Today we mourn all the dead of the war and the tyranny. In particular we commemorate the six million Jews who were murdered in German concentration camps. We commemorate all nations who suffered in the war, especially the countless citizens of the Soviet Union and Poland who lost their lives. As Germans, we mourn our own compatriots who perished as soldiers, during air raids at home, in captivity or during expulsion. We commemorate the Sinti and Romany Gypsies, the homosexuals and the mentally ill who were killed, as well as the people who had to die for their religious or political beliefs. We commemorate the hostages who were executed. We recall the victims of the resistance movements in all the countries occupied by us. As Germans, we pay homage to the victims of the German resistance— among the public, the military, the churches, the workers and trade unions, and the Communists. We commemorate those who did not actively resist but preferred to die instead of violating their consciences.
>
> Alongside the endless army of the dead, mountains of human suffering arise—grief over the dead, suffering from injury or crippling or barbarous compulsory sterilization, suffering during the air raids, during flight and expulsion, suffering because of rape and pillage, forced labor, injustice and torture, hunger and hardship, suffering because of fear of arrest and death, grief at the loss of everything which one had wrongly believed in and worked for. Today we sorrowfully recall all this human suffering. . . .
>
> At the root of the tyranny was Hitler's immeasurable hatred against our Jewish compatriots. Hitler had never concealed this hatred from the public, but made the entire nation a tool of it. Only a day before his death, on April 30, 1945, he concluded his so-called will with the words: "Above all, I call upon the leaders of the nation and their followers to observe painstakingly the race laws and to oppose ruthlessly the poisoners of all nations: international Jewry." Hardly any country has in its history always remained free from blame for war or violence. The genocide of the Jews is, however, unparalleled in history.

The perpetration of this crime was in the hands of a few people. It was concealed from the eyes of the public, but every German was able to experience what his Jewish compatriots had to suffer, ranging from plain apathy and hidden intolerance to outright hatred. Who could remain unsuspecting after the burning of the synagogues, the plundering, the stigmatization with the Star of David, the deprivation of rights, the ceaseless violation of human dignity? Whoever opened his eyes and ears and sought information could not fail to notice that Jews were being deported. The nature and scope of the destruction may have exceeded human imagination, but in reality there was, apart from the crime itself, the attempt by too many people, including those of my generation, who were young and were not involved in planning the events and carrying them out, not to take note of what was happening. There were many ways of not burdening one's conscience, of shunning responsibility, looking away, keeping mum. When the unspeakable truth of the holocaust then became known at the end of the war, all too many of us claimed that they had not known anything about it or even suspected anything.

There is no such thing as the guilt or innocence of an entire nation. Guilt is, like innocence, not collective, but personal. There is discovered or concealed individual guilt. There is guilt which people acknowledge or deny. Everyone who directly experienced that era should today quietly ask himself about his involvement then.

The vast majority of today's population were either children then or had not been born. They cannot profess a guilt of their own for crimes that they did not commit. No discerning person can expect them to wear a penitential robe simply because they are Germans. But their forefathers have left them a grave legacy. All of us, whether guilty or not, whether old or young, must accept the past. We are all affected by its consequences and liable for it. The young and old generations must and can help each other to understand why it is vital to keep alive the memories. It is not a case of coming to terms with the past. That is not possible. It cannot be subsequently modified or made not to have happened. Anyone who closes his eyes to the past is blind to the present. Whoever refuses to remember the inhumanity is prone to new risks of infection.[17]

There is no such thing as the guilt or innocence of an entire nation. Guilt is, like innocence, not collective, but personal.

Anyone who closes his eyes to the past is blind to the present. Whoever refuses to remember the inhumanity is prone to new risks of infection.

CONNECTIONS

What did Weizsaecker mean when he said that "anyone who closes his eyes to the past is blind to the present"? Do you agree?

According to Weizsaecker, what are the consequences of "not burdening one's conscience, of shunning responsibility, looking away, keeping mum"? Give examples from your own experience or your reading that support his view. Give examples that call his view into question.

Is Weizsaecker right to believe that guilt, like innocence, is personal rather than collective? Can a whole nation be guilty?

In August of 1993, fifty years after World War II left more than twenty million people dead in Asia, Japan finally took some responsibility for the brutal policies that brought on the suffering. "I myself believe it was a war of aggression, a war that was wrong," said Prime Minister Morihiro Hosokawa in a deceptively simple statement. Individuals often find it hard to apologize. Why is it a difficult thing to do? Why do nations find it even harder to admit that they were wrong?

Russia has also found it difficult to admit it was wrong. For years, it refused to acknowledge that in September of 1941, at Babi Yar —a ravine outside Kiev, in the Ukraine—the Nazis gunned down over thirty-three thousand Jews. On the twentieth anniversary of the murders, Russian poet Yevgeny Yevtushenko wrote:

> No monument stands over Babi Yar
> The steep precipice is the only gravestone
> I am afraid.

Only after Jews and non-Jews spontaneously remembered the victims on the 25th anniversary of the event did the Communists place a small granite stone at the site to honor "victims of Fascism." In 1976, they unveiled a more heroic monument and set aside the area as a memorial. The plaque noted that "100,000 victims of Fascism" died at Babi Yar but failed to mention that many were Jews. Then in 1991, on the 50th anniversary of Babi Yar, the last president of the Soviet Union, Mikhail Gorbachev, told a crowd:

> Among tens of millions of dead, there were almost six million Jews—representatives of a great nation, dispersed by fate across the planet. Babi Yar is testimony that both on our soil and everywhere in Europe, Jews were always among the Nazis' first victims.
>
> The Nazis speculated on the vilest feelings—envy, nationalist intolerance and hatred. Antisemitism was their main tool of poisoning people's consciousness with chauvinism and racism.

After acknowledging that Stalin used antisemitism to strengthen his own power, Gorbachev noted that the ceremony at Babi Yar "brings hope that we, our renewing society, are able to draw lessons from tragedies and mistakes of the past." Why do you think Gorbachev chose Babi Yar to condemn antisemitism? How was his speech similar to Weizsaecker's? What differences seem most striking?

READING 7

Education and Memory

President Richard von Weizsaecker said of himself and other Germans, "All of us, whether guilty or not, whether old or young, must accept the past. We are all affected by its consequences and liable for it." Yet many young Germans know little or nothing about their country's history. Jane Kramer wrote of one group of teenagers:

> The [skinheads] say "Heil Hitler!" but they know nothing about Hitler, or the war, beyond the fact that Hitler exterminated people who were "different," which is what they would like to do themselves. They do not even know about the "ethnic cleansing" going on a few hundred miles away in Bosnia now. They do not read newspapers. They read killer comic books and listen to Oi music, which is a kind of heavy-metal rock about the pleasures of genocide. Some of them think that Oi comes from the British skins, the Paki (for "Pakistani") bashers, whom they admire as the first skins; they think that it means "original idea." Some of them think that it comes from "joy." And some of them think that it comes from the "oi" in "Doitschland." They go to Oi concerts. They do not know that other people think of Oi as a Yiddish word. They do not know Jews or anything about Jews, but Jews are certainly on their hit list, along with Turks, refugees, and asylum seekers, anybody "foreign." They try to attack Jews when they can find them. The last time skins in Germany attacked a Jew—they killed him—it turned out the Jew may have been a Christian. They said later that he "looked" Jewish.[18]

Bodo Franzmann, a German publisher, has responded to the failure of German schools to teach about the Nazi era by producing a comic book that graphically describes key events in World War II, including the Holocaust. The book clearly indicates that the German public knew what Hitler stood for when he took office in 1933. It also shows how Hitler's "euthanasia" program was carried out. Eight pages are devoted to the Holocaust itself. And the author notes that while Germans "registered that Jews were disappearing, nobody asked where they were going and nobody wanted to know."

Before one community piloted the materials, high school students were questioned about their views of Germany's Nazi past. About 25 percent thought future generations would give Hitler a "fairer judgment." The same percentage believed that a man such as Hitler was needed to improve Germany's standing in the world. According to Hermann Nink, a teacher in Worms, "The most common misconception the youngsters had was that only one man, Hitler, was guilty for everything that happened. The comic

All of us, whether guilty or not, whether old or young, must accept the past. We are all affected by its consequences and liable for it.

helped them understand how and why he came to power and how many people helped him commit the terrible crimes."[19]

After students had read the comic, many more realized that Germans cannot escape blame for voting for the Nazis. "What impressed the young readers was learning the details of how Hitler came to power—realizing he was not born a Nazi but how he became one," said Nink. "This is the most important lesson they could learn—to realize how it is happening to people today."[20]

CONNECTIONS

Weizsaecker says that we must accept the past because we are affected by its consequences and liable for it. How does this reading support his belief? How does it challenge his views?

In France, Serge Klarsfeld spent twenty years trying to persuade officials to revise the nation's history textbooks. As a result of his efforts, students in France no longer learn that the Germans rounded up French and foreign Jews and then deported them. They are now confronted with the truth: it was not the Germans but the French who deported the Jews. Klarsfeld believes that the battle for more complete and truthful accounts in textbooks is important. Would German educators agree? Do you agree?

Can textbooks have blind spots? To find out, check the way two or three different books treat one or more of the following topics: Native American histories, the Atlantic slave trade, the "winning" of the West, the placement of Japanese Americans in internment camps during World War II, the Vietnam War. What similarities do you notice? What differences seem most striking?

How is education linked to memory? Does that education have to take place in school? Where else do students learn about the past?

READING 8

Denial and the Holocaust

The sense of urgency many survivors feel about telling their story is inspired in part by teenagers like those described in the previous reading. It is also fueled by those who deny that there was a Holocaust. Saul Friedlander, an historian born in Czechoslovakia, explains:

At the end of the war, Nazism was the damned part of Western civilization, the symbol of evil. Everything the Nazis had done was condemned, whatever they touched defiled; a seemingly indelible stain darkened the German past, while preceding centuries were scrutinized for the origins of this monstrous development. A sizable portion of the European elites, who two or three years before the German defeat had made no secret of their sympathy for the new order, were struck dumb and suffered total amnesia. Evidence of adherence, of enthusiasms shared, the written and oral record of four years of coexistence with it, and indeed of collaboration, often vanished. From one day to the next, the past was swept away, and it remained gone for the next twenty-five years.

By the end of the Sixties, however, the Nazi image in the West had begun to change. Not radically or across the board, but here and there, and on the right as well as the left, perceptibly and revealingly enough to allow one to speak of the existence of a new kind of discourse.[21]

Among the leaders of that "new kind of discourse" are the so-called "revisionists"—individuals who insist that there was no Holocaust. Yet most reputable scholars ignored their writings and speeches until 1979. That year, Willis Carto, the treasurer of an antisemitic political group called the Liberty Lobby, founded the Institute for Historical Review. Based in California, the institute published a journal, organized conferences, and acted as a clearinghouse for the "revisionists." On the surface, the group seemed respectable. The word *revisionist* is a familiar one to scholars. They use it to refer to those who question accepted theories. The writers' university ties and many publications added to their respectability.

Then in 1979, the Institute for Historical Review offered $50,000 to anyone who could prove that Jews had been murdered in the gas chambers at Auschwitz. Holocaust survivors were stunned. One survivor, Mel Mermelstein, decided to fight back. Mermelstein had been a prisoner in Auschwitz and several members of his family were gassed there. He did not rely, however, just on his own experiences. He also provided pages of documentation, including eyewitness testimony. When the Institute for Historical Review refused to accept his proof, he filed suit against them. At a preliminary hearing on October 19, 1981, the Los Angeles Superior Court ruled that Mermelstein did not have to prove that the Nazis gassed Jews at Auschwitz. He had to prove only that he had not been compensated as promised and suffered emotional stress as a result. In July, 1985, two weeks before the trial was to begin, the Institute settled out of court. It paid Mermelstein $90,000 ($50,000 for the reward and $40,000 for emotional damages) and formally apologized to him and to the court.

Despite the apology, the following year the group charged Mermelstein with libel for statements he made about the incident. When Mermelstein fought back, the charges were withdrawn. Nevertheless, he countersued, charging that the original suit was filed solely to harass him. He also charged that the Institute and its affiliates had ties to the Nazi party. Eight years later, the case was still in the courts.

The Institute and a number of other "revisionist" groups base many of their arguments on the claim that it was technically impossible for large numbers of people to be gassed at Auschwitz-Birkenau or Majdanek. In France, Serge Klarsfeld, the son of a survivor of the Holocaust, and his wife Beate, the daughter of a German soldier, asked Jean-Claude Pressac to critique reports that purported to substantiate those claims. Pressac, the author of a widely respected article on the crematoria at Auschwitz-Birkenau, described revisionist reports as "based on misinformation, which leads to false reasoning and misinterpretation of data."

Pressac's views are of interest not only because his own report is considered definitive but also because he himself once had "revisionist" leanings. In the process of collecting background information for a novel, Pressac went to Auschwitz to gather information about Nazi extermination techniques. Surprised at the lack of physical and documentary evidence, he spent the next eight years studying and analyzing the minute technical details of the Auschwitz crematoriums. His extensive review of blueprints, work orders, and inventories exposed inconsistencies between the stated purpose of the "showering" or "fumigation" chambers and their actual design. For example, when Pressac studied the plans for a chamber in Crematorium II at Birkenau, he found the inventory of the room listed over twenty showerheads but not a single water pipe. And in the written instructions to the workers who built the chamber, Pressac discovered references to *"gasdichte Tueren"* (gas-tight doors), a *"Vergasungskeller"* (gassing chamber), gas-detection devices, and four chutes for introducing Zyklon B into the chamber.

Pressac's second book, *The Auschwitz Crematoria: The Machinery of Mass Slaughter*, provides additional evidence from recently opened K.G.B. archives in Russia. In a telephone interview, Pressac told journalist Timothy Ryback, "In my first book, I worked with twenty documents from the archives of the Auschwitz Museum. The Moscow archives provided me with another sixty documents. This has allowed me to create a complete chronology of the extermination process at Auschwitz and a complete history of the instruments of destruction—when they were built, what their capacity was, when they broke down or malfunctioned. The Holocaust is no longer written in sand. Now it is written in concrete."[22]

CONNECTIONS

If it takes so much effort to refute the claims of revisionists fifty years after the end of World War II, how much harder will it be after another fifty years pass?

Pressac's first book was published in 1989. Ryback says of it, "Through his research, Pressac has provided incontrovertible evidence, based on objec-

The Holocaust is no longer written in sand. Now it is written in concrete.

tive technical detail, that the Germans developed and implemented an industrial-style process for the killing of human beings." Yet the "revisionists" have continued to claim the Holocaust never happened. Chapter 2, Reading 8 described a study made by the German Anthropological Society in the late 1800s. It established that there were no "racial differences" between Jewish and "Aryan" children. Historian George Mosse was quoted as saying of the study:

> This survey should have ended controversies about the existence of pure Aryans and Jews. However, it seems to have had surprisingly little impact. The idea of race had been infused with myths, stereotypes, and subjectivities long ago, and a scientific survey could change little.

How do responses to both studies support the view that what people believe is true is more important than the truth itself? What do they suggest about the power of a lie? What other parallels do you see between the two studies? What differences seem most striking?

Discrediting "revisionists" and their claims is one way to refute denials of the Holocaust. Serge Klarsfeld maintains that four other strategies are needed as well: accurate, well-researched histories; eyewitness accounts to enrich those histories; trials of war criminals along with efforts to educate people about the Holocaust; and films that document the reality of the Holocaust. Which strategy do you consider most effective?

The two lengthy but gripping documentaries Klarsfeld recommends are *Hotel Terminus* and *The Sorrow and the Pity*. Both are the work of French filmmaker Marcel Ophuls. Each raises questions not only of complicity and resistance in France during World War II but also about history and memory. In a third film, *The Memory of Justice*, Ophuls considers the Nuremberg trials and then compares World War II with the wars for independence in Algeria and Vietnam. What film would you select as the best to counter a denial of the Holocaust? What books or documents would you recommend to accomplish the same purpose?

In 1979, the United States government established the Office of Special Investigations (OSI) in the Department of Justice to hunt Nazis. These men and women were able to enter the nation only by illegally concealing facts about their past. If the OSI can prove they were Nazis, their citizenship can be revoked and they can be deported. How important is it to track down Nazi war criminals? What are the short-term consequnces of *not* doing so? The long-term consequences?

➤➤Mermelstein used his own money to fight the Institute for Historical Review in court. Why do you think he chose to do so? What does his story suggest about how one person can make a difference? A video entitled *Never Forget* is available from the Facing History Resource Center. Also available are records of Mermelstein's first court case.

The First Amendment and Denial

Holocaust deniers play upon contemporary society's tendency toward historical amnesia, and its muzzy notion of "tolerance" that cannot distinguish between an open mind and an empty mind.

The revisionists are not interested in truth, writes a judge in France, but in "the destruction of the dead's only 'grave,' that is, our memory, and the erosion of all awareness of the crime itself."[23] In her book, *Denying the Holocaust: The Growing Assault on Truth and Memory*, Deborah Lipstadt provides detailed evidence in support of that view. She shows that denial activities usually spring from antisemitism rather than a concern for the truth. But Lipstadt did not write her book just to counter "revisionists." She had another reason as well. Columnist George Will explained it when he related an incident that took place at an interview Lipstadt gave to publicize the book.

> Holocaust deniers play upon contemporary society's tendency toward historical amnesia, and its fuzzy notion of "tolerance" that cannot distinguish between an open mind and an empty mind. Thus a young reporter for a respected magazine interviewing Lipstadt (without reading her book) asked this question: "What proof do you include in your book that the Holocaust happened?" That reporter passed through college unmarked by information about even the largest events of the century, but acquired the conventional skepticism of the empty-headed: When in doubt, doubt.[24]

The attitude Will describes can also be seen in the way college newspapers responded to ads placed by a group known as the Committee for Open Debate on the Holocaust. Two professors at Rutgers University in New Jersey, historian David Oshinsky and political scientist Michael Curtis, commented on those responses:

> College newspapers are facing a dilemma that pits free speech against historical deception. A group calling itself the Committee for Open Debate on the Holocaust has sent an advertisement to at least a dozen leading campus dailies. The ad contends that the Holocaust never occurred.
>
> Newspapers at Harvard, Yale, Brown, the University of Pennsylvania, and the University of Southern California have refused to run it. Those at Northwestern, Cornell, Duke, and the University of Michigan have published it amid protests from students, faculty and members of their own editorial boards. At Rutgers, the ad was printed free of charge on Dec. 3 as a "guest commentary," surrounded by rebuttals.
>
> The ad attempts to prey on students' ignorance about the Holocaust. It insists, without evidence, that there were no mass killings

of Jews and no "execution gas chambers in any camp in Europe that was under German control." It claims the so-called execution chambers were "fumigation chambers," used "to delouse clothing. . . and prevent disease." It is "from this life-saving procedure," the ad says, "that the myth of extermination gas chambers emerged."

The slickly done ad does not use the violent language common to the literature of racist and nativist groups. It wraps itself in concepts of free speech and open inquiry, arguing that all points of view deserve to be heard. Timed to exploit the controversy about political correctness, the ad says "elitist" and "Zionist" groups have stifled debate on the Holocaust in order "to drum up world sympathy" for Jewish causes and Israel.

The ad was written by Bradley R. Smith, a political soulmate of the California-based Institute for Historical Review, the principal promoter of "Holocaust revisionism." . . . Bradley Smith's committee apparently believes that its theories will be tolerated by some on First Amendment grounds and accepted by others out of ignorance or worse. The Duke student newspaper naively repeated the committee's description of itself as a group of revisionist scholars. Duke's history department was appalled and responded with a statement that distinguished between those who revise history and those who deny it.

Most college editors seem aware of the committee's intentions. Their decision to print its ad is based on principle: an aversion to censorship or a belief that hate material should be aired and publicly refuted. Surely their right to publish such ads should not be questioned. They alone must decide what good purpose, if any, is served by printing ads that are intentionally hurtful and obviously false.

The ads should be rejected. If one group advertises that the Holocaust never happened, another can buy space to insist that American blacks were never enslaved. The stakes are high because college newspapers may soon be flooded with ads that present discredited assertions as if they were part of normal historical debate. If the Holocaust is not a fact, then nothing is a fact, and truth itself will be diminished.[25]

> If one group advertises that the Holocaust never happened, another can buy space to insist that American blacks were never enslaved.

CONNECTIONS

Why does George Will call the saying "When in doubt, doubt" the "conventional skepticism of the empty-headed"? Do you agree?

Lucy Dawidowicz, the author of *The War Against the Jews,* was asked to appear on a radio program with a French "revisionist" who calls the gas chamber and genocide "one and the same lie." When she refused to do so, she was asked if she was against discussing "controversial" issues on the radio. What does the question imply? How is it like the one directed at Lipstadt? Did Dawidowicz do the right thing?

Why do you think the advertisers called their group the *"Committee for Open Debate on the Holocaust"*? What does the name imply? Why might it have special appeal to educated people?

Bradley Smith's committee believes that its theories will be tolerated by some people on First Amendment grounds and "accepted by others out of ignorance or worse." Research the First Amendment to the Constitution. How does it apply to this case? Do people have the right to tell lies? To teach lies? To promote hate?

"If you have a hundred books in the world today that are all devoted to teaching that the Holocaust did not happen, imagine the seeds that can fall on unsuspecting minds," Bill Moyers said in an interview. "Unless we keep hammering home the irrefutable and indisputable facts of the human experience, history as it was experienced by people, we are going to find ourselves increasingly unable to draw distinctions between what was and what we think was."[26] How does this reading support Moyers's point of view? Why do you think Moyers views education as the solution? Do you agree?

In critiquing a crusade against hate speech, Henry Louis Gates, Jr., an African American scholar, insists, "Beliefs that go untested and unchallenged cannot prosper." What does he mean by that statement? Should there be limits on free speech?

Judith Miller writes, "Only a tiny group of malevolent cranks contends that the Holocaust did not take place, but the more subtle forms of revisionism are evident in battles over how history should be taught, in jokes, in literature, and in the popular culture, in television and films."[27] How do the examples of revisionism in this reading support her opinion? Call it into question? Look for other examples in newspapers, television, and films.

➤Canada has a law that makes hate a crime. In 1982, James Keegstra, a high-school history teacher, was charged with violating that law after a student told his mother what he learned in history class. According to the boy, Keegstra taught students that "the Jews received this idea for communism. He said the person who told them how to use communism to control the world was a man named Baal." When asked who Baal was, Keegstra replied, "The devil, Satan." Students were also taught that the French Revolution and the American Civil War were "international Jewish conspiracies." In a class on World War II, Keegstra referred to Jews as "treacherous," "subversive," "sadistic," "money-loving," "child-killers," and "gutter-rats."

When the boy's mother, Susan Maddox, complained to school officials, they ignored her at first. So did her neighbors. Later they began to harrass her. After all, Keegstra was a well-liked teacher with considerable support in the community. But Maddox would not be silenced. After a long battle to "set kids straight," she managed to get Keegstra suspended. Why do you think Susan Maddox chose to take a stand even though her position was not a popular one? *Evil at Clearwater*, a television docudrama of the case, is available from the Facing History Resource Center, as is an investigative report on the Keegstra case entitled *Lessons In Hate*. It provides an excellent summary of the case and includes an interview with Keegstra.

READING 10

A Living Past

In 1939, as Hitler planned the murder of the Jews, he asked, "Who after all speaks today of the annihilation of the Armenians?" What happens to a history that has not been judged or even acknowledged? Are the survivors left isolated and alone? Laura Akgulian offers some insights into the ways an unacknowledged history shaped the lives of members of her own family. She discovered that history on a visit to an aunt.

"Make yourself at home, honey. You wanna take a shower?"

Auntie Parouz's suggestion made me vaguely uneasy. Would she think me uncouth if I didn't wash up? I had traveled only an hour by plane and another hour by limo—hardly enough to work up a sweat. I decided to risk falling a notch in her esteem. "No, thanks, Auntie— maybe later."

I didn't intend to converse much with Auntie the weekend I stayed at her house. But when the man I had flown to Massachusetts to interview could not see me until late afternoon, extra time suddenly materialized. I sat on a couch beside Auntie, and she told me a remarkable story.

The ironies of Auntie's life began 76 years ago. As she celebrated her ninth birthday, hundreds of Armenian intellectuals and community leaders were rounded up and executed by Turkish soldiers. Life for Armenians in Turkey was shattered. Parouz and more than one million other Armenians were driven from the land their ancestors had tended for centuries. Hundreds of thousands perished. Parouz's birthday –April 24– had become her people's day of mourning.

It was early summer, 1915. Parouz and the other Armenians from her village of Yenikhan were given 24 hours to pack. They could take only what they could carry on their backs. Parouz's family packed bread and water. Her mother concealed as much jewelry and money as she could on herself and Parouz; they then buried the rest in their yard.

The Turkish gendarmes never explained what was happening. "Dey said, 'You gonna come back.'" Parouz's voice is so soft and husky it almost seems a whisper. "Dat was foolish—dat we believed it."

In 1939, as Hitler planned the murder of the Jews, he asked, "Who after all speaks today of the annihilation of the Armenians?" What happens to a history that has not been judged or even acknowledged?

The soldiers prodded the marchers up and down mountains, past unfamiliar villages. At each stopping point, more Armenians were forced into the ragtag procession. Few Armenian men marched, the soldiers having, early on, shot them or thrown them into gorges.

If the Armenians didn't walk fast, soldiers on horseback would whip them. Parouz saw one of them slit a woman's face from ear to ear. The woman had to press one hand down on the top of her head and the other under her chin to hold her face together.

The marchers were robbed at every turn. One soldier ripped a gold earring from Parouz's ear; her left earlobe still hangs in two pieces. It was commonly thought that Armenians swallowed their valuables for safekeeping. Parouz remembers how a Turkish soldier looking for gold had sliced open a pregnant woman, scooped out the baby, and tossed it aside.

For eight months, Parouz and her mother endured this nightmarish journey to nowhere. Parouz's bare feet had such deep cracks that her mother tore fabric from Parouz's raggedy dress, cleaned out the pebbles imbedded in her heels, and stuffed the cracks with cloth.

Everywhere they would trip over dead Armenians. The dehydrated, malnourished corpses were swollen like balloons. Parouz noticed puddles where the bodily fluids were draining.

They screamed as Parouz's little brother was carried off by a horseman. They wept as pretty Armenian girls were raped and kidnapped. Her fair skin, blue-gray eyes, and auburn tresses made Parouz herself a likely victim, so her mother shaved her head and eyebrows and smeared her with dirt. Despite these precautions, a soldier grabbed her and was about to ride off when a young girl threw sand in his eyes. Blinded, he dropped Parouz. The rescuer grew up to be my grandmother.

One would expect Parouz to be bitter. Yet she is love incarnate. Sobbing quietly, she thanks God—for her mother's companionship on the march. For the good-hearted Arab woman who hid her for three years. For happy childhood memories, like picking daffodils near Yenikhan. She doesn't condemn Turks as a group: many of them were undoubtedly decent, she says; the government was awful.

While telling her story, she apologizes to her daughter Alice and me: "I'm sorry, I'm makin' you cry." She forgives my gruesome questions ("What do you remember about the corpses, Auntie?"); our brief visit has so pleased her that she exclaims, between sobs, "I'm enjoyin' every minute!"

Parouz is slipping toward eternal sleep; terminal illness rages within her. Perhaps my most vivid memory is how she still suffers over water. No matter where our conversation meandered, it returned, like a parched traveler, to fountains and flowing rivers. Armenians, filthy and dying of thirst, weren't permitted to touch water. Children died diving into wells. People licked grass. They lapped up mud. For five gold coins her mother bought a cup of water from a Turkish villager; her family gathered around to sip it.

A few months ago, hospitalized after a stroke, Parouz couldn't have liquids. She became so desperate that one night she begged the nurse to empty the flowers from a vase so she could drink the water. Ironically, since the stroke, her eyes no longer water—she literally has no more tears to shed.

She can't bear to see water wasted. "If anything drips," Alice says, "she'll about go crazy." Only after leaving did it dawn on me why she kept urging, "Take a shower, make you-self comfortable." Her most precious possession is running water—enough to lavish on someone else. Forgive me, Auntie Parouz, I didn't know you had offered me the ultimate luxury.[28]

CONNECTIONS

Why is Laura Akgulian's aunt unable to forget the past? How is Akgulian's reaction to her aunt's story similar to that of Donia Clenman's family (Reading 4)? What differences seem most striking?

A personal account is not a history. Yet many historians regard personal accounts as invaluable. What is the difference between memory and history? What can you learn from a personal account that you cannot learn from a history book?

➤The Facing History Resource Center has a packet of materials on the Armenian Genocide, including the memoirs of survivors, news accounts of the genocide, and three videos that provide a general introduction to the Armenian Genocide: *Not Everyone is Here* (the way post-genocide generations have dealt with the legacy of genocide); *The Armenian Genocide* (an overview of the genocidal policies of the Young Turks); and *Return to Ararat* (the experiences of a survivor who returns to historic Armenia). The Resource Center also has class sets of the memoir *Road from Home* by David Kherdian and a video interview with the author.

Truth: The Last Victim of Genocide

Vigen Guroian, an expert on the Armenian Genocide, recounts the following story to illustrate the dangers of a history that is unacknowledged and unjudged.

And so year by year, person by person, the genocide blurs, doubt corrodes it, and the easy word, "alleged" creeps in to mock the Armenian anguish.

In May 1983, Richard Cohen wrote an article in the Washington Post entitled "Killing Truth." Cohen in a previous piece had made a passing reference to the Armenian Genocide. He had done so "thinking," as he said, "that it was a given—that no one could possibly dispute that it had happened." In "Killing Truth" Cohen returns to the subject of the Armenian Genocide after a meeting at the Turkish embassy arranged by the Turkish Ambassador Sukru Elekdag. Though he does not say so, Cohen leaves no doubt that he was invited to the embassy because of this mention of the Armenian Genocide in his column. He writes:

"I found myself sitting at one end of an enormous table in the embassy of Turkey. At the other end was the ambassador himself and what he was telling me was that the crime I had always thought had happened, simply had not . . .

"What the world persisted in calling a genocide was actually a civil war—one with atrocities on both sides and one in which the central government in Constantinople lost control of its own troops and could not protect the Armenians. There never was a policy to exterminate the Armenians."

Cohen admits that his confidence was shaken. He was left wondering whether that which he thought for so long was simply a matter of historical record had veracity. For during their conversation the ambassador had dismissed adroitly the sources to which Cohen referred as proof of the genocide, claiming they were distortions "based on hearsay" and allied propaganda of the time. "I read some more about Armenia and talked to some more people," writes Cohen, "but the fact is the ambassador dented my confidence." Cohen found himself in a position not uncommon to so many others whose lives in one way or another have been touched by the Armenian Genocide and its denial. He did not have the time or the requisite linguistic skills to read further. He found himself a part of the problem. "And so year by year, person by person," Cohen reflects, "the genocide blurs, doubt corrodes it, and the easy word, 'alleged' creeps in to mock the Armenian anguish."

Cohen in this article proves to be a conscientious human being who has also learned the destructive power of a lie. He is unwilling to rest at ease with a process which threatens to dispose of all clarity about the first genocide of this century. Letting bygones be bygones will not do, he insists, at least not in the case of the Armenian Genocide or the Holocaust or the Cambodian massacres. For the denial of such occurrences is not simply an attempt to rewrite the past. It is, as he so rightly observes, a deliberate effort "to control the present and shape the future." . . . Cohen ends his article with the disturbing thought that perhaps "the last victim of any genocide is truth."[29]

The last victim of any genocide is truth.

CONNECTIONS

The Turkish ambassador told Cohen that "what the world persisted in calling a genocide was actually a civil war—one with atrocities on both sides." Is he denying the genocide, explaining it, or rationalizing it? What are the consequences of each course of action? What effect does he assume his statement will have on Cohen?

What did Cohen mean when he wrote that "and so year by year, person by person, the genocide blurs, doubt corrodes it, and the easy word, 'alleged' creeps in to mock the Armenian anguish"? Why does he call *alleged* an "easy word"? What is the "destructive power of a lie"? What does it destroy? How does it affect the teller? The victim? Generations to come? Why did it shake Cohen's confidence?

What does the expression "let bygones be bygones" mean? Should bygones always be bygones?

Cohen concludes by saying that "the last victim of any genocide is truth." Judith Miller says that "denial, the least sophisticated form of suppression, is the easiest to combat." How do accounts like Reading 10 support her view? What happens when the last witness is gone?

READING 12

The Politics of Denial

Many believe that "history submits to politics." That is, they maintain that politicians and some historians promote new interpretations of history for reasons that have little to do with the event itself and everything to do with their nation's economic, political, or social concerns. The history of the Armenian Genocide is a good example. When the Allies divided up the old Ottoman Empire after World War I, Turkey was in the midst of a civil war. When the war ended in 1923, the nation had a new leader, Mustafa Kemal Pasha, who took the name Kemal Ataturk. He set out to

For the millions of
Armenians around the
globe . . . , the wounds . . .
remain open, they have
not been closed, and the
hurt's not been able to
heal, because the world
has not faced up to the
truth of the suffering of the
Armenian people in this
period from 1915 to 1923.

build a modern Islamic state. From the start, that state was deeply affected by world politics. The Allies were now united only in their opposition to the new Soviet Union. They saw Turkey, which bordered Russia, as a barrier against communism. So when Kemal Ataturk, an anti-communist nationalist, insisted that there was no Armenian Genocide, no world leader challenged his statement. He did not deny that Armenians suffered during the war. But, he insisted, others had suffered as well.

In time, Kemal Ataturk's view of the massacres became the one most people accepted. Some historians now argued that the Armenians, as a non-Muslim minority with co-religionists in Russia, were rightly seen as a threat to the survival of the Ottoman Empire. Others debated the number of deaths. They claimed that the original estimates of a million to 1.5 million were too high. No more than six hundred thousand died and those deaths were the result of civil war rather than genocide.

A debate in the United States Senate in February, 1990, revealed how successful the Turks have been in their efforts to attach the word *alleged* to the Armenian Genocide. As the seventy-fifth anniversary of the massacres approached, Senator Robert Dole of Kansas sponsored a resolution designating April 24 as a "National Day of Man's Inhumanity to Man." Fifteen years earlier, a similar resolution passed without debate. This time, however, the measure prompted considerable controversy. In his newscast, TV journalist Roger Mudd tried to help Americans understand why:

> No one seems to doubt that a staggering number of Christian Armenians died at the hands of the Moslem Turks between 1915 and 1922. But how they died, claims the modern Turkish Government, was not genocide, it was starvation and resettlement and guerrilla warfare, and to call that genocide would be not only insulting but would also undermine U.S./Turkish relations. . . .
>
> The Armenian resolution comes from Senator Dole, who makes no secret of his debt to an Armenian orthopedic surgeon, Hampar Kalikian of Chicago, who helped nurse him back to health mentally and physically from his terrible World War II wounds. Three of Kalikian's sisters died in the Armenian killings—genocide.
>
> *Sen. Dole (Feb. 21, 1990):* Action on this resolution will not open old wounds. For the millions of Armenians around the globe including nearly one million in this country, the wounds have been opened for almost seventy-five years, and they're open, remain open, they have not been closed, and the hurt's not been able to heal, because the world has not faced up to the truth of the suffering of the Armenian people in this period from 1915 to 1923.
>
> *Mr. Mudd:* At one point last fall, Dole had sixty other sponsors on his resolution, but that number has now dropped to forty-nine because of, says Dole, the lobbying clout of the Turkish Government and its refusal to compromise.

Sen. Dole: Can a million and a half people disappear and say, oh, well, we don't want, certainly don't want to harm our relations with the Turks? We're talking about the Ottomans, and keep in mind, they were on the side of the Germans. They weren't helping us in 1915 to 1923. And as I said yesterday, there is no effort, no attempt in any way to implicate the Republic of Turkey.

Mr. Mudd: Lined up with Dole are six of the Senate's eight Jewish senators, men like Carl Levin of Michigan [a Democrat], who find little difference between genocide and holocaust.

Sen. Levin: Mr. President, Hitler asked when he was planning the final solution of the Jews, "Who remembers the Armenians?" Let us prove Hitler wrong again and by adoption of this resolution remember the Armenian genocide.

Mr. Mudd: Also in favor of the resolution is Republican Pete Wilson now running for Governor of California, which is where roughly twenty-five per cent of Armenian-Americans live.

Sen. Wilson: It was the genocide, and there can be no lesser word for what occurred, the slaughter of a million and a half people, innocent men, women and children. It is language that simply calls upon us to observe with a day of remembrance that tragedy. And the only offense that it gives would be to those actually responsible for that genocide, those long dead, I might say.

Mr. Mudd: Leading the opposition is Robert Byrd of West Virginia, the Senate's senior Democrat, who has since his first days in the Congress been one of Turkey's reliables.

Sen. Byrd: Mr. President, we're not here to determine what is right and what is wrong. This is for the courts to do. And we have created an instrument under the Genocide Convention to determine what is right and what is wrong. Is this Senate going to set itself up as the instrument whereby genocide is to be determined and where the crime of genocide is to be determined where the nation or group that commits the crime is to be labeled, is to be accused of a crime called genocide?

Mr. Mudd: Add to Byrd's opposition that of Sam Nunn, the influential chairman of the Armed Services Committee.

Sen. Nunn: If I thought this resolution could wipe out the tears, the suffering and tragedy of the Armenian people, then my perspective on it would be different. But I'm afraid that we're going to inflame a situation now that does not need inflaming. And I think we're going to cause additional problems if this resolution passes. Mr. President, the Turkish government has made it clear that passage of the resolution before us will cause serious damage to the partnership between the United States and Turkey that we've worked so hard to build. . . .

Mr. Mudd: Late this afternoon as the Senate approached a second vote to cut off debate, Byrd and Dole squared off with one another.

> If I thought this resolution could wipe out the tears, the suffering and tragedy of the Armenian people, then my perspective on it would be different. But I'm afraid that we're going to inflame a situation now that does not need inflaming.

> *Sen. Dole:* We're saying that we can't talk about this genocide; it might embarrass somebody. We can only talk about genocides from here on that don't embarrass anybody. You find me somewhere where they've killed a million people or five hundred thousand or a hundred thousand and if they don't embarrass anybody and don't threaten any American company's profit margin and don't require a few hours studying the facts, then we'll bring it up and pass it.
>
> *Sen. Byrd:* We may be doing the Armenian people a great disservice. Who knows? We may be helping to inflame passions right on this floor, where too much has already been said, and too many have branded Turkey as a criminal.
>
> *Mr. Mudd:* On the vote to close down the filibuster, Dole lost further ground this afternoon, falling twelve votes short of the needed two-thirds. Dole must now decide whether to give up his Armenian crusade or start offering the genocide resolution as an amendment to other legislation.[30]

CONNECTIONS

The overview to this chapter identifies four ways people suppress the truth. Find examples of all four in this reading. Judith Miller views rationalization and relativization as "the most common, insidious, and hence problematic forms of the suppression of memory." How do the examples you identified support her point of view?

How important is it that this Armenian history be called a *genocide*? How important is it that the Holocaust be called a *genocide*? Do the names we give events matter?

Summarize the arguments on both sides in the Senate debate. Are the two sides debating the same question or is each basing its position on a different issue?

Why is Hitler quoted in the debate? What do his remarks suggest about the importance of remembering the past?

What does Senator Nunn mean when he says, "If I thought this resolution could wipe out the tears, the suffering and tragedy of the Armenian people, then my perspective on it would be different. But I'm afraid that we're going to inflame a situation now that does not need inflaming." Do you agree?

Richard Hovannisian, a professor of history at the University of California at Los Angeles, describes the successes the Turks had in their efforts to rewrite history during the Cold War.

Illustrative of this success was an affair relating to plans by MGM Studios to film a motion picture based on Franz Werfel's The Forty Days of Musa Dagh, a saga of some 4,000 Armenian villagers near the Mediterranean Sea who in 1915 resisted the deportation decrees and endured great hardship with legendary courage until they were miraculously rescued by Allied naval vessels. News that a script for the film was being prepared elicited formal protests from the Turkish government, intercession by the Department of State, and pressure on MGM and the Motion Picture Producers and Distributors of America. These channels were ultimately sufficient to force MGM to shelve the project, and all subsequent efforts to revive it were met by a repetition of protest, intercession, pressure, and cancellation.[31]

Why would a foreign government want to stop an American movie about an event that took place long ago? Why would the State Department help the Turks do so? What do your answers suggest about the politics of history? Could it happen today?

➤ The Facing History Resource Center has copies of articles and documents prepared by the Armenian Assembly to refute Senator Byrd and his supporters. Also available is a video tape of a talk by Richard Hovannisian. It is summarized in *Elements of Time,* pages 350-352.

READING 13

What About My History?

The Germans and the Turks are not the only people to have difficulty facing the truth about their past. Americans have had similar problems in confronting their history. In 1941, Richard Wright, a noted novelist wrote:

We black folk, our history, and our present being, are a mirror of all the manifold experiences of what America *is*. If we black folk perish, America will perish. If America has forgotten her past, then let her look into the mirror of our consciousness and she will see the *living* past living in the present, for our memories go back, through our black folk of today, through the recollections of our black parents, and through the tales of slavery told by our black grandparents, to the time when none of us, black or white, lived in this fertile land. The differences between black folk and white folk are blood or color, and the ties that bind us are deeper than those that separate us. The common road of hope which we all traveled has brought us into a stronger kinship than any words, laws, or legal claims.

Fifty years later, John B. Diamond, a college student, wrote:

> Black history week in elementary school was what I like to call a "feel-good" affair. It was a time for all of the white teachers and students to show that they were concerned about "Black" issues and to express their pride in how far we had come as a nation from those horrible days of slavery. It seemed that the only Black leaders we talked about were those who had helped to free Blacks from slavery. For Europeans, history went far beyond this country; for Blacks, however, it seemed to reach only to slavery. No one mentioned the fact that Africans had built the pyramids or had cultures long before the Europeans had moved out of caves. No one mentioned that the Greeks had stolen Egyptian philosophy or that the foundations of science all come from Black Africa. I guess this was just too controversial.
>
> We learned about the slave trade coming from the western coast of Africa. One point that my teachers made sure to emphasize was that Africans interned other Africans and sold them to the white man. This statement served to remove blame from whites and place it on the Africans. It was their way of saying that the blame for slavery doesn't rest only on the white man's shoulders. It wasn't the white man's fault for murdering … Black people and oppressing them: it was their own African brothers who had caused them to face this plight. My teachers denied me an enormous part of my history prior to slavery; they placed much of the blame for slavery on the Black man; and they downplayed my people's contributions to the building of this country.[32]

CONNECTIONS

What is Richard Wright saying about the nation and the importance of confronting its history? About the links between black Americans and white?

In the overview to this chapter, Judith Miller listed four ways individuals and groups suppress or deny memory. The African Americans quoted in this reading believe their history has been suppressed or denied. How do they think it has been suppressed or denied? For what reasons?

In a televised interview with Bill Moyers, poet Rita Dove said, "I think people can hear the truth. I think in fact we long for it. We long for the truth in all of its contradictions, because there is no simple truth either and [we know] that truth means sacrifice, but it also means the enriching of one's inner life, and I think the American people want that, and they know that very often they don't get it." What does Dove mean when she speaks of "truth in all of its contradictions"? To what history do you think she is referring? How does she think the American people will respond to truth about their history—that is, the negative as well as the positive aspects of that history?

I think people can hear the truth. I think in fact we long for it. We long for the truth in all of its contradictions, because there is no simple truth either. [We know] that truth means sacrifice, but it also means the enriching of one's inner life, and I think the American want that, and they know that very often they don't get it.

Robert F. Drinan, a Jesuit priest who served on the Massachusetts Advisory Committee to the U.S. Commission on Civil Rights in the 1960s, recently reviewed two books that describe the "humiliations, the alienation and the suffering that every black person in America must endure." In his view, the "race question" will never subside or be resolved until the nation as a whole learns about and then reacts to that pain. What evidence can you find in this chapter in support of Drinan's argument? What evidence can you find that calls it into question? How do you think Richard Wright, John Diamond, or Rita Dove would respond to Drinan's statement? What do you think?

Celebrating "Black History Week" and including African Ameican heroes in United States history textbooks are some ways of making United States history more inclusive. Many think that even though books are important, they are not as critical as the attitudes and values of the teacher. Based on your own experiences, what advice would you give a teacher who wants to teach a history course that includes everyone's experiences?

Langston Hughes once asked, "What happens to a dream deferred?" He wondered, "Does it sag like a heavy load? Or does it explode—like a raisin in the sun?" How do you think Wright would answer the questions? Diamond? Rita Dove? How would you respond?

READING 14

Acknowledging the Past

Many African Americans today are demanding that their history be acknowledged and that amends be made for past injustices. Only then, they argue, can the nation move forward. In 1990, Julius Lester wrote:

> The summer of 1986 saw the observance of the one-hundredth birthday of the Statue of Liberty. It was a time of national celebration. Newspapers and television carried stories and interviews with immigrants recounting their coming to America, their thoughts and emotions on first seeing the statue. How painful it was to read and listen to such stories; how maddening to listen to immigrants express with deep sincerity and in tears how much they loved America, how America had given them opportunities they would not have had otherwise. . . .

I could not watch the televised Fourth-of-July festivities for very long and when I saw photographs of fireworks exploding around the illuminated Statue of Liberty, I was dismayed that the nation could so celebrate itself and not know that its celebration was a rebuke and an insult to that 10 percent of its population which had its beginnings in the killing arrogance of white people who thought they had divine sanction to steal other human beings by force, to enslave them, use them for their own aggrandizement and profit, and sell them or kill them when they refused to be so used.

America had a birthday party, but I could not attend; and America did not notice my absence, which means it did not care that I was not present. [33]

After noting that the President of the United States marked the occasion with a speech, Lester writes:

> America has a large and frightening shadow that it refuses to look at and refuses to claim as its own. Until America claims that shadow as its own, we will continue to be a nation of children forever claiming that we have done nothing wrong and that all the wrongs that have been done—well, they just kind of happened and we don't know how. Black people know that the wrongs didn't just happen.

I would have liked the president to apologize to black Americans on behalf of all the immigrants and their descendants, of whom he is one, for the fact that that beacon of liberty has not shone her torch on blacks, and that, as painful as it is to acknowledge, immigrants owe some of their success to the fact that one of the rungs on their climb up the ladder of success was the backs of black people. I wanted the president to make it clear that he was speaking in the generality, that he was speaking not about individual immigrants—some of whom, certainly, did all they could within the contexts of their lives to alleviate racism and prejudice—but rather, about the forces in American life that allow racism to flourish like vegetation in a rain forest. I would've liked it very much if the president had gone on to reveal that he felt black suffering and had made it part of him, for we are not bound together as human beings because we all succeed. We do not, and that is an unchangeable part of how things are. What binds us together as human beings is that we all suffer, and the suffering that has brought immigrants to America as a refuge from suffering should have made them feel empathy for the suffering of blacks and generous toward them. What is so painful, what is almost unforgivable, is how ready immigrants and their descendants have been to add to black suffering.

I should have been especially moved if the president had also acknowledged the original inhabitants of his land and their brutal displacement and degradation, which have been enshrined in American history as the "winning of the West." What this nation of immigrants did to native Americans cannot be undone, but there must be a public acknowledgment of what was done and a public asking of forgiveness for the fact that this nation created itself by destroying the people who were already here.

If the president could've made such a speech, it would've meant that America had, at long last, matured into a nation that accepted responsibility for all of its history rather than seizing on a portion and glorifying it as the whole. America has a large and frightening shadow that it refuses to look at and refuses to claim as its own. Until America claims that shadow as its own, we will continue to be a nation of children forever claiming that we have done nothing wrong and that all the wrongs that have been done—well, they just kind of happened and we don't know how. Black people know that the wrongs didn't just happen.[34]

CONNECTIONS

Compare Lester's remarks about the way Americans regard their past with Barnett's remarks about the way Germans view theirs. What similarities do you notice? What differences seem most striking?

Compare the speech Lester wishes an American president would make with the one the president of West Germany actually made (Reading 6). What similarities do you notice? What differences seem most striking?

What does Lester mean when he describes the United States as "a nation of children forever claiming that we have done nothing wrong and that all the wrongs that have been done—well, they just kind of happened and we don't know how"? What would "a nation of adults" be like? What principles would it embody?

In 1923, a mob of white citizens went on a rampage after failing to find a black man accused of assaulting a white woman. Over the course of a week, eight people were killed and nearly every building in the African-American town of Rosewood, Florida, was burned to the ground. In 1994, the Florida state legislature passed a bill that would pay $150,000 to each survivor of the riot and his or her family. A state senator who supported reparations told reporters, "Rosewood has become a symbol of the countless secret deaths and atrocities that took place throughout this era. It is time for us to make Florida fair to all its citizens." How do you think Lester would regard the state's action? How do you think Ida B. Wells would have viewed it? (Chapter 2, Reading 10) To what extent is the bill a legacy of her work?

Opponents of the action by the Florida state legislature feared it would set a precedent for other victims of racial violence. Are their fears justified? How important is it for a government to acknowledge its mistakes? Apologize for wrongdoing? Make amends? How important is it for an individual to acknowledge mistakes? Apologize? Make amends?

Black and White Americans Confront the Past

Never before
[Reconstruction]—never
since—had there been so
much hope. A black
mother knew that her boy
could become governor.
The evidence of things
seen, the evidence of
things heard fired millions
of hearts.

*I*s the denial of African American history by many white Americans the result of a lacuna or blind spot? Or is it a part of the legacy of racism? The way historians have interpreted the years after the Civil War suggests there are no simple answers.

Historians agree on the basic facts. After the Civil War, the nation passed three Constitutional amendments that abolished slavery and gave former slaves all of the rights and privileges of citizenship, including the right to vote and hold political office. Most of the newly formed state governments in the South were unwilling to enforce those laws. Therefore Congress sent federal troops to the South to do the job. While those troops were present, African American men were able to take advantage of their rights as citizens. After those troops were withdrawn in 1877, one state after another passed laws that limited or denied African Americans their constitutional rights. And historians agree that the federal government did not challenge those state laws. Indeed many in government applauded them. The disagreement lies in what Reconstruction—the years between 1867 and 1877—was really like.

Lerone Bennett, Jr., an African American historian, says of Reconstruction, "Never before had the sun shone so bright." He goes on to list the progress the South made during those years—including the establishment of public schools, the expansion of voting rights, and judicial reforms that resulted in more democratic court systems. He also names the African Americans who helped shape these and other laws. Among them were Congressmen and members of state legislatures. And Bennett identifies blacks who helped run states, cities, and colleges in the South. Then noting that "these things were happening on the higher levels," he asks, "What of the masses? How was it with them?"

> They were struggling, as they had always struggled, with the stubborn and recalcitrant earth. But now there was hope. Never before—never since—had there been so much hope. A black mother knew that her boy could become governor. The evidence of things seen, the evidence of things heard fired millions of hearts. Black mothers walked ten, fifteen and twenty miles to put their children in school. They sacrificed and stinted. They bowed down and worshipped the miraculous ABCs from whom so many blessings flowed. The sky or at the very least the mountaintop was the limit. Had not Blanche Bruce [a United States senator from Mississippi] been suggested as a possible vice-presidential candidate? Was it not clear that a black boy could go as far as nerve, energy, and ability would carry him? Black mothers,

bending over washtubs, could hope. Black boys, in cotton fields, could dream. The millennium hadn't come, of course, but there were some who believed it was around the next turning.

A man in this age went to mail a letter, and the postmaster was black. A man committed a crime, and, in some counties, was arrested by a black policeman, prosecuted by a black solicitor, weighed by a black and white jury and sentenced by a black judge.[35]

W. E. B. Du Bois, a noted African American writer and thinker, offered a more somber summary of those years. "The slave went free; stood a brief moment in the sun; then moved back again toward slavery." For a long time, many white historians painted a very different picture of Reconstruction. Eric Foner, a white American historian, describes that view and its consequences in *Reconstruction: America's Unfinished Revolution.*

By the turn of the century, as soldiers from the North and South joined to take up the "white man's burden" in the Spanish-American War, Reconstruction was widely viewed as little more than a regrettable detour on the road to reunion. To the bulk of the white South, it had . . . been a time of "savage tyranny" that "accomplished not one useful result, and left behind it, not one pleasant recollection." Black suffrage, wrote [one historian], was now seen by "all thoughtful men" as "the greatest political crime ever perpetrated by any people." In more sober language, many Northerners . . . concurred in these judgments. "Years of thinking and observation" had convinced [the former commissioner of the Freedman's Bureau] "that the restoration of their lands to the planters provided for [a] future better for the negroes.". . .

This rewriting of Reconstruction's history was accorded scholarly legitimacy—to its everlasting shame—by the nation's fraternity of professional historians. Early in the twentieth century, a group of young Southern scholars gathered at Columbia University to study the Reconstruction era under the guidance of Professors John W. Burgess and William A. Dunning. Blacks [according to Burgess and Dunning], were "children" utterly incapable of appreciating the freedom that had been thrust upon them. The North did "a monstrous thing" in granting them suffrage, for "a black skin means membership in a race of men which has never of itself succeeded in subjecting passion to reason, has never, therefore, created any civilization of any kind." No political order could survive in the South unless founded on the principle of racial inequality. The students' works on individual Southern states echoed these sentiments. Reconstruction, concluded the study of North Carolina, was an attempt by "selfish politicians backed by the federal government. . . to Africanize the State and deprive the people through misrule and oppression of most that life held dear." The views of the Dunning School shaped historical writing for generations, and

To the bulk of the white South, [Reconstruction] had . . . been a time of "savage tyranny" that "accomplished not one useful result, and left behind it, not one pleasant recollection."

achieved wide popularity through D. W. Griffith's film *Birth of a Nation* (which glorified the Ku Klux Klan and had its premiere at the White House during Woodrow Wilson's Presidency). . . .

Few interpretations of history have had such far-reaching consequences as this image of Reconstruction. As Francis B. Simkins, a South Carolina-born historian, noted during the 1930s, "the alleged horrors of Reconstruction" did much to freeze the mind of the white South in unalterable opposition to outside pressures for social change and to any thought of breaching Democratic ascendancy, eliminating segregation, or restoring suffrage to disenfranchised blacks. They also justified Northern indifference to [laws that contradicted] the Fourteenth and Fifteenth Amendments. Apart from a few white dissenters like Simkins, it was left to black writers to challenge the prevailing orthodoxy. In the early years of this century, none did so more tirelessly than former Mississippi Congressman John R. Lynch, then living in Chicago, who published a series of devastating critiques of the racial biases and historical errors [in popular acccounts of Reconstruction]. "I do not hesitate to assert," he wrote, "that the Southern Reconstruction Governments were the best governments those States ever had." In 1917, Lynch voiced the hope that "a fair, just, and impartial historian will, some day, write a history covering the Reconstruction period, [giving] the actual facts of what took place."

Only in the family traditions and collective folk memories of the black community did a different version of Reconstruction survive. Growing up in the 1920s, Pauli Murray was "never allowed to forget" that she walked in "proud shoes" because her grandfather, Robert G. Fitzgerald, had "fought for freedom" in the Union Army and then enlisted as a teacher in the "second war" against the powerlessness and ignorance inherited from slavery. When the Works Progress Administration sent agents into [the South] during the [1930s] to interview former slaves, they found Reconstruction remembered for its disappointments and betrayals, but also as a time of hope, possibility, and accomplishment. Bitterness still lingered over the federal government's failure to distribute land or protect blacks' civil and political rights. "The Yankees helped free us, but they let us be put back in slavery again." Yet coupled with this disillusionment were proud, vivid recollections of a time when "the colored used to hold office." Some pulled from their shelves dusty scrapbooks of clippings from Reconstruction newspapers; others could still recount the names of local black leaders. . . . Younger blacks spoke of being taught by their parents "about the old times, mostly about the Reconstruction, and the Ku Klux." "I know folks think the books tell the truth, but they shore don't," [said] one eighty-eight-year old former slave. . . .[36]

Many young African Americans in other parts of the nation did not know this history until they joined the civil rights movement in the 1960s.

Vincent Harding traces his own interest in African American history to the women and men he met in small towns and large cities throughout the South. In the introduction to *There Is a River; The Black Struggle for Freedom in America*, he says of them:

> It was they—in their lives, in their quiet courage, in their songs and their silences—who first told us that there was a significant history behind what we called "The Movement," a long time of surging toward freedom. It was they who called to see a movement older and deeper than any one life, any one generation. It is with them that I must keep faith, for it was among them, in the 1960s, that the informal, largely unconscious research for this work began. Their churches and homes, the marching lines, the confrontations with sheriffs and deputies in front of the county courthouses, the cars on the treacherous back-country roads, the jails and cemeteries—there were my first archives, my first living sources for the story of our river.[37]

CONNECTIONS

How did African Americans remember Reconstruction? How did many white Americans recall it? Why does Foner believe that "few interpretations of history have had such far-reaching consequences as this image of Reconstruction"? Do you agree?

Foner writes, "Only in the family traditions and collective folk memories of the black community did a different version of Reconstruction survive." What does it mean to have your history denied? To what extent were the issues of identity African Americans faced at the turn of the century like those of the Bear in *the bear that wasn't* (Chapter 1, Reading 1)?

How does a nation's history reflect who is "in" and who is "out"? How might a history written by those who are "out" differ from one written by the "in" group? Bill Moyers believes that "if the state can banish the history of inconvenient facts, . . . we are at the mercy of the official view of reality: or as Big Brother in *1984* explains, the state will 'squeeze you empty and fill you with ourselves.'" Therefore he argues, "We have got to have the ugly facts in order to protect us from the official view of reality. Otherwise, we are squeezed empty and filled with what other people want us to think and feel and experience."[38] Is it the government that protects people from ugly facts? Or is it their own reluctance to confront those painful facts?

Daniel Goleman believes that "questions that can't—or won't—be asked are a sure sign of a lacuna." What questions did white historians at the turn of the century fail to ask about Reconstruction? How important was their failure to do so?

Reread Bennett's assessment of Reconstruction. Whom does he leave out? Is his omission evidence of another lacuna in American history?

➤The Facing History Resource Center has a number of videos that deal with the years after Reconstruction. One of the most powerful is *Assault at West Point*, the story of the first African American cadet. The interview with Maya Angelou included on a video entitled *Facing Evil with Bill Moyers* also offers insights into this period in history and its legacies.

READING 16

Memorials and Monuments

One way a people remembers the past is by building monuments that honor its heroes or commemorate its tragedies.

One way a people remembers the past is by building monuments that honor its heroes or commemorate its tragedies. In creating any memorial, the individuals involved must answer a variety of questions. Some deal with the purpose of the memorial; others focus on its audience; and still others consider who will be remembered and why.

In 1884, the Municipal Council of Calais, France, addressed those very questions, when the group decided to erect a monument to a tragic event in the town's history. In 1346, the English had laid siege to Calais. After eleven months of hunger and suffering, six burghers—prominent citizens of the town—decided to end the blockade by offering themselves as hostages. Jean Froissart, a French writer, created a poem commemorating the event. It tells of how the six leading citizens of Calais marched out of town with "bare heads and feet, with ropes round their necks, and the keys of the town and castle in their hands." Their sacrifice saved the city and its people.

The poem caught the imagination not only of the Municipal Council but also of a famous sculptor, Auguste Rodin. Hired to create a memorial, Rodin researched the story carefully and then decided to depict the six burghers at the very moment they surrendered themselves to King Edward III of England. A historian says of the six statues the artist created:

> Dressed in garments which fall in heavy folds and add a physical burden to their gestures and uncertain bearing, they seem in transition between life and death, between sleeping and waking. . . . Powerless to alter the inevitable consequence of their decision, united only by their common resolve, each participant enacts his own drama, irresolute, deeply self-absorbed, and infinitely sad.[39]

Members of the town's monument committee were disappointed. They expected a more heroic view—one that featured the most famous of the burghers. They also visualized a memorial that would prompt passers-by to look up in awe. Instead Rodin placed his statues at eye-level. Each resembled an ordinary man caught in a tragic dilemma.

The artist and the committee battled over the work for months. When the finished product was finally unveiled in June of 1895, the compromises each side made were clearly visible. Rodin had succeeded in overcoming the Committee's objections to the way the figures looked. But he was unable to persuade them to place the monument in front of the Town Hall so that it could be integrated into daily life in the community. Instead, the committee located the memorial on the edge of a public garden and surrounded it with an iron grill. Only in 1925 were the statues moved to Town Hall Square.

CONNECTIONS

In designing a memorial, architects and other artists must consider: What is the purpose of the memorial? What is its audience—that is, who will visit it and why? Who will be remembered and for what reasons? How did Rodin answer those questions?

How did the townspeople want the burghers remembered? How did Rodin want them remembered? Why does the truth make some people feel uncomfortable? What is the significance of that discomfort?

Is a hero someone who stands "above" ordinary people? Or is he or she an ordinary person who does an extraordinary deed? Add to the working definition of the word *hero* you started in Chapter 8.

In creating any memorial, the individuals involved must answer a variety of questions. Some deal with the purpose of the memorial; others focus on its audience; and still others consider who will be remembered and why.

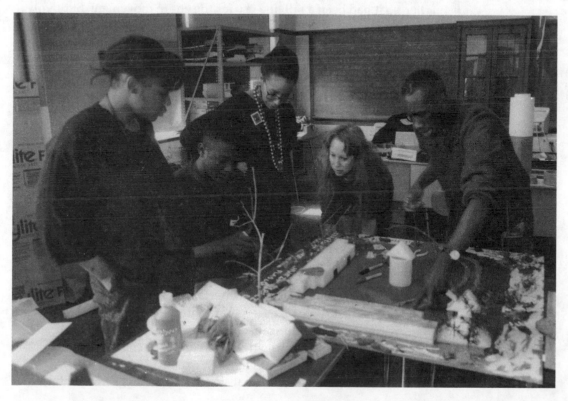

Facing History students show the monuments they created.

In Commemoration

Unlike the Vietnam Memorial which covers a specific period of time that's over, I wanted the Civil Rights Memorial to deal not only with the past but with the future—with how far we still have to go in a continuing struggle.

Nearly one hundred years after Rodin designed his memorial, the Southern Poverty Law Center in Montgomery, Alabama, invited Maya Ying Lin to design a memorial to commemorate another great sacrifice. The center wanted to honor the men and women who lost their lives in the struggle for civil rights. Morris S. Dees, the co-founder and executive director of the Center, selected her for the job because of her work on the Vietnam Memorial in Washington, D.C.

In creating a design, Maya Lin, like Rodin, studied the history of the event she was asked to commemorate. In doing so, she was particularly moved by a quotation Dr. Martin Luther King, Jr., used in a number of speeches. Paraphrasing the Book of Amos, he often said, "We will not be satisfied until justice rolls down like waters and righteousness like a mighty stream." She told an interviewer:

> The minute I hit that quote I knew that the whole piece had to be about water. I learned that King had used the phrase not only in his famous "I have a dream" speech at the Washington civil rights march in 1963 but at the start of the bus boycott in Montgomery eight years earlier, so it had been a rallying cry for the entire movement. Suddenly the whole form took shape and half an hour later I was in a restaurant in Montgomery with the people from the Center, sketching it on a paper napkin. I realized that I wanted to create a time line: a chronological listing of the movement's major events and its individual deaths, which together would show how people's lives influenced history and how their deaths made things better.[40]

The interviewer described the completed monument:

> The memorial has two components, both of black Canadian granite. The first part is a nine-foot-high wall, on the face of which are carved the words:

> . . . until justice rolls down like waters
> and righteousness like a mighty stream.
> —Martin Luther King, Jr.

> Water spills down the wall at waterfall speed. Although the passage from the Prophet Amos as paraphrased by King actually begins with "We will not be satisfied," Maya Lin told me that she started where she did because the word "until" catches the second purpose of the monument. "Unlike the Vietnam Memorial which covers a specific period of time that's over," she said, "I wanted the

Civil Rights Memorial to deal not only with the past but with the future—with how far we still have to go in a continuing struggle."

The second part of the memorial, resting on an asymmetrical pedestal nearby, is a circular tabletop, almost 12 feet in diameter. Around its perimeter, incised in the stone, somewhat in the manner of a sundial, are 53 brief entries, chronologically arranged. Twenty-one of them report landmark events in the movement. . . .The other entries describe 40 individual deaths. . . . Extra space after King's [assassination] shows that this is where the story ends on the memorial. It also therefore shows where the story begins—on May 17, 1954, the Supreme Court's *Brown* decision—and that's where most visitors start their visit, walking slowly around the table and touching the names beneath the water, which arises from a hole in the tabletop and flows over it evenly. The table is only 31 inches high, deliberately accessible to children.

"The water is as slow as I could get it," Maya Lin told me. "It remains very still until you touch it. Your hand causes ripples, which transform and alter the piece, just as reading the words completes the piece. The sound of the water is also very calming. Sound is important to me as an architect."[41]

The monument was even more powerful than the young architect expected. She told the reporter, "At the dedication ceremony, I was surprised and moved when people started to cry. Emmett Till's mother was touching his name beneath the water and crying, and I realized her tears were becoming part of the memorial."[42] Till is one of the Americans the monument honors.

CONNECTIONS

Like Rodin, Maya Lin considered such questions as: What is the purpose of the memorial? Who is its audience—that is, who will visit it and why? Who will be remembered and for what reasons? How did she answer those questions? How were her responses similar to Rodin's? What differences seem most striking?

The memorial Maya Lin created is a memorial to courage and the fight for justice. People also build monuments to injustice. Journalist Dwight Young asks:

What should a monument to injustice look like? Should it be tall, threatening, and sharp-edged, gleaming black and blood-red? Or should it be smaller, more slithery, a poisonous menace half-hidden among rocks and shadowy vines?

Or might it take the form of an isolated valley dotted with scrubby bushes where clouds of wind-borne grit sometimes blot out the rugged mountains looming on all sides?

That's how Manzanar looks.[43]

Manzanar, which lies west of Death Valley in California, was the first of ten facilities the United States built to house Japanese Americans during World War II. (See Connections, Chapter 9, Reading 11.) Manzanar was recently designated a National Historic Site. Therefore a team of architects has been considering the following questions:

- How do you encourage visitors to stare into the ugly face of hate and prejudice?

- Can you show the dark side of history in a way that neither sugarcoats it nor makes people turn away unmoved and unengaged?

- Is it possible to make people think about the unthinkable?

Research the way those questions were answered at Auschwitz in Poland. You may also want to research the way the questions were answered by those who created the memorial to the horrors of the Middle Passage and the Atlantic slave trade at Goree, an island off the coast of West Africa. Or research the ways Native Americans and other groups have chosen to commemorate their experiences with injustice. What similiarities do you find among the way various groups have answered the questions? What differences seem most striking? How would you answer these questions?

➤Many students build a monument as a culminating activity or as part of a class project. In a complete unit on monuments, available from the Facing History Resource Center, Barbara Traietti Hearne describes ways students can make monuments to ideas, persons, and events. This activity allows students to clarify their thoughts and feelings as they manipulate wire, clay, and plaster. The monuments students have created in the past take many forms and use a variety of symbols. A packet of additional materials on monuments—how to build them, observe them, and interpret them—is also available from the Facing History Resource Center. Included with the packet are several videos, one of which features an interview with Maya Lin.

READING 18

Education and the Future

Maya Lin also designed the Vietnam Memorial in Washington, D.C. After seeing it, an anonymous veteran wrote the following poem.

> I didn't want a monument
> not even one as sober as that
> vast black wall of broken lives
> I didn't want a postage stamp.
> I didn't want a road beside the Delaware
> River with a sign proclaiming:
> Vietnam Veterans Memorial Highway.
> What I wanted was a simple recognition
> of the limits of our power as a nation
> to inflict our will on others
> What I wanted was an understanding
> that the world is neither black-and-white nor ours.
> What I wanted was an end to monuments.

What I wanted was an understanding that the world is neither black-and-white nor ours. What I wanted was an end to monuments.

Many believe that the best way to achieve that goal is through education. By studying the terrible events of twentieth-century genocide, we are vividly reminded of the power of the individual to make decisions that affect not only oneself and one's neighbors but also the survival of the entire world. After seeing the destruction the atomic bomb wrought on Nagaski, Japan, at the end of World War II, Jacob Bronowski experienced "a moment that dwarfed his imagination." He called it a "universal moment." Amid the terrible ashes of the city, he wrote that all decisions about disarmament and other issues which weigh the fate of nations "should be made within the forbidding context of Nagasaki; only then could statesmen make realistic judgments of the problems which they handle on our behalf."[44]

Bronowski was never able to convince his colleagues in government and the United Nations of the merits of his idea. They told him that "delegates would be uncomfortable" there. Confronting the history of genocide is always uncomfortable, but it is important work. By denying people access to that history, we fail to honor their potential to confront, to cope, and to make a difference today and in the future. A school principal expressed that idea more eloquently in a letter he sent out on the first day of the school year.

> Dear Teacher:
> I am a survivor of a concentration camp. My eyes saw what no man should witness:
> Gas chambers built by learned engineers.

Children poisoned by educated physicians.

Infants killed by trained nurses.

Women and babies shot and burned by high school and college graduates.

So, I am suspicious of education.

My request is: Help your students become human. Your efforts must never produce learned monsters, skilled psychopaths, educated Eichmanns.

Reading, writing, arithmetic are important only if they serve to make our children more humane.

Help your students become human. Your efforts must never produce learned monsters, skilled psychopaths, educated Eichmanns. Reading, writing, arithmetic are important only if they serve to make our children more humane.

CONNECTIONS

It has been said that the last battles fought in every war are over memory—over the way that war will be remembered. How has World War II been remembered in the United States? In other countries involved in the conflict? How have those memories changed over time? What prompts changes in the way a war is remembered?

The Vietnam War was one of the most controversial wars in American history. Americans today are still divided over how the war ought to be remembered. You may wish to research the controversy over Maya Lin's Vietnam Memorial to find out more about that struggle over memory. You may also want to find out how memories of the Vietnam War affect the way Americans respond to crises in the world today.

How does the way an event is labeled affect the way it is recalled? In 1949, communist-controlled North Korea invaded South Korea. At the request of the United States, the United Nations sent troops to assist the South Koreans. Many Americans referred to the war that followed as a "conflict" or "military action." Why do you think they chose not to call it a war? How important are labels to the way people view an event? To the way the event is remembered?

What would you include in a curriculum that addresses concerns expressed in this reading and in this course as a whole? What readings would you insist students read? What films would you require them to see? What speakers would you invite? What would you omit? Add? How would you begin the course? How would you end it?

In designing a curriculum, decisions have to be made. Whose history should be included? Whose might be left out? If everyone's history is included, what may be lost? How do you discover universal lessons from a particular history without trivializing that history?

The title of this course is "Facing History and Ourselves." What does that title mean to you? How has it been reflected in this course? In the way you have come to perceive the past? In the way you approach the future?

NOTES

[1] Quoted in Terence DesPres, *The Survivor: An Anatomy of Life in the Death Camps* (Oxford University Press, 1976), 35.

[2] Vartan Hartunian, Introduction to Abraham Hartunian, *Neither to Laugh nor to Weep, A Memoir of the Armenian Genocide.*

[3] Judith Miller, *One by One, by One: Facing the Holocaust* (Simon & Schuster, 1990), 287.

[4] Alexander Donat, *The Holocaust Kingdom*, 183.

[5] Based on an interview with Rose Murra by Margot Stern Strom.

[6] Excerpt from *Fragments of Isabella: A Memoir of Auschwitz* by Isabella Leitner, edited and with an Epilogue by Irving A. Leitner. (Thomas Y. Crowell, Publishers) copyright © 1978 by Isabella Leitner and Irving A. Leitner. Reprinted by permission.

[7] Ibid.

[8] Timothy W. Ryback, "Evidence of Evil," *The New Yorker*, 15 Sept., 1993, 68-69.

[9] Ibid.

[10] Daniel Goleman, *Vital Lies, Simple Truths: The Psychology of Self-Deception* (Simon & Schuster), 228.

[11] Nancy Sommers, "Being Personal and Being Academic," Harvard University, 1994.

[12] Letter to the Editor, *New York Times.*

[13] Donia Blumenfeld Clenman, "I Dream in Good English Too," *Poems by Donia Blumenfeld Clenman* (Flowerfield and Littleman, 1988).

[14] Victoria Barnett, *For the Soul of the People*, 295-296.

[15] Marvin Kalb, "'New' SS Wreaths, Old Anti-Semitism," *New York Times*, 14 May, 1985. Copyright © 1986 by The New York Times Company. Reprinted by permission.

[16] Press Release, "The Nasty Girl," Miramax Films, 8-9.

[17] Reprinted in *Bitburg in Moral and Political Perspective*, ed. Geoffrey H. Hartman, (Indiana University Press, 1986), 262-273.

[18] Jane Kramer, "New-Nazis: A Chaos in the Head," *The New Yorker*, 14, June, 1993.

[19] Christine Toomey, "Hitler Comic Fights New Nazism in German Schools," *The Times of London*, 1993.

[20] Ibid.

[21] Saul Friedlander, *Bitburg in Moral and Political Perspective*, ed. Geoffrey H. Hartman.

[22] Timothy W. Ryback, Evidence of Evil," *The New Yorker*, 15 Sept., 1993, 72-73.

[23] Ibid., 70.

[24] George Will, "Perils of Perceived History," 1993.

[25] David Oshinsky and Michael Curtis, *New York Times*, 11 December, 1991. Copyright © 1991 The New York Times Company. Reprinted by permission.

[26] Margot Stern Strom, "An Interview with Bill Moyers," *Facing History and Ourselves News*, Fall, 1986.

[27] Judith Miller, *One by One, by One*, 11-12.

[28] Laura Akgulian ,"Fountains and Flowing Rivers, Before the Mourning," *International Herald Tribune*, 24, April, 1991.

[29] Vigen Guroian, "The Litmus of Bitburg and the Armenian Genocide Resolution," *Holocaust and Genocide Studies*, 1988, 305-322.

[30] Roger Mudd, "Senate Debate on a Resolution Identifying April 24 as a Day of Remembrance," *Newscast*, Public Broadcasting System, February, 1990.

[31] Richard Hovannisian, "The Armenian Genocide," (unpublished speech, Facing History and Ourselves).

[32] John B. Diamond, "Inner Strength: Being African and American." In *In Separate Worlds*, ed. D. Schoem, 185.

[33] Julius Lester, *Falling Pieces of the Broken Sky*, 150.

[34] Ibid., 155-157.

[35] Lerone Bennett, Jr., *Before the Mayflower*, (Johnson Publishing Co., 1982), 215.

[36] Eric Foner, *Reconstruction: America's Unfinished Revolution 1863-1877* (Harper & Row, 1988), 608-611.

[37] Vincent Harding, *There Is a River* (Harcourt Brace, 1981), xiv.

[38] Margot Stern Strom, "An interview with Bill Moyers."

[39] Abraham Lerner, Introduction to *Auguste Rodin: The Burghers of Calais* (Museum Press, Inc., 1976).

[40] William Zinsser, "I Realized Her Tears Were Becoming Part of the Monument," *Smithsonian*, Sept. 1991, 35.

[41] Ibid., 38.

[42] Ibid., 35.

[43] Dwight Young, "The Back Page," *Historic Preservation News*, April/May 1994.

[44] Jacob Bronowski *Science and Human Values* (Harper & Row, 1956), 3–4.

11. *Choosing to Participate*

Each time a man stands up for an ideal,
or acts to improve the lot of others,
or strikes out against injustice,
he sends forth a tiny ripple of hope.

ROBERT F. KENNEDY

O V E R V I E W

The history of the Weimar Republic provides valuable insights into how and why democracies fail. Chapter 11 looks at what is needed for democracy to succeed. Over 140 years ago, Abraham Lincoln found one answer in these words: "We hold these truths to be self-evident, that all men are created equal; that they are endowed by their Creator with certain unalienable rights; that among these rights are life, liberty, and the pursuit of happiness." He believed that a society based on those truths should be the goal of every citizen. It was, in his view, a goal that ought to be "constantly looked to, constantly labored for, even though never perfectly attained, constantly approximated, and thereby constantly spreading and deepening its influence and augmenting the happiness and value of life to all people of all colors everywhere."

In reflecting on efforts to build democracies in Eastern Europe after the fall of Communism, Czech President Vaclav Havel reached a similar conclusion. He stressed the need for a "civil society"—one that promotes "a climate that would encourage people to act as citizens in the best sense of the word." Without that climate, democracy cannot survive. Weimar Germany is a good example. Although it had all of the trappings of democracy, it was not a "civil society." Too many Germans were too eager to find simple answers to complex questions. And too often, those answers were rooted in false ideas about "race" and "racial" differences. Those who knew better chose to look the other way—even when their neighbors were threatened. It was easier to compromise than it was to take a stand. It was easier still to believe that individuals had no choice in the matter, especially if they were not in the habit of participating in community life.

Choosing to Participate, published by Facing History and Ourselves, elaborates on many of the themes developed in this chapter. Some teachers use the book as the basis for a citizenship course that stresses community involvement and volunteerism.

The attitudes and values that destroyed the Weimar Republic exist in every society, including our own. Many of the issues Germans struggled with then are the same ones confronting Americans today. David Schoem, a sociology professor, says:

> The effort it takes for us to know so little about one another across racial and ethnic groups is truly remarkable. That we can live so closely together, that our lives can be so intertwined socially, economically, and politically, and that we can spend so many years of study in grade school and even in higher education and yet still manage to be ignorant of one another is clear testimony to the deep-seated roots of this human and national tragedy. What we do learn along the way is to place heavy reliance on stereotypes, gossip, rumor, and fear to shape our lack of knowledge.[1]

Chapter 11 explores individual efforts to bridge that isolation, end our reliance on "stereotypes, gossip, rumor and fear," and honestly confront the issues that divide us. It also considers what it takes to be a good citizen. History suggests that "people become brave by doing brave acts. People become compassionate by doing compassionate acts. People become good citizens by engaging in acts of good citizenship."[2] Many of the individuals highlighted in this chapter have become good citizens by engaging in acts of good citizenship. They have no easy answers to the tough problems that plague our communities and our nation. They do, however, offer insights into the process of growth and change. And they help us understand what it takes to make a democracy work.

READING 1

"America's Best Self"

*I*n the course of American history, there have been many individuals who made a positive difference in their communities. Each inspired the generations that followed to demand justice, right wrongs, or simply offer a helping hand. Marian Wright Edelman is among those who were inspired by caring, compassionate women and men. As a result, she never had a doubt that she could make a difference. As a college student, Edelman challenged laws that excluded African Americans. She later helped register black voters in Mississippi and in 1965 became the first African American woman to practice law in the state. About twenty years ago, she founded the Children's Defense Fund, which has since become the nation's leading research and lobbying group devoted to the needs of children. Edelman has eloquently described the people who inspired her efforts:

South Carolina is my home state and I am the aunt, granddaughter, daughter, and sister of Baptist ministers. Service was as essential a part of my upbringing as eating and sleeping and going to school. The church was a hub of Black children's social existence, and caring Black adults were buffers against the segregated and hostile outside world that told us we weren't important. But our parents said it wasn't so, our teachers said it wasn't so, and our preachers said it wasn't so. The message of my racially segregated childhood was clear: let no man or woman look down on you, and look down on no man or woman.

We couldn't play in public playgrounds or sit at drugstore lunch counters and order a Coke, so Daddy built a playground and canteen behind the church. In fact, whenever he saw a need, he tried to respond. There were no Black homes for the aged in Bennettsville, so he began one across the street for which he and Mama and we children cooked and served and cleaned. And we children learned that it was our responsibility to take care of elderly family members and neighbors, and that everyone was our neighbor. . . .

We learned early what our parents and extended community "parents" valued. Children were taught—not by sermonizing, but by personal example—that nothing was too lowly to do. I remember a debate my parents had when I was eight or nine as to whether I was too young to go with my older brother, Harry, to help clean the bed and bedsores of a very sick, poor woman. I went and learned just how much the smallest helping hands and kindness can mean to a person in need. . . .

I was fourteen years old the night my daddy died. He had holes in his shoes but two children out of college, one in college, another in divinity school, and a vision he was able to convey to me as he lay dying in an ambulance that I, a young Black girl could be and do anything; that race and gender are shadows; and that character, self-discipline, determination, attitude, and service are the substance of life.

I have always believed that I could help change the world because I have been lucky to have adults around me who did—in small and large ways. Most were people of simple grace who understood what Walker Percy wrote: You can get all A's and still flunk life. . . .

I and my brothers and sister might have lost hope—as many young people today have lost hope—except for the stable, caring, attentive adults in our family, school, congregation, civic and political life who struggled with and for us against the obstacles we faced and provided us positive alternatives and the sense of possibility we needed. . . .

Too many people—of all colors, and all walks of life—are growing up today unable to handle life in hard places, without hope, without adequate attention , and without steady internal compasses to navigate the morally polluted seas they must face on the journey to adulthood.

As a result, we are on the verge of losing two generations of Black children and youths to drugs, violence, too-early parenthood, poor

Never could I have envisaged the positive changes I have seen since my youth. But my parents and elders dreamed of them and never lost hope. So neither will I lose hope that America's best self will overcome growing racial and class divisions.

health and education, unemployment, family disintegration—and to the spiritual and physical poverty that both breeds and is bred by them. Millions of Latino, Native American, and other minority children face similar threats. And millions of white children of all classes, like too many minority children, are drowning in the meaninglessness of a culture that rewards greed and guile and tells them life is about getting rather than giving. . . .

There are a whole lot of mornings when I can barely face the work I know I must do and feel discouraged and hopeless about whether America is ever going to finish the business of ensuring racial and economic and gender justice. . . .

I am terrified by the escalating violence in our country and the apathy and ignorance that feed it. But I ask myself if I believe in my vision of America any less than the hatemongers and those who support them do theirs. And I remember everything I have been given and all the chances each of us in this country has been given to make a difference.

My life is one of the countless lives that attest to the vibrancy of the American Dream under circumstances harder than today's. The segregated world of my childhood in the 1940s and 1950s seemed impenetrable. Never could I have envisaged the positive changes I have seen since my youth. But my parents and elders dreamed of them and never lost hope. So neither will I lose hope that America's best self will overcome growing racial and class divisions.[3]

> There was never a time when I was growing up that we were not involved and not aware. We always thought we could change the world, and that sense of empowerment is something that has to begin young.

CONNECTIONS

Marian Wright Edelman believes children must "be given a voice and a way to participate." She goes on to say, "There was never a time when I was growing up that we were not involved and not aware. We always thought we could change the world, and that sense of empowerment is something that has to begin young." What opportunities do young people have to speak out in your community? To participate? How might those opportunities be expanded?

Edelman tells interviewers, "One of the things I am tired of is people telling me how much they admire me, and 'Keep it up.' I keep saying 'Help!' Everybody's got to help. It's not about other people doing things. Everybody's got to assign themselves to building a more decent community, to healing our communities, and to saving our children." Even the very young can help. "Children writing to politicians matters. We had boxes and boxes of letters and drawings from children when we were trying to pass the national child care bill, and that made a big difference. And I hope that we can do the same thing on the issue of school readiness. I hope children will invite their congressmen to come out and visit them and ask question about what their representatives are doing for kids."

Like Marian Edelman, Jane Addams, a reformer in the late 1800s and early 1900s, also fought for laws that would protect the rights of children. She once wrote, "May I warn you against doing good to people, and trying to make others good by law? One does good, if at all, with people, not to people." What point was she trying to make? Would Edelman agree? For more on Jane Addams and her work, see *Choosing to Participate.*

When Edelman was a child, she was surrounded by adults who affirmed her worth and protected her from the negative messages of the outside world. Noting that many kids today don't have such adults in their lives, Edelman believes that "the good people's silence" can be "as damaging as the bad people's actions." How does your study of the events that led up to the Holocaust support her view? What can ordinary people do to break the silence? For example, who in your community speaks out strongly and consistently against racism? Against hate crimes? Against injustice? Invite those individuals or groups to speak to your class. Find out how they got involved and what others can do to support their work.

Edelman sees a link between "the escalating violence in our country" and "apathy and ignorance." From what you have read so far in this book, how are they linked? How can that link be broken?

The opening to this chapter quotes Robert F. Kennedy as saying, "Each time a man stands up for an ideal, or acts to improve the lot of others, or strikes out against injustice, he sends forth a tiny ripple of hope." How do his remarks apply to Edelman? To the men and women who inspired her efforts? Who are the people in your life who send forth "tiny ripples of hope"?

READING 2

Fighting Violence and Terror

*I*n earlier chapters, we saw that some people are fearful of changes. They are all too eager to hold *them* responsible for all the evil in the world, while *we* remain blameless. False ideas about "racial" differences often give legitimacy to those ideas and encourage violence toward the "other." In the 1960s, for example, even as people like Marian Wright Edelman were working to end segregation, other Americans were fighting to preserve it. Some of them used violence to intimidate African Americans whenever they tried to vote, integrate public schools, or even have a cup of coffee at a lunch counter. By the 1970s, tough new laws and determined enforcement of those laws had put an end to the lynchings and murders—or so many people thought.

Then one morning in the spring of 1981, the residents of Mobile, Alabama, awoke to discover a mutilated body hanging from a tree. The lynching of Michael Donald, a nineteen-year-old African American, shocked people everywhere. A few citizens, however, chose to do more than just express their horror or offer sympathy to the young man's family. They chose instead to channel their outrage into preventing similar crimes. One of those individuals was Morris Dees, the executive director of the Southern Poverty Law Center (SPLC) in Montgomery, Alabama.

Dees traces his interest in fighting social justice to his first court appearance as a witness for an African American farm worker. Dees, then a high-school student, recalls, "I thought all I had to do was go in there, as a white boy, and tell the [justice of the peace] what happened, and that would be the end of it," Dees said. "But the state troopers were white, too, and later I realized that the [justice of the peace] only got paid if he found Clarence (the black defendant) guilty."[4]

Years later, Dees with the help of a fellow lawyer, Joseph Levin Jr., would fight and win a case that resulted in the outlawing of that system. Justices of the peace in Alabama are no longer paid *only* if they find a defendant guilty. That case, in turn, led to the founding of the SPLC in 1971. The two men hoped the new group would change the South by fighting "a few important cases with the right facts." Both believed that the civil rights laws passed in the 1960s were meaningless unless someone was willing to challenge any violation of those laws. Aware that most people lacked the legal knowledge, time, or money to do so, they decided to take on the job themselves.

By 1981, the SPLC had initiated and assisted in a number of important civil and criminal cases, but increasingly, its main focus was the Ku Klux Klan. To monitor and investigate the Klan's activities, the group established Klanwatch. It provided the FBI, state troopers, and local police officers with information about Donald's murder that led to the arrest of two young members of the United Klans of America.

In 1983, James "Tiger" Knowles and Henry Hays were brought to trial. A legal journal summarized Knowles's testimony.

> Several Klansmen from Mobile unit 9 had gathered at Henry Hays's house on the evening of Friday, March 20, 1981, to await the 10 P.M. television news for details of the verdict in a local criminal case. Joseph Anderson, a black man accused of killing a white Birmingham policeman, was being retried at the Mobile county courthouse. The first trial had ended with a jury of 11 blacks and one white deadlocked.
>
> Knowles calmly testified that on the drive to the Hays house he was "tying a hangman's noose for the purpose of hanging somebody." Soon after they arrived a report came over the news that the jury had again failed to arrive at a verdict. Henry Hays and Knowles bolted outside and drove to a predominantly black neighborhood "looking for someone to hang," Knowles told the jury. The two men saw an elderly

black man but decided against him because he was too far from the car and was using a public telephone. Later they came upon Donald. "He seemed like a good victim and no one was around," said Knowles.[5]

The jury found the two men guilty. Hays was sentenced to death. Knowles, who was only seventeen at the time of the murder, was given life in prison because of his age and the help he offered federal authorities. When the trial finally ended, the district attorney told reporters that the case was closed. Dees strongly disagreed. In his experience, members of the Klan rarely act on their own. Their activities are usually planned and directed by local councils. Dees also believed that even if the Klan was not directly involved in Donald's murder, it had created the atmosphere of violence and terror that fostered the crime. Therefore he felt that the state had an obligation to put the Klan itself on trial. Since the district attorney was unwilling to do so, he developed an alternative strategy. It required the help of Beulah Mae Donald, Michael Donald's mother, and her lawyer, Michael Figures.

In June, 1984, Dees and Figures filed a civil suit against the United Klans of America, its local councils, and several of its leaders on behalf of the Donald family and the NAACP (acting as a representative for all African Americans in Alabama). In the suit the plaintiffs charged that the murder was part of a long-standing conspiracy to threaten and intimidate blacks in the state of Alabama. They also noted that the Klan, as a nonprofit group, is liable for its members' actions.

After three years of painstaking investigation by the SPLC and the NAACP, the case came to trial in February 1987. The two attorneys won their first victory before the hearing even began: the United Klans agreed that it would no longer harass African Americans in Alabama. The only remaining question was whether the group and its leaders were liable in the death of Michael Donald.

Dees and Figures maintained that the murder was just one in a series of crimes directed by the Klan. James Knowles's testimony supported that argument. Under oath, he described the propaganda that led him to believe that he not only had a right but even a duty to kill African Americans. He also testified that top Klan officials issued the orders that resulted in Donald's death. Knowles concluded his testimony by pleading with the all-white jury to hold him and the other defendants responsible for the murder. He then asked Beulah Mae Donald to forgive him for killing her son.

The jury found the defendants guilty and awarded the Donalds $7 million in damages. The verdict sent a powerful message to the Klan and similar groups. From then on, any organization that encouraged its members to commit hate crimes would be held accountable for those crimes. Indeed, the verdict almost destroyed the United Klans. When it could not raise enough money to pay damages, the court turned over the group's assets and the paychecks of its leaders to the Donald family.

The goals of the SPLC are based on a strong commitment to the First Amendment to the Constitution. That amendment protects not only freedom of speech but also freedom of assembly—the right to form groups and associations. Therefore even though the SPLC opposes aims and methods of the Klan, it supports the right of individuals to join the Klan if they wish to do so. It attacks the group only when it promotes hatred and violence. Therefore the SPLC continues to keep a close watch on the Klan to make sure that the group stays within both the letter and the spirit of the law.

CONNECTIONS

Compare and contrast the methods of the Klan to those of the Nazi party. How did each use propaganda to win members? Rituals and uniforms to create a sense of belonging? Hate as a way of uniting *us* against *them*? Terror as a weapon?

At the time of the murder, some people were wondering how far the nation had come in its struggle to ensure equal rights for all Americans. How would you respond? In answering, take into account the way the Southern Poverty Law Center took advantage of the new laws to pursue justice. Would the verdict in either the criminal or civil suit have been possible in the early 1900s? In the 1950s or 1960s?

How did Beulah Mae Donald channel her rage and grief? Why were she and her children willing to risk their lives by challenging the Klan? Why was Dees willing to do so? Would they have been able to work together in similar ways in the late 1800s? In the early 1900s? (Consult *Choosing to Participate*, Part I of Chapter 2, for more information.)

Members of the Klan hide behind hoods and costumes when they burn crosses and commit other acts of violence. How do you account for their secrecy? Their use of terror as a weapon? Make an identity chart for a member of a Klan.

Although Morris Dees supports the right of the Klan to speak and assemble peacefully, he has formed a group to closely monitor the Klan's activities. How do you account for his position? Do you agree?

How does the First Amendment to the Constitution help build the kind of "civil society" Havel defined in the overview to this chapter?

The SPLC is one of many groups working for social equality. Among those groups are the NAACP, particularly its Legal Defense Fund, the Urban League, the Anti-Defamation League, and a variety of local associations. Learn more about the goals and tactics of one of these groups and share your findings with the class. You may be surprised to find out how many independent associations there are in the United States. Each provides avenues for civic participation that go well beyond voting.

➤The documentary, *The Klan Youth Corps* offers insights into the ways the Klan has used propaganda to indoctrinate young people. Compare the way the Klan indoctrinates young people with what you have read about Nazi indoctrination. Describe the range of decisions made by youth shown in this film. What are the consequences of their choices?

➤Available from the Facing History Resource Center is the comprehensive television documentary on the Civil Rights Movement, *Eyes on the Prize*. The first six segments focus on the years from 1954-1965. *Eyes on the Prize II: America at the Racial Crossroads* covers the period from 1965 to 1985 and focuses on a shift in strategy in achieving equality for all and a shift in the nation's temperament.

READING 3

Breaking Isolation

*I*n times of political, social or economic stress, many people look for someone to blame. For many years, C. P. Ellis was such a person. He tried desperately to find someone that he could hold responsible for his troubles. As a result, he was attracted to groups that offered simple answers to complex questions. He says of those years:

> I was workin' a bread route. The highest I made one week was seventy-five dollars. The rent on our house was about twelve dollars a week. I will never forget: outside of this house was a 265-gallon oil drum. What I would do every night, I would run up to the store and buy five gallons of oil and climb up the ladder and pour it in that 265-gallon drum. I could hear that five gallons when it hits the bottom of that oil drum, splatters, and it sounds like it's nothin' in there. But it would keep the house warm for the night. Next day you'd have to do the same thing.
>
> I left the bread route with fifty dollars in my pocket. I went to the bank and I borrowed four thousand dollars to buy the service station. I worked seven days a week, open and close, and finally had a heart attack. Just about two months before the last payments of that loan. My wife had done the best she could to keep it runnin'. Tryin' to come out of that hole, I just couldn't do it.
>
> I really began to get bitter. I didn't know who to blame. I tried to find somebody. I began to blame it on black people. I had to hate somebody. Hatin' America is hard to do because you can't see it to hate it. You gotta have somethin' to look at to hate. (Laughs.) The natural person for me to hate would be black people, because my father before

me was a member of the Klan. As far as he was concerned, it was the savior of the white people. It was the only organization in the world that would take care of the white people. So I began to admire the Klan.

I got active in the Klan while I was at the service station. Every Monday night, a group of men would come by and buy a Coca-Cola, go back to the car, take a few drinks, and come back and stand around talkin'. I couldn't help but wonder: Why are these dudes comin' out every Monday? They said they were with the Klan and have meetings close-by. Would I be interested? Boy, that was an opportunity I really looked forward to! To be part of somethin'. I joined the Klan, went from member to chaplain, from chaplain to vice-president, from vice-president to president. The title is exalted cyclops.

Ellis recalled how he felt the day he took the oath:

After I had taken my oath, there was loud applause goin' throughout the buildin', musta been at least four hundred people. For this one little ol' person. It was a thrilling moment for C. P. Ellis.

It disturbs me when people do not really know what it's all about are so very critical of individual Klansmen. The majority of 'em are low-income whites, people who really don't have a part in something. They have been shut out as well as the blacks. Some are not very well educated either. Just like myself. We had a lot of support from doctors and lawyers and police officers.

Maybe they've had bitter experiences in this life and they had to hate somebody. So the natural person to hate would be the black person. He's beginnin' to come up, he's beginnin' to learn to read and start votin' and run for political office. Here are white people who are supposed to be superior to them, and we're shut out.

I can understand why people join extreme right-wing or left-wing groups. They're in the same boat I was. Shut out. Deep down inside, we want to be part of this great society. Nobody listens, so we join these groups.

As tensions mounted between African Americans and whites in Ellis's community, both groups attended city council meetings and school board hearings. At one meeting, Ellis was unexpectedly asked to co-chair a committee. He laughingly remembered:

A Klansman and a militant black woman, co-chairmen of the school committee. It was impossible. How could I work with her? But after about two or three days, it was in our hands. We had to make it a success. This give me another sense of belongin', a sense of pride. This helped this inferiority feelin' I had. A man who has stood up publicly and said he despised black people, all of a sudden he was willin' to work with 'em. In spite of all my hatred for blacks and Jews and liberals, I accepted the job. Her and I began to reluctantly work together. (Laughs.) She had as many problems workin' with me as I had workin' with her.

One night I called her: "Ann, you and I should have a lot of differences and we got 'em now. But there's somethin' laid out here before us, and if it's gonna be a success, you and I are gonna have to make it one. Can we lay aside some of these feelin's?" She say: "I'm willing if you are." I said: "Let's do it."

My old friends would call me at night: "C. P., what the hell is wrong with you? You're sellin' out the white race." This begin to make me have guilt feelin's. Am I doing' right? Am I doin' wrong? Here I am all of a sudden makin' an about-face and tryin' to deal with my feelin's, my heart. My mind was beginnin' to open up. I was beginnin' to see what was right and what was wrong. I don't want the kids to fight forever.

As C. P. and Ann went out into the community, they found that people were not responding to their message.

Some of 'em was cussin' us out. "You're sellin us out, Ellis get out of my door. I don't want to talk to you." Ann was gettin' the same response from blacks: "What are you doin' messin' with that Klansman?"

One day Ann and I went back to the school and we sat down. We began to talk and just reflect. Ann said: "My daughter came home cryin' every day. She said her teacher was makin' fun of me in front of the other kids." I said: "Boy, the same thing happened to my kid. White liberal teacher was makin fun of Tim Ellis's father, the Klansman. In front of other peoples. He came home cryin'." At this point—(he pauses, swallows hard, stifles a sob)—I begin to see, here we are, two people from the far ends of the fence, havin' identical problems, except hers bein' black and me bein' white. From that moment on, I tell ya, that gal and I worked together good. I begin to love the girl, really. (He weeps.)

The amazing thing about it, her and I, up to that point, had cussed each other, bawled each other, we hated each other. Up to that point, we didn't know each other. We didn't know we had things in common.

We worked at it, with the people who came to these meetings. They talked about racism, sex education, about teachers not bein' qualified. After seven, eight nights of real intense discussion, these people, who'd never talked to each other before, all of a sudden came up with resolutions. It was really somethin', you have to be there to get the tone and feelin' of it.

At this point I didn't like integration but the law says you do this and I've got to do what the law says, okay? We said: "Let's take these resolutions to the school board." The most disheartening thing I've ever faced was the school system refused to implement any one of these resolutions. These were recommendations from the people who pay taxes and pay their salaries.

The whole world was openin' up, and I was learnin' new truths that I had never learned before. I was beginnin' to look at a black person, shake hands with him, and see him as a human bein'.

When the school board refused to hear the committee's recommendations, Ellis decided to run for the board. Although he lost the election, the race changed his feelings about himself and others.

> The whole world was openin' up, and I was learnin' new truths that I had never learned before. I was beginnin' to look at a black person, shake hands with him, and see him as a human bein'. I hadn't got rid of all this stuff. I've still got a little bit of it. But somethin' was happenin' to me.
>
> It was almost like bein' born again. It was a new life. I didn't have these sleepless nights I used to have when I was active in the Klan and slippin' around at night. I could sleep at night and feel good about it. I'd rather live now than at any other time in history. It's a challenge.

As Ellis took charge of his life, he went back to school to earn a high school diploma. He also helped form a union at work, even though "my daddy was anti-labor, too."

> I tell people there's a tremendous possibility in this country to stop wars, the battles, the struggles, the fights between people. People say: "That's an impossible dream. You sound like Martin Luther King." An ex-Klansman who sounds like Martin Luther King. (Laughs.) I don't think it's an impossible dream. It's happened in my life. It's happened in other people's lives in America.
>
> When the news came over the radio that Martin Luther King was assassinated, I got on the telephone and begin to call other Klansmen. We just had a real party at the service station. Really rejoicin' 'cause that son of a bitch was dead. Our troubles are over with. They say the older you get, the harder it is for you to change. That's not necessarily true. Since I changed, I've set down and listened to tapes of Martin Luther King. I listen to it and tears come to my eyes 'cause I know what he's sayin' now. I know what's happenin'.[6]

CONNECTIONS

In the overview to this chapter, David Schoem referred to isolation as a "human and national tragedy." How did the isolation Schoem describes shape the values and beliefs of C. P. Ellis? His opportunities for knowing others? For learning their ways? What does it suggest about the kind of leaders needed in a democracy?

Schoem writes that as a result of our isolation we learn "to place heavy reliance on stereotypes, gossip, rumor, and fear to shape our lack of knowledge." How did "stereotypes, gossip, rumor, and fear" shape Ellis' attitudes? At what point did his attitude toward Ann change? Toward African Americans as a group? Why did they change? What does the change suggest about the way groups that regard one another as enemies can be brought together?

As an African American, Marian Wright Edelman was taught that segregation is "not about you; it's about them." How does C. P. Ellis's story support that view?

Earlier, Albert Camus was quoted as saying "I know that the great tragedies of history often fascinate men with approaching horror. Paralyzed, they cannot make up their minds to do anything but wait. So they wait, and one day the Gorgon devours them. But I should like to convince you that the spell can be broken, that there is an illusion of impotence, that strength of heart, intelligence and courage are enough to stop fate and sometimes reverse it." How did Ellis break that "illusion of impotence"? What opportunities are there in your life for overcoming that illusion and breaking the spell?

Draw an identity chart for Ellis when he joined the Klan. Draw a similar chart after he left the Klan and then compare the two charts. What differences seem most striking?

Why did Ellis and his fellow Klansmen need someone to blame for their troubles? Why would they regard the "black person" as the "natural person to hate"?

READING 4

Role Models in a Democracy

*T*oo many young people today are growing up the way C. P. Ellis did — "unable to handle life in hard places, without hope, without adequate attention, and without steady internal compasses to navigate the morally polluted seas they must face on the journey to adulthood."

The Reverend Michael Haynes is among those who have devoted their lives to helping those young people find their way. He began his career in social work as a youth-group leader and summer-camp counselor at a settlement house in a predominantly African American neighborhood. Haynes later recalled the philosophy he learned there:

> My mandate . . . was to spend as much time as I could with these kids, to guide their lives, to be concerned about what's going on in their schools, to get to know their families and to guide their leisure lives. In those days, settlement house workers in the black community were responsible for those kids. They were ours. There was no 9-to-5. I had to hang with them.[7]

Too many people. . . are growing up today unable to handle life in hard places, without hope, without adequate attention, and without steady internal compasses to navigate the morally polluted seas they must face on the journey to adulthood.

Haynes took those ideas with him, when he joined the staff of Norfolk House, a Boston settlement, in the 1950s.

> . . . Norfolk House was looking for a link between the white kids still in the neighborhood, already tense about the arrival of blacks, and the blacks who were entering a new environment. That's when the Exquisites began. The neighborhood houses had weekly parties and dances, basketball and football leagues, tutoring and arts and crafts. Kids just naturally flocked there. It was the perfect place to begin.
>
> We would get a group of about 10 to 15 kids, wherever there was a nucleus of kids who hung around who seemed to have some kind of potential, and we would form a club and concentrate on them. We started at the junior high level and followed these kids everywhere they went—to college if they went to college and to jail if they went to jail.[8]

Carl McCall met Haynes at a local pool hall. McCall, who had skipped school that day to hang out, still recalls their encounter:

We recognized how dependent upon each other we really were. . . . We learned there was nothing wrong with needing each other. And there was nothing wrong with achieving.

> He wanted to know what I was doing there. Right away, he told me I could be doing more than that. And he was a friend, father figure, mentor from then on. He encouraged and assisted me in applying to college, put me in contact with people who could help me get scholarships. And while I was in school, I'd get $5 from Mike every now and then to get my laundry done.
>
> Mike Haynes is a very special and terribly unselfish individual. He was just there for a lot of people. He encouraged us to get involved in the community and church and made sure we met people in politics, in business, people who were doing important things. And when we got to meet these people, most of them were black—they looked just like us. That was hard to forget. [9]

As a result of Haynes's efforts and his own determination, McCall finished not only high school but also college. And after earning a bachelor's degree from Dartmouth, he went on to study at the University of Edinburgh in Scotland. He later became president of the New York City Board of Education.

Albert Holland also belonged to the Exquisites. Now a superintendent within Boston School Department, he recalls that "there was nothing like being an Exquisite. I felt I belonged to an organization that had some goals and direction. It was something to be proud of. Mike got us into the Exquisites and then used the group to steer us. Even when we were away from home and needed lifting, we could pick up a phone and he'd be there. But the key was exposure. He made sure we saw success."[10]

Peter Parham, yet another member of the group, is the executive vice president of the National Center for Neighborhood Enterprise. He has also served as special assistant to U.S. Senator Edward Kennedy and as Director of Human Services for the city of Washington, D.C.

In all of the positions I've held, I drew upon strength I'd gotten as an Exquisite. I believed I could do anything, and I had a huge family reinforcing that idea. I can remember writing speeches for Sen. Kennedy and calling Mike for help, or Al Holland coming down from Boston to help me with fund raising for the 20th anniversary March on Washington. We recognized how dependent upon each other we really were. One might have talent in one area, say academic, but we learned that in order to be able to give something back, other talents were needed. We learned there was nothing wrong with needing each other.

And there was nothing wrong with achieving. I remember the trip the Exquisites took to Washington in 1963, and when I came back 13 years later as an assistant to Sen. Kennedy, there was clearly a bridge. I had no plans to end up working with him, but it wasn't beyond my dreams and perceptions. When you talk about making a dream reality, you first have to think it's possible. The Exquisites made my dream possible.[11]

Not every member of the Exquisites had success. Some got into trouble and lost their way. One of those young men, now a counselor for public housing residents, was in and out of prison seven times before he put his life together. He credits Haynes with his turn-around.

I was tired of people telling me when to do things and how to do them, tired of being considered a leader behind prison walls when I knew I should be a leader on the outside. I was scared to come out, but I made the decision to go straight from Walpole [maximum security prison] to a treatment program. I didn't call Rev. Haynes to tell him I was getting it together, I wanted to show him. I'm continuing his work in my own way.[12]

Norfolk House and the Exquisites no longer exist. The settlement house closed its doors in the 1970s because of funding problems. Michael Haynes reflected on the consequences of that loss:

I think we're paying the price now for the loss of the settlement houses—the violence, the inability to reach out and influence kids. Some of the community and youth leaders are beginning to realize that these components are missing and are trying to reestablish them. I think we're losing two whole generations of kids. The prisons reflect it.[13]

In what ways did Michael Haynes and his staff address Marian Edelman's concern that "Too many people—of all colors, and all walks of life—are growing up today unable to handle life in hard places, without hope, without adequate attention , and without steady internal compasses to navigate the morally polluted seas they must face on the journey to adulthood"? How did the group keep members from feeling shut out, the way C. P. Ellis did?

Carl McCall says of Michael Haynes, "He encouraged us to get involved in the community and church and made sure we met people in politics, in business, people who were doing important things. And when we got to meet these people, most of them were black—they looked just like us. That was hard to forget." What is a *role model*? How does a role model help young people "navigate the morally polluted seas they must face on the journey to adulthood"? Was Michael Haynes such a role model? To what extent were the people the Exquisites met through their association with Haynes role models? Who are your role models? How do they help you navigate "morally polluted seas"?

Compare the Exquisites with the Klan Ellis joined. How does each group satisfy the need of its members to belong? To be a part of something? What differences seem most striking?

At the end of the reading Michael Haynes discusses what the closing of places like Norfolk House means to young people and to the community as a whole. Do you share his concerns? To find out more about the work of settlement houses, see *Choosing to Participate*, Chapter 3, Part 1.

Haynes says of the young people he worked with at his first job, "They were ours. There was no 9-to-5." How is his sense of responsibility similar to that of the adults Edelman recalls from her childhood? How important is that sense of caring and responsibility to a community?

READING 5

American Dreams and Urban Realities

Young people are motivated to join gangs to "meet" the same developmental needs that all youth are seeking—a sense of connection, belonging, and self-definition.

*I*n Chapter 1, we saw that people everywhere live in groups. In groups, they meet their most basic needs and satisfy their yearning to belong. If they do not feel welcome in the larger society, many tend to form smaller groups of their own. Not surprisingly, those groups often challenge the values and beliefs of the larger society. Gangs are a good example. Young people, particularly those who belong to minority groups, have been forming them for hundreds of years. In the 1920s, members were primarily

European immigrants and their children—usually Poles, Italians, Irish, Slavs, and Jews. Today, most gang members are African Americans, Latinos, or Asians. Members continue to be, in the words of one researcher, "tough and resourceful kids, who have committed violence and had violence committed upon them. Most of their bodies show the scars. In their world, a youngster proves manhood by fighting other gang members or by fearlessly confronting outsiders."

The reasons for joining a gang have not changed much over the years but the violence associated with gangs has increased. In 1989, Leon Bing published a study of two of Los Angeles's most prominent gangs—the Crips and the Bloods. When she asked members why they joined, one young man told her:

> I wasn't in it at first. I was just young, about 12 years old, and I started talking about gangbanging [activities of a gang] and all that. Then they started breaking my stuff and all that, you know, so you figure, well, what's the use, it's protection. So you thinking about it and then somebody socks you when you not looking and then you fight 'em back and you end up in their set [a neighborhood affiliate of the Bloods or Crips].[14]

Other members offered other reasons for joining:

> Li'l Monster: Say we're white and we're rich, we're in high school and we been buddies since grammar school. And we all decide to go to the same college. Well, we all on the same street, all those years, and we all just decide to—
> Rat-Neck: —join the gang.
> Tee: What I think is formulating here is that human nature wants to be accepted. A human being gives less of a damn of what he is accepted into. At that age—11 to 17—all kids want to belong. They are un-people.[15]

Bing also asked members what gang life meant to them.

> Tee: It's the same everywhere. A sorority, a fraternity, the Girl Scouts, camping club, hiking club, LAPD, the Los Angeles Raiders, are all the same. Everything that you find in those groups and institutions you find in a gang.
> Bing: So are you saying there's no difference between the motives of you guys joining a gang, and say, a young WASP [White, Anglo-Saxon, Protestant] joining a fraternity?
> Rat-Neck: You got a lot of gangbangers out there who are smart. They want it. They got what it takes. But the difference is they got no money....
> Bing: And how do drugs figure into this?
> Li'l Monster: Wait a minute. I just want to slide in for a minute. I want to set the record straight. People think gangs and drugs go hand in hand, but they don't. If I sell drugs does that make me a

gangbanger? No. If I gangbang, does that make me sell drugs? No. See, for white people—and I am not saying for all white people, just like what I say about black people is not for all black people—they go to college, the stepping-stone to what they want to get. And some black people look to drugs as a stepping-stone to get the same thing.

B-Dog: They want to live better. To buy what they want. To get a house.

Rat-Neck: Not worry about where the next meal comes from.

Tee: To live comfortable and get a slice of American pie, the American Dream.

B-Dog: There it is.

Tee: The army came out with a hell of a slogan: "Be all you can be." And that's it.

We all want the same thing. We've been taught by television, the silver screen, to grow up and have a chicken in every pot, two Chevys, 2.3 kids in the family. So we have been the same thing that you have been taught, but there is certain things that we can hold on to and other things that—we see them, but we cannot reach them. Most of us are dealing with the reality of surviving as opposed to, "Well, my dad will take care of it."

Bing: Are you saying that gangbanging is just another version of the American Dream?

Li'l Monster: It's like this. You got the American Dream over there, and you reaching for it. But you can't get it. And you got dope right here, real close. You can grab it easy. Dealing with the closer one, you might possibly make enough money to grab the other one. Then you throw away the dope. That's a big if.[16]

Martin Sanchez Jankowski, a sociologist, studied thirty-seven gangs in Los Angeles, New York City, and Boston over a ten-year period. He, too, interviewed members on a wide range of topics, including the role that violence plays in their lives. An 18-year-old Puerto Rican from New York told him, "Yeah, I smashed the windshield of this white preppy's Jag [Jaguar automobile]. I dropped a brick on it. . . . I did it because I hate those a—. They got everything 'cause they're white and their fathers were rich and bloodsuckers. And you know, after I do it, I feel a little better that I made them hassled just a little."[17]

A nineteen-year-old who belongs to an Irish gang in Boston said:

"I torched the inside of that blue's [blue blood's] car, so what? I hate them, just like I hate the niggers. They think we're scum. You know they keep us in these low-paying jobs and these row houses and go off to their fancy houses in the suburbs which they bought by ripping us off from good wages. Hell, I won't be getting a job to get me out of this because I won't get the opportunity, they'd rather give it to the niggers. So I think they're scum, and when I get the chance to make it a little hard for them, I take it! And you know what? I feel better afterward.[18]

An eighteen-year-old New Yorker told Jankowski: "See, I and a lot of other guys have inflicted a lot of hurt on people over the years, but we was commanded at various times by the gang to inflict hurt on people. We did it and did it mercilessly. . . . Nobody felt guilty about it because since the whole gang thought it was the right thing, it was the right thing. Plus it was an order and you have to follow orders."[19] A sixteen-year-old Mexican American in Los Angeles stated:

> Check it out, I got me a lot of shooting in and I hit a lot of people. . . . Yeah, I can remember when I first was told [by the gang] to shoot somebody. I was nervous, but I had this automatic rifle, and when I started to shoot, man, it was easy. That's what makes it easy, it's fast and there's nothing personal in it like when you use a knife. . . Hey, you know what I like about carrying this pistol, you get respect no matter who you are or how big you are cause it evens everything up.[20]

Both Bing and Jankowski have tried to understand what motivates gang members to choose violent responses. Bing wrote:

> I'd heard a lot about the gangs and the drive-by shootings. But I'd never read anything about these guys as people. There are well over 10,000 of these kids in L.A. These are American kids! They're drifting into gangs at eight or nine, some becoming killers by the time they're 12. I wondered. What do they think? What makes them hate each other?
>
> They're killing each other, and it's getting worse all the time. Their lives are so desolate, they have so little hope, and they are taking it out on people like themselves. Their parents, some of them, are on crack or other drugs. They have nothing you would recognize as family life, too little food, no future. Many of them are abused as children. Nobody cares about them. They are afraid to walk to the store alone, or to go to their friend's house without protection.
>
> . . . [All] the time homeless children turn up in gang neighborhoods knocking on doors, saying, "I want to claim. I want to be from this 'hood." And the gangs let them in. . . gang members are among the quietest people you will ever meet. You know, gangs are like families. Little kids get disciplined in gangs. When a little kid drifts into a gang, he doesn't just get a gun thrust into his hands. He's gonna get homeboy love, which is pretty potent.
>
> [These] kids are not monsters. They are growing up against all odds in poisonous soil. I cannot judge them. And I cannot fix it for them, this horrible world they live in. All I can do is describe it. And try to stop the denial [by American society].[21]

In the conclusion to his book on gangs, Jankowski wrote:

> . . . Much too often we have thought of gang members as the lowest of the lower class, individuals with low intelligence, psychological

There are well over 10,000 of these kids in L.A. These are American kids! They're drifting into gangs at eight or nine, some becoming killers by the time they're 12. I wondered. What do they think? What makes them hate each other?

disorders (like sadism) and or no initiative to work for a living. This view is simply not accurate. A great range of individuals are in gangs, but the vast majority are intelligent and quite capable of developing and executing creative enterprises.[22]

CONNECTIONS

The individuals quoted in this reading cannot possible speak for the thousands of young people who belong to gangs. They do, however, offer some insights into why some young people are attracted to gangs. What reasons do members give for joining? How are those reasons similar to those given for joining such groups as the Exquisites? The Klan? How are those reasons different?

Write a working definition of the word *gang*. What positive meanings does the word have? What negative meanings does it have? One gang member compared a gang to other groups in American society. How valid is his comparison?

Review the comments of the gang members who told of why they committed violent acts. What do their explanations have in common? Can you understand *why* they did what they did? What is the difference between understanding behavior and excusing it?

At the age of fifteen, poet Luis Rodriguez joined an East Los Angeles gang. He soon learned that the companionship and respect the gang offered came at a very high price. By the time he was eighteen, he writes, "25 of my friends had been killed by rival gangs, police, drugs, car crashes, and suicides." In the fall of 1993 Rodriguez reflected on what young people can learn from his experiences with gangs. He told an interviewer from *Teaching Tolerance*:

> One of the things I keep coming back to is a sense of control. I think what happens when you join gangs is you end up in prison, and prison is the place where everything is controlled; nothing belongs to you. Right now they have more control than they'll ever have in their lives, and they need to know how powerful and beautiful it is to have that control within yourself and be able to make choices.
>
> They need to know they have options and that they can do something about their community. When I ask them what they want to change, they usually say they don't like the violence, they don't like bullets flying through the windows. They want to be able to fix the streets which are crumbling, they want to fix the schools. I tell them that's good; we can do something about it. We can make our own history.
>
> To me, the most important change is internal—when you change within yourself to get through some of the terrible things happening outside of you. But you have to be working on the things outside of you, too. Even with my son Ramiro—we have built up a very strong relationship, but I know that as soon as he walks out the door, he

confronts society. So we have to do things about society, too. It can't just be an individual thing. We have to work together.

According to Rodriguez, what do people need to understand about the consequences of their choices? Many gang members are aware of statistics like those Rodriguez cites. Why then do they often find it hard to accept the need to change their behavior? What does Rodriguez see as the relationship between the individual and society? Do you agree?

It would be wrong to assume, however, that most urban teens or most Latinos or African Americans belong to gangs. Most, in fact, do not. What differentiates gang members from non-gang members? How might a research-based answer to that question be helpful in developing a program to stop gang activities and prevent violence?

It goes without saying that both Leon Bing and Martin Jankowski condemn the violent acts committed by gang members. Yet both try to understand what causes that violence. Bing says of gang members, these "kids are not monsters" but they are growing up in "poisonous soil." What does she mean by that statement? How does she explain why young people join gangs? Is she right to say that most Americans try to deny problems posed by gangs?

Several gang members refer to the American Dream. Jankowski notes that their vision of that dream mirrors the values of American society as a whole. "[The] vast majority of gang members are quite energetic and are eager to acquire many of the same things that most members of American society want: money, material possessions, power, and prestige. Indeed, because they want the "good life," they energetically seek entrepreneurial opportunities that might lead them to it." How do you think Marian Wright Edelman would respond to that vision of the American Dream? How might the Reverend Michael Haynes respond? How do you respond? Leon Bing says that she cannot judge gang members. If she cannot, who can judge and condemn their violent acts?

Gang members do not see themselves as empowered in the way Haynes empowered the young men he worked with. How might gang members be made to feel that they can make a positive difference in their own lives? How can they learn to feel that they are a part of a larger community? Think about those questions as you continue reading the chapter.

➤The video *Beyond Hate,* a useful companion to this reading, is available from the Facing History Resource Center. Also available is a video interview with Carl Washington, a minister who was awarded the Reebok Human Rights Award in 1993 for his efforts at arranging a truce between the Crips and the Bloods in Los Angeles.

Breaking the Bonds of Hate

How does one break out of the cycle of anger and violence that marks gang life? Virak Khiev, a Cambodian immigrant, offers one answer:

> Most Americans believe the stereotype that immigrants work hard, get a good education and have a very good life. Maybe it used to be like that, but not anymore. You have to be deceptive and unscrupulous in order to make it. If you are not, then you will end up like most immigrants I've known. Living in the ghetto in a cockroach-infested house. Working on the assembly line or in the chicken factory to support your family. Getting up at 3 o'clock in the morning to take the bus to work and not getting home until 5 P.M.
>
> If you're a kid my age, you drop out of school to work because your parents don't have enough money to buy you clothes for school. You may end up selling drugs because you want cars, money and parties, as all teenagers do. You have to depend on your peers for emotional support because your parents are too busy working in the factory trying to make money to pay the bills. You don't get along with your parents because they have a different mentality: you are an American and they are Cambodian. You hate them because they are never there for you, so you join a gang as I did.
>
> You spend your time drinking, doing drugs, and fighting. You beat up people for pleasure. You don't care about anything except your drugs, your beers, and your revenge against adversaries. You shoot at people because they've insulted your pride. You shoot at the police because they are always bothering you. They shoot back and then you're dead like my best friend Sinerth.
>
> Sinerth robbed a gas station. He was shot in the head by the police. I'd known him since the sixth grade from my first school in Minneapolis. I can still remember his voice calling me from California. "Virak, come down here, man," he said. "We need you. There are lots of pretty girls down here." I promised him that I would be there to see him. The following year he was dead. I felt sorry for him. But as I thought it over, maybe it is better for him to be dead than to continue with the cycle of violence, to live with hate. I thought, "It is better to die than live like an angry young fool, thinking that everybody is out to get you."
>
> . . . When I was like Sinerth, I didn't care about dying. I thought that I was on top of the world, being immortalized by drugs. I could see that my future would be spent working on the assembly line like most of my friends, spending all my paycheck on the weekend and being broke again on Monday morning. I hated going to school because

I couldn't see a way to get out of the endless cycle. My philosophy was "Live hard and die young."

I hated America because, to me, it was not the place of opportunities or the land of "the melting pot" as I had been told. All I had seen were broken beer bottles on the street and homeless people and drunks using the sky as their roof. I couldn't walk down the street without someone yelling out, "you f—ing gook" from his car. Once again I was caught in the web of hatred. I'd become a mad dog with the mind-set of the past: "When trapped in the corner, just bite." The war mentality of Cambodia came back: get what you can and leave. I thought I came to America to escape war, poverty, fighting, to escape the violence, but I wasn't escaping; I was being introduced to a newer version of war—the war of hatred.

I was lucky. In Minneapolis, I dropped out of school in the ninth grade to join a gang. Then I moved to Louisiana, where I continued my life of "immortality" as a member of another gang. It came to an abrupt halt when I crashed a car. I wasn't badly injured, but I was underage and the fine took all my money. I called a good friend of the Cambodian community in Minneapolis for advice (she'd tried to help me earlier). I didn't know where to go or whom to turn to. I saw friends landing in jail, and I didn't want that. She promised to help me get back in school. And she did.

Since then I've been given a lot of encouragement and caring by American friends and teachers who've helped me turn my life around. They opened my eyes to a kind of education that frees us all from ignorance and slavery. I could have failed so many times except for those people who believed in me and gave me another chance. Individuals who were willing to help me have taught me that I can help myself. I'm now a 12th grader and have been at my school for three years; I plan to attend college in the fall. I am struggling to believe I can reach the other side of the mountain.[24]

[American friends and teachers] opened my eyes to a kind of education that frees us all from ignorance and slavery.

CONNECTIONS

Compare Virak Khiev's view of the American Dream with those of the gang members quoted in Reading 5. How are they similar? What differences seem most striking? What is your view of the American Dream?

What does Khiev mean when he writes that his teachers "opened my eyes to a kind of education that frees us all from ignorance and slavery"? What kind of education does that?

According to Albert Camus, "strength of heart, intelligence and courage are enough to stop fate and sometimes reverse it." How does this reading support that view? What part did Virak Khiev's friends and teachers play in stopping fate or even reversing it? What part did Khiev play?

Jane Addams once said that "one does good, if at all, with people, not to people." Would Virak Khiev agree?

➤ A video interview with Arn Chorn, a survivor of the Cambodian Genocide, is available from the Facing History Resource Center.

R E A D I N G   7

Pride and Prejudice

On April 29, 1992, a jury acquitted a group of Los Angeles police officers accused of beating Rodney King, an African American. Many people were shocked by the verdict. After viewing a video of the beating that a bystander made, they were convinced that the police had acted improperly. Within hours of the announcement, angry African Americans took to the streets to express their outrage. Gregory Alan-Williams, who is also an African American, witnessed the rioting. He later described how he felt as he saw the overturned cars, smashed windows, and smoldering fires:

> I understood clearly what was happening and why it was happening. A part of me wanted it to happen, spurred by the remaining shards of self-righteous indignation that scraped at my insides. But if I had raised my hand against another, when my rage was spent, and I could no longer recall with sufficient clarity the justifications that had driven me to such brutality and horror, what would I do? How would I survive the shame and self-hatred which would overtake me as the battered faces of my brothers bled and pleaded in my memory?[25]

At an intersection, Alan-Williams saw a Japanese American try desperately to drive through the area only to be stopped by a barrage of bricks and bottles. Even after the man lost consciousness, the attacks continued. As Williams watched, he recalled an incident that took place when he was one of two black students in his junior high school:

> I was a few feet from the auditorium doors, engaging in some good-natured banter with another student, when some hard object— like a rock—slammed against my mouth: the flesh burst into bleeding pulp against my teeth. The strength of the blow, combined with the downward incline of the aisle, sent me reeling backward into the

students behind me. They parted like the Red Sea. I fell over some seats, righted myself, and touched two trembling fingers to the pain in my mouth. I could feel the flesh hanging from where my bottom lip had been.

Dazed and bleeding, I staggered back and forth across the aisle, unable to understand what had happened. I caught a blurry glimpse of someone standing laughing in the middle of the aisle. I couldn't make out his face but he was huge. . . . Some kids were standing at the edges of the aisle, others had gathered up ahead and were watching from the double doors of the auditorium. A few joined my assailant in laughter. . . . I was hoping desperately that someone upon this "enlightened landscape" would help me. Help me get away from the huge laughing figure, away from my shame and those who watched as I staggered about, bloody and afraid.

Gregory Alan-Williams speaks to Facing History students.

A few days later, as I sat, stitched and swollen, in the vice principal's office, I came to understand what had happened, for the vice principal said that I had come to his school "walking too tall" and holding my head "a little too high and many of the students resented it. So," he said to my mother, "of course, what could you expect?". . .

Now the vivid memory of that beating and abandonment, some twenty-five years ago, propelled me into the intersection. I remembered too well the feelings I had had, the hurtful words and images—I could not accept this attack, the suffering of this human being. It seemed that he and I had become one, that his suffering and mine had fused, and with one loud and silent voice now cried for help within this single irretrievable moment.

My conscience heard our cry, and carried me forward to preserve justice for him and to reclaim justice for myself.

I moved neither slowly nor quickly, not in anger but in extreme sorrow. Sorrow for those who were seeing, but who could not see; sorrow for the ones who saw but who had lost the ability to feel.

It seemed that he and I had become one, that his suffering and mine had fused, and with one loud and silent voice now cried for help within this single irretrievable moment.

> Sorrow for the hated and for those who nurtured hate with their silence. Although the man in the intersection was being robbed of his existence, my sorrow was not for death, but for the prevailing misery of life and grew from a remembrance of the ache that comes with knowing that one has been exiled from the human heart.[26]

CONNECTIONS

What does Alan-Williams mean when he says that in helping the man attacked by the mob, he was reclaiming "justice for myself"?

How does Williams' story reflect Maya Angelou's belief that the "courage to confront evil and turn it by dint of will into something applicable in the development of our evolution, individually and collectively is exciting, honorable"? (See Chapter 1, Reading 5.)

After the riots in Los Angeles, two African Americans were brought to trial for pulling Reginald Denny, a white truck driver, from his cab and battering him. At their trial, the prosecutors featured the story of four other African Americans who came to Denny's rescue. Columnist Meg Greenfield commented "as one who has watched some of the rescuers' testimony and been absolutely knocked out by it." She wrote that "what they did . . . was not about being a member of any particular race. It was about being human and moral. Remember human and moral?" What is she saying about the way each of us is connected to other human beings? About the importance of that connection?

➤ A videotape of a talk by Alan-Williams at the Ninth Annual Facing History Conference is available from the Facing History Resource Center, as are classroom sets of his autobiography, *A Gathering of Heroes*.

READING 8

Finding Alternatives to Violence

*I*n many schools throughout the United States, students are learning to deal with the anger Khiev and Alan-Williams describe in more positive ways. In one program, for example, students are taught to analyze their behavior and weigh the consequences of their actions. As part of that curriculum, they watch a videotaped argument between two students, David and Lisa. David wants Lisa to go to a party with him. When she refuses, David pressures her to change her mind. He reminds her that as his girlfriend, she is obligated to spend time with him. Their increasingly angry voices attract a group of onlookers. Some are David's friends, while others support Lisa.

David's friends fan the argument by suggesting that Lisa is interested in someone else. At the same time, Lisa's friends tell her that she does not need a domineering boyfriend. Then, as the tension builds, Leon walks into the room and initiates a conversation with Lisa who clearly enjoys the attention. Her behavior provokes David who, in turn, demands that Leon leave. Leon refuses. Once again, David's friends fuel the quarrel by urging him to take action. He responds by shoving Leon aside. The video ends with Leon grabbing a chair just as David seems to be pulling a knife from his pocket.

As students watch the quarrel build in intensity, many laugh nervously even though they know it is a simulation. After all, the scene could easily have taken place in their own school or in thousands of others around the country. The program, called *Violence Prevention*, was developed by a physician, Deborah Prothrow-Stith. Used in over five thousand schools in forty-eight states, it grew out of her belief that violence has become a national public health emergency. Statistics bear her out.

- The United States ranks fifth in the world and first among industrialized nations (including nations at war) in recorded homicide rates.
- Serious assaults increased 400 percent in the nation's cities from the mid 1970s to 1990.
- In the past 30 years, the death rate has decreased for every age group except one—15-24 year olds.
- In the 1980s the arrest rate for juveniles accused of violent offenses shot up 27 percent. The increases hold true for young people of all races and social classes.
- Homicide—the intentional killing of one person by another—is the second leading cause of death for 15 to 24 year olds. For African-American males in the same age group, it is the leading cause of death.

Deborah Prothrow-Stith's interest in violence prevention began in the early 1980s when she worked in the emergency room at two Boston hospitals. In an interview, she recalled:

> It hit me—all we did was stitch them up and send them out, stitch them up and send them out. We did nothing to prevent more violence.
>
> Now that wasn't true of any other disease or injury we treated there. We never sent a heart attack victim home to just have another heart attack. We taught him about diet and exercise and stress. We never sent a suicide attempt home to just try it again. We offered counseling, support—we always did something to prevent them coming back in again. But victims of violence? We did nothing.[27]

It hit me—all we did was stitch them up and send them out, stitch them up and send them out. We did nothing to prevent more violence. . . . We never sent a suicide attempt home to just try it again. We offered counseling, support—we always did something to prevent them coming back in again. But victims of violence? We did nothing.

The doctor's experiences convinced her that something had to be done. "Young Black boys are overrepresented in homicide statistics. They're five percent of the population and forty percent of homicide victims. But what's becoming obvious to us is that, if you think homicide is the tip of the iceberg, it's not just a poor, urban problem. The homicide rate is higher in poor urban areas, but the assault rate [in suburban middle-class areas] isn't very different."[28]

Prothrow-Stith believes that American society as a whole has allowed itself to become "infatuated with violence." The media in particular has glamorized violence so that many young people see it not only as a legitimate way of resolving conflicts but the only way of doing so. Again, statistics support her view. A study by the American Psychological Association revealed that "the average child witnesses 8,000 murders [on television] by the time he or she graduates from elementary school and sees more than 100,000 other acts of violence." And TV is not the only place that young people are exposed to violence. They also see it in movies, video games, books, and magazines. Other studies suggest a link between aggressive acts and an individual's exposure to violence. Students who spend many hours watching brutal acts on TV are more likely to commit spontaneous acts of aggression than those less exposed to violence.

Prothrow-Stith found that television had another effect as well: Many young people did not connect the pain of an injury with a violent act. Marcy Kelly of Mediascope, an organization that monitors violence in the entertainment industry, echoes that observation. "Many young people who wind up in hospitals having been shot say they are surprised that it hurts because it doesn't hurt on television." Prothrow-Stith also found that many teens "knew from their own experience of suffering and grief how much violence can hurt, but they had no idea how to avoid it. Don't you have to fight if someone insults you? they asked. Unless they spend a lot of time at church, or their parents actively taught them nonviolent methods of resolving conflicts, their teachers were television, movies and other kids."[29]

Such conversations convinced the physician that a violence-prevention program ought to emphasize the importance of analyzing the consequences of every action. In the one she developed, students learn to weigh the risks involved in using violence to settle disputes. They are also introduced to other ways of resolving differences and to techniques that help them channel their anger into more positive actions. For example, students are expected to watch each video several times. And each time they are instructed to look for ways of defusing the situation. This technique encourages them to reflect on what causes conflicts to escalate. They become particularly aware of the roles friends can play in a crisis. They also come to realize that fear of what a friend may say can lead an individual to take more extreme action than he or she might otherwise consider.

Prothrow-Stith believes that her techniques empower students to break "the cycle of violence" even when they are confronted with flagrant injustice. She offers an example to underscore her point.

One young Black man told me he was angry because he saw his best friend stabbed in an argument. It took the ambulance 20 minutes to get to the scene of the stabbing. His friend was dead on arrival.

He was angry at the ambulance driver's tardiness. I gave him a litany of reactions: slash the tires of the ambulance, beat up the driver, hold his anger inside and do nothing, beat up a sibling or a pet or write a letter of protest to the company that owns the ambulance.

He said he wouldn't do any of these.

Then I said: "I hope you are so angry that you decide to finish high school and become a professional ambulance driver." I told him he had a right to be angry but anything less than this would be self-destructive.

The suggestion opened up a new possibility. He expressed immediate relief that he had an option in a long term struggle. He told me the suggestion made him feel less trapped.[30]

CONNECTIONS

Prothrow-Stith and other researchers maintain that American society glamorizes violence. Test their opinion by critically viewing television programs popular among your friends. Look for scenes that involve threats of violence or actual violence. What prompts the violence? How do the actors respond? Do they regard the violence as an out-of-the-ordinary occurrence or as a matter of course? Compare your findings with those of your classmates. What patterns or trends do you see?

Much of Facing History and Ourselves has focused on the consequences of seeing the "other" as an enemy. How does the tendency to label *them* as enemies promote acts of violence?

Reread the description of David and Lisa's quarrel. What factors contributed directly to the fight? What factors contributed indirectly? For example, what part did gender play—what is considered appropriate behavior for males and females in our society? What other factors were involved? Then list ways a fight might have been prevented.

Prothrow-Stith knows that her curriculum is only a beginning. Why does she feel it is important for students to learn less violent ways of resolving conflicts? How do those feelings affect the advice she gave the young man who lost a friend?

➤The video *Facing History and Ourselves: Chicago Students Confront Hatred and Discrimination* shows how a group of students views violence. Compare their views to your own. The video is available from the Facing History Resource Center. Also available is a videotape of a presentation Deborah Prothrow-Stith gave at the Ninth Annual Facing History Conference.

Students Organize

People say it's only vandalism. This isn't vandalism. It's the message. They're not out to destroy the property. They're out to destroy the people.

Wellesley, Massachusetts, is an attractive, prosperous suburb ten miles west of Boston. On the surface it seems far removed from the violence associated with large urban areas. Yet, on the night of October 7, 1989, the people of Wellesley discovered that hate crimes are not limited to inner-city neighborhoods. That night someone painted racist graffiti on dozens of cars, homes, and shops. The next morning, residents awoke to such messages of hate as "Hitler's Children," "Nazi Youth," "White Power," "The Final Solution," "Whites Only," and "I Hate Niggers, Chinks, and Spics." A local reporter reflected the sentiments of most people in the community, "No one thought this could happen here. Even five days after anti-Semitic and racial slurs were scrawled throughout the town, the community is still coming to grips with a problem it believed Wellesley was immune to."[31]

Some speculated that the incident was the work of a neo-Nazi hate group outside the community. Others noted that the vandalism seemed to be random; no one group was singled out even though most of the graffiti was clearly racist. Yet many people in Wellesley did not view the vandalism as an isolated event. After seeing the business district, an African American student at Wellesley College told the reporter that she had seen swastikas spray-painted over two posters at the college just a week earlier. A passerby supported that view: "Racist feelings definitely exist here. I have had incidents happen. When people find out you are Jewish, they pull away. I just don't think some people know how to handle differences."[32]

Wellesley was not the only community in Massachusetts to experience a hate-related incident that summer. The Anti-Defamation League reported more racially motivated incidents in the state that summer than in the entire previous year. The number of hate crimes also rose dramatically across the country. They occurred not only in large cities but also on college campuses and in suburbs like Wellesley. Few of those crimes were the work of outsiders. Almost all were committed by people who lived in the community where the crime took place. Wellesley proved to be no exception.

A few days after the incident, the police charged two nineteen-year-olds with twenty-six counts of malicious destruction of property and two counts of intimidating individuals based on their religion—a violation of the state's civil rights law. Both men pleaded guilty. Although the two had grown up in Wellesley and attended local schools, reporters and residents alike labeled them as "odd" or "loners." They were said to like "heavy metal music" and one was said to sport a punk-style hair cut. People seemed to find comfort in viewing the two men as "different" from everyone else in the community.

One Wellesley resident was bothered by that response. Tory Garner, then a senior at Wellesley Hills High School, knew the vandals personally. She had grown up with them and was convinced that they were not so different from others in the community. She therefore concluded that the incident revealed that something was wrong not just with the two men but also with the community in which they grew up. In an interview, she described Wellesley as "an incredibly sheltered town. The fact that I myself thought this could not happen in Wellesley, I think that says a lot. We, the town, think we are different just because we are wealthy, that we are safe from these 'outside attacks.'"[33]

Tory Garner did not want herself or others to shrug off the incident. Therefore she, with the help of two classmates, Brian Doyle and Marissa Kramer, organized a candlelight rally to protest racism. About a thousand people attended. The students also bought a full-page ad in a local newspaper to publicly condemn hate crimes. But they did not stop there. They set out to educate themselves and others about the causes and consequences of those crimes. Doyle, as president of the student council, helped organize a special day-long workshop. Among the experts he invited was Deputy Superintendent William Johnston, then of the Community Disorders Unit, a special section in the Boston Police Department that investigates hate crimes. Johnston told the students and their teachers, "People say it's only vandalism. This isn't vandalism. It's the message. They're not out to destroy the property. They're out to destroy the people."

By the end of the day, Doyle realized that the program was for everyone, including himself. "At times I think I actually take racism and discrimination too easily. I was the type of kid who would laugh at the jokes that were prejudiced. I didn't see the problems behind the jokes. I thought everybody was the same, and these were funny jokes. This has made me look at the deeper meaning."[34] Other students had a similar response. In reflecting on what she learned from the experience, Tory Garner said:

> Everything I did and the reverberations made me realize so much more how individual differences meant so much. The whole thing was not about condemning those two guys but about condemning their attitudes and the things that stem from those kind of attitudes. So I believe it always makes me think a lot more about what I say. Sometimes people say or do things that offend me by way of offending other people. I think before I would have been offended, but I would not have said anything. And now I find myself when people start telling racist jokes, I say, "Could you tell this another time when I am not here or could you just not tell them." I am not so scared of offending people when they do those things.
>
> I have always been tagged a leader, but I never did such a thing on such a large scale. I surprised myself. [35]

I was the type of kid who would laugh at the jokes that were prejudiced. I didn't see the problems behind the jokes. I thought everybody was the same, and these were funny jokes. This has made me look at the deeper meaning.

CONNECTIONS

Why did many residents think Wellesley was immune to hate crimes? Why were they wrong? What did Tory Garner and Brian Doyle learn about prejudice and discrimination in their community? In themselves?

Garner was able to convert her sense of outrage into a constructive plan of action. How do you think she learned to do so? Think back to other readings in this chapter that described role models or mentors who influenced individuals' choices. How do those individuals shape the way we respond to the world around us?

Many people will attend a rally or march after an incident like the one described in this reading. Fewer are willing to work toward preventing such incidents. How can people from different backgrounds be brought together? What kinds of activities promote an atmosphere in which diversity is respected rather than one that demands conformity? List as many ideas as you can. Then as a class, discuss ways you might implement those ideas. What risks do you take if you try to bring about change? What risks do you take if you fail to do so?

How do you account for the fact that most hate crimes are committed by men and women under the age of twenty-five?

Brian Doyle says of himself, "I was the type of kid who would laugh at the jokes that were prejudiced. I didn't see the problems behind the jokes. I thought everybody was the same, and these were funny jokes. This has made me look at the deeper meaning." What is that "deeper meaning"? What is the connection between the jokes and the vandalism? Between vandalism and hate crimes?

➤A video of a talk by Deputy Superintendent William Johnston of the Boston Police Department is available from the Facing History Resource Center.

READING 10

Taking a Stand

Tory Garner and her friends learned that it is important to speak out when someone tells a racist joke or makes a derogatory remark. But taking a stand requires courage. It is not easy to go against the group, even when you believe you are right. Monica Braine discovered just how tough it was when she protested her school's choice of a mascot.

Indiana Area Junior High, like many schools in the United States, has an Indian mascot, "Chief Tommyhawk." His picture is everywhere in the school. It even decorates the school's floor mats. After noting that below his picture is the motto, "Our school is Drug and Alcohol Free," the ninth-grader told a reporter:

> "Apparently, it's not racist mascot free," said Monica Braine, an Assiniboine Sioux, who is a freshman at the school this fall. She has stood her ground and spoken out on the mascot issue, telling the school it is wrong, but so far she is one against a tidal wave of students and community members who take pride in their "Chief Tommyhawk" and their "squaw."
>
> "At sports events such as the football games, the cheerleaders dance around in typical stereotypical 'Indian' dances. The chief and squaw are doing the same.
>
> "At volleyball games, the walls are splashed with posters that say Fight'um and Go Injuns, and before they begin to play they stand in a circle and say 1-2-3 scalp 'um," she said.
>
> "In the lunchroom they serve Big Indian Burgers," Miss Braine said.
>
> "I had no idea this kind of ignorance existed.
>
> "My mother has talked to the cheerleaders, and I wrote in the school newspaper that the mascots are derogatory and racist. But the administration seems to be deaf," she said.
>
> "The entire school was furious with me and I was not popular at the time, but I stood my ground, and I learned who my real friends are. There was even a few threats by some students that they were going to beat me up."
>
> Principal Rodney Ruddock said the mascot issue must be looked at from both points of view, those who want it changed and those who feel just as strongly that the mascot shouldn't be changed. [36]

CONNECTIONS

How difficult is it to take an unpopular stand? To go against the group? Review Chapter 1. What advice do you think Monica Braine would offer the Bear in *the bear that wasn't*? Miriam Thaggert? Eve Shalen? What advice might they have given her?

In the previous reading, Brian Doyle, a high-school student, says of himself, "I was the type of kid who would laugh at the jokes that were prejudiced. I didn't see the problems behind the jokes. I thought everybody was the same, and these were funny jokes. This has made me look at the deeper meaning." How do his comments apply to Monica Braine's efforts to ban her school mascot? What is the deeper meaning in this case? How important is that meaning?

In 1993, the Wisconsin state assembly passed a resolution urging that public schools consider dropping American Indian logos and mascots if they are found to be offensive. A representative who opposed the measure believed it would encourage censorship. Is he right? Or does the use of such mascots threaten what Vaclav Havel calls a "civil society"? Use ideas and information you recorded in your journal to support your point of view.

R E A D I N G   1 1

City Year

The common ground is service. People have lost the sense that they can make a difference. Everything is so imposing: the homeless problem, drugs, the ghettos. What can I do as one person? This shows people that they *can* make a difference.

Michael Brown and Alan Khazei shared a vision when they graduated from Harvard Law School in 1987. They wanted to create a year-long program that would provide students with opportunities for public service. As Brown explained in an interview, "The idea behind City Year is to bring together young people from diverse backgrounds - rich, middle class, and poor, from different city neighborhoods as well as from the suburbs - for one year to concentrate on what they have in common and to work for the common good."[37] To raise money for the project, they spent months seeking donations from private corporations and wealthy individuals. Their determination paid off.

Once they had enough money to set up a program, the men established guidelines. Recruits were to be between the ages of seventeen and twenty-two. Each was to have an "excellent attitude." And each was expected to register to vote, obtain a library card, prepare a resume, complete a workshop on tax preparation, and if not already a high-school graduate, earn a GED by the end of the year. For nine months of community service in the Boston area, each recruit would earn $100 a week and a $5,000 scholarship. The first year, fifty young people signed up. By 1992, there were 220 recruits.

After observing the program, Anthony Lewis, a columnist for the *New York Times*, wrote:

> The Mason School in Roxbury, a largely black area of Boston, has problems typical of an inner-city school: not enough money, an old building, children who speak different languages. But it has a determined principal in Mary Russo, respected teachers and 10 young men and women helping out as aides. They come from a service group known as City Year.
>
> One of the City Year aides, Lucius Graham, is in the first-grade classroom. Three children—Andrea, Shamekia and Alvin—hang on to him, hugging his legs. He talks with them, then goes to the corner and helps three girls paint T-shirts with colors that glow in the dark.
>
> Lucius, 18 years old, dropped out of high school in the 11th grade, last year. "The school had too many problems," he said. "You were labeled as part of a gang. I went every day with a weapon to protect myself."
>
> How did he end up in City Year, helping in the Mason School?

"There was a City Year group building a little park in our neighborhood. The more I watched, the more I liked it."

Now he is in high school equivalency classes that City Year offers its corps members. If he keeps up with the work, and most do, he will get a diploma.

Stephen Noltemy, 21, got his diploma that way, as a City Year corps member, and now teaches in the diploma program. He comes from South Boston, the white stronghold of working-class Boston. He was in trouble, in a halfway house, when he joined City Year.

"I didn't care about too many things then," Steve said. "I was angry, prejudiced, negative. I was less than zero.

"City Year saved my life. I don't want to sell anything to you, but there it is. I like to wake up in the morning—know what I mean?"

One day last week I watched City Year at work and talked with staff and corps members. Like Steve Noltemy, I feel I should discount it and say I am not trying to sell anything. But what I saw was impressive, even moving—and quite without what I had been half afraid I would find, the aroma of do-goodism.

Daina Sutton, 19, had a baby in 1991 and dropped out of school. The father was arrested in June 1992.

"I really didn't want to do anything," she said. "Except I wanted to do something for my son. City Year wasn't a big deal at first. Now it's everything."

The team Daina was on started by making a garden in a run-down area. Then she helped 225 school kids train at the Boston Ballet. Now the team is at a school in East Boston, giving an environmental curriculum it helped design: "basics like what to do with litter."

"One of the people on my team was a rich white girl," Daina Sutton said. "I thought, I don't want to be her welfare case. But we got really close."

Diversity is a major theme of City Year. Teams are mixed in race, class, education. About a quarter of the 220 young people in the corps are dropouts, a third in college or on the way.

Black and white, rich and poor spoke of how daunting it had been at first to be with different people.

"It was not just skin color," said Andre Berry, 20, a black corps member who is now on the staff as a team leader. "One girl on my team had a parent who was a brain surgeon! It was weird to me: Someone who's got money—what's she doing here? But she became one of my close friends."

Lisa Schorr, 22, of Washington, D.C., a graduate of Sidwell Friends School and Harvard, is a corps member this year. "I started out skeptical," she said. "I thought the diversity would be forced and superficial. But it isn't."

Alan Khazei explained to Lewis why City Year works despite the initial skepticism. "The common ground is service. People have lost the sense that they can make a difference. Everything is so imposing: the homeless problem, drugs, the ghettos. What can I do as one person? This shows people that they *can* make a difference: bring life to a community under siege, build a playground, improve a school, rehab housing for the homeless."[38]

Michael Brown told another interviewer, "Essentially, City Year is a community of idealism." A corps member said of his own experience:

> City Year has given me a chance to do something positive with my life. Before this year, I was in a gang, hanging out on street corners. This year, I worked as a teacher's aide at the Blackstone School in my own neighborhood, I renovated green spaces in Chelsea, and organized my own project to work with elderly people. I want to always serve the community because this year I have seen that I can be a positive role model—that I can change other people's lives the way City Year has changed mine.

A young man from an affluent suburb near Boston agrees:

> Being part of City Year has been an experience not to be matched anywhere. There are no neighborhoods, no workplaces, no social groups, no places anywhere, where such a diverse group of people work so closely together. I've learned a lot at City Year about Boston's neighborhoods and its problems. But I have learned the most from my teammates.[39]

CONNECTIONS

In Chapter 1, Reading 5, Maya Angelou spoke of the legacy her uncle Willie left. What is the legacy of City Year? How is it like Uncle Willie's legacy? How is it unique?

Groups similar to City Year have existed in other periods of the nation's history. Research the Civilian Conservation Corps of the 1930s as well as the Peace Corps and Vista. How are they like City Year? What differences seem most striking? How do you account for those differences? (*Choosing to Participate* may be a useful place to begin your research.)

How do Khazei and Brown view the role of a citizen in a democracy? How are their views similar to those of people like Marian Wright Edelman? Jane Addams? Michael Haynes? What differences seem most striking?

To what extent does City Year break down the isolation and barriers that exist between individuals from different racial, ethnic, and economic backgrounds? How might City Year serve as a model for other communities, including your own?

A number of corps members refer to the difficulties of forging friendships with people whose backgrounds are different from their own. What are some of those difficulties? Why is it important that those friendships or alliances be based on mutual respect and equality? How does the philosophy of City Year tackle the problem?

If you could design the ideal service project, what would it be like? What issues would it tackle? How would it address those issues? How would it build a sense of common purpose among participants?

Suppose you had an opportunity to ask Khazei and Brown a question. What would you ask? What other individuals or groups you encountered in the course of this curriculum would you like to interview? What questions would you ask of them?

READING 12

Individuals Can Make a Difference

When Ervin Staub wrote, "Heroes evolve; they aren't born," he was describing rescuers during the Holocaust. But his comments also apply to Americans like those Robert Coles, an author and psychiatrist who teaches at Harvard University, interviewed for his book, *The Call of Service:*

> "I started community service in junior high," said Doris, a woman in her middle thirties, describing the evolution of a life that brought her, a physician, to work in a clinic in a dangerous ghetto neighborhood. Her first encounter with people whose lives were different from her own was at a nursing home, on a visit with her junior high class, when she was twelve.
>
> "I can still remember the first visit to the home: all the people just sitting there, some of them staring into space, and some staring at the television as if it was on, when it was actually off! I don't remember anyone saying hello to us. I remember our teacher clearing her throat and her voice *loud* to get their attention. We'd done this skit, and we were going to perform for them and sing for them. We knew our parts cold, and the songs, too, but those people were scary to us at first. It was as if we'd gone to another planet! We got nervous, and we didn't do too well. I remember this man sitting right up front—he was shaking and drooling. Today I know he had Parkinson's disease. Back then, I believed the man was weird, dangerous, out of his mind: that was the direction of my thinking.
>
> "The teacher took us aside when we got back to school and asked us what we felt about the trip there. We were all totally silent. She knew! Then she gave us a talk, and she apologized for not speaking

with us *before* we went there. To tell the truth, *that* impressed us more than anything—a teacher apologizing for a mistake. We didn't hear *that* all the time! We started telling her it was okay, and we'd like to go back. We were feeling sorry for her—she was upset—instead of feeling sorry for ourselves. That was a big first step in getting out of ourselves and into someone else's shoes, first the teacher's, then the old folks'."

Doris continued with an account of the work she did in high school, bringing food to shelters for the homeless, and in college, tutoring children and working on a psychological crisis hot line. In her senior year she decided that she wanted to be a physician. She took premed courses for two years after she graduated, while working intensively at the crisis hot line and a follow-up counseling center. She also volunteered at a shelter for battered women, where she encountered a most impressive husband-and-wife team of doctors who combined a career in academic medicine with a major commitment of time to a free clinic for the poor.

"I began to see what was possible by watching how others [those two doctors especially] spent their time," she explained, though she did more than merely observe. "From the beginning [of medical school] I was impatient with the usual routine of grinding away in the lab and with the books. I had learned to work with people—that's why I'd decided to go to medical school—but during the first two years there's very little of that kind of contact. So, I kept doing the [volunteer] work I'd been doing in college. When I did start seeing patients, I still wanted to be in touch with the kind of people we otherwise wouldn't see. Remember, in a teaching hospital you get to see the more exotic patients, or those brought in by the staff. What about the people on the streets or in shelters? They didn't come to our hospital. I guess it was in my blood by then—to reach out. I'd been doing it so long, I had a 'reach out' reflex!"

So even during the extremely demanding and exhausting years of her residency in internal medicine Doris found a few hours each week to work with those two doctors, whom she described as her inspiration, her mentors, and her guides. She encouraged other medical students to find ways of working with the hurt and ailing people who live at the edge of society. Under her direction those students, and some college students headed for medicine, connected themselves to shelters and soup kitchens and emergency wards and neighborhood clinics to assist people whose lives had fallen apart.

When her residency was over and she was married to a high school teacher with similar concerns, she created her own version of a public service medical career. She worked in a women's shelter and in the ghetto clinic. Even though the neighborhood was dangerous, her white skin and white jacket never seemed to put her in harm's way: "I stop and talk with the kids. Some of them, boys under ten, are [drug] runners, I know. Others (teenagers) belong to gangs and are hustling drugs—and girls. I hear it all from my patients inside the clinic and sometimes outside. Look, these may be my famous last words, but those guys know my car, and they know me and what I'm doing there, and they leave me alone. They even come up to me and ask me if there's anything I need! You know what I said to one guy, a real powerhouse character, who drives a Mercedes-Benz and doesn't have any job so far as anyone knows? I said, 'I need for more and more of the children around here to grow up and go to school and graduate and go to college and make something of their lives." You know what he said? "What's it to you, doc? Why are you so worried about the kids here?" I looked right at him, and I said, "We're all Americans. This is my country, and it's yours, and theirs, and we're in it together, all of us."

"He kept looking at me, and I got nervous. I figured I hadn't, to my way of thinking, said anything bad or wrong, but there was plenty of tension coming across, and maybe from his viewpoint I was being an outsider delivering a sermon I hadn't the right to deliver. But I also thought to myself, This is my life that I spend here, and dammit, it's *my* neighborhood, too, in a certain way, so I'd better keep talking with him, and anyone else, or I'm through here! Once fear makes me bite my tongue and not say what obviously needs to be said, then I might as well pack up my stethoscope and hammer and go someplace else."

In fact, that confrontation cleared the air, and Doris began to have rap sessions with some of the gang members who were keeping residents of the streets near the clinic in constant terror. They offered her "tons of money" for whatever equipment she wanted to buy, but she said no. They asked her once what *she* thought they should do with the money they were making. She said they should stop making it that way and try other ways of making a living. They asked her whether she minded not making more money when surely she could do so. She told them she wanted to have enough money to live a comfortable life and satisfy some of her hobbies and interests—but she had to sleep at night and have some respect for herself during the day *and* she did have certain values that meant a lot to her.

Such talks didn't by any means rid the neighborhood of violence, drugs, or prostitution, nor did they lower the high crime rate, and soaring school dropout rate. But two members of a gang and their girlfriends did come to see her one afternoon and asked for her help lest they become addicts, lest they die. She was able to arrange for them to live elsewhere in the city, enroll in an educational program, and find work.

That moment brought both fulfillment and gloom, and prompted her to look inward at the purposes she cherished and tried to uphold from day to day: "When they came to see me I wasn't as happy as you might think. I knew they were already in danger; they were being watched because they'd started objecting to certain deals the guys did, and to the use of little kids as runners. It was a matter of time, they knew, before they had their heads blown off. It was also a matter of

[The kids there are] only a little older than my daughter. They're all part of the same generation. They'll all soon be Americans living in the twenty-first century. I owe it to my daughter and my country—and to myself—to stay there.

time before I got into trouble—that's what crossed my mind as I sat there hearing those terrible, terrible stories.

"I talked with my husband. I talked with my mother—she was putting in a lot of time with my little daughter while I worried about these other children, whose mothers somehow hadn't been able to bring them up to say no to self-destruction. I told her, 'Mom, there are days when I want out—out. I want to walk away from that whole ghetto world, from my place in it, from that clinic, and never come back, never. I want to stay in our nice home and be with my husband and daughter, and with you, and maybe have a small private practice, or work in a suburban hospital and teach medical students. I get tired of the big odds against the people there—and that means the big odds against me and the work I do amounting to anything. But then I'll think of the kids I get to know, and the progress some of them are making. They come and see me for their cold and stomachaches, and they tell me they're doing better in school, and they try to remember what I told them—and I sure remember what they tell me. I think to myself, They're only a little older than my daughter. They're all part of the same generation. They'll all soon be Americans living in the twenty-first century. I owe it to my daughter and my country—and to myself—to stay there. If I wasn't there, I wouldn't be able to sleep at night; and thank God, my husband is one hundred percent for me to be doing this work; and Mother, you and Dad *both* got me into this, you really did, and I thank you.'"

She was embarrassed by the emotional and sentimental tone of her remarks, which she characterized as an "outburst"—a consequence of high anxiety (and no small amount of fear) she had been experiencing.[40]

CONNECTIONS

How does Doris illustrate Staub's comment that heroes are not born but evolve? Who were her role models? What values underlay her commitment to others?

Create an identity chart for Doris. How is she like rescuers such as Marion Pritchard (Chapter 8, Reading 9)? Activists like Marion Wright Edelman (Reading 1)? In what ways is she unique?

Doris wonders whether her efforts will make a difference. How would you answer her question? What is her legacy to her daughter? To the children she sees every day? To the community in which she lives? To the nation? A young lawyer who spent her childhood in Harlem and then attended a private school, Harvard College, and Harvard Law School, offers one answer to Doris's question. She told Coles about the difference one person made in her life.

He was a frail-looking Jewish kid with thick glasses, and at first I didn't know what we'd even talk about. But I'll tell you, he saved me, that's the word, *saved*. He was kind and thoughtful, and he loved reading and he taught me to love reading. He was the one who said to me, You can get out of all this, you can, and you don't need a lot of money to do it, the way the drug dealers and pimps con people into believing. All you need is to reach for a good book: it's your passage out. Boy, do I remember that phrase, "your passage out." I just wonder how many others will take the passage; I wonder how to reach them and persuade them. At the time, I wasn't all that interested in leaving, making the passage, but he sure turned me on. Of course, you hear those voices calling you every bad name—traitor!—for making the passage.[41]

Today that young lawyer does legal services work and tutors children in a ghetto neighborhood. What does her life suggest about the legacy of that "frail-looking Jewish kid"? How is his legacy similar to the one left by Maya Angelou's uncle Willie?

READING 13

The World's Conscience

Doris focuses on problems close to home. Elie Wiesel is a Holocaust survivor who has long focused on problems wherever they occur in the world. In 1986, he was awarded the Nobel Peace Prize. In presenting the award, Egil Aarvik, the chairman of the Norwegian Nobel Committee, said of Wiesel:

His mission is not to gain the world's sympathy for the victims or the survivors. His aim is to awaken our conscience. Our indifference to evil makes us partners in the crime. That is the reason for his attack on indifference and his insistence on measures aimed at preventing a new holocaust. We know that the unimaginable has happened. What are we doing now to prevent its happening again?

Through his books Elie Wiesel has given us not only an eyewitness account of what happened, but also an analysis of the evil powers which lay behind the events. His main concern is the question of what measures we can take to prevent a recurrence of these events.[42]

In the early 1990s, Wiesel expressed that concern by traveling to war-torn countries to call attention to violations of basic human rights. Shortly after returning from one such trip, he was asked why students should care about events in distant places. In response, he wrote:

Dear Students,

It is because of you I went to Sarajevo. Have you seen pictures of emaciated children in Somalia? And of wandering orphans in Sarajevo? Look at them. If they don't move you to rage or compassion, look at them again.

I know: You will say, "What can we do about them? If great powers and the United Nations are helpless, what impact could our response have on their fate?"

Your question is valid but its implicit conclusion is not. From past experience we have learned that whenever people speak up on behalf of their more unfortunate fellow human beings, their protest does have an effect. . . . But even if our efforts left the tormentors indifferent, they would still be fruitful, for they bring comfort and consolation to their victims.

In other words: It may very well be that you are powerless to change the course of history on a decision-making level but it is incumbent upon you to improve the psychological condition of those who suffer. . .

Find a way, any way, to give voice to your outrage at the young racists in Germany, to your abhorrence of bigotry on our own streets, to your solidarity with the prisoners in former Yugoslavia and to your determination to combat hunger in Somalia.

Do not tell me you are voiceless. . . . There are adolescents in Somalia who will die if help does not arrive soon. They are younger than you.

It is because of young students like you—and for you—that I went to Sarajevo.[43]

From past experience we have learned that whenever people speak up on behalf of their more unfortunate fellow human beings, their protest does have an effect. . . . But even if our efforts left the tormentors indifferent, they would still be fruitful, for they bring comfort and consolation to their victims.

CONNECTIONS

How does Wiesel define his role in the world? What are the boundaries of his community? Whom does he regard as his neighbors? How might Wiesel respond to those who argue that one person cannot make much difference in the world? How would you respond? Why?

After reading Elie Wiesel's books, Ali Carter told the author:

I don't know what it is about hate and violence that people like so much. Whenever there is a fight at my school hundreds of kids run to see someone get beat up. I've seen kids climb in trees to get a better view. No one tries to break it up until a teacher or security guard comes around. Who knows what makes people like violence. Maybe it's television, maybe it's the violence in the streets, maybe it's human nature.

Professor Wiesel, in light of the violence we see around us, do you think that something like the Holocaust could happen in today's society?[44]

How do you think Wiesel would answer her question? How would you answer it? Give reasons in support of your answers.

READING 14

The Road Not Taken

Two roads diverged in a yellow wood,

And sorry I could not travel both

And be one traveler, long I stood

And looked down one as far as I could

To where it bent in the undergrowth;

Then took the other, as just as fair,

And having perhaps the better claim,

Because it was grassy and wanted wear;

Though as for the passing there

Had worn them really about the same,

And both that morning equally lay

In leaves no step had trodden black.

Oh, I kept the first for another day!

Yet knowing how way leads on to way,

I doubted if I should ever come back.

I shall be telling this with a sigh

Somewhere ages and ages hence:

Two roads diverged in a wood, and I—

I took the one less traveled by,

And that has made all the difference.[45]

–Robert Frost

NOTES

[1] David Schoem, *Inside Separate Worlds* (The University of Michigan Press, 1991), 3.

[2] Ervin Staub, *The Roots of Evil.*

[3] Marian Wright Edelman. *The Measure of Our Success* (Beacon Press, 1992), 3-4, 7-9, 15, 32-33.

[4] "Seeking Justice." (Southern Poverty Law Center, 1988), 1.

[5] Frank Judge, "Slaying the Dragon," *The American Lawyer,* Sept. 1987, 84.

[6] Studs Turkel, *American Dreams: Lost and Found* (Ballantine Books, 1980) 221-223.

[7] Patricia A. Smith, "From Roxbury with Love," *Boston Globe,* 7 July, 1992, 30.

[8] Ibid.

[9] Ibid.

[10] Ibid.

[11] Ibid.

[12] Ibid.

[13] Ibid..

[14] Leon Bing, "Reflections of a Gang Banger," *Harper's Magazine*, March, 1989, 26.

[15] Ibid., 53.

[16] Ibid., 59.

[17] Martin Sanchez Jankowski, *Islands in the Street: Gangs and American Urban Society* (University of California Press, 1991), 159.

[18] Ibid., 159.

[19] Ibid., 171.

[20] Ibid., 172.

[21] Quoted in Janice Castro, "In the Brutal World of L. A.'s Toughest Gangs," *Time,* 16 March, 1992, 12-16.

[22] Martin Jankowski, *Islands in the Street*, 312.

[23] The Summary Report of the American Psychological Association Commission on Violence and Youth, 28-29.

[24] Virak Khiev, "Breaking the Bonds of Hate," *Newsweek,* 27 April, 1992, 8.

[25] Gregory-Alan Williams, *A Gathering of Heroes: Reflections on Rage and Responsibility* (Academy Chicago Publishers, 1994), 76.

[26] Ibid., 82-85.

[27] Quoted in Sasha Cavander, "Doctor Seeks to Cure Violence by Battling It Like Any Other Disease," *Los Angeles Times*, 1991.

[28] Martha Southgate, "Deborah Prothrow-Stith: Dealing with Deadly Consequences," *Essence*, January 1992, 42.

[29] Christina Robb, "A Clear, Passionate Case for Teaching Children How to Avoid Violence," *Boston Globe*, 5 July, 1991.

[30] Marian Christy, "Deborah Prothrow-Stith: A Powerful Voice Against Youthful Violence," *Boston Globe*, 7 August, 1991.

[31] John P. Muldoon, "Town Confronts Bigoted Graffiti," *Wellesley Townsman,* 12 Oct., 1989.

[32] Jerry Thomas, "Two Plead Innocent to Painting Hate Graffiti in Wellesley," *Boston Globe*, 5 July, 1991

[33] Interview with Alan Stoskopf, Facing History and Ourselves, 18, Oct., 1990.

[34] Irene Sage, "Wellesley Students Learn How Bigotry Stings," *Boston Globe,* 18 Sept., 1991.

[35] Interview with Alan Stoskopf.

[36] Avis Little Eagle, "Student Stands Alone in Fight Against Mascots" (*Native Monthly Reader*, Vol. 5, Issue 1, 1993-1994, 7.

[37] Gloria Negri, "100 Enlist to Care," *Boston Globe,* 18 Sept., 1991.

[38] Anthony Lewis, "Making a Difference," *New York Times,* 15 March, 1993. Copyright © 1993 The New York Times Company. Reprinted by permission.

[39] "Corps Members Speak Out on Service," *City Year*, 1992.

[40] Robert Coles, *The Call of Service* (Houghton Mifflin, 1993), 266-271.

[41] Ibid., 276.

[42] Egil Aarvik, "The Nobel Peace Prize, 1986," 4-5.

[43] *Newsday*, date unknown.

[44] *A Discussion with Elie Wiesel: Facing History Students Confront Hatred and Violence.* (Facing History and Ourselves, 1993).

[45] From *The Poetry of Robert Frost*, ed. Edward Connery Latham, Copyright 1916, © 1969 by Holt, Rinehart and Winston. Copyright 1944 by Robert Frost. Reprinted by permission of Holt, Rinehart and Winston.

Available from the Facing History Resource Center. Lectures, speeches, and Facing History interviews are indexed by the speaker's name.

For a more complete and current listing of audio-visual materials, contact the Facing History Resource Center.